Understanding Medical Coding

A Comprehensive Guide

Fourth Edition

Fourth Edition

Understanding Medical Coding

A Comprehensive Guide

Sandra L. Johnson,
MS, CPC, CMA (AAMA)

Robin I. Linker,
CHCA, CHCAS, CPC-I, CCS-P,
CPC-H, MCS-P, CPC-P, CHC, COC

CENGAGE
Learning®

Australia • Brazil • Mexico • Singapore • United Kingdom • United States

CENGAGE
Learning

Understanding Medical Coding:
A Comprehensive Guide, Fourth Edition
Sandra L. Johnson
Robin I. Linker

SVP, GM Skills & Global Product Management:
Dawn Gerrain

Product Director: Matthew Seeley

Product Manager: Jadin Kavanaugh

Senior Director, Development:
Marah Bellegarde

Product Development Manager: Juliet Steiner

Content Developer: Kaitlin Schlicht

Product Assistant: Mark Turner

Vice President, Marketing Services:
Jennifer Ann Baker

Marketing Manager: Jessica Cipperly

Senior Production Director: Wendy Troeger

Production Director: Andrew Crouth

Senior Content Project Manager:
Kara A. DiCaterino

Senior Art Director: Benjamin Gleeksman

Cover image(s):
© Excellent backgrounds/Shutterstock.com
© Hluboki Dzianis/Shutterstock.com

Notice to the Reader

Publisher does not warrant or guarantee any of the products described herein or perform any independent analysis in connection with any of the product information contained herein. Publisher does not assume, and expressly disclaims, any obligation to obtain and include information other than that provided to it by the manufacturer. The reader is expressly warned to consider and adopt all safety precautions that might be indicated by the activities described herein and to avoid all potential hazards. By following the instructions contained herein, the reader willingly assumes all risks in connection with such instructions. The publisher makes no representations or warranties of any kind, including but not limited to, the warranties of fitness for particular purpose or merchantability, nor are any such representations implied with respect to the material set forth herein, and the publisher takes no responsibility with respect to such material. The publisher shall not be liable for any special, consequential, or exemplary damages resulting, in whole or part, from the readers' use of, or reliance upon, this material.

The 2016 versions of CPT, ICD-10-CM, and ICD-10-PCS were used in preparation of this product.

CPT copyright 2015 American Medical Association. All rights reserved. CPT is a registered trademark of the American Medical Association. Applicable FARS/DFARS Restrictions Apply to Government Use. Fee schedules, relative value units, conversion factors and/or related components are not assigned by the AMA, are not part of CPT, and the AMA is not recommending their use. The AMA does not directly or indirectly practice medicine or dispense medical services. The AMA assumes no liability for data contained or not contained herein.

This program has the prior approval of the American Academy of Professional Coders (AAPC) for 3 continuing education hours. Grant of prior approval in no way constitutes endorsement by the AAPC of the program content or program sponsor. For more information on obtaining CEUs, please go to www.aapc.com.

For product information and technology assistance, contact us at
Cengage Learning Customer & Sales Support, 1-800-354-9706

For permission to use material from this text or product,
submit all requests online at **www.cengage.com/permissions**
Further permissions questions can be e-mailed to
permissionrequest@cengage.com

Library of Congress Control Number: 2015958580

Book Only ISBN: 978-1-305-66615-3

Package ISBN: 978-1-305-66612-2

Cengage Learning
20 Channel Center Street
Boston, MA 1432
USA

Cengage Learning is a leading provider of customized learning solutions with employees residing in nearly 40 different countries and sales in more than 125 countries around the world. Find your local representative at **www.cengage.com**

Cengage Learning products are represented in Canada by Nelson Education, Ltd.

To learn more about Cengage Learning, visit **www.cengage.com**

Purchase any of our products at your local college store or at our preferred online store **www.cengagebrain.com**

Printed in the United States of America
Print Number: 01   Print Year: 2016

Table of Contents

List of Tables

Preface

Introduction

Health care facilities and providers depend on the knowledge, expertise, and resourcefulness of medical coders to correctly code procedures and office visits for reimbursement. With annual revisions to the coding guidelines and changes in payor requirements, medical coding is an ever-changing and challenging industry. A successful career as a medical coder starts in the classroom, with the right materials and an enthused instructor. The fourth edition of *Understanding Medical Coding: A Comprehensive Guide* provides a solid groundwork for understanding how to code, the intricacies of reimbursement and billing, and many more pertinent topics that will enhance and promote well-rounded and knowledgeable medical coders.

Understanding Medical Coding: A Comprehensive Guide, Fourth Edition, is a practical and relevant guide for the modern health care environment. With coverage of all the major coding systems—HCPCS Level II, ICD-10-CM, and CPT—this textbook is comprehensive, yet offers practical and easy-to-understand explanations and coding examples.

Organization of This Textbook

This textbook is organized into 16 chapters:

- Chapter 1 provides an introduction to the profession of medical coding, its purpose in the health care system, and its impact in insurance and billing. Professional organizations and their importance in future career endeavors are discussed. The chapter concludes with an in-depth introduction to the different coding systems of ICD-10-CM, CPT, and HCPCS Level II.

- Chapters 2 through 4 cover the main coding systems introduced at the end of Chapter 1. Chapter 2 contains in-depth coverage of ICD-10-CM. Beginning with the history and usage of ICD-9-CM and ICD-10-CM, Chapter 2 covers the basics on how to find a code and the official coding guidelines. Chapter 3 provides coverage of HCPCS Level II codes and their use in medical coding. Current Procedural Terminology (CPT) coding is explained in Chapter 4. These three chapters provide a comprehensive and logical presentation of the main coding systems used in the health care industry, specifically outpatient coding.

- Chapter 5 is dedicated to Evaluation and Management codes and their importance and relevancy in accurate coding.

- Chapters 6 through 12 are categorized by coding sections of the CPT and ICD-10-CM coding manuals, including general surgery, the integumentary system, orthopedics, the cardiovascular system, obstetrics, and medicine. These chapters thoroughly cover the coding intricacies associated with these sections, while also providing step-by-step explanations.

- Chapter 13 contains information about CPT and HCPCS modifiers. This chapter was included to allow for better understanding of the purpose and use of these modifiers in medical coding.

- Chapter 14 delves into the particulars of insurance and billing in medical care facilities and practices, specifically for the ambulatory setting. It instructs on proper billing procedures and payment collection.

- Chapter 15 continues the discussion of insurance and reimbursement with in-depth coverage of how to file the claim form, using the CMS-1500 form. There are numerous examples throughout this chapter covering Medicare and Medicaid, other government insurance programs, HMOs, and various Blue Cross Blue Shield insurance policies.

- Chapter 16 contains detailed descriptions of payment cycles and strategies to receive proper reimbursement, and also discusses audit procedures and compliance concepts.

Features

Textbook chapters contain the following elements:

Key Terms are listed alphabetically at the beginning of each chapter and appear in the side margin with the definition upon the first appearance in the text.

Learning Objectives are also included at the start of each chapter. These objectives address concepts the student should understand.

Practice Exercises utilizing CPT, ICD-10-CM, and HCPCS can be found throughout the content and appear after core concepts have been introduced. These exercises are included to challenge the student's knowledge and application of the material presented and to facilitate problem solving.

Examples are included throughout chapters to explain step by step how to code procedures, diseases, and challenging areas for professionals.

Coding Tips serve as advice to help code complex situations unique to medical specialties.

Highlights focus on the essential skills and information coders will need to excel on the job.

Official Coding Guidelines present coding guidelines from the *ICD-10-CM Official Guidelines for Coding and Reporting* published by the Centers for Medicare and Medicaid Services (CMS) and National Center for Health Statistics (NCHS).

Official CPT Guidelines appear in appropriate chapters to highlight important coding guidelines from the *AMA Current Procedural Terminology 2016 Professional Edition* published by the American Medical Association.

HIPAA alert icons help students become aware of these Health Insurance Portability and Accountability Act of 1996 regulations.

Each chapter includes a **Summary,** which synthesizes chapter content and highlights main points. Also found at the end of each chapter is a **References** list, which students or instructors may utilize for further inquiry.

The **Glossary** included at the end of the textbook gives a complete listing of all key terms for quick reference.

New to the Fourth Edition

The fourth edition and its ancillaries has been updated to reflect the latest ICD-10-CM, CPT, and HCPCS Level II code sets and official guidelines. ICD-9-CM content, examples, and exercises have been replaced with ICD-10-CM throughout the text. The CMS-1500 forms have also been updated with the 02/12 version to support submission of ICD-10-CM codes. In addition to these updated codes and forms throughout, additional changes for each of the chapters are listed below.

Chapter 1 contains the following new and updated content:

- Updated information on the transition to ICD-10-CM

- Expanded information on federal laws governing Medicare fraud and abuse

- Updated information on penalties for not using the Physician Quality Reporting Systems (PQRS)

Chapter 2 contains the following new and updated content:

- Updated entire chapter to reflect ICD-10-CM coding for morbidity, implemented in the United States on October 1, 2015

- Updated official coding guidelines are included throughout the chapter

Chapter 3 contains the following new and updated content:

- Revised information on submission requests for code changes

- Expanded information on providing origin and destination modifiers

- Revised information on C codes

- Additional exercise providing practice for HCPCS Level II and ICD-10-CM code assignment

Chapter 4 contains the following new and updated content:

- Updates to information about the current CPT code book to make sure the most relevant information is in the chapter

- Revised Highlights, Coding Tips, and Exercises are embedded in the chapter to bring attention to important coding situations and procedures for CPT

- Updated information on each CPT appendix, A through O, and its impact in coding

Chapter 5 contains the following new and updated content:

- New information on Care Management Services (99487, 99489, 99490), Transitional Care Management Services (99495–99496), and Advanced Care Planning (99497–99498)

Chapter 6 contains the following new and updated content:

- Expanded information on anesthesia services, anesthesia time, and calculating an anesthesia charge

- Expanded information on coding proctosigmoidoscopies, sigmoidoscopies, and colonoscopies

- Brand new table explaining the codes for diagnostic procedures and therapeutic procedures for colonoscopies

- Brand new exercise to practice ICD-10-CM coding for general surgery

Chapter 7 contains the following new and updated content:

- Updated and expanded information on skin grafts

Chapter 8 contains the following new and updated content:

- Updated and expanded information on coding injuries

- New content on placeholder character X and 7th characters

- New content on use of encounter codes exclusive to fractures

Chapter 9 contains the following new and updated content:

- New content for coding hypertension with ICD-10-CM

- Explanation of Z codes to indicate tobacco use

- Updated Category II codes

Chapter 10 contains the following new and updated content:

- Updated content on coding for HIV encounters

- Guidelines on pregnancy trimesters from Chapter 15 of the ICD-10-CM

- Updated content on termination of pregnancy, spontaneous abortions, and alcohol and tobacco use

Chapter 11 contains the following new and updated content:

- New content about the Food and Drug Administration (FDA), Center for Medicare and Medicaid Services (CMS), and the Center for Disease Control (CDC) and their role with Clinical Laboratory Improvement Amendments (CLIA 1988)

- Updated information on drug assays

- New content about molecular pathology

Chapter 12 contains the following new and updated content:

- Additional instruction for coding infusions

Chapter 13 contains the following new and updated content:

- Revisions to certain modifier descriptions noting other qualified health care professionals who are qualified to use

- Information regarding Medicare's new HCPCS Level II modifiers

- NCCI modifier updates

- Clearer examples for modifier application

Chapter 14 contains the following new and updated content:

- Coverage of the Affordable Care Act (ACA)

- Expanded content on electronic medical records (EMRs), including a flowchart

- New practice exercises

Chapter 15 contains the following new and updated content:

- The 02/12 revision of the CMS-1500 form and explanations of each item on the form to accommodate submission of ICD-10-CM codes

- Information related to the Affordable Care Act

- Expanded content on Welcome to Medicare and Annual Wellness Visit

- New and revised exercises

Chapter 16 contains the following new and updated content:

- Revisions to the Medicare appeals process and latest thresholds

- Revised ABN form for Medicare

- Clarity on incident-to with example

Supplements

- Instructor Companion Website

- NEW! MindTap

- EncoderPro Expert free online 59-day trial

Instructor Companion Website

(ISBN 978-1-305-66614-6)

Spend less time planning and more time teaching with Cengage Learning's Instructor Companion Website to accompany the fourth edition of *Understanding Medical Coding: A Comprehensive Guide*. As an instructor, you will have access to all of your resources online, anywhere, and at any time. All instructor resources can be accessed by going to http://www.cengagebrain.com to create a unique user log-in. The password-protected instructor resources include the following:

- An electronic format of the Instructor's Manual for access at any time.
  - Introductory materials consist of:
    - A Note to the Instructor on how to use the text in tandem with the core text
    - Teaching a Basic Medical Coding Course
    - Teaching an Advanced Medical Coding Course
  - The manual is organized based on the chapter organization of the text:
    - Chapter Overview
    - Coverage of core chapter concepts
    - Answers to Chapter Exercises
    - ICD-10-CM: Coding Challenge with answers. The Coding Challenge introduces students to ICD-10-CM codes that are not seen or used in most medical practices. These questions are perfect for an in-class game with students.
- *Cengage Learning Testing Powered by Cognero* is a flexible, online system that allows you to author, edit, and manage test bank content from multiple Cengage Learning solutions. You can also create multiple test versions in an instant, and deliver tests from your learning management system (LMS), classroom, or elsewhere.
- Customizable instructor support slide presentations in PowerPoint® direct classroom study on core chapter content.
- A conversion guide between editions will be available from *Understanding Medical Coding,* third edition to the fourth edition, to ease course planning.
- A competitor conversion guide will also be available for Carol Buck's *Step-by-Step Medical Coding* matching up with the fourth edition of *Understanding Medical Coding*.

MindTap

ISBNs: 978-1-305-66656-6 (electronic access code)/ 978-1-305-66659-7 (printed access card)

New: Johnson and Linker's *Understanding Medical Coding,* fourth edition, on MindTap is the first of its kind in an entirely new category: the Personal Learning Experience (PLE). This personalized program of digital products and services uses interactivity and customization to engage students, while offering instructors a wide range of choice in content, platforms, devices, and learning tools. MindTap is device agnostic, meaning that it will work with any platform or Learning Management System and will be accessible anytime, anywhere: on desktops, laptops, tablets, mobile phones, and other Internet-enabled devices.

This MindTap includes:

- An interactive eBook with highlighting, note-taking and more
- Flashcards for practicing chapter terms
- Computer-graded activities and exercises
- Self-check and application activities, integrated with the eBook
- Case studies
- Easy submission tools for instructor-graded exercises

About the Authors

Sandra Johnson, MS, CPC, CMA (AAMA), has worked 35 years in the health care field, with 25 years of teaching experience in medical assisting, medical coding, and medical transcription courses. She is an active member of the American Association of Medical Assistants and the American Academy of Professional Coders. She was awarded the Indiana Medical Assistant of the Year (1993), the Golden Apple Educator Award in 2003, and served as the president of the Indiana Society of Medical Assistants (1993–1994). She has been a multiple nominee for Who's Who Among America's Teachers, and was the recipient of the Glenn W. Sample Award for Instructional Excellence in 1996 and 2004 from Ivy Tech State College. She is a professor in biology and an allied health instructor at Indiana University Southeast, and holds a master's degree in Human Resource Development with a specialization in health and safety management from Indiana State University.

Robin Linker, CHCA, CHCAS, CPC-I, CPC, CPC-H, CCS-P, MCS-P, CPC-P, CHC, COC, is executive director of Operations and Auditing for the Association of Health Care Auditors and Educators (AHCAE) and CEO of Robin Linker & Associates, Inc. Considered a leading expert with over 30 years in health care, Robin has provided consulting and education in most areas of health care coding and billing.

Robin is the former director of Education and Technical Development for the American Academy of Professional Coders (AAPC), where she wrote and presented numerous specialty related coding and training programs nationwide. She has been a frequent guest speaker for AHIMA, AAPC, HFMA, and HCCA, as well as numerous medical societies and health care organizations. Robin is also a past member of the Provider Outreach and Education Advisory Group for CMS and is the current president of the Northern Colorado Health Information Management Association (NCHIMA). She assists various health care venues, including attorneys, providers, and facilities in the areas of coding, auditing, and fraud and abuse assistance, and has served as an expert case witness on behalf of physicians. She is an experienced IRO assisting providers and organizations under mandated OIG Corporate Integrity Agreements. As a speaker, author, and educator for the American Medical Association, she provides annual CPT updates and ICD-10-CM trainings for the AMA. She first started teaching ICD-10 in 2002. As a true advocate in the health care industry, Robin has dedicated her career to her clients by increasing industry awareness and contributing to systems improvement. She is a member of the National Speakers Association and has provided thousands of educational and keynote presentations throughout the United States and, on occasion, internationally over the past 20 years.

Reviewers

Yehia Aly, MBA, CPC, CHTS
Professor
Florida Technical College
Orlando, Florida

Barbara Marchelletta, BS, CMA (AAMA), RHIT, CPC, CPT, AHI
Program Director, Allied Health
Beal College
Bangor, Maine

Cheryl A. Miller, MBA/HCM
Program Director/Assistant Professor
Westmoreland County Community College
Youngwood, Pennsylvania

Lori Warren Woodard, MA, RN, CPC, CPC-I, CCP, CLNC
Medical Department Co-Director
Spencerian College
Louisville, Kentucky

Special thanks also to technical reviewer:

Carline Dalgleish, BS, MA, RHIA, AHIMA Approved ICD-10-CM/PCS Trainer.

Dedications

Sandy's Dedication

To all my students—past, present, and future: You look to me for guidance and inspiration; instead you inspire me. Little do you know, I learn as much from you as you learn from me as you bring your experiences, hopes, and dreams into the classroom. My success is helping you reach your goals and seeing you succeed.

Robin's Dedication

I want to thank God and my family for all your love and support throughout the years. Your encouragement and support continue to be core in my career. To my colleagues and students, a special thank you for entrusting me as your educator and mentor. I remain humbled and overjoyed of having had the opportunity to be a part of your journey in your new career path!

How to Use the EncoderPro Free Online Trial

Optum360's *www.EncoderPro.com Expert* is a powerful medical coding software solution that allows you to locate CPT, HCPCS, ICD-10-CM, and ICD-10-PCS codes. The software provides users with fast searching capabilities across all code sets, it greatly reduces the time needed to build or review an insurance claim, and it helps improve overall coding accuracy. The software includes additional features such as ICD-10-CM and ICD-10-PCS crosswalks for ICD-9-CM codes and coding guidance (e.g., 1995 E/M guidelines). This software can be used to assign codes to any of the exercises in the *Understanding Medical Coding: A Comprehensive Guide* textbook.

How to Access the Free Trial of *www.encoderpro.com Expert*

Information about how to access your 59-day trial of *www.EncoderPro.com Expert* is included on the printed tear-out card located in the front cover of this textbook. The card contains a unique user access code and password. Once you log in, scroll down to the bottom of the *License Agreement* page and click the *I Accept* link. Then, click the *I Accept* link on the *Terms of Use* page.

Introduction to Coding

Learning Objectives

Upon successful completion of this chapter, you should be able to:

- Define coding and its purpose in health care.
- Differentiate between insurance abuse and insurance fraud and list examples of each.
- Recognize professional associations and credentials offered by each.
- Identify the legal implications and ramifications of incorrect coding and the rules to follow for compliance and protection.
- Name the resources available for coders.
- List the types of codes used in health care and define each one.

Key Terms

American Academy of Professional Coders (AAPC)

American Health Information Management Association (AHIMA)

Association of Health Care Auditors and Educators (AHCAE)

authorization

Centers for Medicare & Medicaid Services (CMS)

confidentiality

consent

disclosure

Electronic Prescribing Incentive Program

Federal Register

Healthcare Common Procedure Coding System (HCPCS)

Health Information Technology for Economic and Clinical Health (HITECH)

Health Insurance Portability and Accountability Act (HIPAA)

insurance fraud

International Classification of Diseases, 9th Revision, Clinical Modification (ICD-9-CM)

International Classification of Diseases, 10th Revision, Clinical Modification (ICD-10-CM)

Office of Inspector General (OIG)

Omnibus Budget Reconciliation Act (OBRA) of 1987

Physician Quality Reporting System (PQRS)

Physicians' Current Procedural Terminology (CPT)

privacy

privileged information

protected health information (PHI)

Quality Improvement Organizations (QIO)

Centers for Medicare & Medicaid Services (CMS): An administrative agency within the Department of Health and Human Services (DHHS) that oversees Medicare, Medicaid, and other government programs.

International Classification of Diseases, 9th Revision, Clinical Modification (ICD-9-CM): Coding system used to report diagnoses, diseases, symptoms, and reason for patient encounters for insurance claims.

Healthcare Common Procedure Coding System (HCPCS): Coding system that consists of CPT codes (level I) and national codes (level II), used to identify procedures, supplies, medications (except vaccines), and equipment.

International Classification of Diseases, 10th Revision, Clinical Modification (ICD-10-CM): Coding system that replaced ICD-9-CM as of October 1, 2015, to report diagnoses, diseases, symptoms, and reason for patient encounters for insurance claims.

Federal Register: The official daily publication for rules, proposed rules, and notices of federal agencies and organizations, as well as executive orders and documents.

Health Insurance Portability and Accountability Act (HIPAA): Federal law mandating regulations that govern privacy, security, and electronic transactions standards for health care information.

Introduction

Coding is defined as the translation of diagnoses, procedures, services, and supplies into numeric and/or alphanumeric components for statistical reporting and reimbursement purposes. Coding occurs when a medical term is cross-referenced into a three-, four-, or five-digit alphanumeric or numeric code. Coders abstract information from a patient record to assign the correct code(s).

Knowledge of medical terminology and anatomy is required to describe accurately the patient's reason for the encounter, which is the diagnosis, symptom, or complaint. Specific terms are also required to describe accurately surgical procedures, diagnostic tests, and medical services provided to the patient. With the passage of the Medicare Catastrophic Coverage Act of 1988, the Health Care Financing Administration (HCFA), now the **Centers for Medicare & Medicaid Services (CMS),** mandated the use of a first set of codes, the **International Classification of Diseases, 9th Revision, Clinical Modification (ICD-9-CM)** to report diagnoses and treatment, plus a second set of codes, the **Healthcare Common Procedure Coding System (HCPCS),** for services and supplies provided relative to those diagnoses. **International Classification of Diseases, 10th Revision, Clinical Modification (ICD-10-CM)** replaced ICD-9-CM on October 1, 2015, and will be covered in Chapter 2 extensively.

Federal Register

The **Federal Register** is the official daily publication for regulations, proposed rules, notices of federal agencies and organizations, as well as final rules and executive orders and documents. It is updated daily by 6 a.m. and published Monday through Friday, except on federal holidays. The proposed rules section contains notices to the public of proposed issuance of rules and regulations in an attempt to allow individuals to participate and comment on rules before the adoption of the final rules. This publication contains rulings for CMS, the **Health Insurance Portability and Accountability Act (HIPAA),** the Occupational Safety and Health Administration (OSHA), and the Drug Enforcement Administration (DEA). An example of these rulings that interest health care providers and personnel is the adoption of the 10th revision of ICD (ICD-10-CM), as modifications were made to the official guidelines and code sets prior to final rules.

A Career as a Medical Coder

The term *coder* may actually be described in many health care arenas a bit differently:

- Billers are not the same as coders. Coders will often perform certain billing functions in conjunction with their coding duties. Those who are employed in physician practices, immediate or urgent care centers, and other providers of medical care for ambulatory patients often find overlap between billing, coding, and insurance specialists.

- Coders in Health Information Administration departments of hospitals and skilled nursing facilities may encompass additional medical record functions.

  Others include:

- Claims processors for government agencies and commercial insurance carriers

- Educators in coding and insurance programs of allied health and vocational schools, community colleges, and universities

- Self-employed consultants who work with medical practices assisting with billing, coding, auditing, and compliance issues

- Writers and editors of informational and continuing education articles in professional journals and newsletters, and medical billing and insurance coding textbooks

The U.S. Department of Labor's Bureau of Labor Statistics projects that careers in health insurance areas noted in the previous list will increase through the year 2022.

What Skills Are Required in Medical Coding?

While many medical coders have been trained on the job, formal training provided by allied health/vocational schools, community colleges, and universities is necessary. Such courses as medical terminology, anatomy and physiology, and basic coding as well as advanced instruction to include both inpatient and outpatient coding essentials provide a good background for employment opportunities and the education necessary for certification. A certificate or degree in medical coding offered by educational institutions prepares an individual for both certification and employment.

Computer skills are required for electronic claims processing and electronic data interchange (EDI) to share information between the provider and the insurance carrier, and the implementation of the electronic medical records. Internet knowledge is needed to explore the numerous websites available to coders. Professional organizations, insurance companies, and government agencies such as Medicare and Medicaid provide professional journals, newsletters, and bulletins via the Internet. Professional organizations also offer continuing education opportunities to their members online. Coding tools are available and listed later in this chapter.

A credential in coding is recommended, and is required by many health care facilities, as certification provides validation of the knowledge and skills necessary to earn respect and recognition in the profession. Recertification is required to maintain the credential and certification status by meeting continuing education requirements established by each association. Membership in a professional association is a benefit to a coder. Publications such as journals and newsletters as well as members-only websites provide continuing education, networking with other coding professionals, and employment and professional development opportunities.

The **American Academy of Professional Coders (AAPC)** is an organization with national certification in the following areas:

American Academy of Professional Coders (AAPC): The professional association for medical coders providing ongoing education, certification, networking, and recognition, with certifications for coders in physicians' offices and hospital outpatient facilities.

- Certified Professional Coder–Apprentice (CPC-A). This certification allows applicants who have not met the medical experience requirement in the physician practice/outpatient setting the opportunity to become certified. The "A" drops off after 2 years of experience have been verified.

- Certified Professional Coder (CPC). This certification is for coders with physician practice work experience and for the CPC-A who meets this requirement.

- Certified Outpatient Coder (COC). This credential replaced the former Certified Hospital/Outpatient (CPC-H) in 2015. This certification is for outpatient facility and hospital services coders.

- Certified Professional Coder—Payor (CPC-P). This credential concentrates on coding and billing after submission to the payor.

- Certified Interventional Radiology Cardiovascular Coder (CIRCC). This certification is for individuals working in the specialized areas of interventional radiology and cardiovascular coding and charging.

Medical coding certification is also available in 19 specialties that are stand-alone credentials with no requirement for a previous CPC credential. Some of these are Internal Medicine, Emergency Department, General Surgery, and Pediatrics. A full list is available at http://www.aapc.com.

The AAPC can also be contacted at 800-626-CODE (2633).

American Health Information Management Association (AHIMA): One of the four cooperating parties for ICD-9-CM. Professional association for health information management professionals throughout the country.

The **American Health Information Management Association (AHIMA)** provides certification in these areas for health information management professionals:

- Certified Coding Associate (CCA). This is certification for entry-level coders.

- Certified Coding Specialist (CCS). This is a certification based on ICD-10-CM and CPT coding performed in the hospital setting.

- Certified Coding Specialist—Physician Based (CCS-P). This is certification for coders based on ICD-10-CM, multispecialty CPT coding, and HCPCS for physician practices.

- Certified Health Data Analyst (CHDA). This is certification based on expertise in health data analysis, particularly in use of electronic health records.

- Certified in Healthcare Privacy and Security (CHPS). This certification is based on the design, implementation, and administration of privacy and security protection programs in all types of health care organizations.

AHIMA can be contacted at http://www.ahima.org or 312-233-1100.

Association of Health Care Auditors and Educators (AHCAE): The national association for auditors, educators, clinicians, and compliance professionals dedicated to a higher level of education and training, auditing certification, recognition, and support in both professional and facility settings.

The **Association of Health Care Auditors and Educators (AHCAE)** is the professional organization that supports health care auditors and educators by providing professional, facility, and surgical chart auditing certifications, education, and recognition to members internationally. Credentials offered are:

- Certified Health Care Chart Auditor—Professional (CHCA)

- Certified Health Care Chart Auditor—Facility (CHCAF)

- Certified Health Care Chart Auditor—Surgical (CHCAS)

AHCAE can be contacted at http://www.ahcae.org or 303-905-2357.

Exercise 1.1

Visit the website for the American Academy for Professional Coders, http://www.aapc.com. Click on the Certification tab to read about the credentials available to coders in physician practices or other outpatient areas. Search the site for AAPC chapters in your state and local area. Where is the chapter nearest you?

What Is Fraud and Abuse?

To accurately assign codes, there must be an understanding of fraud and abuse and the rules of confidentiality. The Health Insurance Portability and Accountability Act (HIPAA) of 1996 defines **insurance fraud** as "knowingly and willfully executing, or attempting to execute, a scheme or artifact: (1) to defraud any health care benefit program; or, (2) to obtain, by false or fraudulent pretenses, representing, or promising, any of the money or property owned by or under the custody or control of a health care benefit program."

insurance fraud: Intentional, deliberate misrepresentation of information for profit or to gain some unfair or dishonest advantage.

Some examples of fraudulent activities are:

- Upcoding purposefully to a higher level of service to increase revenue
- Submitting claims for services not medically necessary
- Kickbacks or receiving rebates or any type of compensation for referrals
- Misrepresenting a diagnosis to justify payment
- Unbundling or billing separately for laboratory tests performed together in order to receive higher reimbursement
- Billing Medicare patients a higher fee than non-Medicare patients
- Billing for services, equipment, supplies, or procedures that were never provided

Insurance abuse, whether commercial or federal, is not acceptable in any aspect and may be deemed as fraudulent practices. Some examples of health care abuse are:

- Overcharging for services, equipment, supplies, or procedures
- Billing for services that were not medically necessary

According to the Centers for Medicare and Medicaid Services (CMS), other federal laws governing Medicare fraud and abuse include the following:

- False Claims Act (FCA)
- Anti-Kickback Statute (AKS)
- Physician Self-Referral Law (Stark Law)
- Social Security Act
- United States Criminal Code

While fraud must be proven in a court of law typically as an intentional, deliberate act, coders and physicians must pay scrupulous attention to details when documenting medical information, coding, and submitting claims. Medical records documentation must be complete, legible, and accurate to appropriately assign codes, and diagnosis codes must be correctly linked to the CPT/HCPCS codes to show medical necessity for the service or procedure provided. If an abusive practice is ignored or continued without correction, an investigation for a potential fraudulent act could occur.

The Health Insurance Portability and Accountability Act of 1996 establishes a formal link between government programs and private insurance companies in an effort to provide recognition and penalties for submission of fraudulent claims. Civil penalties include a $5,500 to $11,000 fine per claim form under the False Claims Act when an individual knowingly and willfully misrepresents information submitted to

Office of Inspector General (OIG): The office that enforces rules and penalties for violations of CMS and federal and state programs.

Omnibus Budget Reconciliation Act (OBRA) of 1987: A federal law outlining numerous areas of health care, establishing guidelines and penalties.

result in greater payment or benefits, plus three times the fraudulent claim amount. Criminal fines and/or imprisonment of up to 10 years can result from conviction of the crime of health care fraud outlined in HIPAA. Imprisonment of up to five years and/or fines of up to $50,000 are imposed for violations of the Medicare and Medicaid Patient and Program Protection Act (informally, the Anti-Kickback Statute). The **Office of Inspector General (OIG)** was formed under HIPAA to identify and eliminate fraud and abuse by undertaking nationwide audits and inspection and review of claim submission and reimbursement methodologies. When fraud is reported, the OIG investigates allegations of an incident, and refers the case to the Department of Justice for criminal and/or civil charges, penalties, and possible prosecution.

There are also civil penalties for fraudulent claims and coding errors contained in the **Omnibus Budget Reconciliation Act (OBRA)** of 1987. OBRA is a federal law requiring providers and facilities to keep copies of any government insurance claims and copies of all attachments for a period of five years. OBRA penalizes the health care provider for errors made by coders in the amount of a $2,000 fine per violation (a single coding error), an assessment in lieu of damages of up to twice the amount of the error submitted on the claim, and exclusion from Medicare and Medicaid programs for up to five years.

To avoid legal implications and ramifications, follow these rules:

- Keep current with coding and billing practices. Purchase new code books annually. Update encounter forms, charge tickets, and computer programs yearly as well.

- Attend educational and informational sessions to stay abreast of changes, revisions, and updates.

- Know and understand coding rules and use them correctly.

- Code only what is documented in the medical record. If there is a question or confusion, ask for clarification. The documentation must always support the diagnosis and services/treatment provided.

- Respond to Explanation of Benefits (EOBs) and other correspondence from insurance companies. Failure to do so can be considered *reckless disregard*.

- Develop and follow a coding compliance program. This includes educating everyone in the practice about the importance of billing and coding policies, and these policies should be in a written format. The compliance plan should include provider credentialing, documentation standards for medical records, and training and education, as well as continuing education and professional development. A compliance officer or officers should be appointed to identify any noncompliance and make the necessary corrections. An internal audit system ensures that precertification authorizations have been completed and documented, and that codes assigned to procedures and services are relevant to the medical record documentation of medical necessity.

Confidentiality

Title II of HIPAA, Administrative Simplification, contains uniform standards to protect confidential health information and place limits on its use.

The health care facility is the owner of the patient medical record. Patients have the right to request access to their individual record and make any amendments. Patients can restrict access to their health information and request the identity of those who have received their health information. Health care facilities, providers, and their employees must understand and practice the rules of confidentiality as they can be held accountable for the inappropriate use or disclosure of health information. The first step in this process is to know and understand the related terminology:

- **Confidentiality:** the maintenance, protection, security, and restriction of patient information

- **Privacy:** the right of individuals to keep information from being released or disclosed to others

- **Disclosure:** to reveal, release, transfer, or divulge information outside of the individual or facility holding the information to other parties

- **Consent:** written or verbal agreement to use, release, or disclose information for treatment, payment, or other reasons

- **Authorization:** formal permission in writing to use or disclose personal health information for reasons other than treatment, payment, or other purposes

- **Protected health information (PHI):** age, gender, health status, or other demographic information that is identifiable to an individual

- **Privileged information:** information related to treatment and progress of the patient

Highlight:

In a medical facility, PHI includes all patient information such as prescriptions, insurance claim forms, encounter forms, x-rays, physician notes, whether in electronic format, written, transcribed, or dictated, or telephone or e-mail messages.

Confidentiality can be waived in certain situations. Some of those are:

- During criminal investigations

- To report communicable diseases

- In suspicious death investigations

- To report domestic violence, child and elder abuse, and certain injuries, such as gunshot wounds

- When an exam is requested by a third-party payor who is responsible for charges, such as workers' compensation

- In response to a court-ordered subpoena or search warrant

Health Information Technology for Economic and Clinical Health (HITECH)

In February 2009, the American Recovery and Reinvestment Act (ARRA) was passed to fund rebuilding of health technology infrastructure and to expand technology in clinical education. As part of ARRA, the **Health Information Technology for Economic and Clinical Health (HITECH)** was passed to govern development within the health

confidentiality: The maintenance, protection, security, and restriction of patient information, to only be disclosed to a third party with patient authorization/consent.

privacy: The right of individuals to keep information from being released or disclosed to others.

disclosure: To reveal, release, transfer, or divulge information outside of the individual or facility holding the information to other parties.

consent: Written or verbal agreement to use, release, or disclose information for treatment, payment, or other reasons.

authorization: Formal written permission to use or disclose personal health information for reasons other than treatment, payment, or other purposes.

protected health information (PHI): Any information identifiable to an individual, such as age, gender, health status, or other demographic information.

privileged information: Any information communicated by a patient to a provider related to treatment and progress of the patient.

Health Information Technology for Economic and Clinical Health (HITECH): Enacted as part of the American Recovery and Reinvestment Act of 2009 to promote the adoption and meaningful use of health information technology.

care industry of health information technology by funding the implementation of electronic health record systems, and the ability to exchange patients' health information anywhere nationwide at any time. This would improve the quality of health care and allow better coordination of patient care with reductions in medical errors and duplicate tests and care. Another goal is to strengthen federal privacy and security laws to protect identifiable health information from misuse as the health care industry increases use of health information technology. Health care facilities and providers receive significant financial incentives through CMS to encourage hospitals and physicians to adopt and use certified electronic health records.

HITECH expands HIPAA coverage by increasing privacy regulations and compliance obligations, and increasing enforcement penalties related to patient medical records. HIPAA privacy and security requirements for business associates such as accounting firms and billing agencies that work with medical facilities, providers, and pharmacies are outlined in HITECH. These associates are now accountable to meet HIPAA security and privacy requirements.

Physician Quality Reporting System (PQRS)

Physician Quality Reporting System (PQRS): An incentive program for physicians, hospitals, and other health care providers for participation in reporting to CMS on quality performance measures.

The 2006 Tax Relief and Health Care Act required the establishment of a physician quality reporting initiative (PQRI) as an incentive payment program for eligible professionals who satisfactorily report data on quality measures for covered professional services provided to Medicare beneficiaries. In 2011, this program was renamed the **Physician Quality Reporting System (PQRS)**, which gives physicians, hospitals, and other health care providers the opportunity for incentives of up to 1 percent of total Medicare allowed charges for participation in reporting to CMS on quality performance measures. In 2015, financial penalties for health care providers who do not participate were implemented. An example of performance measure areas is screening for unhealthy alcohol use and tobacco use and cessation counseling. As of January 1, 2015, providers who do not use the PQRS program will see a negative payment adjustment. This promotes the reporting of quality information by individual providers and group practices. Coders do not typically code these, as the measures are determined by the provider of service and they are entered into the system for reporting. Electronic medical record systems may also have the measures built in, providing an easier reporting method by the provider as they click and fill in their measure templates.

Electronic Prescribing Incentive Program

Electronic Prescribing Incentive Program: A program developed by the Centers for Medicare & Medicaid Services (CMS) to offer incentives to health care providers to use a qualified electronic prescribing system.

Another quality improvement program developed by CMS is the **Electronic Prescribing Incentive Program**, or e-scribing. Providers who do not participate with electronic reporting will see a reimbursement decrease from those who participate with e-scribing.

Quality Improvement Organizations (QIOs)

Quality Improvement Organizations (QIOs): Organizations contracted by CMS in each state to review medical care, help beneficiaries with complaints, and work to improve the quality of care provided to Medicare beneficiaries by any health care provider or facility.

Quality Improvement Organizations, known as **QIOs,** are contracted by CMS to serve in each state to review medical care, help beneficiaries with complaints, and work to improve the quality of care provided to Medicare beneficiaries by hospitals, physician offices, nursing facilities, and, in general, any facility that provides medical care. QIOs were previously known as peer review organizations. QIOs are private, mostly not-for-profit organizations staffed by physicians and other health care professionals trained to review medical necessity and the appropriateness of care provided, whether inpatient or outpatient. Medical documentation plays a major role in the event of a QIO review.

Tools of the Trade

When it comes to coding and billing, the proper tools are essential for optimal reimbursement. Be sure the following resources are available in the workplace:

- Current ICD-10-CM manual (issued and effective every October). ICD-9-CM will still be necessary for past claims and those entities not covered by the HIPAA ruling, such as auto carriers and some workers' compensation agencies. Claims dates of service prior to October 1, 2015, required utilization of ICD-9-CM diagnosis codes. Various audit programs may necessitate the reviews of claims (post-reviews) as far back as seven years, which would have required ICD-9-CM coding.

- Current CPT manual. This is issued and effective every January.

- Current HCPCS manual (issued every January). Periodic releases throughout the year may warrant earlier implementation for some new HCPCSII codes.

- Medical dictionary. Also include supplemental resources for medical abbreviations and acronyms.

- Carrier bulletins, newsletters, and websites.

Recommended Resources for Coders

- American Academy for Professional Coders (AAPC)—http://www.aapc.com
- American Health Information Management Association (AHIMA)—http://www.ahima.org
- Association of Health Care Auditors and Educators (AHCAE)—http://www.ahcae.org
- American Medical Association (AMA) and the *AMA CPT Assistant*, a monthly newsletter published by the American Medical Association (AMA)—http://www.ama-assn.org
- Centers for Medicare and Medicaid Services (CMS) and National Correct Coding Initiative (NCCI)—https://www.cms.gov
- Office of Inspector General (OIG)—http://www.oig.hhs.gov
- Center for Disease Control—http://www.cdc.gov

Exercise 1.2

Visit the website for the American Health Information Management Association (AHIMA) at http://www.ahima.org. Click on About AHIMA to learn about the health information management profession, credentialing, and certification.

Types of Coding

In 1983, Medicare created the Healthcare Common Procedure Coding System (HCPCS) (pronounced "hick-picks"). HCPCS codes for certain services are required when reporting services and procedures provided to Medicare and Medicaid beneficiaries. HCPCS codes are composed of level I—CPT codes and level II—national codes or HCPCS. In this publication, level II national codes will be referred to as HCPCSII.

Level I—CPT Codes

Physicians' Current Procedural Terminology (CPT): Numeric codes and descriptors for services and procedures performed by providers, published by the American Medical Association.

The **Physicians' Current Procedural Terminology (CPT)**, published by the American Medical Association, is a listing of descriptive terms with codes for reporting medical services and procedures performed by health care providers. CPT provides uniformity in accurately describing medical, surgical, and diagnostic services for effective communication among physicians, patients, and third-party payors. CPT was introduced in 1966, and has undergone editing and modification to the current revision. The greatest change in CPT, which has had a major impact on coders, occurred in 1992 when evaluation and management services were created. This CPT section requires practitioners to make a decision as to level of service for offices, hospitals, nursing home services, and other providers.

Chapters in CPT include Evaluation and Management, Anesthesia, Surgery, Radiology, Pathology and Laboratory, and Medicine. Coding guidelines and concepts are discussed in later chapters of this textbook, as well as in the appendices in CPT.

Level II—National Codes (Referred to as HCPCSII)

Level II consists of alphanumeric "national codes" supplied by the federal government. These codes supplement CPT codes, enabling providers to report nonphysician services such as durable medical equipment, ambulance services, supplies, and medications, particularly injectable drugs. When billing Medicare and Medicaid for supplies and medications, avoid using CPT code 99070 (supplies and materials provided by the physician over and above those usually included with the office visit or other services). Level II codes list supplies and medications, especially injectable drugs, in more detail.

> EXAMPLES OF LEVEL II CODES:
>
> Injection, dimenhydrinate, up to 50 mg J1240
>
> Slings A4565

Modifiers

Level II also contains modifiers that are either alphanumeric or letters that can be used with all levels of HCPCS codes.

> EXAMPLES:
>
> LT—used to identify procedures performed on the left side of the body
>
> RR—used to identify durable medical equipment to be rented

A listing of HCPCS Level II codes is available for purchase as an individual publication updated annually.

Chapter 3 of this textbook covers HCPCSII in detail.

Exercise 1.3

Visit the American Medical Association (AMA) website (http://www.ama-assn.org) to learn more about CPT, including immunization and other periodic updates to CPT codes.

ICD-10-CM Codes

The International Classification of Diseases, 10th Revision, Clinical Modification (ICD-10-CM) is a modification of ICD-10, which was created by the World Health Organization (WHO) based in Geneva, Switzerland. ICD-10-CM was implemented in the United States on October 1, 2015. The ICD-10-CM is a morbidity classification published by the United States for classifying diagnoses and reason for visits in all health care settings. ICD-10 has been used in the United States since 1999 solely for the purpose of coding death certificates. One who codes death certificates is referred to as a *nosologist.* More than 90 countries have implemented ICD-10 for morbidity purposes. ICD-10-CM replaces ICD-9-CM, which was the diagnostic coding system used for reporting in the United States prior to October 1, 2015.

ICD-10-CM contains an Alphabetic Index, a tabular, and additional tables that are very crucial for coding. Chapter 2 will cover ICD-10-CM in depth. All health care facilities utilize the ICD-10-PCS (Procedural Coding System), which has taken the place of ICD-9-CM, Volume 3. Hospitals use ICD-10-PCS to report inpatient procedures for capturing the facility portion. CPT is used to report the physicians' and other reporting providers' services regardless of where the procedure/service takes place (e.g., procedures performed in physician offices, ambulatory care centers, nursing homes, and hospital inpatient and outpatient departments).

ICD-10-CM requires assignment of the most specific code to represent the diagnosis or problem being treated by the provider. This means the primary or first-listed diagnosis should be the one for the reason or condition indicated within the medical record, that best describes the main reason the patient sought medical care.

ICD-10-CM serves three major functions for insurance purposes:

1. It justifies procedures and services rendered by the physician.

2. It assists in establishing medical necessity for services and procedures performed by the physician.

3. It serves as an indicator in measuring the quality of health care delivered by the physician provider.

ICD-10-CM is discussed in detail in Chapter 2, and will be covered in other chapters throughout this textbook.

Transitioning from ICD-9-CM to ICD-10-CM

Between 1979 and October 1, 2015, the United States used ICD-9-CM to provide a diagnostic coding system for the compilation and reporting of morbidity and mortality statistics for reimbursement purposes in the United States. Similar to

ICD-10-CM, it allowed for the reporting of conditions, injuries, and traumas, along with complications and circumstances occurring with the illness or injury, and the reason for patient care. The basic guidelines for ICD-10-CM have remained very similar in many areas, but with a robust growth for specificity.

The major differences between ICD-10-CM and ICD-9-CM are as follows:

- ICD-10-CM has fewer nonspecific (NOS) codes than ICD-9-CM. Codes are more specific, with details such as which side of the body may be affected by a condition or if the encounter is the patient's first visit for the condition.

- ICD-10-CM codes have up to seven characters as opposed to five in ICD-9-CM, using both alpha and numeric characters.

- ICD-10-CM categorizes diagnoses differently. For example, ICD-9-CM groups codes for injuries primarily by the type of injury sustained; ICD-10-CM codes are grouped primarily by body region or area.

The format for ICD-10 is as follows:

- The tabular is the final stopping point in searching for the appropriate diagnostic code. It is the list that contains the alphanumeric listing of diseases classified by etiology and causes of injury, as well as a classification of other reasons for encounters and causes of injury. The tabular is used by all health care providers and facilities.

- The Alphabetic Index is typically located in the front sections of most book resources and is the starting point of locating the appropriate ICD-10-CM. It is then confirmed in the tabular listing. The Alphabetic Index and the tabular index are used much greater in concert than were the prior ICD-9-CM tabular and Alphabetic Index. The Official ICD-10-CM Guidelines for Coding and Reporting typically precede the Alphabetic Index.

- ICD-10-PCS: The ICD-10-PCS is a procedure classification published by the United States for classifying procedures performed in hospital inpatient health care settings. These codes are not reported by the physicians; they are reported by the facilities where the services are provided. The greatest difference between ICD-9-CM and ICD-10-CM is that the ICD-10-CM codes are alphanumeric, with more detailed descriptions. ICD-9-CM contains more than 13,000 codes; ICD-10-CM contains more than 68,000 codes, with approximately a third of the growth due to laterality (right, left, and bilateral).

Some examples of ICD-10-CM codes are:

- Type I diabetes mellitus with diabetic neuropathic arthropathy—E10.610

- Diverticulitis of large intestine with perforation and abscess with bleeding—K57.21

- Malignant neoplasm of lower-outer quadrant of right female breast—C50.511

- Foreign body in cornea, left eye, subsequent encounter—T15.02XD

Exercise 1.4

Visit the following websites to learn more about ICD-10-CM.

- CMS at https://www.cms.gov
- Centers for Disease Control and Prevention (CDC) at http://www.cdc.gov
- World Health Organization (WHO) at http://www.who.int

Summary

The ultimate goal in coding is to present a clear picture of medical procedures and services performed (CPT codes), linking the diagnosis, symptom, complaint, or condition (ICD-10-CM codes), thus establishing the medical necessity required for reimbursement.

Continuing education is a must for medical coders and billers. Staying current and up-to-date on all billing and coding regulations is mandatory. Civil and criminal penalties are imposed for convicted acts of fraud and abuse. All health care personnel must practice confidentiality diligently to protect, secure, and maintain patient personal and health information.

One example is CMS's enforcement of Evaluation and Management (E/M) Documentation Guidelines, developed by CMS with input from the American Medical Association (AMA) and various specialty organizations. These guidelines outline documentation required in a patient's medical record for the E/M code submitted on the claim form, giving requirements for certain elements that comprise the specific levels of service. The goal is to provide consistency and uniformity in medical record documentation for evaluation and management services. The transition to ICD-10-CM from ICD-9-CM is relatively straightforward from a coding perspective, as the process, many guidelines, and some conventions remain the same. The robust growth in the number of codes within ICD-10-CM, however, has posed a challenge for some providers and coders who were well versed in the ICD-9-CM code set.

References

American Academy for Professional Coders (AAPC). Retrieved from http://www.aapc.com.

American Health Information Management Association (AHIMA). Retrieved from http://www.ahima.org.

American Medical Association (AMA). Retrieved from http://www.ama-assn.org.

Association of Health Care Auditors and Educators (AHCAE). Retrieved from http://www.ahcae.org.

Centers for Medicare & Medicaid Services (CMS). Retrieved from https://www.cms.gov.

Green, M. & Rowell, J. (2010). *Understanding health insurance: A guide to professional billing and reimbursement* (10th ed.). Clifton Park, NY: Cengage Learning.

CHAPTER 2

ICD-10-CM

Learning Objectives

Upon successful completion of this chapter, you should be able to:

- Apply ICD-10-CM rules and regulations and code accurately.
- Identify the correct principal and primary diagnoses.
- Demonstrate the use of Z codes to assign the correct codes in those circumstances.
- Describe the appropriate use of External Cause codes (V00–Y99) and their applications.
- Utilize resources including code books, the Internet, and available organizations to increase coding accuracy.

Key Terms

Alphabetic Index

American Hospital
  Association (AHA)

category

cooperating parties

diabetes mellitus

diagnosis-related
  groups (DRG)

eponym

etiology

first-listed diagnosis

ICD-10-PCS

main term

manifestation

National Center for
  Health Statistics
  (NCHS)

neoplasm

principal diagnosis

sequela

sequencing

subcategory

subclassification

tabular list

transient

Introduction

ICD-10-CM is the diagnostic classification system that describes the reasoning "why" a medical service is rendered. Every procedure or service reported must have a corresponding diagnosis code to justify the medical necessity. The best way to use this chapter is to have the ICD-10-CM code book while reviewing the material. Work through the examples as the information is discussed to have a thorough understanding of the material as it is presented. Refer to the ICD-10-CM Official Coding Guidelines often to become familiar with any additional instruction or rules.

History and Usage of ICD-10-CM

ICD-10-CM stands for *International Classification of Diseases, 10th Revision, Clinical Modification*. It is used for coding and classifying diagnoses and procedures by an alphanumerical system. Classifying diseases by their cause has been done in various forms for many years, even as far back as the ancient Greek civilization.

The ICD system has been around for many years, and as the "10th revision" implies, it has been updated many times to reflect changes in medicine. The ICD classification was developed and is updated by the World Health Organization (WHO). It was modified by the United States in the 1970s to provide greater specificity for use in classifying both diseases and procedures for hospital and physician usage. On October 1, 2015, ICD-10-CM was finally implemented to replace ICD-9-CM for use in the United States.

ICD-10-CM was not developed for use as a reimbursement system; however, on October 1, 2008, CMS converted to a MS-DRG or Medicare severity (MS) **diagnosis-related groups (DRG)** system. It was designed for statistical collection. It is a classification system that continues to group discharges for hospital stays, diagnoses, and procedures into various classes. MS-DRGs assist CMS with determining and paying hospitals more for the severely ill patients and to provide reduced reimbursement to hospitals for those who are not as severely ill.

diagnosis-related groups (DRG): The method of prospective payment used by Medicare and other third-party payors for hospital inpatients.

The *International Classification of Diseases* code book is updated every year with changes effective October 1 of that year, with implementation of the 10th revision on October 1, 2015. It is essential that code books and coding software be updated with the new system and reviewed annually to update any revisions.

The Cooperating Parties

The ICD-10-CM is based on the ICD-10, the statistical classification of disease published by the World Health Organization (WHO). The guidelines for ICD-10-CM have been approved by four agencies known as the **cooperating parties** that have the responsibility for maintaining and updating ICD-10-CM. These are the **American Hospital Association (AHA)**, the **National Center for Health Statistics (NCHS)**, the Centers for Medicare & Medicaid Services (CMS), and the American Health Information Management Association (AHIMA). Each agency has varying responsibilities, as shown in Table 2–1.

cooperating parties: Four agencies who share responsibility for maintaining and updating ICD-10-CM.

American Hospital Association (AHA): One of the four cooperating parties for ICD-10-CM.

National Center for Health Statistics (NCHS): National Center for Health Statistics, one of the four cooperating parties for ICD-10-CM.

Table 2-1 Responsibilities of the Cooperating Parties for ICD-10-CM

NCHS	Maintains and updates the diagnosis portion of ICD-10-CM
CMS	Maintains and updates the procedure portion (ICD-10-PCS)
AHA	Maintains the Central Office on ICD-10-CM to answer questions from coders and produces the *Coding Clinic for ICD-10-CM*
AHIMA	Provides training and certification for coding professionals

The ICD-10-CM Coordination and Maintenance Committee is made up of various federal interdepartmental representatives from the Centers for Disease Control (CDC), Centers for Medicare and Medicaid Services (CMS), and the National Center for Health Statistics (NCHS). Although requests may be made for change discussion, the committee is responsible for any modifications, approval, addendums, and errata development.

Coordination and Maintenance Committees

Each spring and fall, the coordination and maintenance committees meet. The typical meeting is a two-day format in which CMS leads the ICD-10-PCS procedural issues on the first day. The CDC leads day two, which is devoted to diagnosis coding issues. Participants of both coding systems are encouraged to attend or submit questions, and are welcome to offer any recommendations for changes. It is important for attendees to know that during these committee meetings, no final decisions are made. The final decisions must be cleared through the Department of Health and Human Services. Information on attending these meetings can be found at www.cms.gov.

Format and Structure of ICD-10-CM

All codes in ICD-10-CM are alphanumeric. Valid three-character codes still exist, with approximately 11,400 being four characters in length. Codes may be three to seven characters long. This information will be covered further in the Categories, Subcategories, and Subclassifications section in the pages ahead.

Sequencing Diagnosis Codes

sequencing: Arranging codes in the proper order according to the definitions of principal or first-listed diagnosis.

principal diagnosis: The reason, after study, which caused the patient to be admitted to the hospital.

first-listed diagnosis: In the outpatient setting, the diagnosis that is the main reason and listed first for the visit. It is usually the diagnosis taking the majority of resources for the visit.

Several of the official coding guidelines in the ICD-10-CM refer to **sequencing** guidelines. Sequencing refers to the selection of the appropriate first diagnosis for the patient's encounter. In the hospital inpatient setting, this is known as the **principal diagnosis**. The principal diagnosis is the condition, after study, that brought the patient to the hospital for care. For example, if after the patient was admitted for chest pain it was found that the chest pain was caused by an acute myocardial infarction, the infarction would be the principal diagnosis.

In the outpatient or physician's office setting, the first diagnosis is known as the **first-listed diagnosis**. It is the primary or main reason that caused the patient to seek treatment for that visit. This may be a symptom such as vomiting, chronic illness, or acute disease, such as gastroenteritis or laceration.

How to Look Up a Term

Alphabetic Index: The ICD-10-CM alphabetic listing of diagnoses.

ICD-10-CM consists of an Alphabetic Index and a tabular list. The **Alphabetic Index** includes a Table of Neoplasm; Table of Drugs and Chemicals; and an external Alphabetic Index. The first step in coding is to locate the diagnostic term in the Alphabetic Index, typically placed at the beginning of the ICD-10-CM book. It is officially called the ICD-10-CM Index to Disease and Injuries, and is alphabetized. For purposes of this publication, we will refer to it as the Alphabetic Index.

Step 1: Locating the Main Term

main term: The patient's illness or disease. In ICD-10-CM the main term is the primary way to locate the disease in the Alphabetic Index. Main terms are printed in boldface type and are even with the left margin on each page.

The first step to looking up a term in the ICD-10-CM book is to look in the Alphabetic Index under the **main term**. The main term is printed in bold type at the left margin, and is the main disease, injury, or condition wrong with the patient. Examples of main terms are: *fracture, pneumonia, disease, injury, enlargement,* and *enlarged.* Anatomical terms such as *kidney* or *shoulder* are *never* main terms in ICD-10-CM. If a coder tries to look up a code by the anatomical site, an instructional note to "See condition" will be found. This means the coder should look up the main condition that is wrong with the patient. This does not mean to look under the main term "condition."

For example, if the patient comes to the physician's office for a sore throat, and the coder looked up the term *throat,* there is a note that says, "See condition." (The throat is not what is wrong with the patient; the soreness is the main issue wrong, or the main condition.) The coder should look under the main term of *sore* to get a code of J02.9.

The Alphabetic Index is cross-referenced extremely well to allow the coder to locate the correct code using several different terms. For example, the diagnosis "Congestive heart failure" can be found under the main term "failure" as well as "congestive." By looking up this diagnosis either way, the coder is led to the correct code of I50.9. In ICD-10-CM, the alphabetic and tabular listing should be used in concert. Often, additional terms may be located in the Alphabetic Index; however, they might not be listed the exact same way in the tabular. Reviewing and learning various subterms will lend to successfully finding the correct code.

Exercise 2.1

Underline the main term in each example.

1. Senile cataract
2. Carcinoma of the breast
3. Mitral valve prolapse
4. Urinary cystitis
5. Hypertensive cardiovascular disease
6. Sudden infant death syndrome
7. Nontoxic thyroid goiter
8. Sickle cell anemia
9. Acute situational depression
10. Upper respiratory tract infection
11. Sore throat
12. Migraine headache
13. Chronic lower back pain
14. Rectal mass
15. Left ureteral calculus

Step 2: Identify Subterms

Below the main terms are indented subterms that further describe the condition. They may describe different sites of the illness, **etiology** (cause), or type of illness. Look in your ICD-10-CM book for the following main term in the Alphabetic Index.

etiology: Cause of the disease or illness.

Bronchiolitis (acute) (infectious) (subacute) J21.9

with

influenza, flu, or grippe *-see* Influenza, with, respiratory manifestations NEC

chemical (chronic) J68.4

In this example, "Bronchiolitis" is the main term. "With" and "chemical" are indented equally under the main term, so both are considered subterms. "Influenza," "flu," or "grippe" are subterms under the subterm "with." When a main term appears with many subterms, the coder might need to use a ruler to ensure correct usage.

eponym: A disease, disorder, or procedure named after the person who researched or identified a particular disease or disorder or developed a procedure.

> ### Highlight:
> **Eponyms** are diseases, disorders, and procedures named after the person who researched or identified a particular disease or disorder or developed a procedure. In addition to locating the code under the main term, you can also locate it by the name. For example, Bell's palsy can be located under both "Bell" and "palsy."

Nonessential Modifiers

Nonessential modifiers are terms in parentheses following main terms. These are modifiers or terms describing the main term whose presence or absence in the diagnostic statement does not change the code assignment. For example:

Intussusception (bowel) (colon) (enteric) (ileocecal) (ileocolic) (intestine) (rectum) K56.1

-appendix K38.8

Intussusception is the main term. "Colon," "enteric," "intestine," and "rectum" are examples of nonessential modifiers. So if the coder's diagnostic statement said *intussusception* only and did not mention the colon, the coder is still correct in using the K56.1 code.

Tabular List

tabular list: ICD-10-CM is a tabular listing (alphanumerical order) of diseases.

"ICD-10-CM Tabular List of Diseases and Injuries" is the **tabular list** of diagnoses. Once a coder has identified a code in the Alphabetic Index, it must be verified in the tabular list. In the tabular list, codes are arranged numerically in 21 chapters and are grouped according to their cause (etiology), such as fractures, or body system, such as digestive system.

Chapter Title	Code Categories
1. Certain Infectious and Parasitic Diseases	A00–B99
2. Neoplasms	C00–D49
3. Diseases of the Blood and Blood Forming Organs and Certain Disorders Involving the Immune Mechanism	D50–D89
4. Endocrine, Nutritional, and Metabolic Diseases and Immunity Disorders	E00–E89

5. Mental, Behavioral and Developmental Disorders   F01–F99

6. Diseases of the Nervous System   G00–G99

7. Disease of the Eye and Adnexa   H00–H59

8. Disease of the Ear and Mastoid Process   H60–H95

9. Diseases of the Circulatory System   I00–I99

10. Diseases of the Respiratory System   J00–J99

11. Diseases of the Digestive System   K00–K95

12. Diseases of the Skin and Subcutaneous Tissue   L00–L99

13. Diseases of the Musculoskeletal System and Connective   M00–M99
    Tissue

14. Diseases of the Genitourinary System   N00–N99

15. Pregnancy, Childbirth and the Puerperium Connective   O00–O9A
    Tissue

16. Certain Conditions Originating in the Perinatal Period   P00–P96

17. Congenital Malformations, Deformations,   Q00–Q99
    and Chromosomal Abnormalities

18. Symptoms, Signs, and Abnormal Clinical Laboratory   R00–R99
    Findings, Not Classified Elsewhere

19. Injury, Poisoning and Certain Other Consequences of   S00–T88
    External Causes

20. External Causes of Morbidity   V00–Y99

21. Factors Influencing Health Status and Contact with Health   Z00–Z99
    Services

> **Highlight:**
>
> Remember:
>
> Category = 3 characters
>
> Subcategory = 4th or 5th character
>
> Codes may be 3, 4, 5, 6, or 7 characters
>
> Example: Code L89.112
>
> L89- = category (pressure ulcer)
>
> L89.1- = subcategory (back)
>
> L89.11- = subcategory (right upper)
>
> L89.112 = Pressure ulcer of right upper back, stage 2

Categories, Subcategories, and Subclassifications

The tabular list of ICD-10-CM is set up in **categories**, **subcategories**, and codes. The ICD-10-CM uses an indented format to assist in easily finding the codes. All categories are three characters. There are only a limited number of three-character codes in which no further subdivision is required. A **subclassification** or a subcategory is either four or five characters. Further, some codes extend to six or seven characters. An example of a category requiring further characters is M16, Osteoarthritis of hip. The category itself is not a code. If, however, we look further, we see where this category allows for description of unilateral, bilateral, or unspecified osteoarthritis of the hip. Code M16.11 is a code that describes unilateral primary osteoarthritis of the right hip. This not only explains the condition but also indicates the specific location and side. The coder must always code to the greatest level of specificity. In other words, *if there is a 4th, 5th, 6th, or 7th character required*, it must be used. We will address the 6th and 7th characters in the Coding Conventions section later in this chapter.

category: Categories are three-digit representations of a single disease or group of similar conditions, such as category E11, diabetes mellitus. Many categories are divided further into subcategories and subclassifications.

subcategory: Four-digit subcategories are subdivisions of diagnostic categories to provide greater specificity regarding etiology, site, or manifestations.

subclassification: Fifth-digit subclassifications are subdivisions of subcategories to provide even greater specificity regarding etiology, site, or manifestation of the illness or disease.

Trusting the Alphabetic Index

Due to space constraints, sometimes a term listed in the Alphabetic Index will not be repeated in the tabular list. In these cases, the coder must trust the Alphabetic Index and use the code listed. The Alphabetic Index uses an indented format with hyphens (-) to assist with following for the full terminology. The use of watermarks (small vertical gray lines) is used by other publishers in the Alphabetic Index in place of the dashes for ease of reference.

Coding Conventions

ICD-10-CM uses several terms, abbreviations, punctuation marks, and symbols to lead the coder to the correct codes. These should be studied carefully and must be followed whenever present in the guidelines. We will touch on just the main conventions of ICD-10-CM.

Punctuation

- **Placeholder character:** ICD-10-CM utilizes a placeholder character X to allow for future expansion if needed. Where a placeholder exists, the X must be used to fill in the empty characters. In some situations, more than one placeholder X may be necessary to allow appendage of any required 7th characters.

- **7th characters:** When certain categories require a 7th character, the 7th character is not optional. The notes within the tabular will instruct the coder for use of the 7th character when required. For example, category O31, Complications Specific to Multiple Gestations, requires a 7th character to indicate the fetus affected. Code O31.01, Papyraceous fetus, first trimester, shows only five characters, meaning the placeholder X will be required to apply the 7th character. If the second fetus was affected, the 7th character 2 would be required. This would be coded as O31.01X2.

- **Brackets** [ ] are used in the tabular list to enclose synonyms, alternative wordings, and explanatory phrases such as:

  J00 Acute Nasopharyngitis [common cold]

  The common cold is just another name for acute nasopharyngitis.

  Brackets are also used in some chapters of the ICD-10 when a specific subcategory character should be used. For example, S04.01 [1,2,9] means that a fifth character of either 1, 2, or 9 is required.

  ○ S04.011   Injury of optic nerve, right eye

  ○ S04.112   Injury of optic nerve, left eye

  ○ S04.119   Injury of optic nerve, unspecified eye

- **Parentheses** ( ), referred to as nonessential modifiers, are used in both the index and tabular listing to enclose supplementary words that may be present or absent in the statement of a disease or procedure without affecting the code to which it is assigned.

- **Colons** : are used in the tabular list after an incomplete term, which needs one or more of the modifiers following the colon to make it assignable to a given category.

Includes and Excludes Notes

The notation *Includes notes* means the entry provides further examples or defines the category. For example, in the tabular list under code J32.0, Chronic Maxillary Sinusitis, the code book gives examples of diagnoses that can be coded using this code, such as chronic antritis.

ICD-10-CM provides two Excludes notes:

- Excludes1 is referred to as a "pure" exclusion meaning, "Not Coded Here." This directs the coder to never use the code referenced in the exclusion information at the same time with the code above to what it's referencing.

- Excludes2 notes reference additional coding information that tells the coder that it's not included with the code in reference however may be appropriate to report at the same time, if applicable.

Example: I77.0, Arteriovenous fistula, acquired

Excludes1:

   arteriovenous aneurysm NOS (Q27.3-)

   presence of arteriovenous shunt (fistula) for dialysis (Z99.2)

   traumatic: see injury of blood vessel by body region

Excludes2:

   cerebral (I67.1)

   coronary (I25.4)

In this example, cerebral aneurysm code I67.1 isn't included but may be used in addition to the I77.0, if applicable. The Excludes1 note, however, will not allow code Z99.2 for the presence of arteriovenous shunt (fistula) for dialysis to be reported in addition to the I77.0.

"Code First," "Use Additional Code," and "In Diseases Classified Elsewhere" Notes

This is referred to as the etiology/manifestation convention. When conditions have both an underlying etiology and multiple body system manifestations due to the underlying etiology or cause of an illness or disease, ICD-10-CM has a coding convention that requires the underlying condition be sequenced first followed by the **manifestation** or an obvious indication or specific evidence that a disease is present. There is a "use additional code" note at the etiology code, and a "code first" note at the manifestation code wherever such a combination exists. These instructional notes indicate the correct sequencing order of the codes. The etiology is first, followed by the manifestation.

manifestation: An obvious indication or specific evidence that a disease is present.

"And"

The word *and* should be interpreted to mean either "and" or "or" when it appears in a title.

"With"

The word *with* is to be interpreted as meaning "due to" or "associated with" when it appears in an instructional note in the tabular list or in a code title. The word *with* in the Alphabetic Index is sequenced immediately following the main term, not in alphabetical order.

Official Coding Guidelines:

In addition to the etiology/manifestation convention that requires two codes to fully describe a single condition that affects multiple body systems, there are other single conditions that also require more than one code. "Use additional code" notes are found in the tabular list at codes that are not part of an etiology/manifestation pair where a secondary code is useful to fully describe a condition. The sequencing rule is the same as the etiology/manifestation pair; "use additional code" indicates that a secondary code should be added.

For example, for bacterial infections that are not included in Chapter 1, a secondary code from category B95, Streptococcus, Staphylococcus, and Enterococcus, as the cause of diseases classified elsewhere, or B96, Other bacterial agents as the cause of diseases classified elsewhere, may be required to identify the bacterial organism causing the infection. A "use additional code" note will normally be found at the infectious disease code, indicating a need for the organism code to be added as a secondary code.

"Code first" notes are also under certain codes that are not specifically manifestation codes but may be due to an underlying cause. When there is a "code first" note and an underlying condition is present, the underlying condition should be sequenced first.

"Code, if applicable, any causal condition first," notes indicate that this code may be assigned as a principal diagnosis when the causal condition is unknown or not applicable. If a causal condition is known, then the code for that condition should be sequenced as the principal or first-listed diagnosis.

> **Highlight:**
>
> The code book frequently provides hints, such as "use additional code" or "code also" to let the coder know that more than one code is necessary. It is important that the coder use additional codes until all components of the diagnosis are fully described.

Abbreviations NEC (Not Elsewhere Classifiable) and NOS (Not Otherwise Specified)

NEC is an abbreviation that means not elsewhere classifiable. This means that a more specific category is not available in ICD-10-CM. In the diagnosis deafness, auditory fatigue, if the coder looks up the main term "deafness," there is a subterm of "auditory fatigue—see Deafness, specified type, NEC." Once you look this up, it shows code subcategory H91.8. In the tabular, subcategory H91.8 requires additional characters.

Official Coding Guidelines:

Codes labeled "other specified" (NEC—not elsewhere classifiable) or "unspecified" (NOS—not otherwise specified) are used only when neither the diagnostic statement nor a thorough review of the medical record provides adequate information to permit assignment of a more specific code.

Use the code assignment for "other" or NEC when the information at hand specifies a condition but no separate code for the condition is provided.

NOS stands for not otherwise specified. It should be interpreted as "unspecified" and is used when the coder has no further information available in the medical record to fully define the condition. Under code R56.9, Unspecified convulsions, one of the examples given is Seizure(s), (convulsions) not otherwise specified (NOS). If the coder had more information regarding the seizures, a more specific code could be appropriately used. If the documentation in the chart only stated "seizures," then code R56.9 would be the correct code assignment.

Official Coding Guidelines:

Other and Unspecified Codes

"Other" or "other specified" codes are used when the information in the medical record provides detail for which a specific code does not exist.

"Unspecified" codes are used when the information in the medical record is insufficient to assign a more specific code. In those categories where an unspecified code is not provided, the "other specified" code can be used.

Combination Codes

Official Coding Guidelines:

A combination code is a single code used to classify:

Two diagnoses, or

A diagnosis with an associated secondary process (manifestation)

A diagnosis with an associated complication

Combination codes are identified by referring to subterm entries in the Alphabetic Index and by reading the inclusion and exclusion notes in the tabular list.

Assign only the combination code when that code fully identifies the diagnostic conditions involved or when the Alphabetic Index so directs. Multiple coding should not be used when the classification provides a combination code that clearly identifies all of the elements documented in the diagnosis. When the combination code lacks necessary specificity in describing the manifestation or complication, an additional code should be used as a secondary code.

At times, the code book provides a combination code that identifies the entire diagnostic statement. For example, for the diagnosis of pneumonia with parainfluenza virus, when the coder looks up the main term "pneumonia," there is a subterm "with parainfluenza virus." Code J12.2 is all that is needed to code both conditions.

Some coders and providers continue to use a cheat sheet that lists many of the common diagnoses and procedures used in their facility or physician practices. While this may save time in coding some diagnoses, it can also lead to many coding errors. ICD-10-CM does provide many combination codes that are to be used when two diagnoses are both present. If a coder is simply reading the code from a cheat sheet, the instructions to use combination codes will not be located. This is also true in the case of a physician simply checking off diagnoses from a fee ticket, superbill, or other standardized coding form. The current CMS-1500 claim form can hold up to 12 ICD-10-CM diagnoses.

Review of the Basic Steps in Coding

To illustrate the steps in coding, the diagnostic statement of "acute cholecystitis with gallbladder calculus" is coded as follows:

1. *Identify the main term(s) of the condition(s) to be coded.*

   The main term is *cholecystitis. Calculus* can be a main term also.

2. *Locate the main terms in the Alphabetic Index.*

   Using the Alphabetic Index, locate the main term "Cholecystitis."

3. *Refer to any subterms indented under the main term.*

   This may be an extensive list, so it is important that the coder uses care in searching the listing. Also refer to any nonessential modifiers, instructional terms, or notes to select the most likely code.

   Next to the bolded main term cholecystitis, code K81.9 is listed. This is considered to be the "default" code. The default code is considered equivalent to the unspecified code. The terms for look-up are as follows:

   Cholecystitis K81.9

   > with
   >
   > > acute (emphysematous) (gangrenous) (suppurative) K81.0 with
   > >
   > > calculus, stones in
   > >
   > > > cystic duct—see Calculus, gallbladder, with cholecystitis, acute
   > > >
   > > > gallbladder—see Calculus, gallbladder, with cholecystitis, acute

   The next step is to review Calculus, gallbladder, with cholecystitis, which brings you to K80.10

   Following ICD-10-CM coding rules, the coder would verify the coding within the tabular list.

4. *Verify the code(s) in the tabular list.*

   The coder would go to the tabular list in numerical order to locate the code K80.10.

5. *Check all instructional terms in the tabular list and be sure to assign all codes to their highest degree of specificity.*

   The coder will find the actual code description for K80.10 as Calculus of gallbladder with chronic cholecystitis without obstruction. Additional terminology such as Cholelithiasis with cholecystitis NOS listed as a subterm under K80.10 provides the description similar to the Alphabetic Index.

6. *Continue coding the diagnostic statement until all of the elements are identified completely.*

   All parts of the diagnostic statement are identified by using this one (combination) code.

> **Coding Tip:**
>
> Notice the following fifth-digit subclassification with category K80.0:
>
> K80.00, Calculus of gallbladder with acute cholecystitis **without** obstruction K80.01, Calculus of gallbladder with acute cholecystitis **with** obstruction.

Exercise 2.2

Assign ICD-10-CM codes to the following diagnoses.

1. Migraine headache _____
2. Congestive heart failure _____
3. Diabetes mellitus, type 1 _____
4. Acute myocardial infarction, anterior wall, initial episode _____
5. Closed fracture of left hip, initial encounter in ED _____
6. Acute gastroenteritis _____
7. Barrett's esophageal ulcer, no bleeding _____
8. Chronic coronary insufficiency _____
9. Bell's palsy _____
10. Hypothyroidism _____
11. Urinary retention _____
12. Early onset Alzheimer's disease _____
13. AIDS _____
14. Syncope _____
15. Tension headache, not intractable _____
16. Acute tonsillitis _____
17. Pain left great toe _____
18. Epistaxis _____
19. Generalized anxiety disorder _____
20. Dermatomyositis _____

ICD-10-PCS: Procedural Coding with ICD-10-CM

ICD-10-PCS, or the International Classification of Diseases, Tenth Revision, Procedure Coding System, is used as a replacement for ICD-9-CM Volume 3 to code hospital inpatient procedures. ICD-10-CM codes are alphanumeric with all codes containing seven characters. ICD-10-CM procedure descriptions are described based on the procedure performed and do not contain any diagnostic information. The disease or diagnosis is described in the diagnosis coding, not in the procedure coding. ICD-10-PCS is not used in the physician's office/clinic setting. Procedures in these settings are coded using the *Current Procedural Terminology (CPT)*. This is discussed in Chapter 4 of this text.

Coding Signs and Symptoms

In many circumstances, the physician may initially not know what the patient's diagnosis is, so the coder may only be able to code the patient's signs and symptoms. It is important to understand the difference between signs and symptoms.

- A sign is visible evidence that the physician can determine objectively (e.g., overactive bowel sounds, laceration to the skin).

- A symptom is a subjective, descriptive term, usually in the patient's own words, such as, "My head hurts."

Exercise 2.3

In the following statements, identify each as a sign or a symptom.

1. Diaper rash _____
2. Chest pressure _____
3. Laceration of forehead _____
4. Fever _____
5. Strep throat _____
6. Swelling of right hand _____
7. Muscle cramping _____
8. Tachycardia _____
9. Abdominal pain _____
10. Elevated blood pressure _____

Coding Tip:

Signs and symptoms must be coded with care. If a sign or symptom is a common occurrence with a particular diagnosis, then it is not coded once the diagnosis has been made. For example, chest congestion is a sign of pneumonia. Only the pneumonia would be coded. In the outpatient setting, it is common to code signs and symptoms until a definitive diagnosis is made.

Official Coding Guidelines:

Conditions That Are an Integral Part of a Disease Process

Conditions that are integral to the disease process should not be assigned as additional codes.

Additional conditions that may not be associated routinely with a disease process should be coded when present.

If a sign or symptom occurs that is not a part of the usual disease process, then that condition is coded. For example, if the patient had a rash on the skin (R21) with gastroenteritis (K52.9), both diagnoses would be coded.

In the emergency room setting, the physician may not be able to make an exact diagnosis, and will recommend that the patient follow up with his or her primary care physician. In these cases, the documentation only substantiates coding of the patient's signs and symptoms. For example, if the patient is seen in the emergency department with dizziness, the ER physician will try to determine the etiology, but may not be able to find a definitive cause. He may refer the patient to an ear, nose, and throat specialist to see if there is an inner ear problem.

> **Official Coding Guidelines:**
>
> **Uncertain Diagnosis**
>
> If the diagnosis documented at the time of discharge is qualified as "probable," "suspected," "likely," "questionable," "possible," or "rule out," code the condition as if it existed or was established.

In hospital inpatient coding, conditions listed as "suspected," "rule out," or "possible" are coded as if the condition exists. In these cases, sometimes the physician will also want the signs and symptoms coded for use in further study.

> **Official Coding Guidelines:**
>
> **Outpatient Services**
>
> Do not code outpatient diagnoses documented as "probable," "suspected," "questionable," "rule out" (often documented as R/O). Rather, code the condition(s) to the highest degree of certainty for that encounter/visit, such as symptoms, signs, abnormal test results, or other reason for visit.
>
> Please note: This is contrary to the coding practices used by hospitals and medical records departments for coding the diagnosis of hospital inpatients.

In those instances where the physician or other health care professional does not document (identify) a definite condition or problem at the conclusion of a patient care encounter/visit, the coder should select the documented chief complaint(s) as the reason for the encounter/visit.

With physician office and outpatient/emergency room coding, the coder may only assign codes to the highest degree of certainty. In these situations, do not code suspected, ruled out, or possible conditions.

For example, if the patient had the diagnosis of "wheezing, rule out pneumonia," and was seen in the physician's office, the coder would only code the wheezing, R06.2. In the inpatient setting, the coder would code both the R06.2 and the J18.9 for the unspecified pneumonia.

Lab reports usually show "normal" values, and when searching through the patient's record, the coder may find a value that is not within normal range. If the patient's potassium level was a bit high, he or she might possibly have hyperkalemia. But the results may not be enough out of the normal limit range to really be significant. It is up to the physician to make this determination. The coder should ask the physician if this is truly hyperkalemia and should not code it without clarification and documentation by the physician with the ICD-10-CM code E87.5. It is important in ICD-10-CM that any findings and methods to rule out any conditions be documented. Abnormal findings in the chart are coded as a secondary code to indicate that these findings have a clinical significance. The coder may refer to "findings" in the alphabetic listing of ICD-10-CM to research the code related to an abnormal reading or value as documented within the medical record.

> **Coding Tip:**
>
> **Abnormal Findings**
>
> A general medical examination that results in an abnormal finding (laboratory, x-ray, pathologic, and other diagnostic results) should be coded as follows: The first-listed diagnosis is the general medical examination with a secondary code for the abnormal finding.

Exercise 2.4

Based on coding rules for outpatient/physician billing, code the following statements.

1. Abnormal EKG, R/O sick sinus syndrome _____
2. Chest pain, R/O myocardial infarction _____
3. Fever of unknown origin _____
4. Positive tuberculin skin test _____
5. Weight loss of undetermined etiology _____
6. Abnormal pulmonary function studies _____
7. Positive serology for HIV _____
8. Cervical pap smear with abnormal findings _____
9. Impaired glucose tolerance test, R/O diabetes _____
10. Positive throat culture, R/O strep _____

Coding Tip:

Bacteremia is the presence of bacteria in the blood, and is coded to R78.81. It can lead to sepsis/septicemia but is not necessarily the same thing.

Highlight:

Sepsis is a severe infection due to bacteria in the blood and is marked by high fever and chills, and can lead to shock and death. Usually, blood cultures (placing a sample of blood in a specially treated dish and watching the sample over a period of time to see if microorganisms grow from the specimen) are taken to determine the type of bacteria causing the severe infection.

Infections

Official Coding Guidelines:

Sepsis, Severe Sepsis, and Septic Shock

- For a diagnosis of sepsis, choose the appropriate code for the underlying systemic infection.

- Two codes are needed to code severe sepsis, first a code for the underlying infection, followed by a code from subcategory R65.2, severe sepsis.

- For sepsis and severe sepsis, if the agent cannot be determined, code A41.9 Sepsis, unspecified organism.

- Septic shock generally refers to circulatory failure associated with severe sepsis. Code the systematic infection first, followed by code R65.21, severe sepsis with septic shock or T81.12, post procedural septic shock. Acute organ dysfunctions would follow.

How to Locate the Code for a Microorganism

If a specific organism causing a patient condition is identified, and the code book directs the coder to "Use additional code, if desired, to identify organism," at times the code book does not give any hints as to where to look to find the code for the organism. The coder can look under the main term "infection" to locate the code for the organism, such as B96.20, *Escherichia coli* [*E. coli*].

For example, if the patient has the diagnosis of urinary tract infection, N39.0, there is a note following the description for code N39.0 in the tabular list of the code book that says, "Use additional code to identify organism, such as *Escherichia coli* [*E. coli*] (B96.20)."

HIV Infections

Human immunodeficiency infection is a condition caused by the human immunodeficiency virus (HIV). This condition gradually destroys the immune system, making it more difficult for the body to fight infections. HIV can be spread through sexual contact and through blood such as in transfusions, accidental needlesticks, or sharing of needles for intravenous drug use. HIV can also be transmitted from a mother to her fetus through shared blood circulation, or to her baby through breast milk. Persons infected with HIV may have no symptoms for up to 10 years, but can still pass the infection on to others. After exposure to the virus, it can take up to three months for the blood test for HIV to change from HIV negative to HIV positive.

Acquired immune deficiency syndrome (AIDS) is a disease of the human immune system caused by HIV. HIV is a chronic medical condition that can be treated but not yet cured. People infected with HIV will develop AIDS if left untreated.

When coding HIV and AIDS, it is important to review the medical record documentation carefully for accurate diagnosis. Physician-documented HIV illness or disease is coded B20. Never use a code from category R75 or Z71 after HIV has been documented. If someone is HIV positive without any symptoms or conditions of HIV infection, the code is Z21. Exposure to someone with HIV is coded Z20.6.

> **Highlight:**
> Whenever dealing with a possible diagnosis of HIV or AIDS, the coder should take extreme care to verify the accuracy of the diagnosis. The coder should always remember the patient behind the codes and must realize that a wrong code placed on a patient's chart can affect the patient's insurance coverage, employment, and life.

Official Coding Guidelines:

Code Only Confirmed Cases of HIV Infection/Illness

In this context, "confirmation" does not require documentation of positive serology or culture for HIV; the physician's diagnostic statement that the patient is HIV positive, or has an HIV-related illness, is sufficient.

Official Coding Guidelines:

Selection of HIV Code

B20 Human Immunodeficiency Virus [HIV] Disease/Infection

Patients with an HIV-related illness should be coded to B20, Human immunodeficiency virus [HIV] disease/infection.

Z21 Asymptomatic Human Immunodeficiency Virus (HIV) Infection

Patients with physician-documented asymptomatic HIV infections who have never had an HIV-related illness should be coded to Z21, Asymptomatic human immunodeficiency virus [HIV] infection.

R75 Inconclusive Laboratory Evidence of Human Immunodeficiency Virus [HIV]

Code R75, Inconclusive evidence of human immunodeficiency virus [HIV], should be used for patients (including infants) with inconclusive HIV test results.

Previously Diagnosed HIV-Related Illness

Patients with any known prior diagnosis of an HIV-related illness should be coded to B20. Once a patient has developed an HIV-related illness, the patient

(continues)

should always be assigned code B20 on every subsequent admission. Patients previously diagnosed with any HIV illness (B20) should never be assigned to R75 or Z21.

Sequencing

The circumstances of admission govern the selection of principal diagnosis for patients with HIV-related illnesses. In other words, "that condition established after study to be chiefly responsible for occasioning the admission of the patient to the hospital for care."

Patients who are admitted for an HIV-related illness should be assigned a minimum of two codes: First assign code B20 to identify the HIV disease and then sequence additional codes to identify the other diagnoses.

If a patient is admitted for an HIV-related condition, the principal diagnosis should be B20, followed by additional diagnosis codes for all reported HIV-related conditions.

If a patient with HIV disease is admitted for an unrelated condition (such as a traumatic injury), the code for the unrelated condition (e.g., the nature of injury code) should be the principal diagnosis. Other diagnoses would be B20 followed by additional diagnosis codes for all reported HIV-related conditions.

Whether the patient is newly diagnosed or has had previous admissions for HIV conditions (or has expired) is irrelevant to the sequencing decision.

HIV Infections in Pregnancy, Childbirth, and Puerperium

During pregnancy, childbirth, or the puerperium, a patient admitted because of an HIV-related illness should receive a principal diagnosis of O98.7-, Other specified infectious and parasitic disease in the mother classifiable elsewhere, but complicating the pregnancy, childbirth, or the puerperium, followed by B20 and the code(s) for the HIV-related illness(es). This is an exception to the sequencing rule stated in the previous HIV code information.

Patients with asymptomatic HIV infection status admitted during pregnancy, childbirth, or the puerperium should receive codes of O98.7- and Z21.

Asymptomatic HIV Infection

Z21, Asymptomatic human immunodeficiency virus (HIV) infection, is to be applied when the patient without any documentation of symptoms is listed as being HIV positive, known HIV, HIV test positive, or similar terminology. Do not use this code if the term AIDS is used or if the patient is treated for any HIV-related illness or is described as having any condition(s) resulting from his/her HIV positive status; use code B20 in these cases.

Encounters for Testing for HIV

Z11.4, Encounter for screening for human immunodeficiency virus (HIV). Additional codes may be assigned for associated high-risk behavior.

Patients with inconclusive HIV serology, but no definitive diagnosis or manifestations of the illness, may be assigned code R75.

If a patient with signs or symptoms is being seen for HIV testing, code the signs and symptoms. An additional counseling code, Z71.7, may be used if counseling is provided during the encounter for the test.

(continues)

When the patient returns to be informed of his/her HIV test results, use code Z71.7, HIV counseling, if the results of the test are negative. If the results are positive but the patient is asymptomatic, use code Z21, Asymptomatic HIV infection. If the results are positive and the patient is symptomatic, use code B20, HIV infection, with codes for the HIV-related symptoms or diagnosis. The HIV counseling code may also be used if counseling is provided for patients with positive test results.

Circulatory System Coding

Chapter 9 of this text covers cardiology in detail. Please refer to that chapter for more information on coding cardiovascular diseases and procedures.

There are many instructional notes used in the circulatory chapter of ICD-10-CM. The coder should review these notes and assign these codes with care.

Hypertension

Hypertension is defined as an increase in systolic blood pressure and in diastolic blood pressure. Benign hypertension is considered to be mild and usually under control with medication. Malignant hypertension is a life-threatening, severe form of hypertension. ICD-10-CM now classifies Essential (primary) hypertension to include descriptions of high blood pressure, hypertension described as arterial, benign, essential, malignant, primary, and systemic with the ICD-10-CM code of I10, Hypertension.

Official Coding Guidelines:

Hypertension with Heart Disease

Certain heart conditions classified to I50.- or I51.4–I51.9 are assigned to a code from category I11 when a causal relationship is stated (due to hypertension) or implied (hypertensive). Use only the code from category I11. Use an additional code from I50, Heart failure, to identify the type of heart failure in those patients with heart failure.

The same heart conditions (I50.-, I51.4–I51.9) with hypertension, but without a stated causal relationship, are coded separately. Sequence according to the circumstances of the admission or encounter.

Coding Tip:

ICD-10-CM makes a distinction between diagnoses "with hypertension" and "due to hypertension." Hypertensive should be interpreted as "due to hypertension" and coded appropriately.

If the patient has CHF (congestive heart failure) due to hypertensive heart disease, the correct code is I11.0, hypertensive heart disease with congestive heart failure, since the causal relationship is specified by the words "due to." Congestive heart failure, with hypertension, on the other hand, would be coded I50.9 and I10 since no causal relationship is stated.

When a patient is diagnosed with hypertensive chronic kidney disease, assign codes from I12 and a condition classifiable to category N18, chronic kidney disease (CKD). Unlike hypertension with heart disease, ICD-10-CM presumes a cause-and-effect relationship and classified chronic kidney disease with hypertension as hypertensive chronic kidney disease.

When both hypertension and chronic kidney disease is documented in the diagnosis, assign codes from category I13, Hypertensive chronic kidney disease (CKD). ICD-10-CM assumes a causal relationship. Code also the stage of CKD from category, N18. If acute renal failure is also documented, assign a code from category N17.

Official Coding Guidelines:

Hypertensive Chronic Kidney Disease

Assign codes from category I12, Hypertensive chronic kidney disease, when conditions classified to category N18, Chronic kidney disease are present. Unlike hypertension with heart disease, ICD-10-CM presumes a cause-and-effect relationship and classifies chronic kidney disease with hypertension as hypertensive chronic kidney disease. Acute renal failure is not included in this cause-and-effect relationship. If a patient has hypertensive chronic kidney disease and acute renal failure, an additional code is required for the acute renal failure.

Official Coding Guidelines:

Hypertensive Heart and Chronic Kidney Disease

Assign codes from combination category I13, Hypertensive heart and chronic kidney disease, when both hypertensive kidney disease and hypertensive heart disease are stated in the diagnosis. Assume a relationship between the hypertension and the chronic kidney disease, whether or not the condition is so designated. If heart failure is present, assign an additional code from category I50 to identify the type of heart failure.

If the patient's diagnosis is renal sclerosis with hypertension, the coder goes to the main term "sclerosis," subterm "renal" "with hypertension (*see also* hypertension, kidney)" and assigns I12.9. No causal relationship must be stated to use this combination code.

Official Coding Guidelines:

Hypertensive Retinopathy

Two codes are necessary to identify the condition. Subcategory H35.0, Background retinopathy and retinal vascular changes should be used with a code from category I10-I15 to include the systemic hypertension. The sequencing is based on the reason for the encounter.

Hypertension Secondary

Secondary hypertension is due to an underlying condition requiring two codes: One to identify the underlying etiology and one from category I10–I15 to identify the hypertension. Sequencing of codes is determined by the reason for the admission or encounter.

Secondary hypertension is different from essential hypertension. Secondary hypertension is due to a disease, such as primary renal disease (I15.1), or other specified (I15.8,).

> **Coding Tip:**
>
> For transient hypertension, assign code R03.0, Elevated blood pressure reading without diagnosis of hypertension, unless patient has an established diagnosis of hypertension. Assign code from category O13.- for gestational hypertension of pregnancy.

Transient means the condition existed only temporarily, based on an elevated blood pressure reading without diagnosis of hypertension, unless the patient has an established diagnosis of hypertension. This would be coded R03.0, Elevated blood pressure reading without diagnosis of hypertension. Transient or gestational hypertension with a subterm "of pregnancy" is to be coded as O13.- for gestational hypertension.

transient: Short-term or disappearing after a short amount of time.

This diagnostic statement usually refers to an existing state of hypertension under control if the patient is currently taking medication or receiving treatment for the hypertension.

> **Coding Tip:**
>
> For controlled hypertension, assign appropriate code from categories I10–I15. This diagnostic statement usually refers to an existing state of hypertension under control by therapy.

> **Coding Tip:**
>
> Uncontrolled hypertension may refer to untreated hypertension or hypertension not responding to current therapeutic regimen. In either case, assign the appropriate code from categories I10–I15 to designate the state and type of hypertension. Code to the type of hypertension.

Sometimes circumstances such as a trauma cause a patient's blood pressure to go up. If the patient has a high blood pressure reading without being diagnosed as having hypertension, coders should assign code R03.0, as indicated in transient hypertension.

> **Coding Tip:**
>
> For a statement of elevated blood pressure without further specificity, assign code R03.0, Elevated blood pressure reading without diagnosis of hypertension, rather than a code from category I10 (essential hypertension).

Myocardial Infarctions

Acute myocardial infarction (AMI) is considered to be in the acute phase during the first four weeks following the infarction. ICD-10-CM defines this as ST elevation myocardial infarction (STEMI) and non-ST elevation myocardial infarction (NSTEMI). The site must be identified, such as anterolateral wall or true posterior wall. For encounters occurring while the myocardial infarction is equal to or less than four weeks old, including transfers to another acute setting or a postacute setting, and the patient requires continued care for the myocardial infarction, codes from category I21 may be reported. After the four-week time frame and the patient is still receiving care related to the myocardial infarction, the appropriate aftercare code should be assigned, rather than a code from category I21. For old or healed myocardial infarctions not requiring further care, code 125.2, Old myocardial infarction, may be assigned.

The physician should specify the site of the MI for proper code assignment. A code of Myocardial infarction, unspecified, may be rejected by the carrier as a nonspecific principal diagnosis. The coder can look at the EKG reports to see if the location is documented in the report, but the site must be verified with the physician.

Another test to look for in documenting an MI is the serum enzyme lab tests (CK, CK-MB, LD). These tests rise and fall at predictable intervals following an MI, and will be ordered and done at specific intervals according to the approximate age of the MI. They may be negative if the patient waits to seek treatment. Elevation of the cardiac enzymes may be indicative of an MI. Again, documentation by the physician or other qualified health care professional is needed.

A previous myocardial infarction is coded to I25.2 when the physician states history of healed or old myocardial infarction presenting no symptoms during the current treatment. If the chart states "history of myocardial infarction," it is always considered relevant and should be coded to I25.2.

If the patient has a previous MI and presents with symptoms of a new AMI within the four-week time frame of the initial AMI, a code from category I22, Subsequent ST elevation (STEMI) and non-ST elevation (NSTEMI) myocardial infarction is assigned in conjunction with a code from category I21.

ICD-10-CM does contain additional codes to identify the following:

- Exposure to environmental tobacco smoke (Z77.22)
- History of tobacco use (Z87.891)
- Occupational exposure to environmental tobacco smoke (Z57.31)
- Tobacco dependence (F17.-)
- Tobacco use (Z72.0)

Angina

Angina pectoris is chest pain with cardiac origin. All chest pains should not be coded to the angina category. Unstable angina should be coded only when documented by the physician, and is also known as "pre-infarct angina." This diagnosis should not be coded with documented evidence of myocardial infarction.

Congestive Heart Failure

Congestive heart failure (CHF) is the condition where the heart cannot pump the required amount of blood, causing fluid buildup in the lungs and other areas, including the lower extremities. One common medication for patients with CHF is Lasix, a diuretic that helps the body rid itself of excessive fluid.

Cerebrovascular Disease

Cerebrovascular disease is coded according to the type of condition, including hemorrhage, occlusion, and other cerebrovascular disease. Category I67.81, Acute cerebrovascular insufficiency, is used only when the diagnosis is stated as cerebrovascular accident (CVA) without further mention of cause. ICD-10-CM code I63.9 is used to indicate a cerebral infarction or stroke that is unspecified.

If the physician lists the diagnosis as CVA, the coder should check the chart for further information as to the cause of the CVA (stroke). A cerebrovascular accident may be caused by many problems, including the following:

- Subarachnoid hemorrhage—A hemorrhage into the subarachnoid space
- Intracerebral hemorrhage—A hemorrhage within the brain
- Subdural hematoma—A localized collection of hemorrhaged blood in the subdural space
- Occlusion—Decreased blood flow of the arteries that supply the brain tissues
- Cerebral thrombosis—An abnormal collection of blood causing an obstruction in the arteries supplying the brain with blood
- Cerebral embolism—Obstruction of the arteries that supply the brain, caused by a blood clot coming from elsewhere in the body

The coder should review the chart for documentation of the cause of a CVA before using code I63.9. This code is considered to be a nonspecific diagnosis and should not be used when a more specific cause can be identified.

> **Coding Tip:**
>
> The codes in category G45.9 are for transient cerebral ischemia (TIA), temporary decreased blood flow to the brain. The symptoms for a TIA are the same as for a CVA, except that the symptoms disappear after about 24 hours. The codes for TIA and CVA should not be used together in a single hospital episode, unless there are two distinct episodes. (For example, the patient had a TIA with symptoms clearing, then four days later had a full-blown CVA.) The coder should be alerted to check with the physician prior to coding both codes.

> **Coding Tip:**
>
> **Coding Clinic Note: Sequelae (Late Effect) of Cerebrovascular Disease**
>
> Category I69 is used to indicate conditions classifiable to categories I60–I67 as the causes of late effects or sequelae (neurologic deficits). The "late effects" include neurologic deficits that persist after initial onset of conditions classifiable to I60–I67. Unlike other late effects, the neurologic deficits caused by cerebrovascular disease are present from the onset rather than arising months later.
>
> Codes from category I69 that specify hemiplegia, hemiparesis, and monoplegia identify whether the dominant or nondominant side is affected.

ICD-10-CM codes in category I69 include the type of residuals (current condition) or sequelae within the code. A code such as I69.841 is for late effects, following cerebrovascular disease, monoplegia of lower limb affecting right dominant side.

Exercise 2.5

Using the ICD-10-CM code book, assign the correct diagnosis code(s) to the following six scenarios.

1. The patient was in the hospital with hemiplegia and aphasia due to acute CVA caused by subarachnoid hemorrhage as noted on CT scan of brain done on admission. On discharge, the aphasia had cleared, but the hemiplegia is present affecting the left dominant side and will require home care.

   Diagnoses: _____

2. The patient was admitted with a two-day history of intolerable abdominal pain. The diagnosis of acute cholecystitis with cholelithiasis was made. The patient is on medication for hypertension, chronic rheumatoid arthritis, and type 2 diabetes. She also had a coronary angioplasty with implant and graft last April. Treatment was laparoscopically assisted cholecystectomy. Patient was discharged two days post-op to be followed by the surgeon in two weeks.

   Diagnoses: _____

3. Mr. Jones came to the clinic today because he was feeling weak and has seen a decrease in urine output over the last two days and has not been able to keep any food down. He is HIV-positive, but has been asymptomatic. Lab results indicate dehydration and gastroenteritis. I am going to send him over to the hospital to be admitted for IV treatment of the dehydration.

   Diagnoses: _____

4. Note to Home Health Nurse: Ms. Swanson is ready to be discharged from the hospital to go home. We have treated her in the hospital for pneumococcal pneumonia due to her AIDS and this is better

   but not completely resolved yet, but she insists on going home. She also has Kaposi's sarcoma of the skin due to AIDS.

   Diagnoses: _____

5.	**Discharge Summary**

History of Present Illness:

The patient is a 54-year-old black male with a five-day history of feeling ill. When his daughter went by his house today to check on him, she found him clammy with a fever and very disoriented. Lab results in the ER showed UTI, probable sepsis, renal insufficiency. BUN, creatinine elevated. WBC was 23,000. The patient was admitted for treatment of probable urinary sepsis.

Findings While in Hospital:

WBCs fell during hospitalization to 9,000. Urine culture grew *E. coli,* blood cultures also grew out *E. coli.* No other abnormalities noted.

Hospital Course:

The patient was started on IV fluid rehydration; electrolytes improved throughout stay. He was started on IV antibiotics and was switched to oral antibiotics the day of discharge. The patient was discharged to his daughter's care at her home until he gets back on his feet again.

Diagnoses: _____

(continues)

Exercise 2.5 (*continued*)

6.   **Discharge Summary**

History of Present Illness:

The patient, a 53-year-old Caucasian male, was admitted through the emergency room with un-stable angina pectoris, diaphoresis, and pain radiating to the left arm. The patient had a previous MI three years ago.

Hospital Course:

Cardiac enzymes were done at 12, 24, and 36 hours and were elevated. Serial EKGs were per-formed, which confirmed the diagnosis of AMI, inferolateral wall. A left cardiac catheterization was performed on the first day of hospitalization with findings of the LAD blocked at 95% and second artery blocked at 100%. We then scheduled the patient for bypass. On the second hospital day he had an aortocoronary bypass, two coronary arteries performed successfully. After two days in CCU, the patient was transferred to a regular hospital bed. The patient was discharged after uneventful recovery period on the sixth day of hospitalization.

Diagnoses: _____

Diabetes Mellitus

Diabetes mellitus is one of the most common diseases of the endocrine system, and one that coders have many problems coding. ICD-10-CM codes E00-E89 include Endocrine, Nutritional, and Metabolic Diseases, which includes diabetes mellitus. These codes are combination codes that include the type of diabetes, the body system affected, and the complications affecting that body system.

diabetes mellitus: A metabolic disease of the endocrine system in which the body does not produce enough insulin, or the cells do not respond to the insulin that is produced.

Diabetes mellitus is a disorder of the pancreas in which the beta cells of the islets of Langerhans of the pancreas fail to produce an adequate amount of insulin, resulting in the body's inability to appropriately metabolize carbohydrates, fats, and proteins. There are three main types of diabetes mellitus:

Type 1 diabetes mellitus results from the body's failure to produce insulin and requires the patient to inject insulin. (It was previously referred to as insulin-dependent diabetes mellitus [IDDM]) and juvenile diabetes.) Type 1, or juvenile type, diabetes mellitus is an autoimmune disease that usually appears in childhood but can occur at any age. This condition is due to genetic factors when the pancreas does not produce insulin in sufficient quantities to regulate blood glucose levels, thus making the patient dependent on insulin or an insulin pump on a regular basis to survive.

Long-term or current use of insulin is indicated by ICD-10-CM code Z79.4. This code is not assigned if insulin is prescribed temporarily to bring a type 2 patient's blood sugar under control during an encounter.

Type 2 diabetes mellitus results from insulin resistance when the cells fail to use the insulin properly. (It was previously referred to as non-insulin-dependent diabetes mellitus [NIDDM] and adult-onset diabetes.) Type 2 diabetes mellitus is a metabolic disorder in which the pancreas does not make enough insulin or use it efficiently. This condition results in insulin resistance when the body produces insulin but the body's cells do not respond appropriately to the insulin. Its etiology is considered to be environmental and it is usually controlled by diet, exercise, and oral medications. The type 2 patient sometimes must be given injections of insulin, but is not dependent on the insulin to survive.

If the type of diabetes is not documented in the medical record, ICD-10-CM code E11.-, Type 2 diabetes, is assigned as a default code.

Gestational diabetes is when pregnant women who have never been diagnosed with diabetes before have a high blood glucose level during pregnancy. In many cases, this condition ends when the pregnancy ends, although it may precede type 2 diabetes mellitus. Gestational diabetes is coded O24.419.

In the event of an abnormal glucose blood test, code R73.09 is assigned until further testing may be ordered to further investigate the possibility of diabetes. It is important not to code diabetes until documentation from the physician is determined. Hyperglycemia is coded R73.9 and hypoglycemia E16.2.

Diabetes insipidus is a metabolic disorder characterized by extreme thirst and increased urination. This is a disorder of the pituitary gland due to a deficiency in the secretion of the antidiuretic hormone. The code for diabetes insipidus is located by researching under "diabetes," then locating "insipidus" under that description.

> **Coding Tip:**
>
> When coding "elevated" or "abnormal" glucose or glucose tolerance test (GTT), refer to "Findings" in the Alphabetic Index of ICD-10-CM. Diabetes should never be coded in these cases until a definitive diagnosis is determined by the physician

Secondary Diabetes Mellitus

Secondary diabetes is a relatively uncommon condition caused by factors other than genetics or environmental factors, and is usually related to other disease processes, past surgical history, or drug therapy.

Coders will still be required to code the specific manifestation of the disease (e.g., diabetic nephropathy or ketoacidosis), whether it is documented to be controlled or uncontrolled, and also the underlying cause of the disease, which requires specific documentation by the physician or medical provider.

The major difference in coding secondary diabetes is the presence of another underlying condition that is determined to be the cause of the diabetes. Examples include:

- Chronic pancreatitis, hemochromatitis (excessive absorption of iron), pancreatic damage due to malnutrition, and other endocrine disorders

- Endocrine disorders such as Cushing's syndrome, hyperthyroidism, and conditions involving excessive levels of growth hormones

- Liver diseases, such as hepatitis C

- Some carcinoid tumors of the lungs, intestines, or stomach, including tumors of the pituitary and adrenal glands where the hormone cortisol is overproduced

- Celiac disease and other autoimmune disorders

- The use of drugs and chemical agents including:

  ○ Antihypertensive diuretics and beta blockers

  ○ Hormone supplements such as estrogen, oral and injected contraceptives, growth hormones, anabolic steroids, and hormones such as those prescribed for prostate cancer

  ○ Antipsychotics, lithium, and some antidepressants

  ○ Antiretrovirals such as drugs used in the treatment of HIV

  ○ Anticonvulsants

- ○ Chemotherapy drugs
- ○ Immunosuppressives, including corticosteroids
- Surgical treatments such as:
  - ○ Pancreatectomy, mainly performed for pancreatic cancer or severe pancreatic disease
  - ○ Orchiectomy performed for testicular cancer or as hormonal drug therapy in the treatment of prostate cancer

These codes are found in the E09.- series of codes located under the Diabetes section of ICD-10-CM and are indicated by "due to drug or chemical or underlying condition."

Exercise 2.6

Using the ICD-10-CM code book, assign code(s) to the following statements.

1. Diabetic gangrene _____
2. Type 2 diabetic with skin ulcer _____
3. Type 2 diabetes mellitus with Kimmelstiel-Wilson disease _____
4. Type 1 diabetes with cataracts _____
5. Diabetes mellitus with type 1 diabetic nephrosis _____
6. Retinal hemorrhage in patient with type 1 diabetes _____
7. Type 1 diabetes mellitus with ketoacidosis _____
8. Gestational diabetes in otherwise nondiabetic woman _____
9. Diabetes in patient second trimester of pregnancy _____
10. Hypoglycemia coma in patient without diabetes _____
11. Diabetes insipidus _____
12. Diabetic nephropathy due to underlying chronic pancreatitis _____
13. Abnormal glucose tolerance test (GTT) _____
14. Diabetes mellitus due to underlying condition with unspecified diabetic retinopathy with macular edema _____
15. Diabetes mellitus, type 2, proliferative retinopathy _____

Using Z Codes (Z00-Z99)

Z codes include factors influencing health status and contact with health services, and can be used as principal and secondary diagnoses. Z codes are used when a person who is not currently sick uses health care services, such as need for a vaccination, or checkup, or when a problem affects the patient's current illness, such as a history of carcinoma, or status post-coronary artery bypass graft. Sometimes it is difficult to locate a needed Z code because of the main terms used in ICD-10-CM. Many common main terms to locate Z codes are as follows:

Admission for, Attention to, Examination, Follow up, History of, Observation for, Screening, Status post, Supervision, Testing

If the patient uses medical facilities and does not have a medical diagnosis, the Z code can be used as the principal or first listed diagnosis. For example, a mother comes in for a six-week checkup following delivery and has no problems. Code Z39.2, Routine postpartum follow-up, is assigned.

Z53.20 is used when a procedure is not done because of the patient's decision. The coder can locate this code in the Alphabetic Index of Diseases by looking under the main term "procedure." Following "procedure," the next term indented is "not done," followed by "because of" and then patient's decision.

To code a patient's encounter for a screening mammogram, use either code Z12.31, Encounter for screening mammogram for malignant neoplasm of breast, or Z12.39, Encounter for other screening for malignant neoplasm of the breast. Any abnormality found on the screening mammogram, such as a lump, should be listed as a secondary diagnosis.

Code a patient encounter for a preprocedural examination using a code from the category Z01.81- as the first diagnosis. The reason for the surgery should be assigned as an additional diagnosis.

If a past condition might affect the current treatment, the Z code can be used as a secondary diagnosis, such as Z98.1, Arthrodesis status (surgical fixation of a joint) or Z98.61.

The use of certain Z codes for encounters for general medical examinations provide code selection for with and without abnormal findings. Should the provider discover an abnormal finding, the abnormal finding would be listed as a secondary code.

For example, a suspicious lesion on the face of a 49-year-old male was found during a routine, general medical exam. The physician diagnosed the condition as actinic keratosis and treated the lesion. Code Z00.01, Encounter for general adult medical examination with abnormal findings, would be used along with the actinic keratosis diagnoses code, L57.1. The appropriate CPT codes would be linked to the corresponding diagnosis code (i.e., 99386 linked to Z00.01 and 17000 linked to L57.1). Z codes are used to distinguish a patient's *exposure* to a disease or condition, and to indicate the disease or condition itself has not been diagnosed. For example, a patient is seen and tested for exposure to HIV. The patient at this point is not diagnosed with HIV, but, rather, the exposure to the disease. The main term to research in the ICD-10-CM code is "exposure," which guides the coder to Z20.6, Contact with and (suspected) exposure to human immunodeficiency virus [HIV].

Highlight:

Check with local carriers as to individual preferences for diagnosis coding of preadmission testing or preoperative examinations, as these may vary by insurance carrier.

Official Coding Guidelines:

Contact/Exposure

Category Z20 indicates contact with, and suspected exposure to, communicable diseases. These codes are for patients who do not show any sign or symptom of a disease but are suspected to have been exposed to it by close personal contact with an infected individual or are in an area where a disease is epidemic.

Category Z77, Other contact with and (suspected) exposures hazardous to health, indicates contact with and suspected exposures hazardous to health.

Contact/exposure codes may be used as a first-listed code to explain an encounter for testing, or, more commonly, as a secondary code to identify a potential risk.

(continues)

Official Outpatient Coding Guidelines—Excerpt

K. Patients receiving diagnostic services only

For patients receiving diagnostic services only during an encounter/visit, sequence first the diagnosis, condition, problem, or other reason for encounter/visit shown in the medical record to be chiefly responsible for the outpatient services provided during the encounter/visit. Codes for other diagnoses (e.g., chronic conditions) may be sequenced as additional diagnoses.

For encounters for routine laboratory/radiology testing in the absence of any signs, symptoms, or associated diagnosis, assign Z01.89, Encounter for other specified special examinations. If routine testing is performed during the same encounter as a test to evaluate a sign, symptom, or diagnosis, it is appropriate to assign both the Z code and the code describing the reason for the non-routine test.

For outpatient encounters for diagnostic tests that have been interpreted by a physician, and the final report is available at the time of coding, code any confirmed or definitive diagnosis(es) documented in the interpretation. Do not code related signs and symptoms as additional diagnoses.

Please note: This differs from the coding practice in the hospital inpatient setting regarding abnormal findings on test results.

L. Patients receiving therapeutic services only

For patients receiving therapeutic services only during an encounter/visit, sequence first the diagnosis, condition, problem, or other reason for encounter/visit shown in the medical record to be chiefly responsible for the outpatient services provided during the encounter/visit. Codes for other diagnoses (e.g., chronic conditions) may be sequenced as additional diagnoses.

The only exception to this rule is that when the primary reason for the admission/encounter is chemotherapy or radiation therapy, the appropriate Z code for the service is listed first, and the diagnosis or problem for which the service is being performed listed second.

ICD-10-CM Official Guidelines list Z codes that may only be reported as the principal or first-listed diagnosis, except when there are multiple encounters on the same day and the encounters are combined or when more than one Z code meets the definition of principal diagnosis. For example, a patient is admitted to home health care for both aftercare and rehabilitation and both are equally presented for the definition of principal diagnosis.

Nonspecific Z Codes/categories

According to ICD-10-CM Official Coding Guidelines, "Certain Z codes are so nonspecific, or potentially redundant with other codes in the classification, that there can be little justification for their use in the inpatient setting. Their use in the outpatient setting should be limited to those instances when there is no further documentation to permit more precise coding. Otherwise, any sign or symptom or any other reason for the visit that is captured in another code should be used." These categories/codes are:

Z02.9	Encounter for administrative examinations, unspecified
Z04.9	Encounter for examination and observation for unspecified reason
Z13.9	Encounter for screening, unspecified
Z41.9	Encounter for procedure for purposes other than remedying health state, unspecified
Z52.9	Donor of unspecified organ or tissue
Z86.59	Personal history of other mental and behavioral disorders
Z88.9	Allergy status to unspecified drugs, medicaments and biological substances status
Z92.0	Personal history of contraception

First-Listed/Principal Diagnosis

The following are Z codes/categories that are only acceptable as first listed or principal diagnosis. This means they should only be listed as first (primary or principal) diagnoses, never as secondary diagnoses.

Z00–Z04, (except Z00.6), Z33.2, Z31.81, Z31.82, Z31.83, Z31.84, Z34, Z38, Z39, Z42, Z51.0-Z51.1, Z52, Z76.1, Z76.2 and Z99.12.

Exercise 2.7

Assign the Z code from ICD-10-CM to the following statements.

1. Physical exam required for nursing school _____
2. Family history of colon cancer _____
3. Exposure to SARS, a communicable viral disease _____
4. Diaphragm fitting _____
5. Family history of ischemic heart disease _____
6. Personal history of allergy to penicillin _____
7. Normal pregnancy visit without complications _____
8. Annual pelvic exam including Pap smear _____
9. Influenza vaccination _____
10. Six-month well-baby check _____
11. Screening for osteoporosis _____
12. Contact with anthrax _____
13. Marriage counseling _____
14. Exposure to blood-tainted emesis while at work _____
15. Blood-alcohol testing _____

Obstetrical Coding

Obstetrical (OB) coding can be quite challenging to some coders. The ICD-10-CM Chapter 15 is dedicated to "Pregnancy, Childbirth, and the Puerperium." This section of codes takes sequencing precedence over all the other chapters of diagnostic coding.

Many conditions that are normally coded in different chapters are considered complications of pregnancy, so they are reclassified to the pregnancy chapter when the patient is pregnant. It is the provider's responsibility according to the guidelines to state that the condition that is being treated is not related to the pregnancy. When this documentation is found, coder's are instructed to use the code of Z33.1, Pregnant state, incidental. Conditions that complicate or are associated with pregnancy are normally listed under the main terms: pregnancy, labor, delivery, puerperium. See Chapter 10 of this book for more information on coding OB procedures and diagnosis.

All ICD-10-CM codes start with the letter "O." These codes are to be used only on the mother's record, not on the newborn's. The majority of codes in the obstetrical section of ICD-10-CM require a final character, which indicates the trimester of pregnancy. The time frames for each trimester can be found at the beginning of the OB Chapter 15 of ICD-10-CM, directly above the chapter blocks.

Trimesters are counted from the first day of the last menstrual period. They are defined as follows:

1st trimester: less than 14 weeks 0 days

2nd trimester: 14 weeks 0 days to less than 28 weeks 0 days

3rd trimester: 28 weeks 0 days until delivery

An additional *gestational age by weeks* code is required to identify the week of the pregnancy. This code is selected from category Z3A, which can be found right after code Z36. When coding from category Z3A, instructions within the section direct the coder to code first any complications of pregnancy, childbirth, and the puerperium.

Official Coding Guidelines:

Selection of trimester for inpatient admissions that encompass more than one trimester

In instances when a patient is admitted to a hospital for complications of pregnancy during one trimester and remains in the hospital into a subsequent trimester, the trimester character for the antepartum complication code should be assigned on the basis of the trimester when the complication developed, not the trimester of the discharge. If the condition developed prior to the current admission/encounter or represents a preexisting condition, the trimester character for the trimester at the time of the admission/encounter should be assigned.

For example, for an insulin-dependent diabetic pregnant patient in her fourth week of pregnancy visiting her physician for the first time, the coder would begin under the main term "pregnancy," subterm "complicated by," "diabetes (mellitus) (conditions classifiable to E10 category)." The principal or first diagnosis listed would be O24.011, Preexisting diabetes mellitus, type 1, in pregnancy, first trimester. There is a note following category O24.0- that reminds the coder to "Use additional code from category E10 to further identify any manifestations." This means that both codes are needed to fully identify the patient's condition. For example, code E10.9 would be used as a secondary diagnosis if there were no complications with the type I diabetes. A third code, Z3A.01 is used to indicate the gestation is less than 8 weeks.

Coding Nonobstetric Conditions

If a woman is pregnant, the treatment decisions for a nonobstetric condition may be different because of the pregnancy. To locate these conditions, the coder should look in the alphabetic section under "Pregnancy, complicated by." If the specific condition cannot be found, and it does affect the pregnancy, then the coder should use a code from category O99, Other maternal diseases classifiable elsewhere, but complicating pregnancy, childbirth and the puerperium, should be used in conjunction with the nonobstetric condition. If a physician treating the nonobstetric condition uses the appropriate codes from the pregnancy chapter, and provides sufficient documentation in the patient's chart, it will indicate that the patient's condition was complicated by the pregnancy. This complication increases the amount of effort, and could increase the number of treatment options for the patient, possibly warranting justification for additional or a higher level of service in CPT.

Code O80

Code O80 is for delivery in a completely normal case, and cannot be used in conjunction with any other code in the pregnancy chapter. This code can only be used when the following criteria are met:

1. Liveborn

2. Term (37 completed weeks but less than 42)

3. Single, normal vaginal birth

4. No complications

5. No instrumentation except episiotomy or artificial rupture of membranes

6. Cephalic or vertex presentation

7. No fetal manipulation (turning or version of the fetus)

If the delivery meets all of these criteria, use code O80. If not, use a code for every factor in the case that does not meet the criteria. For example, the patient delivers a single liveborn infant at 38 weeks' gestation with cephalic (head) presentation. A small episiotomy was performed. Using the previous list, the coder can determine that all criteria are met, so code O80 is used for the delivery. If the patient delivered liveborn twins at 36 weeks by cesarean section, this case does not meet criteria numbers 2, 3, and 5. The coder would code at least three diagnosis codes: one for each criteria not met and one for the outcome of delivery.

- O60.14X2, Preterm labor third trimester with preterm delivery third trimester

- O30.003, Twin pregnancy, unspecified number of placenta and unspecified number of amniotic sacs, third trimester

- Z3A.36, 36 weeks gestation of pregnancy

- Z37.2, Twins, both liveborn

> **Official Coding Guidelines:**
>
> **Selection of Principal Diagnosis**
>
> When a delivery occurs, the principal diagnosis should correspond to the main circumstances or complication of the delivery. In cases of cesarean deliveries, the principal diagnosis should correspond to the reason the cesarean was performed, unless the reason for admission was unrelated to the condition resulting in the cesarean delivery.

Guidelines instruct the use of a code from the Z37 category to identify outcome of delivery on the mother's chart. These codes specify if the baby was liveborn, single, twin, stillborn, and so on, and are not used on the baby's chart. Z37.0, for example, would be used for a single liveborn outcome of delivery.

Codes from category Z34.0-, Supervision of normal first pregnancy, and Z34.8-, Supervision of other normal pregnancy, both require specification of the trimester. These codes are used for routine prenatal care and should not be used in conjunction with any other code from the pregnancy chapter.

Procedures having to do with labor or delivery are commonly located under the main term "delivery." All deliveries should be coded with a corresponding procedure code.

> **Official Coding Guidelines:**
>
> **Fetal Conditions Affecting the Management of the Mother**
>
> **Codes from categories O35 and O36**
>
> Codes from categories O35, Maternal care for known or suspected fetal abnormality and damage, and O36, Maternal care for other fetal problems, are assigned only when the fetal condition is actually responsible for modifying the management of the mother, that is, by requiring diagnostic studies, additional observation, special care, or termination of pregnancy. The fact that the fetal condition exists does not justify assigning a code from this series to the mother's record.

If the fetus was known to have spina bifida, for example, this would require additional studies and additional observation and probable cesarean delivery to prevent trauma to the fetus. In this case, it would be appropriate to use code O35.00, Maternal care for (suspected) central nervous system malformation in fetus, on visits prior to the delivery, then a code from the Q05- Spina bifida section as one of the diagnoses after delivery to be coded onto the baby's record.

There are many codes to be used on the baby's chart noting problems with the mother that affected the baby. These should not be confused with pregnancy codes, and are usually codes in the P00–P96 category range. For example, for an issue with twins during delivery, go to the Alphabetic Index under the main term " newborn" and there is a subterm for "affected by," then "maternal (complication of)," then multiple pregnancy. The code shown is P01.5, Newborn (suspected to be) affected by multiple pregnancy. This code is only to be used on the baby's chart, and only if the twin pregnancy somehow affected the newborn(s).

Pregnancy with abortive outcome is coded with codes from O00–O08. A Missed abortion code, O21.1, is used for early fetal death before completion of 20 completed weeks of gestation, with retention of fetal demise. Code category O03 is for spontaneous (miscarriage), whether complete or incomplete, and contains several codes that include complications. The diagnosis of abortion, spontaneous, with excessive hemorrhage, incomplete, for example, would be coded O03.1.

Delivery of Infants and Congenital Anomalies

The Z codes for newborns (which is the newborn's principal diagnosis) are included in the Z code section. These codes describe delivery codes for the initial birth record, which are not for use on the mother's chart.

Official Coding Guidelines:

Principal Diagnosis for Birth Record

When coding the birth episode in a newborn record, assign a code from category Z38, Liveborn infants, according to place of birth and type of delivery, as the principal diagnosis. A code from category Z38 is assigned only once, to a newborn at the time of birth. If a newborn is transferred to another institution, a code from category Z38 should not be used at the receiving hospital.

A code from category Z38 is used only on the newborn record, not on the mother's record.

When coding the newborn's medical stay, the principal diagnosis is always a code from Z38 to show that the baby was born during this episode of care. Any complicating factors or anomalies would be coded secondarily. These codes are only used once on the newborn's chart, and are not used by a secondary hospital where the newborn was transferred.

Official Coding Guidelines:

Certain Conditions Originating in the Perinatal Period (P00-P96)

For coding and reporting purposes, the perinatal period is defined as before birth through the 28th day following birth. The following guidelines are provided for reporting purposes. All clinically significant conditions noted on routine newborn examination should be coded. A condition is clinically significant if it requires any of the following:

- Clinical evaluation

- Therapeutic treatment

- Diagnostic procedures

- Extended length of hospital stay

- Increased nursing care and/or monitoring

- Situation with implications for future health care needs

Note: The perinatal guidelines listed here are the same as the general coding guidelines for "additional diagnoses," except for the final point regarding implications for future health care needs. Codes should be assigned for conditions that have been specified by the provider.

For example, if the infant is a term liveborn, born in this hospital by vaginal delivery the code is Z38.00 for the newborn record. Any complications upon birth, such as respiratory distress, would be documented in addition. Code P22.0 for respiratory distress syndrome of newborn would be noted on the newborn record. For the fetal distress, first noted during labor, the code O77.9, Labor and delivery complicated by fetal stress, unspecified, would be listed on the mother's record.

Highlight:

Z38, Liveborn infants according to place of birth and type of delivery

This category is for use as the principal code on the initial record of a newborn baby. It is to be used for the initial birth record only. It is not to be used on the mother's record. Following are just a sample of some of the codes required for use on the birth record.

- Z38.00, Single liveborn infant, delivered vaginally

- Z38.01, Single liveborn infant, delivered by cesarean

- Z38.1, Single liveborn infant, born outside hospital

- Z38.2, Single liveborn infant, unspecified as to place of birth

- Z38.30, Twin liveborn infant, delivered vaginally

- Z38.31, Twin liveborn infant, delivered by cesarean

Official Coding Guidelines:

Congenital Anomalies (Q00–Q99)

Assign an appropriate code(s) from categories Q00–Q99, Congenital malformations, deformations, and chromosomal abnormalities, when a malformation/deformation or chromosomal abnormality is documented. A malformation/deformation or chromosomal abnormality may be the principal/first-listed diagnosis on a record or a secondary diagnosis.

When a malformation/deformation/or chromosomal abnormality does not have a unique code assignment, assign additional code(s) for any manifestations that may be present.

When the code assignment specifically identifies the malformation /deformation / or chromosomal abnormality, manifestations that are an inherent component of the anomaly should not be coded separately. Additional codes should be assigned for manifestations that are not an inherent component.

Codes from Chapter 17 may be used throughout the life of the patient. If a congenital malformation or deformity has been corrected, a personal history code should be used to identify the history of the malformation or deformity. Although present at birth, malformation/deformation/or chromosomal abnormality may not be identified until later in life. Whenever the condition is diagnosed by the physician, it is appropriate to assign a code from codes Q00–Q99. For the birth admission, the appropriate code from category Z38, Liveborn infants, according to place of birth and type of delivery, should be sequenced as the principal diagnosis, followed by any congenital anomaly codes, Q00–Q99.

Highlight:

Congenital heart conditions can be extensive and should be coded with great care. They are divided between cyanotic and acyanotic defects. Cyanotic defects occur when the defect allows for mixing of oxygenated and deoxygenated blood within the heart. Here are two of the most common cardiac defects:

1. *Ventricular septal defect* (an opening in the ventricular septum allowing the blood to go from the left to right ventricle). The appropriate code is Q21.0. *Figure 2–1 shows a ventricular septal defect.*

2. *Patent ductus arteriosus* is a condition in which the fetal blood vessel connecting the aorta and pulmonary artery that allows blood to bypass the fetal lungs remains open (patent). This should close within the first few hours after birth. If it remains open, heart failure and pulmonary congestion result, and surgical repair is almost always needed. The code for the patent ductus arteriosus is Q25.0.

Congenital heart disease
Ventricular septal defect

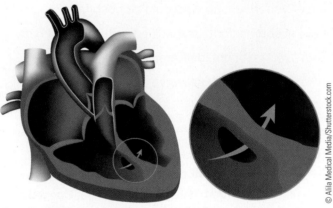

© Alila Medical Media/Shutterstock.com

Figure 2-1 Congenital heart disease: ventricular septal defect

Official Coding Guidelines:

Providers utilize different criteria in determining prematurity. A code for prematurity should not be assigned unless it is documented. Assignment of codes in categories P05, Disorders of newborn related to slow fetal growth and fetal malnutrition, and P07, Disorders of newborn related to short gestation and low birth weight, not elsewhere classified, should be based on the recorded birthweight and estimated gestational age. Codes from category P05 should not be assigned with codes from category P07.

When both birth weight and gestational age are available, two codes from category P07 should be assigned, with the code for birth weight sequenced before the code for gestational age (P05.-).

Sub category P05.0- is to report Newborn light for gestational age, often referred to simply as "light-for-dates." Several codes can be found in this category, such as P05.04, Newborn light for gestational age, 1000–1249 grams. The actual weight of the newborn is specified in the description.

If the baby's weight is recorded in pounds, the coder will need to use a conversion chart for appropriate coding (500 grams is equivalent to approximately one pound, one and two-thirds ounces). Subcategory P05.1-, Newborn small for gestational age, is similar in that the actual weight is specified within the code (e.g., P05.15, Newborn small for gestational age, 1250–1499 grams).

Exercise 2.8

Using the ICD-10-CM code book, code the following diagnoses.

1. Thirty-three-year-old white female with history of multiple miscarriages, now at 27 weeks' gestation, is put on bed rest by physician for remainder of gestation. Home care to see patient on weekly basis to monitor mother and child.

   Diagnoses: _____

2. This 27-day-old infant was seen today in the clinic for jaundice. Radiology report shows congenital obstruction of the bile duct. We are going to refer the parents to the pediatric surgery clinic for surgical evaluation.

   Diagnoses: _____

3. Progress note: This baby was born prematurely this morning at 36 weeks' gestation at home and is admitted for observation. Weight is 2456 grams.

   Diagnoses: _____

4. Final diagnoses: Uterine pregnancy, term. Spontaneous delivery of single liveborn infant, cephalic presentation. Postpartum hemorrhage, onset 32 hours following delivery.

   Diagnoses: _____

Neoplasms

The term **neoplasm** literally means "new growth." Types of neoplasms or tumors are identified as follows:

- Adenoma—usually a benign tumor found in glandular epithelial tissue

- Carcinoma—a malignant tumor of epithelial tissue

- Fibroma—a benign encapsulated tumor of connective tissue

- Glioma—a malignant tumor comprised of neurological cells of the brain

- Lipoma—a benign tumor of adipose or fatty tissue

- Melanoma—a malignant tumor of the skin

- Osteoma—a malignant tumor of the bone

- Sarcoma—a malignant tumor found in connective tissue such as bone or muscle

- Leukemia is cancer of the blood and lymphoma is cancer of lymphatic tissues.

Figure 2–2 shows various cell types of lung cancers, or carcinomas.

A common error made by many people is to think that all neoplasms are malignant, or cancerous. It is important that the correct code assignment be made,

neoplasm: Any new and abnormal growth of tissue in some part of the body, specifically one in which cell multiplication is uncontrolled and progressive, that may be benign or malignant.

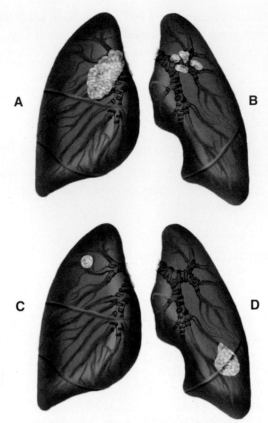

Figure 2-2 Different types of lung cancers: (A) small-cell carcinoma; (B) squamous-cell carcinoma; (C) adenocarcinoma; (D) large-cell carcinoma

especially in dealing with a disease such as cancer, and the coder must be sure of the correct diagnosis. An incorrect malignancy coded on a patient's chart can cause long-term problems, such as the loss of insurance, denial of life insurance policies, and increased rates. The final coding of a suspect mass or tumor should not be completed until after review of the pathology report.

Neoplasm Table

ICD-10-CM has provided an extensive table that is used to code most neoplasms. Figure 2–3 shows a partial sample of this table. It is located in the Alphabetic Index under the main term Neoplasm. The table is divided into sites, then into codes to show the neoplasm's behavior.

When coding malignancies, it is easiest to start with the neoplasm table. There are three available choices for malignancies, which are represented in the first three columns of the neoplasm table (Figure 2–3):

- *Primary* is the site where the neoplasm originated.

- *Secondary* is the site to which the primary site has spread, either by metastasis (movement to another body location), direct extension to an adjacent organ, or invasion into the blood or lymph system.

- *In situ* is where the cells are malignant, but have not spread to (invaded) the basement membrane of the structure.

There are three other choices of other behavior:

- *Benign* is when the tumor is not spreading or invasive into other sites.

- *Uncertain behavior* is the diagnosis when the pathologist is unable to determine whether the neoplasm is malignant or benign.

- *Unspecified* can be used when the documentation does not support a more specific code. This may be used when the patient is transferred to another facility or is discharged without further workup done on the neoplasm.

	Malignant Primary	Malignant Secondary	Ca in situ	Benign	Uncertain	Unspecified Behavior
Note: The list below gives the code number for neoplasms by anatomical site. For each site there are six possible code numbers according to whether the neoplasm in question is malignant, benign, in situ, of uncertain behavior, or of unspecified nature. The description of the neoplasm will often indicate which of the six columns is appropriate; e.g., malignant melanoma of skin, benign fibroadenoma of breast, carcinoma in situ of cervix uteri. Where such descriptors are not present, the remainder of the Index should be consulted where guidance is given to the appropriate column for each morphological (histological) variety listed; e.g., Mesonephroma - see Neoplasm, malignant; Embryoma (see also Neoplasm, uncertain behavior); Disease, Bowen's - see Neoplasm, skin, in situ. However, the guidance in the Index can be overridden if one of the descriptors mentioned above is present; e.g., malignant adenoma of colon is coded to C 18.9 and not to D12.6 as the adjective "malignant" overrides the Index entry "Adenoma (see also Neoplasm, benign)." Codes listed with a dash -, following the code have a required 5th character for laterality. The tabular list must be reviewed for the complete code.						
Neoplasm, neoplastic	C80.1	C79.9	D09.9	D36.9	D48.9	D49.9
abdomen, abdominal	C76.2	C79.8 – ☑	D09.8	D36.7	D48.7	D49.89
cavity	C76.2	C79.8 – ☑	D09.8	D36.7	D48.7	D49.89
organ	C76.2	C79.8 – ☑	D09.8	D36.7	D48.7	D49.89
viscera	C76.2	C79.8 – ☑	D09.8	D36.7	D48.7	D49.89
wall — *see also* Neoplasm, abdomen, wall, skin	C44.509	C79.2	D04.5	D23.5	D48.5	D49.2
connective tissue	C49.4	C79.8 – ☑	—	D21.4	D48.1	D49.2
skin	C44.509	—	—	—	—	—
basal cell carcinoma	C44.519	—	—	—	—	—
specified type NEC	C44.599	—	—	—	—	—
squamous cell carcinoma	C44.529	—	—	—	—	—
abdominopelvic	C76.8	C79.8 – ☑	—	D36.7	D48.7	D49.89
accessory sinus — *see* Neoplasm, sinus						
acoustic nerve	C72.4 – ☑	C79.49		D33.3	D43.3	D49.7

Figure 2-3 Partial ICD-10-CM Neoplasm Table

How to Code a Neoplasm

- *Step 1:* The coder should first go to the neoplasm table unless the histological term, such as carcinoma, adenoma, leiomyoma, etc., is referenced first.

- *Step 2:* If using a histological term, go to the Alphabetic Index first, and look for a subterm that describes the site found in the diagnostic statement. If a code is located, that is as far as the coder must search to describe the condition. For example, if the patient has microcystic adenoma of the pancreas, the coder would look under the main term "adenoma" and find the subterms "cystic" and "pancreas." The coder can go directly to the tabular list to verify the code found, D13.7.

- *Step 3:* If the site is not listed as a subterm in the Alphabetic Index, under the main term for the histological type there should be an instruction to "*See also* Neoplasm, by site, behavior" (such as benign, malignant, etc.). For example, a search for papillary adenoma in the Alphabetic Index leads to the instruction "See also, Neoplasm, benign, by site."

- *Step 4:* The coder should then turn to the neoplasm table and locate the appropriate code. The neoplasm table is located immediately after the end of the Alphabetic Index.

- As always, a code found in the Alphabetic Index or in the neoplasm should be verified in the tabular index.

For example, if the patient had a diagnosis of "liposarcoma of the right shoulder," the coder would begin under the main term "liposarcoma." There is no subterm for shoulder, but a note located next to the main term tells the coder to "*see also* Neoplasm, connective tissue, malignant." This note directs the coder to go to the neoplasm table to locate the code. In the neoplasm table, search for "connective tissue," then the subterm "shoulder." Once that is located, the next step is to locate the appropriate malignant column (the "See" instruction in the Alphabetic Index included the word *malignant*). Since there is no mention of secondary malignancy or metastasis, the code would be C49.1-. Once confirmed in the tabular index, code C49.11 provides laterality. The full code description for C49.11 is Malignant neoplasm of connective and soft tissue of right upper limb, including shoulder.

> **Coding Tip:**
>
> ICD-10-CM Guidelines state the neoplasm table in the Alphabetic Index should be referenced first. However, if the histological term is documented, that term should be referenced first, rather than going immediately to the neoplasm table, in order to determine which column in the neoplasm table is appropriate. For example, if the documentation indicates "adenoma," refer to the term in the Alphabetic Index to review the entries under this term and the instructional note to "see also neoplasm, by site, benign." The table provides the proper code based on the type of neoplasm and the site.

Highlight:

Neoplasm coding tips:

- If a malignant neoplasm has been removed, but has recurred at the primary site, code the recurrence as a primary site.

- Be careful of the word *metastatic*. It can be used to describe both a primary and secondary site. Metastatic from the breast means the breast is the primary site. Malignancy, breast metastatic to the liver, means the breast is the primary site and the liver is the secondary site.

- Code C80.1, Malignant (primary) neoplasm, unspecified, equates to Cancer, unspecified. This code should only be used when no determination can be made as to the primary site of a malignancy. This code should rarely be used in the inpatient setting. If the patient has had a malignancy removed and is still in the initial stage of treatment, such as chemotherapy or radiation therapy, the cancer should be coded as if it was still present.

- If the patient has had a malignancy removed and is back for follow-up to look for further signs of cancer, and there is none, then a "history of malignant neoplasm" code is used from the Z85 section.

- If the patient is undergoing testing because a family member has or previously had cancer, a code from category Z80 can be used to show "family history of malignant neoplasm."

Principal Diagnosis

Neoplasms often cause problems to the coder when trying to determine the correct principal diagnosis. The following official coding guidelines provide sequencing guidance:

Official Coding Guidelines:

Neoplasms

A.   Treatment directed at the malignancy.

If the treatment is directed at the malignancy, designate the malignancy as the principal diagnosis. The only exception to this guideline is if a patient admission/encounter is solely for the administration of chemotherapy, immunotherapy or radiation therapy, assign the appropriate Z51.–code as the first-listed or principal diagnosis, and the diagnosis or problem for which the service is being performed as a secondary diagnosis.

B.   Treatment of secondary site.

When a patient is admitted because of a primary neoplasm with metastasis and treatment is directed toward the secondary site only, the secondary neoplasm is designated as the principal diagnosis even though the primary malignancy is still present.

C.   Coding and sequencing of complications.

Coding and sequencing of complications associated with the malignancies or with the therapy thereof are subject to the following guidelines:

(1)   Anemia associated with malignancy.

When admission/encounter is for management of an anemia associated with the malignancy, and the treatment is only for anemia, the

(continues)

appropriate code for the malignancy is sequenced as the principal or first-listed diagnosis followed by the appropriate code for the anemia (such as code D63.0, Anemia in neoplastic disease).

(2) Anemia associated with chemotherapy, immunotherapy, and radiation therapy.

When the admission/encounter is for management of an anemia associated with an adverse effect of the administration of chemotherapy or immunotherapy and the only treatment is for the anemia, the anemia code is sequenced first, followed by the appropriate codes for the neoplasm and the adverse effect (T45.1X5, Adverse effect of antineoplastic and immunosuppressive drugs).

When the admission/encounter is for management of an anemia associated with an adverse effect of radiotherapy, the anemia code should be sequenced first, followed by the appropriate neoplasm code and code Y84.2, Radiological procedure and radiotherapy as the cause of abnormal reaction of the patient, or of later complication, without mention of misadventure at the time of the procedure.

(3) Management of dehydration due to the malignancy.

When the admission/encounter is for management of dehydration due to the malignancy or the therapy of a combination of both, and only the dehydration is being treated (intravenous rehydration), the dehydration is sequenced first, followed by the code(s) for the malignancy.

(4) Treatment of a complication resulting from a surgical procedure.

When the admission/encounter is for treatment of a complication resulting from a surgical procedure, designate the complication as the principal or first-listed diagnosis if treatment is directed at resolving the complication.

D. Primary malignancy previously excised.

When a primary malignancy has been previously excised or eradicated from its site and there is no further treatment directed to that site and there is no evidence of any existing primary malignancy, a code from category Z85, Personal history of malignant neoplasm, should be used to indicate the former site of the malignancy. Any mention of extension, invasion, or metastasis to another site is coded as a secondary malignant neoplasm to that site. The secondary site may be the principal or first-listed, with the Z85 code used as a secondary code.

E. Admissions/Encounters involving chemotherapy, immunotherapy, and radiation therapy.

(1) Episode of care involves surgical removal of neoplasm.

When an episode of care involves surgical removal of a primary site or secondary site malignancy followed by adjunct chemotherapy or radiation treatment during the same episode of care, the code for neoplasm should be assigned as principal or first-listed diagnosis.

(2) Patient admission/encounter solely for administration of chemotherapy, immunotherapy, and radiation therapy. If a patient admission/encounter

(continues)

is solely for the administration of chemotherapy, immunotherapy or radiation therapy assign code Z51.0, Encounter for antineoplastic radiation therapy, or Z51.11, Encounter for antineoplastic chemotherapy, or Z51.12, Encounter for antineoplastic immunotherapy as the first-listed or principal diagnosis. If a patient receives more than one of these therapies during the same admission more than one of these codes may be assigned, in any sequence.

The malignancy for which the therapy is being administered should be assigned as a secondary diagnosis.

(3) Patient admission for radiotherapy/chemotherapy and immunotherapy and develops complications.

When a patient is admitted for the purpose of radiotherapy, immunotherapy, or chemotherapy and develops complications such as uncontrolled nausea and vomiting or dehydration, the principal or first-listed diagnosis is Z51.0, Encounter for antineoplastic radiation therapy, or Z51.11, Encounter for antineoplastic chemotherapy, or Z51.12, Encounter for antineoplastic immunotherapy followed by any codes for the complications.

F. Admission/encounter to determine extent of malignancy.

When the reason for admission/encounter is to determine the extent of the malignancy, or for a procedure such as paracentesis or thoracentesis, the primary malignancy or appropriate metastatic site is designated as the principal or first-listed diagnosis, even though chemotherapy or radiotherapy is administered.

G. Symptoms, signs, and abnormal findings listed in Chapter 18 associated with neoplasms.

Symptoms, signs, and ill-defined conditions listed in Chapter 18 characteristic of, or associated with, an existing primary or secondary site malignancy cannot be used to replace the malignancy as principal or first-listed diagnosis, regardless of the number of admissions or encounters for treatment and care of the neoplasm.

See section I.C.21, Factors influencing health status and contact with health services, Encounter for prophylactic organ removal.

H. Admission/encounter for pain control/management.

See Section 1.C6.a.5 for information on coding admission/encounter for pain control/management.

I. Malignancy in two or more noncontiguous sites.

A patient may have more than one malignant tumor in the same organ. These tumors may represent different primaries or metastatic disease, depending on the site. Should the documentation be unclear, the provider should be queried as to the status of each tumor so that the correct codes can be assigned.

See additional information in the Official ICD-10-CM Guidelines for Neoplasms, Chapter 2, sections I through R.

Exercise 2.9

Using ICD-10-CM, code the following diagnoses.

1. Malignant carcinoma of appendix with appendectomy and resection of cecum
   Diagnoses _____

2. Metastatic carcinoma to pelvic bone from prostate
   Diagnoses _____

3. Hodgkin's disease with cervical lymph node biopsy
   Diagnoses _____

4. Recurrent papillary carcinoma of bladder, low-grade transitional cell
   Diagnoses _____

5. Carcinoma of the brain metastatic from the lungs
   Diagnoses _____

6. Carcinoma in situ of the cervix uteri
   Diagnoses _____

7. Carcinoma of the right breast, lower-outer quadrant with metastasis to the lung
   Diagnoses _____

8. Benign neoplasm of tongue
   Diagnoses _____

9. Malignant neoplasm of tongue
   Diagnoses _____

10. Carcinoma of anterior bladder wall metastatic to rectum and colon
    Diagnoses _____

External Cause

External causes of injury codes are used as secondary codes to show the cause of the injury whenever it is known, such as a fall or automobile accident. Most external cause codes are not mandatory, but it is recommended that they be used wherever possible to fully describe the patient's condition. There is a separate External Cause Alphabetic Index (in the Alphabetic Index section of the code book located behind the table of drugs and chemicals) to facilitate locating the appropriate code. They include type of injury (fall, motor vehicle accident [MVA]), place of accident or occurrence, specific person involved (pedestrian, driver of car), and codes for late effects. Some states are now beginning to mandate the use of all External Cause codes for certain conditions. The use of the External Cause codes helps to tell the whole story behind what happened to the patient. If an accident or injury code is used, payment on a claim may be delayed prior to investigation of the facts surrounding the injury. By using the External Cause code to tell the cause of the injury, the coder has given the carrier all of the information needed to pay the claim.

Chapter 19 of ICD-10-CM, Injury, Poisoning, and Certain Other Consequences of External Causes (S00-T88), contains codes for the following:

- Injuries
- Fractures (traumatic)

- Burns and corrosions

- Adverse effects, poisoning, underdosing, and toxic effects

- Adult and child abuse, neglect, and other maltreatment

- Complications of care

New in ICD-10-CM is the application of 7th characters in most categories of Chapter 19. Most categories have three 7th-character values (with the exception of fractures). These characters are located with cross-referencing the condition in the alphabetic listing with the tabular listing where the appropriate 7th character can be determined and added to the code.

Coding Tip:

An appropriate 7th character is assigned to an ICD-10-CM code to identify the encounter of the service or procedure. The 7th character must always be in 7th-character position. If a code contains fewer digits, placeholder X must be used to fill in or "hold" the empty characters.

A initial encounter

D subsequent encounter

S sequel

Chapter 20 of ICD-10-CM, External Causes of Morbidity (V00–Y99) contains codes intended to provide data for injury research and evaluation of injury prevention strategies. These codes are intended to describe the cause of the injury or health condition, the intent, whether accidental, unintentional, or intentional, such as suicide or assault, the place of occurrence at the time of the event, and the person's status, such as civilian or military. There is no requirement for mandatory reporting of these external cause codes unless mandated by a particular payor.

EXAMPLE: A man injured his left thumb while using a circular saw at home in his garage workshop. The wound lacerated the thumb damaging the nail. He was taken by car to the emergency department, where the injury was evaluated and repaired.

First, code the laceration of the left thumb S61.112A.

The 7th character "A" is assigned to indicate Initial Encounter

Second, code appliance, implement, etc. that caused the accident (the circular saw) W31.2XXA.

The 7th character is added for the initial encounter. Since the actual code is only four digits (W31.2), placeholders (XX) must be used to add the 7th character to the code (A).

Third, code where the accident occurred, in his garage workshop at his home. Y92.015 is coded, private garage of single-family (private) house

Note: The location is important to verify where the accident happened in relation to work, home, or other area.

Highlight:

To code lacerations in ICD-10-CM, the coder is referred directly to the Alphabetic Index, Laceration, listed by site, then the tabular index for additional 6th character for specificity/laterality, and 7th character to indicate whether initial or subsequent encounter, or sequela to correctly code the repair.

Place of occurrence codes are located in the Alphabetic Index to External Causes.

EXAMPLE: Here is an example for an accident involving a fracture. A patient had a comminuted nondisplaced fracture of the shaft of the right femur due to crashing the snowmobile he was driving into a tree in a field of his grandfather's farm.

First code the fracture (traumatic), S72.354A.

To show the cause of the fracture, code V86.52XA. Locate the correct code by checking the External Cause Alphabetic Index under the main term "Accident," subterm transport," then locate snowmobile, driver, V86.52. When the coder verifies this code in the External Cause tabular list, a 7th character is required to indicate encounter. The X placeholder would be added before the 7th character, so the correct code would be V86.52XA.

The third code would be the place of occurrence or the location of the accident. Y92.73 would be added to show a farm field as the place of occurrence of the accident.

Highlight:

The coder should review the facility's policy on the use of External Cause codes and follow it consistently. External cause codes are *never* assigned as principal or primary diagnoses.

Official Coding Guidelines:

Place of Occurrence Guidelines

Use an additional code from category Y92 to indicate the Place of Occurrence as secondary codes for use after other external cause codes to identify the location of the patient at the time of injury or other condition. The Place of Occurrence describes the place where the event occurred and not the patient's activity at the time of the event.

Highlight:

A place of occurrence code is used only once at the initial encounter for treatment. It is to be used as a secondary code after other external cause codes to identify the location of the patient at the time of the injury or other condition. No 7th characters are used for category Y92. Only one code from Y92 should be recorded on a medical record.

While External Cause codes are not required, they do provide further information about the cause of the patient's injury. In other words, if the patient was injured on the job in a factory, the coder could use code Y92.63 for Factory (building) (premises). This would most likely be a workers' compensation case.

Official Coding Guidelines:

Multiple Cause External Cause Code Coding Guidelines

If two or more events cause separate injuries, an External Cause code should be assigned for each cause.

Cataclysmic events are those related to forces of nature, such as hurricanes, tornadoes, earthquakes, and floods. These codes are listed in category X30–X39.

> **Official Coding Guidelines:**
>
> External Cause codes for transport accidents take priority over all other External Cause codes except cataclysmic events, child and adult abuse, and terrorism.

According to the ICD-10-CM book, a transport accident is defined as "any accident involving a device designed primarily for, or being used at the time primarily for, conveying persons or goods from one place to another." Examples of transport accidents are those in airplanes, cars, trains, and boats.

> **Official Coding Guidelines:**
>
> The first listed External Cause code should correspond to the cause of the most serious diagnosis due to an assault, accident, or self-harm, following the order of hierarchy listed in the previous section.
>
> **Child and Adult Abuse Guidelines**
>
> When the cause of an injury or neglect is intentional child or adult abuse, neglect, or other maltreatment, sequence first the appropriate code from category T74.- (Adult and child abuse, neglect, and other maltreatment, followed by any accompanying mental health or injury code. If the documentation in the medical record states abuse or neglect, it is coded as confirmed T74.-). If it is documented as suspected, it is coded T76.-. If the perpetrator(s) of the abuse is/are known, refer to Index of External Causes of Injury, Perpetrator, for additional External Cause code. An extensive list of identified perpetrators is listed using Y07.- codes.

Injuries

Many injuries are classified according to the general type of injury, such as wound, injury, internal, or injury, superficial. Superficial injuries such as abrasions or contusions are not reported when associated with more severe injuries of the same site. Traumatic injury codes (SOO–T14.9) are not to be used for normal healing surgical wounds or to identify complications of surgical wounds.

> **Official Coding Guidelines:**
>
> **Multiple Injuries**
>
> When multiple injuries exist, the code for the most severe injury, as determined by the attending physician, is sequenced first.
>
> **Coding for Multiple Injuries**
>
> When coding multiple injuries such as fracture of tibia and fibula, assign separate codes for each injury unless a combination code is provided, in which case the combination code is assigned. Multiple injury codes are provided in ICD-10-CM, but should not be assigned unless information for a more specific code is not available.
>
> - The code for the most serious injury, as determined by the physician, is sequenced first.

(continues)

- Superficial injuries such as abrasions or contusions are not coded when associated with more severe injuries of the same site.

- When a primary injury results in minor damage to peripheral nerves or blood vessels, the primary injury is sequenced first with additional code(s): Injury to nerves and spinal cord, such as category S04, or S15, Injury to blood vessels. When the primary injury is to the blood vessels or nerves, that injury should be sequenced first.

Exercise 2.10

Assign ICD-10-CM codes to the following, including E codes.

1. Concussion sustained from traffic/motor vehicle accident to driver in collision with bicycle on Main Street; no loss of consciousness. _____

2. Struck by falling tree limb during severe thunderstorm on the golf course, lacerating right eyebrow _____

3. Puncture wound to left index finger due to accidental stick with hypodermic needle in physician's office lab _____

4. Struck by lightning in a public swimming pool _____

5. Follow-up encounter for reevaluation of facial bruises after being trampled by a crowd during a rock concert _____

Fractures

Fractures are classified according to whether they are traumatic or pathological. Pathological fractures occur due to a disease rather than a trauma. If the fracture is stated to be "pathological," "spontaneous," or "due to disease," it is coded as a pathological fracture. Pathological fractures are coded to Diseases of the Musculoskeletal System, M00–M99. It is necessary to also code the disease as the underlying cause of the fracture. For example, the patient has a fracture of the left hip due to osteoporosis. Under the main term "fracture," the coder would find the subterm "pathological," subterm "hip," referring the coder to Fracture, femur, neck, with the appropriate code assignment of M84.651-, Pathologic fracture of left femur. with 7th character to indicate encounter for the fracture. The coder should also code the osteoporosis, M80.852- with 7th character to indicate the encounter for the fracture.

Traumatic fractures are those caused by an injury and not a disease or condition. They are coded to Injury, Poisoning, and Certain Other Consequences of External Causes, specifically categories beginning with S. Fractures of specified sites are coded individually by site in accordance with both the provisions within categories S02, S12, S22, S32, S42, S49, S52, S62, S72, S79, S82, S89, S92, and the level of detail furnished by medical record content.

A fracture not indicated as open or closed should be coded to closed. A fracture not indicated whether displaced or nondisplaced should be coded to displaced. A closed fracture is one where there is no open wound into the skin. An open fracture is a fracture where there is an open wound into the skin. If the diagnostic statement does not identify whether the fracture is open or closed, it is coded as closed. Examples of closed fractures are comminuted, greenstick, simple, and impacted. Examples of open fractures are compound, infected, puncture, and with foreign body. Refer to Chapter 8 of this text for more information on orthopedics.

All fracture codes require the use of a 7th character to describe the encounter. Unlike the three encounter types mentioned earlier, there are 16 choices, depending on the type of encounter (initial, subsequent, or **sequela**), the type of fracture, and any complication that may exist regarding the fracture, such as a subsequent encounter for a closed fracture with delayed healing (D), initial encounter for closed fracture (A), or subsequent encounter for open fracture type IIIA, IIIB, or IIIC, with malunion (R). For fracture codes less than six characters in length, a placeholder (X) must be added, as appropriate.

sequela: A residual or late effect after the acute phase of an illness or injury.

Official Coding Guidelines:

Fractures

The principle of multiple coding of injuries should be followed in coding fractures. Fractures of specified sites are coded individually by site with both the provisions within categories S02, S12, S22, S32, S42, S49, S52, S62, S72, S79, S82, S89, S92 and the level of detail documented in the medical record.

- A fracture not indicated as open or closed should be coded to closed. A fracture not indicated whether displaced or nondisplaced should be coded to displaced.

- Traumatic fractures are coded using the appropriate 7th character extension to indicate encounter (A, B, C) while the patient is receiving active treatment for the fracture.

- The appropriate 7th character extension for subsequent care relates to encounters after the patient has completed active treatment of the fracture and is receiving routine care for the fracture during the healing or recovery phase, such as cast change or removal, removal of external or internal fixation device, medication adjustment, and follow-up visits following fracture treatment.

- Care for complications of surgical treatment for fracture repairs during the healing or recovery phase should be coded with the appropriate complication codes.

- Care of complications of fractures, such as malunion and nonunion, should be reported with the appropriate 7th character extensions for subsequent care, with nonunion (K, M, N), or subsequent care with malunion (P, Q, R).

- Pathologic fractures are coded from category M80, not a traumatic fracture code.

- Multiple fractures are sequenced in accordance with the severity of the fracture.

Exercise 2.11

Assign ICD-10-CM codes to the following statements.

1. Closed fracture, displaced, great toe, right foot _____
2. Initial encounter for multiple compression fractures of vertebrae due to age-related osteoporosis _____
3. Fracture of left ilium in patient with type 2 diabetes _____
4. Multiple fractures, distal end, medial condyle, right femur, nondisplaced _____
5. Open fracture maxilla _____
6. Motor vehicle accident/collision with another vehicle to passenger in car. Examination revealed greenstick fracture of the shaft of the right ulna and laceration of the forehead. _____
7. Nondisplaced spiral fracture of the shaft of humerus, left arm, from fall from day care playground swing _____
8. Follow-up visit for recheck of nondisplaced lateral epicondyle fracture of the right elbow with normal healing _____
9. Stress fracture of the right ankle _____
10. Dislocation of left acromioclavicular joint in child, age 3, seen in ED. Child abuse suspected of the mother (perpetrator). _____

Burns

A burn is classified according to first, second, or third degree. For two degrees of burn in the same location, the coder should only code to the highest degree. For example, if the patient has second- and third-degree burns of the lower back due to exposure to sofa fire due to burning cigarette, the coder would assign code T21.34-, Third-degree burn, lower back, with code X08.01- to further identify exposure to sofa fire due to burning cigarette. A 7th character is assigned to indicate the encounter, using X for placeholder. Figure 2–4 shows an image of the Lund-Browder chart, which is a method for estimating the extent and total body surface area affected in patients with burns that allows for the varying proportion of body surface in persons of different ages. Chapter 7 of this text contains extensive information on coding burns.

Official Coding Guidelines:

ICD-10-CM differentiates between burns and corrosions. The burn codes are assigned for thermal burns, except sunburns, that occur from a heat source, such as a fire or hot appliance, and also for burns resulting from electricity and radiation.

Corrosions are burns due to chemicals. They both follow the same guidelines.

Current Burns

Current burns (T20–T25) are classified by depth, extent, and, by agent (X code). By depth burns are classified as first degree (erythema), second degree (blistering), and third degree (full-thickness involvement). Burns of the eye and internal organs (T26–T28) are classified by site, not by degree.

Sequence first the code that reflects the highest degree of burn when more than one burn is present.

(continues)

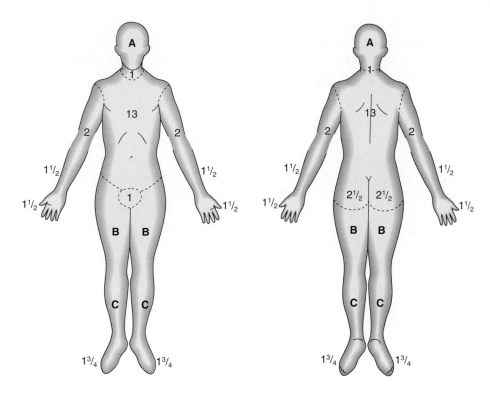

Figure 2-4 Lund-Browder chart

Body Part	Age					
	0 yr	1 yr	5 yr	10 yr	15 yr	Adult
a = 1/2 of head	9 1/2	8 1/2	6 1/2	5 1/2	4 1/2	3 1/2
b = 1/2 of one thigh	2 3/4	3 1/4	4	4 1/4	4 1/2	4 3/4
c = 1/2 of one lower leg	2 1/2	2 1/2	2 3/4	3	3 1/4	3 1/2

- All burns are coded with the highest degree of burn sequenced first.

- Classify burns of the same local site (three-character category level (T20–T28) but of different degrees to the subcategory identifying the highest degree recorded in the diagnosis/documentation.

- Nonhealing burns are coded as acute burns. Necrosis of burned skin should be coded as a nonhealed burn.

  o Sequencing of burns and related condition codes

    Sequence first the code that reflects the highest degree of burn when more than one burn is present.

    a When the reason for the admission or encounter is for treatment of external multiple burns, sequence first the code that reflects the burn of the highest degree.

    b When a patient has both internal and external burns, the circumstances of admission govern the selection of the principal diagnosis or the first-listed diagnosis.

(continues)

> c When a patient is admitted for burn injuries and other related conditions such as smoke inhalation and/or respiratory failure, the circumstances of admission govern the selection of the principal or first-listed diagnosis.
>
> o An external cause code should be assigned with burns and corrosions to identify the source and intent of the burn, as well as the place where it occurred.
>
> • Category T31, Burns classified according to extent of body surface involved, T32, Corrosions classified according to body surface involved, are used when the site of the burn is not specified or when there is a need for additional data, such as the evaluation of burn mortality usually needed by burn units. Category T31 can also be used as an additional code for reporting a third-degree burn involving 20 percent or more of the body surface. These categories are based on the classic "rule of nines" or Lund-Browder diagram in estimating body surface involved with differences noted between adults, infants, and children.
>
> • When appropriate, both a code for a current burn or corrosion with 7th character "A" or "D" to indicate initial or subsequent encounter or 7th character "S" may be assigned to indicate sequelae of a healed burn or corrosion.

Exercise 2.12

Assign ICD-10-CM codes to the following statements.

1. Second-degree burn of palm of right hand, first-degree burn of back of left hand while preparing french fries at a local fast-food restaurant _____

2. Chemical (corrosion) burn of mouth, pharynx, and esophagus due to splashing of solvent degreaser used in cleaning floor of commercial garage _____

3. Severe sunburn of face, arms, and shoulders, second degree _____

4. Burn to right upper leg due to cigarette _____

5. First-degree burns of head, face, and neck due to exposure to mattress fire _____

Poisoning Versus Adverse Effects

The Table of Drugs and Chemicals is located following the Alphabetic Index of Diseases and is used to code poisonings and adverse reactions.

Poisoning

A poisoning is a condition caused by drugs, medicines, and biological substances when taken improperly or not in accordance with the physician's orders. Examples of poisonings are:

• Wrong dosage given in error

• Wrong medication given or taken by patient

• Overdose

• Prescription drugs taken in conjunction with alcohol

• Prescription drugs taken with over-the-counter medications not prescribed by the physician

Official Coding Guidelines:

(b) Poisoning

When coding a poisoning or reaction to the improper use of a medication (e.g., overdose, wrong substance given or taken in error, wrong route of administration), first assign the appropriate code from categories T36–T50. The poisoning codes have an associated intent as their 5th or 6th character (accidental, intentional self-harm, assault, and undetermined). Use additional code(s) for all manifestations of poisonings.

If there is also a diagnosis of abuse or dependence of the substance, the abuse or dependence is assigned as an additional code.

Examples of poisoning include:

(i) Error was made in drug prescription. Errors made in drug prescription or in the administration of the drug by provider, nurse, patient, or other person.

(ii) Overdose of a drug intentionally taken. If an overdose of a drug was intentionally taken or administered and resulted in drug toxicity, it would be coded as a poisoning.

(iii) Nonprescribed drug taken with correctly prescribed and properly administered drug. If a nonprescribed drug or medicinal agent was taken in combination with a correctly prescribed and properly administered drug, any drug toxicity or other reaction resulting from the interaction of the two drugs would be classified as a poisoning.

(iv) Interaction of drug(s) and alcohol. When a reaction results from the interaction of a drug(s) and alcohol, this would be classified as poisoning. See Section I.C.4. if poisoning is the result of insulin pump malfunctions.

(c) Underdosing

Underdosing refers to taking less of a medication than is prescribed by a provider or a manufacturer's instruction. For underdosing, assign the code from categories T36–T50 (5th or 6th character "6").

Codes for underdosing should never be assigned as principal or first-listed codes. If a patient has a relapse or exacerbation of the medical condition for which the drug is prescribed because of the reduction in dose, then the medical condition itself should be coded.

Noncompliance (Z91.12-, Z91.13-) or complication of care (Y63.6–Y63.9) codes are to be used with an underdosing code to indicate intent, if known.

(d) Toxic Effects

When a harmful substance is ingested or comes in contact with a person, this is classified as a toxic effect. The toxic effect codes are in categories T51–T65.

Toxic effect codes have an associated intent: accidental, intentional self-harm, assault, and undetermined.

How to Code Poisonings

Poisonings are coded by looking in the Table of Drugs and Chemicals (see Figure 2–5) for the drug or causative agent. Codes in categories T36–T65 are combination codes that include the substance that was taken as well as the intent. No additional external cause code is required for poisonings, toxic effects, adverse effects, and underdosing codes. An example of a poisoning is a child brought to the ER in a coma after ingesting his mother's Thorazine. The coder would go to the Table of Drugs and Chemicals and find the poisoning code for Thorazine, T43.3X1, Poisoning by phenothiazine antipsychotics and neuroleptics, accidental(unintentional). Then the coder would select the appropriate code for the coma from the R40.2 category.

Substance	Poisoning, Accidental (unintentional)	Poisoning, Intentional Self-harm	Poisoning, Assault	Poisoning, Undetermined	Adverse Effect	Under-dosing
14-Hydroxydihydromorphinone	T40.2X1	T40.2X2	T40.2X3	T40.2X4	T40.2X5	T40.2X6
1-Propanol	T51.3X1	T51.3X2	T51.3X3	T51.3X4	—	—
2,3,7,8-Tetrachlorodibenzo-p-dioxin	T53.7X1	T53.7X2	T53.7X3	T53.7X4	—	—
2,4,5-T (trichlorophenoxyacetic acid)	T60.1X1	T60.1X2	T60.1X3	T60.1X4	—	—
2,4,5-Trichlorophenoxyacetic acid	T60.3X1	T60.3X2	T60.3X3	T60.3X4	—	—
2,4-D (dichlorophenoxyacetic acid)	T60.3X1	T60.3X2	T60.3X3	T60.3X4	—	—
2,4-Toluene diisocyanate	T65.0X1	T65.0X2	T65.0X3	T65.0X4	—	—
2-Deoxy-5-fluorouridine	T45.1X1	T45.1X2	T45.1X3	T45.1X4	T45.1X5	T45.1X6
2-Ethoxyethanol	T52.3X1	T52.3X2	T52.3X3	T52.3X4	—	—
2-Methoxyethanol	T52.3X1	T52.3X2	T52.3X3	T52.3X4	—	—
2-Propanol	T51.2X1	T51.2X2	T51.2X3	T51.2X4	—	—
4-Aminobutyric acid	T43.8X1	T43.8X2	T43.8X3	T43.8X4	T43.8X5	T43.8X6
4-Aminophenol derivatives	T39.1X1	T39.1X2	T39.1X3	T39.1X4	T39.1X5	T39.1X6
5-Deoxy-5-fluorouridine	T45.1X1	T45.1X2	T45.1X3	T45.1X4	T45.1X5	T45.1X6
5-Melhoxypsoralen (5-MOP)	T50.991	T50.992	T50.993	T50.994	T50.995	T50.996
8-Aminoquinoline drugs	T37.2X1	T37.2X2	T37.2X3	T37.2X4	T37.2X5	T37.2X6
8-Methoxypsoralen (8-MOP)	T50.991	T50.992	T50.993	T50.994	T50.995	T50.996
ABOB	T37.5X1	T37.5X2	T37.5X3	T37.5X4	T37.5X5	T37.5X6
Abrine	T62.2X1	T62.2X2	T62.2X3	T62.2X4	—	—
Abrus (seed)	T62.2X1	T62.2X2	T62.2X3	T62.2X4	—	—
Absinthe	T51.0X1	T51.0X2	T51.0X3	T51.0X4	—	—
beverage	T51.0X1	T51.0X2	T51.0X3	T51.0X4	—	—
Acaricide	T60.8X1	T60.8X2	T60.8X3	T60.8X4	—	—
Acebutolol	T44.7X1	T44.7X2	T44.7X3	T44.7X4	T44.7X5	T44.7X6
Acecarbromal	T42.6X1	T42.6X2	T42.6X3	T42.6X4	T42.6X5	T42.6X6
Aceclidine	T44.1X1	T44.1X2	T44.1X3	T44.1X4	T44.1X5	T44.1X6
Acedapsone	T37.0X1	T37.0X2	T37.0X3	T37.0X4	T37.0X5	T37.0X6

Figure 2-5 Partial ICD-10-CM Table of Drugs and Chemicals

Exercise 2.13

Assign ICD-10-CM codes to the following statements.

1. Ingestion of Clorox by 18-month-old child _____

2. Hemorrhaging due to accidental overdose of prescribed Coumadin _____

3. A patient is seen in the ER complaining of dizziness. The patient had recently started a prescription of Trazodone and this evening had three vodka tonics. The patient had been cautioned by both the physician and the pharmacist against drinking alcohol while taking medication. The Trazodone had been taken as prescribed. _____

4. Coma due to acute barbiturate intoxication, attempted suicide _____

5. Two-year-old patient ingested unknown quantity of mother's Enovid, suffering severe vomiting _____

Adverse Effects

Adverse effects of drugs are when the patient is given or takes the medication properly, but has a side effect due to the medication, such as anaphylactic shock due to penicillin.

Official Coding Guidelines:

Adverse Effect

When coding an adverse effect of a drug that has been correctly prescribed and properly administered, assign the appropriate code for the nature of the adverse effect followed by the appropriate code for the adverse effect of the drug (T36–T50). The code for the drug should have a 5th or 6th character "5" (for example T36.0X5-). Examples of the nature of an adverse effect are tachycardia, delirium, gastrointestinal hemorrhaging, vomiting, hypokalemia, hepatitis, renal failure, or respiratory failure.

How to Code Adverse Effects

To code an adverse effect, first code the effect itself, such as shock or tachycardia. Then locate the drug in the Table of Drugs and Chemicals and select the code from the Adverse Effect column. Sequencing of these codes is very important. If a patient had vomiting and diarrhea due to prescribed erythromycin, the coder would first code the vomiting (R11.10) and diarrhea (R19.7), and then use the External Cause code from the Adverse Effect column, code T36.3X5 to show the adverse effect caused by the medication.

Highlight:

The coder should always check the documentation in the record very carefully, and should not use any assault or attempted suicide codes unless the physician specifically states the cause as such.

Exercise 2.14

Assign ICD-10-CM codes for the following statements.

1. Hypokalemia resulting from reaction to increased dosage of Diuril prescribed by the physician _____

2. Urticaria secondary to allergy to tetracycline prescribed p.o. _____

3. Excessive drowsiness due to side effects of Chlor-Trimeton taken as prescribed _____

4. Tachycardia due to h.s. OTC antihistamines _____

5. Anaphylactic shock after IM injection of penicillin (no known allergy to PCN) _____

Complications

ICD-10-CM distinguishes between different types of complications, which can be found throughout various sections. Intraoperative and postprocedural complication codes are found within the body system chapters. The codes in this section are specific to the organs and structures of that system. These codes should be sequenced first, followed by a code(s) for the specific complication. On occasion, a complication of care code might have the external cause included in the code descriptor. The nature of the complication as well as the type of procedure that caused the complication is listed. For these codes, no external cause code is necessary.

Official Coding Guidelines:

Documentation of Complications of Care

Code assignment is based on the provider's documentation of the relationship between the condition and the care or procedure. The guideline extends to any complications of care, regardless of the chapter the code is located in. It is important to note that not all conditions that occur during or following medical care or surgery are classified as complications. There must be a cause-and-effect relationship between the care provided and the condition, and an indication in the documentation that it is a complication. Query the provider for clarification, if the complication is not clearly documented.

How to Code Complications

To code a complication, first look under the main term for the condition and see if there is a complication code, such as toxic gastroenteritis due to radiation therapy. To find this code, start with the complication: gastroenteritis, toxic. The code referenced is K52.1. Next, verify in the tabular and the following information will be provided.

K52.1 Toxic gastroenteritis and colitis

- This is for drug-induced gastroenteritis and colitis.

- Code first (T51–T65) to identify toxic agent.

- Use additional code for adverse effect, if applicable, to identify drug (T36–T50 with 5th or 6th character 5).

- Refer to the table of drugs and chemicals for the "Radioactive drug" to report the adverse effect from the radiation (T50.8X5).

This scenario would be coded in the following order.

1. K52.1 Toxic gastroenteritis and colitis
2. T50.8X5 Adverse effect of diagnostic agents

Exercise 2.15

1. Assign the appropriate ICD-10-CM code(s). The patient's chief complaint was itching and redness around the pacemaker site implanted two months ago. After examination, diagnosis was made of local infection inflammation of the pacemaker site. The patient was started on antibiotics and is to be rechecked in one week. _____

Sequela (Late Effects)

A previous illness or injury may cause a late-effect (sequela) condition or problem, a long-lasting residual or side effect that may not show up for a period of time. The late effect is often identified in the documentation by such statements as "residual of," "sequela of," "due to previous illness," and others. There is no time limit on when a residual effect can occur, but an effect is considered a residual if the initial (acute) illness or injury has resolved or healed. For example, a cerebrovascular accident (CVA) can result in symptoms that occur months or years later.

> **Official Coding Guidelines:**
>
> **Sequela (Late Effects)**
>
> A sequela is the residual effect (condition produced) after the acute phase of an illness or injury has terminated. There is no time limit on when a sequela code can be used. The residual may be apparent early, such as in cerebral infarction, or it may occur months or years later, such as that due to a previous injury. Examples of sequela include scar formation resulting from a burn, deviated septum due to a nasal fracture, and infertility due to tubal occlusion from old tuberculosis. Coding of sequela generally requires two codes sequenced in the following order: The condition or nature of the sequela is sequenced first. The sequela code is sequenced second.
>
> An exception to the above guidelines are those instances where the code for the sequela is followed by a manifestation code identified in the tabular list and title, or the sequela code has been expanded (at the 4th, 5th, or 6th character levels) to include the manifestation(s). The code for the acute phase of an illness or injury that led to the sequela is never used with a code for the late effect.

Some conditions that can produce late effects (sequela) are:

- Adverse or toxic reactions to drugs
- Bacterial and viral infections
- Burns
- Cerebrovascular disease
- Childbirth
- Fractures
- Lacerations

How to Code Sequela

There are several late effect codes for use in ICD-10-CM, and these can be located under the main term "sequelae."

This main term also directs the coder to "*see also* condition" because some common late effects have been included under the "condition" main term.

Two codes are commonly used to completely code the late effect:

1. The residual (current condition affecting the patient)
2. The original cause, illness, or injury that is no longer present in acute form

Another example of coding a late effect is scar on the face due to a previous third-degree burn. The scar, or residual, would be coded to L90.5 first, then the code for the late effect (sequelae), T20.30XS, Burn of third degree of head, face, and neck, unspecified site, sequela. The code for the late effect starts with "sequelae" then "burn," which states, "Burn and corrosion—code to injury with 7th character S." The coder looks up the third-degree burn to the face and selects the 7th character of "S" to indicate late effect.

> **Coding Tip:**
>
> Category I69 is used to indicate conditions classifiable to categories I60–I67 as the causes of sequela (neurologic deficits), themselves classified elsewhere. These "late effects" include neurologic deficits that persist after initial onset of conditions classifiable to categories I60–I67. The neurologic deficits caused by cerebrovascular disease may be present from the onset or may arise at any time after the onset of the condition classifiable to categories I60—I67.

Exercise 2.16

Assign ICD-10-CM codes to the following statements.

1. Residuals of poliomyelitis _____
2. Cerebrovascular accident (CVA) two years ago with residual hemiplegia of the dominant side _____
3. Traumatic arthritis, right ankle, following fracture of ankle _____
4. Bilateral neural deafness resulting from childhood measles 10 years ago _____
5. Brain damage following cerebral abscess seven months ago _____

Official Coding Guidelines

All diagnoses that affect the current encounter must be coded. In the hospital inpatient setting, the principal diagnosis, which by definition is "the condition established after study to be chiefly responsible for the admission of the patient to the hospital for care," must be listed first. The circumstances of the admission to the facility always determine the order of diagnoses.

In the outpatient, physician's office, or clinic setting, the first-listed diagnosis should be the main reason for the visit that day. For example, if the patient has hypertension and was seen in the clinic today for the complaint of shortness of breath, the shortness of breath would be the first-listed diagnosis. The hypertension would also be coded if it was still being treated.

Previous or history of illnesses or injuries should not be coded unless they affect the patient's current treatment.

Official Inpatient Coding Guideline Excerpts:

B. Two or more interrelated conditions, each potentially meeting the definition for principal diagnosis.

When there are two or more interrelated conditions (such as disease in the same ICD–CM chapter or manifestation characteristically associated with a certain disease) potentially meeting the definition of principal diagnosis, either condition may be sequenced first, unless the circumstances of the admission, the therapy provided, the tabular list, or the Alphabetic Index indicate otherwise.

C. Two or more diagnoses that equally meet the definition for principal diagnosis

In the unusual instance when two or more diagnoses equally meet the criteria for principal diagnosis as determined by the circumstances of admission, diagnostic workup and/or therapy provided, and the Alphabetic Index, tabular list, or another coding guideline does not provide sequencing direction, any one of the diagnoses may be sequenced first.

D. Two or more comparative or contrasting conditions

In those rare instances when two or more contrasting or comparative diagnoses are documented as "either/or" (or similar terminology), they are coded as if the diagnoses were confirmed and the diagnoses are sequenced according to the circumstances of the admission. If no further determination can be made as to which diagnosis should be principal, either diagnosis may be sequenced first.

E. A symptom followed by contrasting/comparative diagnoses

GUIDELINE HAS BEEN DELETED EFFECTIVE OCTOBER 1, 2014

F. Original treatment plan not carried out

Sequence as the principal diagnosis the condition, which, after study, occasioned the admission to the hospital, even though treatment may not have been carried out due to unforeseen circumstances.

Official Coding Guidelines:

Section I.B.8. If the same condition is described as both acute (subacute) and chronic and separate subentries exist in the Alphabetic Index at the same indentation level, code both and sequence the acute (subacute) condition first.

Official Coding Guideline Excerpts:

Section I. B.

11. Impending or Threatened Conditions

Code any condition described at the time of discharge as "impending" or "threatened" as follows:

- If it did occur, code as confirmed diagnosis.

- If it did not occur, reference the Alphabetic Index to determine if the condition has a subentry term for "impending" or "threatened" and also reference main term entries for Impending and for Threatened.

- If the subterms are listed, assign the given code.

- If the subterms are not listed, code the existing forerunner condition(s) and not the condition described as impending or threatened.

12. Reporting Same Diagnosis Code More than Once

Each unique ICD-10-CM diagnosis code may be reported only once for an encounter. This applies to bilateral conditions when there are no distinct codes identifying laterality or two different conditions classified to the same ICD-10-CM diagnosis code.

13. Laterality

Some ICD-10-CM codes indicate laterality, specifying whether the condition occurs on the left, right, or is bilateral. If no bilateral code is provided and the condition is bilateral, assign separate codes for both the left and right side. If the side is not identified in the medical record, assign the code for the unspecified side.

15. Syndromes

Follow the Alphabetic Index guidance when coding syndromes. In the absence of Alphabetic Index guidance, assign codes for the documented manifestations of the syndrome. Additional codes for manifestations that are not an integral part of the disease process may also be assigned when the condition does not have a unique code.

Section IV. Diagnostic Coding and Reporting Guidelines for Outpatient Services (Hospital-Based and Physician Office)

The terms "encounter" and "visit" are often used interchangeably in describing outpatient service contacts and, therefore, appear together in these guidelines without distinguishing one from the other.

Coding guidelines for outpatient and physician reporting of diagnoses will vary in a number of instances from those for inpatient diagnoses, recognizing that:

The Uniform Hospital Discharge Data Set (UHDDS) definition of principal diagnosis applies only to inpatients in acute, short-term, general hospitals.

Coding guidelines for inconclusive diagnoses (probable, suspected, rule out, etc.) were developed for inpatient reporting and do not apply to outpatients.

A. Selection of first-listed condition

In the outpatient setting, the term *first-listed diagnosis* is used in lieu of *principal diagnosis*.

In determining the first-listed diagnosis, the coding conventions of ICD-10-CM, as well as the general and disease-specific guidelines, take precedence over the outpatient guidelines.

Diagnoses often are not established at the time of the initial encounter/visit. It may take two or more visits before the diagnosis is confirmed.

(continues)

The most critical rule involves beginning the search for the correct code assignment through the Alphabetic Index. Never begin searching initially in the tabular list, as this will lead to coding errors.

1. Outpatient Surgery

When a patient presents for outpatient surgery (same day surgery), code the reason for the surgery as the first-listed diagnosis (reason for the encounter), even if the surgery is not performed due to a contraindication.

2. Observation Stay

When a patient is admitted for observation for a medical condition, assign a code for the medical condition as the first-listed diagnosis.

When a patient presents for outpatient surgery and develops complications requiring admission to observation, code the reason for the surgery as the first reported diagnosis (reason for the encounter), followed by codes for the complications as secondary diagnoses.

B. Codes from A00.0 through T88.9, Z00–Z99

The appropriate code(s) from A00.0 through T88.9, Z00–Z99 must be used to identify diagnoses, symptoms, conditions, problems, complaints, or other reason(s) for the encounter/visit.

C. Accurate reporting of ICD-10-CM diagnosis codes

For accurate reporting of ICD-10-CM diagnosis codes, the documentation should describe the patient's condition, using terminology that includes specific diagnoses as well as symptoms, problems, or reasons for the encounter. There are ICD-10-CM codes to describe all of these.

D. Codes that describe symptoms and signs

Codes that describe symptoms and signs, as opposed to diagnoses, are acceptable for reporting purposes when a diagnosis has not been established (confirmed) by the provider. Chapter 18 of ICD-10-CM, Symptoms, Signs, and Abnormal Clinical and Laboratory Findings Not Elsewhere Classified (codes R00-R99), contain many, but not all codes for symptoms.

E. Encounters for circumstances other than a disease or injury

ICD-10-CM provides codes to deal with encounters for circumstances other than a disease or injury. The Factors Influencing Health Status and Contact with Health Services codes (Z00–Z99) are provided to deal with occasions when circumstances other than a disease or injury are recorded as diagnosis or problems.

See Section I.C.21, Factors Influencing Health Status and Contact with Health Services.

F. Level of Detail in Coding

1. ICD-10-CM codes with 3, 4, 5, 6, or 7 characters

ICD-10-CM is composed of codes with 3, 4, 5, 6, or 7 characters. Codes with three characters are included in ICD-10-CM as the heading of a category of codes that may be further subdivided by the use of 4th, 5th, 6th, or 7th characters to provide greater specificity.

2. Use of full number of characters required for a code

A three-character code is to be used only if it is not further subdivided. A code is invalid if it has not been coded to the full number of characters required for that code, including the 7th character, if applicable.

(continues)

G. ICD-10-CM code for the diagnosis, condition, problem, or other reason for encounter/visit

List first the ICD-10-CM code for the diagnosis, condition, problem, or other reason for encounter/visit shown in the medical record to be chiefly responsible for the services provided. List additional codes that describe any coexisting conditions. In some cases, the first-listed diagnosis may be a symptom when a diagnosis has not been established (confirmed) by the physician.

H. Uncertain diagnosis

Do not code diagnoses documented as "probable," "suspected," "questionable," "rule out," or "working diagnosis" or other similar terms indicating uncertainty. Rather, code the condition(s) to the highest degree of certainty for that encounter/visit, such as symptoms, signs, abnormal test results, or other reason for the visit.

Please note: This differs from the coding practices used by short-term, acute care, long-term care, and psychiatric hospitals.

I. Chronic diseases

Chronic diseases treated on an ongoing basis may be coded and reported as many times as the patient receives treatment and care for the condition(s).

J. Code all documented conditions that coexist

Code all documented conditions that coexist at the time of the encounter/visit, and require or affect patient care treatment or management. Do not code conditions that were previously treated and no longer exist. However, history codes (categories Z80–Z87) may be used as secondary codes if the historical condition or family history has an impact on current care or influences treatment.

K. Patients receiving diagnostic services only

For patients receiving diagnostic services only during an encounter/visit, sequence first the diagnosis, condition, problem, or other reason for encounter/visit shown in the medical record to be chiefly responsible for the outpatient services provided during the encounter/visit. Codes for other diagnoses (e.g., chronic conditions) may be sequenced as additional diagnoses.

For encounters for routine laboratory/radiology testing in the absence of any signs, symptoms, or associated diagnosis, assign Z01.89, Encounter for other specified special examinations. If routine testing is performed during the same encounter as a test to evaluate a sign, symptom, or diagnosis, it is appropriate to assign both the Z code and the code describing the reason for the non-routine test.

For outpatient encounters for diagnostic tests that have been interpreted by a physician, and the final report is available at the time of coding, code any confirmed or definitive diagnosis(es) documented in the interpretation. Do not code related signs and symptoms as additional diagnoses.

Please note: This differs from the coding practice in the hospital inpatient setting regarding abnormal findings on test results.

L. Patients receiving therapeutic services only

For patients receiving therapeutic services only during an encounter/visit, sequence first the diagnosis, condition, problem, or other reason for encounter/visit shown in the medical record to be chiefly responsible for the outpatient services provided during the encounter/visit. Codes for other diagnoses (e.g., chronic conditions) may be sequenced as additional diagnoses. The only exception to this rule is that when the primary reason for the admission/encounter is chemotherapy or radiation

(continues)

therapy, the appropriate Z code for the service is listed first, and the diagnosis or problem for which the service is being performed is listed second.

M. Patients receiving preoperative evaluations only

For patients receiving preoperative evaluations only, sequence first a code from subcategory Z01.81, Encounter for pre-procedural examinations, to describe the pre-op consultations. Assign a code for the condition to describe the reason for the surgery as an additional diagnosis. Code also any findings related to the pre-op evaluation.

N. Ambulatory surgery

For ambulatory surgery, code the diagnosis for which the surgery was performed. If the postoperative diagnosis is known to be different from the preoperative diagnosis at the time the diagnosis is confirmed, select the postoperative diagnosis for coding, since it is the most definitive.

O. Routine outpatient prenatal visits

See Section I.C.15, Routine outpatient prenatal visits.

P. Encounters for general medical examinations with abnormal findings

The subcategories for encounters for general medical examinations, Z00.0-, provide codes for with and without abnormal findings. Should a general medical examination result in an abnormal finding, the code for general medical examination with abnormal finding should be assigned as the first-listed diagnosis. A secondary code for the abnormal finding should also be coded.

Q. Encounters for routine health screenings

See Section I.C.21. Factors influencing health status and contact with health services, Screening.

Procedures in ICD-10-CM

ICD-10-CM does not contain a procedure index. The Centers for Medicare and Medicaid Services (CMS) funded a project with 3M Health Information Systems to develop a replacement for Volume 3 of ICD-9-CM, known as the *International Classification of Diseases, 10th Revision Procedure Classification System,* or **ICD-10-PCS**. ICD-10-PCS is used for facility reporting of inpatient procedures. (Medical offices and other outpatient areas use CPT to code encounters and procedures.) The following general guidelines were followed in the development of ICD-10-PCS:

ICD-10-PCS: International Classification of Diseases, 10th Revision, Procedure Classification System.

- Diagnostic information is not included in the procedure description. Any description of the disease or disorder is in the diagnosis code, not the procedure code.

- The elimination of the Not Otherwise Specified option requires a minimum level of specificity to achieve the code assignment, making the option unnecessary.

- Not Elsewhere Classified is limited, as all possible components of a procedure are included.

- The combination of the seven alphanumeric characters allows all possible procedures to be defined, resulting in greater specificity in coding.

The goal of ICD-10-PCS is the same as that of ICD-10-CM: to improve accuracy and efficiency in coding and allow the capability for expansion of new codes. Characteristics include:

- Completeness—All substantially different procedures will have a unique code.

Highlight:

The Official Coding and Reporting Guidelines of ICD-10-CM can be found at http://www.cdc.gov.

- Expandability—Adding new medical procedures with new codes will be easier with the increase in the number of code characters.

- Standardized terminology—Each character has a standard meaning that will contribute to the accuracy of the code assigned.

- Multiaxial—Use of seven characters with a standard meaning within and across all procedure sections will result in more accuracy and precision when assigning a procedure code.

Each character has up to 34 different values. The 10 digits 0–9 and the 24 letters A–H, J–N, and P–Z comprise each character. Procedures are divided into sections that relate to the general type of procedure (e.g., medical and surgical, imaging, etc.). The first character of the procedure code always specifies the section. The second through 7th characters have a standard meaning within each section but may have different meanings across sections. In most sections, one of the characters specifies the precise type of procedure being performed (e.g., excision, revision, etc.), while the other characters specify additional information such as the body part on which the procedure is being performed. Codes can be located in an Alphabetic Index based on the type of procedure being performed. In medical and surgical procedures, the seven characters are as follows:

1. Section

2. Body system

3. Root operation (such as MRI, incision, and drainage)

4. Body part

5. Method or approach

6. Device (such as a pacemaker or implant—remains in the body after the procedure is completed)

7. Qualifier—additional information pertinent to the individual procedure, such as diagnostic or partial

The index for ICD-10-PCS provides the first three characters of the code. The coder is then referred to the tabular list to locate the remaining four characters needed. The index contains an alphabetical list of primary entries of root operations and composite terms, which are multiple aspects of a procedure. The secondary entries are specific to the root operation and may include body parts, devices used, or a root operation for revision.

For example, code 095HBYZ is the ICD-10-PCS code for Dilation eustachian tube, right, with Device, NEC, transorifice intraluminal. Following the meanings listed above, the seven digits show:

0 means the code falls in the Medical Surgical section

9 refers to the body system of ear, nose, sinus

5 shows the procedure is a dilation

H is the eustachian tube, right

B is the transorifice intraluminal approach

Y means this is a device NEC (not elsewhere classifiable)

Z means there is no qualifier

Another example is code 021OOZ4, Bypass, one coronary artery to right internal mammary artery, open.

0 means the code falls in the Medical Surgical section

2 refers to the body system, heart and great vessels

1 is the root operation of bypass

O is the body part, the coronary artery

O is the approach, which is open

Z indicates that no device was used

4 is a qualifier for right internal mammary artery

History of the Transition of ICD-9-CM to ICD-10-CM

ICD-9-CM, the 9th revision of the International Classification of Diseases, was used for many years in the coding and classification of diagnoses and procedures by a numerical system. The implementation of ICD-10-CM allows greater coding accuracy and specificity with space to accommodate future expansion in the advancement in medicine and technology. ICD-10-CM codes will provide better-quality information for measuring the quality, safety, and efficiency of health care services.

ICD-10-CM is built on the current ICD-9-CM coding system with modified conventions and the incorporation of a new code format and nomenclature, or naming, system. Table 2–2 outlines a comparison between ICD-9-CM and ICD-10-CM.

Table 2–2 Comparison of ICD-9-CM and ICD-10-CM

ICD-9-CM	ICD-10-CM
Consists of three to five characters	Consists of three to seven characters
Approximately 14,500 codes	Approximately 70,000 codes
First character is numeric or alpha (E or V); characters 2–5 are numeric	First character is alpha; 2nd and 3rd characters typically are numeric; characters 4–7 are alpha or numeric
Always contains at least three characters with no more than 5 characters	Always contains at least three characters. May expand further in the future if necessary to add new codes. ICD-10-CM will require greater documentation for coding specificity.
Decimal is placed after the first three characters when code extends further.	Decimal is placed after the first three characters when code extends further.

Even with the implementation of ICD-10-CM, ICD-9-CM will remain active in the health care facility as billing systems will continue to process claims and payments based on ICD-9-CM codes until the closing of these accounts. Many health care facilities with the assistance of their electronic medical record software programs are cross-walking ICD-9-CM codes with ICD-10-CM codes for a smoother transition.

Websites Related to ICD-10-CM

The following websites contain information on ICD-10-CM and ICD-10-PCS and maintain updates as to the progress of this revision.

Centers for Medicare and Medicaid Services (CMS) **https://www.cms.gov**

National Center for Health Statistics (NCHS) **http://www.cdc.gov/nchs**

Official Coding and Reporting Guidelines of ICD-10-CM **http://www.cdc.gov**

World Health Organization (WHO) **http://www.who.int**

Summary

ICD-10-CM is the *International Classification of Diseases, 10th Revision, Clinical Modification,* and is used to uniformly classify diagnoses and procedures. HIPAA requires the usage of ICD-10-CM diagnoses for billing of patients in the inpatient, outpatient, clinic, and physician office setting. The procedure section of ICD-10-PCS is not used in the clinic/physician office setting; it is for inpatient use only. Official coding guidelines for all users of ICD-10-CM and ICD-10-PCS are published at the CDC and CMS websites.

Coding has six basic steps:

1. Identify the main term(s) of the condition to be coded.

2. Locate the main term in the Alphabetic Index.

3. Refer to any subterms indented under the main term. Refer to any nonessential modifiers, instructional terms, or notes to select the most likely code.

4. Verify the code(s) in the tabular list. Never code directly from the Alphabetic Index.

5. Check all instructional terms in the tabular list and be sure to assign all codes to their highest degree of specificity.

6. Continue coding the diagnostic statement until all of the elements are identified completely.

Coders should be familiar with tools available, such as books and publications, organizations, and Internet sites, that can help to increase knowledge and awareness of coding rules, guidelines, new medical techniques, and changes to the coding systems.

References

Bowie, M. (2014). *Understanding ICD-10-CM and ICD-10-PCS: A worktext,* (2nd ed.). Clifton Park, NY: Cengage Learning.

Centers for Medicare & Medicaid Services (CMS) and National Center for Health Care Statistics (NCHS). (2015). *ICD-10-CM official guidelines for coding and reporting (FY 2016).* Retrieved from http://www.cms.gov.

D'Amato, C. & Melinda, S. (2008). *Coding secondary diabetes mellitus.* Advance for Health Information Professionals, Vol. 18, No 11.

Green, M. & Rowell, J. (2015). *Understanding health insurance: A guide to professional billing and reimbursement* (12th ed.) Clifton Park, NY: Cengage Learning.

ICD-10-CM expert for hospitals 2016 edition. (2015). Salt Lake City, UT: Optum360.

MedlinePlus. (2015). HIV infection. Retrieved from http://www.nlm.nih.gov.

Office of Inspector General, U.S. Department of Health and Human Services. *Work Plan: Fiscal Year 2015.* Retrieved from http://www.oig.hhs.gov.

HCPCS Level II

Learning Objectives

Upon successful completion of this chapter, you should be able to:

- Select HCPCSII codes to identify procedures, supplies, medications, and equipment items.
- Identify the structure of HCPCSII codes and applicable modifiers.
- Understand the placement position of the HCPCSII codes and modifiers on the claim.
- Blend the use of CPT codes and HCPCSII for accurate description of the care.

Key Terms

DMEPOS

enteral

Healthcare Common
   Procedure Coding
   System Level II
   (HCPCSII)

inhaled solution (INH)

injection not otherwise
   specified (INJ)

intra-arterial (IA)

intramuscular (IM)

intrathecal (IT)

intravenous (IV)

orally (ORAL)

other (OTH)

parenteral

subcutaneous (SC)

Table of Drugs

various (VAR)

Introduction

Codes from the **Healthcare Common Procedure Coding System Level II** is commonly referred to by the acronym HCPCS. Since CPT is considered HCPCS level I, we have distinguished the two in this publication by referring to HCPCS level II as HCPCSII. Sections or specific HCPCSII codes are used more frequently by certain specialties and health care entities, depending on the types of services provided. Many physician practices and coders lack familiarity with its codes, structure, and development processes. The HCPCSII codes are updated annually with periodic changes throughout the year as warranted by government policy. This chapter will introduce the coder to the importance of the HCPCSII codes and modifiers. Federally funded claims (e.g., CMS, Medicaid, Railroad Retirement, federal employees, and TRICARE/CHAMPVA) and other payors may reject claims if the HCPCSII codes and modifiers are not properly reported.

History of HCPCS

Healthcare Common Procedure Coding System Level II (HCPCSII): The second level of the coding system created by CMS for reporting of procedures, services, supplies, medications, equipment, and items.

Healthcare Common Procedure Coding System (HCPCS) is now a two-level coding system, originally created in 1983 (see Table 3-1). HCPCSII codes are required for all health insurance plans since the inception of HIPAA. In 2000, HIPAA implemented HCPCS level II codes as the standard coding system for describing and identifying health care equipment and supplies that are not included in CPT.

The HCPCS level I is synonymous with the American Medical Association Current Procedural Terminology (CPT) codes. This chapter of *Understanding Medical Coding* will focus on the proper selection of the HCPCS level II codes.

Table 3-1 Code Level Descriptions per CMS

Level	Definition
HCPCS I	American Medical Association Current Procedural Terminology
HCPCSII	National Codes
	• The American Dental Association has the copyright for the D code chapter.
	• Blue Cross Blue Shield (BCBS) contributes to the S code chapter. CMS works with other insurance plans for the remainder of the code chapters.

DMEPOS: Durable medical equipment, prosthetics, orthotics and supplies created by CMS. Examples include wheelchairs, walkers, braces, and colostomy supplies.

HCPCSII codes were created to identify products, procedures, services, supplies, medications (except vaccines), ambulance services and durable medical equipment, prosthetics, orthotics and supplies (**DMEPOS**). This coding system is maintained by the Centers for Medicare & Medicaid Services (CMS). The original goal in developing and introducing HCPCSII codes in the 1980s was the lack of CPT code existence for a variety of services and supplies identified by Medicare and other insurers necessary for claims processing. In reality, the code system was broadened to include code sets for Dental and Transportation. Further, the HCPCS system assists in tracking various policies set forth by Congress, such as the screening and vaccine services that were authorized under the 1997 Balanced Budget Act.

According to CMS, there are currently more than 4,000 separate categories of like items or services representing millions of products by various manufacturers. The code descriptors typically do not specify the particular product, brand, or trade names.

The HCPCSII codes are used by the following health care professionals, as well as by others:

Coding Tip:

HCPCSII codes are frequently created to assist CMS in tracking, reporting, and implementing policies that were created under the Social Security Act. When Congress introduces a health care policy, CMS will create HCPCSII code if a CPT code does not exist. Policy typically follows shortly thereafter.

> Physicians
>
> Advanced nurse practitioners (ANP, NP)
>
> Physician assistants
>
> Therapists
>
> Home health
>
> Outpatient departments
>
> Ambulance providers
>
> Dentists
>
> Durable medical goods companies

At the time of this publication, most insurance plans have adopted the HCPCSII codes. Workers' compensation and auto insurance plans are recognizing and using HCPCSII codes more frequently than in years past. Whenever reimbursement for a code is established, assigning pricing to the individual code is essential for claims payment. When a coder has determined that a HCPCSII code is not available, the coder may default to the CPT code 99070 for the supply or items that are not typically an inherent part of the procedure or visit. Using code 99070 typically causes the claim to be suspended for manual review and pricing. The carrier must determine what the 99070 represents and often requests additional information, such as a copy of the invoice and documentation to accompany the claim.

Format

The code format layout is relatively simple. The first digit is an alpha character (A through V), followed by four numeric digits, for example A4770. Each chapter of most HCPCSII code books has a brief descriptive paragraph related to the code section. There are now more than 8,700 HCPCSII codes. Some HCPCSII code publications include additional instruction and appendices for many of the payment rules. Coders should take caution, as many of these publications do not include all of the policies that may be associated with the code. The information often includes such topics as the Medicare Carriers Manual, Hospital Outpatient Prospective Payment System, Coverage Issues Manual, Physician Fee Schedule, and the Ambulatory Surgical Center rules. Research is often required to determine the coverage policies for the HCPCSII code.

> **Coding Tip:**
>
> Medicare and other payors have established limitations such as units or specific time frames (e.g., once per two years) on certain HCPCSII codes. For Medicare patients, if the quantity is exceeded or the service performed more frequently than allowed by policy, for coverage, the physician practice may need to prepare and provide an Advance Beneficiary Notice (ABN). The ABN advises the patient in advance of the reason that a particular service, medication, device, or item may not be covered by Medicare. The ABN also provides an estimate of the charges, and if the patient still desires the service, the patient signs the form and acknowledges that he or she may be responsible to pay for the service.

Familiarity with the HCPCSII code book and the various symbols will greatly assist coders in accurate code selection, and typically improves the profitability of a health care practice. Examples of medication codes and common dosages and their potential reimbursements are covered later in this chapter.

Fact versus Fiction

Most health care practices today use HCPCSII codes. A common compliance risk is the use of outdated HCPCSII codes. All federally funded providers (e.g., Medicare, Railroad Retirement, Medicaid, federal employees) require applicable HCPCSII codes for all health insurance claim forms that are submitted electronically. This code set is not optional for reimbursement purposes when a HCPCSII code exists or Medicare policy requires it. It might be mandatory for accurate claim submission, regardless of the amount of reimbursement anticipated.

The unlisted codes are selected as the last option. For example, prior to assigning an unlisted code for medications, coders should first investigate the medication being used, and check the package insert and perhaps the package box to determine the exact substance (item) that is being given. A code may be located in an area of the code book that you are less familiar with. If there is no code for the item, service, or medication in the HCPCSII code set, an unlisted code may be necessary.

The *National Correct Coding Initiative (NCCI) Manual* gives some detail for the selection of HCPCSII codes. The HCPCSII edits may or may not be published in the CMS policies. Coders should review the edits for NCCI that are released quarterly by visiting the NCCI page at http://www.cms.gov.

HCPCSII Hierarchy

When the documentation reflects duplicate descriptions, how does a coder know whether it is appropriate to select a HCPCSII or a CPT code?

There is duplication of some descriptions for both HCPCSII and CPT code. The hierarchy for selecting codes is as follows:

- If the descriptions match exactly between the HCPCSII code and the CPT code, use the CPT code unless Medicare or a specific payor states otherwise.

- If the descriptions do not match exactly between the HCPCSII code and the CPT code, check with the insurance plan prior to reporting the code. The policies may identify distinguishing criteria exceptions for each code.

Index

The index is typically located in the front of the HCPCSII code book, along with a combination of medical terminology and insurance terms. Many medications and some equipment items are listed by both brand name and generic (or chemical) name in the index. The **Table of Drugs** is typically located in the back of the HCPCSII book as an appendix. This table is alphabetized and extremely helpful as a starting point for determining the drug code selection.

Table of Drugs: A comprehensive list of non-oral drugs by both technical and brand names that include the route of administration and dose information for reporting purposes.

The principles for selecting the code are:

1. Read the documentation to determine the service, item, or supply.

2. Look in the index first.

   a. Start with the index, which is alphabetical. The table of contents or the Table of Drugs may provide further guidance for you.

   b. Keep in mind that the descriptions relate less to medical terminology than to insurance terms.

   c. "Examination" is a common term describing many services.

   d. "Screening" is another common term describing many services.

3. Locate the code in the HCPCSII code book chapter. Read the guidelines of the chapter first. This will especially be helpful in coding for supplies provided

at various facility locations, such as a physician office versus an ambulatory surgical center.

4. Double-check the details, symbols, and small print. This is probably the single most important skill for coding HCPCSII. If sufficient details are not available, more information must be sought from the physician, and documentation must be obtained prior to selecting the code.

5. Check the payment rules for the code if applicable or available.

6. Review and append modifiers when applicable.

7. Select the code for claim submission.

HCPCSII codes require a diagnosis to be linked to the code the same way a diagnosis is linked to a CPT service. It is important that the medical record document the medical necessity of the claim with sufficient detail, particularly when reimbursed according to a policy.

Code Revisions

CMS allows submission requests for code changes from anyone. Details for the HCPCSII process can be found at http://www.cms.gov. CMS has an ongoing and continuous HCPCS workgroup. There are three types or categories of coding revisions that can be requested:

1. Addition of a new permanent code

2. Language change or description modification

3. Recommended deletion of an existing code

The CMS internal workgroup for HCPCS is composed of CMS and various agency representatives, which include Medicaid and Pricing, Analysis, Data, and Coding (PDAC).

Exercise 3.1

As part of learning to use the index, table of contents, and Table of Drugs, answer the following questions.

1. Select the range of codes in the index for an amputee's wheelchair.

   Wheelchair _____

   Amputee _____

2. Select the code range for a latex, urinary leg bag sent home with the patient.

   Leg bag _____

   Urinary _____

3. For birth control, Depo-Provera 150 mg (medroxyprogesterone acetate) is given. _____

HCPCSII Chapter Details

The HCPCSII code book is organized by chapters, A0000 through V5999. For each of the chapters in the HCPCSII code book, the paragraphs located at the beginning of each chapter and prior to a group of codes usually outline the type of codes the section represents.

A0000–A0999 Transportation Services Including Ambulance

The A0000 section begins the series of codes designated by CMS for HCPCSII; the first actual code is A0021. This section provides codes to support emergency and nonemergency transportation services (ambulance and patient transport) and their related fees.

Coders reporting ambulance services should visit the CMS website to review "The Medical Conditions List" and instructions. This list can be found in the Medicare Claims Processing Manual, Chapter 15, Section 40, and is available at http://www.cms.gov. Previously, ambulance suppliers needed to sufficiently document the medical necessity for transport services. This documentation may still assist claims and benefit clarifications.

Building a modifier is often a term used when learning ambulance coding. Special single-digit modifiers are located within this chapter and must be used when reporting patient transports. The first digit of the modifier describes the origin; the second digit modifier describes the destination.

> **EXAMPLE:** A diabetic patient in distress is in need of an ambulance. The ambulance picks the patient up from her home and takes her to the hospital nearby. In this example, modifier RH would be used. The "R" is for the origin, picking the patient up from their residence (home). The "H" is the second character that provides the destination of the transport to the hospital.

Caution must be taken when providing origin and destination modifiers. HCPCSII modifiers may have an actual modifier once the coder builds the transportation modifier, which might cause confusion while learning. The difference is that the building of a modifier only applies to transportation services, and once payors receive the claim, they will know how to identify that this is an origin and destination character.

A4206–A4306 Medical and Surgical Supplies

The next section of the A0000 series is the medical surgical supply codes. It includes a little bit of everything. In selecting a code, it is important to distinguish the supplies, device, and components of the device, apart from the maintenance and professional services for use of the device.

Claims for HCPCSII codes may or may not be sent to the Medicare Part B carrier. Some of the codes are submitted and paid as part of another division, and are sent to the durable medical equipment regional carrier (DMERC). In order to send a claim to the DMERC, a separate enrollment and a simple practice assessment are required.

A4310–A4434 Incontinence, External Urinary, Ostomy A4310–A4434 is still listed under medical and surgical supplies. Supplies needed for permanent,

Coding Tip:

Prior to implementing a new supply in your practice, investigate payor policy or authorization. Sales information from the vendor or manufacturer is not always accurate for code selection or for anticipated reimbursements.

indefinite, and long-term incontinence are automatically covered by Medicare. Commercial plans might have alternative coverage policies. Local carriers will determine supply payment policies of temporary incontinence items that are provided at the physician's office.

> **Coding Tip:**
>
> An A4550 surgical tray is commonly used in providing a service at a physician office. CPT surgical guidelines state that when a supply tray beyond the typical type is needed, additional codes are to be selected. There are still some insurance plans and carriers that may accept code A4550 for reporting of surgical trays. Reimbursement will vary. Medicare and most payors will rarely reimburse for a surgical tray separately as they consider trays to be an inherent part of performing the surgical procedure.

A6000–A7527 Dressings

Medicare requests that for a dressing for an implanted device, the claim is sent to the local carrier. If the dressing is not for an implanted device, the claim is sent to the DMERC, not the local carrier.

Medical records will often describe a brand name for a dressing, rather than the specific description. The physician should be queried for appropriate details.

B4034–B9999 Enteral and Parenteral Therapy

Enteral therapy is within the intestine, and **parenteral** therapy is by injection through some route other than the alimentary canal, such as subcutaneous, intramuscular, or intravenous (IV). Enteral therapy, for example, is provided through a gastrostomy tube (G-tube); parenteral is through a feeding tube typically inserted into one side of the nares. The feeding may be for temporary or long-term use. Feeding may also be supplied via IV therapy.

enteral: The patient receives feeding or medication into the small intestine.

parenteral: The patient receives feeding or medication by injection route such as intravenously, subcutaneously, etc., not through the alimentary canal.

The codes in this area are used to report tube feedings and other nutritional items. The documentation may indicate a brand name but not be clearly identified for the code descriptions. The physician should be queried so the coder may determine the matching code description for the formula that is given.

The dose must be calculated accurately, and the quantity per code selected. Some code descriptions include the administration set, whereas other codes do not. Additional J codes for medications that might be given via the tube or parenteral method are often required, as are additional CPT codes for the professional services for placing the tube.

C1300–C9899 Outpatient Prospective Payment System (OPPS)

This chapter is CMS-specific and is rarely used by commercial plans. Even though C codes were intended for temporary use, many have been in place since 2001.

The C codes are reported for device categories, new technology procedures, and drugs, biologicals, and radiopharmaceuticals that do not have other HCPCSII code assignments. Non-OPPS hospitals such as Critical Access Hospitals (CAHs) and some Indian Health Service Hospitals (IHS) may report these codes at their discretion.

D0000–D9999 Dental Procedures

The HCPCSII codes are selected for dental services, often correlating to the dental insurance benefits and coverage. The place of service and the service the professional performed inform the code selection.

The D0000 code series is the Current Dental Terminology (CDT), which is created, maintained, and modified by the American Dental Association. The national panel for HCPCSII does not oversee the D codes. Since the CDT codes are a copyright of the American Dental Association, certain HCPCSII publications may not include the D codes within the resource.

There are some codes listed in the CDT that are duplicated in the CPT code book. It is usually necessary to contact the insurance plan to verify the correct code required for the care. For example, a physician might perform a surgical procedure that is covered under the patient's dental insurance, rather than the patient's health insurance. The dental insurance plan may accept the CDT code rather than the CPT code for the surgical procedures.

Many services in the D chapter are not a covered benefit for the federally funded programs. Since the services are not a covered benefit, the Advance Beneficiary Notice is not a requirement. Informing the patient prior to the care being rendered if the patient does not have coverage, however, would constitute good customer service.

Highlight:

Selecting a code that is simply "close" for equipment items may be a consideration of potential fraud risk. Accuracy for equipment coding is just as important as CPT or ICD-10-CM code selection.

E0100–E9999 Durable Medical Equipment

The durable medical equipment codes identify items and medical equipment. The E codes are very detailed specific descriptions of various equipment items. Many of the codes have multiple coverage rules for Medicare and other insurance plans.

Within this chapter, there are very few unlisted or unspecified options. The description must be matched for accurate code selection.

Chapter G0008–G9999 Procedures/Professional Services (Temporary)

This chapter is frequently used for many physician services. Although described as temporary, some of the codes have been active for many years. Policies surrounding the codes change frequently and often list specific criteria for use.

CMS creates the G codes and their descriptions. The codes may be used in addition to various CPT codes or, in some cases, in lieu of CPT codes. It is especially important to frequently review the policies associated with the use of G codes.

As discussed previously, the HCPCSII codes, including the G code chapter, may or may not be used by commercial insurance plans. Determining the insurance benefits and the medical necessity and then choosing the correlative codes will assist in accurate claims.

The NCCI's *National Correct Coding Manual* states that G0101 may be selected in addition to separately identifiable evaluation and management (E/M) services at the same encounter. Modifier 25 is added to the E/M code for this example. In Chapter 10 of this textbook, an example of an OB/GYN claim is prepared to assist in understanding the application of the codes. The G code coverage issues vary. For example, according to the NCCI, G0102 may *not* be selected in addition to an E/M service at the same encounter, and modifier 25 would not be applicable. This logic, however, is not consistent with CPT guidelines and rules.

Exercise 3.2

Colorectal cancer screening by flexible sigmoidoscopy is performed in the GI lab on a 51-year-old Medicare patient.

Select only the HCPCSII Code: _____

Coding Tip:

Depending on the HCPCSII book, if you look up occult blood, you might not find the code on the first try. The documentation should give you more detail so you can locate the correct code. If the documentation states, "The examination is performed on fecal material, or stool," you might have a bit of a challenge at first, but knowing that this is a screening type of service is helpful.

- If you look up the term "fecal," you may be guided to the code, depending on the HCPCSII resource used.

- Looking up "examination" may or may not guide you effectively.

- If you look up "screening," you would have to also know the test is a colorectal cancer–screening test, which is often included in the index as one of many choices listed with a range of codes.

EXAMPLE: A preventive examination is performed for prostate cancer, and a blood sample is obtained by the physician and sent to the lab for a PSA test.

Questions the coder needs to consider:

What insurance plan does the patient have?

What was the exact date of the previous tests?

Has the patient experienced any symptoms since the previous date?

These questions will guide the coder to the coverage of the benefits and the code selection.

If the patient has Medicare coverage, the code G0102 for prostate cancer screening, digital rectal examination, is selected. The physician practice would not indicate G0103 for the PSA, since this code reports the laboratory services and not the services for obtaining the sample. The physician would report 36415 for obtaining the blood sample. It is possible that additional CPT codes might be required along with G0102, depending on the documentation and the actual care provided.

For the "Welcome to Medicare, Initial Preventive Physical Examination (IPPE)," and also the digital rectal exam (DRE), both the G0402 and the G0102 codes are selected if performed.

Selecting the proper CPT, G, and Q codes, and linking to the ICD-10-CM as described in the medical record, is one of the most tedious aspects of coding. As the policies create instructions for coverage, the complexity of coding is growing, creating challenges for physicians and coders.

Coding Tip:

Typically behind every G or Q code is a memorandum or policy that should be reviewed. Coders should take caution when reviewing the policies, as many have numeric requirements for exam elements and specific FDA references for drugs.

H0001–H2037 Alcohol and Drug Abuse Treatment Services

This chapter is specifically for use by Medicaid agencies under mandated state law to establish separate identification for mental health services. Most other insurance payors do not activate the codes in this chapter.

Alcohol and Drug Abuse Treatment Services Guidelines

The descriptions are very site specific, often reported by health care professionals to describe mental health care. There are no miscellaneous or unlisted code options.

J0120–J9999 Drugs Administered Other than Oral Method

This is an important chapter in the HCPCSII coding, requiring special attention for accuracy.

The heading of the chapter is no longer quite accurate. The oral immunosuppressive drugs are now assigned J codes. As drugs are approved by the FDA, they are assigned a J code by CMS. Therefore, "other than oral method" of administration is no longer totally accurate.

Another important detail is that vaccines and immunizations are reported using CPT codes located within the Medicine section. This is one of the few supply type codes that are contained within CPT. CMS covers only a few vaccine and immunization codes, which can be found in the HCPCSII code set. Codes are selected when the physician practice has purchased the medication, representing a cost to the physician practice. If the physician practice has not yet purchased the medication, report only the administration codes (either HCPCSII or CPT, as appropriate). When reporting a code for medications administered, a fee representing a cost to the physician for the supply should not be listed unless one was actually incurred.

Drugs Administered

Administered drugs are considered those that cannot ordinarily be self-administered. There are exceptions and specific policies for insulin and diabetes, but most others have limitations. A drug with limitations, for example, is epinephrine jet injections, used for allergic reactions.

The following are listed as drugs:

- Chemotherapy

- Immunosuppressive therapy

- Inhalation solutions

- Other drugs and solutions

The drugs may have an associated policy limiting the quantity or units that are covered benefits. Most drugs have a quantity limitation, although the associated policy may not be published for each drug code. Selecting the specific code and also the exact amount of medication that was given requires extreme caution. Details of importance include units, such as mg versus mcg; and wording such as "per" and "up to." When necessary, query the physician for missing details required prior to reporting the code.

Coding Tip:

At least every six months, obtain a listing of all medications that are stored in the back office of the practice, including the refrigerator, and inventory each. Copy the package insert or box and keep it with the internal tracking sheet. Then, create a list or table that includes each drug by generic and by brand name, with the correlated HCPCSII code.

Medication Tracking Sheet (Example)

Technical Drug Name	Generic/Brand Name	Number of Vials	Doses per Vial	Route of Admin.	HCPCSII/CPT Code	Date & Initials

This will assist the staff in correct dosage documentation and, ultimately, in correct code selection.

Exercise 3.3

The provider administered Dexone to a patient. To select the code, make the following determinations:

1. Technical drug name referenced as Dexone
2. Route of administration
3. Drug dosage

   Select the HCPCSII code(s): _____

Highlight:

The main index of the HCPCSII code book includes many medications, but it is not as thorough as the Table of Drugs (see the appendix).

- Look up Rocephin and you are quickly guided to J0696.

- Look up the technical term for this medication, ceftriaxone sodium, and note how similar this name is to another medication. Be careful to select the codes based on the exact generic terms. Frequently, you will see terms with the addition of "acetate"; this is not the same substance. Do not select a code that is similar—they must match exactly.

- Now turn to the Table of Drugs. Rocephin or ceftriaxone sodium is commonly (not required to be) rendered either IM or IV, listed as per 250 mg. The table guides you to J0696.

- J0696 Rocephin quantity 1 is for 250 mg. If you give 1 gm, this equals 1000 mg; therefore a quantity of 4 is to be indicated on the claim form in the units field to accurately reflect the dosage administered.

EXAMPLE: Methylprednisolone acetate is given. Look at J1020, J1030, and J1040. Determine what dose was given and the exact concentration of the medication for correct code assignment.

Within the J codes chapter are multiple options for unlisted, not otherwise classified, drugs and solutions. Not every medication that is manufactured and listed in the *Physicians' Desk Reference* or *Red Book* (two popular medical resources) has an HCPCSII code listed. Some plans require the actual National Drug Classification or NDC number found in the *Red Book*. Consider all unlisted options in the specific area of the chapter prior to final selection of the code.

J3490 Unclassified drugs

J3590 Unclassified biologics

J8999 Prescription drug oral, chemotherapeutic, not otherwise specified

J9999 Not otherwise classified, antineoplastic drugs

Exercise 3.4

Select the HCPCSII code(s) and indicate the units based on the quantity given.

1. Injection of 3 mg Diazepam _____
2. Propofol 10 mg is injected _____
3. IM injection octreotide depot, 180 mg _____
4. IM cephalothin, 1 gm given _____

K0000–K0999 Temporary Codes

This chapter was created for purposes when permanent national codes do not include codes to implement a durable medical equipment Medicare administrative carrier (DME MAC) medical review policy. Physician offices do not typically report these codes.

Review the policies carefully prior to selecting the codes in this chapter. Medical necessity documentation in the medical record is always required.

L0100–L9900 Orthotic Procedures

The L0000 series codes describe various items, devices, and procedures, listed by anatomical sites. Only certain codes are used and dispensed by physician practices, depending on the specialty. For example, an orthopedic practice may provide a patient with a walking boot.

Prosthetic Procedures

The items listed from L5000 through L9999 are considered as *base* or *basic procedures* or *prosthetics* codes. It is not uncommon to report multiple codes for this chapter when applicable. For example, code L5624, Addition to lower extremity, test socket, above knee, could be used with code L5535, Preparatory, below knee "PTB" type socket code.

Coding Tip:

Use the Abbreviations and Acronyms appendix in the HCPCSII code book, if included. If your publication does not contain a special appendix, look for the abbreviations in the front of the book. Most abbreviations included in the HCPCSII are standard.

M0000–M0301 Medical Services

Medical Services are physician office services that are not listed elsewhere. In reality, the codes are mostly obsolete services, with the exception of M0064, Brief office visit for changing of mental psychoneurotic and personality disorder drug prescription. The documentation will guide the accurate code selection of these uncommon services.

Per NCCI, do not select M0064 and also 908 ___ series CPT codes for the same service.

P0000–P9999 Pathology and Laboratory Services

These codes are for the laboratory processing the studies. This section includes codes for chemistry, toxicology, microbiology, and miscellaneous services such as blood products. A commonly used code is P3000, Screening Papanicolaou smear, by technician under physician supervision. The lab would indicate this code for the performance and report of the actual specimen received for testing.

Q0035–Q9968 Temporary Codes

The codes in this chapter were intended to be temporary, according to Medicare. However, some have been in place for many years. Q codes describe many types of services, medications, and items that have not been authorized within other chapters of the HCPCSII code book and for which there is no CPT code. Careful consideration should be given for these codes, as Medicare often provides specific policy and guidance for correct use.

Coding Tip:

Section 4103 of the Accountable Care Act (ACA) allows coverage and payment for an annual wellness visit after January 1, 2011, for an individual who is more than 12 months past the effective date of his or her first Medicare Part B coverage period, and who has not received either an IPPE or an annual wellness visit within the past 12 months. Codes G0438 (first visit) and G0439 (subsequent visit) were established to report these annual wellness visits for Medicare patients. The following criteria, however, must be met:

- This visit includes a health risk assessment (HRA) and creates a personalized prevention plan (PPP). A PPP includes the following services:

  1. Establish or update an individual medical and family history.

  2. Establish a list of current providers and suppliers and medications prescribed for the individual.

  3. Measure height, weight, body mass index (BMI) or waist circumference, and blood pressure (BP).

  4. Detect any cognitive impairment, and establish or update an appropriate screening schedule for the next 5–10 years.

  5. Establish or update list of risk factors and condition (including mental health condition).

  6. Furnish personalized health advice and referral as appropriate to health education or prevention counseling services or programs.

CMS has added depression screening and functional status screening as elements of the first annual wellness visit only.

Here are some commonly used codes for many physician practices:

- Q0091 Screening Pap smear; obtaining, preparing, and conveying of cervical or vaginal smear to the lab. The code may be reported in addition to various G codes and/or CPT codes as described in the documentation.

- Q0111 Wet mounts, including preparation of vaginal, cervical, or skin specimens.

- Q0112 KOH preparations, all potassium hydroxide preps.

Per NCCI, some Q codes such as Q0091 may be selected in addition to Evaluation and Management services when significant, separately identifiable care is provided at the same encounter. Modifier 25 is added to the E/M code for this example.

Exercise 3.5

A physician provided home health care to a 92-year-old patient in an assisted living facility. The patient is quite alert for his age; however, he suffers from chronic diastolic congestive heart failure. Assign the appropriate HCPCSII and ICD-10-CM codes for the service.

HCPCSII: _____

ICD-10-CM: _____

R0070–R0076 Diagnostic Radiology Services

The three codes in this chapter are used for transporting equipment (portable x-ray and EKG) from one place to another, when medically required.

S0012–S9999 Temporary National Codes

Although the heading for this chapter indicates temporary national codes, the intent is to allow insurance plans *other than* Medicare to standardize systems by adopting a national code structure.

The S codes and their descriptions are created by BCBS and the Health Insurance Association of America (HIAA) for implementation by local insurance plans. BCBS then implements the codes locally. The state Medicaid offices are also now selectively implementing the S codes. Other insurance plans may choose whether or not to implement. The S chapter is used for BCBS, HIAA, and by the Medicaid program. Policies must be obtained for each insurance plan for accurate code selection, as these are not universally implemented. S codes are used for drugs, services, and supplies.

Here are some commonly used codes for many physician practices:

- S0610 Annual gynecological examination; new patient

- S0612 Annual gynecological examination; established patient

The documentation requirements, the ICD-10-CM linking of the diagnoses to the listed S codes above are necessary.

T1000–T9999 National Codes Established for State Medicaid Agencies

These codes are mostly tracking codes created at the request of various Medicaid programs, and may also be used by other insurance plans. They are not applicable for Medicare.

V0000–V2999 Vision Services

The codes up to V2999 are for vision purposes, usually for eyeglass sales departments. The use of multiple codes is likely for these services.

Reading the descriptions carefully will be required. The hierarchy for these codes may be one of the following:

- V code instead of a CPT code

- CPT code instead of a V code

- S code instead of a V or CPT code, if BCBS

V5000–V5999 Hearing Services

The V5000–V5999 are for hearing services, speech tests, and supplies. It is important to check the policies, as many screening services for hearing are considered bundled into another examination or noncovered benefits.

HCPCSII Modifiers

The HCPCSII modifiers are two digits, either alphanumeric or alpha/alpha. HCPCSII codes and modifiers may be updated, deactivated, or activated quarterly; however, most publishers print their code book annually. AMA/CPT announces annually the CPT modifiers that are nationally accepted for all claims, while other insurance plans create their own policies for activating the remaining modifiers. Just because a modifier is listed in the code book does not necessarily authorize standardized use of the modifier on the claim. HCPCSII modifiers will be addressed further in Chapter 13.

Table of Drugs

This is a highly utilized section of HCPCSII codes. It lists medications alphabetically by generic and brand name, along with the associated dose, common route, and the code.

The Route of Administration column lists the *most common* routes, not necessarily the only routes that are acceptable. Orally administered medications are not listed as these are often considered to be self-administered by many payors' payment policies. Different drugs will require different routes of administration. If the route is listed as IV, for example, the drug must be administered into the vein (intravenous). If it requires an arterial administration, an indicator of IA would be listed: SC for subcutaneous and IM for intramuscular, for example. If the medication is administered in a method other than that listed on this chart, additional investigation is warranted. Read the description of the code and the policies (if listed) to determine if there are special circumstances for coding. The abbreviations for the route of administration are included in the Table of Drugs.

Exercise 3.6

Match the abbreviation with the proper route of administration:

IA   Variously, into joint, cavity tissue, or topical _____

IV   Into catheter or suppositories _____

IM   Subcutaneous _____

IT   Orally by drops _____

SC   Injection not otherwise specified _____

INH   Intramuscular _____

INJ   Intra-arterial _____

VAR   Intravenous _____

OTH   Intrathecal _____

ORAL   Inhaled solution via IPPB _____

intra-arterial (IA): The patient receives through the artery system.

intravenous (IV): The patient receives through the venous system.

intramuscular (IM): The patient receives an injection into the muscular system. This is the most common method of administration.

intrathecal (IT): The patient receives through the membrane.

subcutaneous (SC): The patient receives an injection into the subcutaneous tissue.

inhaled solution (INH): The patient inhales the medication; may use respiratory equipment commonly known as the Intermittent Positive Pressure Breathing treatment.

injection not otherwise specified (INJ): The patient receives an injection other than the options listed, such as intradermal or an injection directly into anatomy.

various (VAR): The patient receives the medication using various, often multiple means.

Coding Tip:

Three common types of IV administration are:

IV Gravity

IV Infusion

IV Push

Medicare Policies

Not every publication includes the Medicare policies that are frequently associated with HCPCSII codes. If they are included, they are often in the back sections of the HCPCSII resource manual. It is important to check regularly on the CMS website and with individual commercial carriers for policies and updates, as coverage rules vary.

HCPCSII Revisions

The revisions give an at-a-glance look at the code revisions for the year. Often, no description will be listed, simply the code, which makes it necessary to review each code for description changes. Some HCPCSII manuals have the changes listed in the front sections, while others list the changes in the back of the book.

Accuracy Tips

It is continually challenging for a health care practice to stay on top of the actual medications and supplies that are rendered in patient care. Frequent and effective communication between the administrative and clinical staff is necessary in order for accurate HCPCSII code selection to be accomplished.

HCPCSII Medication: Questions and Tips to Consider

1. The physician documents and orders the specific medication.

   - Is the medication medically necessary for the condition or reason the patient is receiving it?

   - Is the medication ordered for an unusual purpose, dose, route, or frequency?

   - Is the medication for a cosmetic, contraceptive, or possible non-FDA-approved purpose?

2. Consider investigating the coverage for the practice's top insurance plans.

3. When purchasing the medication, consider:

   - Is the brand name or generic drug purchased?

   - What concentration is purchased?

4. For Medicare patients, obtain an ABN if necessary.

5. Does the chart state who administered the drug?

6. Is the route of administration and dose documented?

7. Does the encounter information (encounter form, charge slip, routing slip, etc.) match the information documented in the medical record for accurate coding?

The HCPCSII code is then selected and reported on the claim form.

other (OTH): The patient receives any other method not listed.

orally (ORAL): The patient receives medication through the mouth (orally).

Summary

It is important to make an accurate selection for HCPCSII services, supplies, and medication. Noting the correct dosage and quantity is crucial. Become familiar with the multiple chapters and appendices that appear in your HCPCSII coding resource. Understand the importance of the HCPCSII codes and modifiers and the role they serve in day-to-day coding.

References

Centers for Medicare and Medicaid Services. (2015). *Alpha-numeric* HCPCS. Retrieved from the HCPCS page found at https://www.cms.gov.

Centers for Medicare and Medicaid Services. (2015). *National correct coding initiative policy manual for Medicare services*. Retrieved from http://cms.gov.

CHAPTER 4

Current Procedural Terminology (CPT) Basics

Learning Objectives

Upon successful completion of this chapter, you should be able to:

- Identify the layout of the CPT code book.
- Study the symbols, the descriptions, and their purpose.
- Understand the proper steps for the selection of a CPT code.

Key Terms

Category II

Category III

CPT guidelines

CPT modifier

diagnostic

National Correct Coding Initiative (NCCI)

therapeutic

Introduction

Physicians' Current Procedural Terminology, referred to as CPT, is published by the American Medical Association (AMA). It identifies in detail the specific medical services and procedures performed by physicians and other health care providers. The descriptions of specific medical, surgical, and diagnostic services translate into a numerical five-digit primary code (referred to as CPT Category I) and two sections of alphanumeric codes (Category II and Category III). CPT codes may be further defined with assistance from two-digit **CPT modifiers** that provide additional information about the procedure or service that was performed (see Chapter 13).

The CPT is a uniform reporting system for procedural and medical services, creating reliable communications nationwide between health care professionals, patients, and insurance companies. It also serves to capture statistical data on quality measures (Category II codes) for the Physician Quality Reporting Initiative (PQRI) as required by the 2006 Tax Relief and Health Care Act. The CPT codes are reflective of services performed in the care of patients in the United States and are therefore reviewed frequently by the American Medical Association's CPT Editorial Panel. Each provider is to obtain the most current edition for selecting codes for billing and reporting purposes. A discussion of how to obtain the semiannual release for certain CPT codes will be covered later in this chapter.

The CPT was introduced in 1966, standardizing a variety of previously regional systems, and is now updated annually with the exception of vaccines and new and emerging technology services, which are released twice a year. Some of the milestone changes that have occurred over the past few years include the implementation of the Transitional Care Management and Chronic Care Management Services found within the evaluation and management section. **Category II** codes are used for data research and quality reporting. They are selected for tracking of services that measure health and, indirectly, the quality of health care delivered. **Category III** codes describe new and emerging technology, which were previously indicated by use of the unlisted codes.

The key to understanding CPT is to keep in mind that the codes are selected to communicate what professional service or procedure a practitioner has performed. The goal is to be as descriptive and inclusive as possible using the code system. Multiple codes may be selected to accomplish this goal, and there are instances when the use of an additional modifier will complete the explanation of the circumstances for the services that are performed. Specific details are essential in determining an appropriate code. The details are found in the providers documentation, which accounts for the care delivered. This information is required to be documented within the patient's medical record. Certain criteria are required for the selection of a code that help to explain the medical services delivered or procedures performed.

CPT modifier: A two-digit number placed after the usual procedural code, which represents a particular explanation to further describe the procedure/service or circumstances involved with the procedure.

Category II: Optional alphanumeric codes for quality measures, statistical data research, and development purposes.

Category III: Required alphanumeric codes for emerging technology instead of unlisted codes.

AMA/CPT Code Book

The American Medical Association publishes the CPT code book in a standard and a professional edition. The professional edition is in color and includes more illustrations than the standard edition. The professional edition also correlates code references to the AMA's newsletter, *CPT Assistant,* and to the annual resource for updates, *CPT Changes: An Insider's View.*

The CPT code book begins with helpful information located inside the front and back covers. The front cover includes a quick-glance, abbreviated listing of the symbols, modifiers, and common HCPCS Level II modifiers (HCPCSII). The AMA added the Place of Service (POS) codes list and descriptions as required by HIPAA for electronic transmission of professional claims. These POS codes are updated as needed by the Centers for Medicare & Medicaid Services (CMS). On the back inside cover of the CPT code book is a listing of common abbreviations that may be found in the patient's medical record, CPT, or other AMA publications.

Other publishers provide unofficial CPT type resources, which might include reimbursement or non-CPT supplemental information. These resources, however, are not approved for certification exams and often paraphrase specific CPT coding descriptors.

Foreword

Annually, the AMA issues an explanation of the changes at its Annual CPT Symposium. This symposium, along with AMA CPT Update Workshops, provides orientation to new codes, revised codes, and deleted codes from the previous year's edition. Many of these changes are reflected throughout the chapters of this publication.

CPT Editorial Panel and Advisory Committee

When coders and physicians have concerns regarding the description for CPT, taking a moment to inquire and bring the information to attention improves the system.

The AMA CPT Editorial Panel reviews information for the annual update of CPT on a quarterly basis. Anyone may write to the AMA/CPT outlining thoughts and changes by downloading the CPT Coding Change Request Instructions and Coding Change Request Forms available at the AMA's CPT website: http://www .ama-assn.org.

The revisions require time for review and discussion. It is advised when gathering information and communicating concerns for change consideration that pertinent parties such as specialty societies and state medical associations be contacted for involvement. Often, the societies and specialty associations will provide a spokesperson to address the CPT Editorial Panel.

CPT Code Book Introduction

CPT codes are composed using the following formats:

- The basic service or procedure has five digits (numbers) (e.g., 99212).

- Additional two-digit modifiers are selected to indicate special circumstances. The modifiers are appended to the procedure code on the claim form in a designated field. In this publication, they will be separated from the basic service or procedure with a dash (e.g., 99212-25).

- Category II and Category III are four digits followed by one alpha character, the letter "F" indicating a Category II code or the letter "T" for a Category III (e.g., 3083F or 0203T).

> **Coding Tip:**
>
> A principal rule (found in the introduction of the AMA's official CPT code book) for professional coders is that the selection of a CPT code does not imply insurance payment or reimbursement. CPT codes are for the accurate identification of the service, procedure, or supply as supported by the medical documentation and not a guarantee that payment will be received.

AMA annually publishes and distributes the revised CPT edition prior to the January 1 implementation of the code changes. Although the Category II and Category III codes are included in the annual publication, they are further updated and distributed on the AMA website each January 1 and July 1.

The evaluation and management (E/M) codes are selected for services performed primarily by physicians of all specialties. For convenience, CPT places this popular E/M chapter at the front of the code book, which results in a numeric sequencing break. Following the E/M chapter, the chapters are sequenced according to numeric value (e.g., Anesthesia codes begin with the number 0, Surgery with 1, etc.). The professional edition has tabbed sections for easy reference and is color coded. Refer to Table 4–1 for an at-a-glance listing of the CPT chapter titles and sections.

In general the CPT code book provides instructions for selecting the accurate CPT code. The instructions consist of the guidelines prior to the section, paragraphs prior to the main terms, references to AMA publications beneath a specific code, and parenthetical tips located before or after the codes. The documentation of the performed professional service must be accurately associated

Table 4–1 CPT Chapter Sections

CPT Sections	Code Ranges
Evaluation and Management (E/M)	99201–99499
Anesthesia	00100–01999 and 99100–99140
Surgery Guidelines	Surgery 10021–69990
Integumentary	10021–19499
Musculoskeletal	20000–29999
Respiratory	30000–32999
Cardiovascular	33010–37799
Hemic and Lymphatic	38100–38999
Mediastinum and Diaphragm	39000–39599
Digestive	40490–49999
Urinary	50010–53899
Male and Female Systems	54000–59899
Endocrine and Nervous	60000–64999
Eye and Ocular/Auditory	65091–69990
Radiology	70010–79999
Pathology and Laboratory	80047–89398
Medicine	90281–99607
Category II	0001F–9007F
Category III	0019T–0357T
Appendices	A–O (*modifiers and other information*)
Index	Instructions for use of index

to the code selection. The CPT code book specifically cautions against selecting approximate or "close match" codes.

CPT also guides physicians of any specialty to select from any area of the CPT code book to indicate the exact services that are performed, although it would be rare for every chapter of codes to be selected to describe professional services of one physician specialty. The Anesthesia codes, for example, are most likely to be performed by anesthesiologists rather than family practice physicians. The CPT code could be selected by any qualified physician or qualified health care professional performing the services.

Although the CPT was created for the purpose of identifying physician services, the health care industry has now expanded such that other qualified health care personnel may provide some of the same services. The CPT code may be selected only if the person who performed the service is clearly qualified. The definition of a qualified physician or health care professional directly correlates to licensure and scope of practice for each state. Some procedure codes specifically state that the service is performed by a specific type of service provider, either a physician or perhaps a therapist, radiologist, or other specialist.

Coding Tip:

According to the CPT instructions, mere approximation of a CPT code is insufficient. It is imperative that accurate code selection reflect the procedure or service that was provided and documented within the medical record.

Exercise 4.1

True or False: It is proper to select the CPT code that merely approximates the service or procedure that was documented.

Symbols

Semicolon ;

Certainly one of the more important rules for CPT is saving space, which is the purpose of the semicolon punctuation. Ignoring the semicolon will cause inappropriate and improper code selection. If a code description is indented, the words in the description prior to a semicolon in the first code above the indented code are the beginning of the indented code's description. This is often referred to as the *common portion*.

EXAMPLE:

00140 Anesthesia for procedures on eye; not otherwise specified

00142   lens surgery

In the code book, next to 00142, only the words "lens surgery" are printed. The common portion is found prior to the semicolon, with the "unique portion" (e.g., lens surgery) following after. In this case, the primary code is 00140 and the common portion is "Anesthesia for procedures on eye." Code 00142 should be read as, "Anesthesia for procedures on eye; lens surgery."

Add-On Codes +

The + symbol indicates that the particular CPT code is a supplemental or additional service to another specifically designated service performed by the same physician. A parenthetical note beneath the code will often state the specific code(s) with which the add-on service is allowed to be reported. The add-on codes are never to be used alone or coded separately. They will always require selection of a primary service to be listed first. Although most add-on codes are linked with the neighboring codes as the primary codes, some may be applied to various CPT codes in other areas of the book.

EXAMPLE: +99356 Prolonged physician service in the inpatient or observation setting, requiring unit/floor time beyond the usual service; first hour (List separately in addition to code for inpatient Evaluation and Management Service).

(Use 99356 in conjunction with 90837, 99218–99220, 99221–99223, 99224–99226, 99231–99233, 99234–99236, 99251–99255, and 99304–99310.)

Modifier 51 indicates a multiple procedure; however, it may not be used with add-on codes (see Chapter 13).

Revised ▲

To assist in alerting users to changes annually, the code book places the triangular alert prior to the CPT code when a substantial change has been made to the descriptor. Upon receipt of the new code book, review Appendix B, Summary of Additions, Deletions, and Revisions, to identify the changes from the previous year's description to the current year's description. In the professional edition, the triangle is blue; in the standard edition, all symbols are in black.

New Code •

The new code symbol signifies the addition of an entirely new code and description for the CPT book from the prior year's edition. The dot is red in the professional edition and black in the standard edition and is removed once the next annual edition is published. Updating coding resources annually will keep coders and physicians current on any additions from previous years.

▶ New or Revised Wording ◀

The sideways triangles alert users to a wording or content change. These are frequently seen in the **CPT guidelines**, which are the paragraphs prior to a series of codes. The impact of these changes may introduce an entirely new section or set of instructional guidelines. The text revision symbols also appear when a mere code within a code range has changed.

CPT guidelines: Within the CPT code book, the guidelines are the pages or paragraphs prior to a series of codes.

Reference to CPT Publications ⊃

In the professional edition, two additional symbols differing only in color guide the reader to AMA references that correlate to the specific CPT code. The red arrow refers to the quarterly newsletter *Clinical Examples in Radiology*. The green arrow refers to the *CPT Assistant* newsletter and the annual *CPT Changes: An Insider's View* book.

Exemptions to Use of Modifier 51 ⊘

To indicate that a code is exempt from the use of modifier 51, CPT uses the symbol ⊘ or a statement within the subsection guidelines and notations. Appendix E of the code book lists all codes with this exemption for quick reference.

For example, code "90281, Immune globulin human, for intramuscular use" does not show the 51-exempt symbol ⊘, as the guidelines for the entire section of immune globulins clearly state exemption of modifier 51 use.

The add-on codes are automatically exempt from the use of modifier 51, as stated previously.

Moderate Sedation ⊙

The symbol with a white circle surrounding a black dot or "bull's-eye" symbol is added to a CPT code for a procedure that is typically performed utilizing moderate conscious sedation (see Appendix G of the code book). The symbol indicates that conscious sedation is included in the performance of the procedure and cannot be additionally selected. If the bull's-eye symbol is not present and moderate conscious sedation is performed by the same provider performing the service, the codes may then be reported separately.

Flash ⚡

The flash symbol is found only in the vaccine section of CPT when a vaccine is pending FDA approval. Vaccines that are expected to be FDA approved within the current year are assigned a CPT code for immediate use upon the approval (see Appendix K of the AMA CPT code book).

Resequenced

The #symbol was added in 2010 and is referred to as a navigational alert by CPT. It is used when a code is not placed in numerical sequence due to lack of number availability but is appropriately located within a particular code family (see Appendix N of the AMA CPT code book for a listing of resequenced CPT codes).

Exercise 4.2

Define the following CPT symbols and list at least one code example for each of the symbols.

1. ▲
2. ⊙
3. +
4. ⚡
5. #
6. ⊘
7. ►◄

Unlisted Codes

Health care technology progresses rapidly, and the implementation of new techniques influences the code selection. For this reason, it is important to review the latest Category III codes from AMA (updated twice a year, not annually). In the absence of a Category III code to describe a service that is not listed in the CPT code book, an unlisted code is selected. There is at least one unlisted code in every chapter section of CPT, with some areas providing multiple unlisted codes.

Sending Medical Record Copies

There are instances where performed services may require additional information (the documentation) to be sent to the insurance company or other agencies. When sending copies of medical records, the CPT guideline states that the *pertinent* components of documentation should include the following:

- Adequate description of the nature, extent, and need for the procedure
- Time, effort, and equipment necessary
- Complexity of symptoms

- Final diagnosis
- Physical findings
- **Diagnostic** and **therapeutic** procedures
- Concurrent findings
- Anticipated follow-up care

diagnostic: To identify or investigate for purposes of determining a condition or diagnosis.

therapeutic: To achieve a therapeutic result or to treat a condition or diagnosis.

Illustrations

The CPT professional edition includes surgical terminology tips and anatomy and procedural illustrations to assist in understanding the code descriptions. A full listing of Anatomical and Procedural Illustrations and corresponding page numbers can be found at the beginning of the CPT book. The actual illustrations can be found within the pertinent sections of CPT.

Evaluation and Management (E/M)

In Chapter 5 you will become familiar with E/M services. This section is well known and used by most providers. This section of CPT includes specific categories of services such as preventive medicine, also known as wellness visits; consultations; newborn care; critical care; and much more. Chapter 5 will also expound on E/M criteria and code selection determination in detail.

Anesthesia

Chapter 6 discusses the Anesthesia code selection and its rather unique concepts in detail. The guidelines prior to the codes describe the code selection criteria and should be reviewed thoroughly. These include guidances for reporting of time and unique physical status modifier usage. An important fact to note is that anesthesiologists and coders utilize an additional coding resource published by the American Society of Anesthesiologists (ASA). This publication gives guidance on relative values, which is to be used for calculating with the actual time being reported.

CPT Surgical Guidelines

The surgical guidelines are located after the Anesthesia section and just prior to the Integumentary codes. The surgical guidelines are unique to procedures (rather than professional services) and apply to every code from the 10000 series to code 69990. It is important to comprehend the surgical guidelines prior to surgical coding, as they set the stage with foundational direction for use with the largest section of the CPT codes. The guidelines within each surgical section and their coding concepts extensively affect reimbursement and provide direction for correct use.

It is helpful to first review the definitions of surgery according to AMA/CPT before getting into the surgical guidelines. The June 1996 issue of *CPT Assistant* defined surgery as incision, excision, amputation, introduction, endoscopy, repair, destruction, suture, and manipulation. All of these terms are included in CPT codes throughout the surgical section of CPT.

Surgical Package

CPT surgical package rules are intended for application with the codes from 10000 through 69990. The CPT defines the surgical package as specific services included in a given CPT surgical code that are not separately reportable outside of the operation. The following descriptions are considered an inherent part of any surgical procedure:

- Evaluation and management service(s) subsequent to the decision for surgery on the date immediately prior to *or* on the same date as the procedure (including history and physical)

- Local infiltration, metacarpal/metatarsal/digital block, or topical anesthesia

- Immediate postoperative care, including dictating operative notes, and talking with the family and other physicians or qualified health care professionals

- Writing orders

- Evaluating the patient in the postanesthesia recovery area

- Typical postoperative follow-up care

National Correct Coding Initiative (NCCI): Established by the Centers for Medicare & Medicaid Services, often referred to as *bundling edits*. Individual payors often follow NCCI.

> **Highlight:**
>
> The **National Correct Coding Initiative (NCCI)** was established by the Centers for Medicare & Medicaid Services and is often referred to as "bundling edits." NCCI is often followed by individual payors that sometimes vary from the CPT definition of the surgical package.

Follow-Up Care for Surgical Procedures

The usual follow-up care for diagnostic procedures includes only those services related to recovery from the diagnostic procedure(s) itself. Therapeutic procedures include only care that is usually a part of the surgical procedure. Any complications, exacerbation, recurrence, or other illnesses requiring additional services may be reported separately. These circumstances will require the use of specific ICD-10-CM codes describing the complication or specific details. Separate payment will vary by insurance carrier.

Multiple Procedures

The use of modifier -51 is to be reported when multiple procedures are performed on the same date. Multiple surgical procedures on the same day are often subject to additional payment reduction after the first procedure and will vary by payer. Modifiers are discussed in detail in Chapter 13.

> **Coding Tip:**
>
> Do not use modifier 51 with the add-on codes, as they are modifier 51 exempt. Reducing charges when submitting multiple procedures is discouraged as this may result in further decrease of your reimbursement. Coders should become familiar with Medicare's National Correct Coding Initiative Edits (NCCI). Edits are updated quarterly and are available on the CMS website.

Materials and Supplies

CPT guides you to select 99070 for any supplies "over and above" those usually included with the procedure. Insurance plans may have various interpretations for the coding for materials and supplies with the physician services.

Select HCPCSII codes for supplies whenever describing items used during procedures beyond the typical care or global surgical package. Xylocaine/lidocaine is not coded when used as topical anesthetic, because topical anesthesia is included in the CPT surgical package definition. However, different medications for other purposes are reported.

Destruction

Surgical destruction is selected if it is separate from the standard management of the problem. Cryosurgery, ablation, electrosurgery, laser, and chemical (silver nitrate) are all common forms of destruction.

> **Highlight:**
> Conscious sedation rules vary among insurance plans. The surgeon must be the same provider performing the procedure and conscious sedation. CPT states that an "independent trained observer" is required to assist the surgeon in the conscious sedation.

Exercise 4.3

A patient presented with a 2 cm laceration to the index finger. Prior to suturing, the physician numbed the finger by performing a digital block and wants to know from the coder if he can report the block separately. What should the coder tell the physician, and where is the answer for the reference?

Radiology, Pathology, and Laboratory Guidelines

Radiology, pathology, and laboratory coding guidelines are discussed in detail in Chapter 11. Both the radiology and the pathology include CPT codes for diagnostic as well as therapeutic services. Only certain laboratory services are allowed to be performed in physician offices without site inspections and special laboratory certifications.

Medicine Section

The medicine section of CPT is often referred to as the "everything else" section. Coders will find a variety of codes starting with immune globulins and vaccines and ending with medical nutrition therapy. In between, services such as physical medicine, psychiatric services, ophthalmology, special services, and reports, plus a plethora of diagnostic services, can be found.

Category II Codes

CMS and the AMA have been encouraging providers to use Category II codes for several years now, even though they remain optional. Using the codes is a way for health care professionals to report measures, reflecting the quality of care delivered to their patients. The codes are four digits followed by the alpha F, currently ranging from 0001F to 9007F. This range of codes continues to grow quickly. CMS released notice that Providers participating with PQRS starting in 2015, will avoid the PQRS negative payment adjustment in 2017 and beyond. To learn more about PQRS and the negative payment adjustment, visit www.cms.gov.

Category II codes are not separately reimbursed and are used for informational (data measure) reporting only.

Category III Codes

Unlike Category II codes, the Category III codes are mandatory to use when a CPT Category I code is not available. The AMA provides the following information in this section: "This is an activity that is critically important in the evaluation of health care delivery and the formation of public and private policy. The use of the codes in this section allow physicians and other qualified health care professionals, insurers, health services researchers, and health policy experts to identify emerging technology, services, and procedures for clinical efficacy, utilization and outcomes."

The Category III codes are four digits followed by an alpha T. The codes are active for no longer than five years, as they are considered for permanent Category I CPT code assignment. The updates are distributed in January and June at http://www.ama-assn.org. The list continues to increase, and it is recommended that coders obtain the listing each January and June as the CPT book is published annually.

Coding Tip:

Prior to selecting an unlisted CPT code, review the Category III codes first. Keep current with new and emerging technology:

- Review the Category III section of CPT upon receipt of the new CPT book.

- Mark your calendar to visit http://www.ama-assn.org on February 1 and July 1 to keep current on any upcoming changes.

- Highlight frequently used codes.

Within the Category I section of CPT, Category III codes can be found listed within parenthetical notes under a particular Category I code when applicable references are made.

Online Medical Evaluation

To keep current on changes to health care delivery, CPT now includes an Online Medical Evaluation and Management service code (99444), sometimes referred to as an *e-visit* with a patient. These codes have specific requirements that must be followed:

- The communication is a response to an *established* patient's online inquiry.

- The response is provided by a qualified health care professional. (CPT has designated an online medical evaluation code for physicians and a separate code for qualified health care professionals.)

- The communication involves the physician or qualified health care professional's personal, timely response to the inquiry.

- The provider must have permanent storage of the entire encounter with retrieval capability.

- The service may not be reported if the inquiry is regarding a pre- or post-E/M service that has been delivered in the previous seven days, or is related to the next soonest available appointment, should the provider decide to address the inquiry in person.

- The inquiry includes all related telephone calls such as prescriptions and diagnostic testing orders for the problem.

- The communication must meet security guidelines according to HIPAA.

- No examination is performed, as these are not face-to-face encounters.

- The codes are not for every e-mail communication sent by the patient, and not for provider- or staff-initiated online inquiries.

CPT Errata

Each year, AMA/CPT publishes an errata identifying any corrections that are necessary after the annual code book is distributed. This information is distributed via the AMA website and, depending on the correction, may affect the code selection or correct use.

Appendix A: Modifiers

The modifiers, found in Appendix A of the CPT code book, are essential, as they assist in painting a clearer picture of the procedure or service that is being performed. Modifiers are often selected to indicate additional information such as special circumstances and are necessary to signal the variance from the description of the base code. Figure 4–1 shows an example of placement for CPT codes and modifiers. See Chapter 13 for a detailed discussion of modifiers.

Appendix B: Summary of Additions, Deletions, and Revisions

This area of the CPT code book offers a great "quick review" of all changes for the year. Many coders go straight to Appendix B when they receive the new CPT code book because it clarifies revisions, additions, and deletions from the previous year of coding. The following is an example from the 2014–2015 CPT code book for code description comparison purposes.

- 2014 Code Description: 27280, Arthrodesis, sacroiliac joint (including obtaining graft)

- 2015 Code Description: (▲) 27280, Arthrodesis, open, sacroiliac joint, including obtaining bone graft, including instrumentation, when performed

Appendix C: Clinical Examples

Most importantly, the clinical examples contained in Appendix C of CPT are not a description of the actual proper documentation. The examples do not list the history, exam, and medical decision-making criteria. They assist in guiding for code selection based on brief descriptions of many specialty-specific options for E/M services.

HEALTH INSURANCE CLAIM FORM

APPROVED BY NATIONAL UNIFORM CLAIM COMMITTEE (NUCC) 02/12

PICA | PICA

1. MEDICARE (Medicare#) MEDICAID (Medicaid#) TRICARE (ID#/DoD#) CHAMPVA (Member ID#) GROUP HEALTH PLAN (ID#) FECA BLK LUNG (ID#) OTHER (ID#)

1a. INSURED'S I.D. NUMBER (For Program in Item 1)

2. PATIENT'S NAME (Last Name, First Name, Middle Initial)

3. PATIENT'S BIRTH DATE MM DD YY   SEX M F

4. INSURED'S NAME (Last Name, First Name, Middle Initial)

5. PATIENT'S ADDRESS (No., Street)

6. PATIENT RELATIONSHIP TO INSURED Self Spouse Child Other

7. INSURED'S ADDRESS (No., Street)

CITY   STATE

8. RESERVED FOR NUCC USE

CITY   STATE

ZIP CODE   TELEPHONE (Include Area Code) (   )

ZIP CODE   TELEPHONE (Include Area Code) (   )

9. OTHER INSURED'S NAME (Last Name, First Name, Middle Initial)

10. IS PATIENT'S CONDITION RELATED TO:

11. INSURED'S POLICY GROUP OR FECA NUMBER

a. OTHER INSURED'S POLICY OR GROUP NUMBER

a. EMPLOYMENT? (Current or Previous) YES NO

a. INSURED'S DATE OF BIRTH MM DD YY   SEX M F

b. RESERVED FOR NUCC USE

b. AUTO ACCIDENT? YES NO   PLACE (State)

b. OTHER CLAIM ID (Designated by NUCC)

c. RESERVED FOR NUCC USE

c. OTHER ACCIDENT? YES NO

c. INSURANCE PLAN NAME OR PROGRAM NAME

d. INSURANCE PLAN NAME OR PROGRAM NAME

10d. CLAIM CODES (Designated by NUCC)

d. IS THERE ANOTHER HEALTH BENEFIT PLAN? YES NO *If yes,* complete items 9, 9a, and 9d.

READ BACK OF FORM BEFORE COMPLETING & SIGNING THIS FORM.
12. PATIENT'S OR AUTHORIZED PERSON'S SIGNATURE I authorize the release of any medical or other information necessary to process this claim. I also request payment of government benefits either to myself or to the party who accepts assignment below.

SIGNED _____ DATE _____

13. INSURED'S OR AUTHORIZED PERSON'S SIGNATURE I authorize payment of medical benefits to the undersigned physician or supplier for services described below.

SIGNED _____

14. DATE OF CURRENT ILLNESS, INJURY, or PREGNANCY (LMP) MM DD YY   QUAL.

15. OTHER DATE QUAL. MM DD YY

16. DATES PATIENT UNABLE TO WORK IN CURRENT OCCUPATION FROM MM DD YY TO MM DD YY

17. NAME OF REFERRING PROVIDER OR OTHER SOURCE   17a.   17b. NPI

18. HOSPITALIZATION DATES RELATED TO CURRENT SERVICES FROM MM DD YY TO MM DD YY

19. ADDITIONAL CLAIM INFORMATION (Designated by NUCC)

20. OUTSIDE LAB? YES NO $ CHARGES

21. DIAGNOSIS OR NATURE OF ILLNESS OR INJURY Relate A-L to service line below (24E)   ICD Ind.

A. ___ B. ___ C. ___ D. ___
E. ___ F. ___ G. ___ H. ___
I. ___ J. ___ K. ___ L. ___

22. RESUBMISSION CODE   ORIGINAL REF. NO.

23. PRIOR AUTHORIZATION NUMBER

24. A. DATE(S) OF SERVICE From MM DD YY	To MM DD YY	B. PLACE OF SERVICE	C. EMG	D. PROCEDURES, SERVICES, OR SUPPLIES (Explain Unusual Circumstances) CPT/HCPCS	MODIFIER	E. DIAGNOSIS POINTER	F. $ CHARGES	G. DAYS OR UNITS	H. EPSDT Family Plan	I. ID. QUAL.	J. RENDERING PROVIDER ID. #
1				99214	25					NPI	
2				12001						NPI	
3										NPI	
4										NPI	
5										NPI	
6										NPI	

25. FEDERAL TAX I.D. NUMBER SSN EIN

26. PATIENT'S ACCOUNT NO.

27. ACCEPT ASSIGNMENT? (For govt. claims, see back) YES NO

28. TOTAL CHARGE $

29. AMOUNT PAID $

30. Rsvd for NUCC Use

31. SIGNATURE OF PHYSICIAN OR SUPPLIER INCLUDING DEGREES OR CREDENTIALS (I certify that the statements on the reverse apply to this bill and are made a part thereof.)

SIGNED _____ DATE _____

32. SERVICE FACILITY LOCATION INFORMATION   a. NPI   b.

33. BILLING PROVIDER INFO & PH # (   )   a. NPI   b.

NUCC Instruction Manual available at: www.nucc.org   **PLEASE PRINT OR TYPE**   APPROVED OMB-0938-1197 FORM 1500 (02-12)

CARRIER

PATIENT AND INSURED INFORMATION

PHYSICIAN OR SUPPLIER INFORMATION

Figure 4-1 Placement of five-digit CPT codes and modifier on CMS-1500 claim form

The clinical examples represent presenting problems frequently encountered by certain specialties. They are, however, just examples.

The purpose of this appendix is to assist physicians with the understanding and meaning of the E/M descriptors. The listed specialties for each of the clinical examples were developed by that particular specialty. Codes that do not have a listing may have clarifications located in other AMA publications such as *CPT Assistant* or the *AMA Principles of CPT Coding*.

Appendix D: Summary of CPT Add-On Codes

Appendix D contains a listing of the add-on + codes. Add-on codes are supplemental or additional procedures commonly carried out in addition to the primary procedure performed. Appendix D further reminds coders not to use modifier -51 with add-on codes.

Appendix E: Summary of CPT Codes Exempt from Modifier -51

Appendix E lists modifier -51 exempt codes other than the add-on codes or codes stating -51 exemption within specific guidelines. CPT codes accompanied by the ⊘ symbol are the only modifier-exempt services listed in Appendix E.

Appendix F: Summary of CPT Codes Exempt from Modifier -63

Appendix F lists codes exempt from modifier -63, which is a modifier for procedures performed on infants less than 4 kg. Although there is no symbol denoting the modifier -63 exemption, there are parenthetical notations with the codes to indicate the exemption beneath certain CPT codes.

Appendix G: Summary of CPT Codes That Include Moderate (Conscious) Sedation

Appendix G provides a list of procedure codes that are accompanied by the ⊙ symbol, indicating that conscious sedation is an inherent part of providing the procedure. Additional instruction for when a second provider assists with conscious sedation services is provided.

Appendix H: Alphabetic Index of Performance Measures by Clinical Condition or Topic

Appendix H of the code book is the Alphabetical Clinical Topics Listing (also called the Alphabetical Listing). It has been removed from the CPT codebook. It can only be accessed on the AMA CPT website (www.ama-assn.org).

Appendix I: Genetic Testing Code Modifiers

Appendix I has been removed from the CPT code set. Physicians and coders are referred to the molecular pathology codes, which can be found at the AMA CPT website (www.ama-assn.org)

Appendix J: Electrodiagnostic Medicine Listing of Sensory, Motor, and Mixed Nerves

To accurately report nerve conduction studies, Appendix J has been provided to assign each sensory, motor, and mixed nerve to the appropriate code.

Appendix K: Product Pending FDA Approval

Appendix K provides a listing of vaccine products anticipating Food and Drug Administration (FDA) approval. CPT assigns a Category I code and identifies these pending vaccines with the lightning bolt ($\mathscr{N}$) symbol.

Appendix L: Vascular Families

Appendix L assists coders with understanding and assigning the appropriate first, second, and third order within vascular families. This table is especially important to those who code interventional cardiovascular and radiology procedures.

Appendix M: Crosswalk to Deleted CPT Codes

The table provided by Appendix M assists with crosswalking, or matching, deleted CPT codes to their respective replacements. This table lists codes that were deleted and renumbered from 2007 to 2009. No additional codes will be added, as the AMA no longer practices the deletion and renumbering method.

Appendix N: Summary of Resequenced CPT Codes

Appendix N is a summary of CPT codes that may be listed out of numerical sequence. The # symbol has been appended to the codes in this list to indicate a break in numeric sequence. The use of this symbol avoids the need to delete and renumber entire code ranges.

Appendix O: Multianalyte Assays with Algorithmic Analyses

This appendix provides administrative codes for MAAA or Multianalyte Assays with Algorithmic Analyses procedures found in the Laboratory and Pathology section of Category I CPT codes. Additions for this section may be released three times per year through the AMA CPT website to assist with immediate use and reporting.

Index

The alphabetic index is designed to guide the user to the correct main text of the CPT code. When selecting a CPT code, the coder should start with the index. Familiarity with the CPT index and the concepts for use will encourage accurate coding and expedite the code selection. The index is streamlined and does not offer multiple, redundant options for each procedure and service.

The index is based on certain concepts to simplify the search process. The main terms are as follows:

- Procedure or service

- Organ or other anatomical site

- Condition

- Synonyms, eponyms, and abbreviations

Beneath the main term, three indented options may be listed. These indented options are modifying terms used to select the code.

Exercise 4.4

1. Which appendix contains the full listing of revised codes from the previous year?
2. To further clarify or describe additional circumstances of a procedure or service, what might be necessary to append?
   a. A category III code
   b. A modifier
3. Using the index, complete the following:
   a. Find and list the term for EKG.
   b. *Following the term, what code is referenced for a rhythm evaluation?*

In an entry with more than one code, the codes will be stated either with a comma to indicate multiple codes or with a dash to indicate a range of codes. It is important to review all of the codes in the listed area prior to making the final code selection.

Tips for Selecting a CPT Code

1. Read the documentation for the care that was provided. Locate all professional services that you believe were rendered, the medications and supplies given, and tests performed at the encounter/session.

2. Using the CPT index, find the possible code(s) to be considered.

3. Review the entire description of the code(s).

4. Review the guidelines of CPT related to the code selection, paying close attention to the surrounding parenthetical notes.

5. Determine if any modifiers are required, including national HCPCSII modifiers.

6. If necessary, seek additional resources for guidance regarding the selection of the code (AMA's *CPT Assistant* newsletter or *CPT Changes: An Insider's View*).

7. If necessary, confirm with or query the physician prior to selecting the code.

8. Once the CPT code is selected, and any appropriate modifiers are determined, the code is ready to be placed on the claim form or sent electronically for claim submission.

Exercise 4.5

1. What term is used to represent the description of information listed after the semicolon symbol?
2. Where are the codes located in the CPT for physician visit services?
3. What codes should be used in lieu of unlisted codes when available?
4. In the CPT index, what section is referenced for reporting an Expired Gas Analysis?
5. Who is the publisher and owns copyright of the entire CPT code set?

Summary

Familiarity with the CPT code book symbols, concepts, guidelines, parenthetical tips, and other details will assist in accurate code selection. Services may be rendered at different facility types and locations, depending on the procedure or service performed. The code descriptions may also vary based on the site for the care. The care rendered and services performed must be documented sufficiently in the medical record to support the code selection. In the absence of appropriate documentation support, it would be improper to select the CPT code.

References

AMA Current Procedural Terminology 2016 professional edition. (2015). Chicago, IL: American Medical Association.

Centers for Medicare and Medicaid Services. Retrieved from http://www.cms.hhs.gov.

Evaluation and Management

CHAPTER 5

Learning Objectives

Upon successful completion of this chapter, you should be able to:

- Discuss the relevance of evaluation and management (E/M) codes.
- Identify the criteria for code selecting from the logic of AMA/CPT, Centers for Medicare & Medicaid Services (CMS) 1995 E/M guidelines, and/or the CMS 1997 E/M guidelines.
- Correctly select E/M codes to match documentation.
- Locate the E/M criteria for visits/encounters in the CPT code book.
- Determine levels of service by key components and the time factor.

Key Terms

chief complaint (CC)	evaluation and management services (E/M)	history of present illness (HPI)	past, family, and social history (PFSH)
consultation		medical decision making	professional services
coordination of care	examination		review of systems (ROS)
counseling	history	nature of the presenting problem (NPP)	

Introduction

The codes for **evaluation and management services (E/M)** were created and released in 1992 when the Resource-Based Relative Value Scale (RBRVS) was introduced. Patient encounters typically begin with an E/M service that is distinguished by the type of service and the location. E/M codes describe visits provided by health care professionals for the "evaluation and management" of patients. The selection process for the type of service performed (e.g., emergency visit, nursing home visit) is fairly straightforward. The specific code selection within the specific sections, however, may be challenging.

The E/M codes are appropriately located in the front of the CPT code book, as they are utilized most frequently by physicians of all specialties. The series of codes begins with 99201 and ends with 99499.

evaluation and management services (E/M): The first section of the CPT coding manual that describes visit and special encounter–type services such as office visits, hospital visits, nursing facility visits, and consultations.

AMA/CPT Evaluation and Management (E/M) Guidelines

The guidelines are located at the beginning of the E/M section prior to the first code, 99201. E/M codes are unique in comparison with other codes as no other section includes categories with a multilevel process. While the CPT contains evaluation and management guidance, the levels of determination are not readily quantifiable. Subjectivity regarding specific elements of an E/M code leads to a vast interpretive platform among health care professionals and auditors. For this reason, additional resources and guidance are frequently used to assist with defensible E/M coding. These other guidelines will be discussed later in this chapter.

Most E/M services delineate a service performed on a specific calendar date. This concept does not always blend clearly with all places of service. For example, a 23-hour stay description by the hospital does not describe the physician services that occur from 11 p.m. of the first date to 1 a.m. of the second date. Service dates are to be reported with the actual date the services were rendered.

The E/M codes are grouped by location and type of care and may have further subdivisions, such as initial and subsequent visits.

Clinical Examples

The CPT code book published by the American Medical Association includes published clinical examples pertinent to specific E/M codes; the examples can be found in Appendix C of the CPT. These clinical examples, or vignettes, describe common scenarios for various specialties. These scenarios do not represent complete documentation; they are merely examples provided to accompany the E/M descriptors contained in the full CPT text.

Prefacing each type of E/M service are informational paragraphs. This information provides additional guidance and clarity for correct code use. Cross-reference information directing the coder to other sections of CPT is prevalent throughout the book.

New Patient Definition

Understanding the definition of a new versus an established patient in procedural coding is a fundamental rule that can have a negative effect if misinterpreted. CPT first distinguishes between new and established patients by defining a professional service.

professional services: A face-to-face service rendered by a physician or qualified health care professional and reported by a specific CPT code.

Solely for the purposes of distinguishing between new and established patients, **professional services** are those face-to-face services rendered by physicians or other qualified health care professional (i.e., nurse practitioner, physician assistant) who may report evaluation and management services reported by a specific CPT code(s). A new patient is one who has not received any professional services from the physician/qualified health care professional or another physician/qualified health care professional of the exact same specialty and subspecialty who belongs to the same group practice, within the past three years.

There are certain key phrases and words that are used throughout the E/M section such as the term "physician" used above. This does not, however, limit the definition to physicians only. On page 4 of the 2015 *CPT Professional Edition,* E/M guidelines state, "E/M services may also be reported by other qualified health care professionals who are authorized to perform such services within the scope of their practice."

If a new patient presents to the office for blood work prior to a face-to-face visit and the following week sees the physician for the first time, the new patient designation is not forfeited. The blood draw is an ancillary service provided by the nurse or medical assistant (MA) and is billable. The fact that the patient has a medical record established does not matter. When the patient returns the following week for the face-to-face encounter, the physician may report the new patient service.

> **EXAMPLE:** New patient presents on 12/3/20XX to the cardiologist's office for EKG and blood work. The patient fills out a history form and medical record is established. The nurse performs standard blood work and EKG. On 12/8/20XX, the patient returns to the office for her first encounter with the physician. The physician reviews the labs and EKG, performs an expanded problem-focused history and exam, and gives the patient BP tracking instructions and hypertensive prescriptions. The patient is to return in three months for follow-up.
>
> 12/3/20XX—Code: 36415, 93000
>
> 12/8/20XX—Code: 99202

Should the provider need on-call coverage, the patient designation for the on-call provider will be the same as it would have been for the provider who was unavailable.

Coding Tip:

Common coding errors occur when patients are first seen in a setting other than the office. If a newborn is seen in the hospital for the first time and then seen at the office for the 10-day visit, the patient is considered an "established patient." The new versus established rule is not site specific; it is dependent on whether or not a face-to-face encounter has occurred with the physician.

Specialty Designations

Most carriers interpret the definition of *same specialty* the same way. A pediatrician who shares a practice with a pediatric urologist is not of the same specialty. Subspecialties can be tricky. CMS provides a crosswalk for health care providers / suppliers to a taxonomy code that is listed by the specialty. This taxonomy code information is what is used when providers enroll with CMS. An orthopedic surgeon who prefers to specialize in hip procedures is still an orthopedic surgeon. If his partner prefers to treat shoulders, that is still the same specialty. Some insurance companies grant certain provisions for specialty division when board certifications or advanced training skills within a specialty are acquired. The provider enrollment department of each insurance plan can assist in defining the subspecialties that are recognized as bundled. For example, according to CMS, medical oncology, radiation oncology, gynecological oncology, and surgical oncology are all designated as different specialties. Most of this chapter will discuss the various types of E/M services and key areas of documentation that are required for selection.

Leveling: Determining Level of Service

Many evaluation and management services include leveling, or level-of-service, criteria within the code descriptor. In determining level selection, specific elements must be considered. Seven elements are provided in CPT, with six used in defining the E/M levels. The first three are referenced as the three key components:

- History
- Exam
- Medical decision making

The next three components are considered to be contributing factors. Although these are important factors, they are not required to be provided at every encounter but may be influential.

- Counseling
- Coordination of care
- Nature of presenting problem (NPP)

Time is the final and 7th component. In coding, this is considered to be an exception to the general E/M rules. Time is only considered in E/M level selection when more than 50 percent is spent in counseling and coordinating care. Code selection for purposes of time criteria will be discussed later in this chapter.

One of the most important contributory factors is the **nature of presenting problem (NPP)**. CPT defines the NPP as a disease, condition, illness, symptom, sign, finding, complaint, or other reason for the encounter with or without a diagnosis at the time of the encounter.

nature of presenting problem (NPP): A presenting problem may be a complaint, disease, illness, condition, sign or symptom, injury, finding or other reason for an encounter.

Nature of Presenting Problem Types

CPT ranks the nature of the presenting problem in severity by providing the following five types:

1. **Minimal:**
   - The problem might not require the presence of the physician, but service is provided under the physician's supervision.

2. **Self-limited or minor:**
   - Prognosis is good with management/compliance.
   - Problem runs a definite and prescribed course, is transient in nature, and is not likely to permanently alter health status.

3. **Low severity:**
   - There is little to no risk of mortality without treatment.
   - Risk of morbidity without treatment is low.
   - Full recovery without functional impairment is expected.

4. **Moderate severity:**
   - There is moderate risk of mortality without treatment.
   - Prognosis is uncertain OR there is increased probability of prolonged functional impairment.
   - Risk of morbidity without treatment is moderate.

5. **High severity:**
   - There is high probability of severe, prolonged functional impairment.

Coding Tip:

The NPP sets the stage for the type of patient encounter the physician may need to perform. From a perspective of determining the level of care provided, the NPP is critical in assisting with medical necessity and is directly related to quality of care.

- ○ Risk of morbidity without treatment is high to extreme.
- ○ There is a moderate to high risk of mortality without treatment.

The E/M criteria for new patient code selection and documentation is greater than for established patients. Likewise, a lower level within a given code category, such as 99213, will require less work than a 99215. Only certain categories distinguish between new and established patients. Emergency room visits and observation services, for example, do not distinguish these categories differently; they have one code set only that can be used regardless of the patient status.

Exercise 5.1

1. Look in CPT at code 99212. Notice the descriptive paragraph that states "which requires at least two of three key components." List the key elements required for this code:

   History: _____

   Exam: _____

   Medical Decision Making: _____

2. Look in CPT at code 99202. List the typical presenting problem type for this code.
   _____

3. Where can providers find clinical examples of specific E/M levels? _____

CPT Criteria for Documentation and E/M Code Selection

This section describes the problem-oriented or "sick visit" type of E/M services. Later in this chapter, preventive medicine examinations and related services will be discussed.

History

Obtaining a clear **history** is imperative. The history provides insight to the problem or concern the patient is presenting with today. The depth or extent of history obtained is based on the nature of the presenting problem and the provider's clinical judgment.

This is the first key component that often begins the leveling process. Similar to peeling an onion one layer at a time, the provider will determine how much history is necessary and how far to go. The history should depict the "detective work," setting the stage for the examination and **medical decision making** that is necessary.

Chief Complaint (CC)

The **chief complaint (CC)** is required on every patient encounter. Typically, the chief complaint is documented in the patient's own words, describing his or her symptoms, problems, condition, diagnosis (if known), or other reason for the visit.

If the chief complaint changes (such as the patient scheduled the appointment for athlete's foot and now wants to have an annual exam), the medical record

history: A record of past events; a systematic account of the medical, psychosocial occurrences in a patient's life and of factors in the family, and environment that may have a bearing on the patient's condition.

medical decision making: The complexity of establishing a diagnosis and/or selecting a management option.

chief complaint (CC): A concise statement describing the symptom, problem, condition, diagnosis, or other factor that is the reason for the encounter, usually stated in the patient's words.

documentation must reflect the rendered services that were chiefly responsible for the visit. The appointment schedule may or may not match what was rendered.

Often the chief complaint is augmented such as when the physician enters the room and the patient provides additional complaints they are wanting addressed. The medical record must reflect all services rendered by the provider. A statement such as "follow-up" or "recheck" without elaboration is not sufficient. The chief complaint must be clearly reflected in the medical record and is often found within the **history of present illness (HPI)**. A simple statement such as "follow-up on hypertension" provides the condition that will be addressed. Not every encounter is illness related. Documentation of "BCP counseling for refill" or "Immunization update" implies and justifies the reason for the visit. An auditor would not accept the statement recheck or follow-up unless the body of the documentation clearly indicated the missing information. Best practices are to obtain a clear chief complaint from the very start.

history of present illness (HPI): A description of the development of the patient's present illness from the first sign and/or symptom to the present.

History of Present Illness (HPI)

The history of present illness often includes the chief complaint. There is not a mandate requiring physicians to document this a certain way. The HPI is defined as a chronological description of the development of the patient's present illness from the first sign and/or symptom to the present. The HPI relates directly to the nature of the presenting problem(s) and includes a description of one or more of the following elements listed in the CPT E/M section:

- Location
- Quality
- Severity
- Timing
- Context
- Modifying factors
- Associated significant signs and symptoms

Coding Tip:

The E/M guidelines expanded an additional element in determining the history of present illness. CPT does not include "duration" as a component; however, it is listed as one of the eight elements of an HPI within both the 1995 and 1997 E/M guidelines and accepted as an additional qualifying component among the majority of auditors.

For example, "The patient presents today with left ankle pain after suffering a fall from her horse earlier today. She applied ice but fears it might be broken." This statement provides information as to "why" (chief complaint) the patient is coming in today. It also provides the chronological description from the first sign of injury. In applying the HPI components above, we can abstract location (ankle—*specific body location*), context (fall from her horse—*how the problem occurred*), modifying factors (applied ice—*what the patient did to try and remedy or make it better*), and duration (earlier today—*onset or length of time patient has had the problem*).

HPI elements are quantified through other source documents such as the 1995 and 1997 *Documentation Guidelines for Evaluation and Management Services,* which are reviewed later in this chapter. These resources are used widely across the medical sector and are the basis for many documentation templates and tools within the electronic medical record.

Review of Systems (ROS)

Often referred to as the "inventory" component, the **review of systems (ROS)** is a question and answer segment between the patient and provider. A history intake form might be completed by the patient or taken by ancillary staff; however, the work component of an E/M requires the physician/qualified health care provider to give evidence that he or she has reviewed the information recorded by others. Reviewing pertinent systems is beneficial for:

- Establishing baseline information or data for possible management options
- Further defining presenting problems
- Clarifying differential diagnosis
- Identifying needed testing or referral

A provider "touching" or "looking" at a problem is examining the patient and is not conducting a systems review.

Documentation of questions and answers for the organ system being reviewed is important. For example, asking, "Have you experienced problems with shortness of breath or difficulty breathing?" is an example of a respiratory systems review. The patient response serves as potential information that may assist the physician with the start of a provisional or definitive diagnosis. When a provider documents information such as, "Patient denies chest pain; however, states an increase of palpitations," a cardiovascular system review has been performed. This information may aid in determining additional services or actions such as ordering tests, performing procedures, referring to a specialist, medication needs and so on.

CPT has established the following elements for ROS:

- Constitutional (fever, malaise, weight loss, pallor)
- Eyes
- Ears, nose, mouth, throat
- Cardiovascular
- Respiratory
- Gastrointestinal
- Genitourinary
- Musculoskeletal
- Integumentary (skin and/or breast)
- Neurological
- Psychiatric
- Endocrine
- Hematologic/lymphatic
- Allergic/immunologic

Past, Family, and Social History

The next area of information gathered during the inquiry is the pertinent **past, family, and social history (PFSH)**. The term *pertinent* is described in the

review of systems (ROS): The obtaining of an inventory of body systems through a series of questions seeking to identify signs and/or symptoms that the patient may be experiencing or has experienced.

past, family, and social history (PFSH): Pertinent inquiry of the patient and family's history of allergies, illness, treatments, and surgeries. Social history relates to the patient's occupation, military, education level, sexual history, drug or alcohol use, and other relevant information that may be beneficial to the encounter.

guidelines, suggesting the importance of the questions correlating to the chief complaint and nature of the presenting problem.

Past History

The past history criteria for the pertinent information to be documented are:

- Past major illnesses and injuries
- Prior operations
- Prior hospitalizations
- Current medications
- Allergies
- Age-appropriate immunization status
- Age-appropriate feeding/dietary status

Family History

The family history criteria for the pertinent information to be documented are:

- Health status or morbidity of parents, siblings, and children
- Specific diseases related to problems identified in the chief complaint, HPI, or ROS
- Diseases of family or hereditary diseases that may place the patient at risk

Social History

The social history criteria for the pertinent information to be documented, for age-appropriate past and current activities, are:

- Marital status and/or living arrangements
- Current employment
- Occupational history
- Military history
- Use of drugs, alcohol, and tobacco
- Level of education
- Sexual history
- Other relevant social factors

Final History Determination

The criteria or elements of history determination include the chief complaint, HPI, ROS, and PFSH.

There are four history levels to select from that pertain to all E/M codes that have a leveling option:

- *Problem focused:* Chief complaint; brief history of the present illness or problem
- *Expanded problem focused:* Chief complaint; brief history of the present illness; problem-pertinent system review
- *Detailed:* Chief complaint; extended history of the present illness; problem-pertinent system review extended to include a review of a limited number of

additional systems; pertinent past, family, and/or social history directly related to the patient's problems

- *Comprehensive:* Chief complaint; extended history of present illness; review of systems that are directly related to the problem(s) identified in the history of the present illness plus a review of all additional body systems; complete past, family, and social history

See Table 5–1 for specific criteria for the E/M history levels.

Table 5-1 Criteria for E/M History

History Types[a]	History of Present Illness (HPI)	Review of Systems (ROS)	Past, Family, Social History (PFSH)
Problem Focused	Brief 1–3 elements	N/A	N/A
Expanded Problem Focused	Brief 1–3 elements	Problem Pertinent 1	N/A
Detailed	Extended 4+ elements	Extended 2–9	Problem pertinent 1
Comprehensive	Extended 4+ elements	Complete 10+	Complete 3

[a] The history service must meet all criteria to qualify for the history type coded.

Permission to reuse in accordance with http://www.cms.gov Website Content Reuse Policy.

> **Coding Tip:**
> AMA/CPT does not publish a number for quantifying purposes to define the terms *brief, expanded,* or *complete* history levels. All criteria contained in history definition must be met or exceeded in order to select the history level. The 1995 and 1997 E/M guidelines began defining the point system that is used today.

Examination

The physician determines the type and extent of the **examination** to perform based on the nature of the presenting problem and his or her clinical judgment. The examination is the "hands-on" component of the E/M encounter, yet it does not always require the physician to physically touch the patient. For example, the physician may note jaundice or icteric sclera appearance or the gait and station from simple visual observance of the patient. The physician might obtain additional history criteria during the examination service, particularly on positive findings.

examination: A critical inspection and investigation, usually following a particular method, performed for diagnostic or investigational purposes and driven by the presenting problem and provider judgment.

It is important to understand that the physician may choose to examine a body area and/or organ system during a visit; however, the extent of the exam should always meet medical necessity. The following body areas and organ systems are recognized in both CPT and are included in the 1995 E/M guidelines. The 1995 and 1997 E/M guidelines also include *constitutional* as an additional exam element:

Body Areas

- Head, including the face
- Neck
- Chest, including breasts and axilla
- Abdomen
- Genitalia, groin, buttocks
- Back
- Each extremity

Organ Systems

- Constitutional (1995 and 1997 E/M guidelines only)
- Eyes

- Ears, nose, mouth, and throat
- Cardiovascular
- Respiratory
- Gastrointestinal
- Genitourinary
- Musculoskeletal
- Integumentary/skin
- Neurologic
- Psychiatric
- Hematologic/lymphatic/immunologic

Final Examination Criteria

In determining the level of exam performed, CPT recognizes four types of examination:

- *Problem focused:* A limited examination of the affected body area or organ system
- *Expanded problem focused:* A limited examination of the affected body area or organ system *and* other symptomatic or related organ system(s)
- *Detailed:* An extended examination of the affected body area(s) *and* other symptomatic or related organ system(s)
- *Comprehensive:* A general multisystem examination *or* a complete examination of a single organ system

Again, the CPT does not identify a specific number of exam elements for each level. The exam component of an E/M service is one of the primary reasons for the additional, external guidelines developed by CMS with input from the AMA and most specialty organizations. Interpreting the definition of a "comprehensive general multisystem exam," for example, will vary from one provider to the next. Specialty exams at a comprehensive level using solely the CPT guidelines are also just as subjective. This book will not address the nuances of "medical record chart auditing" for E/M services; rather it will introduce the reader to the essential concepts, intent, and components of the E/M foundation. Regardless of the methodology used to interpret or select a level, the documentation must support the level criteria. See Table 5–2 for the CPT examination criteria and Table 5–6 for a comparison of different guidelines.

Table 5-2 Examination Criteria According to E/M in CPT

Examination Types	Body Area or Organ System	Other Symptomatic or Related Organ System
Problem Focused	Limited exam of affected body area or organ system	N/A
Expanded Problem Focused	Limited exam of affected body area or organ system	Limited exam to include other symptomatic or related organ system(s)
Detailed	Extended exam of affected body area(s)	Extended exam to include other symptomatic or related organ system(s)
Comprehensive	Complete general multisystem exam or complete single organ system exam	

Exercise 5.2

Using Table 5–2, select the appropriate level of exam for the following scenarios.

1. The pharynx is red and swollen. Mild wheezing is heard at the base of the right lower lobe.
_____

2. Blood pressure is 130/90 today. _____

3. Constitutional: Well-nourished 44-year-old female in NAD. Weight is down to 145 lbs, B/P is 110/70. Abdomen: Normal bowel sounds. No abdominal masses or tenderness. No guarding on palpation. No hepatomegaly. Pt is 4 months post appendectomy—site is healing nicely and free of any discharge, scaling, or erythema.
_____

Coding Tip:

The 1995 and 1997 E/M guidelines both include the following documentation guidance (DG):

- DG: Specific abnormal and relevant negative findings of the examination of the affected or symptomatic body area(s) or organ system(s) should be documented. A notation of "abnormal" without elaboration is insufficient.

- DG: Abnormal or unexpected findings of the examination of any asymptomatic body area(s) or organ system(s) should be described.

- DG: A brief statement or notation indicating "negative" or "normal" is sufficient to document normal findings related to unaffected area(s) or asymptomatic organ system(s).

Medical Decision Making

This component represents the complex process the physician must go through in establishing a diagnosis and in selecting necessary management options for the patient. For code selection, the complexity of the decision-making process must be reflected within the documentation. The information should correlate to the chief complaint and any other issues addressed during the encounter.

Medical decision-making criteria are assessed by:

- The number of possible diagnoses and/or the number of management options that must be considered

- The amount and/or complexity of medical records, diagnostic tests, and/or other information that must be obtained and reviewed or analyzed

- The risk of significant complications, morbidity, and/or mortality, as well as comorbidities associated with the patient's presenting problem(s), the diagnostic procedure(s), and/or the possible management options

While it appears there are only three options listed, the terms within each description refer to *and/or*, expanding the possible selection. CPT provides a table to assist in determining the level of decision making. For a selection of the medical decision-making level, two of the three criteria must meet or exceed the required elements. Table 5–3 helps make this selection at a glance. For example, if the documentation reflects a limited number of management options during the encounter, a moderate amount of data reviewed, and a moderate risk of complications, the overall level of decision making would be moderate. This scenario reflects two of the three criteria being met within the moderate level.

Table 5-3 Medical Decision Making

Number of Diagnoses or Management Options	Amount and/or Complexity of Data to Be Reviewed	Risk of Complications, Morbidity, or Mortality	Type of Decision Making
Minimal	Minimal or none	Minimal	Straightforward
Limited	Limited	Low	Low complexity
Multiple	Moderate	Moderate	Moderate complexity
Extensive	Extensive	High	High complexity

Current Procedural Terminology ©2015 American Medical Association. All Rights Reserved.

counseling: The act of providing advice and guidance to a patient and his or her family.

coordination of care: The arrangement and/or organization of patient care to include necessary referral or contact with other health care providers.

Highlight:

Additional components for E/M are **counseling** and **coordination of care**. The nature of the presenting problem indirectly affects the level of code selection. While the NPP is an important factor, it is not a quantifiable component. The NPP provides guidance for overall selection of the specific code level and is beneficial for patient management.

Procedures performed are not included in the E/M services codes. Additional codes are selected for procedures or services that are performed over and above the E/M service being reported. The provider's review of the results, when documented, is captured within the portion of the E/M coding that covers medical decision making and complexity of data to be reviewed, as previously discussed.

Counseling and Coordination of Care: Time Factor

In the real world, not every encounter "fits" into the history, examination, and medical decision-making services. For this reason, CPT provides an alternative method of reporting services in the event that counseling and coordination of care dominate the encounter. This mode of determination is referred to as the *time factor*.

Official CPT Guidelines:

When counseling and/or coordination of care dominates (more than 50 percent) the physician/patient and/or family encounter (face-to-face time in the office or other outpatient setting or floor/unit time in the hospital or nursing facility), then time shall be considered the key or controlling factor to qualify for a particular level of E/M services. This includes time spent with parties who have assumed responsibility for the care of the patient or decision making, whether or not they are family members (e.g., foster parents, person acting in loco parentis, legal guardian). The extent of counseling and/or coordination of care must be documented in the medical record.

Time Factor Example

The test results of a biopsy have been returned to the physician and the patient is asked to come to the office to discuss the results. The biopsy is positive for malignant breast adenocarcinoma. At this appointment the physician informs the patient of the results, and then discusses the options for treatment, including a referral to a surgeon, a medical oncologist, and a radiation oncologist. The patient asks her spouse to join in on the discussion. They decide to defer the surgical option, and initiate the care with the oncology and radiation oncologist. The physician refers the patient for this care plan, and requests the patient return in one month for a follow-up appointment. Total physician face-to-face time for the encounter was approximately 40 minutes, of which the total was spent counseling and coordinating care.

The documentation in this example does not include much history or exam. It is solely an encounter dedicated to counseling and patient management regarding treatment for the adenocarcinoma. The documentation states the extent of the counseling and/or coordination of care and the time spent.

Three typical styles of acceptable documentation for this example:

1. *Documenting total time for 100 percent counseling visit. For example:*

   "Spent the total visit, approximately 40 minutes, with the patient and spouse in counseling regarding treatment options and mortality risks regarding breast adenocarcinoma. Patient understands her options, as does her spouse, and they wish to defer surgical intervention at this time and start with chemotherapy and radiation treatment."

2. *Documenting visit dominated by counseling/coordinating care:*

   CC: F/Up Biopsy Results

   History: Patient presents for follow-up regarding her recent biopsy. She states she's been feeling well but is still having pain at the surgical site. She's trying to remain positive in light of the news.

   Exam: Vitals: Wt. 168 lbs; B/P 108/70. Heart: RRR. Lungs: Clear to auscultation. Skin: Appears to be healing nicely with no sign of infection over the surgical site or surrounding area.

   Assessment: Breast Adenocarcinoma

   Plan: I told her that tenderness is expected for the next few weeks and to continue to keep the area covered until next week when we remove the sutures. I had a lengthy discussion with the patient and her spouse regarding treatment options and mortality risks for her type of cancer.

   Counseling: I spent 40 minutes with the patient and spouse, greater than 50 percent of which was spent counseling on the above. Patient understands her options as does her spouse and they wish to defer surgical intervention at this time and start with chemotherapy and radiation treatment. We will set up a referral to the medical oncologist before she leaves.

For the same documentation in example 2, the counseling section includes a specific amount of time: "I spent 40 minutes with the patient and spouse, of which 30 minutes were spent counseling on. . . ."

This example proves the CPT requirement of which greater than 50 percent of the total face-to-face encounter in the outpatient setting, or unit-floor-time in the inpatient setting, was fulfilled. Time now would be the key or controlling factor, regardless of the extent the "key" components might have been performed.

Selecting the Level Based on the Time Factor

To determine the level of CPT code based on the time factor, there is no regard for the history, exam, or medical decision-making key components. Look at the AMA's description of CPT code 99215:

99215   **Office or other outpatient visit** for the evaluation and management of an established patient, which requires at least two of these three key components:

- **A comprehensive history**
- **A comprehensive examination**
- **Medical decision making of high complexity**

Counseling and/or coordination of care with other providers or agencies are provided consistent with the nature of the problem(s) and the patient's and/or family's needs.

Usually, the presenting problem(s) are of moderate to high severity. Physicians typically spend 40 minutes face-to-face with the patient and/or family.

Notice the paragraphs below the medical decision-making component that describe the counseling and coordination of care service, and then the next paragraph, which states, "Usually, the presenting problem(s) are of moderate to high severity. Physicians typically spend 40 minutes face to face with the patient and/or family." The code selected for the above example is 99215. This typical time was established in the event that *greater than 50 percent or more* of face-to-face time was spent counseling or coordinating care.

In reviewing Table 5–4 for new patient office E/M services, note that the time factor is higher for code 99205 than the example above for the established patient code 99215.

Table 5-4 New Patient Office/Outpatient E/M Level of Service

New Patient: Requires 3/3 Key Components				
E/M Code	History	Exam	Medical Decision Making	*Time Factor
99201	Problem Focused	Problem Focused	Straightforward	10
99202	Expanded	Expanded	Straightforward	20
99203	Detailed	Detailed	Low	30
99204	Comprehensive	Comprehensive	Moderate	45
99205	Comprehensive	Comprehensive	High	60

*Use only if counseling and coordinating care dominate greater than 50 percent of total face-to-face time counseling.

Source: Association of Health Care Auditors and Educators, Quick View Series.

Applying Counseling and Coordination of Care

Here are tips for applying Counseling and Coordination of Care concepts:

- Counseling and Coordination of Care concepts apply for the treatment and management of an illness or disease. The rule does not apply for risk management, prevention, or other health improvement concepts, as the 99401 series are for these purposes.

- Often the encounter begins with a history and possibly part of an examination, and then converts to a counseling session. The documentation needs to clearly reflect that counseling and coordination of care dominate more than 50 percent of the encounter, with a statement on time when this instance occurs.

- Psychotherapy sessions are not reported by using evaluation and management service codes. For psychotherapy services, see codes 90832–90853.

- Ineligible inpatient or nursing facility locations, Counseling and Coordination of Care documentation must capture the time based on the floor/unit total time, and does include time with parties who have assumed responsibility for care or decision making. The time the physician is located on the unit and at the bedside rendering care for that particular patient is included. Also included is the time spent reviewing the data, writing orders, and communicating with other professionals and the family while on the unit. It does not include time spent by other personnel assisting the physician. The time away from the unit in other areas of the facility is not captured, nor is the rule for telephone discussion counseling.

- The Counseling and Coordination of Care exception is limited to eligible codes only. Not every E/M leveling service allows this rule. Look up 99281, Emergency department visit, and notice that the description in the paragraph does not include any time options. The code is not eligible for the counseling rule.

- Time that staff members spend with the patient or proxies is not included in time for Counseling and Coordination of Care. Only time with the physician or other health care professional managing the encounter is eligible.

- Pre and post time is not separately counted for code selection inclusion, for purposes of the time factor.

How to Select the E/M Code

First, review the medical record:

1. What: Determine the type of service that was rendered (e.g., emergency room visit, office visit, preventive service, etc.).

2. Where: Determine the place of service or the setting where the care was rendered (e.g., hospital, nursing home).

3. Who: Determine if the patient is new or established, or if such criteria are not applicable to the code (e.g., ER services can be either new or established).

Then, review the CPT code book.

1. First, go to the category related to the documentation you are reviewing in the CPT index and turn to the pertinent section. Usually this is the place of service or the type of care (outpatient, hospital or critical care, preventive).

2. Next, review the guidelines that are located just prior to the codes in that category for any special circumstances that correlate to the case.

3. Determine the key component requirements if applicable (three of three or two of three key components) for each of the codes in the category. *Compare to the medical record* documentation for code selection.

4. If there is no history, or exam, or if the service is dominated by (greater than 50 percent) counseling and coordination of care, the level of service may be selected based on the total time. In the absence of the time documentation, the level of determination will fall back onto the key component method.

E/M Selection of Level Example

Using Table 5–5, the example shows the provider performed a comprehensive history, detailed exam, and a moderate level of medical decision making. Since new patient services require 3/3 key components, the elements must meet or exceed the criteria within each level prior to selection. Even though codes 99204 and 99205 both share a comprehensive history element, the other elements must be met for level selection. Code 99204 just fell short of the final selection because of the exam component. On any level code requiring 3/3 key components, the level will always fall to the weakest link. In this example, the provider may not report higher than a level 99203. The time factor in this case is not applicable. If this were an established patient, the criteria are less stringent: Only 2/3 key components would need to be met or exceeded in order to select the level of service.

Table 5-5 New Patient Office/Outpatient E/M Selection of Level

New Patient: Requires 3/3 Key Components				
E/M Code	History	Exam	Medical Decision Making	*Time Factor
99201	Problem Focused	Problem Focused	Straightforward	10
99202	Expanded	Expanded	Straightforward	20
99203	Detailed	Detailed	Low	30
99204	Comprehensive	Comprehensive	Moderate	45
99205	Comprehensive	Comprehensive	High	60

*Use only if counseling and coordinating care dominate greater than 50 percent of total face-to-face time counseling.

Source: Association of Health Care Auditors and Educators, Quick View Series.

Introduction to 1995 and 1997 *Documentation Guidelines for Evaluation and Management Services*

After the introduction of E/M services in 1992, it became clear that quantifying the levels based on the CPT criteria alone was widely variable. CMS, AMA, and multiple specialties joined forces to further clarify the level criteria and published the 1995 *Documentation Guidelines for Evaluation and Management Services*. These were used for a few years for additional clarification, but more work needed to be done. Attempting to further clarify, CMS, the AMA, and other organizations came together once again and developed the 1997 *Documentation Guidelines for Evaluation and Management Services*. Although the guidelines were adopted, they were not mandatory for physicians to use. The leveling criteria for the higher-level E/M services created widespread discord, with many physicians claiming, for example, that they would never qualify for a comprehensive exam.

Determining Which Guidelines to Use

Rather than definitively replacing the 1995 E/M guidelines with the 1997 E/M guidelines, a final attempt to clarify level criteria was reviewed in 2000. The margin of discrepancy lessened but not enough. CMS nixed the proposed 2000 E/M guidelines and instructed its contractors to continue reviews using both the 1995 and 1997 Documentation Guidelines for E/M services. They further stated that whichever method proves more advantageous to the physician during the review is the methodology they are to use. According to the Association of Health Care Auditors and Educators, the majority of auditors use the same guidance as CMS. For this reason, AHCAE recommends and requires testing on both methods in its auditing certification exams. The area of most difference between the 1995 and 1997 E/M guidelines is that regarding the examination criteria. Only one slight clarification in the history was included in the 1997 guidelines, and absolutely no change was made to the medical decision-making component.

Bullet elements and shaded box information are contained within the specialty organ system table descriptors in the 1997 E/M guidelines. It would be necessary to reference the full 1997 set of guidelines to relate this language to the specific examination being performed. Table 5–6 shows only a side-by-side comparison of each of the exam leveling differences.

Table 5-6 CPT and 1995 and 1997 E/M Examination Comparison

Exam Levels CPT and 1995 Criteria	1997 Multisystem Exam	1997 Single Organ System Exam
Problem Focused A limited examination of the affected body area or organ system	**1 to 5** elements are identified by a bullet in one or more organ system(s) or body area(s).	**1 to 5** elements are identified by a bullet, whether in a shaded or unshaded box.
Expanded Problem Focused A limited examination of the affected body area or organ system and other symptomatic or related organ system(s)	**At least 6** elements are identified by a bullet in one or more organ system(s) or body area(s).	**At least 6** elements are identified by a bullet, whether in a shaded or unshaded box.
Detailed An extended examination of the affected body area(s) and other symptomatic or related organ system(s)	**At least 2** elements are identified by a bullet **from each of 6 areas/systems**; OR **At least 12** elements are identified by a bullet **in 2 or more areas/systems**.	**At least 12** elements are identified by a bullet, whether in a shaded box or unshaded border. Eye and psychiatric: **At least 9** elements are identified by a bullet, whether in a shaded or unshaded box.
Comprehensive A general multisystem examination or a complete examination of a single organ system **1995 Guideline:** *The medical record for a general multisystem examination should include findings about 8 or more of the 12 organ systems.*	Perform **all elements** identified by a bullet in **at least 9** organ systems or body areas. Document **at least 2** elements identified by a bullet **from each of 9 areas/systems**.	Perform **all** elements identified by a bullet, whether in a shaded or unshaded box. Document **every** element in each shaded box and at least 1 element in each unshaded box.

Source: Association of Health Care Auditors and Educators, Quick View Series.

> ### General Principles of Medical Record Documentation
>
> The principles of documentation listed here apply to all types of medical and surgical services in all settings. For evaluation and management (E/M) services, the nature and amount of physician work and documentation vary by type of service, place of service, and the patient's status. The general principles may be modified to account for these variable circumstances in providing E/M services:
>
> 1. The medical record should be complete and legible.
> 2. The documentation of each patient encounter should include:
>   - Reason for the encounter and relevant history, physical examination findings, and prior diagnostic test results
>   - Assessment, clinical impression, or diagnosis
>   - Plan for care
>   - Date and legible identity of the observer
> 3. If not documented, the rationale for ordering diagnostic and other ancillary services should be easily inferred.
> 4. Past and present diagnoses should be accessible to the treating and/or consulting physician.
> 5. Appropriate health risk factors should be identified.
> 6. The patient's progress, response to and changes in treatment, and revision of diagnosis should be documented.
> 7. The CPT and ICD-10-CM codes reported on the health insurance claim form or billing statement should be supported by the documentation in the medical record.

The information in the first column is extremely nonspecific, while the 1997 columns are very specific. The difference between an expanded problem focused and a detailed exam for 1995 is vague, whereas the 1997 difference is twice as much criteria (6 bullet elements to 12).

Each set of guidelines includes general principles of medical record documentation. The following information prefaces both the 1995 and 1997 *Documentation Guidelines for Evaluation and Management Services* and is referenced by the coverage determination rules of many private, local, and national insurers. It is used as a foundation by most major insurance companies and cited frequently by coders, auditors, malpractice carriers, and quality-of-care organizations.

Table of Risk

For levels of medical decision making, the three criteria categories are the same in CPT and the 1995 and 1997 guidelines except for the inclusion of a Table of Risk (see Table 5–7) found only in the 1995 and 1997 guidelines. This table information augments the criteria for levels of medical decision making for further clarification and example.

Table 5-7 Table of Risk

Level of Risk	Presenting Problem(s)	Diagnostic Procedures Ordered	Management Options Selected
Minimal	• One self-limited or minor problem (e.g., cold, insect bite, tinea corporis)	• Laboratory tests requiring venipuncture • Chest x-rays • EKG/EEG • Urinalysis • Ultrasound (e.g., echocardiography) • KOH prep	• Rest • Gargle • Elastic bandages • Superficial dressings
Low	• Two or more self-limited or minor problems • One stable chronic illness (e.g., well-controlled hypertension or non-insulin-dependent diabetes, cataract, BPH) • Acute uncomplicated illness or injury (e.g., cystitis, allergic rhinitis, simple sprain)	• Physiological tests not under stress (e.g., pulmonary function tests) • Noncardiovascular imaging studies with contrast (e.g., barium enema) • Superficial needle biopsies • Clinical laboratory tests requiring arterial puncture • Skin biopsies	• Over-the-counter drugs • Minor surgery with no identified risk factors • Physical therapy • IV fluids without additives
Moderate	• One or more chronic illnesses with mild exacerbation, progression, or side effects of treatment • Two or more stable chronic illnesses • Undiagnosed new problem with uncertain prognosis (e.g., lump in breast) • Acute illness with systemic symptoms (e.g., pyelonephritis, pneumonitis, colitis) • Acute complicated injury (e.g., head injury with brief loss of consciousness)	• Physiological tests under stress (e.g., cardiac stress test, fetal contraction stress test) • Diagnostic endoscopies with no identified risk factors • Deep needle or incisional biopsy • Cardiovascular imaging studies with contrast and no identified risk factors (e.g., arteriogram, cardiac catheterization) • Obtain fluid from body cavity (e.g., lumbar puncture, thoracentesis, culdocentesis)	• Minor surgery with identified risk factors • Elective major surgery (open, percutaneous, or endoscopic) with no identified risk factors • Prescription drug management • Therapeutic nuclear medicine • IV fluids with additives • Closed treatment of fracture or dislocation without manipulation
High	• One or more chronic illnesses with severe exacerbation, progression, or side effects of treatment • Acute or chronic illnesses or injuries that pose a threat to life or bodily function (e.g., multiple trauma, acute MI, pulmonary embolus, severe respiratory distress, progressive severe rheumatoid arthritis, psychiatric illness with potential threat to self or others, peritonitis, acute renal failure) • An abrupt change in neurological status (e.g., seizure, TIA, weakness, or sensory loss)	• Cardiovascular imaging studies with contrast with identified risk factors • Cardiac electrophysiological tests • Diagnostic endoscopies with identified risk factors • Discography	• Elective major surgery (open, percutaneous, or endoscopic) with identified risk factors • Emergency major surgery (open, percutaneous, or endoscopic) • Parenteral controlled substances • Drug therapy requiring intensive monitoring for toxicity • Decision not to resuscitate or decision to de-escalate care because of poor prognosis

Permission to reuse in accordance with http://www.cms.gov Website Content Reuse Policy.

The official 1997 *Documentation Guidelines for Evaluation and Management Services* are available at http://www.cms.gov. Readers are encouraged to review this information to determine correct leveling prior to code selection.

Exercise 5.3

Using your CPT book, answer the following questions.

1. What is the definition of a new patient?
2. List the key components in selecting the proper level of evaluation and management service.
3. What are the contributory components?
4. In documenting, what information is typically contained in the chief complaint?
5. What is the term for the chronological description of the patient's present illness from the first sign and/or symptoms to today?
6. List each of the components for HPI.
7. What does ROS stand for?
8. At what level of risk is a patient who presents with a newly found breast lump?
9. What level of E/M service would be selected for an established patient who received an expanded problem-focused history and a detailed exam, and was given a prescription for a medication to treat osteoporosis?
10. Identify the modifying factor from the following history: A patient presents with lower back pain, subsequent to a recent urinary tract infection. The location of the pain is over the flank on the right side and is spontaneous. Pain does not improve with Tylenol.

E/M Categories

E/M services are represented by multiple types and place of service codes. Each category provides subsection reference information to assist with correct code application.

Coding Tip:

Typical patterns for leveling are obvious throughout the E/M section. For example, the following criteria are consistent throughout:

- 3/3 Key components are required for: New patient services, Initial (e.g., inpatient and observation) services, Consultations, and Emergency Department

- 2/3 Key components are required for: Established patient services and subsequent services

The E/M coding section starts with Office or Outpatient Services and ends with Other E/M services.

Office or Outpatient Services (99201–99215)

The codes in this series of CPT are selected for the typical physician office place of service and occasionally are used for other outpatient locations.

There are two options for code selection based on whether the patient is a new patient (99201–99205) or an established patient (99211–99215). The criteria are simpler for an established patient, requiring only two of the three key components.

Exercise 5.4

Select the appropriate CPT code.

New patient office visit:

1. Comprehensive history, straightforward medical decision, problem-focused exam

   CPT(s) _____

2. Comprehensive history, detailed exam, low-complexity medical decision making

   CPT(s) _____

3. Comprehensive history, detailed exam, straightforward medical decision making

   CPT(s) _____

Established patient in the office:

4. Expanded problem history, detailed exam, moderate-complexity decision-making

   CPT(s) _____

5. Detailed history, expanded problem-focused exam and low-complexity medical decision making

   CPT(s) _____

Observation Care (99217–99220, 99224–99226)

The observation codes are not sequential in the code book. The first code in this section is for discharge from observation (99217), followed by the initial (99218–99220) and subsequent observation code options. Subsequent observation care codes (99224–99226) are out of numerical sequence, as indicated by the # resequencing symbol.

Codes for observation should be selected when the patient is designated as "observation status," regardless of the physical space where the patient is located. For example, some facilities have a designated observation area; however, other facilities do not. The patient may be in the Obstetrics Department, with monitoring device recordings, rather than in the Emergency Department (ED). The status is still observation, yet the patient is located in the OB department with other patients who have been admitted as inpatients.

The 99217 code, Observation discharge, describes the final examination of the patient, the home instructions, and the documentation *that occurs on a different date than the admission to the observation care.* The "per calendar date," midnight-to-midnight

> **Highlight:**
>
> Per NCCI, the E/M services include cleansing of wounds, closure of wounds with adhesive strips (Band-Aids), basic dressings, counseling, and instructions associated with the illness/problem.

concept applies for this code. The initial observation care series of codes does not offer the same breakdown availability as the office/outpatient codes. There are three initial codes and three subsequent codes. The concept of new versus established patient does not apply. The criteria for the codes require all three key components to be met or exceeded. Also note, the components provide "detailed or comprehensive" and "straightforward or low" for code 99218. The initial observation service is for the physician admitting and overseeing the care of the patient in observation. If the physician is not the attending physician but was called in to see the patient, outpatient consultation codes 99241–99245 or subsequent observation codes 99224–99226 would be applicable, depending on the situation.

When the physician sees the patient in observation at 2 a.m., then admits the patient to the hospital at 3 a.m., all of the history, exam, and decision making are grouped together for the same date of service. The initial inpatient hospital services codes 99221–99223 would be selected. If the two services are performed on separate dates, a code is selected for the observation and another for the hospital admission service.

Highlight:

The CPT manual reflects that typical E/M reporting does not include multiple E/M leveling services by the same provider, on the same day. Exceptions to this rule are for add-on codes and other E/M service types that are periodically performed on the same date such as critical care services and an inpatient visit.

Coding Tip:

Observation care is typically provided for short stays up to 48 hours. In the circumstance where the patient stays for three calendar days, the following would apply.

Day 1: Initial observation care (99218–99220)

Day 2: Subsequent observation care (99224–99226)

Day 3: Observation discharge (99217)

E/M services that stem from other settings, such as office visits on the same day that the patient is later admitted to observation by the same provider, are not reported separately. All related E/M services on the same date are rolled up into the observation admission. Any other services such as diagnostics, labs, x-ray, treatment, and so on may be reported for the other sites of service.

Exercise 5.5

1. The physician visits a patient in step-down room for observation at 5 a.m. and then visits the patient again at 11 a.m. First visit was an expanded problem focused (EPF) history, EPF exam, straightforward medical decision. Second visit was augmented to detailed history, detailed exam, straightforward medical decision.

   CPT(s) _____

2. The physician sees his patient in observation on day two and provides a detailed history, detailed exam, and low-complexity decision making prior to sending him home.

   CPT(s) _____

3. The physician admits a 32-year-old patient to the observation area at 5 a.m. A comprehensive history, detailed exam, and low-complexity decision making are documented. At 3 p.m., the patient is significantly better and is discharged.

   CPT(s) _____

Inpatient Hospital Care (99221–99223)

These codes are to be selected when the physician provides care for the patient who is admitted to "inpatient" status, or partial hospital. Regardless of new versus established patient, these initial codes require three of three components and are to be used by the admitting physician only.

The initial care includes all related E/M care provided to the patient on the same date, from all other sites. For physicians other than the admitting physician, either subsequent hospital care or consultation services (if the criteria are met) would be selected. This rule differs for Medicare. Medicare does not recognize consultation services and directs physicians to the option of "initial" or "subsequent" hospital care services for their first encounter. The admitting physician must use HCPCSII modifier "AI," which will distinguish that physician from the other providers potentially using the initial codes. Modifier AI stands for "Principal Physician of Record."

Occasionally, a patient is admitted to either observation or inpatient status and discharged on the same date (midnight to midnight). When this occurs, select from the combination codes 99234–99236 rather than the initial observation or inpatient care codes.

Notice there are no lower levels for problem focused or expanded problem focused history or exam key components. The lowest level requires a detailed or comprehensive history and physical.

Exercise 5.6

Select the appropriate CPT code.

Initial hospital visit, new patient:

1. Detailed history, detailed exam, straightforward medical decision

   CPT(s) _____

Initial hospital visit, established patient:

2. Expanded problem focused history, detailed exam, straightforward medical decision

   CPT(s) _____

Initial hospital visit, established patient:

3. Comprehensive history, comp exam, low-complexity medical decision

   CPT(s) _____

Established patient, second-day hospital visit:

4. Expanded problem focused history, problem-focused exam, low-complexity medical decision

   CPT(s) _____

Subsequent Hospital Care (99231–99233)

The codes in this series are selected for inpatient care, after the admission service date. These are also selected by other physicians who see the patient yet do not meet the consultation criteria. In general, these codes are selected once per date, per physician visit.

Notice that these include the lower level of key components. In the event the service performed is beyond the detailed level of 99233, prolonged service add-on codes might be applicable.

Combination Admission and Discharge on the Same Date (99234–99236)

Codes 99234–99236 are selected when the patient is admitted and discharged on the same calendar date from either observation status or as an inpatient in the hospital. These codes require 3/3 key components and the same concepts apply as discussed earlier. All related E/M services on the same date are grouped together to select the appropriate level of admit/discharge code 99234–99236.

If the admit occurs on a different date, these codes would not be used.

The counseling and coordination of care concepts do not have time allocations for these codes.

Discharge Services (99238–99239)

One of the most important facts surrounding the discharge codes is that they are categorized according to 30 minutes or less, or more than 30 minutes. This time descriptor is to be documented in the medical record; otherwise, it will always default to discharge service, 99238. The 2015 CPT Professional Edition provides the following discharge information on page 18:

> The hospital discharge day management codes are to be used to report the total duration of time spent by a physician for final hospital discharge of a patient. The codes include, as appropriate, final examination of the patient, discussion of the hospital stay, even if the time spent by the physician on that date is not continuous, instructions for continuing care to all relevant caregivers, and preparation of discharge records, prescriptions, and referral forms.

These hospital discharge codes are not used for discharging a patient from a nursing facility, as there are separate codes.

Consultations (99241–99255)

Consultation encounters (whether provided at the physician office or other locations) have very detailed criteria for documentation and code selection. It is important to understand that these criteria have been established by the AMA for optimal patient care purposes. Medicare no longer recognizes consultation services and will deny the claim if consultation codes are submitted for processing.

The **consultation** is defined as a type of evaluation and management service provided by a physician at the request of another physician or appropriate source to do one of the following:

- Recommend care for a specific condition or problem

consultation: A type of service provided by a physician (usually a specialist) whose opinion or advice regarding evaluation and management of a specific problem is requested by another physician or other appropriate source.

- Determine whether to accept responsibility for ongoing management of the patient's entire care or for the care of a specific condition or problem

    Coders can remember consultation requirements by the three Rs:

- **Request** and document specific opinion and or advice.

- **Render** the service (opinion/advice).

- **Respond** in writing.

A "consultation" initiated by a patient and/or family is not reported using the consultation codes but may be reported using the office visit, home service, or domiciliary/rest home care codes as appropriate.

Coding Tip:

The term "other appropriate source" for consultation referrals means someone other than a physician, including a physician assistant, nurse practitioner, doctor of chiropractic, physical therapist, occupational therapist, speech-language pathologist, psychologist, social worker, lawyer, or insurance company.

There must be documentation of the request for consult (written or verbal) in the patient's medical record. A written report is also required to go back to the requesting provider along with the opinion/advice and any procedures or services that were performed or ordered.

Exercise 5.7

The consultation criteria are specific. Review the following examples and indicate Yes or No if you agree these requests meet criteria.

1. "Medical or Surgical consult" or "ENT consult" requested by M.D. _____
2. RN requested consultation regarding management of diabetes. _____
3. Patient requests a second opinion regarding gallbladder surgery. _____
4. PCP requested endocrinology consult regarding management of patient's uncontrolled diabetes evaluation for possible thyroid nodule. _____
5. A consultant may initiate diagnostic treatment at the encounter. _____

Procedures that are performed at the time of the consultation encounter will require additional codes. These additional services are often diagnostic testing or procedures.

Follow-up visits that are initiated by the consultant at the office location are coded with 99211–99215. Follow-up visits by the consultant at the hospital location are coded with subsequent observation codes 99224–99226 or subsequent hospital services 99231–99233.

Exercise 5.8

Answer the following questions.

Office consultations

1. What are the three Rs for coding consultations?

   R: _____   R: _____   R: _____

2. Provide the level for a comprehensive history, comprehensive exam, low-complexity medical decision making.

   CPT(s) _____

Inpatient consultation

3. Provide the level for a comprehensive history, comprehensive exam, low-complexity medical decision making.

   CPT(s) _____

Emergency Department Care (99281–99285)

The codes 99281–99285 are for both new and established patients. They have five levels of service, which require three of three components. These services do not have a time factor component. The codes may only be used when an encounter is provided in the hospital Emergency Department (ED), defined as a facility that must be open 24 hours a day.

> **Coding Tip:**
>
> Insurance plans have various interpretations and policies regarding who may use the ED codes. Some allow only the ED physician use of these codes. Further, many direct that any other physician who sees a patient in the ER on the same date should select from outpatient codes 99201–99215 or outpatient consult codes 99241–99245. This logic is not the CPT standard.

When critical care services are provided in the ED, codes 99291–99292 are selected. Procedures may also be performed in the ED (setting a fracture, for example) and are separately reported.

Other Emergency Services (99288)

Occasionally, two-way voice communication is used for a physician to direct the management of patient care by ambulance personnel. This service is reported with a single code, 99288, Physician direction of emergency medical systems (EMS) emergency care, advanced life support.

Critical Care (99291–99292)

Understanding correct use of critical care codes has often been a challenge to physicians. Defining critical care is truly key.

> **Official CPT Guidelines:**
>
> **CPT Definition–Critical Care**
>
> "A critical illness or injury acutely impairs one or more vital organ systems such that there is a high probability of imminent or life threatening deterioration in the patient's condition. Critical care involves high complexity decision making to assess, manipulate, and support vital system function(s) to treat single or multiple vital organ system failure and/or to prevent further life threatening deterioration of the patient's condition. Examples of vital organ system failure include, but are not limited to: central nervous system failure, circulatory failure, shock, renal, hepatic, metabolic, and/or respiratory failure."
>
> (AMA CPT 2015 Professional Edition, page 23)

The location of the patient is not a factor for adults; it is the condition of the patient. Codes 99291 and 99292, for example, may be used for the following situations:

- An adult is critically ill or critically injured and meets the CPT criteria, regardless of location (outpatient or inpatient).

- A neonate or pediatric patient meets critical care criteria in the outpatient setting only.

- If a neonate or pediatric patient is seen in the outpatient setting and critical care was performed and the patient was admitted on the same day, codes 99291–99292 will roll into the inpatient neonatal and pediatric intensive care services (99468–99476) "per day" codes, only if the service is provided by the same provider.

- Just because a patient is located in the ICU, NICU, MICU, or SICU does not automatically qualify the service as critical care. The patient may simply be in the ICU because of hospital protocol, a need for additional nursing care, or possibly bed availability. For a patient in the ICU who is not critical, the subsequent hospital care codes or inpatient consultation services, if applicable, should be used.

- Critical care involves care of the critically ill or injured patient, which often requires highly complex decision making. It is imperative that time be documented when reporting critical care. If multiple visits (critical care services) are necessary on the same day, the total critical care time (unit/floor time) for the date, midnight to midnight, is added together with code(s) selected thereafter.

- Critical care codes 99291–99292 are selected based on total time. If under 30 minutes, use the subsequent hospital codes.

Table 5–8 will help you in selecting the correct units for reporting critical care. The time includes the unit and floor time related to managing the patient's care. This includes nursing station, reviewing tests, discussing with other professionals, and documentation time.

Key fact: If the patient is not able to participate in the discussions, the time with the family or decision makers obtaining the history and discussing condition, prognosis, and treatment options are all coded as critical care time *if this time directly correlates to the care/management of the patient.* If the discussions occur away from the unit/floor, this criterion is not met. If the discussions do not bear on the care of the patient, the time does not count for the critical care time.

Table 5-8 Critical Care Time Table (99291 and 99292)

Total Duration Must Be Documented	Critical Care Codes
Less than 30 minutes	Use the appropriate E/M code
30–74 minutes	99291 × 1
75–104 minutes	99291 × 1 AND 99292 × 1
105–134 minutes	99291 × 1 AND 99292 × 2
135–164 minutes	99291 × 1 AND 99292 × 3
165–194 minutes	99291 × 1 AND 99292 × 4
195 minutes or longer	99291 × 1 AND 99292 as appropriate

The time necessary to perform procedures that are not included in the CPT critical care description is to be subtracted out, as these procedures will be reported separately. For example, if the physician is managing a respiratory failure episode and inserts the laryngoscope, the charting should reflect time and management:

> Time in 8:01 a.m. Respiratory failure, patient remains on the ventilator. Blood gases show . . . X-rays reviewed . . . Orders . . . Laryngoscope inserted with ease
>
> Time out 8:55 a.m.
>
> Total critical care time, 51 minutes exclusive of procedures (Laryngoscope insertion).

Total critical care time thus far for this date is 51 minutes. If the physician provides additional critical care on the same date, it would be added to the initial time prior to selecting the codes.

If critical care codes are selected and reported on the claim in addition to any other E/M services provided by the same physician, modifier -25 may be required.

For reporting by professionals, the following services are included in critical care when performed during the critical period by the physician(s) providing critical care:

- The interpretation of cardiac output measurements (93561, 93562)
- Chest x-rays (71010, 71015, 71020)
- Pulse oximetry (94760, 94761, 94762)
- Blood gases, and information data stored in computers (e.g., ECGs, blood pressures, hematologic data [99090])
- Gastric intubation (43752, 43753)
- Temporary transcutaneous pacing (92953)
- Ventilatory management (94002–94004, 94660, 94662)
- Vascular access procedures (36000, 36410, 36415, 36591, 36600)

Any services performed that are not included in this listing should be reported separately. Facilities may report the above services separately.

Highlight:

- For the emergency placement of endotracheal tube by laryngoscopy, select only the code for the endotracheal tube placement. The reason for the placement must be documented.

- Performance of CPR is reported with code 92950. The time for this service is not included in the critical care time.

- Routine monitoring is part of critical care services; do not select additional monitoring codes. If significant review and monitoring are required, document the time specifically required for the service.

- Ventilation management and continuous positive airway pressure (CPAP) are included in critical care services.

- Physician transportation with a critically ill patient, other than the pediatric age, uses the critical care codes.

Exercise 5.9

The physician indicates on the hospital card that she performed CPR for a 32-year-old patient on the regular floor. Time is 12:10 p.m. She managed the code, performed cardiac output measurements, reviewed EKG strips, put in the IV and pushed meds, stabilized the patient for transport to ICU. She admitted the patient to ICU. Time out: 1:20 p.m. Time in: 7:30 p.m. Later in the day, she revised the IV orders, reviewed data. Time out: 8:15 p.m. Total time spent for this day was 1 hr 55 min, exclusive of CPR. Code this encounter for the physician services.

CPT(s) _____

Nursing Facility Care (99304–99310)

Nursing facilities now include skilled nursing facilities, intermediate care facilities and long-term care facilities, and psychiatric residential treatment centers. It is anticipated that additional definitions for care facilities will also be included here.

All codes are for the new or established patient, yet the service selection is determined by whether the encounter is an initial or subsequent visit. Nursing facility (NF) care includes the physician completing a resident assessment instrument, with a minimum data set of information.

When the patient is admitted to the NF, all other related E/M services are grouped together, selecting a single NF code for the date performed. *However,* hospital discharge or observation discharge on the date of a nursing facility admission or readmission can be reported. This is very different from other E/M leveling code guidelines.

Nursing Facility Discharge (99315–99316)

The codes 99315–99316 are selected based on documented time for all E/M services performed on the date of discharge, including final record preparation, instructions, final examination, and so on. Codes are separated for reporting and distinguished by 30 minutes or less (99315) or more than 30 minutes (99316). The code would be reported for a death as well, which would commonly include exam, death pronouncement, paperwork, and so on.

Domiciliary, Rest Home, Custodial Care (99324–99337)

Domiciliary, rest home, and custodial care are also known as adult foster care or companion care. This type of location does not provide a medical care component. The physician may provide a visit at the location; there are five separate levels for new patients and four levels for established patients. Typical times have been established should counseling and coordination of care dominate the encounter. Codes 99339–99340 are for care plan oversight services for patients in this setting. These are not face-to-face services and are reported once per 30 days (calendar month). Typically, these patient records are flagged internally as the time accumulates during the month and is billed at month's end. Policy regarding operational issues and billing functions for these services is always recommended. Physicians must document whom they spoke with, the date, time spent, nature of call discussion, management/treatment changes, orders, and so on.

Home Visits (99341–99350)

The codes in the 99341 series are for provider visits at a private residence, whether a home owned by the patient or not. Any facility that is considered a residence qualifies as a home. These services are fashioned similar to the other new and established E/M leveling codes. Five levels are used for new and five for established patient services. Home visits are becoming somewhat rare, however; they occur more in rural areas. Counseling and coordination of care descriptors pertaining to the time factor are present within this code set.

Prolonged Service With Direct Patient Contact (99354–99357)

Prolonged services are divided into two categories. The first is when direct patient contact (face-to-face) occurs. Codes 99354 and 99355 are for reporting prolonged services in the office or other outpatient setting. Codes 99356 and 99357 are unit/floor time for the inpatient setting. These are considered to be companion codes as they are an additional service used for reporting prolonged care provided to the patient in addition to the basic E/M. If the prolonged service is under 30 minutes, it is not separately reportable.

Table 5–9 will assist with time reporting for prolonged physician services in the office setting.

Table 5-9 Prolonged Services Time Table (99354 and 99355)

Total Face-to-Face Time	Prolonged Service Code(s)
Less than 30 minutes	Not reported separately
30–74 minutes	99354 × 1
75–104 minutes	99354 × 1 AND 99355 × 1
105 minutes or more	99354 × 1 AND 99355 for each additional 30 minutes

Most insurance plans will pay for prolonged services with face-to-face care if the medical record reflects the medical necessity and ICD-10-CM codes.

Prolonged Service Without Direct Patient Contact (99358–99359)

Another option for prolonged service code includes codes 99358–99359. Unlike the face-to-face service codes, these prolonged services are to be considered stand-alone codes and require the same time consideration; however, they are not required to be reported on the same day as a face-to-face encounter or unit-floor-time encounter. An example of when this type of service may be reported is the necessity of extensive records review. This service often is provided on a date other than a visit date and may be reported if the time threshold is met.

> **Highlight:**
>
> The uniqueness of codes 99358–99359 is that they are for non-face-to-face services, so they may be reported on a *different date than the primary service*. For example, extensive record review may relate to a previous evaluation and management service and commence upon receipt of past records. However, it must relate to a service or patient where direct (face-to-face) patient care has occurred or will occur and relate to ongoing patient management.

EXAMPLE: A patient went to see her new primary care provider (PCP) to establish care and get medication refills. While she was there, the provider requested her old records be sent. The patient filled out the request form and the office faxed it to her previous provider. Three days later, the patient's records were received by the provider. He spent approximately 1.5 hours reviewing all the information and preparing a thorough summary. In this example, the PCP reported an E/M service three days prior. The service for today is reported with codes 99358 and 99359. This service also relates to a prior E/M service that was provided and reported separately.

Physician Standby Services (99360)

The standby concept is described as a provider who receives a request from another physician to stand by (e.g., for cesarean section, high-risk delivery, or frozen section). These are potentially urgent situations, and the physician on standby may not be providing any other services to other patients during this period. Standby is not separately reportable by the standby provider if the standby period ends with performance of a procedure subjective to the surgical package. The code is reported for each 30-minute increment.

Case Management Services (99363–99368)

Case management is for the physician who is responsible for direct care of the patient including managing, coordinating services, and providing care plan oversight.

Anticoagulation management (99363–99364) is specifically managing outpatient warfarin therapy. Specific INR (international normalized ratio for blood clotting time) testing information is provided in the guideline section along with several code reference notes for further clarification. Double dipping is sometimes an issue, as providers may not use the anticoagulation management services as a basis for reporting an E/M during the reporting period. In other words, if the provider is seeing the patient for warfarin (Coumadin) therapy services and a different E/M is generated, the same time period cannot also include anticoagulation management codes 99363–99364.

Medical Team Conference codes have a qualifying "team" requirement that at least three qualified health care professionals from different specialties participate. For code 99366, Medical Team Conference, Direct (face-to-face) contact with patient and/or family, 30 minutes are required with the team, and the participant using this code must be a nonphysician qualified health care professional. This includes active participation and involvement in health care services needed by the patient.

Code 99367 is for the physician providing medical team conferences *without* direct face-to-face patient contact. Code 99368 shares the same descriptor except the code is for nonphysician qualified health care professionals.

Workers' compensation or auto insurance policies may accept and encourage the use of the codes. Typically, whoever is reporting the service must have seen the patient in a face-to-face encounter within the previous 60 days of any team conference. No more than one individual from the same specialty may report 99366–99368 at the same encounter. Guidelines state that the team conference starts at the beginning of the individual review and ends at the conclusion of the patient review. The time for record reporting and recording is not countable time, nor is the time to be used for reporting other services at the same time.

Care Plan Oversight Services (99374–99380)

For care plan oversight provided by "physicians" to patients with direct face-to-face contact, providers are instructed to report the appropriate evaluation and management level of service. This likely would be a level selected based on the time factor and counseling/coordinating care. This series of codes is selected based on the location of the patient, such as the home health agency, hospice setting, or nursing facility. Each setting has two codes to report care plan oversight (CPO) services. Codes 99374, 99377, and 99379 are all defined as 15–29 minutes of CPO service provided over a 30-day period (patient not present). Codes 99375, 99378, and 99380 are for 30 or more minutes within their respective settings. These codes are selected by the supervising physician assuming the responsibility for the patient care plan, providing plan establishment and revision, reviewing of reports and studies, assessment of care with health care professionals, and so on. It is for the physician time, not the MA, nurse, or ancillary staff time. Services are documented and timed with accumulative totals gathered at the end of the 30-day period (month-to-month) for reporting.

Exercise 5.10

1. Is a physician allowed to report anticoagulation services code 99364 in addition to an E/M service on the same day?

2. What code should be used to report 45 minutes of care plan oversight services for a patient in the hospice setting for a 30-day period?

Preventive Medicine Services (99381–99397)

Preventive medicine services do not have the same focus as a problem-oriented encounter/visit. Their purpose is for prevention, screening, and overall well-being.

Management of chronic illness is not preventive care. If the patient has a stable, chronic illness being treated by the physician today (perhaps with an ongoing treatment plan or regime), the problem-oriented E/M codes should be used instead of the preventive care codes.

Preventive services span codes 99381 to 99397. They are based on new and established patients, and upon the age of the patient. Medicare statutorily excludes these preventive service codes but has ample screening and diagnostic services that can be found in the HCPCSII section. A comprehensive history and physical are expected when using preventive service codes.

The "comprehensive" terminology is not synonymous with that of a problem-oriented comprehensive service. These are age and gender specific. Some of the specialty associations such as the American Academy of Family Physicians or American Academy of Pediatrics have recommended guidelines for age and gender. The preventive care codes are to include risk factor reduction interventions, guidance, and education for the patient. The counseling regarding risk factors is included in the 99381–99397 codes. Counseling regarding illness may be considered separately if it is significant and separately identifiable.

Multiple codes are anticipated on the claim with preventive services. Additional services and procedures are to be separately reported. For example, a visual screen examination is coded with 99173, the tympanometry is 92567, a urinalysis (UA) dipstick is 81002, and the EKG is 93000. If immunizations or vaccines are rendered, the vaccine/toxoids codes (90476–90749) and the administration(s) 90460–90474 are coded in addition.

Now for the tricky part: what to do if the preventive service starts to become a sick visit, or if both a sick visit and a wellness visit are performed at the same encounter. This is a fairly regular occurrence, but whether separate reimbursement occurs is variable. The second paragraph in the CPT preventive (AMA CPT 2015 Professional Edition, page 35) provides the following instruction:

- If an abnormality/ies is encountered or a preexisting problem is addressed in the process of performing this preventive medicine evaluation and management service, *and* if the problem/abnormality is significant enough to require additional work to perform the key components of a problem-oriented E/M service, then the appropriate Office/Outpatient code 99201–99215 should also be reported. Modifier 25 should be added to the Office/Outpatient code to indicate that a significant, separately identifiable evaluation and management service was provided by the same physician on the same day as the preventive medicine service. The appropriate preventive medicine service is additionally reported.

- An *insignificant or trivial problem*/abnormality that is encountered in the process of performing the preventive medicine evaluation and management service and that does not require additional work and the performance of the key components of a problem-oriented E/M service should not be reported.

EXAMPLE: The 55-year-old hypertensive patient (Pt) presents to her primary care provider (PCP) for her physical prior to joining the health club. It has been two years since her last annual exam and Pap smear and she is anxious to get a clean bill of health. The physician did a comprehensive, age-appropriate history including review of the patient intake form, and performed a comprehensive exam. Breast and pelvic exam were negative and a Pap smear was obtained. Her blood pressures are stable. Pt requests a refill on her HTN (hypertension) medication, which the provider gives. In this scenario, a written script itself does not constitute an additional E/M service. There needs to be "significant" work performance in the history and exam in order to capture a problem-oriented visit at the same time. This example would be reported with code 99396.

CMS provides additional codes for screening services for Medicare beneficiaries. For example, for women, the HCPCSII code G0101, "Cervical or vaginal cancer screening; pelvic and clinical breast exam," is defined by specific criteria. This code comes with additional Medicare policy attached that specifies approved diagnosis, the frequency allowed, and any coinsurance or deductible payments that might be due. This code defines the examination of seven of eleven body areas. The code G0101 does not include a preventive history nor any risk factor reduction. If the physician provides these additional services (as stated in the specific code selection), the E/M preventive services or problem-oriented E/M code would be reported in addition with modifier 25.

The G0101 has frequency limitations, as well as high-risk or low-risk diagnosis purposes. An advance beneficiary notice (ABN) is required prior to the service being performed for the G0101 aspect of the care, outlining any reasons for Medicare nonpayment for the patient. The Advanced Beneficiary Notice (ABN) is not required for the preventive services 99381–99397 as they are statutorily excluded. The code Q0091, "Screening Pap smear; obtaining, prep and conveyance to lab," is additionally coded, along with the G0101 when applicable. Medicare will allow the modifier 25 to append to G0101. Again, the high-risk or low-risk diagnosis and the frequency limitations (one time per three years) are to be considered. Offer the ABN if necessary for this service and include the reason with estimated fees.

Another area of HCPCSII is the S series of codes that may be required for BCBS or some Medicaid patients. The policies may vary among plans, so it is best to check with your plans in your area. The S code may or may not include the CPT preventive services. S0610 is an annual GYN exam for a new patient.

For both men and women, G0402 is the Welcome to Medicare Physical Examination discussed in Chapter 3.

If the patient has requested a preventive examination that is the service they expect to be rendered. Fortunately, most insurance benefits now cover preventive care services.

Exercise 5.11

Select the appropriate CPT code.

1. The established 45-year-old patient presents for her annual exam. Upon seeing the patient, the physician refills prescriptions and orders a chest x-ray for preventive purposes only.
   CPT(s) _____

2. An established patient, 45 years old, requests an annual exam. Upon examining the patient, the physician notes abnormal lung sounds in the lower lobe. Patient has a personal history of breast cancer. The physician completes the preventive exam and then provides an additional detailed history, expanded exam, and low-complexity decision making.
   CPT(s) _____

Risk Factor Reduction, Behavior Change Intervention, Telephone Services, Medical Evaluation Online (99401–99444)

The codes in the 99401–99412 range are used for preventive medicine counseling services. Both individual and group codes are listed with time elements. Specific codes for smoking and tobacco use cessation counseling and alcohol and/or substance abuse screening codes will warrant review of the subsection guidelines. Non-face-to-face services not previously mentioned, such as telephone services (99441–99443), are used to respond to an established patient inquiry that cannot be related to an E/M reported within the previous seven days or at the next soonest available appointment. The codes are listed by time, with the lowest level, 99441, requiring 5 to 10 minutes of medical discussion. Although these codes have been completely restructured, they still remain reimbursed infrequently.

Code 99444 is for the online electronic medical evaluation, which is a non-face-to-face E/M service by a provider in response to the patient's online inquiry. This mode of evaluation requires permanent storage of the data or hard copy of the encounter. It also cannot be related to a previous E/M service that was rendered within the previous seven days, nor can it relate to an E/M provided within the next soonest available appointment. The physician's response is expected to be timely. Some carriers advise to use the "online request" date as the date of service and others state to use the "online response" date. Carriers should be contacted prior to billing online medical evaluation services. Malpractice carriers often provide valuable input and warnings regarding online medical evaluation services.

Special Evaluation and Management Services (99450–99456)

Codes 99450–99456 are selected for life insurance and disability examinations. The examinations may be performed at various settings (home, physician office, or other sites) and are not site specific. These codes are not defined by new or established patient but rather are based on the treating versus a nontreating physician.

Newborn Care Services (99460–99465)

The 99460–99465 codes refer to newborn care in the hospital, birthing room, or other setting. Two initial newborn care services, 99460 for birth in the hospital or birthing center, and 99461 for initial care in settings other than hospital or birthing center, are the two initial codes used most frequently. Code 99463 is in the rare event the newborn is admitted and discharged on the same (calendar) day. Subsequent hospital services or daily newborn visits are coded with 99462. The final day of discharge includes all the E/M services. The hospital discharge services 99238–99239 are selected and are based on the documented time.

Code 99454 is for attendance at delivery when requested by the delivering physician for potential stabilization of a newborn. Code 99465 is for birthing room/ delivery room resuscitation services. Code 99465, Newborn resuscitation, and 99464 Attendance at delivery, may not be reported together.

Inpatient Neonatal and Pediatric Critical Care Services (99466–99476, 99485–99486)

Transport

Codes 99466–99467 are used to report critical care transport services for pediatric and neonatal patients. These codes require the physician's presence by personally accompanying the patient and providing face-to-face care during an interfacility transport. As for the other critical care services, coders should review the guidelines in this section carefully to identify the services that are typically included in these codes.

Codes 99485–99486, Supervision by a control physician of interfacility transport care of the critically ill or injured patient, are resequenced codes added to this section of CPT in 2013. They only apply to patients that are 24 months of age or younger, include the data interpretation and report and require at least 30 minutes to be reported. Should the patient be older than 24 months, CPT states to use code 99288.

Inpatient Neonatal and Pediatric Critical Care (99468–99476)

The codes in this area are selected once per date of service, rather than by accumulated hours. The neonatal or pediatric critical care codes are selected in addition to other services provided on the same date that are not included in the code section descriptors.

A neonate is defined as 28 days of age or younger. After the critical care service is completed, the codes for follow-up while in the hospital are either intensive birth weight codes (99478–99480) or the subsequent hospital visit codes (99231–99233) if the patient is not a low-birthweight baby.

The infant or young child is defined as 29 days through 24 months. If the child is over 24 months of age, select codes 99291–99292 for critical care and document the time. If the critical care is provided in a setting other than the inpatient setting, select the critical care codes 99291–99292. If critical care is provided at both the outpatient and the inpatient setting on the same date, group all of the services together and select only the inpatient pediatric critical care code for the date of service. Pediatric and neonatal critical care services include criteria listed in 99291–99292 and the following services and management:

- Invasive or noninvasive electronic monitoring of vital signs
- Vascular access procedures
  - Peripheral vessel catheterization (36000)
  - Other arterial catheters (36140, 36620)
  - Umbilical venous catheters (36510)
  - Central vessel catheterization (36555)
  - Vascular access procedures (36400, 36405, 36406)
  - Vascular punctures (36420, 36600)
  - Umbilical arterial catheters (36660)
- Airway and ventilation management
  - Endotracheal intubation (31500)
  - Ventilatory management (94002–94004)

- ○ Bedside pulmonary function testing (94375)
- ○ Surfactant administration (94610)
- ○ Continuous positive airway pressure (CPAP) (94660)
- Monitoring or interpretation of blood gases or oxygen saturation (94760–94762)
- Car seat evaluation (94780–94781)
- Transfusion of blood components (36430, 36440)
- Oral or nasogastric tube placement (43752)
- Suprapubic bladder aspiration (51100)
- Bladder catheterization (51701, 51702)
- Lumbar puncture (62270)

Any services performed that are not listed above may be reported separately.

Critical care services provided by a second physician of a different specialty not reporting a 24-hour global code can be reported with the critical care codes 99291, 99292.

Initial and Continuous Intensive Care Services (99477–99480)

Code 99477 is for the initial hospital care service for E/M of the neonate 28 days of age or younger who is not critically ill but requires frequent interventions, intensive observation, and other intensive care type services. This is not for the initiation of normal newborn care services or for the critically ill neonate/pediatric patient. Codes 99478–99480 are separated by body weight. Code 99478 is for body weight that is less than 1500 grams, code 99479 for 1500–2500 grams, and code 99480 for 2501–5000 grams. The codes are to be reported once per day.

Care Management Services (99487, 99489, 99490)

Patient management services provided by physicians have historically been difficult to quantify and report. The concept of care management has gradually made its way into the CPT allowing for various reporting opportunities. While CPT provides codes to report Chronic Care and Complex Chronic Care Management services, the guidelines are detailed and stringent, with multiple requirements outlined within the guideline subsections.

These care management services are management and support services provided by clinical staff, under the direction of a physician or other qualified health care professional, to a patient residing at home or in a domiciliary, rest home, or assisted living facility.

Transitional Care Management Services (99495–99496)

Transitional Care Management or "TCM" commences upon the date of discharge and continues for the next 29 days. These services are for the patient whose medical and/or psychosocial problems require moderate- or high-complexity medical decision making during transitions in care from an inpatient hospital setting (see CPT for various setting qualification), partial hospital, observation status in a hospital, or skilled nursing facility/nursing facility to the patient's community setting (home, domiciliary, rest home, or assisted living). These codes provide specific guidance and requirement for services and documentation to qualify for reporting. The guidelines will need to be thoroughly reviewed.

Advanced Care Planning (99497–99498)

Planning is the key phrase to report these services, no action is necessary on the patient's part during this encounter. It is to establish advanced directives and to plan or appoint an agent to carry out the patient's wishes, should they lack decision-making capacity at a future date. Durable Power of Attorney for Health Care and Living Will are just a few examples of written advanced directives.

1997 Documentation Guidelines for Evaluation and Management Services

As discussed previously, the 1995 E/M guidelines are very similar to the CPT guidelines. The 1997 E/M guidelines were created to fill the interpretation void and provide instruction for specific exam levels. Originally, the hope was to replace and eliminate the 1995 E/M guidelines with the 1997 E/M guidelines. Once the guidelines were released, provider disagreements could not be resolved. For this reason, CMS allows the use of either set of E/M guidelines for providers to use. The vast majority of differences between the two guideline sets are in the examination portion. The information contained within the parenthetical statements of both the General Multisystem Exam tables and the Single Organ System Exam specialty tables are critical for both providers and coders to review. This information is of vital importance for providers in assisting with clinical documentation and is important for coders that may move into the world of health care auditing. Table 5–10, discussed below, is an example of the General Multisystem Exam taken from the 1997 E/M guidelines.

Table 5-10 1997 General Multisystem Table

System/Body Area	Elements of Examination
Constitutional	• Measurement of any three of the following seven vital signs: (1) sitting or standing blood pressure, (2) supine blood pressure, (3) pulse rate and regularity, (4) respiration, (5) temperature, (6) height, (7) weight (May be measured and recorded by ancillary staff) • General appearance of patient (e.g., development, nutrition, body habitus, deformities, attention to grooming)
Eyes	• Inspection of conjunctivae and lids • Examination of pupils and irises (e.g., reaction to light and accommodation, size, and symmetry) • Ophthalmoscopic examination of optic discs (e.g., size, C/D ratio, appearance) and posterior segments (e.g., vessel changes, exudates, hemorrhages)
Ears, Nose, Mouth, and Throat	• External inspection of ears and nose (e.g., overall appearance, scars, lesions, masses) • Otoscopic examination of external auditory canals and tympanic membranes • Assessment of hearing (e.g., whispered voice, finger rub, tuning fork) • Inspection of nasal mucosa, septum, and turbinates

(continues)

Table 5-10 (continued)

System/Body Area	Elements of Examination
	• Inspection of lips, teeth, and gums
	• Examination of oropharynx: oral mucosa, salivary glands, hard and soft palates, tongue, tonsils, and posterior pharynx
Neck	• Examination of neck (e.g., masses, overall appearance, symmetry, tracheal position, crepitus)
	• Examination of thyroid (e.g., enlargement, tenderness, mass)
Respiratory	• Assessment of respiratory effort (e.g., intercostal retractions, use of accessory muscles, diaphragmatic movement)
	• Percussion of chest (e.g., dullness, flatness, hyperresonance)
	• Palpation of chest (e.g., tactile fremitus)
	• Auscultation of lungs (e.g., breath sounds, adventitious sounds, rubs)
Cardiovascular	• Palpation of heart (e.g., location, size, thrills)
	• Auscultation of heart with notation of abnormal sounds and murmurs
	Examination of:
	• Carotid arteries (e.g., pulse amplitude, bruits)
	• Abdominal aorta (e.g., size, bruits)
	• Femoral arteries (e.g., pulse amplitude, bruits)
	• Pedal pulses (e.g., pulse amplitude)
	• Extremities for edema and/or varicosities
Chest (Breasts)	• Inspection of breasts (e.g., symmetry, nipple discharge)
	• Palpation of breasts and axillae (e.g., masses or lumps, tenderness)
Gastrointestinal (Abdomen)	• Examination of abdomen with notation of presence of masses or tenderness
	• Examination of liver and spleen
	• Examination for presence or absence of hernia
	• Examination (when indicated) of anus, perineum, and rectum, including sphincter tone, presence of hemorrhoids, rectal masses
	• Obtain stool sample for occult blood test when indicated
Genitourinary	MALE:
	• Examination of the scrotal contents (e.g., hydrocele, spermatocele, tenderness of cord, testicular mass)
	• Examination of the penis
	• Digital rectal examination of prostate gland (e.g., size, symmetry, nodularity, tenderness)
	FEMALE:
	Pelvic examination (with or without specimen collection for smears and cultures), including:
	• Examination of external genitalia (e.g., general appearance, hair distribution, lesions) and vagina (e.g., general appearance, estrogen effect, discharge, lesions, pelvic support, cystocele, rectocele)
	• Examination of urethra (e.g., masses, tenderness, scarring)
	• Examination of bladder (e.g., fullness, masses, tenderness)
	• Cervix (e.g., general appearance, lesions, discharge)
	• Uterus (e.g., size, contour, position, mobility, tenderness, consistency, descent or support)
	• Adnexa/parametria (e.g., masses, tenderness, organomegaly, nodularity)

(continues)

Table 5-10 (*continued*)

System/Body Area	Elements of Examination
Lymphatic	Palpation of lymph nodes in two or more areas: • Neck • Axillae • Groin • Other
Musculoskeletal	• Examination of gait and station • Inspection and/or palpation of digits and nails (e.g., clubbing, cyanosis, inflammatory conditions, petechiae, ischemia, infections, nodes) Examination of joints, bones and muscles of one or more of the following six areas: (1) head and neck; (2) spine, ribs and pelvis; (3) right upper extremity; (4) left upper extremity; (5) right lower extremity; and (6) left lower extremity. The examination of a given area includes: • Inspection and/or palpation with notation of presence of any misalignment, asymmetry, crepitation, defects, tenderness, masses, effusions • Assessment of range of motion with notation of any pain, crepitation, or contracture • Assessment of stability with notation of any dislocation (luxation), subluxation, or laxity • Assessment of muscle strength and tone (e.g., flaccid, cog wheel, spastic) with notation of any atrophy or abnormal movements
Integumentary/ skin	• Inspection of skin and subcutaneous tissue (e.g., rashes, lesions, ulcers) • Palpation of skin and subcutaneous tissue (e.g., induration, subcutaneous nodules, tightening)
Neurologic	• Test cranial nerves with notation of any deficits • Examination of deep tendon reflexes with notation of pathological reflexes (e.g., Babinski) • Examination of sensation (e.g., by touch, pin, vibration, proprioception)
Psychiatric	• Description of patient's judgment and insight Brief assessment of mental status including: • Orientation to time, place, and person • Recent and remote memory • Mood and affect (e.g., depression, anxiety, agitation)

Parenthetical examples have been provided and are helpful in defining specific exam elements. Elements that have a specific number must meet the stated requirement. Elements without a specific numeric, such as examination of liver and spleen, require at least one element to be documented. The full 1997 E/M Guideline document can be located at http://www.cms.gov.

General Multisystem Examination

Table 5–10 demonstrates the content and documentation requirements for the General Multisystem Examination guide to selecting the examination level. For the detailed exam, it is more common to have documentation of two elements from six areas, rather than 12 elements from only two body areas. Note that the comprehensive level requires two elements from nine areas to be documented.

Exercise 5.12

1. A patient arrives with a sore throat he has had for the past two days. The throat is reddened and streaked to the palate, the tonsils and adenoids are enlarged, the lymph nodes are swollen in the front of the neck, normal in the back of the neck. The lungs are clear. What level of exam is this using the General Multisystem exam table?

2. A patient arrives with a sore throat he has had for the past two days. The throat is reddened and streaked to the palate, the tonsils and adenoids are enlarged, tympanic clear, canals red and tenderness upon exam noted, the lymph nodes are swollen in the front of the neck, normal in the back of the neck. The lungs are clear. Cardiac sounds are normal, regular pulse rate. Mother states that patient had a slight rash on the chest yesterday. Temperature 102. What level of exam is this using the ENT exam table located in the official 1997 E/M guidelines?

3. A patient arrives with a sore throat he has had for the past two days. The throat is reddened and streaked to the palate, the tonsils and adenoids are enlarged, nares clear, tympanic clear, canals red and tenderness upon exam noted, sinuses stuffy, conjunctivae of eyelids red and crusty, the lymph nodes are swollen in the front of the neck, normal in the back of the neck. The lungs are clear. Cardiac sounds are normal, regular pulse rate. Mother states that patient had a slight rash on the chest yesterday, no rash visible today. Temperature 102. (Gastrointestinal, genitourinary, musculoskeletal, neurological, psychiatric are noncontributory today.)

   a. What level of exam is this using the ENT table?

   b. What level of exam is this using the general multisystem table?

4. What are the three factors to consider when determining the level of medical decision making?

5. If a patient is gravely ill, does this automatically qualify for high-complexity decision making?

6. This established patient was recently diagnosed with cancer of the breast, and the physician spent 25 minutes counseling her in his office during a 35-minute encounter to determine the treatment plan and management options.

   a. What component type(s) are used to select the code?

   b. What CPT code should be used to report this service?

Summary

E/M codes are commonly performed by most physician specialties. These services are commonly audited by federal, state, and private insurance plans. Learning the details of E/M is necessary as more coders move into the world of auditing. The criteria (key components) must be accurately followed for the selection of the E/M codes. Frequently visiting the 1995 and 1997 *Documentation Guidelines for Evaluation and Management Services* is a must. The time factor component is only considered relevant in the event that 50 percent or more of the encounter (face-to-face for office/outpatient or unit/floor time for inpatient) is spent counseling and coordinating care.

Coders should become familiar with both the 1995 and the 1997 *Documentation Guidelines for Evaluation and Management Services* and have them readily available for referencing. The exam tables provided in the 1997 E/M guidelines are very helpful in becoming familiar with specific exam elements that are necessary when learning to quantify the exam for level determination. A valid ICD-10-CM code will be required for reporting of any CPT code, including the evaluation and management service codes to support medical necessity of the rendered service. Both the Official 1995 (15-page document) and the 1997 E/M *Documentation Guidelines for Evaluation and Management Services* (51-page document) are available for download in their entirety at http://www.cms.gov.

References

AMA CPT Assistant Archives. (2004–2009). Chicago, IL: American Medical Association.

AMA Current Procedural Terminology 2016 professional edition. (2015). Chicago, IL: American Medical Association.

Centers for Medicare and Medicaid Services. *1995 Documentation Guidelines for Evaluation and Management Services.* Retrieved from http://www.cms.gov.

Centers for Medicare and Medicaid Services. *1997 Documentation Guidelines for Evaluation and Management Services.* Retrieved from http://www.cms.gov.

Evaluation and Management Level of Determination Tools. (2015). Aurora, CO: Association of Health Care Auditors and Educators.

HCPCS Level II Expert. (2015). Salt Lake City, UT: Optum360.

ICD-10-CM expert for hospitals 2016 edition. (2015). Salt Lake City, UT: Optum360.

Anesthesia and General Surgery

Learning Objectives

Upon successful completion of this chapter, you should be able to:

- Identify how and when anesthesia codes are used.
- Identify the physical status modifiers and know how they apply.
- Identify the organs upon which general surgery is performed.
- Identify the major procedures performed within general surgery.

Key Terms

achalasia

anesthesia

anesthesiologist

aphakia

base units

catheter

certified registered
  nurse anesthetist
  (CRNA)

endoscopy

epidural

fissure

fistula

general anesthesia

local anesthesia

moderate (conscious)
  sedation

physical status modifier

regional anesthesia

sphincter

Introduction

This chapter reviews the codes used by physicians performing **anesthesia** for surgeries performed by another physician, and the codes used by surgeons describing general surgical procedures.

An **anesthesiologist** is a physician specializing in the evaluation and preparation of a patient for surgery. Preoperative care includes meeting the patient prior to surgery to get a medical history in order to plan the anesthesia that is right for the patient. During the surgical procedure, there are three phases of anesthesia. First is the induction or introduction of the anesthetic. Second is the maintenance phase. During this phase, the anesthesiologist monitors blood pressure, heart rate, breathing, and level of consciousness, and makes adjustments to control pain. The emergence phase is bringing the patient out of the anesthetic and providing postoperative care while the patient is in the recovery room.

A **certified registered nurse anesthetist (CRNA)** is a registered nurse who is licensed by the state of practice and has completed a nurse anesthesia program meeting the criteria of the Council on Accreditation of Nurse Anesthesia Educational Programs, and is credentialed as a CRNA.

anesthesia: The pharmacological suppression of nerve function.

anesthesiologist: A physician specializing in the evaluation and preparation of a patient for surgery, the introduction of the anesthesia for the procedure, the maintenance phase, and the emergence and postoperative phase.

certified registered nurse anesthetist (CRNA): A registered nurse licensed by the state of practice who has completed a nurse anesthesia program, credentialed as a CRNA, who provides the same anesthesia services as an anesthesiologist.

general anesthesia: A state of unconsciousness, produced by anesthetic agents, with absence of pain sensation over the entire body.

regional anesthesia: The production of insensibility of a part by interrupting the sensory nerve conductivity from that region of the body.

local anesthesia: Anesthesia confined to one part of the body.

moderate (conscious) sedation: A decreased level of consciousness during a procedure without being put completely to sleep. The patient is able to respond to verbal instructions and stimulation.

Anesthesia

Anesthesia is defined as pharmacological suppression of nerve function and can be administered by general, regional, or local method. The CPT codes for anesthesia are used to report the administration of anesthesia by or under the responsible supervision of a physician. They are reported only by the physician who is administering the anesthesia, and only if that physician is not performing the surgery. If a physician provided anesthesia for a surgery that he or she performed, the appropriate codes from the surgery section would be applied with a modifier of -47, anesthesia by surgeon, except in the case of conscious sedation (see the Chapter 12 section Moderate (Conscious) Sedation). General, regional, and local anesthesia and other supportive services are included in the anesthesia codes.

Types of Anesthesia

General anesthesia provides an unconscious state during a procedure that is extensive or when regional anesthesia is not an option. Usual means of administration are inhalation, intramuscular, rectal, or intravenous. Inhalation anesthesia is introduced through the respiratory system by way of nose and trachea. Rectal anesthesia is administered in the form of a retention enema. Intramuscular anesthesia is given as an injection directly into the muscle. Intravenous anesthetics are introduced into the vein and are generally used as a light anesthetic, sometimes prior to an inhalant being administered. In endotracheal anesthesia, a gaseous drug is administered by inserting a tube into the mouth or nose. General anesthesia puts the patient into a deep sleep, blocks any memory of the surgery, and prevents the brain from perceiving pain. All vital signs must be closely monitored during the procedure, and a breathing tube may also be inserted.

Regional anesthesia provides insensitivity to pain or a field or nerve block in a particular area of the body. These anesthetics can be administered by injection or a topical application to the skin or mucous membranes. A nerve block is when a local anesthetic is injected directly into or in close proximity to the nerve to desensitize or numb the surrounding tissue. This type of anesthesia is common for pain control following hip or knee replacement. Field block is administered by injecting the area around the surgical site with a local anesthetic. Caudal anesthesia used in childbirth is dripped through a needle inserted into the spinal canal at the sacrum. The needle is left in place during delivery so the anesthetic can drip in gradually. Epidural anesthesia is administered by injection of the anesthetic into the epidural space given at the thoracic or lumbar area (Figure 6–1). A catheter can be inserted if needed to allow for repeated injections. This method is commonly used in childbirth.

Local anesthesia desensitizes a particular area undergoing a procedure and is administered by injecting the anesthetic subcutaneously. A local anesthetic can also be topically applied directly to the body surface to provide desensitization.

Moderate (conscious) sedation provides a drug-induced decreased level of consciousness without putting the patient completely to sleep. This enables the patient to breathe without assistance. The patient is also able to respond to verbal instructions and stimulation. The physician performing the procedure can provide moderate (conscious) sedation as long as there is a nurse or other health care professional to observe the patient. The following services are included and not reported separately:

- Assessment of the patient (not included in intra-service time)
- Establishment of IV access and fluids to maintain status of patient

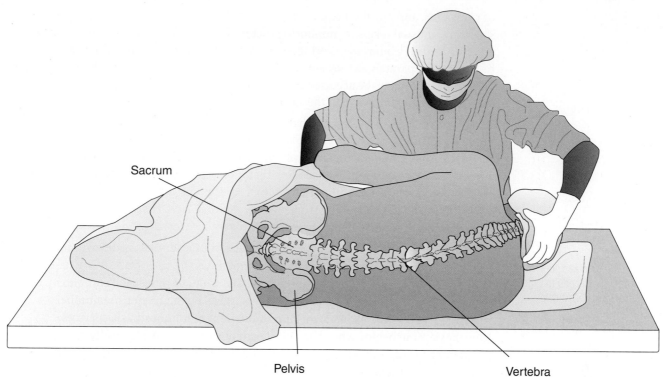

Sacrum

Pelvis

Vertebra

Figure 6-1 A common type of anesthesia is epidural anesthesia, which is administered via injection between the vertebrae of the spine. It is commonly used during childbirth.

- Administration of medications used

- Maintenance of sedation

- Monitoring of blood pressure, heart rate, and oxygen saturation

- Recovery time (not included in intra-service time)

Intra-service time starts with the administration of the sedation medications, requires continuous face-to-face attendance and monitoring, and ends at the conclusion of the procedure and personal contact with the physician providing the sedation.

When a physician performs a procedure and provides conscious sedation for the procedure, codes are assigned from the Medicine section of CPT (codes 99143–99150). These codes describe moderate sedation services provided by the same physician performing the service, or a physician other than the health care professional performing the service. Codes are also selected based on the age of the patient and intra-service time.

As in coding any procedure, ICD-10-CM codes must also be assigned to support the medical necessity for the procedure performed.

Anesthesia Coding

Most anesthesia codes, with the exception of moderate (conscious) sedation codes, are found in the Anesthesia section of the CPT (00100–01999). Preoperative and postoperative visits by the anesthesiologist, care during the procedure, monitoring of vital signs, and any fluid administration are also included in the anesthesia codes. There are unusual forms of monitoring that may be required from the anesthesiologist (such as central venous monitoring or Swan-Ganz catheterization), which should be reported separately as they are not normally part of the anesthesia services. The anesthesia codes may be accessed in the index under the key word anesthesia, and then by body site upon which the surgery is performed.

Anesthesia codes are applied based on the body site being operated on, and are not based on the type of anesthesia administered. In the Anesthesia chapter of CPT, the subheadings are the different body sites that could be operated on. Select the appropriate code under the subheading that represents the surgery being performed on that body site. Keep in mind that codes from this chapter are applied only for the anesthesia that is being performed for surgery in that area. The surgeon would assign codes from the surgery chapter to represent his or her work.

base units: Values assigned to each anesthesia CPT code to reflect the difficulty of the anesthesia service, including preoperative and postoperative care and evaluation.

The fee schedule for reimbursement of anesthesia services is determined by the American Society of Anesthesiologists and includes the use of **base units**. Base unit values are assigned to each anesthesia CPT code to reflect the complexity of the surgery. The more complex or difficult the surgery is, the higher the number of base units. Time is a key factor in reimbursement for anesthesia services. Anesthesia time begins when the anesthesiologist or CRNA physically prepares the patient for the induction of anesthesia and ends when the anesthesia service is concluded and the patient is safely under postoperative care.

Anesthesia codes in CPT are submitted in 15-minute increments or time units. Each minute is considered one unit of service with a fraction rounded up or down.

Medicare and other carriers consider integral parts of the anesthesia service and are included in the procedure. These services are reimbursed as part of the base unit and not billed separately:

- Transporting, positioning, prepping, and draping of the patient
- Placement of external devices necessary for cardiac monitoring, oximetry, temperature, EEG, etc.
- Placement of peripheral intravenous lines necessary for administration of fluids and medications
- Placement of an airway
- Placement of naso-gastric or oro-gastric tube
- Intraoperative interpretation of monitored functions
- Interpretation of lab determinations
- Nerve stimulation for determination of level of paralysis or localization of nerve
- Insertion of urinary bladder catheter
- Blood sampling

Calculating an Anesthesia Charge

The formula generally used to calculate an anesthesia charge is:

(Base units + Time units + Modifying units) × Conversion factor
= Anesthesia charge.

The total number of units (base, time, and modifying units) is multiplied by the conversion factor to calculate the charge.

Each anesthesia procedure has a base unit value. The base unit reflects how difficult the procedure is to perform, and how much skill it takes. The more difficult it is, the higher the number of base units. The number of base units for each anesthetic procedure is fixed and does not change.

The anesthesia charge also includes the amount of time it took to provide the anesthesia. These time units are usually 15 minutes in length. For example if anesthesia is provided for 45 minutes, 3 time units would be included in the formula for calculating the anesthesia charge.

The modifying unit accounts for special conditions that may affect the anesthesia. This could include the patient's health or if the anesthesia was provided in an emergency.

EXAMPLE: A healthy patient (no modifying units apply) received anesthesia for gallbladder surgery, which is valued at 7 base units, for 75 minutes (5 time units). The patient was treated in a location with a conversion factor of $70. The anesthesia charge would be calculated as follows:

(Base units + Time units + Modifying units) × Conversion factor = Anesthesia charge.

(7 base units + 5 time units + 0 modifying units) × $70 = $840 charge

Table 6–1 demonstrates the conversion from minutes to units used by insurance carriers.

Highlight:
The units of service are entered in Box 24G of the CMS-1500 claim form.

Table 6-1 Conversion from Minutes to Time Units for Anesthesia

Minutes	Units	Minutes	Units
1–2	0.1	16–17	1.1
3	0.2	18	1.2
4–5	0.3	19–20	1.3
6	0.4	21	1.4
7–8	0.5	22–23	1.5
9	0.6	24	1.6
10–11	0.7	25–26	1.7
12	0.8	27	1.8
13–14	0.9	28–29	1.9
15	1.0	30	2.0

Current anesthesia conversion factors and anesthesia base units can be found on the CMS website. An exception to recognition of time units for anesthesia codes in CPT is 01996.

Exercise 6.1

Match the term in column A with the definition in column B.

Column A

_____ 1. Caudal anesthesia

_____ 2. Epidural anesthesia

_____ 3. Nerve block

_____ 4. Topical anesthetic

_____ 5. Field block

_____ 6. Endotracheal anesthetic

Column B

A. Injected into area around surgical site

B. Used in childbirth via drip into spinal canal at sacrum

C. Injected into or in close proximity to the nerve to numb surrounding tissue

D. Gaseous drug inserted via oral or nasal tube

E. Injection into spaces between vertebrae

F. Injected subcutaneously or topically

Exercise 6.2

Assign the following moderate (conscious) sedation codes.

1. 45 minutes of moderate (conscious) sedation for closed treatment with manipulation of a dislocated shoulder, patient age 29 years _____

2. One hour of moderate (conscious) sedation for closed treatment of a Bennett fracture of the left thumb, age 3 years _____

3. A 10-year-old patient receives 30 minutes of moderate (conscious) sedation for a tonsillectomy. _____

4. A 71-year-old patient undergoes a colonoscopy for bleeding control using bipolar cautery, 45 minutes of moderate (conscious) sedation. _____

5. A surgeon administers moderate (conscious) sedation to a patient undergoing a diagnostic bronchoscopy in his office. The patient is a 55-year-old female in generally good health except for a history of smoking since age 21. The intraservice time is 30 minutes. _____

Anesthesia Modifiers

physical status modifiers:
A two-digit amendment to the anesthesia CPT codes that describes the physical status of the patient who is receiving anesthesia.

All anesthesia services require the use of the five-digit CPT code plus an additional two-digit modifier to indicate the physical status of the patient. The **physical status modifiers** are consistent with the American Society of Anesthesiologists (ASA) ranking of a patient's physical status. The anesthesiologist provides the ASA ranking, or physical status of the patient, as the risk is identified for anesthesia provided for the procedure. This can usually be found on the anesthesia graph. These modifiers consist of the letter P followed by a single digit from 1 to 6, as outlined in Figure 6–2.

For example, an anesthesiologist who provides general anesthesia for a patient who is undergoing a corneal transplant would select the five-digit code 00144, Anesthesia for procedures on eye: corneal transplant. Included in that code is a preoperative evaluation during which the anesthesiologist discovers that the patient

P1—A normal healthy patient
P2—A patient with mild systemic disease
P3—A patient with severe systemic disease
P4—A patient with severe systemic disease that is a constant threat to life
P5—A moribund patient who is not expected to survive without the operation
P6—A declared brain-dead patient whose organs are being removed for donation

Figure 6-2 Physical status modifiers

has a severe systemic disease. The five-digit code of 00144 should be appended with the modifier P3 to indicate the physical status of the patient.

Carriers that do not recognize these physical status modifiers will not assign base units to the anesthesia if included in the claim.

Medicare's definition of anesthesia time is as follows:

Anesthesia time is defined as the period during which an anesthesia practitioner (physician, CRNA, AA, etc.) is present with the patient. It starts when the anesthesia practitioner begins to prepare the patient for anesthesia services in the operating room or an equivalent area and ends when the anesthesia practitioner is no longer furnishing anesthesia services to the patient; that is, when the patient may be placed safely under postoperative care (www.cms.gov).

Anesthesia time begins when the anesthesiologist begins to prepare the patient for the induction of anesthesia in the operating room or in an equivalent area, and requires the continuous presence of the anesthesiologist or CRNA when medically directing.

- Anesthesia start and stop times must be reported in actual minutes and not rounded up or down.

- It is important to document the transfer time to recovery room personnel.

Highlight:

Sometimes anesthesia is provided under particularly difficult qualifying circumstances. These qualifying circumstances may be the condition of the patient, notable operative conditions, or unusual risk factors. It would be appropriate to add a code from 99100 to 99140 to indicate these qualifying circumstances. These codes are never to be used alone, but in association with the code for the anesthesia procedure or service. Patients of extreme age (under 1 year or over 70) and emergency conditions are examples of unusual risk factors.

Other CPT modifiers specific to anesthesia care are as follows:

-22 Increased Procedural Services: Assigned when work required to provide a service is substantially greater than typically required. Documentation must support and give reason for the additional work (e.g., increased intensity, time, technical difficulty of procedure, severity of patient's condition, physical and mental effort required).

-23 Unusual Anesthesia: Assigned when a procedure that normally requires no anesthesia or local anesthesia must be performed under general anesthesia because of unusual circumstances.

-59 Distinct Procedural Service: Assigned to indicate that a procedure or service was distinct or independent from other non-E/M services performed on the same day. These services are not normally reported together but are appropriate under certain circumstances. Documentation must support a different session, procedure, or surgery, different site or organ system, separate incision or excision, separate lesion, or separate injury not normally encountered or performed on the same day by the same individual.

HCPCS modifiers related to anesthesia services are:

-AA: Anesthesia services personally performed by the anesthesiologist

-AD: Medical supervision by a physician; more than four concurrent anesthesia services

-G8: Monitored anesthesia care (MAC) for deep complex, complicated, or markedly invasive surgical procedure (an informational modifier, does not affect reimbursement)

-G9: Monitored anesthesia care (MAC) for at-risk patient with history of severe cardiopulmonary condition (an informational modifier, does not affect reimbursement)

-QK: Medical direction of two, three, or four concurrent anesthesia procedures involving qualified individuals

-QS: Monitored anesthesia care (an informational modifier, does not affect reimbursement)

-QX: CRNA service with medical direction by a physician

-QY: Medical direction of one CRNA by a physician

-QZ: CRNA service without medical direction by a physician

> **Highlight:**
>
> Modifier -59 is only used with non-E/M services. Modifier -25 is used with an evaluation/management CPT code to report a distinct, significantly separate service by the same physician on the same day of the procedure or other service.

Exercise 6.3

Assign the CPT code that an anesthesiologist would report for the following. Code the physical status modifier, if indicated.

1. General anesthesia provided for a patient with mild systemic disease who is undergoing a ventral hernia repair _____

2. Anesthesia for patient, 51 years old, for closed treatment of femoral fracture, in good health _____

3. Anesthesia for 6-month-old infant, for repair of cleft palate _____

4. Anesthesia vaginal hysterectomy, age 42, with benign essential hypertension _____

5. Anesthesia for diagnostic arthroscopy of right shoulder, patient is Type 2 diabetic, well controlled with medication _____

6. Anesthesia for pneumocentesis, 81-year-old patient with mild COPD _____

7. Anesthesia for laparoscopic cholecystectomy on 45-year-old with benign hypertension _____

(continues)

Exercise 6.3 *(continued)*

8. Anesthesia for blepharoplasty, age 69, with malignant hypertension _____

9. Anesthesia for corneal transplant, age 71, with Type I diabetes, controlled _____

10. Anesthesia for patient, age 66, terminally ill, diagnosed with metastatic bladder carcinoma
_____

General Surgery

General surgery refers to operations performed on the following body systems: respiratory, cardiovascular, hemic and lymphatic, mediastinum and diaphragm, digestive, urinary, male genital, female reproductive, endocrine, nervous, eye and ocular adnexa, and auditory. The female reproductive system will be covered separately in Chapter 10 of this text. Subsections within each system list the specific organ followed by the procedure performed on each of these organs.

CPT codes and the use of modifiers are used extensively in the surgical section. As outlined in Chapter 2 and following chapters, ICD-10-CM codes must be listed to support the medical necessity for any procedure submitted to third party payer for reimbursement.

A modifier describes a specific circumstance or an unusual event that alters the definition of the procedure. Unilateral surgery performed on organs that have a definite right and left side are reported with either the -LT (left side) or -RT (right side) modifier. Codes for surgery performed on eyelids, fingers, and toes should be modified using the list in Table 6–2 to prevent erroneous denials when duplicate HCPCS codes are billed reporting separate procedures performed on different anatomical sites or different sides of the body. A complete list of modifiers, including specific HCPCS modifiers as demonstrated in Table 6–2, are located in Appendix A of CPT.

Table 6-2 HCPCS Level II Modifiers

-E1 Upper left, eyelid	-F8 Right hand, fourth digit
-E2 Lower left, eyelid	-F9 Right hand, fifth digit
-E3 Upper right, eyelid	-TA Left foot, great toe
-E4 Lower right, eyelid	-T1 Left foot, second digit
-FA Left hand, thumb	-T2 Left foot, third digit
-F1 Left hand, second digit	-T3 Left foot, fourth digit
-F2 Left hand, third digit	-T4 Left foot, fifth digit
-F3 Left hand, fourth digit	-T5 Right foot, great toe
-F4 Left hand, fifth digit	-T6 Right foot, second digit
-F5 Right hand, thumb	-T7 Right foot, third digit
-F6 Right hand, second digit	-T8 Right foot, fourth digit
-F7 Right hand, third digit	-T9 Right foot, fifth digit

The Respiratory System

The respiratory system is divided into upper and lower tracts (Figure 6–3). The organs of the upper tract include the nose, nasal cavity, nasopharynx, oropharynx, laryngopharynx, and larynx. The lower tract includes the trachea and the bronchi, bronchioles, and alveoli that comprise the lungs. The respiratory section in the CPT code book is subdivided into the following categories: nose, accessory sinuses, larynx, trachea and bronchi, and lungs and pleura.

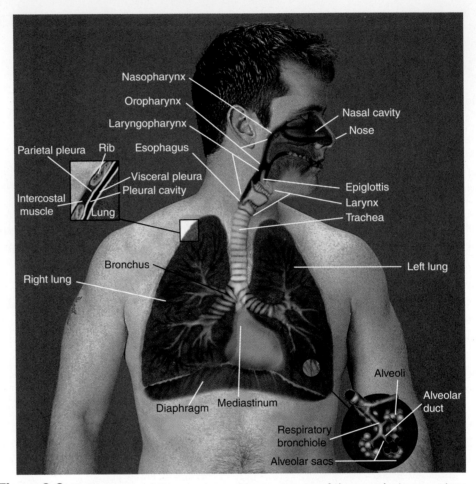

Figure 6-3 The organs of the upper and lower tracts of the respiratory system

Nasal Polyps

An excision of nasal polyps, simple, means that there was just one polyp on one side of the nasal cavity. An extensive procedure involves the excision of multiple nasal polyps on one side. Use the bilateral modifier (-50) to report the excision of nasal polyps from both sides of the nasal cavity only if the same degree of excision is performed on both sides.

General Sinus Surgery

For repair codes on the nasal sinus (30400–30630), primary repair refers to the first repair of any structure. Secondary repair is a repair performed subsequent to a primary repair. Minor revision rhinoplasty, or plastic surgery of the nose, involves only nasal cartilage. Intermediate revision rhinoplasty involves an osteotomy, or the cutting of bone. Major revision rhinoplasty includes both cartilage (work on the nasal tip) and an osteotomy.

Code 30520 is reported for a septoplasty or submucous resection, with or without cartilage scoring, contouring, or replacement with graft. This is the only code assigned if the cartilage used for the graft is obtained from the immediate surgical area. If, however, the physician must go outside of the septum to obtain enough cartilage for the graft, it would be appropriate to add the code 20912, Cartilage graft, nasal septum.

In order to correctly code the control of nasal hemorrhage, the following questions must be answered:

1. Was the hemorrhage anterior (the forward or front part of the body or body part) or posterior (the back part of the body or body part)?

2. If it was anterior, was the hemorrhage simple or complex?

3. If it was posterior, was the control an initial or a subsequent procedure?

The physician should document in the medical record if the procedure was simple or complex.

Paranasal sinuses are spaces that contain air and are lined with mucous membranes. There are four sinus cavities on each side of the face:

* Frontal, on each side of the forehead, above each eye medially

* Maxillary (also called antrum), located in the cheekbones below each eye

* Sphenoid, located behind the nasal cavity

* Ethmoid, located between the nose and the eye

Laryngoscopy

Laryngoscopy codes are subdivided into diagnostic and surgical. Diagnostic involves viewing only, while surgical involves any excision, destruction, repair, or biopsy. A surgical laryngoscopy always includes a diagnostic laryngoscopy, so the two codes would not be assigned together. A direct laryngoscopy involves passing a rigid or fiber-optic endoscope through the mouth and pharynx to allow for direct visualization of the larynx. An indirect laryngoscopy uses a light source and two mirrors, one positioned at the back of the throat, and the other held in front of the mouth. The tongue is grasped and held out as far as possible and the larynx is observed.

Bronchoscopy

A surgical bronchoscopy includes a diagnostic bronchoscopy. If a biopsy is taken, a foreign body is removed, or a tumor or blockage is destroyed, it is considered a surgical bronchoscopy and the appropriate code applied. It would be inappropriate to assign 31622, Bronchoscopy, diagnostic, in addition to the surgical bronchoscopy.

Exercise 6.4

Assign the appropriate CPT code for the following statements.

1. Control by packing of anterior nasal hemorrhage, simple _____

2. Extensive cauterization of nasal hemorrhage, left nares _____

3. Simple excision of nasal polyps, bilateral _____

4. Nasal/sinus endoscopy, surgical, to control hemorrhage _____

5. Laryngoscopy, direct, operative with biopsy _____

6. Bronchoscopy, flexible, diagnostic _____

7. Thoracentesis for pneumothorax with insertion of tube with syringe to the catheter for removal of air
_____

8. Unilateral sinusotomy of the frontal, maxillary, and ethmoid paranasal sinuses _____

9. Laryngoscopy, direct, operative to remove foreign body _____

10. Lung transplant, bilateral, with cardiopulmonary bypass _____

Highlight:

Assign the code that fully describes all procedures performed.

The Cardiovascular System

The cardiovascular system involves the heart and blood vessels. Some heart surgery requires the use of cardiopulmonary bypass (heart lung machine). A pericardiectomy without the use of cardiopulmonary bypass would be coded 33030, whereas the use of cardiopulmonary bypass during a pericardiectomy would be coded 33031 because the use of cardiopulmonary bypass is stated within the code. The same holds true for repair of wounds of the heart and great vessels (33300–33335).

Pacemakers

A pacemaker system includes a pulse generator and one or more electrodes (leads) inserted through a vein (transvenous) or on the surface of the heart (epicardial). A single chamber device includes the generator and one electrode inserted into either the atrium or ventricle of the heart. A dual chamber device includes the generator and electrodes inserted into *both* the atrium and the ventricle of the heart. A pacemaker with atrial and ventricular leads is shown in Figure 6–4. The changing of a battery is actually the replacement of a generator. This procedure requires the code for the removal of the old generator and a second code for the insertion of the new generator. Any repositioning or replacement within the first 14 days after initial insertion of the pacemaker is included in the code assignment. Insertion of a temporary pacemaker (33211) is a separate procedure and therefore would not be assigned if the reason for the temporary pacer was for the performance of other heart surgery. Often the temporary pacemaker is inserted to ensure the steady rhythm of the heart while other surgery is being performed. In this case, the temporary pacemaker is inherent in the major procedure and would not be coded separately. There is a specific code for the upgrade of a single chamber system to

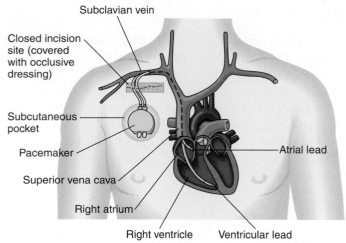

Figure 6-4 Artificial pacemaker with atrial and ventricular leads

a dual chamber system (33214). This code includes the removal of the previously placed generator, the testing of the existing lead, the insertion of a new lead, and the insertion of a new pulse generator.

Coronary Artery Bypass Graft

Veins and/or arteries can be used for the performance of coronary artery bypass graft (CABG) surgery (Figure 6–5). There are separate code ranges for the use of veins, arteries, or a combination of veins and arteries for the graft. If only the veins are used, a code from 33510–33516 must be applied. If only arteries are used, a code from 33533–33545 is applied. When a combination of both veins and arteries are used, it is necessary to report two codes: (1) the appropriate combined Arterial-venous graft code (33517–33523), and (2) the appropriate Arterial graft code (33533–33536). The procurement of the saphenous vein for grafting is included in the description of the code for the venous grafting.

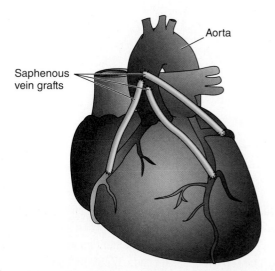

Figure 6-5 Coronary artery bypass surgery is performed by placing vein grafts to bypass blocked arteries.

Catheters

catheter: A tubular, flexible instrument for withdrawal of fluids from, or introduction of fluids into, a body cavity.

A **catheter** is defined as a flexible, tubelike instrument used to pass through body channels for withdrawal of fluids from a body cavity or to introduce fluids into a body cavity. The insertion of catheters into the venous system can be especially difficult to code because there are many types and uses of catheters. Codes are assigned as to the location of the area where inserted and the technique, not by brand name of the catheter. These sites include catheters inserted in the jugular, femoral, cephalic, subclavian, or umbilical vein. See Figure 6–6 for an example of commonly used catheters.

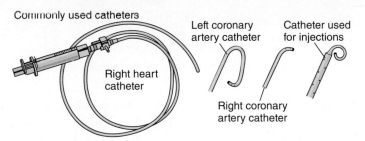

Figure 6-6 Commonly used catheters

Central Venous Catheter

Central venous catheters (CVCs) are placed in a large vein, such as the jugular, femoral, or subclavian, with a needle and syringe. The catheter is left in place for blood draws for analysis; or IV fluids, medication, or chemotherapy substances can be directly administered into the vein. Peripherally inserted central catheters (PICC) are inserted into superficial veins, usually in the arms, legs, or feet. Percutaneous catheters are placed through the skin. A cutdown catheter is made by an incision into the side of the vein in order to access the vein in the arm or upper leg. The most common types of CVCs (codes 36555–36556, 36568–36569, 36580, 36584) are:

- Broviac
- Hickman
- Hydrocath
- Groshong
- Dual lumen
- Triple lumen

> **Coding Tip:**
> There is no CPT code used to report the removal of a catheter when it requires only the removal of the skin suture holding it in place. To report a simple removal of a catheter, refer to the appropriate Evaluation and Management code. If a catheter becomes embedded and must be removed, assign code 37799 (unlisted vascular procedure) and provide supporting documentation.

Vascular Access Devices

Vascular access devices (VADs) are devices that provide prolonged vascular access for chemotherapy, IV fluids, medications, and the withdrawal of blood for sampling. VADs are designed to provide long-term access to the vascular system without the necessity and trauma of repeated needlesticks. VADs are surgically implanted, creating a subcutaneous pocket to house the portal. A simple venous catheter does not contain a portal; therefore a subcutaneous pocket is not created. Several CPT codes describe the insertion of an implantable venous access port (36557–36561, 36565–36566, 36570–36571). Some of the common types are:

- Infuse-a-Port
- Medi Port
- Dual Port
- Groshong Port
- Port-a-Cath
- Q-Port
- Perm-a-Cath

The removal of a vascular access device is code 36589. The removal of an old vascular access device and the insertion of a new device is considered a revision and is coded to 36575–36578, 36581–36583, or 36585.

The Hemic and Lymphatic Systems

The hemic system consists of the spleen and the bone marrow. The harvesting of bone marrow or peripheral stem cells is reported using 38205, 38206, or 38230. The transplantation of these cells is reported using 38240, or 38241, depending on whether the bone marrow or stem cells are allogenic (donated) or autologous (from the patient). Bone marrow aspiration for biopsy purposes would be coded using 38220.

The lymphatic system contains the lymph nodes and the lymphatic channels. The biopsy or excision of a single or random lymph nodes is coded to 38500–38555. A radical lymphadenectomy (38700–38780) is the removal of all or most of the lymph nodes in a certain area. The code for the excision of internal mammary nodes (38530) is a separate procedure, meaning it is not to be assigned if it is commonly carried out as an integral component of another procedure. For example, it is common to excise some internal mammary nodes during a breast biopsy or mastectomy. In this case, the code 38530 would not be applied separately. This code may be applied if it is carried out independently or is considered to be unrelated or distinct from other procedures provided at that time. Figure 6–7 outlines the organs of the lymphatic system.

The Mediastinum and Diaphragm

Procedures on the Mediastinum and diaphragm are reported using codes 39000–39599. Diaphragmatic hernias are repaired by transthoracic approach or by abdominal approach. Code selection depends on the approach used to repair

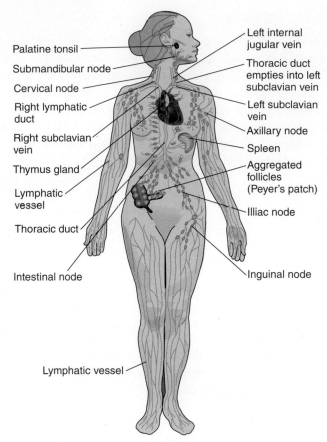

Figure 6-7 The lymphatic system

the hernia. In the event that a physician repairs the hernia by some other method (endoscopic repair), the unlisted code for procedures on the Diaphragm (39599) would be assigned.

The Digestive System

The digestive system is composed of the following organs and structures: the mouth, pharynx, esophagus, stomach, large intestine, and small intestine. Accessory organs of the digestive system include the teeth, salivary glands, liver, gallbladder, and pancreas (see Figure 6–8 for a diagram of the main structures and accessory organs of the digestive system). The main functions of the digestive system are the digestion, absorption, and elimination of food. Physicians who specialize in the diagnosis and treatment of disorders of this body system are called gastroenterologists. *Gastro* is the root word meaning stomach. Figure 6–9 shows the structures of the large intestine.

Similar to the other body system areas of CPT, the digestive system subsection is organized by body site and includes codes for the abdomen, the peritoneum, and the omentum (a double fold of the peritoneum that hangs down over the small intestine and lies between the liver and the lesser curvature of the stomach). Codes for hernias and **endoscopy** are also included in this subsection.

For procedures done on the lips (40490–40761), the vermilion refers to the part of the lip between the outer skin and the moist oral mucosa of the mouth. It is sometimes

endoscopy: Inspection of organs or cavities by use of a tube through a natural body opening or through a small incision.

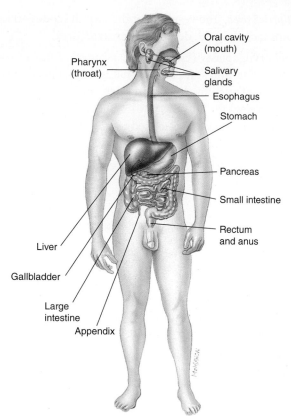

Figure 6-8 The major and accessory organs of the digestive system

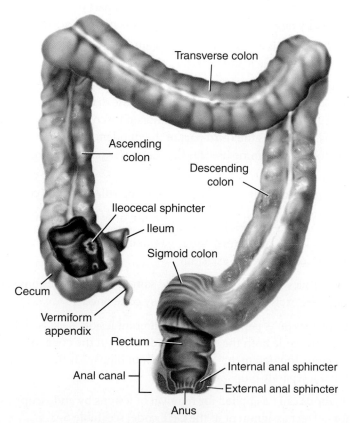

Figure 6-9 Anatomy of the large intestine

referred to as the *lipstick area*. The vestibule of the mouth (codes 40800–40845) refers to the oral cavity, not including the dentoalveolar structures.

A uvulopalatopharyngoplasty (UPPP) is the removal of mucosa and muscle from the pharyngeal walls, uvula, and soft palate. What is left is a permanent, noncollapsing, oropharyngeal airway that attempts to correct sleep apnea of the obstructive type. The correct code assignment for UPPP is 42145. The same procedure done by laser or thermal, cryotherapy, or chemicals is coded to 42160. This procedure is often completed in the physician's office since it is minimally invasive; it has been referred to as the snore-cure.

Tonsillectomy

A tonsillectomy is coded in conjunction with an adenoidectomy when appropriate.

Coding Tip:

It is essential to know the age of the patient receiving the tonsillectomy and/or adenoidectomy. The surgery performed on children under the age of 12 is assigned one set of codes, while the procedure performed on a patient age 12 or older is coded with a different set of codes.

Endoscopy

A surgical endoscopy always includes a diagnostic endoscopy. Diagnostic refers to viewing only. Once surgery is performed during an endoscopy procedure, it would not be appropriate to use the diagnostic code, as viewing is part of the surgery. Code the diagnostic endoscopy only if a surgical procedure was not performed.

An upper endoscopy is a scope passed through the mouth into the esophagus and in some cases into the stomach and even into the duodenum.

An esophagoscopy is limited to the study of the esophagus. An esophagogastroscopy is when the endoscope passes the diaphragm. An esophagogastroduodenoscopy (EGD) is when the endoscope traverses the pyloric channel. An ileoscopy passes the third part of the duodenum. It is essential to read the operative report to determine how far the scope was passed in order to assign the correct code.

When coding a surgical endoscopy, the following rules must be considered:

1. If a single lesion is biopsied but not excised, use only the biopsy code.

2. If a biopsy of a lesion is obtained and the remaining portion of the same lesion is then excised, code only the excision.

3. If multiple biopsies are obtained (from the same or different lesions) and none of the lesions are excised, use only the biopsy code once.

4. If a biopsy of a lesion is performed and a different lesion is excised during the same procedure, code both the excision and biopsy, if the code for the excision does not include the statement "with or without biopsy." If this statement is included, use a separate biopsy code.

Several methods can be applied for removal of lesions by endoscopy that must be understood for correct assignment of the CPT code; see Table 6–3.

Table 6-3 Methods for the Removal of Lesions by Endoscopy

Hot biopsy	Forceps use an electrical current that excises and fulgurates the polyp simultaneously. Forceps may be passed through a scope to remove tissue for biopsy.
Ablation	Involves the elimination or control of a hemorrhage of a tumor or mucosal lesion.
Electrocautery	Destroys the remaining tissue after a specimen is obtained.
Snare	A loop is slipped out of a long plastic tube and closed down around the lesion to remove it.
Bipolar cautery	Electrosurgery using a pair of electrodes. The tissue that lies between the electrodes is coagulated using a flow of current from one electrode to another.
Cold biopsy	The same method as hot biopsy except that it is not hooked up to the fulgurator and is used for smaller specimens.

Bleeding can be controlled using several different methods, all of which are reported using one single code.

For the esophagus, strictures and **achalasia**, or the inability of muscles to relax, can be treated using esophageal dilation. Using an instrument, the orifice is expanded or enlarged to relieve the obstruction.

achalasia: The inability of muscles to relax.

Proctosigmoidoscopy is the examination of the rectum and may include examination of a portion of the sigmoid colon.

Sigmoidoscopy is the examination of the entire rectum and sigmoid colon, and may include examination of a portion of the descending colon.

Colonoscopy is an exam used to detect changes or abnormalities in the large intestine (colon) and rectum. During a colonoscopy, a long, flexible tube (colonoscope) is inserted into the rectum. A tiny video camera at the tip of the tube allows the physician to view the inside of the entire colon. If necessary, polyps or other types of abnormal tissue can be removed through the scope during a colonoscopy. Tissue samples (biopsies) can be taken during a colonoscopy as well. Table 6–4 demonstrates the diagnostic procedure versus the therapeutic procedure, indicating CPT codes and any required modifiers.

Table 6-4 Codes for Colonoscopies

Procedure Type	Extent of Procedure	Defined As	Code
Diagnostic	Does not reach splenic flexure	Flexible sigmoidoscopy	45330
Diagnostic	Beyond splenic flexure, but not to the cecum	Colonoscopy	45378, modifier 53
Diagnostic	To cecum	Colonoscopy	45378, no modifier
Therapeutic	Does not reach splenic flexure	Flexible sigmoidoscopy	45331-45347
Therapeutic	Beyond splenic flexure, but not to the cecum	Colonoscopy	45379-45398, modifier 52
Therapeutic	To cecum	Colonoscopy	45379-45398, no modifier

Moderate (conscious) sedation is used to perform most endoscopic procedures. Chapter 12, Medicine, of this textbook addresses coding for this type of sedation, as anesthesia codes are not assigned for these procedures.

Patients that cannot get enough nutrition by mouth can have a percutaneous endoscopic gastrostomy (PEG) tube placed. This is a procedure in which the endoscope is passed into the stomach, and a gastrostomy tube is placed percutaneously through the wall of the stomach as the endoscopist visualizes the insertion from inside. The code assignment for a PEG is 43246.

Highlight:
Several factors need to be considered for proper coding of esophageal dilation. These factors involve the type of endoscopy involved, the method of dilation, and direct or indirect visualization. Direct visualization implies an endoscopic procedure. It is important to read the operative report to determine if the esophagus alone was examined, or if the scope was inserted all the way to the duodenum. Types of dilators that can be used include balloon, guide wires, bougie, or retrograde dilators.

Endoscopic Retrograde Cholangiopancreatography

sphincter: Muscles that constrict an orifice.

Endoscopic retrograde cholangiopancreatography (ERCP) is the injection of contrast medium into the papilla to visualize the pancreatic and common bile ducts by radiographic examination. As implied by the name, this is an endoscopic procedure, meaning that a scope is passed through the patient's mouth and into the duodenum where dye is instilled and then x-rays are taken. Before the endoscope is removed, many other procedures can be performed. A diagnostic ERCP includes the taking of specimens by brushing or washing. If a biopsy is obtained by other methods, the correct code would be 43261. If the ERCP is done and a sphincterotomy (incision of the **sphincter**) is performed, use code 43262. Pressure measurements can be made of the sphincter of Oddi and would be coded to 43263. Stones are often removed with such devices as a basket or balloon, and code 43264 should be applied. If the stones are too large for simple removal, a device known as a lithotriptor can be passed through the endoscope and into the bile duct to crush the stones. The use of the lithotriptor necessitates the use of 43265. A drainage tube may be left in place to allow these crushed stones to pass, and code 43274 should be applied. If indicated, a stent may be placed. A stent is an indwelling device that is left in position for long-term drainage. Stents are coded to 43274. A replacement of a stent is code 43275 and removal and exchange of a stent 43276. When it is necessary to do a dilation of the bile or pancreatic duct, code 43277 would be applied (Table 6–5).

It is considered unbundling to assign the code for ERCP, diagnostic, when any of these procedures are done at the same operative episode.

Table 6-5 Procedures That Can Be Performed in Conjunction with ERCP, Using One CPT Code

ERCP	43260
ERCP with biopsy	43261
ERCP with sphincterotomy/papillotomy	43262
ERCP with pressure measurement	43263
ERCP with removal of stones	43264
ERCP with lithotripsy	43265
ERCP with placement of stent into biliary or pancreatic duct	43274
ERCP with removal of foreign body or stent/removal and exchange of tube or stent	43275/43276
ERCP with balloon dilation	43277
ERCP with ablation of lesion, polyp, or other lesion	43278

Endoscopic Procedures:

Proctosigmoidoscopy is the examination of the rectum and sigmoid colon.

Sigmoidoscopy is the examination of the entire rectum, sigmoid colon, and may include a portion of the descending colon.

Colonoscopy is the examination of the entire colon, from the rectum to the cecum, and may include the terminal ileum.

Many of these procedures are performed under moderate (conscious) sedation, and these are indicated in CPT with the symbol ⊙

Highlight:

When a patient is fully prepped for a colonoscopy, but the colonoscopy cannot be completed and is documented as an incomplete procedure, assign the code for the colonoscopy with modifier -52 and provide documentation. If the procedure was performed in an ambulatory surgical center (ASC), the appropriate modifiers would be -73 or -74.

Hemorrhoidectomy

A hemorrhoid is an abnormal enlargement of a vein or veins in the lower rectum or anus. A hemorrhoid could be either internal, occurring above the internal sphincter of the anus, or external, appearing outside the anal sphincter. To code a hemorrhoidectomy, selection of the CPT code is based on the location of the hemorrhoid or hemorrhoids (external or internal), and whether there is a single column or group versus two or more columns or groups. If a **fistula** or **fissure** is present (Figure 6–10) and treated at the same time as a hemorrhoidectomy, the use of the combination code (hemorrhoidectomy with fistulectomy or fissurectomy) is necessary. Use the code for subcutaneous fistulectomy if the procedure does not involve the muscle. A submuscular fistulectomy involves the division of muscle. A fistulectomy is considered complex if multiple fistulas are excised.

fistula: An abnormal tubelike passage from a normal cavity to another cavity or surface.

fissure: A groove, split, or natural division.

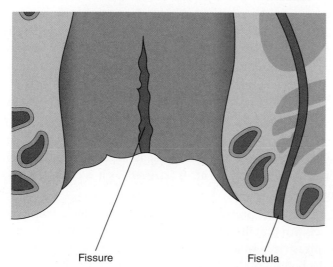

Fissure   Fistula

Figure 6-10 An example of an anal fissure (left) and fistula (right)

> **Highlight:**
>
> Note the difference between fissure and fistula. Refer to Figure 6–10.
>
> Fissure—a sore, crack, or groove in the skin or mucous membrane, such as an anal fissure.
>
> Fistula—an abnormal passageway between two tubular organs (e.g., rectum and vagina) or from an organ to the body surface.

Liver Biopsy

A percutaneous or needle biopsy of the liver is a closed procedure done percutaneously through the skin. A liver biopsy is considered to be open if it is an excisional biopsy or a wedge biopsy. A closed liver biopsy can be accomplished even during an open abdominal procedure. If, during another procedure in which the abdomen is open, the operative report indicates that a needle or trochar is used to obtain liver tissue, it is considered to be a closed liver biopsy. If the operative report indicates that a wedge of liver tissue was excised, it is considered an open biopsy. Normally, an open biopsy of the liver requires the use of a suture after the removal of the tissue. For example, a fine needle aspiration of the liver is coded from the General Surgery section (codes 10021 or 10022). For laboratory and pathology evaluation of a fine needle aspirate, refer to the Laboratory and Pathology chapter of the CPT book (codes 88172, 88173).

Cholecystectomy

A cholecystectomy is the surgical removal of the gallbladder. Use codes 47600–47620 for an open procedure. For laparoscopic procedures, see codes 47562–47564.

Hernia Repair

A hernia is the projection or protrusion of an organ through the wall of the cavity that normally contains it. Reducible hernias can be corrected by manipulation. Nonreducible hernias cannot be reduced by manipulation, but are fixed in the hernial sac, allowing for no mobility of the hernia. An incarcerated hernia is one that is constricted, confined, or imprisoned in the hernia sac, and thus is nonreducible. Strangulation is the most serious complication of a hernia. When the hernia strangulates (or cuts off the blood supply to the herniated part), the result is tissue ischemia or death. A recurrent hernia is one that has been surgically treated prior to the current treatment.

Hernias are classified based on the location (Figure 6–11). An inguinal hernia is the most common form of hernia, and is a protrusion of the abdominal contents through the inguinal canal, or groin area. A lipoma of the spermatic cord is frequently excised during a hernia repair. A separate code for the lipoma excision is not applied when an inguinal hernia is repaired, as it is considered a normal part of the procedure.

A femoral hernia is the protrusion of intestine through the femoral canal, next to the femoral vessels. An umbilical hernia is a protrusion of part of the intestine at the umbilicus. An epigastric hernia is the protrusion of fat or a peritoneal sac between the umbilicus and the bottom of the sternum. The sac may be empty or contain an internal organ that cannot be easily reduced.

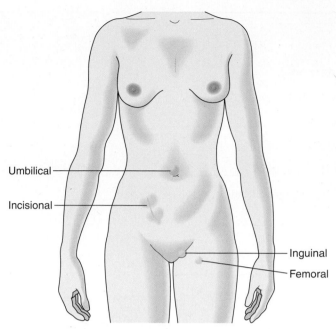

Figure 6-11 Common locations for hernias

An incisional hernia occurs at the incision site from previous surgery. A hernia may develop at the site of an incision when the wound is new, recent, or even if it is an old wound. Ventral hernias are coded as incisional.

Often the repair of the hernia includes the implantation of mesh or other prosthetic material to hold the surrounding tissue in place. The only time that an additional code is used to indicate the use of mesh (49568) is when an incisional or ventral hernia is repaired. The other types of hernia repairs do not require an additional code to indicate the use of mesh or other prostheses.

If repair or excision is completed to the strangulated organs or structures from a hernia, an appropriate code for the excision or repair should be applied in addition to the hernia repair. For example, if a portion of the sigmoid colon needs to be removed because it is strangulated into the hernia sac, the code for the sigmoid resection would be applied in addition to the hernia repair.

Highlight:

The key elements in the coding of hernia repair are as follows:

   The age of the patient

   The type of hernia being repaired

   The stage of the hernia (initial or recurrent)

   The clinical presentation (reducible or incarcerated/strangulated)

   The method of repair (open or laparoscopic)

Codes for bilateral hernia repairs do not exist, so the use of the modifier -50 "bilateral procedure" is imperative when a hernia is repaired on both sides.

Exercise 6.5

Assign CPT codes to the following statements.

1. Flexible colonoscopy diagnostic with biopsy _____

2. Tonsillectomy with adenoidectomy, age 18 _____

3. Hemorrhoidectomy by rubber band procedure _____

4. Esophageal dilation, balloon method, retrograde _____

5. Right inguinal hernia repair, initial, age 56, using Marlex mesh, reducible _____

6. Laparoscopic cholecystectomy _____

7. Cholecystectomy with cholangiography _____

8. Appendectomy with generalized peritonitis _____

9. Flexible colonoscopy to remove polyps by snare technique _____

10. ERCP with pressure measurement of sphincter of Oddi _____

The Urinary System

Urinary system coding includes procedures performed on the kidney, ureter, bladder, and urethra. Included in this section are also procedures on the prostate that are performed by the transurethral method. Open procedures on the prostate are in the male genital system section. The parts of the urinary system are shown in Figure 6–12.

A nephrostomy is the creation of an artificial fistula into the renal pelvis. If the nephrostomy is completed with a nephrotomy (incision into the kidney), assign code 50040. If the procedure is a percutaneous nephrostomy, use code 50395. A nephrolithotomy (50060–50075) is the surgical removal of stones from the kidney through an incision in the body of the kidney. A nephrostolithotomy is a percutaneous procedure used to establish a passageway from the kidney through which stones can be extracted. The code assignment is based on the size of the stone. If a stone that is 2 centimeters or less is extracted through a nephrostolithotomy, assign code 50080. If the stone extracted through the nephrostolithotomy is over 2 centimeters, assign code 50081. Sometimes the passageway for removing stones already exists from a previous procedure (nephrostomy or pyelostomy) and a physician will remove a stone through it. In this case assign code 50561 because a new nephrostomy has not been created in this operative episode.

Many codes in this section state "exclusive of radiological service." Several procedures on the urinary system are done in conjunction with a radiological procedure to further visualize the organs being examined. The codes in this section do not include the taking of the radiological images. An additional code from the radiology section of the CPT code book must be assigned in order to classify the radiological service performed.

For the surgical removal of stones from the ureter through a direct incision into the ureter, use codes 50610–50630, depending on what portion of the ureter was incised, the upper one-third, the middle one-third, or the lower one-third.

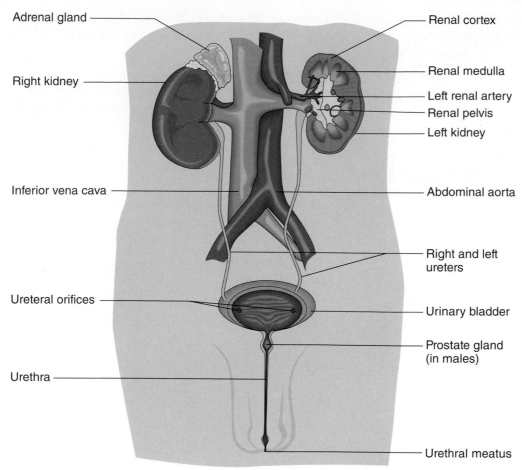

Adrenal gland

Right kidney

Inferior vena cava

Ureteral orifices

Urethra

Renal cortex

Renal medulla

Left renal artery

Renal pelvis

Left kidney

Abdominal aorta

Right and left
ureters

Urinary bladder

Prostate gland
(in males)

Urethral meatus

Figure 6-12 The primary organs of the urinary system are shown here in a diagram of a male.

Indwelling ureteral catheters are inserted into the renal pelvis through the ureter to allow drainage from the renal pelvis when something is impinging on the ureters. The most common types of ureteral stents are Gibbons and double-J stents. The approach for the insertion of the catheters determines the code assignment. Insertion of indwelling ureteral catheters through established nephrostomy is code 50553 while those through established ureterostomy is code 50953.

An ileal conduit is a method of diverting the urinary flow by making a conduit with the ureter through a segment of the ileum and out the abdominal wall. A special receptacle collects the urine. This procedure is usually performed when a bladder carcinoma or pelvic tumor is obstructing the ureter so that the patient is unable to pass urine.

The insertion of temporary stents during diagnostic or therapeutic cystourethroscopic interventions is included in 52320–52334 and should not be reported separately. Use code 52332 in addition to the primary procedure and add modifier -51, multiple procedures, when the stents are self-retained and indwelling, not just temporary during the time of the procedure. Because code 52332 is considered a unilateral procedure, assign the modifier -50, bilateral procedure, if the procedure was performed on both ureters. The removal of indwelling ureteral stents is coded to 52310 (simple procedure) or 52315 (complicated procedure) with the modifier -58, staged or related procedure or service by the same physician during the postoperative period. The operative report should substantiate the use of the complicated removal of ureteral stents.

All minor procedures done concurrently with endoscopic or transurethral surgeries are included in the main procedure and are not to be coded separately (see instructional notes under Endoscopy-Cystoscopy, Urethroscopy, Cystourethroscopy in the CPT book).

The Male Genital System

The male genital system contains the penis, testes, epididymis, tunica vaginalis, vas deferens, scrotum, spermatic cord, seminal vesicles, and prostate (Figure 6–13).

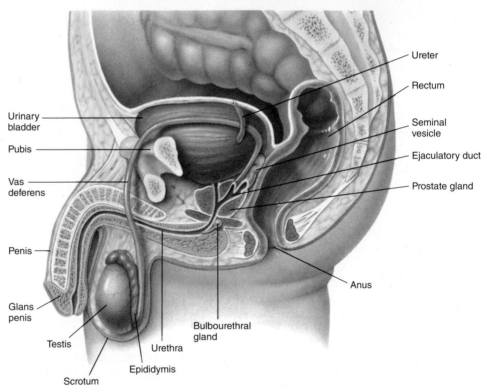

Figure 6-13 Structures of the male genital system and reproductive organs

Codes 54050–54065 are used for the destruction for condylomas, papillomas, molluscum contagiosums, and herpetic vesicle lesions. All other lesions of the penis are coded in the integumentary system of CPT. Simple destruction of the lesion of the penis is coded based on the method of the destruction (electrodesiccation, cryosurgery, laser surgery, or surgical excision). If the physician states that the procedure was extensive, assign code 54065, regardless of the method used.

The excision of a hydrocele from the tunica vaginalis is code 55040 and the excision of a hydrocele from the spermatic cord is code 55500. For a hydrocelectomy that is performed with an inguinal hernia repair, see codes 49505 or 49507 and 54840 or 55040.

Vasectomies are reported using code 55250. The code description states unilateral or bilateral, therefore the modifier -50, bilateral procedure, would be inappropriate for use with this code. Note that included in this code is any postoperative semen examination(s), no matter how many are performed.

Prostate biopsies are codes 55700–55705. The code assignment is based on the type of biopsy performed (needle or punch, or incisional). The description of the code indicates that any approach used is included in the code assignment. For fine needle aspiration of the prostate, refer to codes 10021 and 10022. Codes for the cytopathology evaluation of the fine needle aspiration are assigned from the Pathology and Laboratory section of CPT.

Laparoscopy and Hysteroscopy

More and more procedures are being performed by laparoscopy on a variety of organ systems in the abdominal and peritoneal region. This less-invasive method greatly reduces the risk to the patient and less recovery time is needed than with open procedures. Procedures that are performed by laparoscopy or hysteroscopy, the inspection of the uterus with a special endoscope, must be reported using codes 58541–58579 (Figure 6–14).

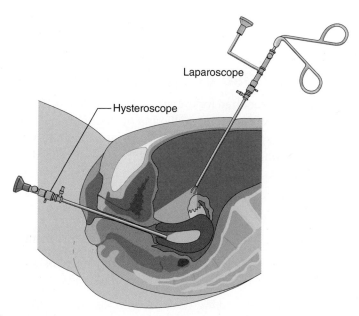

Figure 6-14 Laparoscopy and hysteroscopy procedures

The Central Nervous System

The central nervous system (CNS) includes the brain and spinal cord. Figure 6–15 shows the major parts of the brain. The peripheral nervous system (PNS) includes the cranial nerves, the spinal nerves, and the autonomic nervous system. The autonomic nervous system is the portion of the nervous system concerned with regulation of the activity of cardiac muscle, smooth muscle, and glands. Twist drill, burr holes, and trephine all refer to the making of small openings into the bone of the skull.

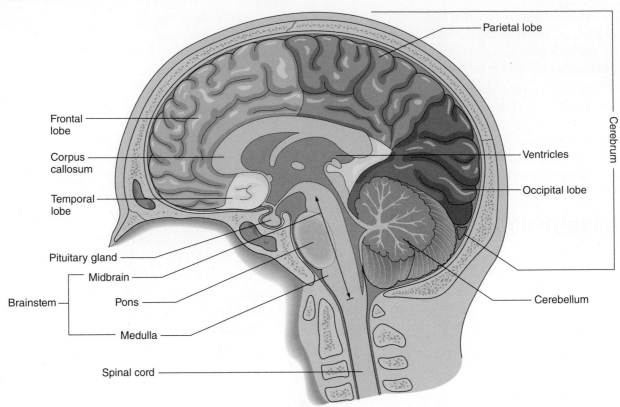

Figure 6-15 Cross section of the brain showcases the major parts of the brain.

Surgery on the Base of the Skull

Several surgeons are often required for the surgical management of lesions involving the base of the skull (base of anterior, middle, and posterior cranial fossae). These physicians from different specialties work together or in tandem (one after the other) during the operative session. These operations are usually not staged because it is necessary to close the dura, subcutaneous tissues, and skin in a definitive way in order to avoid serious infections. These procedures fall into three categories:

1. The approach or anatomical area involved

2. The definitive procedure, biopsy, excision, resection, or treatment of lesions

3. Repair/reconstruction of defect—reported separately if extensive, such as ural grafting, cranioplasty, pedicle flaps, or extensive skin grafts

The *Physicians' Current Procedural Terminology* book states, "When a surgeon performs the approach procedure, another surgeon performs the definitive procedure, and another surgeon performs the repair/reconstruction procedure, each surgeon reports only the code for the specific procedure performed."

Use of Operative Microscope

Code 69990 is assigned for use of the surgical or operative microscope during a microsurgical procedure when anatomical structure or pathology is too small for adequate visualization otherwise. It is an add-on code used in addition to the code for the primary procedure performed. Do not add 69990 when the operating or surgical microscope is included in the procedure.

Lumbar Puncture

In a lumbar puncture, an anesthetic is first injected, then a spinal needle is inserted between the spinous processes of the vertebrae (usually between the third and fourth lumbar vertebrae). The stylet is removed from the needle, and cerebral spinal fluid (CSF) drips from the needle. The CSF pressure is measured and recorded. The physician also evaluates the appearance of the CSF. After the specimen has been collected, a final pressure reading is taken, and the needle is removed.

A blood patch is performed if the spinal fluid continues to leak after the patient has had a spinal puncture or **epidural** anesthesia. The leakage causes the patient to suffer from headaches. The blood patch involves injecting the patient's blood into the site where the spinal puncture catheter originally was inserted. This injection of blood forms a patch and, as a result, stops the leakage of the spinal fluid.

epidural: Located over or on the dural.

Catheter Implantations

Codes 62350, 62351, and 62355 are not percutaneous procedures. Percutaneous procedures are coded to 62270–62273, 62280–62284, and 62310–62319. Report two codes when a spinal reservoir or pump is implanted or replaced. Assign a code for the catheter implantation and a code for the reservoir or pump. The refilling of implantable pumps is reported with codes 95990–95991 in the Medicine chapter of CPT.

Laminotomy/Laminectomy/Decompression

These codes are determined based on the surgical approach, the exact anatomical location within the spine, and the actual procedure performed. For a laminotomy (hemilaminectomy), note that the codes are based on one interspace in a specific area of the spine. If the procedure is performed on more than one interspace, then additional codes should be applied.

The Eye and Ocular Adnexa

The Eyeball

Evisceration refers to a partial enucleation wherein the white of the eye, the scleral shell, is left intact but the intraocular contents are removed. Exenteration is a radical procedure that is performed for malignant, invasive orbital tumors. The procedure involves the removal of the eye, the orbital contents, the extraocular muscles, the orbital fat, and lids.

Secondary Implants

Secondary implants into the eye are inserted subsequent to the initial surgery of eyeball removal. If the implant is put in at the same time as the initial removal, it is reported with a combination code (65093, 65103, or 65105). Ocular implants are placed inside the muscular cone. Orbital implants are placed outside the muscular cone. Note that these are not intraocular lens implants for cataracts and refer to codes 66983–66986.

Removal of Foreign Body

It is important to determine if the slit lamp (an operative lamp used in the operative field) is used on patients with removal of foreign body from the cornea, as it affects the code assignment (see codes 65220 and 65222). Equally important is to determine if a magnet is used to remove a foreign body from the posterior segment of the eye as the codes specifically state "magnetic extraction" or "nonmagnetic extraction" (see codes 65260 and 65265).

Anterior Segment of the Eye

The anterior segment of the eye involves the cornea, the anterior chamber, the anterior sclera, the iris, and the lens itself. Keratoplasty is a corneal transplant. If the transplant involves the outer layer of the cornea only, it is coded as lamellar, code 65710. If the transplant includes all layers of the cornea, it is considered penetrating. If the keratoplasty is penetrating, be sure to identify if aphakia or pseudophakia are present, as it affects the code assignment (see codes 65730–65755). The operative report should state if aphakia or pseudophakia was encountered. If no mention is made, assume that neither is present.

Glaucoma is a condition in which the aqueous humor is unable to drain correctly through the trabecular meshwork. The fluid stays in the eyeball and causes pressure within the eye. In goniotomy, the surgeon uses a gonioknife to release the pressure from glaucoma. In trabeculotomy ab externo the surgeon uses a trabeculotome from outside the eye (ab externo) to release the aqueous. A trabeculoplasty by laser surgery does not use an incision technique. This procedure is done in a series of single treatment sessions and evaluation is done in between sessions to determine the effect of the treatment. This code is applied only once for the treatment series. Each session would not be coded separately. See the instructional note in the CPT book about the establishment of a new treatment series and the use of a modifier.

Codes 66150–66172 are used for glaucoma filtering surgery. Sometimes medication and laser treatment fail to adequately control the glaucoma. In these cases, a tiny opening can be made into the sclera, which establishes a new pathway for the fluids in the eye. Use code 66170 for a trabeculectomy on an eye that has not had previous surgery. Use code 66172 when a trabeculectomy is performed on an eye that has scarring from previous surgery or injury. Examples of previous surgery are history of failed trabeculectomy, history of cataract surgery, history of strabismus surgery, history of penetrating trauma to the eyeball, and conjunctival lacerations.

Iris and Ciliary Body

An iridectomy is the penetrating of the iris, usually for excision of lesions beyond the iris. A cyclectomy goes deeper, going through the iris into the ciliary body.

Lens

aphakia: Absence of the crystalline lens of the eye.

A cataract is the opacity of the lens of the eye. To correct this abnormality, the lens of the eye is removed and an artificial one is implanted. This is known as intraocular lens or IOL. When a lens is removed, the patient is said to have **aphakia**, the absence of the lens. When a new lens is inserted, the patient is said to have pseudophakia, an artificial lens. There are two basic types of cataract extractions, intracapsular cataract extraction (ICCE) and extracapsular cataract extraction (ECCE). An ICCE is the surgical removal of the entire lens along with the front and back of the lens capsule. An ECCE is the surgical removal of the front portion and the nucleus of the lens, leaving the posterior capsule in place (Figure 6–16). This is sometimes called an endocapsular cataract extraction. If the physician does not clearly state if an ICCE or an ECCE procedure was performed, carefully review the operative report to determine if the posterior capsule was excised.

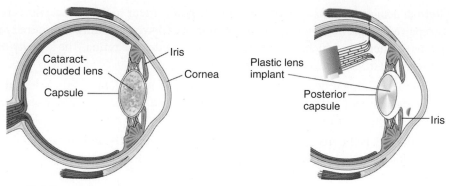

Figure 6-16 Extracapsular cataract extraction (ECCE)

Phacofragmentation and phacoemulsification are the two methods used to destroy the lens for removal.

When an intraocular lens is inserted within the same operative episode as a cataract extraction, one code is used to describe both procedures. However, if the insertion of the IOL was subsequent to the initial removal of the cataract, the code assignment would be 66985. Make sure that aphakia is present if you assign the code 66985.

For a list of procedures that are considered part of the cataract surgery, refer to the CPT code book under the cataract subsection.

When the hospital provides the IOL, it receives the ambulatory surgical center payment, plus a designated amount for the lens. If a physician provides the lens, the appropriate HCPCS code should be reported for proper reimbursement (see codes V2630–V2632).

Posterior Segment

A vitrectomy is the removal of the vitreous humor from the eye. An anterior vitrectomy is performed through the front of the eye. A posterior vitrectomy is performed through the core of the vitreous. Sometimes, during other surgery on the eye, a partial vitrectomy is necessary because the vitreous is in the surgical field, or impedes the operation. When a code exists to describe the primary surgery and the vitrectomy, use only that code. A cataract removal is a good example because it states "with or without vitrectomy." An additional code for the vitrectomy would be inappropriate. Figure 6–17 shows both the anterior (A) and posterior (B) segments of the eyeball.

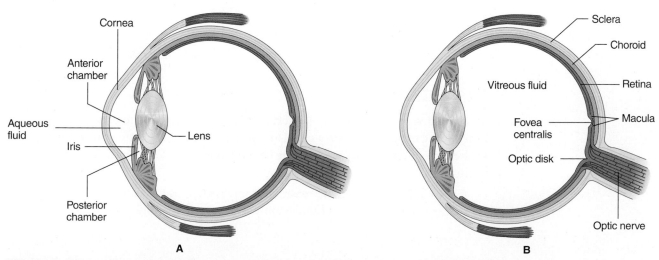

Figure 6-17 (A) The anterior segment of the eyeball; (B) the posterior segment of the eyeball

Retinal detachments usually start as a break, hole, or tear in the retina, which is easily repaired by laser or cryoretinopexy. A more extensive procedure is required for retinal detachments in which fluid has accumulated under the retina. The severity of the detachment determines which procedure is used.

A scleral buckling procedure is the suturing of an elastic sponge to the sclera at the site of the detachment. A band can also be placed around the circumference of the eye, depending on the severity of the detachment.

Cryotherapy is the freezing of tissue to destroy abnormal tissue and cause the retina to adhere back to the eye. Diathermy causes the same result but uses heat to burn through the back of the eye.

Ocular Adnexa

Strabismus surgery is used to correct a misalignment of the eyes. These codes are divided into initial surgery and repeat surgery. The reoperation on strabismus requires more physician effort and skill.

Recession is the lengthening of the muscle and resection is the shortening of the muscle. Strabismus surgery is coded based on the operation being performed on the horizontal muscles or the vertical muscles of the eye. The following chart defines which eye muscles are horizontal and which are vertical:

Inferior oblique—vertical

Inferior rectus—vertical

Lateral rectus—horizontal

Medial rectus—horizontal

Superior oblique—vertical

Superior rectus—vertical

Codes 67320, 67331, 67332, 67334, 67335, and 67340 are add-on codes that are added to the strabismus surgery currently being performed. The add-on codes clarify the specific circumstances and show additional physician work.

Strabismus surgery is considered to be unilateral, so be certain to add the modifier -50 "bilateral procedure," when indicated.

The Auditory System

The auditory system consists of the external, middle, and inner ear (Figure 6–18).

The External Ear

For surgeries performed on the external ear, be certain that the procedure is being done on the external auditory canal and not the skin of the outer ear. Procedures on the skin of the outer ear would be coded from the Integumentary System section.

Code 69220, Debridement, mastoidectomy cavity, simple, is for routine cleaning in patients who have had a mastoidectomy. This type of cleaning usually needs to

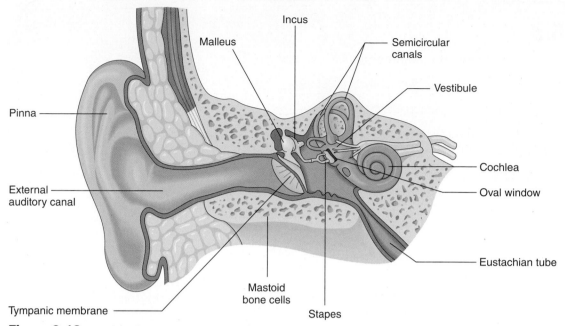

Figure 6-18 Cross section of the structures of the external, middle, and inner ear

happen every three to six months. For patients who require extensive cleaning, or cleaning that is more than just routine cleaning, code 69222 would be applied.

The Middle Ear

The inflation of the eustachian tube by placing a catheter through the nose to force the air into the eustachian tube, and the catheterization of the eustachian tube through an incision and raising of the eardrum are all coded 69799, unlisted procedure, middle ear.

A myringotomy is also called a tympanotomy. It is an incision into the eardrum. Notice that code 69424 indicates that it is assigned for the removal of the ventilating tube when it was originally inserted by another physician. The removal of the tube by the same physician is considered part of the surgical package and would be paid as such. Therefore, when the tube is removed by the physician who inserted it, a code from this section is not applied.

A tympanostomy is the creation of an artificial opening into the eardrum by the insertion of tubes. Use care in selecting a code for the tympanostomy because the selection of the code is based on the type of anesthesia used (local or general). This is often done as a bilateral procedure, so be certain to add the modifier -50, bilateral procedure.

The Inner Ear

Fenestration (69820) creates a new window and sound pathway, bypassing the fixed stapes and oval window.

Exercise 6.6

Assign CPT codes for the following statements.

1. Cystoscopy for transperineal needle biopsy of prostate _____

2. Vasectomy including postop semen examination _____

3. Extracapsular cataract removal with insertion of intraocular lens prosthesis, left eye
   _____

4. Removal of impacted cerumen, bilateral _____

5. Ear piercing _____

6. Myringotomy with eustachian tube inflation _____

7. Orchiectomy, simple, complete _____

8. Lithotripsy, extracorporeal shock wave _____

9. Stereotactic implantation of depth electrodes into the cerebrum for long-term monitoring of seizure activity _____

10. Hemilaminectomy with nerve root compression, including partial facetectomy, foraminotomy, and excision of herniated intervertebral disk, one interspace, lumbar _____

Exercise 6.7

Assign the ICD-10-CM code for the following exercises.

1. Crohn's disease   _____

2. Fecal impaction   _____

3. Foreign body in right ear canal, initial encounter   _____

4. Deviation of nasal septum, acquired   _____

5. Amputation of right great toe, recheck   _____

6. Nosebleed   _____

7. Nystagmus   _____

8. Internal bleeding hemorrhoids   _____

9. Pleural effusion   _____

10. Carpal tunnel syndrome   _____

11. Impacted cerumen both ear canals   _____

12. Acute appendicitis with peritonitis   _____

13. Chronic viral hepatitis Type B   _____

14. Carcinoma of left testis   _____

(continues)

Exercise 6.7 (*continued*)

15. Intracranial abscess _____

16. Morbid obesity _____

17. Hematoma of epididymis _____

18. Urinary retention _____

19. Carcinoma of tongue, posterior third _____

20. Allergic rhinitis _____

21. Acute bronchitis with bronchospasm _____

22. Nontoxic thyroid goiter _____

23. Cholelithiasis with cholecystitis _____

24. Retinal hemorrhage, right eye _____

25. Chronic bilateral serous otitis media _____

Summary

Anesthesia codes are used to report the administration of anesthesia by or under the responsible supervision of a physician. Anesthesia codes are always followed by a physical status modifier that must come from the physician. When general surgery is performed, the operative report will identify the organ on which surgery is performed, and the procedure performed. Experience at reading and interpreting operative reports will assist the coder in the correct code assignment. Modifiers are used extensively in the surgery section of CPT to describe a special circumstance or unusual event that alters the definition of the procedure.

References

AMA Current Procedural Terminology 2016 professional edition. (2015). Chicago, IL: American Medical Association.

Association of Surgical Technologists. (2014). *Surgical technology for the surgical technologist: A positive care approach* (4th ed.). Clifton Park, NY: Cengage Learning.

Centers for Medicare & Medicaid Services (CMS). (2014). *Medicare claims processing manual.* Retrieved from http://www.cms.gov.

CPT Assistant. (2015). Chicago, IL: American Medical Association.

Dorland's illustrated medical dictionary (32nd ed.). (2011). Philadelphia, PA: W.B. Saunders.

Ehrlich, A., & Schroeder, C. (2009). *Medical terminology for health professions* (6th ed.). Clifton Park, NY: Cengage Learning.

ICD-10-CM expert for hospitals 2016 edition. (2015). Salt Lake City, UT: Optum360.

Jones, B. D. (2011). *Comprehensive medical terminology* (4th ed.). Clifton Park, NY: Cengage Learning.

Keir, L., Wise, B., Krebs, C., & Kelley-Arney, C. (2008). *Medical assisting administrative and clinical competencies* (6th ed.). Clifton Park, NY: Cengage Learning.

Orion HealthCorp. (2011). *Anesthesiology billing: How to ensure proper reimbursement and avoid a RAC audit.* Retrieved from www.orionhealthcorp.com.

Scott, A., & Fong, E. (2013). *Body structures & functions* (12th ed.). Clifton Park, NY: Cengage Learning.

Tamparo, C. D., & Lewis, M. A. (2011). *Diseases of the human body* (5th ed.). Philadelphia, PA: Davis.

The Merck manual, professional edition (19th ed.). (2011). Rahway, NJ: Merck.

White, L., Duncan, G., & Baumle, W. (2011). *Foundations of nursing* (3rd ed.). Clifton Park, NY: Cengage Learning.

Integumentary System

Learning Objectives

Upon successful completion of this chapter, you should be able to:

- Assign ICD-10-CM diagnosis codes to various diseases involving the integumentary system.
- Assign CPT procedure codes to describe procedures performed on the skin and subcutaneous structures, nails, or breast.
- Identify common terminology related to disorders of the integumentary and dermatology procedures.
- Apply official coding guidelines in the assignment of codes.

Key Terms

benign lesion	dermatitis	malignant lesion	pedicle flap
biopsy	dermis	mastectomy	provisional diagnosis
burns	epidermis	Mohs surgery	removal
contralateral	excision	muscle flap	repair
debridement	fascia	myocutaneous flap	skin tag
decubitus ulcer	fasciocutaneous flap	pedicle	ulcer
definitive diagnosis			

Introduction

The integumentary system includes the skin, or integument, and its specialized structures including the nails, hair, sebaceous and sweat glands. The skin is composed of three layers: the epidermis or outer layer, the dermis or middle layer, and the subcutaneous or inner layer (Figure 7–1). The epidermis is a layer of squamous epithelial cells. Through keratinization, specialized epithelial cells called keratinocytes produce keratin, a tough, fibrous protein. Keratin serves as a barrier repelling bacteria and other substances. The epidermal cells on the palms of the hands or the soles of the feet, for example, contain large concentrations of keratin. The epidermis also contains cells called melanocytes that produce melanin, the pigment giving skin its color. The dermis is connective tissue made up of collagen and elastic fibers, blood, lymph vessels, nerves, sweat and sebaceous glands, and hair roots. The subcutaneous layer consists of connective and adipose tissue

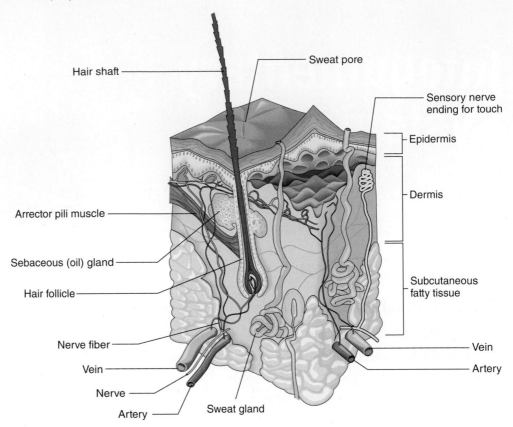

Figure 7-1 Structures of the skin

fascia: The tissue that connects muscles.

and is where the skin attaches to the muscles and bones. The **fascia** and muscles are located below the subcutaneous layer.

The skin performs many functions, including protecting internal body organs, regulating body temperature, helping maintain fluid and electrolyte balance, excreting certain body wastes, and producing vitamin D.

This chapter discusses codes used for the procedures performed on the integumentary system, with a focus on CPT. Codes for ICD-10-CM are introduced where appropriate, and the exercises may incorporate both types of codes.

ICD-10-CM Code Selection

How do you select the code for screening dermatology examinations? How do you select the code for reviewing the final pathology report? How do you select the code if the specimen is not sent for pathology?

These three skills are important for the integumentary (skin) system and will guide you toward accurate claim submission. You will soon learn that the code selection for the integumentary system requires frequent review of the medical record and potentially an addendum documented by the physician.

HIPAA identifies ICD-10-CM as the standard set of codes to be selected in reporting diagnostic physician and outpatient care services. The Official Coding Guidelines are for the use of ICD-10-CM list interpretation, sequencing, and proper selection principles for the specific codes; however, the Official Coding Guidelines are not specifically identified within the HIPAA rules.

> **Highlight:**
> The medical record must support and substantiate the ICD-10-CM code that is selected and reported on the claim. If the ICD-10-CM code submitted is not for an item or service in the medical record, the claim could border on a "false claim" situation, and at the very least it is "not medically supported." On post review, the carrier would likely collect the money back; and if a state or federal program is involved, a substantial fine and penalties could be enforced.

Coding for **benign lesions** or potential cosmetic services (e.g., PUVA light treatments for acne) often result in the beneficiary being responsible for the service. Making a list of the procedures that are likely to require prior approval or services that will most likely result in denial is very helpful to the practice. Providers are also encouraged to implement policy within the practice for determining when to present an advance beneficiary notice (ABN) form for dermatological procedures.

benign lesions: A noncancerous injury, wound, or infected patch of skin.

Rules for workers' compensation or auto insurance may vary from state to state and plan to plan. If the purpose of the visit is for an accident or an injury, it is possible that HIPAA rules, HIPAA privacy policies, and patient release forms are not required. The state laws or specific rules may have adopted the concepts of HIPAA within the workers' compensation or auto insurance, but the plans are not covered by the federal HIPAA rules. Check the state laws to determine the privacy policies, electronic claim transmission rules, and security rules for workers' compensation and auto insurance benefit claims.

When various types of encounters are performed on the same date of service, and multiple payers are involved, the documentation must indicate separate entries within the medical record based on the care rendered. For example, a preventive examination and a therapeutic treatment for workers' compensation care on the same day would be separate entries. Providers sometimes keep auto or work-related injury notes/information in a separate section within the chart, as they are frequently requested for claims processing.

Official Coding Guidelines for Integumentary

The Official Coding Guidelines for ICD-10-CM now include Chapter 12: Diseases of the Skin and Subcutaneous Tissue. The diagnostic code range is L00–L99 and is dedicated for the time being to pressure ulcers. At the time of this publication, ICD-10-CM Guidelines in Chapter 12 are very similar to those in ICD-9-CM and are limited to pressure ulcers as well with fewer subsections within the guidelines than ICD-10-CM.

ICD-10-CM Guidelines: Skin Screening: Section IV-F. Encounters for Circumstances Other Than a Disease or Injury

When the chief complaint documented for the office visit is charted as screening for an illness or disease, select a code from the Z00–Z99 series.

Index Tip:

1. Look up "Screening."

2. Specific Reason (e.g., screening (for)).

3. Review subentries for the "Condition" or "Skin Condition."

   a. Both of these subentries refer to code Z13.9, Encounter for screening, unspecified. This is the most general screening code.

4. If the screening was for a basal cell carcinoma, the screening subentry to look up in the Alphabetic Index would be "malignant neoplasm" and its indented subentry "skin." Code Z12.83 is referenced. Confirming in the tabular index of Volume 1, coders will find the description for Z12.83 is Encounter for screening of malignant neoplasm of other sites, skin.

Always double-check the indented print in the tabular section for additional codes and/or relationships to other illness.

EXAMPLE: The patient is healthy, has no known history of illness and no family history of skin disorders; however, her best friend was recently diagnosed with melanoma, which prompted her to get her skin screened today for melanoma. A head-to-toe skin exam reveals no problems, only healthy skin. Patient is advised to continue proper use of sunscreen, trained to self-examine, given an educational brochure for skin-care safety, and asked to return every two years in the future unless she finds a discoloration or lump.

Z12.83 Encounter for screening for malignant neoplasm of skin

The documentation of the purpose for the examination is very important. If the examination documented was other than melanoma or malignancy, the code might be selected for other skin conditions.

ICD-10-CM Guidelines: "History of" Rule: Section IV-J. Code All Documented Conditions That Coexist

There are two important details in this rule. First, the word *documented* means clearly indicated in the medical record. Second, the rule tells us to select codes if *both:*

- The condition coexists at the time of the visit, *and*

- It requires or affects patient treatment or management.

The coder will look for the documentation's specific details and will review to determine what is treated or managed at this encounter before assigning ICD-10-CM code(s).

Index Tip:

1. Look up "History of."

2. You will find a selection for "Personal."

3. Review the subentries for "Personal history," as they are numerous.

   a. Find "malignant neoplasm (of)."

   b. Scroll further to "skin" and you will find two codes, Z85.820, Personal history of malignant melanoma of the skin, and code, and Z85.828, Other malignant neoplasm of the skin, not elsewhere classified (NEC).

4. "Family history" has a subentry that relates to the patient's family history of certain skin conditions or illnesses.

   a. The family history is indicated with code Z80.9, which identifies only Family history of malignant neoplasm, unspecified.

Double-check the tiny print in the tabular section for additional codes and/or relationship with the original illness.

Highlight:

Do not select codes for previously treated illness that no longer exist. This is a common coding error. For example, last year a malignant neoplasm was excised and treated. Patient returns for examination today and is found to have no further problems and has had no additional treatment since last year from basal cell carcinoma. The patient is not taking any medications. It would be erroneous to select the malignant neoplasm code because the patient is and has been clear of disease. The proper coding would be, as the Index Tip example depicts, Z85.828, History, personal, of malignant neoplasm of the skin, conditions classifiable to C44, Other and unspecified malignant neoplasm of skin.

ICD-10-CM Guidelines: Rule Out Issues: Section IV-H. Uncertain Diagnosis

ICD-10-CM Guidelines state not to code diagnoses documented as "probable," "suspected," "questionable," "rule out," "working diagnosis," or other similar terms indicating uncertainty. Rather, code the condition(s) to the highest degree of certainty for that encounter/visit, such as symptoms, signs, abnormal test results, or other reason for the visit. The first area of importance for this guideline is that it applies to physician/provider coding only. It does not equal the coding principal diagnosis for hospital facility code selection. Next, it is proper to select the code for the sign, symptom, or test results. **Provisional diagnosis** is defined as the physician care that is rendered prior to determining the exact, final diagnosis. Upon the physician reviewing all information, which may be collected over a period of multiple visits or dates, the determination of the **definitive diagnosis** professional opinion occurs. During the provisional diagnosis time, the codes selected are signs and symptoms. At the point of physician documentation of the definitive diagnosis, the disease or illness codes are then selected.

provisional diagnosis: Preliminary diagnosis, including the present signs and symptoms.

definitive diagnosis: Diagnosis based on physician findings; the determination of the illness or disease is made by the physician.

> **EXAMPLE:** Patient has a purulent rash extending from the hemicenter of the back to the thighs. Confirmation test is ordered and performed. Possible herpes zoster versus exposure to nettle plants while hiking Tuesday. See patient again in 48 hours.
>
> For this first encounter, code L08.0, Other local infections of skin and subcutaneous tissue. After the physician reviews the test results and documents a diagnosis, then you may select the code for the definitive diagnosis. In this case, the test results indicate nettle rash and the code would be 7 L50.9, Urticaria, unspecified, which would be used at the next encounter, when the patient returns.

This same logic is proper for lumps that are excised. The ICD-10-CM Index uses the term *mass* to describe superficial (localized) lumps with code R22.9. Note that there are specific ICD-10-CM codes based on location of the lump or mass to allow more specific description. If the physician excises the lump without submitting a pathology report, this might be the proper code. However, in many circumstances, when the specimen is sent to pathology, in order to properly select the CPT code, it is necessary to await the pathology report. *Do not* select an ICD-10-CM code from the Malignant Neoplasm Table or chapter without the final pathology report to document this finding. It is also recommended that the coder confirm the final diagnosis for malignancies with the physician.

> ### Coding Tip:
>
> - Use the Neoplasm Table in the index only when your physician has reviewed and signed off on the pathology report. The surgeon may not always agree with the pathologist and may request a second pathology review *prior* to determining the definitive or final diagnosis.
>
> - If the documentation states malignant with another term, select the code under malignant.
>
> - The Neoplasm Table provides an asterisk (*) to guide to the use of skin codes, then the anatomical site.
>
> - Do not get caught in the risky trap of coding from a preliminary finding, and always confirm a malignancy diagnosis with the provider, as the clinical findings from the pathology report may be difficult to interpret with respect to coding terms.

Erroneous ICD-10-CM codes submitted on claims cannot be retracted with ease. In other words, you cannot reverse the harm that you might cause if you report the patient as having a positive malignancy and later the physician determines it to be nonmalignant. The patient will already have the erroneous diagnosis listed on his or her database of claim information.

Never select a code based on whether the claim will be paid. Everyone responsible for code selection is liable under the False Claims Act, particularly the provider, who attests that all the information is accurate and correct. Besides the high risk for fraudulent activity, miscoding undermines the purpose of utilizing ICD-10-CM codes for the accurate indication of the illness, disease, or reason for the visit. The patient's insurance benefits may or may not pay for the **removal** (**excision**, destruction, and cryosurgery) of nonmalignant skin lesions, for example. Do not select malignant ICD-10-CM codes in order to process the claim as a covered insurance benefit. Use ICD-10-CM codes for signs and symptoms until the diagnosis is determined.

removal: Removal of lesions can be by excision, destruction, shaving, or ligation. A biopsy only removes a portion of a lesion.

excision: Removal by cutting out.

ICD-10-CM Guidelines: Section IV-I. Chronic Diseases

Chronic diseases treated on an ongoing basis may be coded and reported as many times as the patient receives treatment and care for the condition(s) according to the guidelines. An example might be a patient with chronic eczema, with the visit coded L30.9, Dermatitis, unspecified. Details that are documented for today's visit will be required for the code selection, such as the patient presenting today with an acute exacerbation of the eczema and **dermatitis** determined by the provider to be caused by a recent tanning bed session. With the details documented, the code selection would be L57.8, Dermatitis due to the tanning bed, L30.9 for the chronic eczema as a secondary code, and W89.1XXA to indicate the tanning bed and the initial encounter to the provider.

dermatitis: An inflammation of the upper layers of the skin (eczema). Drugs taken internally can also cause skin reactions, which are considered adverse reactions. Sunburn is classified as dermatitis in ICD-10-CM.

If the dermatitis is due to accidental cause (e.g., side effect from an antibiotic), an additional code is selected to indicate the cause. If multiple medications caused the illness, then use an external cause code for each medication or substance from the Table of Drugs and Chemicals.

EXAMPLE: Allergic rash developed as a reaction to ampicillin 250 mg properly taken.

> L50.0 Allergic urticaria

> T36.0X5 Adverse effect of penicillin (The penicillin caused the allergic or hypersensitivity reaction.)

Injury Code Rules

Select the injury code by anatomical site and the type of the injury, based on the highest level of specificity. A laceration of the left wrist would not warrant an additional code for the superficial skin injury caused by the laceration, as this would be redundant. Superficial injuries are not coded; instead, select the code for the more complicated or serious injury of the same site. Multiple injuries treated on different anatomical sites, such as left wrist and right cheek, would warrant additional codes.

Fracture

The displaced fracture code for the anatomical site injured would include the care for the skin, and therefore a separate code is not necessary. Displaced fracture is typically a clean break to the bone (Figure 7–2). Displaced fracture, upper end of the right tibia alone, is coded as S82.101, with the additional external cause code for the accidental cause and location if documented. It is not necessary to add an ICD-10-CM code for the **repair** of the skin that is caused by the fracture injury, as this is included in the displaced fracture treatment.

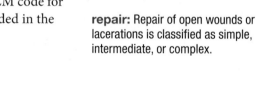

repair: Repair of open wounds or lacerations is classified as simple, intermediate, or complex.

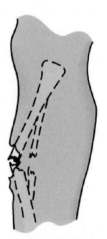

Figure 7-2 A compound fracture

Burns

There are three important required documentation facts that are necessary before selecting an ICD-10-CM code for **burns**. It is also likely that most burn injuries will require the use of external cause codes to describe circumstances of the injury.

1. What is the depth of the burn? (first, second, or third)

2. What is the extent of the burn? (total body surface calculation—Lund-Browder Diagram and Classification Table)

3. What caused the burn? (flame, chemical, sun, etc.)

burns: A burn is an injury to tissue resulting from heat, chemicals, or electricity. The depth or degree of burns is identified as first degree, second degree, and third degree.

> **Coding Tip:**
> Dermatitis, eczema, and other conditions often consider the cause of the skin effect. Look in the documentation for "due to," "exposure to," or "reaction to." These details guide the accurate code selection for skin outbreaks.

For the burn codes, the ICD-10-CM codes that are selected must be sequenced. The guidelines are:

- Select the highest degree of burn (depth question) first.

- If there are multiple burns of the same anatomical site, select the code for the highest degree per anatomical site. For example, if there are first-, second-, and third-degree burns of the right arm, select a code for the third-degree burn, right arm. Each site is coded, if documented.

- Infected burns are coded as a complicated open wound for the site.

Evaluation and Management Services for Integumentary/Skin

Mohs surgery: A highly effective treatment for certain types of skin cancer where the surgeon performs both surgical excision of the skin cancer and microscopic examination of the surgical margins to ensure that all skin cancer cells have been removed.

Integumentary system procedures in CPT are a subsection of the Surgery section and fall in the code range 10030–19499. This range includes procedures on the skin and subcutaneous tissue such as incision and drainage, debridement, paring, biopsy, removal of skin tags, shaving, excision and destruction of lesions, repair of lacerations, **Mohs surgery**, and skin grafts. Other plastic procedures involve skin grafts, cosmetic procedures, treatment of burns, and excision of pressure ulcers. The term *plastic surgery* refers to procedures that involve tissue transplantation and repositioning. Nail procedures include debridement, excision, and reconstruction of the nail bed. Procedures on the breast include biopsy, mastectomy, and reconstruction.

Evaluation and management services (E/M) are used most frequently for patient encounters. Dermatologists, plastic surgeons, and other specialties may perform an E/M prior to or with a skin procedure if warranted. Physicians and providers may use either the 1995 or 1997 *Documentation Guidelines for Evaluation and Management Services*. These guidelines were developed by CMS and the American Medical Association to define documentation elements to determine the level of examination. Primary care and general practitioners generally use the 1995 guidelines based on multisystem examinations. Specialists who perform organ- or body-area-specific examinations typically use the 1997 guidelines. The 1997 guidelines for elements of specialty skin examinations are very helpful for coders and may be reviewed in Table 7–1.

Table 7-1 Skin Examination

Body Area	Examination
Constitutional	• Measurement of any three of the following: blood pressure, pulse rate and regularity, respiration, temperature, height, weight • General appearance of patient
Eyes	• Inspection of conjunctivae and lids
Ears, nose, mouth, and throat	• Inspection of lips, teeth, and gums • Examination of oropharynx
Neck	• Examination of thyroid
Cardiovascular	• Examination of peripheral vascular system by observation and palpation

(continues)

Table 7-1 (continued)

Body Area	Examination
Gastrointestinal (abdomen)	• Examination of liver and spleen • Examination of anus for condyloma and other lesions
Lymphatic	• Palpation of lymph nodes in neck, axillae, groin, and/or other location
Extremities	• Inspection and palpation of digits and nails

Skin	• Palpation of scalp and inspection of hair of scalp, eyebrows, face, chest, pubic area, and extremities. Inspection and/or palpation of skin and subcutaneous tissue (e.g., rashes, lesions, ulcers, susceptibility to and presence of photo damage) in eight of the following 10 areas:
	
	    Head, including the face
	    Neck
	    Chest, including breasts and axillae
	    Abdomen
	    Genitalia, groin, buttocks
	    Back
	    Right upper extremity
	    Left upper extremity
	    Right lower extremity
	    Left lower extremity
	
	NOTE: For the comprehensive level, the examination of at least eight anatomical areas must be performed and documented. For the three lower levels of examination, each body area is counted separately. For example, inspection and/or palpation of the skin and subcutaneous tissue of the right upper extremity and the left upper extremity constitute two elements.
	
	• Inspection of eccrine and apocrine glands of skin and subcutaneous tissue with identification and location of any hyperhidrosis, chromhidrosis, or bromhidrosis

Neurological/psychiatric	Brief assessment of mental status including: • Orientation to time, place, and person • Mood and affect (e.g., depression, anxiety, agitation)

Preoperative Component

In the CPT surgical package concept, when a surgical procedure is on the same day as or the day after the E/M encounter in which surgery is decided on, modifier -57 is attached to the E/M code. Proper documentation is needed for the history, exam, and decision making at the E/M encounter.

Highlight:

Modifier -57 has a bit different interpretation from CPT. The National Correct Coding Initiative (NCCI) states the modifier -57 is attached to the E/M for the decision for *major* surgery. Although the definition is not specifically listed, the interpretation of major is understood as those CPT services listed with a global period of 90 postoperative days. The term "global period" refers to the total period defined for a particular surgery, which includes the typical pre, intra, and post surgery follow-up for the procedure. Many of the CPT services in the integumentary system do not have 90 postop days.

For 0- to 10-day global postoperative days, the decision for surgery is included in the surgical preoperative component of the surgical code.

Operative Surgical Day Component

Most commonly, the surgical date is considered the date the procedure is rendered, from midnight to midnight. In the rare event a procedure continues after midnight, the operative date progresses to that date. However, verification might be necessary, as not all insurance plans have the same definitions.

CPT Appendix A guides the coder to attach modifier -25 to the E/M code if documentation shows that on the date of a surgical procedure a significant, separately, identifiable service beyond the usual pre- and postoperative service is performed. If the decision for major surgery was made on the same day as the E/M, modifier -57 would be appropriate. Modifier -25 is used when procedures with 0–10 global days are performed in addition to the E/M service. What is significant, separate, identifiable? This is documentation that is over and above the typical information that correlates to the surgical procedure. In addition, CPT states a second diagnosis is not required, although many payers may have the expectation for multiple diagnosis codes.

Highlight:

The most up-to-date quarterly National Correct Coding Initiative information can be found on the CMS website https://www.cms.gov by searching for NCCI and selecting the most current version. There are three important areas for review about service codes: the mutually exclusive edit quarterly listing, the Column 1/Column 2 edit quarterly listing, and the National Correct Coding Initiative manual (updated October annually) rules. If you choose to purchase a private non-CMS publication, make certain the quarterly effective dates are implemented immediately and accurately for optimal compliance and reimbursement. In the past, for example, the NCCI may have bundled services during the first quarter of the year, and reversed the bundling in the second quarter, paying physicians for multiple services. Physicians are allowed to rebill those services if the action is backdated.

The first step for proper compliance is to clearly understand the CPT rules, as HIPAA has identified CPT as the standard code set for physician procedural services.

Every insurance plan does not necessarily follow the National Correct Coding Initiative edits, as published by CMS. Each insurance plan may have policies and payment rules that are more or less stringent than NCCI. This is especially true for the integumentary system claims.

Postoperative Component

CPT does not list the global postoperative days. Each insurance plan has a listing, as do the federally funded programs (Medicare, Railroad, Medicaid, TRICARE, federal employees), which are published annually in the *Federal Register* and may update throughout the year. Many procedures within the integumentary section of CPT are 0 to 10 global postoperative days. Postoperative complications vary by coverage and often depend on the work involved for the complication. For example, Medicare will not cover a postoperative complication unless it requires a return trip to the operating room. See additional information in Chapter 13, Modifiers.

Highlight:

Care for the integumentary system is frequently considered cosmetic or screening services by many insurance benefit plans and often requires preauthorization. If the physician is participating or choosing to accept assignment with the insurance plan, it is recommended that the practice effectively determine the patient's benefits with written details of coverage *prior* to performing the service.

Surgical Guidelines for Integumentary

In Chapter 4, CPT Basics, the surgical guidelines as determined by the AMA are described in detail. Familiarity with the surgical package concepts and the definition for biopsy and destruction will be required for coding the integumentary services.

Coding Tip:

- Most supplies for integumentary services are not indicated with a code; they are included with the surgical service. If there is an HCPCSII code, review the policy prior to selecting.

- A common rule to remember for supplies in procedures is that the typical materials required to perform a procedure are inclusive. For example, a laceration repair cannot be performed without the tissue adhesives, sutures, or staples. A sterile tray is also necessary but rarely reimbursed separately. A bandage or dressing applied is not only necessary to keep the wound site clean but is also an inherent part of the procedure and is not separately reported. Special supplies and dressings will vary for additional coverage by individual payers.

Destruction

CPT's definition of destruction:

> *Destruction* means the ablation of benign, premalignant, or malignant tissues by any method, with or without curettement, including local anesthesia, and not usually requiring closure.

> Any method includes electrosurgery, cryosurgery, laser, and chemical treatment. Lesions include condylomata, papillomata, molluscum contagiosum, herpetic lesions, warts (e.g., common, plantar, flat), milia, or other benign, premalignant (e.g., actinic keratoses), or malignant lesions. (AMA/CPT 2015 Professional Edition)

Guidelines further instruct that different methods of destruction are not ordinarily listed separately unless the technique substantially alters the standard management of a problem or condition.

Incision and Drainage (10040–10180)

Incision and drainage procedure codes (range 10040–10180) are further specified by the terms *simple* and *complicated.* The CPT book does not include defined criteria for the use of these terms, and their use is subjective by the physician. However, "complicated" can be substantiated by the difficulty in performing a procedure that may include the presence of infection with an unusual length of time and/or depth.

Terminology is of utmost importance for the accurate code selection. For example, *incision,* which means to "cut into," differs from other terms, such as *excision* or *destruction.* The codes correlate to the type of procedure that is performed: incision, excision, resection, reconstruction, and shaving, to name a few. If you have questions regarding the terms used within the medical record documentation, research the answer or query the physician prior to selecting codes.

> ### Index Tip:
> Incision and drainage (a cut into the site with a scalpel or other sharp item) is performed to drain a paronychia.
>
> 1. The term "incision and drainage" is the key term to look up in the CPT index.
>
> 2. Within the index under incision and drainage, the subheading of "skin" provides a code range of 10060–10061.
>
> 3. Since the codes specify single/simple or complicated/multiple, documentation would need to be more specific for the coder to select complicated/multiple; otherwise the code defaults to the simple.
>
> The CPT index is helpful in providing guidance for the proper code range selection for greater accuracy than directly coding from the CPT section by habit.

> ### Coding Tip:
> When the procedure performed progresses to excise (or resect, remove, etc.) the site, select the excision code and do not select the incision and drainage codes during the same session. If a separate area is involved, modifier -59 may be reported on the additional services but only if no other, more appropriate modifier is available.

The incision and drainage services include the placement of a drain, wick, or other item that may be left in the opening after the procedure. Incision and drainage services do not include a closure or repair. For most of these codes, it is anticipated that the services do not require a repair, or the wound will not be surgically closed. If a closure is documented and necessary, select the additional repair code.

Debridement (11000–11047)

debridement: A procedure where foreign material and contaminated or devitalized tissue are removed from a traumatic or infected lesion or wound until the surrounding healthy tissue is exposed.

Debridement is a procedure where foreign material and contaminated or devitalized tissue is removed from the wound until the surrounding healthy tissue is exposed. The indication may be for injuries, infections, wounds, or ulcers. The notes in CPT instruct the coder to another subcategory, Active Wound Care Management (97597–97598) if the debridement is for the skin (e.g., epidermis and dermis) only. For debridement of the nails or for burn treatment, specific sections are indicated. Some of the codes in this subcategory refer to debridement of the subcutaneous tissue, the fascia, muscle, and bone.

Debridement codes (11042–11047) are not reported with the active wound care codes (97597–97602).

Paring or Cutting (11055–11057)

Paring or cutting involves a superficial removal of a benign hyperkeratotic lesion. These are corns or calluses, described by patients. The cutting or paring may be performed using a razor, shaving, or scissors. These codes are not used if the benign lesion is removed using destruction methods (see 17110).

Biopsy (11100–11101)

Biopsy is the removal of tissue for microscopic review, which assists in diagnosing the disease. The physician may choose to use a punch, curette, or other instruments to obtain the sample.

biopsy: Tissue or organ removal for study or examination.

When a lesion is removed in its entirety by an excision, the biopsy service is included and not separately coded. When this is documented, do not code it as a biopsy; use the excision of lesion codes (either benign or malignant based on the pathology report). The surgeon's documentation and the pathology should be equal, both describing that the complete lesion was obtained.

If a biopsy is performed on one anatomical site, and an excision is performed at another, separate incision, then both codes are reported. The modifier -59 is used to signal this on the claim, along with the RT/LT modifiers if applicable.

The simple closure is included in the biopsy code. If an intermediate or complex closure were documented, the closure would be additionally reported.

Removal of Skin Tags (11200–11201)

A **skin tag**, or *acrochordon,* is a small, flesh-colored, benign outgrowth of epidermal and dermal tissue that generally appears on the eyelids, neck, and armpits (Figure 7–3). A physician may remove a skin tag through a variety of methods,

skin tag: Small, soft, flesh-colored skin flap that appears mostly on the neck, armpits, or groin.

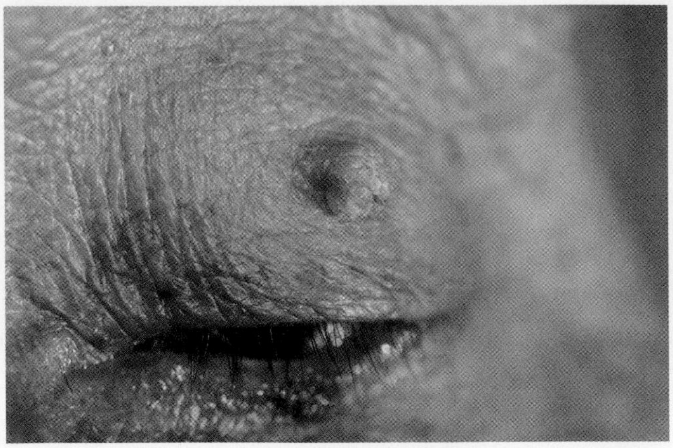

© ARZTSAMUI/Shutterstock.com.

Figure 7-3 Skin tags are a common benign outgrowth of epidermal and dermal tissue.

including scissoring, ligature strangulation, electrosurgical destruction (electrosurgery, cryosurgery, laser, or chemical treatment), or a combination of these. The coder should read the patient's medical record carefully to see the number of skin tags removed, since choosing the correct code is based on the number removed.

Shaving of Epidermal or Dermal Lesions (11300–11313)

Shaving of lesions is done topically, with a horizontal cut, and typically no closure (suturing/stapling) is required. The physician may use a straight razor blade or another instrument. A dressing or butterfly closure is commonly used. The code selection is determined by the shaving technique used for excision, the lesion size, and the anatomical location.

Lesion Removal or Destruction

Skin lesions are growths that can be either benign or malignant. Lesions may be primary or secondary. Examples of primary lesions include macules, papules, nodules, wheals, and tumors. Secondary lesions generally develop from primary lesions and include ulcers, excoriations, fissures, and scars.

Criteria for Measuring and Proper Documentation for Lesion Size

The lesion size is measured prior to the infusion of the anesthetic. See Figure 7–4 for the CPT measurement and documentation criteria. Measure the lesion and the narrowest margins together. If the margins are irregular, the lesion should be described with the greatest diameter of the lesion utilized when measuring the size. The measurements are documented in centimeters (Table 7–2).

The anatomical site is documented specifically (note face versus scalp). If the incision is extended during the lesion removal, the wound is measured for the potential repair code selection.

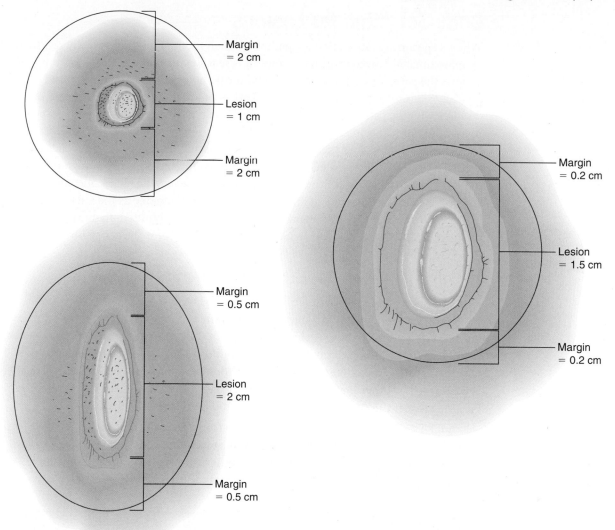

Margin = 2 cm

Lesion = 1 cm

Margin = 2 cm

Margin = 0.2 cm

Lesion = 1.5 cm

Margin = 0.2 cm

Margin = 0.5 cm

Lesion = 2 cm

Margin = 0.5 cm

Figure 7-4 Examples of measuring and coding the removal of a lesion

Table 7-2 Metric Conversions

1 mm = 0.1 cm
10 mm = 1 cm
1 inch = 2.54 cm
0.3937 inch = 1 cm
3/16 inch = 0.5 cm

Coding Tip:

When determining the total size in centimeters for a lesion, the narrowest margin required to adequately remove the lesion is included. For example, a 2 cm lesion needs to be removed. The physician documented the necessity to remove 0.5 cm on each side to fully excise the lesion. The total size of 3 cm (2 cm + 0.5 cm + 0.5 cm) would be selected for correct coding.

Code Selection for Lesions

When a specimen is submitted for pathology analysis, the report is typically returned in approximately two to three days unless it is sent stat or frozen section. The surgeon reviews the pathology report, findings, and the pathologist's final diagnosis, and then typically signs the report and notifies the patient of the results. Should the surgeon disagree with the pathology report, the surgeon may then either contact the pathologist, review the slides/specimen personally, or request a second opinion prior to determining the definitive diagnosis of the lesion site. In the absence of a final definitive diagnosis, the ICD-10-CM codes selected are the signs and symptoms only, not benign or malignant. When coding for the surgeon's procedure, select the CPT code after the surgeon has documented the definitive diagnosis when possible as the CPT categories are separated by benign or malignant. If no specimen is submitted, there is no proof of malignancy. This would always result in a benign category for the procedure.

Excision—Benign Lesions (11400 series)

Excision of benign lesions falls within code range 11400–11471. Excision is the full-thickness removal of a lesion, which includes a simple closure. Benign lesions are harmless and nonrecurring. A closure other than simple (e.g., layered) would be coded in addition to the lesion removal. Types of wound closure are discussed later in this chapter. A plastic repair (e.g., skin graft) includes the lesion removal. If lesion excision is performed by other methods (e.g., electrosurgical destruction, laser, cautery), the CPT notes refer the coder to the destruction codes (17000–17999).

A CPT code assigned without verification from the pathology report is very risky to the provider, especially if the provider wants to assign a malignancy. Pathology is the only definitive way to determine if a lesion is benign or malignant and usually requires supporting documentation to the insurance carrier.

> ### Coding Tip:
>
> - Excision of benign lesions includes the local anesthetic and simple closure.
> - Regional block (except for digital block) anesthetic services are additionally coded.
> - Intermediate and/or complex closure procedures are additionally coded.
> - Repair with grafting of the secondary defect is additionally coded.
> - Each lesion site is coded, using modifier -51 or modifier -59 when appropriate.
> - RT/LT modifiers may assist in payment of claims.
> - Modifier -22 may also be indicated for increased procedural circumstances (often requiring additional time and effort as documented in the report).

Highlight:

In most circumstances, excision of a cyst is coded to a benign lesion. However, the CPT index will refer the coder to the correct anatomical section for certain sites, such as Breast cyst (19120–19126), Ganglion cyst of wrist (25111 or 25112), or Mucous cyst of finger (26160).

Frequently, the benign lesion removals are not covered benefits. Investigate the benefits and properly complete an advance beneficiary notice for Medicare patients prior to providing the care if it seems likely to be denied. Indicate the GA modifier (advance beneficiary notice on file) when applicable.

Excision—Malignant Lesions (11600 series)

A **malignant lesion** grows worse over time and often resists normal treatment. When a lesion is removed, the physician may not know if it is benign or malignant. If the lesion is malignant, usually further wide excision or resection is done to determine if the lesion has spread to its margins.

malignant lesion: Having the properties of nearby invasive and destructive tumor growth and metastasis; changes in the tissues.

Figure 7–4 shows that an excision extends beyond the lesion to include additional margins of excision. The entire distance that is documented will be calculated for the CPT code selection.

Did the surgeon sign the pathology report? The surgeon determines the definitive diagnosis, after reviewing and authorizing the pathology report. Once the physician has determined the definitive diagnosis, the CPT and the ICD-10-CM codes can then be selected accurately.

Coding Tip:

- Excision of malignant lesions includes the local anesthetic and simple closure.

- Regional block (other than digital block) anesthetic services are additionally coded.

- Intermediate and/or complex closure procedures are additionally coded.

- Repair with grafting of the secondary defect is additionally coded.

- Each lesion site is coded, using modifier -51 or modifier -59 when appropriate.

- RT/LT modifiers may assist in payment of claims.

- Modifier -22 may be indicated for reporting increased procedural circumstances (often requiring additional time and effort as documented in the report).

- Multiple margin excisions during the same session for the same lesion are coded one time for the total margin centimeters. If more excisions occur at another session, use 11600–11646 with modifier -58 for the re-excision.

Exercise 7.1

Using your CPT and ICD-10-CM coding books, assign the ICD-10-CM code and the CPT procedure code to the following:

Postoperative final diagnosis: Pigmented, ulcerated lesion, face.

Measurement: 6 mm pigmented, ulcerated lesion on the right cheek. Margins of 1 cm × 0.5 cm.

Procedure: Excisional biopsy RT cheek lesion. Lidocaine injected then elliptically excised. The epidermal is closed using 5-0 nylon interrupted sutures.

Pathology: Specimen-RT cheek face lesion. Specimen consists of an ellipse of skin measuring 0.9 × 0.6 cm. The epidermal surface shows a 5 mm en-block granular lesion. Diagnosis Actinic keratosis per pathologist, reviewed and signed by the surgeon.

ICD-10-CM code(s) _____

CPT code(s) _____

Exercise 7.2

Using your CPT and ICD-10-CM coding books, assign the ICD-10-CM code and the CPT procedure code to the following:

Diagnosis: Hydradenitis of the right axilla.

Procedure: The cystic structure in the axilla was excised and skin was sutured.

Pathology: Specimen-skin, right axilla. The specimen shows inflammatory changes consistent with chronic hydradenitis.

ICD-10-CM code(s) _____

CPT code(s) _____

Nails (11719–11765)

The 11719 series of codes include procedures on the nail(s) and nailbed. Read the code descriptions carefully, as most describe per individual nail or nailbed.

Biopsy of a nail unit (11755) is only reported once, regardless of the number of biopsies done per individual nail. If procedures are performed on different nails, these can be identified by the HCPCSII anatomical modifiers and/or the number of different nails listed in the units column on the claim.

For a nail injury, the health insurance plan may not cover the care. Review the insurance benefits and provide the advance beneficiary notice for Medicare patients.

Use the HCPCSII modifiers for each anatomical site treated today. These national HCPCSII modifiers are listed in the CPT code book with the other modifiers and are also conveniently found in the HCPCSII book.

F1–F4, FA Left Hand Digits and Left Thumb (F1 index finger; F4 "pinky")

F5–F8 Right Thumb and Right Hand Digits (F5 thumb; F6 index finger; F8 "pinky")

T1–T4, TA Left Foot Digits and Left Great Toe (T1 toe next to great toe; T4 "pinky")

T5–T9 Right Great Toe and Right Foot Digits (T5 great toe, T6 toe next to great toe; T9 "pinky")

The HIPAA Administrative Simplification Act identifies the HCPCSII modifiers as one of the standards to report on electronic claims. These anatomical modifiers must be used properly.

Coding Tip:

The documentation of the involvement of the nail plate versus the matrix guides the proper selection of the codes.

Ask yourself, is the service incision and drainage, debridement, excision, or repair? Code 11765, Wedge excision of skin or nail fold for ingrown toenails, is commonly performed.

The *National Correct Coding Initiative Policy Manual* states that for nail debridement and paring or cutting of a benign hyperkeratotic lesion on the same anatomical site, only the debridement code (11720) is selected. The anatomical site modifiers must be used for these codes. If performing nail debridement on one site (T5) and excision of lesion on another site (T6), modifier -59 is used to indicate separate anatomical sites.

Injections (11900–11983)

Codes in the 11900 series refer to the injection of lesions, tattooing, collagen injection, insertion/replacement/removal of tissue expanders or contraceptive capsules.

Code 11900 or 11901 is reported for the number of lesions, regardless of the number of injections performed.

Tissue expansion involves creating extra soft tissue and skin for use in reconstruction procedures. In this procedure, a fluid-filled bag is inserted under the skin to which saline is added at intervals to slowly expand the skin. This creates extra skin that may be used for a subsequent skin grafting procedure or a reconstruction. The codes referenced here are for tissue expansion of skin other than the breast.

Repair (Closures)

The professional service of closing a wound may be performed using sutures, staples, or tissue adhesives, or in conjunction with adhesive strips (butterfly closure). Figure 7–5 displays a close-up graphic of the types of simple repair closures that may be performed, but does not depict intermediate nor complex repairs. If only adhesive

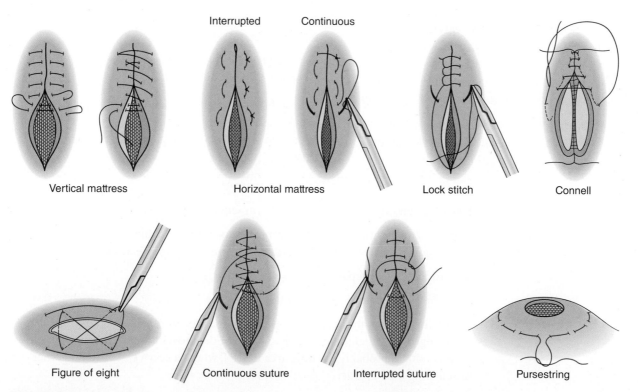

Figure 7-5 Types of wound closure

strips (Band-Aid, butterfly, etc.) are applied to close the wound, the service is not coded and is included in the typical E/M code services. In other words, use the E/M codes to report the professional physician service of closing a wound *without* the use of suture, staples, or tissue adhesives.

Highlight:

The NCCI rules are equal to CPT for the simple, intermediate, and complex closure concepts. There are many details that directly affect the code selection for closure services.

Simple repair is a one-layer closure and is used to close superficial tissue, and it includes:

- Local anesthesia
- Chemical or electrocautery methods

Intermediate repairs are either:

- Layered closure of one or more of the deeper layers of subcutaneous and superficial (nonmuscle) fascia, plus the dermal and epidermal layer
- Single-layer closure after extensive cleaning of a heavily contaminated opening or removal of matter

Complex repair is more than a layered closure, and scar revision, debridement, extensive undermining, stents, or retention sutures.

Coding Tip:

- Where the documentation reflects various types of sutures (Vicryl, chromic, Dexon, or gut), it may be an indication the repair is beyond simple closure. Verify the anatomical levels of the skin to determine whether the closure is intermediate or complex, and if necessary query the physician.

- Physicians and coders frequently overlook complex closure. The surgical package includes normal, uncomplicated closure, not the complex closure that may be provided by the physician. If the repair is measured and the anatomical site documented, the complex codes would also be reported.

- Excision of a scar is included with the repair code, not an additional code.

- The term plastic closure does not guide to the level of skin that is closed, nor the type of closure. More documentation is required for the proper selection of the closure CPT code.

Steps for measurement and proper documentation for repair:

1. Measure and record the length in centimeters. Refer to Table 7–2 for the conversion of inches to centimeters, to assist in the code selection.

2. Record the type of repair (e.g., curved, angular, stellate).

3. State the exact anatomical site for the repair.

4. Group the same anatomical sites with the same type of repairs and add the total lengths together, unless the ICD-10-CM diagnoses are not the same for all repairs. This is probably the only area of CPT where a service is added together in selecting a CPT code.

5. Sequence the most complicated repair code first, followed by lesser repair codes with modifier -59 as applicable.

6. Prolonged debridement (if documented) is separately coded.

7. Debridement without closure is coded.

8. Repair of nerves, blood vessels (not simple ligation), and tendons *are* coded for complex repairs. Use modifier -59 on each, as applicable.

9. Simple ligation of blood vessels is included in all repair codes.

10. Simple exploration of nerves, blood vessels, or tendons through an open site is not coded.

11. For extensive enlargement, dissection, see 20100–20103 codes. If a separate incision is required with more dissection, then separate codes from other chapters of CPT may apply.

Exercise 7.3

Using your CPT and ICD-10-CM coding books, assign the ICD-10-CM code and CPT procedure code to the following:

Simple repair of multiple lacerations after playing baseball and falling against a window, which broke. The repairs consist of the left leg, 8.5 cm; left forearm, 5.5 cm; and left hand, 2.5 cm. There was also a superficial abrasion of the left hand, which was cleansed and covered with Steri-Strip bandage.

ICD-10-CM code(s) _____

CPT code(s) _____

Exercise 7.4

Using your CPT and ICD-10-CM coding books, assign the ICD-10-CM code and CPT procedure code to the following:

Patient presents to urgent care with a 3 cm laceration on the top of the left mid-thigh. Patient accidentally cut it on the tailgate of a truck. The wound extends down to the subcutaneous level, but does not appear to be a deep penetrating laceration. Wound was cleansed with saline and closed with 5-0 Vicryl in the subcutaneous twice and 4-0 Prolene horizontal mattress skin sutures.

ICD-10-CM code(s) _____

CPT code(s) _____

Skin Graft Concepts and Tips

A skin graft is a patch of skin that is removed by surgery from one area of the body and transplanted, transferred, or attached to another area of the body. Skin grafts are commonly used after serious injury where the skin is damaged, such as:

• Infected areas where there is a large amount of skin loss

• Burns

- Skin cancer surgery

- Venous, pressure, or diabetic ulcers that do not heal

- Very large wounds

- Surgeries that require skin grafts to heal

- Surgeries where a wound cannot be closed properly or may result in an excessive amount of scarring

- Cosmetic or reconstructive surgeries where there is skin damage or skin loss

Skin grafting serves two purposes:

- To reduce the course of treatment needed and any time in the hospital

- To improve the function and appearance of an area of the body which receives the skin graft

Donor Site

Healthy skin is taken from a place on the body called the donor site. The donor site can be any area of the body, often it is an area that is hidden by clothes, such as the buttocks or inner thigh and is usually selected to match skin tone. Common donor sites for full-thickness skin grafts include the chest wall, abdominal wall, or the back. It is important the donor site be dressed and kept clean as any other wound as it can also become infected.

Many tips throughout the AMA/CPT code book guide the proper selection of each of the potential components surrounding the grafting procedures. Review the documentation and highlight the components prior to finalizing the code selection, exercising caution to avoid missing all service codes that have been provided. Some information to look for in the documentation:

Preparation code: (15002) How was the recipient site prepared?

Debridement

Excision

Harvest code: What type of graft was obtained?

Graft types:

Adjacent tissue transfer or rearrangement. Involves the transfer or transplantation of healthy, flat sections of skin or other tissue adjacent to a wound, scar, or other lesion. The flaps of skin remain connected at the borders and moved to an adjacent or nearby defect and attached in their entirety to the new location and commonly referred to as local flaps.

Split thickness. A skin graft including the epidermis and part of the dermis with the thickness depending on the donor site and patient needs. These are commonly used to cover large areas.

Full thickness. A skin graft consisting of the epidermis and the entire thickness of the dermis. The donor site can be closed by suture or covered by a split-thickness skin graft.

Composite. A small graft containing skin and underlying cartilage or other tissue.

Pedicle. Attached, bridgelike, dependent on the mainland.

pedicle: In skin grafting, it is the stem that attaches to a new growth.

A *bilaminate artificial* can also be used as a tissue substitute, usually described by the brand name of the product, such as Integra.

Autograft or autologous italics. The donor skin is taken from a different site on the same individual's body.

Allograft or homograft italics. The donor skin is taken from another of the same species, usually cadaver, however, could be a transplant from a living donor.

Xenograft or heterograft. The donor (and recipient are = from another species, often porcine (pig) skin.

Experimental procedures are being tested using stem cells to treat burn victims. Stem cells are applied to the burn area with a skin cell gun.

How Was the Graft Obtained?

The most common instrument to obtain and harvest the skin is the dermatome. The physician may also "mesh" the graft, thereby allowing it to expand to cover more area upon placement at the prepared site. The skin is harvested at different depths of the **dermis**, hence split thickness skin graft (STSG) or full thickness skin graft (FTSG). Watch for details of documentation to identify the type of graft that is being obtained. Refer to Figure 7–1 and Figure 7–6 for important anatomical identifications.

dermis: The middle layer of the integument, or skin.

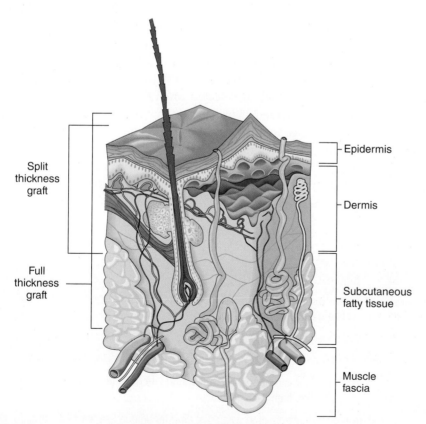

Figure 7-6 Integumentary layers and depths of grafts

Another common simple procedure is the punch graft. The instrument captures a small, tunnel-like portion of tissue, and is frequently used for hair transplant or other purposes using the dermal layer.

Pedicle grafts are often performed over a period of time. The surgeon often creates a tube or connects the anatomical sites directly, placing vascularity of both the donor site and the recipient site together to heal over time. The blood vessel area, capillary refill, and color help to determine when the two anatomical sites will be surgically separated. The use of modifier -58 is common for these procedures.

Modifier -58 is frequently used with these procedures, to indicate staged components of the care extending over multiple sessions and dates of service. The donor component may occur at one session, whereas the placement may occur over multiple sessions, as the recipient site is properly prepared and ready to receive the graft. For placement of the graft on the recipient site, the operative note may use terms such as granulation tissue, adequate blood supply or color, and noninfected pertaining to the recipient site.

Recipient or Placement Site (Graft)

If the CPT code states microvascular within the description of the code, the microvascular service includes the use of the operating room microscope, and 69990 cannot be added.

> **Coding Tip:**
>
> An allograft and/or xenograft at the same placement site as any other graft is not additionally coded.

Adjacent Tissue Transfer or Rearrangement

An adjacent tissue transfer relocates flap of healthy skin from a donor site to an adjacent laceration, scar, of other discontinuity. A portion of the flap is left intact to supply blood to the grafted area. This may be due to repair of traumatic skin wounds, lesion excision, or rearrangement/reconstruction of tissue by Z-plasty, W-plasty, V-Y plasty, rotation flaps, advancement flaps, or other methods. The codes in this range (14000–14350) are selected when the tissue (skin) slides over to provide an effective closure. Table 7–3 provides many details of the procedures and terminology that may be encountered while reviewing the operative reports. One additional note to Table 7–3 is that the small autograft may be described as either a pinch or a punch graft. The excision work of the primary lesion with the tissue transfer is included. If an additional lesion were removed, it would be reported with modifier -59.

Table 7-3 Examples of Tissue Transfer/Rearrangement

Adjacent Tissue Transfer	
Types of Tissue	**Description**
Advancement flap	Nearby skin is stretched over a wound
Melolabial flap	Flap from the medial cheek used as a rotational flap to repair a defect on the side of the nose
Pedicle flap or double-pedicle flaps	Flaps of the entire skin and subcutaneous tissue transferred to a clean tissue bed
Rotation flap	A semicircular flap of skin that is rotated over the wound site (may also be called transpositional or interpolation flap)
Sliding flaps	Flap that is transferred to a new position using a sliding technique (similar to advancement technique)

(continues)

Table 7-3 (continued)

Adjacent Tissue Transfer	
Types of Tissue	**Description**
V-Y-plasty	An incision is made in the shape of a V, and sutured in the shape of a Y
W-plasty	Similar to a Z-plasty, but used for less linear scar/wound repair
Y-V-plasty	An incision is made in the shape of a Y, and sutured in the shape of a V
Z-plasty	A scar is lengthened, straightened, or realigned

Free Skin Grafts	
Type of Graft	**Description**
Allograft	Skin graft is transplanted between two individuals. These are temporary and may be used to cover large burn areas as new skin grows beneath it.
Autograft	Skin graft is transferred from a donor site to a recipient site in the same individual.
Full thickness graft	A graft containing an equal and continuous portion of both epidermis and dermis layers.
Split graft	A graft containing both epidermis and dermis layers.
Xenograft	Skin graft is transplanted between an animal and a human. These are temporary grafts used to cover large areas.

If tissue is rearranged to repair a laceration, the rearrangement must be medically necessary in order to repair the site, and the documentation needs to reflect the surgeon's work. When the rearrangement is incidentally performed, do not select the codes from this area; instead, use the repair codes only. The adjacent tissue transfer or rearrangements are commonly performed on anatomical sites that are not flat and may need more tissue for movement (e.g., axilla, elbow) or for nonlinear lacerations. Z-plasty is two incisions of approximately equal length, usually one above and one below the area for repair. W-plasty is a zigzag tissue flap, usually on both sides of the area for repair. In V-Y-plasty the V incision is made, shaping to a Y closure.

Split thickness or full thickness skin graft codes may also be selected when the defect area requires additional coverage grafting.

Highlight:

The laceration simple repair may be a covered benefit, yet complex repair or grafting may not be a covered benefit. Verify the insurance benefits before performing the service and properly complete the advance beneficiary notice. Also, workers' compensation carriers may vary in their policies.

Exercise 7.5

Using CPT and ICD-10-CM code books, assign the proper codes:

Preoperative Diagnosis: RT ear tumor

Postoperative Diagnosis: Malignant carcinoma RT ear

Procedure: Excision of RT ear tumor with advancement tissue transfer

Measurement: 1.3 cm × 1 cm × 1.5 cm ulcerated lesion located on the helix of the RT auricle

The RT ear is prepped and draped and locally anesthetized using 1 percent Xylocaine with epinephrine injection. Initial incision with scalpel is made around the lesion at the helical rim, minimizing the resection

(continues)

Exercise 7.5 (*continued*)

of cartilage. It is noted that the lesion depth on the anterior lateral side includes a small aspect of the cartilage. A 3 mm margin is then obtained surrounding the lesion site. The specimen is sent for pathological determination. A skin flap is marked 1.5 cm × 2.0 cm and raised in the postauricular region to cover the entire defect nicely. The graft is extended and secured. No cartilage graft is required to fill the minimal cartilage defect. The wound and graft are closed using 5-0 Novofil suture. Antibiotic ointment was applied to the wound, then covered with nonadherent gauze, fluff gauze, and secured with Kerlix. The patient tolerated the procedure well. Estimated blood loss minimal.

Pathology Report: (signed by surgeon accepted)

Specimen A: RT ear tumor

Description: Consists of skin ellipse measuring 2.0 cm × 1.0 cm × 0.3 cm. The ulcerated area is 0.8 cm × 0.5 cm, identified as invasive differentiated squamous cell carcinoma into the tissue. Normal cartilage is seen. The margins are not clear.

Diagnosis: Invasive differentiated squamous cell carcinoma of RT auricle.

ICD-10-CM code(s) _____

CPT code(s) _____

Skin Replacement Surgery and Skin Substitutes

Surgical Preparation

Subheadings for this section start with Surgical Preparation (15002–15005), which describes services related to preparation of a graft, flap, or skin substitute or replacement. It also pertains to negative pressure wound therapy. Codes are based on the anatomical location and defect size. Guidelines state:

> In all cases, appreciable nonviable tissue is removed to treat a burn, traumatic wound, or necrotizing infection. The clean wound bed may also be created by incisional release of a scar contracture resulting in a surface defect from separation of tissues.

Application of Skin Replacements and Skin Substitutes

The codes 15100–15278 are not intended to be reported for simple graft application alone or for simple dressing stabilization. The code is based on the type of skin or skin substitute or replacement. CPT guidelines provide the following definition for correctly applying codes within this section for referencing "100 sq cm or 1% of body area": "*The measurement of 100 sq cm is applicable to adults and children age 10 and older; percentages of body surface area apply to infants and children younger than 10 years of age. When square centimeters are indicated, this refers to 1 sq cm up to the documented amount.*" Measurements apply to the recipient area size. Simple debridement is always included in the application. Modifier -58 should be used for staged or related application procedures.

> **Measurement Tips:**
> - Size is measured in square centimeters. (Table 7–2 assists in conversion from inches to cm; then a calculation may be necessary to convert to square cm.)
> - Anatomical site of the defect is to be documented in square centimeters for flaps and grafts. When a measurement in square centimeters is listed within the code, it refers to a range from 1 sq cm up to the stated code (e.g., first 100 sq cm or less).

> **Coding Tip:**
> 1. Simple debridement is always included. Only if extensive work is documented and the code description allows, then a separate code may be listed in addition.
> 2. Select one code per anatomical site for the preparation from 15002–15005.
> 3. Select a second code for the graft placement based on the type of graft applied (15100–15278).
>
> Note: Only if the donor site harvested requires a graft or flap would an additional code be selected. Refer to the guideline subsections of CPT for additional rules.

Exercise 7.6

Using CPT and ICD-10-CM coding books, assign the ICD-10-CM code and CPT procedure code to the following:

Diagnosis: Return encounter for nonhealing wound, tip of nose measuring 3 cm × 2 cm

Operation: Split thickness skin graft, nose

Procedure: Borders of granulation tissue are debrided and skin edges freshened. Due to the defect, skin approximation cannot be accomplished. Using a dermatome, a split thickness skin graft is harvested from the right thigh. The graft is placed onto the nose defect and secured with interrupted 5-0 Prolene sutures. The donor site is examined and reveals good hemostasis.

ICD-10-CM code(s) _____

CPT code(s) _____

Flaps (Skin and/or Deep Tissues) (15570–15738)

Flaps may be performed over multiple sessions. The regions within this section do not refer to the donor site; they pertain to the recipient area. Donor site repair requiring a skin graft or local flap may be coded as an additional procedure. The first session often forms the pedicle flap, keeping the blood vessels intact to "feed" the future graft. The first service is usually coded with 15570–15576 or the delay of flap 15600–15630.

A delayed flap is a flap detached from its donor area in two or more stages to increase its chances of survival after transfer. With an adjacent tissue transfer, the flap is developed immediately next to the defect and then rotated or advanced into that area. A pedicle flap is developed from an area that is a short distance from the defect and once elevated, the flap remains attached to a pedicle that maintains the blood supply into that flap to keep it viable. Once the pedicle flap has been transferred into the wound, it is sutured into place and can then be divided releasing it form the area where it was harvested. CPT codes 15570–15576 series would be coded as a one-stage procedure wherein the direct pedicle was formed and a transfer was accomplished. CPT codes 15600–15630 are used to code the delay of the flap or sectioning of flap (division and insert). Immediate transfer of any pedicle flap, often referred to as a "walking tube," is coded with 15650 for the abdomen to wrist, any location. For the face, which includes the eyelids, nose, ears, or lips, code selection would be made from the appropriate anatomical area.

When special devices are placed to secure the flap or for extensive immobilization, the instrumentation or casting services are additional codes. However, simple dressings are included in the flap code.

pedicle flap: A flap of skin that is lifted from a healthy site, a portion of which is grafted to a new site but remains attached to its blood supply.

muscle flap: A layer of muscle is dissected and moved to a new site.

myocutaneous flap: A muscle flap that contains overlying skin.

fasciocutaneous flap: The fasciocutaneous is fibrous tissue beneath the skin; it also encloses muscles and groups of muscles, and separates their several layers or groups. The flap is the placement of portion of tissue or skin and may or not include the fascio. Pedicle, local, or distant are all commonly used flap terms.

Pedicle flap	A flap of skin is lifted from a healthy site and a portion is immediately grafted to a new site. Part of the graft, or the pedicle, remains temporarily attached to the original site and blood supply.
Muscle flap	A layer of muscle is dissected and moved to a new site.
Myocutaneous flap	A muscle flap that contains overlying skin is grafted.
Fasciocutaneous flap	A muscle flap that contains overlying skin and connective tissue.

Measurement Tips:
- The code is selected per the anatomical recipient area/region.
- A repair of a donor site requiring a skin graft or local flaps is considered an additional separate procedure.

Index Tip:

Skin Graft and Flap

Refer to Skin Graft and Flap for direction as to Type of Flap (island pedicle, pedicle, pinch, punch) and Formation, Delay of Flap, or Transfer

Coding Tip:
- Select an additional code for any casting or fixation services.
- Select the code for the service that is performed today (formation, delay, or transfer).
- Select the code based on the recipient region, rather than on the donor site.
- Only if the donor site requires a graft or flap would an additional code be selected.

Per CPT and the NCCI, if a lesion is excised incidentally at the same site as the flap graft, no additional excision code is selected.

Other Flaps and Grafts

This area of the code book describes complex or combination methods. Read the descriptions carefully and match to the operative notes.

> **Coding Tip:**
>
> 1. Many of the codes in the series include the use of an operating room microscope. Do not add the 69990 code if the procedure description states microvascular or if the code selected for the procedure is listed as included within the parenthetical notes of code 69990.
>
> 2. Only if the donor site (harvested site) requires a graft or flap would an additional graft or flap code be selected.
>
> 3. A composite graft is a combination of tissue and another part of the anatomy, cartilage being the most frequent.
>
> 4. Dermafascia fat grafts combine fat and muscle.
>
> 5. Punch grafts for hair transplant, code 15775, are coded based on 1–15 punch grafts. If there are more than 15 punch grafts, code 15776 should be used alone.

Other Procedures

Various plastic surgery services are listed in this area of the CPT code book. Notice that many descriptions state the purpose as well as the procedure. Do not report the procedure code if the description does not match the documentation of the service performed.

Suture removal codes 15850 and 15851 describe removal of sutures under anesthesia by the same or other surgeon. A commonly asked coding question is if removing the sutures is not under anesthesia, how is this reported? Suture removal at the physician office provided by the nonsurgeon is coded using E/M codes for the correct level of office service. This example is described in the CPT code book in Appendix C: Clinical Examples of CPT.

Dermabrasion, chemical peels, blepharoplasty, are likely to be considered cosmetic services unless medical necessity can be proven (e.g., blepharoplasty due to obstructed visual field from excessive skin). Obtain preauthorization from the carrier prior to performing the service to determine coverage and payment responsibility.

Pressure Ulcers (Decubitus Ulcers)

A pressure ulcer, or **decubitus ulcer**, is a sore caused by extended pressure on an area of the body that interferes with circulation. Pressure from an appliance, such as a splint, may also cause an **ulcer** to develop. Decubitus ulcers may also be called pressure sores, dermal ulcers, or bedsores. They commonly occur in areas of the body where the bones come close to the surface of the skin, such as the elbows, hips, heels, shoulders, ankles, sacrum, and knees. See Figure 7–7.

Use code range 15920–15999 to code excision of pressure ulcers. Excision of pressure ulcers at sites other than the coccyx, sacrum, ischium, or trochanter are

decubitus ulcer: A pressure ulcer; also known as a bedsore or pressure sore. These result from a lack of blood flow and irritation to the skin over a bony projection. As the name indicates, decubiti occur in bedridden or wheelchair-bound patients or from a cast or splint.

ulcer: Loss of a portion of the skin, penetrating the dermis. Gangrene can be associated with skin ulcers. These are usually due to a vascular disease, as in diabetes.

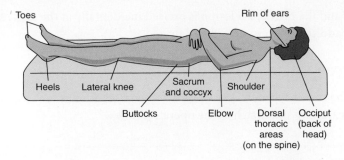

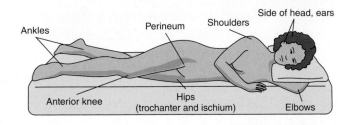

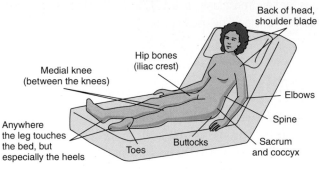

Figure 7-7 Common sites for potential pressure ulcers for patients in bed

reported with an appropriate code such as debridement, closure, or flap, based on the documentation of the procedure performed.

The 15920 series of codes is selected to report the surgical repair service. If additional defect repair (commonly a full thickness flap) is performed, an additional code is selected. The active wound management 97597–97610 codes are frequently performed prior to the surgical repair services.

Typically the surgeon will excise and debride the **ulcer** site, followed with a graft repair. The graft selected will be determined based on the depth of the ulcer site, from a split thickness graft to a full delayed pedicle flap. Figure 7–7 lists common terms for the areas where pressure ulcers may be found on the patient as described in operative notes.

> **Index Tip:**
>
> **Pressure Ulcer Excision**
>
> Then select the repair of the defect type of graft (split thickness, full thickness, pedicle, etc.).

Burns, Local Treatment

Burns are identified by degree as follows (refer to Figure 7–8):

epidermis: The outer layer of the integument, or skin.

First degree	Erythema and redness, affecting the superficial skin layer
Second degree	Blistering and oozing, affecting the **epidermis** layer (also known as a partial thickness burn)
Third degree	Destruction of epidermis and dermis (also known as a full thickness burn)

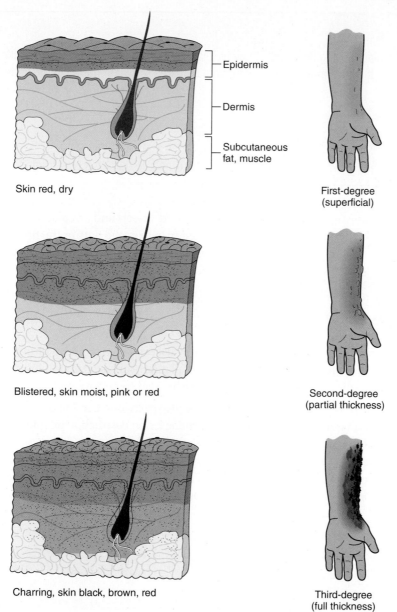

Epidermis

Dermis

Subcutaneous fat, muscle

Skin red, dry

First-degree (superficial)

Blistered, skin moist, pink or red

Second-degree (partial thickness)

Charring, skin black, brown, red

Third-degree (full thickness)

Figure 7-8 The degree of burns is identified by the layers of skin affected. The levels range from first degree (superficial burn), to second degree (partial thickness), to the most severe, third degree (full skin thickness).

To assist in the calculation of the total body surface area (TBSA), use the Lund-Browder Diagram and Classification Method for Burn Estimations (see Figure 2–4). Documentation that clearly indicates this criterion will be necessary for selection of the CPT and the ICD-10-CM code.

The codes in series 16000 are for the treatment of the burned surface only. If other professional services (E/M services such as office or hospital visits, critical care visits, IV placement, etc.) are performed, select the additional services. Supplies such as special dressings and antibiotic ointments for burn treatment services provided by the physician (at the provider's expense) may be separately reportable for some carriers.

Coding Tip:

Total body surface area (TBSA) burned is calculated using the Lund– Browder Diagram and Classification Method Table (refer to the CPT illustration of calculation of TBSA in the burn treatment section). Note that the calculation for an infant varies from that for an adult.

- Document degree of burn (e.g., first, second, third).

- Select appropriate code from 16000–16030 as applicable.

- Select the ICD-10-CM code(s) giving special consideration to the amount of third-degree burn that was treated if any.

Escharotomy is performed to relieve the blood vessels and circulation beneath the burned necrotic binding tissue. This is frequently performed within the first few days of the injury, and may require multiple incisions. Code 16035 is for the initial incision only. Use code 16036 for each additional incision.

Destruction

The destruction services represent a commonly used series of codes within the integumentary chapter, for example, common plantar wart destruction by cryotherapy. Table 7–4 describes various methods that may be used to remove by destruction.

Select 17000 code series for destruction of skin-type lesions. See Table 7–5 for common types of lesions that may be destroyed. If performing lesion destruction on internal or other anatomical sites, select from the other chapters of CPT. *Watch closely for the terms "up to" or "each" in the description of the CPT code.* If the word "each" is in the description, enter the total number on the quantity line on the claim form. Do not select a code from the 17000 series codes for skin tags and fibrocutaneous tags; see codes 11200–11201.

Table 7-4 Common Descriptions for Destruction Procedures

Destruction	Ablation
	Electrosurgery
	Cryosurgery (cold)
	Laser (any type)
	Chemical
	Surgical curettement
	Chemosurgery

Table 7-5 Common Skin Lesion Types Destroyed

Common Destruction Codes	Common Lesion Types
Premalignant Lesion Destruction (17000–17004)	Premalignant lesions (e.g., actinic keratosis)
Benign Lesion Destruction (17110–17111)	Benign lesions, common or plantar warts, molluscum contagiosum, milia, or other benign lesions other than skin tags or vascular proliferative lesions
Malignant Lesion Destruction (17260–17286)	Malignant skin lesions, basal cell carcinoma, squamous cell carcinoma, etc.

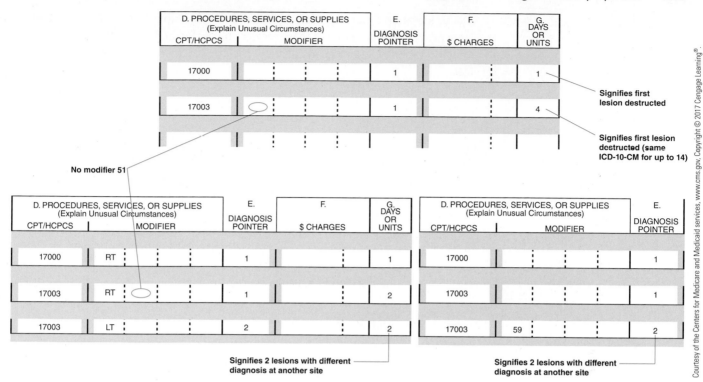

Figure 7-9 Claim examples with CPT, ICD-10-CM, and quantity

Figure 7–9 can assist in understanding the link reasoning of the ICD-10-CM to CPT, the quantities, the modifier use, and the necessity of entering line-item details.

Note that 17004 is modifier -51 exempt and not subject to the typical multiple procedure reduction. One-hundred percent of the payment allowable would be expected from the insurance plan, even if this service is in addition to code 17000.

Do not select chemical cauterization if excision of the same lesion is performed (blood vessel cautery would be included in the surgical service). For combinations of removal such as excision and destruction at the same time, the excision code includes the destruction, as CPT guidelines prior to the surgery section state that surgical destruction is a part of a surgical procedure.

When performing destruction service with biopsy of a separate anatomical site lesion at the same session, use modifier -59. If the destruction and biopsy are of the same anatomical site, only one code is selected and no modifier -59 is reported.

> **Index Tip:**
>
> If you look up the various types of destruction, you will be guided to the other chapters for the internal anatomical sites. The quickest method to find the skin service is to begin with the word "destruction."
>
> Destruction
>
> Skin
>
> (Use this sequence rather than looking up "lesion.")

Mohs Micrographic Surgery

Mohs micrographic surgery (code range 17311–17315) is used for the treatment of complex or ill-defined skin cancer where the physician acts in two integrated but separate capacities, as the surgeon and pathologist.

If a repair is performed, a separate code is assigned for the repair, flap, or graft codes. These codes are reported by stages and the number of specimens (tissue blocks) reviewed. A tissue block is considered to be an "individual tissue piece embedded in a mounting medium for sectioning." Tumor tissue is removed in stages and the specimen mapped and divided into pieces. Add-on codes are available for additional stages and for each additional tissue block over five. Documentation must be sufficient to support the code assignment.

Documentation describing the surgical and the pathology work is required from the same provider. Should one of these services be performed by another provider, the Mohs codes may not be used. Not all physicians are qualified to perform these services.

> ### Coding Tip:
> Biopsy of the same site for the initial pathology diagnosis performed (because there was no prior pathology confirmation of a diagnosis) on the same date is selected as 11100–11101 with 88331 for frozen section pathology and with modifier -59 appended. (If more than one tissue block is biopsied, use 88332 as appropriate.)

If the surgeon needs to obtain a diagnostic biopsy for the decision for surgery, select the Mohs CPT code and also modifier -58 for staged procedure. Otherwise, the frozen section is not additionally selected, according to the NCCI.

Other Procedures

Codes in range 17340–17999 refer to acne procedures and electrolysis.

Breast Procedures

It is especially important to use the CPT index for the breast procedure code selection if coders are unfamiliar with this area. Fine needle aspiration and stereotactic radiological services are two examples that guide you to other areas throughout the code book.

mastectomy: Excision of the breast.

Surgical procedures such as **mastectomy**, implants, or mammoplasty may be performed on either male or female patients.

Personal identification of patient information associated with any procedure or service (elective and nonelective) should always be held in strict confidentiality. In the office, use caution in discussion of patient care; cover the reports to prohibit "glance" opportunities; and minimize computer screens whenever they are not in use, as examples of extra protection. It is appropriate to discuss care, billing, and operations with professionals; however, it is advised to exercise common privacy techniques and not to discuss patient information with other patients or family members. Offices are required to give patients a HIPAA privacy statement, disclosure, or policy acknowledgment to sign, which provides the patient with an understanding of what personal information may be used and how.

> ### Highlight:
> Breast procedure codes are selected based on the services performed.
>
> When the decision for surgery (excision or resection) depends on the biopsy results from a previous session, the excision or resection service may be coded with modifier -58 to indicate a staged or related procedure. All breast excision codes are inclusive of the closure. Reconstruction and/or repair services are reflected with codes 19316–19396.

Incision

Breast cysts are common and may be aspirated. Imaging is allowed should the surgeon decide radiology services are needed. When radiology services such as imaging guidance are performed by the surgeon (often using the equipment at an outpatient facility) for puncture aspiration of a breast cyst, for example, select code 19000 with the appropriate imaging guidance service and append modifier -26 to indicate the professional component for the radiological service.

Excision

Biopsy may be percutaneous (needle core) or open (scalpel) and may or may not use imaging guidance.

> Biopsy codes are 19100–19101.

> Excisional surgeries (removal of cysts, tumors, or lesions) for the breast include:

- Certain biopsy procedures

- Surgical treatment of malignances

> Partial mastectomy includes open excisions of breast tissue *with* surgical margin work documentation:

- Lumpectomy

- Tylectomy

- Quadrantectomy

- Segmentectomy

> There are specific code descriptions for the type of mastectomy that is documented, often with the excision of additional anatomy such as pectoral muscles and lymph nodes. Select the codes carefully and verify within the operative note by reading the entire note.

> Chest wall excision describes excision of any lesions (not simply breast invasion) that extend into the bone or mediastinal lymphadenectomy in the operative note. These are involved cases, typically requiring extensive work, and may also involve the lungs.

> If a physician performs a breast implant at the time of the mastectomy, additional codes are selected. This implant service is usually a covered medical necessity and paid as a covered benefit by most insurance plans. Indicating the illness (reason) as the diagnosis code for the implant is key for showing medical necessity.

> **Coding Tip:**
>
> Use modifier -50 with the codes in this series if performed bilaterally.
>
> Additional services that should be coded are for imaging and placement of clips or markers.

Introduction

The codes in this series are selected to report needle, wire, or other items used to mark the lesion. They also include placement of radiotherapy after loading brachytherapy and expandable catheters. If the physician performs the radiological supervision and interpretation for the preoperative placement of needle localization wire only, supervision and interpretation codes may also be applied from the radiology section. If the physician is qualified to provide radiation elements, the additional codes are selected for this service as well.

Mastectomy Procedures

Codes 19300–19307 are representative of various mastectomy procedures. Radical mastectomy 19305 includes pectoral muscles and axillary lymph nodes. Delayed or immediate insertion of implant cross references are given beneath most of these services. Radiotherapy after loading placement for brachytherapy is also referenced.

Repair and/or Reconstruction

Modifier -50 is frequently used with repair and/or reconstruction codes. These are commonly considered cosmetic surgery codes when performed for non-medically necessary purposes such as a mastopexy (19316). For the reduction mammoplasty, insurance plan benefits often cover the procedure if the condition is causing other health concerns and symptoms such as neck and back pain. The specific weight (or grams) to be removed, along with certain preoperative examinations and findings, are typically required during the preauthorization period.

Highlight:

Obtain insurance plan preauthorizations in writing with specificity. A general statement of "will cover if medically necessary upon review" does not indicate the policy payment after the procedure has been performed. Counseling the patient regarding the potential financial implications is often necessary prior to scheduling the procedure.

Cancer and malignant breast excisions may require reconstructive surgery with breast implantation. The reconstruction and implant may be performed at the same time as the initial primary procedure or may be planned, staged, or scheduled sometime in the future. The reconstruction and breast implant are usually covered benefits with most insurance plans.

Code 19364, Breast reconstruction with TRAM flap, includes the harvest of the flap, microvascular transfer, closure of the donor site, and inset shaping of the flap. This varies from the previous skin graft logic of coding.

Mastectomy procedures may progress during the same session for additional services, such as reconstruction (implantation of prosthesis, spreader insertion, invasive to other sites). When this occurs, the additional services are coded. Combination services may also have co-surgeons involved, modified with -62 on the codes that are jointly provided. Many procedures may be performed using staged or delayed technique. If the description of the code does not state delayed, the modifier -58 is added to the codes when documented as delayed or staged.

Highlight:

- Sentinel node biopsy codes of the same breast are selected in addition to local excision without lymphadenectomy.

- **Contralateral** (opposite side) services are coded with RT or LT as appropriate on each line.

- Also, if there are various pathology diagnoses, each line reflects the proper diagnosis by site. (Excision RT may be malignant; excision LT may be benign.)

contralateral: The opposite side.

Exercise 7.7

Using your CPT and ICD-10-CM coding books, assign the code for the surgeon:

Diagnosis: Primary malignant carcinoma LT breast

Pre-op procedure in Radiology: Mammogram guided wire needle placement

Operation: Open excision LT breast lesion, identified by marker

History: The female patient had a stereotactic biopsy of the left breast the week prior, which confirmed the carcinoma of primary malignant carcinoma. Patient is having biopsy to remove any remaining calcifications. The patient was first taken to the Radiology Department for the left breast needle localization.

Procedure 1: Utilizing mammographic guidance, a Kopan's needle is inserted into the upper outer LT breast. After confirmation that the needle was within the calcifications, the patient was transported to the surgical suite.

Procedure 2: An elliptical incision was made and carried down through the skin and subcutaneous tissue to the breast tissue. A block of breast tissue was removed to include for specimen mammogram. Specimen was then sent to pathology.

ICD-10-CM code(s) _____

CPT code(s) _____

Summary

When coding for integumentary system services, document the condition being treated, type of services performed, and specific location. Debridement guidelines are explicit to the type and depth. Measure and document size of lesions in centimeters and flaps/grafts in square centimeters. Code pathology after the surgeon has reviewed the findings and agrees. Identify the type of repair that is documented as simple, intermediate, complex, or grafting. Determine what is included in the surgical package according to CPT, then determine all the services performed, giving consideration to potential bundling edits and modifiers.

References

AMA Current Procedural Terminology 2016 professional edition. (2015). Chicago: American Medical Association.

American Society for Mohs Surgery. (n.d.) *American Society for Mohs Surgery (ASMS).* Retrieved from www.mohssurgery.org.

Centers for Medicare & Medicaid Services. *1997 evaluation and management documentation guidelines.* Retrieved, from https://www.cms.gov.

Centers for Medicare and Medicaid Services. (2015). *National correct coding initiative policy manual for Medicare services.* Retrieved from https://cms.gov.

ICD-10-CM expert for hospitals 2016 edition. (2015). Salt Lake City, UT: Optum360.

mdStrategies. (2014, September). *Flaps (skin and/or deep tissue).* Retrieved from https://mdstrategies.com/ml_0914.html.

U.S. National Library of Medicine. *MedlinePlus.* Retrieved from www.nih.gov.

Orthopedics

Learning Objectives

Upon successful completion of this chapter, you should be able to:

- Explain the proper application of coding rules and conventions in the ICD-10-CM and CPT classification systems as applied to orthopedics and use them to solve any coding problem.
- Demonstrate clinical knowledge of the normal structure and function of the musculoskeletal tissues by always referencing the proper body system in CPT and ICD-10-CM.
- Explain the most common diseases, disorders, and injuries of the musculoskeletal system and be able to differentiate between similar conditions with different codes.
- Accurately and completely classify diagnoses and procedures applicable to orthopedics without overcoding or undercoding the case.

Key Terms

arthropathy	dislocation	open reduction internal fixation (ORIF)	osteomyelitis
carpal tunnel syndrome	internal derangement		radiculopathy
closed fracture	open fracture	orthopedics	

Introduction

Orthopedics (orthopaedics) is a medical specialty concerned with the prevention, investigation, diagnosis, and treatment of diseases, disorders, and injuries of the musculoskeletal system. The orthopedic specialty is a major provider in injuries related to trauma: work-related injuries, motor vehicle accidents, and falls. V and Y codes, external cause codes, are necessary to assign to the diagnosis code to describe the reason for the injury and to help determine liability for the charges. Figures 8–1A, 8–1B, and 8–1C present an overview of the musculoskeletal system. The specialty may employ medical, surgical, physiological, pathological, and other related sciences in the scope of diagnosis and treatment.

This chapter covers the broader concepts and most common themes seen in the field of orthopedics. It is designed to provide a better understanding of the most common diagnoses and procedures as well as the classification rules in ICD-10-CM and CPT. It presents an opportunity to see and use some code designations that may be new or unfamiliar, to learn more about the details of the many diagnoses and

orthopedics: A medical specialty concerned with the prevention, investigation, diagnosis, and treatment of diseases, disorders, and injuries of the musculoskeletal system.

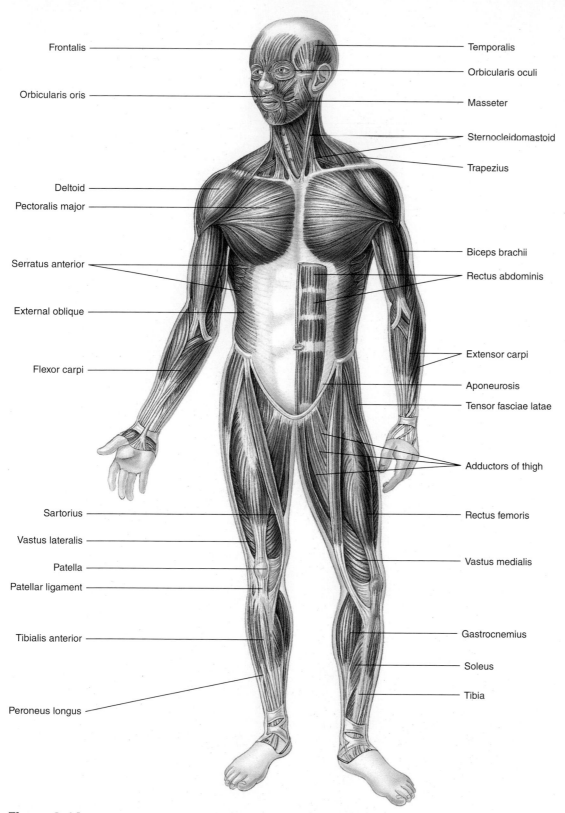

Frontalis

Orbicularis oris

Deltoid

Pectoralis major

Serratus anterior

External oblique

Flexor carpi

Sartorius

Vastus lateralis

Patella

Patellar ligament

Tibialis anterior

Peroneus longus

Temporalis

Orbicularis oculi

Masseter

Sternocleidomastoid

Trapezius

Biceps brachii

Rectus abdominis

Extensor carpi

Aponeurosis

Tensor fasciae latae

Adductors of thigh

Rectus femoris

Vastus medialis

Gastrocnemius

Soleus

Tibia

Figure 8-1A Anterior view of superficial muscles of the body

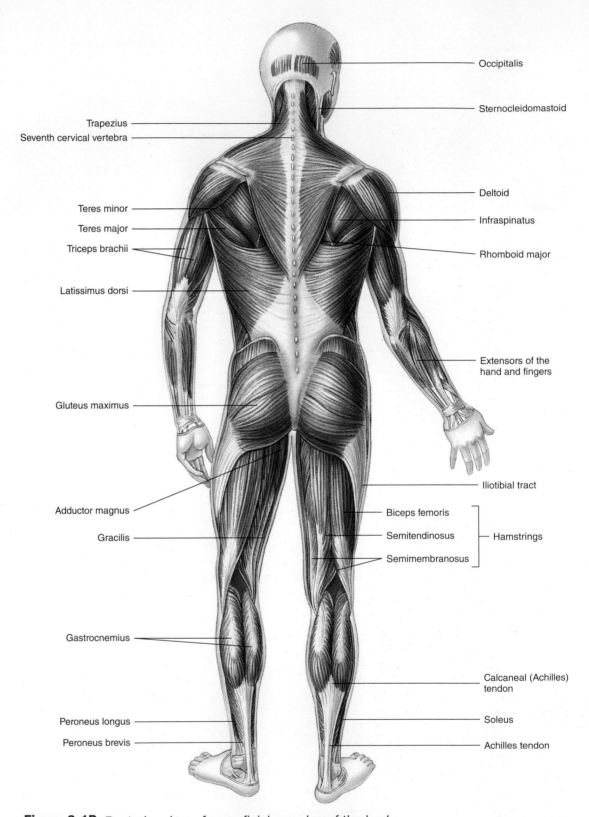

Figure 8-1B Posterior view of superficial muscles of the body

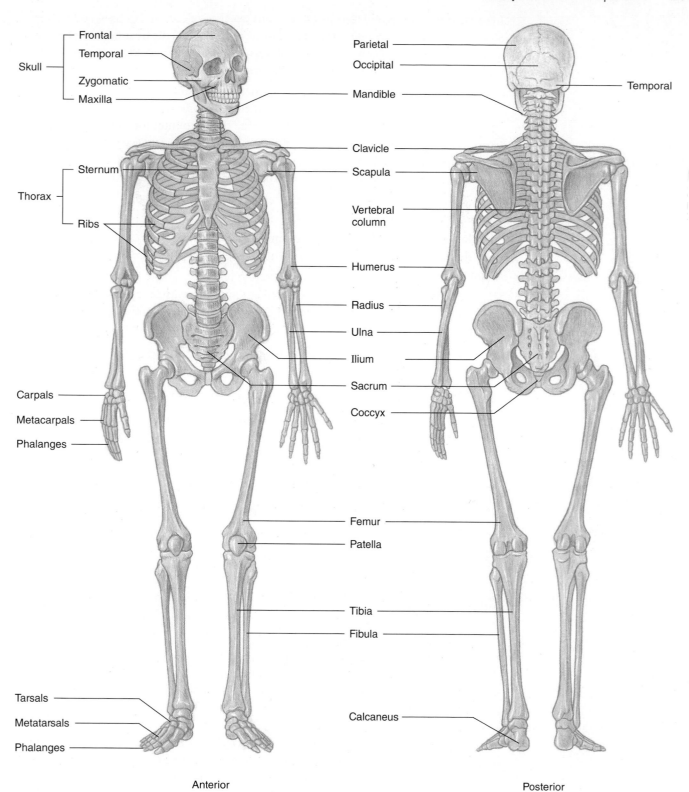

Figure 8-1C Anterior and posterior views of the human skeleton

procedures available in the classification systems, and to gain practical knowledge of how to handle some difficult orthopedic classification issues.

Most orthopedic diagnoses will fall into the ICD-10-CM Chapter 13, Diseases of the Musculoskeletal System and Connective Tissue, code range M00–M99, and Chapter 19,

Injury and Poisoning, and Certain Other Consequences of External Causes, code range S00–T88. Some other conditions that are amenable to orthopedic treatment can be found in other chapters, such as malignant neoplasms of bone in the Neoplasms chapter, and musculoskeletal anomalies found in the Congenital Anomalies chapter.

ICD-10-CM further expands with specificity in site and laterality designations in coding injuries, wounds, fractures, and other pathology and trauma using an appropriate 7th digit character added to indicate the encounter for the visit or treatment. If an ICD-10-CM code requires the 7th character and there are only five digits of the code, placeholder character X is used to allow for future expansion of the code. This will be discussed and demonstrated further in this chapter.

CPT classifies most orthopedic procedures within the Musculoskeletal System chapter, code range 20000–29999.

The next section of this chapter examines the most common conditions and procedures encountered in orthopedics, and reviews the proper coding and reporting of these in ICD-10-CM and CPT.

The musculoskeletal system is a combination of the muscles and bones of the body. The following terminology is helpful to understand the components of the musculoskeletal system and the conditions related to it.

- Bone: connective tissue that forms the framework of the body and protects the internal organs

- Muscle: tissue that is able to contract to allow movement of body parts and organs

- Joint: the place of union between two or more bones to allow movements (also referred to as articulations)

- Tendon: tissue that attaches muscle to bone

- Ligament: tissue that connects joints

- Fascia: connective tissue that covers, supports, and separates muscles

- Bursa: a fibrous sac filled with synovial fluid to cushion the area to allow movement

- Synovia: fluid that serves as a lubricant for a joint, tendon sheath, or bursa

Fractures

A fracture is a break or disruption in an organ or tissue that accounts for a large number of patients treated in the orthopedic specialty. In orthopedics, fractures of the bone are classified in ICD-10-CM as pathological fractures (M00–M99 category) or traumatic fractures (S00–T88). They refer to a structural break in the continuity of bone as a result of physical forces exerted beyond its ability to accommodate by resistance, elasticity, or bending. Fractures can occur as a result of direct injury such as being hit in the upper arm with a heavy object, or by indirect injury such as a fracture of the clavicle as a result of falling upon an outstretched hand, where the initial force is transmitted indirectly through one or more joints (Figure 8–2). Muscular contractures, stress, and pathology can also result in fractures.

Fractures are classified by various methods. A compound fracture is called an **open fracture** because of the open skin and has a high risk of bone infection. If there is no opening of the skin, the fracture is described as closed or simple. A complete fracture goes completely through the bone. An incomplete fracture is when the bone is fractured but not in two portions. An example of a common incomplete fracture is a greenstick

open fracture: One in which the fracture site communicates with the outside environment.

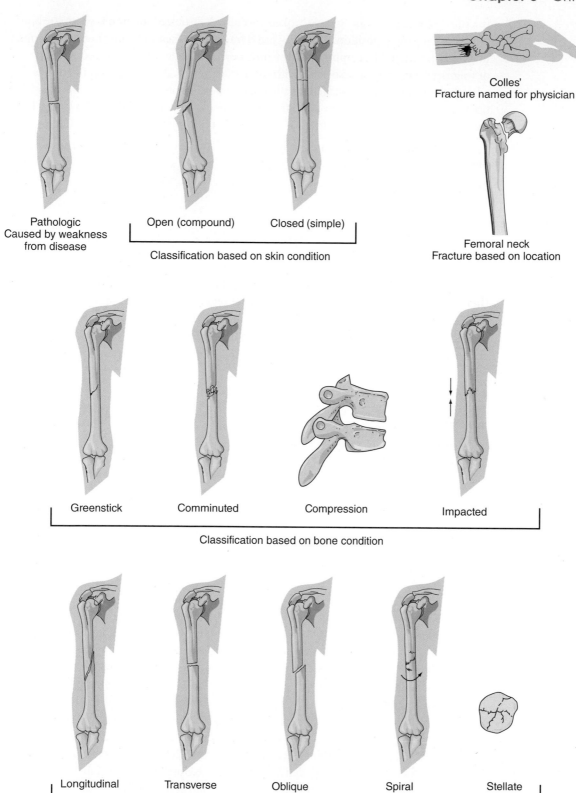

Pathologic
Caused by weakness
from disease

Open (compound)   Closed (simple)

Classification based on skin condition

Colles'
Fracture named for physician

Femoral neck
Fracture based on location

Greenstick   Comminuted   Compression   Impacted

Classification based on bone condition

Longitudinal   Transverse   Oblique   Spiral   Stellate

Classification based on position of fracture line

Figure 8-2 Types of bone fractures

fracture because it appears to have broken partially. A displaced fracture is when the bone fragments are out of position. A nondisplaced fracture is when the bone fragments remain in correct position. In a comminuted fracture, bone is broken into two or more pieces or fragments and may be associated with soft tissue trauma. A compression fracture is when bone is squeezed or wedged together at one side. A common site for a compression fracture is in a vertebra. An impacted fracture occurs when an end of bone is wedged into the opposite end. A greenstick fracture is a break in only one cortex of bone.

To properly classify fractures in ICD-10-CM, the coder must have four important pieces of information:

1. The site of the fracture

2. Whether the fracture is open or closed

3. The laterality (right, left, bilateral, or unspecified)

4. The encounter

The site of the fracture is first classified by the name of the fractured bone, and then by the anatomical subclassification of the region, section, or part of the bone where the fracture occurred. A fracture not indicated as displaced or nondisplaced should be coded to displaced. A fracture not indicated as open or closed should be coded to closed (Table 8–1).

Table 8-1 Open and Closed Fracture Terms

Closed Fracture Terms		Open Fracture Terms
Comminuted	Impacted	Compound
Depressed	Linear	Infected
Elevated	Simple	Missile
Fissured	Slipped epiphysis	Puncture
Fracture, unspecified	Spiral	With foreign body
Greenstick		

closed fracture: One in which the fracture site does not communicate with the outside environment.

It is important to remember that some of the terms for **closed fractures** can sometimes indicate either a closed or an open fracture, depending on the circumstances, and the terms in the table do not take precedence over the clinical presentation. An open fracture may puncture the skin and contaminate the wound with foreign materials, such as glass, dirt, or bone fragments. Debridement codes may be needed to remove the foreign material and clean the wound. Codes 11010–11012 and 11042 are assigned from the integumentary system of CPT and billed with the treatment code for the fracture with modifier -51 to indicate multiple procedures. Thus, it is possible, for example, to have a depressed skull fracture that is classified as an open fracture, if the fracture site has a wound over it that is deep and communicates the fracture site with the outside environment. Open fractures are sometimes graded according to the Gustilo classification, the most commonly used system to classify open fractures, as illustrated in Table 8–2.

Note that a grade IIIc open fracture will require additional codes to classify the vascular injury and any subsequent repair. Grade III fractures with extensive soft tissue damage and/or devitalized tissue may require a wound debridement procedure in addition to fracture reduction and fixation. The tabular index of ICD-10-CM contains this classification system to assign the appropriate 7th character to further describe these types of fractures.

Table 8-2 Gustilo Classification of Open Fractures

Type	Description
Grade I	An open fracture with a wound less than 1 cm in diameter with minimal soft tissue injury
Grade II	An open fracture with a wound greater than 1 centimeter and less than 10 cm in diameter, but without extensive soft tissue loss or devitalization, and no vascular injury
Grade III	An open fracture with a high-energy wound with extensive damage to soft tissues, including muscle, skin, and neurovascular structures, or one in which there has been a major vascular injury
Grade IIIa	A grade III injury, but one without extensive periosteal stripping or a vascular injury requiring repair
Grade IIIb	A grade III injury accompanied by extensive periosteal stripping and exposure of the bone with massive contamination
Grade IIIc	A grade III injury accompanied by a major vascular injury requiring repair

Pediatric Fractures

Children's fractures differ from those seen in the adult because of the presence of a growth plate called the physis, or cartilago epiphysialis in long bones. Whenever the fracture involves this growth plate, the Salter-Harris Classification of Pediatric Fractures is used to describe the extent and severity of the fracture as shown in Table 8–3. The tabular index of ICD-10-CM contains information to assign the appropriate 7th character to further describe these types of fractures.

Table 8-3 Salter-Harris Classification of Pediatric Fractures

Type	Description
Type I	The fracture line goes directly through the physis.
Type II	The fracture line is mostly through the physis, but it exits one cortex such that a small fragment of metaphysis is included with the fracture fragment containing the physis and epiphysis.
Type III	The fracture line is mostly through the physis, but it exits one cortex such that a small fragment of epiphysis is included with the fracture fragment containing the metaphysis and diaphysis.
Type IV	The fracture line crosses the physis such that both the fragments contain portions of the metaphysis, physis, and epiphysis.
Type V	In this injury, there is no definite fracture line. Like the type I fracture, it cannot be easily diagnosed radiographically. The injury involves a crush injury to the physis, in which the metaphysis and epiphysis are acutely affected one another.

Head, Skull, and Facial Injuries (S00–S09)

Skull and facial fractures are classified in ICD-10-CM to category S02. If a concussion occurs, ICD-10-CM category S06.0 contains codes related to state of consciousness based in time measurements. A concussion is a traumatic injury to soft tissue, usually the brain, as a result of a violent blow, shaking, or spinning. Consciousness is a general state of wakefulness and perception and awareness of one's surroundings. There are different levels of altered consciousness, ranging from slight drowsiness to a reduction in intensity or sensitivity, to light coma, to deep coma. Conditions seen in the awake (conscious) patient that are sometimes confused with a loss of consciousness include inattention, confusion, delirium, hallucinations, and delusions. Another clinical feature that the coder needs to determine is whether or not the skull fracture is accompanied by an intracranial injury. Contusion, laceration, bleeding, and any other term indicating trauma to the meninges, the brain, or the brain stem affect code selection and may require additional code.

Neck Injuries (S10–S19)

Code categories S10–S19 are used to report injuries to the neck, supraclavicular region, and throat, including cervical vertebral column (C-spine) fractures, with code category S12 covering the larynx, trachea, and other parts of the neck, including the hyoid bone and thyroid cartilage.

Injuries to the Thorax (Codes S20–S29)

Injury locations in this category include the breasts, chest wall, and thoracic vertebrae. These injuries include fractures, subluxation and dislocations, open wounds, superficial injuries, and crush injuries. Code selections are found in S20–S29.

Injuries to the Abdomen, Lower Back, Lumbar Spine, Pelvis, and External Genitalia (S30–S39)

Injury locations in this category include the abdominal wall, anus, buttocks, external genitalia, flank, and groin, and includes injuries to organs located in the abdominal cavity: kidneys, ureters, bladder, fallopian tubes, and the uterus. This category of codes includes fractures and dislocations of the lumbar spine and pelvis, superficial injuries, contusions, open wounds, and lacerations.

Injuries of the Upper Extremity (Codes S40–S69)

This code range includes injuries to the shoulder, arm, elbow, wrist, and hand, including fingers, with codes significant to right or left side as well as bilateral. This section contains codes for fractures, superficial wounds, lacerations, and open wounds. It also includes injuries to muscles and tendons of the shoulder area.

Injuries of the Lower Extremity (Codes S70–S99)

This code range includes injuries to the hip (femur), thigh, knee, lower leg, ankle, foot, and toes and includes fractures, dislocations, and muscle injuries.

Traumatic hip fractures classified to category S72 are very common in the elderly population, and may also involve an impaction type fracture of the acetabulum, code range S32. Because of the stresses placed on this joint and the weakness of the bones in the elderly population, the most common method of treating these fractures is by partial or complete joint replacement. A total hip replacement involves the replacement of both the femoral head and the acetabulum, and a partial hip replacement involves either the acetabulum or the femoral head, although the femoral head is most common. When referencing procedures in CPT for total or partial hip replacement, look under index terms such as arthroplasty, reconstruction, and replacement. The elderly are also subject to pathological hip fractures, and the classification of these fractures is discussed later in the chapter.

Pathological Fractures (M84)

Code category M84 classifies pathological fractures. A pathological fracture is any fracture through diseased bone, but for classification purposes it has been further defined as without any identifiable trauma or following only minor trauma. In order for a fracture to be classified as pathological, the qualifying terms of *pathological* or *spontaneous* should be documented, or the chart should document a cause-and-effect relationship between the fracture and some underlying pathology. In the latter instance, there should always be a code reported for bone pathology with the pathological fracture code to complete the coding profile.

Fractures not specified as pathological, spontaneous, or due to an underlying bone disease are classified to the code category range S00–S99 as if they were due to injury or trauma. For this reason, when a pathological fracture is implied but not clearly stated in the medical record, the responsible physician should be queried as to whether or not this represents a pathological fracture. Situations that imply a pathological fracture include those in which the fracture seems out of proportion to the degree of injury or trauma, and those in which a disease is present that is often associated with pathological fractures, but no cause and effect is documented. Etiologies for pathological fractures include:

- Metastatic bone disease
- Osteoporosis
- Osteopenia
- Disuse atrophy
- Hyperparathyroidism
- Osteitis deformans
- Avascular necrosis of bone
- **Osteomyelitis**
- Osteogenesis imperfecta
- Osteopetrosis
- Neuromuscular disorders with disuse osteoporosis

Note that multiple myeloma also causes pathological fractures, but as they are an integral part of the disease process, only the code for multiple myeloma subcategory (C90) is assigned. Although virtually all pathological fractures involve some degree of precipitating trauma or injury, a code from category range S00–S99 is never assigned with a code from subcategory M84 for the same fracture.

Placeholder Character X for Fractures

ICD-10-CM utilizes a placeholder character X used to "hold the place" at certain codes to allow for future expansion. Where a placeholder exists, the X must be used in order for the code to be considered a valid code.

> **Highlight:**
> Reporting and sequencing of multiple fractures in acute care hospitals are based on the Uniform Hospital Discharge Data Set (UHDDS) definitions and generally take into account the severity of the fractures. In the outpatient setting, the UHDDS definitions do not apply, and the reason for the outpatient encounter should be based on the condition chiefly responsible for the outpatient encounter.

osteomyelitis: Infection or inflammation of the bone or bone marrow. It may be acute, subacute, or chronic.

Seventh Characters

Certain ICD-10-CM categories have applicable 7th characters. The applicable 7th character is required for all codes within the category, or as the notes in the Tabular List instruct. The 7th character must always be the 7th character in the data field. If a code that requires a 7th character is not six characters, a placeholder X must be used to fill in the empty characters.

The Tabular List of ICD-10-CM contains the appropriate 7th character to be added to each code from category S02:

A   initial encounter for closed fracture

B   initial encounter for open fracture

D   subsequent encounter for fracture with routine healing

G   subsequent encounter for fracture with delayed healing

K   subsequent encounter for fracture with nonunion

P   subsequent encounter for fracture with malunion

S   sequel

These 7th characters are also added when coding pathological fractures, with the exception of "B" to indicate initial encounter for open fracture.

EXAMPLE: Traumatic fracture of the angle of the mandible seen for delayed healing of the fracture. Additional x-rays will be ordered to determine cause.

ICD-10-CM directs the coder to S02.65XG. The required 7th character is G to indicate subsequent encounter for fracture with delayed healing. The X is assigned as the placeholder.

Fracture Procedures

There are many different ways to treat a fracture. It depends on the fracture's clinical presentation, which includes its severity, the bones involved, the type and number of fractures, and even related factors such as the age of the patient and underlying bone pathology.

Reduction and Fixation Procedures

Reduction and fixation are the two most common procedures associated with fractures. A reduction of a fracture is a procedure in which the physician aligns fractured bones and bone fragments back into their normal anatomical alignment. Except in very rare instances, a reduction will be performed whenever there is a displaced fracture. Nondisplaced fractures and fractures in which the displacement is minimal and judged to be insignificant do not require reduction. Fixation is a procedure where the fractured bones or bone fragments are secured in their normal anatomical alignment. Fixation may or may not occur following a reduction. Sometimes the fixation is done to stabilize a nondisplaced fracture.

The terms *open* and *closed* as they apply to fracture procedures have specific meanings that are unrelated to whether or not the fracture itself is open or closed. Coders must be careful when reviewing medical record documentation not to confuse statements relating to the diagnosis with statements relating to the procedure. The fact that a fracture is open or closed has no bearing upon whether or not the procedures to treat the fracture will be open or closed.

A closed reduction is one in which the physician manually, or through the use of traction devices, realigns the bone ends or fragments without surgically exposing the fracture site. In an open reduction, the fracture site is exposed during the reduction procedure, and it is normally performed in an operating room. If the fracture was an open fracture, the operative report may describe the procedure with terms such as *reopening, debriding,* or *exploring* the wound down to the fracture site prior to reduction. In some cases, a closed reduction is followed by an open reduction. In the case of a failed closed reduction, no code is assigned for closed reduction. If the closed reduction was accomplished and later judged to be suboptimal, or if the bones or bone fragments fell out of alignment at a later time, then codes for both the initial closed reduction and the subsequent reduction (which may be open or closed) may be assigned.

Open reduction is indicated when one or more of the following conditions are met:

- Fractures irreducible by manipulation or closed means.

- Displaced intra-articular fracture, where the fragments are sufficiently large to allow internal fixation.

- Certain displaced injuries such as displaced Salter III and IV injuries.

- Major avulsion fractures with significant disruption of an important muscle or ligament. These include fractures of the greater tuberosity of the humerus, the greater trochanter, the olecranon, the patella, the intercondylar eminence of the tibia, and the tibial tubercle.

- Nonunion of a fracture that has received adequate treatment by a closed method.

- Replantations of extremities or digits. In this case, rigid fixation is necessary to protect the repair of the neurovascular structures (Canale, 2013).

Internal fixation is the process of directly securing bone ends or fragments together by means of surgical hardware, such as with nails, screws, plates, and rods. In directly securing the bone ends or fragments, some part of the hardware will come in contact with the fracture site, in the same way that a carpenter's nail driven through two wooden boards will come in contact with both boards to directly connect them together (Figure 8–3). Although Steinmann pins and Kirschner wires are normally associated with external fixation, they can also be used for internal fixation. For this reason, the coder should be careful to review the medical record documentation to. determine exactly which type of fixation is being performed and not make assumptions based on a piece of hardware's typical usage. Orthopedic surgeons can be very creative in their use of hardware. For example, intra-articular phalangeal fractures involve the joint surface. If displaced, they are often treated with **open reduction and internal fixation (ORIF)** using fine Kirschner wire as the fixation hardware. ORIF is a method of surgically repairing a fractured bone, generally involving the use of plates and screws or an intra-medullary rod to stabilize the bone.

open reduction internal fixation (ORIF): A method of surgically repairing a fractured bone, generally involving the use of places and screws or an intra-medullary rod to stabilize the bone.

Internal fixation can be performed without the need for a fracture reduction. This occurs in two instances. First, the fracture may be in good anatomical alignment so no reduction is necessary. In this case, the internal fixation is performed to stabilize the fracture site. The internal fixation can also be used to revise or replace a previous internal fixation, such as in the case where the original internal hardware has become displaced or broken.

External fixation is any method of securing the bone ends or fragments in their proper anatomical alignment without directly connecting them with hardware. Simply put, in

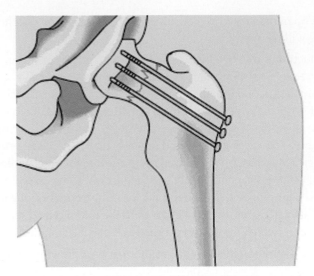

Figure 8-3 Internal fixation screws are used to stabilize the fracture of the femoral neck. These pieces of hardware are not removed once the bone has healed.

external fixation the bone ends or fragments are held together without nailing, screwing, rodding, plating, or wiring the bone ends or fragments together at the point of fracture. Casts, wraps, splints, and similar immobilization devices are some external fixation devices and should not be confused with the more complex external fixation devices such as pins, wires, and screws. The key difference between external and internal pins, wires, and screws is that the external ones are used solely to hold the bone ends or fragments in their normal anatomical position. They do not connect bone (fragment) to bone (fragment) and the fracture site is not touched. Small incisions are normally made near the fracture site to secure them to the adjacent bone. Care must be exercised not to confuse these minor procedures with the surgical procedure of internal fixation. In external fixation, the hardware does not come in contact with or cross the fracture site. Internal and external fixation should not be coded concurrently for the same fracture during the same operative episode as surgeons do not incorporate both methods of fixation at the same time.

The tarsals and metatarsals are made up of 12 bones as shown in Table 8–4 and Table 8–5. Figure 8–4 and Figure 8–5 are representations of the bones in the human hands and feet.

Table 8-4 Carpal and Metacarpal Bones

Carpals	Metacarpals
Scaphoid (navicular)	First metacarpal
Lunate (semilunar)	Second metacarpal
Triquetral	Third metacarpal
Pisiform	Fourth metacarpal
Trapezoid (lesser multangular)	Fifth metacarpal
Capitate	
Trapezium (greater multangular)	
Hamate	

Table 8-5 Tarsal and Metatarsal Bones

Tarsals	Metatarsals
Talus (astragalus)	First metatarsal
Calcaneus	Second metatarsal
Navicular	Third metatarsal
Cuboid	Fourth metatarsal
Medial cuneiform	Fifth metatarsal
Intermediate cuneiform	
Lateral cuneiform	

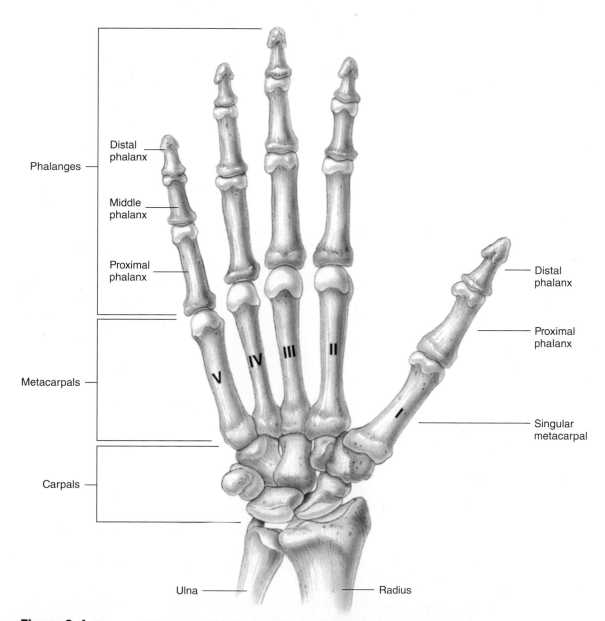

Figure 8-4 Bones of the lower left arm, wrist, and hand

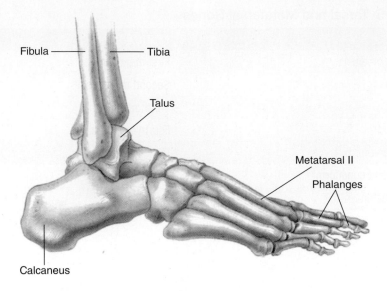

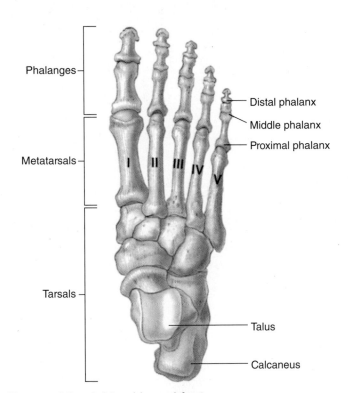

Figure 8-5 Bones of the right ankle and foot

Be wary of preoperative anesthesia notes, nursing notes, and consent forms when doing chart reviews. Often these forms will routinely refer to any fracture surgery as ORIF (open reduction with internal fixation), when in fact the operative report will describe a different classifiable procedure.

Nonsurgical treatments of fractures include casting, taping, splinting, bandaging, immobilization, and traction.

CPT Procedure Codes for Fractures and Dislocations

Codes for reporting fracture procedures can be found throughout the CPT chapter on the Musculoskeletal System. As in ICD-10-CM, the codes differentiate between closed or open treatment, but add "percutaneous skeletal fixation" as a third alternative. Closed treatment is used to describe procedures where the fracture site is not surgically opened. It may be used in conjunction with the following methods of treating the fracture: with manipulation, without manipulation, or with or without traction. Open treatment is used when the fracture site is surgically opened; the fracture site is visualized and internal fixation may be used. Percutaneous skeletal fixation describes fracture treatment in cases in which the fracture is not exposed, but fixation is placed across the fracture site, usually under x-ray imaging.

The term *manipulation* is used synonymously with reduction in CPT. It is the actual restoration or attempted restoration of a fracture or joint dislocation to its normal anatomical alignment. Note that codes indicating manipulation can be assigned in CPT, even if a fracture reduction is not accomplished. When a closed treatment is done without manipulation, it usually means that no attempt to reduce the fracture has been made, and a cast, splint, bandage, or other traction or immobilization device has been applied. CPT does not classify reductions with open procedures, and the use of internal or external fixation is normally found within the code narrative for the open procedure. When an external fixation is done and it is not listed in the code narrative for the basic fracture or dislocation procedure, select either code 20690 or 20692 as an additional code assignment. If an adjustment or revision of the external fixation device is performed, code 20693 is assigned.

Some CPT procedure codes for fractures and dislocations use anesthesia as a decision point in determining the correct code. Anesthesia is the pharmacological suppression of nerve function and can be general, regional, or local. It should not be confused with sedation (calming), analgesia (pain reduction), or topical anesthetics (ointments, salves), which are not included in CPT as anesthesia.

Multiple codes can be assigned in CPT for fixation devices and fracture procedures, depending on the number of fractures and the clinical circumstances involved, just as in ICD-10-CM. Some important differences do exist, however, such as the global services concept for most surgical procedures. For fracture procedures such as subsequent suture removal and casting, strapping, or other immobilization revision or removal, the surgeon performing the service should not bill for these minor procedures at a later date. Certain fracture procedures encourage multiple reporting of the same code by using the terms *each, single,* or *one* in the code narrative. Code 26600 for "Closed treatment of metacarpal fracture, single; without manipulation, each bone," requires the coder to assign this code as many times as necessary to report each metacarpal bone treated in this manner. The bones may be on one or both hands.

CPT surgical package guidelines define the following services always included in addition to the operation:

- Local infiltration, metacarpal/metatarsal/digital block, or topical anesthesia

- Subsequent to the decision for surgery, one related E/M encounter on the date immediately prior to or on the date of the procedure (including history and physical examination)

- Immediate postoperative care, including the dictation of operative notes, discussion with family and/or other physicians
- Writing orders
- Evaluating the patient in the postanesthesia recovery area
- Usual postoperative follow-up care

Dislocations

dislocation: A complete separation of the bone from its normal position in a joint.

A **dislocation** is a complete separation of the bone from its normal position in a joint. It is synonymous with the term *luxation*. In a true dislocation, there is a complete loss of congruity between the articular surfaces of a joint. An incomplete dislocation is called a *subluxation*, but the two terms are sometimes used interchangeably (and incorrectly). ICD-10-CM classifies both dislocations and subluxations with the same codes. Figure 8–6 gives a visual comparison of a dislocation and a subluxation of a shoulder joint. When a dislocation is associated with a fracture, only the fracture code is assigned. In a fracture/dislocation, the fracture is located near the joint where the disarticulation took place. It is possible to have a fracture and a dislocation of the same bone, without its being classified as a fracture/dislocation. For example, a patient may have a dislocation of the proximal femur (at the hip joint) and a fracture at the distal femur (at the knee joint). In this case, the fracture and the dislocation have occurred at different sites and two codes can be assigned.

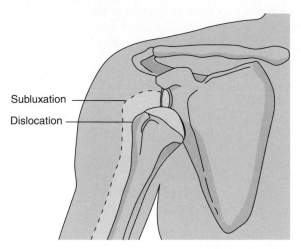

Subluxation
Dislocation

Figure 8-6 Subluxation and dislocation shown on a posterior view of the left shoulder

The terminology and coding rules for dislocations are virtually the same as they are for fractures. Dislocations and subluxations are classified to ICD-10-CM category range S43–S63, and the terms *open* and *closed* as discussed in the section on fractures have basically the same meaning. Three types of dislocations are not classified to this area:

1. Congenital dislocations (Q65)—those existing at birth
2. Pathological dislocations (M24), which might be due to an underlying disease or disorder, and include spontaneous dislocations
3. Recurrent dislocations (M24), frequently occur in a major joint such as the shoulder or hip, due to a lack of integrity of the soft tissues of the joint capsule

Dislocation Procedures

The terms for open treatment, closed treatment, and percutaneous skeletal fixation have the same meaning for dislocations as they do for fractures. The code ranges classifying different parts of the skeletal system in the Musculoskeletal System chapter of CPT are inconsistent with regard to how dislocations are coded. The terminology of the code ranges may appear in the following five ways:

1. *Bones that are part of a fixed cartilaginous joint and thus not typically described as a dislocation.* These codes may be listed with the subtitle "Fracture and/ or Dislocation," even though the term *dislocation* is not present in any of the code descriptions. For example, fractures of the ribs are classified within the code range 21805–21825. The subtitle of this code range is "Fracture and/or Dislocation" but none of these codes mention the term *dislocation,* only the fracture.

2. *Combination fracture and/or dislocation codes.* These codes will describe fractures alone, dislocations alone, or fracture/dislocations. Example: 27217, Open treatment of anterior pelvic bone fracture and/or dislocation with internal fixation (includes pubic symphysis and/or rami).

3. *Fracture/dislocation codes.* These codes specifically classify fractures associated with dislocations. Example: 26665, Open treatment of carpometacarpal fracture dislocation, thumb (Bennett fracture), with or without internal or external fixation.

4. *Dislocation only codes.* These codes specifically classify treatment of dislocations alone. Example: 27250, Closed treatment of hip dislocation, traumatic; without anesthesia.

5. *Specified clinical types of dislocations.* Example: 27265, Closed treatment of post hip arthroplasty dislocation; without anesthesia.

   From these varied code narratives, it is easy to see why it is so important to thoroughly read and understand the code narrative before assigning a code.

> **Highlight:**
> ORIF is the acronym for open reduction internal fixation.

Exercise 8.1

Assign ICD-10-CM codes first for the diagnosis, and then the CPT procedure codes.

1. Fracture of the left humerus, upper end, with closed reduction and internal fixation of same, initial encounter.
   ICD-10-CM   _____
   CPT   _____

2. Open reduction without internal fixation of closed left navicular and cuboid bone ankle fractures, nondisplaced, initial encounter.
   ICD-10-CM   _____
   CPT   _____

3. Closed fracture of the right forearm (Colles type) with percutaneous reduction and mini-fixation, initial encounter.
   ICD-10-CM   _____
   CPT   _____

(continues)

Exercise 8.1 (*continued*)

4. Dislocated right patella, lateral, initial encounter. Dislocation reduced under intravenous sedation.
   ICD-10-CM   _____
   CPT   _____

5. Fracture of the right hip with slight degree of subluxation, due to age-related osteoporosis, initial encounter. Closed reduction under regional nerve block.
   ICD-10-CM   _____
   CPT   _____

6. Intertrochanteric right hip fracture, closed, with internal fixation replacement using methylmethacrylate cement, initial encounter.
   ICD-10-CM   _____
   CPT   _____

7. Closed treatment without manipulation of small, nondisplaced fracture of the shaft of the second proximal phalanx, right foot, initial encounter.
   ICD-10-CM   _____
   CPT   _____

8. Open fracture of the left lower fibular shaft with closed treatment without manipulation, initial encounter.
   ICD-10-CM   _____
   CPT   _____

9. Closed reduction with manipulation for a compound fracture of the right talus neck, displaced, initial encounter.
   ICD-10-CM   _____
   CPT   _____

10. Treatment of spontaneous left ischium dislocation by splint without manipulation; senile osteoporosis.
    ICD-10-CM   _____
    CPT   _____

Arthropathy

arthropathy: A vague, general term meaning pathology affecting a joint.

Arthropathy is a vague, general term meaning pathology affecting a joint. There are many different descriptive types, which overlap each other, including infective, rheumatoid, degenerative, and internal derangements. This next section will examine the most common types seen by orthopedic physicians.

Infective Arthropathy

Infective arthropathy is any arthritis, arthropathy, polyarthritis, or polyarthropathy associated with an infective agent and is classified to category M00-M99 in ICD-10-CM. The agent is most often bacterial, but can also be viral, fungal (mycotic), mycobacterial, parasitic (micro and macroparasites), or helminthic (worms). It should not be confused with infective osteomyelitis, which is an infection of the bone and/or bone marrow classified to category M86. But both infective arthropathy and infective osteomyelitis can occur concurrently.

Pyogenic arthritis is arthropathy due to a specific bacterial organism known to produce suppuration. It is important to reference the ICD-10-CM index carefully when coding bacterial arthropathy for specific location of the site of the arthropathy and type, such as staphylococcal or streptococcal. Coders should first determine from the chart documentation the name of the specific bacteria-caused arthropathy, and then read and be guided by the index entries under the main term Arthritis. One code will describe both the site of the arthropathy and the bacteria.

Rheumatoid Arthropathy

A distinction needs to be made between arthropathy that falls into the general category of rheumatoid arthritis, and arthropathy associated with acute rheumatic fever. Rheumatic fever is an acute inflammatory disease that attacks the connective tissue in the heart, blood vessels, and joints of children. It is due to infection by group A hemolytic streptococci. Due to the transient nature of the joint lesions and the effectiveness of antibiotics, arthropathy associated with rheumatic fever is considered symptomatic and rarely leads to permanent joint pathology.

Rheumatoid arthritis (unspecified) as classified to subcategory M06.9 is a chronic, systemic, inflammatory connective tissue disease. Unlike osteoarthritis that is related to wear and tear damage to the joints, rheumatoid arthritis primarily attacks the peripheral joints and surrounding muscles, tendons, ligaments, and blood vessels (Figure 8–7). The severity and frequency of exacerbations can vary greatly from patient to patient. The etiology of rheumatoid arthritis is unknown, but it is considered an autoimmune disorder that affects the entire body. A blood test called the rheumatoid factor can test for the antibody for rheumatoid arthritis. However, this factor can be detected in the blood of normal individuals and of those with other autoimmune disorders, such as lupus erythematosus and Sjogren's syndrome, and can be found in individuals diagnosed with hepatitis and mononucleosis. ICD-10-CM classifies subcategory M05, Rheumatoid arthritis with rheumatoid factor, and M06,

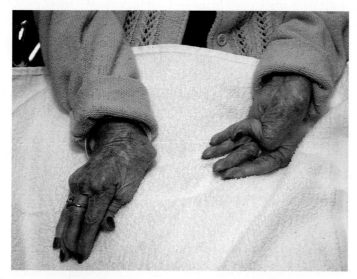

Figure 8-7 A female patient displaying deformities caused by rheumatoid arthritis

Rheumatoid arthritis without rheumatoid factors. The disease also goes by the names of primary progressive arthritis and proliferative arthritis.

Juvenile rheumatoid arthritis, also known as juvenile idiopathic arthritis, is the most common type of arthritis in children under the age of 17. Symptoms include joint pain, swelling, and stiffness, and they can lead to serious complications such as growth problems and eye inflammation. Symptoms can last a few months, while others may continue to have symptoms the rest of their lives. Juvenile rheumatoid arthritis codes in ICD-10-CM are classified to subcategory M08 (with or without rheumatoid factor).

Subcategory code M05.00, Felty's syndrome, is rheumatoid arthritis associated with splenomegaly and leukopenia. Mild anemia and thrombocytopenia may accompany the severe neutropenia, and skin and pulmonary infections are frequent complications. Specific categories in ICD-10-CM classifies rheumatoid arthritis with extra-articular lesions of connective tissue disease in the cardiovascular, reticuloendothelial, digestive, and respiratory systems. Category code M08 classifies a number of juvenile chronic polyarthritic diseases, which are rheumatoid-like disorders affecting children, but have a much better prognosis than the adult-onset diseases. Category code M12.00, Chronic postrheumatic arthropathy, is a form of arthropathy affecting the hands and feet caused by repeated attacks of rheumatic arthritis. Rheumatoid lung disease, code M05.10, is a disease of the lung associated with rheumatoid arthritis. It is sometimes seen in Caplan's syndrome, a disease that features rheumatoid pneumoconiosis.

As evidenced by the information in the preceding paragraph, rheumatoid arthritis can be associated with a wide variety of concomitant clinical conditions. It can be quite difficult for the coder to determine which concomitant conditions need to be classified separately, and which are integral to the disease processes classifiable to subcategories and subclassifications under category M05. When in doubt, the responsible physician should be consulted before the variables of rheumatoid arthritis are broken into individual codes.

Degenerative Arthritis (Osteoarthritis)

ICD-10-CM code category M19 classifies degenerative arthritis, also known as degenerative joint disease, osteoarthritis, senescent arthritis, and hypertrophic arthritis (Figure 8–8 illustrates the effects of osteoarthritis). The term *arthritis* may also be further specified as polyarthritis when more than one joint is involved. Category M47 classifies degenerative arthritis when it involves the bones of the spinal column. This condition is sometimes referred to as spondylosis or spondylarthritis. Arthritis of the spine will be discussed later in this chapter under vertebral disorders. Degenerative arthritis is a condition marked by a deterioration of articular cartilage, hypertrophy, and remodeling of the subchondral bone, and secondary inflammation of the synovial membrane.

Within category M19, there are qualifying terms that must be understood to properly assign codes to the fourth-digit level:

- *Generalized:* A form of arthritis involving multiple joints that is almost always characterized as a primary osteoarthritis.

- *Primary osteoarthritis:* Degeneration of the joints without any known preexisting abnormality but considered "wear and tear" related to the aging process. It is sometimes referred to as idiopathic and commonly affects joints in the spine, knees, hips, and joints of the hands and feet.

- *Secondary arthritis:* Degeneration of the joints due to an identifiable initiating factor. The factors can include obesity, trauma, congenital malformations, foreign bodies, malalignments of joints, fibrosis and scarring from previous inflammatory

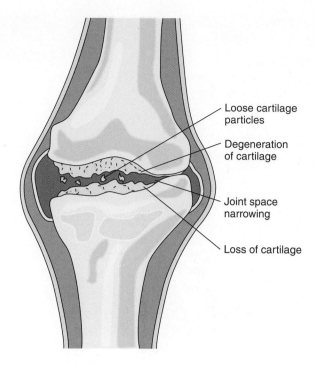

Loose cartilage
particles

Degeneration
of cartilage

Joint space
narrowing

Loss of cartilage

Figure 8-8 Damage caused by osteoarthritis to the knee joint

disease or infection, metabolic or circulatory bone diseases, and iatrogenic factors
such as continuous pressure put on joint surfaces during orthopedic treatment of
congenital anomalies.

- *Gouty arthritis, or gout:* Recurrent arthritis of the peripheral joints in which
  excessive uric acid in the blood is deposited in the joints.

Internal Derangements

An internal derangement of a joint is usually related to previous trauma or injury to
the joint. ICD-10-CM category code M23 classifies internal derangements of the knee,
and category M24 classifies other types of internal derangements involving other joints.
The term **internal derangement** refers to a range of injuries of the joint involving the
soft tissues such as the synovium, cartilage, and ligaments. It is important to differentiate
between pathology and acute injuries classified to sprains, strains, and other acute
injuries in ICD-10-CM Chapter 19, Injury, Poisoning, and Certain Other Consequences
of External Causes. Acute injuries of the joints are always classified to Chapter 19, even
if the physician uses the term internal derangement. The acute phase of the injury is
variable depending upon the joint involved and the severity of injury, but typically lasts
between two and six weeks. Conditions classifiable to categories M23 and M24 refer to
lasting or old internal derangements, and most often with degenerative changes.

internal derangement: A range
of injuries of the joint involving the
soft tissues, such as the synovium,
cartilage, and ligaments.

Arthropathy Procedures

A wide variety of procedures are used to treat arthropathy. The following is a
discussion of the most common joint procedures:

- *Arthrotomy:* Incision into a joint. This procedure may be performed to drain a
  joint of blood, synovial fluid, or purulence. When documented as the approach
  to further surgery, it should not be coded.

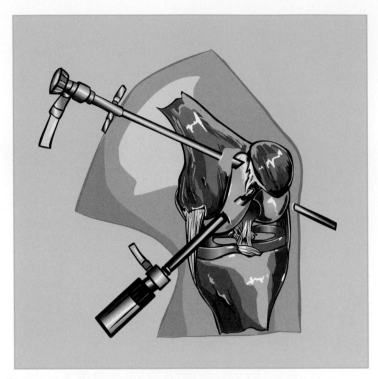

Figure 8-9 Use of arthroscope in viewing the knee joint

- *Arthroscopy:* The viewing of a joint by means of an endoscope (arthroscope). Refer to Figure 8–9. As with arthrotomy, when the arthroscopy is used to gain entrance to a joint in order to perform further surgery, it is considered an operative approach and not coded.

- *Biopsy:* The removal of a tissue sample for examination. When the entire lesion or tissue is removed, an excision code is used rather than a biopsy code.

- *Arthrocentesis:* The puncture of a joint with a needle to withdraw fluid for diagnostic testing, to remove fluid from joints to relieve pain, or to inject medications.

- *Arthrodesis:* The process of making a joint immobile by binding it together, usually by grafting bone or bone chips to the joint. The term is used synonymously with fusion.

- *Arthroplasty:* An operation to restore the integrity and function of a joint. An arthroplasty may or may not involve the use of prosthetics and artificial materials.

- *Replacement:* The removal of diseased or deranged joint tissue or bone and replacement with artificial materials, allograft, or autograft tissue.

- *Revision:* Surgery on a joint that has already undergone a primary repair procedure. A revision may make minor repairs to the existing joint, or repeat steps of the primary repair procedure right up to a complete redo of the primary repair procedure.

- *Trigger point:* A painful, tense, irritated muscle or knot in a muscle that causes localized or referred pain that can mimic pinched nerves in the lower back or neck. Muscle injuries, repetitive movements, secondary conditions such as a herniated disc, or even poor posture can cause trigger point pain. Injections of local anesthetic agents or cortisone may be given into the area of the trigger point to relax the muscle spasm, and can be performed as a series of injections. These are usually performed in the physician office or outpatient setting.

CPT organizes all of its procedures in the chapter of the Musculoskeletal System according to the anatomical part, and then by the type of procedure involved. The way the procedures are listed is fairly consistent throughout the chapter. For example, under the subheading of Forearm and Wrist, the following order of procedures is found:

- Incision

- Excision

- Introduction or Removal

- Repair, Revision, and/or Reconstruction

- Fracture and/or Dislocation

- Arthrodesis

- Amputation

- Other Procedures

Other types of procedures such as Grafts or Replantations are added to certain anatomical sites, whereas some procedures just listed are eliminated from other anatomical sites.

Careful attention must be given when coding amputations. Specific codes are listed in CPT for amputation at knee (below-knee amputation) or at the thigh through the femur (above-knee amputation). Figure 8–10 shows the different levels of amputation of the lower extremity.

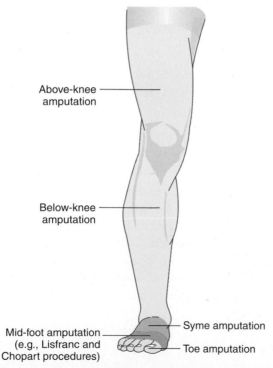

Figure 8-10 Different levels of amputation of the lower extremity

It is important to note that Endoscopy/Arthroscopy is found at the end of the chapter in code range 29800–29999. CPT does not follow the same coding rules for arthroscopic procedures that ICD-10-CM uses. All CPT arthroscopic procedures will be found at the end of the chapter when the operative approach is documented as arthroscopic (endoscopic). The code assigned will be chosen from this list. When a procedure is converted from endoscopic to an open procedure, the code for the endoscopic procedure may be assigned according to what was done under arthroscopy, and a separate code may be assigned for the open procedure. Some payors will require adding modifier -51 to the arthroscopy procedure to identify it as a multiple procedure performed on the same day.

A common error arises because some of the arthroscopic procedures in this chapter, particularly those of the knee, are easy to unbundle (separate). The National Correct Coding Initiative (NCCI), developed and used by the Centers for Medicare & Medicaid Services, has many edits to prevent unbundling these codes. To begin with, all surgical endoscopies include a diagnostic endoscopy. When assigning more than one knee procedure code for a particular surgery, be sure that the additional codes are not integral parts of the main procedure. For example, code 29880, is for Arthroscopy, knee, surgical with meniscectomy (medial AND lateral, including any meniscal shaving) including debridement/shaving or articular cartilage (chrondroplasty), same of separate compartment(s), when performed. Figure 8–9 shows an arthroscopic procedure of the knee. In reading through the operative report, you may notice mention of any or all of the following:

- Minor synovectomy
- Fat pad resection
- Articular shaving
- Removal of loose bodies
- Evacuation of debris
- Shaving of meniscus or cruciate stump
- Splinting or Casting

All of these procedures are integral parts of an arthroscopic knee meniscectomy and should not be coded and reported separately. They are all found in the NCCI billing editing software as well.

Vertebral Disorders

ICD-10-CM, Tabular Index, code categories M45-48 classify disorders of the vertebral column (Figure 8–11), along with some other related pathology of the spinal musculature and the spinal cord and spinal roots. Acute injuries of the vertebral column are not classified here, and should be classified to ICD-10-CM, Chapter 19, through the specific type of injury as referenced in the ICD-10-CM index. The terms *spondylosis* and *spondylitis* refer, respectively, to degeneration and inflammation of the vertebrae. Spondylarthritis is an inflammation of the vertebral articulations.

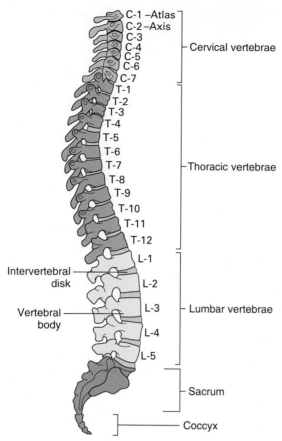

C-1 –Atlas
C-2 –Axis
C-3
C-4
C-5
C-6
C-7 — Cervical vertebrae

T-1
T-2
T-3
T-4
T-5
T-6
T-7
T-8
T-9
T-10
T-11
T-12 — Thoracic vertebrae

Intervertebral disk

L-1
L-2
L-3
L-4
L-5 — Lumbar vertebrae

Vertebral body

Sacrum

Coccyx

Figure 8-11 Lateral view of the vertebral column

Exercise 8.2

Assign ICD-10-CM codes first for the diagnosis, and then the CPT procedure codes.

1. Acute pseudomonas mallei infection of the left shoulder and wrist. Incision and drainage of both joints.
   ICD-10-CM _____
   CPT _____

2. Bucket handle tear of right lateral meniscus, current injury, subsequent encounter for surgical intervention. Lateral meniscectomy with partial synovectomy and debridement of the patella under endoscopic control.
   ICD-10-CM _____
   CPT _____

3. Arthritis of the left proximal humerus due to multiple myeloma, not currently in remission. Radical resection of tumor, proximal humerus.
   ICD-10-CM _____
   CPT _____

4. Degenerative joint disease localized in both knees and hips due to morbid obesity. Bilateral total knee replacement of both knee joints.
   ICD-10-CM _____
   CPT _____

(continues)

Exercise 8.2 (*continued*)

5. Internal derangement of the knee, following bicycle accident this morning. Incision and drainage of bloody effusion of the left knee.

    ICD-10-CM   _____

    CPT   _____

6. Bilateral arthrotomy temporomandibular joints for patient with TMJ pain.

    ICD-10-CM   _____

    CPT   _____

7. Injection of cortisone into both thumb joints (carpometacarpal) for treatment of primary degenerative arthritis, without ultrasound guidance.

    ICD-10-CM   _____

    CPT   _____

8. Arthroscopy of left elbow with limited debridement to remove gravel after superficial injury from fall from playground swing.

    ICD-10-CM   _____

    CPT   _____

9. Rheumatology consultation to discuss disease-modifying anti-rheumatic drugs (DMARDs) for severe juvenile rheumatoid arthritis. Consultation is documented as comprehensive history, and exam with moderate-complexity medical decision making.

    ICD-10-CM   _____

    CPT   _____

10. Amputation of right leg through tibia and fibula due to peripheral arterial occlusion.

    ICD-10-CM   _____

    CPT   _____

Important qualifying terms used in the subcategories for spinal arthritis include:

- *Myelopathy:* Pathology of the spinal cord due to the arthritic changes of the vertebrae. Paresthesia, loss of sensation, and loss of sphincter control are the most common forms of myelopathy.

- *Cervical:* Referring to the seven cervical vertebrae. The first and second cervical vertebrae are also known as the atlas and axis, respectively.

- *Thoracic:* Referring to the 12 thoracic vertebrae.

- *Lumbar:* Referring to the five lumbar vertebrae.

- *Sacral:* Referring to a single fused bone made up of five segments.

- *Coccyx:* Referring to a single fused bone at the end of the spinal column made up of three to five segments.

- *Lumbosacral:* Referring to one or more lumbar vertebrae in conjunction with the sacrum.

- *Enthesopathy:* Pathology occurring at the site where muscle tendons and ligaments attach to bones or joint capsules.

ICD-10-CM category M47 classifies spondylosis, excluding those infective and inflammatory spondylopathies of the vertebral column that are classified to category M46. Categories M50 and M51 classify intervertebral disk disorders with myelopathy and radiculopathy. For coding purposes, myelopathy includes any symptomatic impingement, compression, disruption, or disturbance to the spinal cord or blood supply to the spinal cord, due to spondylosis in category M47 or intervertebral disk disorder in categories M50 and M51. It is possible for a patient to concurrently have conditions classifiable to both categories. Figure 8–12 demonstrates a normal intervertebral disk as well as a herniated disk.

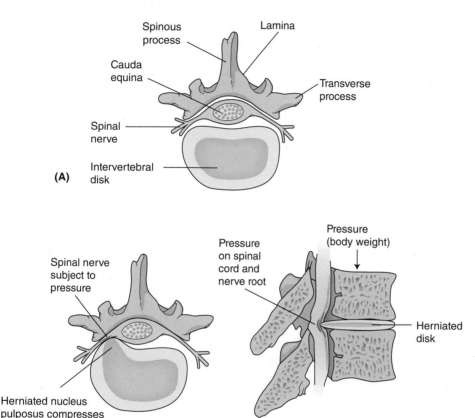

Figure 8-12 (A) Normal intervertebral disk (B) Two views of a herniated disk

Sometimes the term *radiculitis* or *radiculopathy* is confused with myelopathy. **Radiculopathy** and radiculitis are diseases and/or inflammation of the spinal nerve roots. The spinal nerves emerge from the spinal cord and can become entrapped, compressed, or irritated by diseased vertebral bodies, or more commonly, displaced intervertebral disks. Radiculopathy manifests itself almost exclusively as sensory symptoms (radicular pain or paresthesia) and/or motor symptoms (painless weakness) and can occur at any level, although involvement of the thoracic vertebrae and coccyx is very rare. In all, there are 31 pairs of spinal nerves: 8 cervical, 12 thoracic, 5 lumbar, 5 sacral, and 1 coccygeal.

radiculopathy: Disease of the spinal nerve roots.

ICD-10-CM category M53 contains codes for other and unspecified dorsopathies, not elsewhere classified. The term *dorsopathy* describes various diseases of the back and/or spine. Some of these terms include spinal instabilities of the various regions of the spine. M54 lists codes for dorsalgia or symptoms affecting regions of the neck and back such as neuralgia, radiculitis, panniculitis, ankylosis, sciatica, and low back pain.

Curvatures and related deformities of the spine can be either congenital (present at birth) or acquired, and ICD-10-CM classifies each type to different chapters.

The congenital deformities are found classified to subcategory Q05–Q06. Acquired deformities are classified to M95. Acquired deformities may be due to a variety of etiologies, including:

- Trauma

- Pathological weakness of bone

- Degenerative joint disease

- Surgical intervention

- Congenital conditions (e.g., congenital shortness of limb, with acquired compensatory defect)

- Paralytic syndromes

- Poor posture

- Muscle spasms

Coders sometimes misinterpret the subterm *traumatic* listed in the ICD-10-CM index under the main term *spondylolisthesis*. Traumatic spondylolisthesis is a congenital defect due to birth or intrauterine trauma and is classified to code Q76.2. Spondylolisthesis due to acute trauma at any time after birth is classified as a current injury with codes S12-. Acquired or degenerative spondylolisthesis is coded from subcategory M43. Spondylolisthesis as a late effect (sequelae) of trauma, such as due to a prior fracture of the vertebrae, is classified as acquired and should also carry the appropriate 7th character added to the ICD-10-CM code for sequela (late effect). For example, Displaced fracture of shaft of first metacarpal bone, right hand, is S62.241S.

Vertebral Procedures

The three most common procedures for disorders of the vertebrae are decompression of the spinal nerve root, vertebral disk excision, and spinal fusion. A decompression of the spinal nerve root is a procedure designed to relieve pressure and irritation of the root that causes radiculopathy. The procedure can be a laminotomy, which is an incision into one or more vertebral laminae; or a laminectomy, which is an excision of vertebral laminae, usually the posterior arch. These procedures can be modified with the prefix *foramen*, meaning at the site of the aperture into the vertebral canal bounded by the pedicles of adjacent vertebrae above and below the vertebral bodies anteriorly, and the articular processes posteriorly.

Spinal fusion is the process of immobilizing two or more vertebrae by fixation or stiffening. Bones grafts and/or orthopedic hardware may be used to accomplish this task.

CPT has many codes to classify spinal nerve decompression and intervertebral disk excision, and they can be found in the code range 63001–63290, Surgery/Nervous System. There are many decision points the coder must be aware of, including:

1. Was the main procedure a laminectomy, laminotomy, or diskectomy?

2. What region (lumbar, thoracic, cervical, sacral) was involved?

3. Was the main procedure accompanied by a facetectomy; foraminotomy; diskectomy; decompression of spinal cord, cauda equina, and/or nerve root; myelotomy; cordotomy; or nerve section?

4. Was the procedure a primary or reexploration?

5. How many interspace levels were involved?

6. Was a concurrent arthrodesis performed?

With so many decision points and the precise language used in the code narratives, it is imperative to read the descriptions and choose only the one that matches precisely what was done.

Arthrodesis is classified to the code range 22532–22819. These codes classify only the arthrodesis; additional codes are needed if a bone graft was obtained (20900–20938) or if hardware was used (22840–22855). Modifier -51 for multiple procedures is not reported with these codes as they are considered add-on procedure codes. CPT classifies arthrodesis by vertebral level and by technique. If a hemidiskectomy was performed with arthrodesis by instrumentation and bone graft, four codes would need to be assigned: one for the hemidiskectomy, one for the arthrodesis, one for the bone graft, and one for the instrumentation. Arthrodesis is also considered a primary procedure if it is performed for a spinal deformity, and these codes are located in the code range 22800–22812. Note that bone grafts and instrumentation are reported in addition to these codes also.

Sprains and Strains

Sprains and strains of joints and adjacent muscles are classified in ICD-10-CM Chapter 19, Injury, Poisoning, and Certain Other Consequences of External Causes (S00–T88). A sprain is defined as a severe stretching of a ligament with minor tears and hemorrhage, without subluxation, dislocation, or fracture. A severe sprain can result in occult joint instability. A strain is a less precise term that applies to any soft tissue injury (joint capsule, ligament, muscle, tendon) that occurs from overexertion. Strains and sprains that occur secondarily to any condition classifiable as a fracture, subluxation, or dislocation are incidental and not coded. Sprains and strains usually require only nonoperative procedures such as casting, strapping, splinting, and so on; and only when there is joint instability and chronic pain will surgery be indicated.

Exercise 8.3

Assign ICD-10-CM codes first for the diagnosis, and then the CPT procedure codes.

1. Cervical spondylosis with severe spinal cord compression. Anterior diskectomy at C1–2 with decompression of spinal cord.
   ICD-10-CM _____
   CPT _____

2. Spinal stenosis due to herniated nucleus pulposus, L1–2, with radiculitis. Foraminotomy, laminectomy, decompression of spinal nerve root L1–2 with partial resection of bony facet.
   ICD-10-CM _____
   CPT _____

3. Degenerative spondylolisthesis. Insertion of Harrington rod, anterolateral technique, thoracolumbar spine spanning four segments.
   ICD-10-CM _____
   CPT _____

(continues)

Exercise 8.3 *(continued)*

4. Aspiration of left knee with blood culture for bacterial septic arthritis.

    ICD-10-CM _____

    CPT _____

5. Hemilaminectomy L4–5 and L5–S1 for herniated disk.

    ICD-10-CM _____

    CPT _____

6. Whirlpool therapy for patient with muscle spasm of neck, shoulders, and upper back.

    ICD-10-CM _____

    CPT _____

7. Posterior arthrodesis for spinal deformity, 10 vertebral segments for scoliosis.

    ICD-10-CM _____

    CPT _____

8. Decompression of sciatic nerve; radiculopathy of lumbosacral spine.

    ICD-10-CM _____

    CPT _____

9. Kyphoplasty of T2–3; congenital kyphosis.

    ICD-10-CM _____

    CPT _____

10. Open treatment of fracture of coccyx for open fracture with other cauda equina injury.

    ICD-10-CM _____

    CPT _____

Other Conditions and Procedures

A few of the other more common orthopedic conditions and procedures are discussed in this section. These include malunion and nonunion of fractures, bone infections, and carpal tunnel syndrome.

Malunion and Nonunion of Fractures

Malunion and nonunion of fractures occur when fractured bones do not heal properly. Malunion is healing of the fracture in an abnormal or nonfunctional position. Nonunion is when the bone does not heal properly. A distinction needs to be made between malunion and nonunion following a traumatic or pathological fracture, and malunion and nonunion of bone following surgery. When a malunion or nonunion occurs following a fracture, ICD-10-CM refers the coder to the fracture, by site. This includes instances in which there has been an open or closed reduction and an internal or external fixation. In cases in which bone has been grafted for either arthrodesis or to further stabilize and strengthen a fracture site, if the grafted bone does not properly join to the graft site, this is considered a postoperative complication, a code from the Complications, mechanical, by site should be selected, such as T84.8, Other specified complications of internal orthopedic prosthetic devices, implants and grafts. The code is selected based on the symptom or condition caused by the device, such as embolism, hemorrhage, pain, or thrombosis

When a malunion of a fracture is surgically repaired, the most common method is to perform osteoclasis. A small amount of debridement or excision of the bone ends may also be done. A nonunion is more likely to be repaired with an arthrodesis. As with other arthrodesis procedures, harvesting of bone for grafting should also be reported. In CPT, codes for malunion and nonunion repair are found in each anatomical subsection in the musculoskeletal system chapter under the heading "Repair, Revision, and/or Reconstruction." For example, a repair of a malunion of the tibia without a graft would be coded 27720.

Bone Infections

Acute osteomyelitis is any acute or subacute infection of the bone or bone marrow. It is usually due to bacteria but can be caused by other infective agents, and is more common among children where the pathogen settles into the metaphyseal bed of the developing long bones. Chronic osteomyelitis is a persistent or recurring infection of the bone, and is extremely difficult to eradicate completely in the chronic stage. Periostitis is the inflammation of the periosteum, the thick fibrous membrane covering the bone surfaces except at the articular cartilage.

Common procedures for these conditions include bone biopsy, local excision of tissue or lesion of bone, sequestrectomy, and bone grafts. In CPT, most procedures for bone infection will be found in each anatomical subsection in the musculoskeletal chapter under the heading "Excision." Here you will find sequestrectomy codes, as well as various types of excisions with or without grafts.

Carpal Tunnel Syndrome

Carpal tunnel syndrome occurs when the tendons and the median nerve that pass through the carpal tunnel in the hands are overused in repetitive movements. The carpal tunnel is a narrow, bony passage under the carpal ligament located below the inner surface of the wrist. Symptoms of carpal tunnel syndrome are pain, burning, tingling, or numbness in the thumb, index finger, and middle finger. Figure 8–13 shows a normal wrist in comparison to one with the nerve pinched due to swelling and inflammation of the tendons. When conservative treatment such as stopping the repetitive motion, rest, splinting, anti-inflammatory medications, and physical therapy fail to relieve the symptoms,

carpal tunnel syndrome: A condition that occurs when the tendons and the median nerve that pass through the carpal tunnel in the hands are overused in repetitive movements.

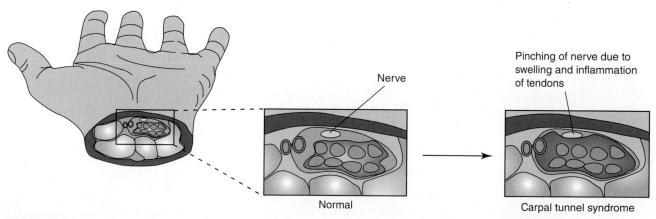

Nerve

Pinching of nerve due to swelling and inflammation of tendons

Normal

Carpal tunnel syndrome

Figure 8-13 Carpal tunnel syndrome

carpal tunnel release may be required. This procedure is the surgical enlargement of the carpal tunnel or cutting of the carpal ligament to relieve nerve pressure. CPT code 64721, Neuroplasty of the median nerve at the carpal tunnel, is used for the decompression or freeing of the nerve. An arthoscopic procedure may be indicated as "Endoscopy, wrist, surgical, with release of transverse carpal ligament," which is CPT code 29848.

Highlight:

When coding orthopedic conditions, remember that infections, malunion/nonunion of fractures, complications with hardware, scarring, and contractures of joints can affect the healing process of the injury. CPT modifiers -58 and -78 can make the difference between reimbursement or rejection of a claim.

- -58 Planned staged procedures (e.g., debridements)

- -78 Assign to procedures due to complications of the injury

Exercise 8.4

Assign ICD-10-CM codes first for the diagnosis, and then the CPT procedure codes.

1. Nonunion of a bone graft to the lumbosacral fusion performed eight weeks prior to admission. Autograft for spine surgery of bone fragment from the left iliac crest to the L1–S1 unstable site using lateral posterior technique.

   ICD-10-CM _____

   CPT   _____

2. Acute osteomyelitis of the radial head due to *E. coli.* Sequestrectomy of right radial head and debridement of surrounding muscle and fascia of the radius, 15 sq. cm.

   ICD-10-CM _____

   CPT   _____

3. Osteotomy with diskectomy of the spine at T9 and T10 levels through anterior approach for scoliosis.

   ICD-10-CM _____

   CPT   _____

4. Sprained left ankle after falling out of bed; walking short leg cast applied.

   ICD-10-CM _____

   CPT   _____

5. Patient with carpal tunnel syndrome undergoes bilateral neuroplasty at right carpal tunnel.

   ICD-10-CM _____

   CPT   _____

6. Trigger point injections, total of six into four muscle groups for reflex sympathetic dystrophy syndrome (Horner Syndrome) in the shoulder.

   ICD-10-CM _____

   CPT   _____

7. Extracorporeal shock wave therapy to treat plantar fasciitis.

   ICD-10-CM _____

   CPT   _____

(continues)

Exercise 8.4 (*continued*)

8. Correction of hammer toe (acquired), left foot, with partial phalangectomy.

   ICD-10-CM _____

   CPT _____

9. Arthroscopy with lateral meniscus repair; tear of lateral right meniscus, initial encounter.

   ICD-10-CM _____

   CPT _____

10. Application of short leg clubfoot cast with molding, bilateral; congenital clubfoot.

    ICD-10-CM _____

    CPT _____

Summary

Coding for the orthopedic specialty includes fractures and dislocations, sprains and strains, and the disease processes of the musculoskeletal system and connective tissue. The orthopedic specialty is the major medical provider for work-related injuries, motor vehicle accidents, and falls. External Causes of Morbidity (V01–Y99) codes are necessary to assign with the ICD-10-CM code to describe the reason for the injury in order to determine liability for the charges. It is important to remember that both the Alphabetic Index and the Tabular List in each classification system must be referenced for accuracy. This is especially necessary to assign additional specificities of a code as well as the 7th character. In some cases, the correct code may be classified in a different section of the code book, as in the case of congenital deformities in ICD-10-CM.

References

AMA Current Procedural Terminology 2016 professional edition. (2015). Chicago: American Medical Association.

American Academy of Orthopaedic Surgeons. (2015). *Complete global services data for orthopaedic surgery*. Park Ridge, IL: American Academy of Orthopaedic Surgeons.

Canale, S. T., & Beaty, J. H. (2013). *Campbell's operative orthopedics* (12th ed.). St. Louis, MO: Mosby/Elsevier.

ICD-10-CM expert for hospitals 2016 edition. (2015). Salt Lake City, UT: Optum360.

Neighbors, M., & Tannehill-Jones, R. (2015). *Human diseases* (4th ed.). Clifton Park, NY: Cengage Learning.

Salter, R. B. (1998). *Textbook of disorders and injuries of the musculoskeletal system*, 3rd ed. Baltimore, MD: Williams & Wilkins.

White, L., Duncan, G., & Baumle, W. (2011). *Foundations of Nursing* (3rd ed.). Clifton Park, NY: Delmar Cengage Learning.

Cardiology and the Cardiovascular System

Learning Objectives

Upon successful completion of this chapter, you should be able to:

- Recognize cardiovascular anatomy, physiology, and terminology.
- Identify common diagnostic procedures.
- Differentiate a diagnostic procedure from a therapeutic service.
- Recognize nuclear cardiology procedures.

Key Terms

angioplasty

aorta

aortic semilunar valve

arrhythmia

atrium

cardiac catheterization

cardiomyopathy

cardioversion

circumflex artery

echocardiography (ECHO)

electrocardiogram (EKG or ECG)

endocardium

implantable cardioverter-defibrillator (ICD)

ipsilateral

mitral valve

multiple gated acquisition (MUGA)

myocardium

occlusion

pacemaker

pericardium

plaque

pulmonary artery

pulmonary semilunar valve

septum

stent

tricuspid valve

vascular families

ventricles

Introduction

Cardiology is the medical specialty dealing with disorders of the heart that includes the diagnosis and treatment of congenital heart defects, coronary artery disease, heart failure, valvular heart disease, and electrophysiology. A cardiologist is the specialist in the diagnosis and treatment of the heart. Other medical specialists in cardiology include cardiac, cardiothoracic, and cardiovascular surgeons, who perform cardiac surgery including operative procedures on the heart and great vessels. Nuclear cardiology uses radioactive procedures to help to diagnose cardiac conditions.

As learned in anatomy, the heart is a muscle that pumps blood throughout the body. The heart can basically be divided into mechanical and electrical functions. Mechanical function is the purpose of the heart to perform as a pump to move blood efficiently throughout the body. Heart failure is a condition in which the mechanical function of the heart has failed, meaning insufficient blood is being circulated. Electrical function is centered on the periodic muscle contraction that is caused by the cardiac pacemaker. Electrocardiography focuses on the electrical conduction system of the heart, which is demonstrated in the **electrocardiogram (EKG or ECG)**. Examples of dysfunctions of the electrical system include **arrhythmias**, atrial or ventricular fibrillation, and heart block. Procedures to correct such problems are pacemakers and cardioverter-defibrillators. Myocardial infarction (MI) or heart attack causes cellular death of the heart, which affects both the mechanical and electrical capabilities of the heart and can lead to death. Cardiac arrest is the cessation of normal systemic circulation of the heart due to failure in proper contraction of the heart, such as ventricular fibrillation.

electrocardiogram (EKG or ECG): The recording of the electrical activity of the heart.

arrhythmia: An irregular heartbeat due to abnormal electrical activity in the heart.

This chapter introduces the many facets of modern cardiology practice. The two common service areas of care are medical (noninvasive) cardiology versus invasive (therapeutic), or interventional, cardiology.

The invasive, or interventional, cardiology procedures are commonly performed through the percutaneous route, or intravascularly, such as the removal of a clot from a blood vessel. The body is entered by breaking the skin to remove the clot or the injection of a substance to dissolve the clot.

This chapter explores various services, procedures, and encounters that are likely to be performed by the cardiology specialty. Accurate selection of codes that are unique and specific for cardiology are discussed, along with related bundling issues. As discussed in other chapters, the term bundling relates to procedures that are typically performed together and reimbursed as a whole rather than billed and reimbursed separately. Table 9–1 contains common cardiology abbreviations with which a coder will need to be familiar.

Table 9-1 Common Cardiology Acronyms

ACVD	acute cardiovascular disease	DOE	dyspnea on exertion
AICD	automatic implantable cardioverter-defibrillator device	DVT	deep vein thrombosis
ASCVD	arteriosclerotic cardiovascular disease	HDL	high density lipoprotein
AMI	acute myocardial infarction	HR	heart rate
AP	anterior posterior	HTN	Hypertension
ASHD	atherosclerotic heart disease	LAD	left anterior descending
BP	blood pressure	LBBB	left bundle branch block
CABG	coronary artery bypass graft	LV	left ventricle
CAD	coronary artery disease	MVP	mitral valve prolapse
CHF	congestive heart failure	MUGA	multiple gated acquisition
COPD	chronic obstructive pulmonary disease	NSR	normal sinus rhythm
CPR	cardiopulmonary resuscitation	PAD	peripheral arterial disease

(continues)

Table 9-1 (*continued*)

PCI	percutaneous coronary intervention	RCA	right coronary artery
PT	prothrombin time	RV	right ventricle
PTCA	percutaneous transluminal coronary angioplasty	SOA	shortness of air
RA	right atrium	VSD	ventricular septal defect
RBBB	right bundle branch block		

Cardiology physician services often begin with an evaluation and management (E/M) visit or encounter. The services are provided at various locations, depending on the individual physician's choice, skill level, and ownership of equipment. For example, the nuclear cardiologist may choose to provide some services at the physician office location and legally be authorized to do so. Or, due to the lack of equipment availability at the physician office, the nuclear cardiologist may perform the same service at the hospital location (either inpatient or outpatient). The place and the level of the service may vary greatly depending on the documented services that were provided.

A patient may see a cardiologist for a variety of symptoms or problems that may include coronary artery disease, arrhythmias, and chest pain such as angina pectoris. During or after the initial encounter, the physician may order and/or personally perform diagnostic services. These services may use conventional radiology or other medical diagnostic testing procedures. The physician may also choose a more invasive diagnostic procedure, in which a catheter is inserted percutaneously (through the skin) into a vessel (arterial or venous) and progresses into the coronary (heart) area, or other organ sites (e.g., renal), or the peripheral (noncoronary) area, or more than one of these. We will discuss the coding combination of each of these procedures.

Many cardiovascular codes are paired or partnered by anatomical sites with the radiological codes. The CPT codes are selected per physician and per service rendered, selecting a "sister" component radiological code plus the diagnostic procedure code.

Codes used in cardiology are found in the 30000, 70000, and 90000 series in the CPT code book, as well as the Category III CPT code series for emerging technology, services, and procedures assigned to allow data collection for these services/procedures. Unlisted CPT codes do not allow for collection of specific data, so if a Category III code is available, this code must be reported instead of a Category I unlisted code to allow data collection to evaluate health care delivery. Since cardiology is a high-tech specialty with new devices, advances in procedures, and new services continuously developing in the field, codes are updated more frequently than in other areas of the CPT. Category II tracking codes may also be selected; however, they are not required to be reported on claims at this time. Accurate code selection will require the coder to query the physician and/or conduct research for detailed information.

Cardiology service claims may be denied if the service does not meet the criteria for medical necessity or does not have FDA approval, and some services are restricted by quantity limitations. It is recommended that insurance coverage always be verified for any service prior to the physician performing the care, or when accepting assignment for an insurance claim. If a service is not covered, the advance beneficiary notice (ABN) is then properly completed. Chapter 15 discusses the advance beneficiary notice in detail.

Cardiac and Vascular Anatomy and Physiology

The heart is a fist-sized organ that weighs approximately 250 to 350 grams. It pumps in excess of 6,800 liters of blood daily, each heartbeat expelling an average of 145 mL. Its primary purpose is to supply blood to all organs and tissues throughout the vascular system, which also furnishes a pathway for nutrients, oxygen, hormones, and immunologic substances. The cardiovascular system not only delivers; it also picks up tissue waste and by products through venous blood return. The venous blood, depleted of oxygen and full of waste products, is routed through the lungs for fresh oxygenation and the removal of carbon dioxide. Blood is then routed through the liver for some metabolic functions and detoxification, and through the kidneys for waste removal and electrolyte balance.

Layers of the Heart Wall Muscle Layers

The heart is a muscle that is extremely rich in nerves and vessels and is made up of three major layers. The **pericardium** is a double layer of fibrous tissue that surrounds the heart. The **myocardium** is the cardiac muscle tissue that makes up the major portion of the heart. The **endocardium** covers the heart valves and lines the blood vessels, providing smooth transit for blood flow. The **septum** is a thick, muscular wall separating the heart into right and left sides.

Also in multiple layers, the outer, fibrous pericardium is loose and elastic. The inner layer, or serous pericardial layer, is also made up of more than one layer of tissue. These are the parietal and the visceral layers. The parietal layer lines the fibrous pericardium while the visceral layer, or epicardium, adheres to the outside of the heart itself. The pericardial space is located between the visceral and parietal layers. It is filled with a clear fluid that lubricates the heart's surface and prevents friction or rubbing from the sac. Though normal fluid retention in this space is 10–30 mL, up to 300 mL of fluid may accumulate before the heart's contractile function is impaired. Figure 9–1 shows all the major cardiac landmarks as well as the muscle of the heart wall discussed previously.

pericardium: Sac surrounding the heart.

myocardium: The muscular tissue of the heart.

endocardium: The innermost layer of tissue that lines the chambers of the heart.

septum: The dividing wall or muscle between the right and left sides of the heart.

Heart Chambers

Four major chambers are found in the heart. The upper two chambers, or the right **atrium** and left atrium, and the lower chambers, called the right and left **ventricles**, represent the four major chambers. Each is designed with a specific task and process. Figure 9–1 also displays the four distinct heart chambers. The right atrium receives systemic or deoxygenated blood from the extremities through the inferior and superior venae cavae (inferior drains the lower body, and the superior drains the upper regions). The right ventricle is divided into inflow and outflow tracts to account for the progress of the blood through this chamber. In the left atrium, oxygenated blood is returned fresh from the lungs. From here, the blood is expelled into the left ventricle. The left ventricle possesses the thickest and most muscular walls in order to propel fresh blood out into the blood's circulatory pathway throughout the body.

atrium: Upper chamber of the heart.

ventricles: The two lower chambers of the heart are called the ventricles. The right ventricle is two to three times thinner in muscle tissue than the left ventricle. The greater thickness and muscle mass of the left chamber are necessary to exert enough pressure and force to propel blood into systemic circulation.

tricuspid valve: Diametrically larger and thinner than the mitral valve, three separate leaflets or cusps are found in this critical valve. The anterior, posterior, and septal leaflets are competent only if the right ventricle's lateral wall functions correctly. The septal leaflet is attached to the interventricular septum and is in close proximity to the AV node.

mitral valve: A two-leafed or cuspid valve shaped like a bishop's miter (head covering), this valve is located between the left atrium and left ventricle. Considered an atrioventricular valve, the mitral valve opens when the atria contract and sends blood into the ventricles. When the ventricles contract, pressure is exerted on the leaflets causing them to balloon upward toward the atria.

pulmonary semilunar valve: A three-leaflet valve, the pulmonic is another semilunar valve. It is situated between the right ventricle and the pulmonary artery. During heart contractions, internal pressure forces this valve to open. Loss of pressure during diastole (heart relaxation) allows the valve to close.

aortic semilunar valve: Located between the junction of the aorta and left ventricle of the heart.

aorta: The main arterial trunk within the circulatory system. All other arteries, except the pulmonary artery, are branches off of this main channel. This vessel originates in the left ventricle of the heart and passes upward toward the neck. The carotid (major artery to the brain) and the coronary (major artery to the heart) are branches of the aorta. Blood that has been cleaned and freshly oxygenated flows through the aorta to the various body organs.

pulmonary artery: A major blood vessel that transports blood between the heart and the lungs for oxygenation. Deoxygenated blood is carried from the right ventricle via this vessel, which forks into the right and left lungs. The pulmonary vein then carries freshly oxygenated blood into the left atrium of the heart for passage into the left ventricle and, subsequently, into systemic circulation.

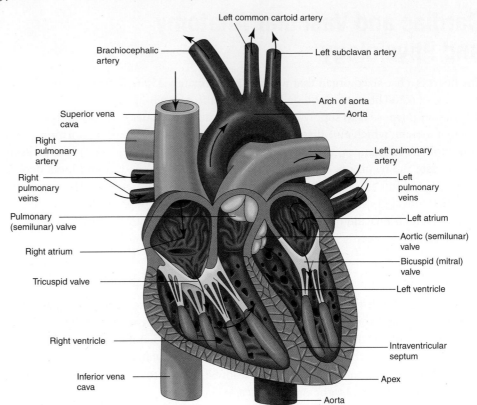

Figure 9-1 Anatomy of the heart with the four chambers, muscle layers, and vessels; the arrows show the proper flow of blood through the heart.

Heart Valves

Two atrioventricular valves and two semilunar valves are found inside the heart's vessels and chambers. The atrioventricular (AV) valves are the **tricuspid valve**, and the bicuspid **mitral valve** (also known as bicuspid valve). The **pulmonary semilunar valve** is located at the opening of the pulmonary artery and allows blood to travel from the right ventricle into the pulmonary artery, and then into the lungs. The **aortic semilunar valve** is at the orifice of the aorta, allowing blood to pass from the left ventricle into the aorta, but not backwards into the left ventricle. These valves are called semilunar due to their resemblance to the shape of the moon (Figure 9–2).

The Cardiac Cycle

During a cardiac cycle, two phases occur. They are systole and diastole. In diastole, there are two phases. Phase 1 of diastole occurs when the atria contract and force the AV valves to open. About 70 percent of the blood is expelled from the atria into the relaxed ventricles. Phase 2 of diastole involves a slowing of blood flow until accelerated atrial contraction forces any remaining blood into the ventricles. In systole, ejection of the blood occurs. Phase 1 of systole forces the AV valves to snap shut and begins the contractile phase of the ventricles. When pressure in the ventricles is greater than that in the **aorta**, the semilunar valves open and blood is expelled into the **pulmonary artery** and the aorta. As the contraction phase subsides, the muscles of the ventricles relax and intraventricular pressure decreases.

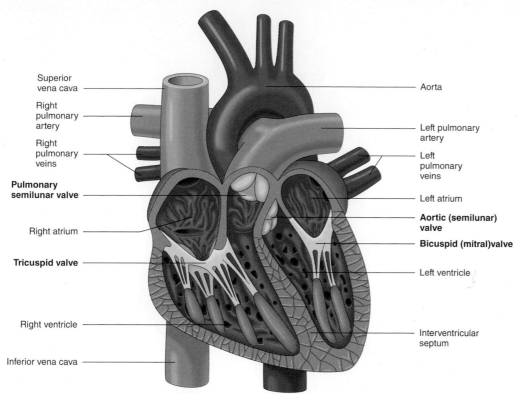

Figure 9-2 Internal view of the heart showing heart valves and pulmonary arteries and veins

Major Cardiac Vessels

The heart receives its blood supply from the coronary arteries. Major coronary vessels include the right coronary artery and two major left coronaries: the left anterior descending (LAD) and the **circumflex artery**. **Occlusion**, or obstructed blood flow, of any of these vessels due to thrombus, or clot, or **plaque** deposits can result in a myocardial infarction, or heart attack. Blood circulates throughout the coronary vasculature all during the cardiac cycle but is decreased with systole and increased during diastole. Figure 9–3 shows the position and location of the major vessels previously discussed.

Electrical Conduction Pathway

As introduced earlier in this chapter, electrophysiology relates to the electrical conduction system of the heart. The heart has a rich electrical conduction relay mechanism. Specialized tissue scattered strategically throughout the cardiac anatomy is designed to relay impulses that provoke the contractile action of the pump. The sinoatrial (SA) node is known as the heart's natural pacemaker. From here, impulses travel over the conduction paths to the atrioventricular (AV) node. The impulse is then transmitted to the bundle of His and terminates at the Purkinje fibers. Figure 9–4 illustrates the conduction pathway.

circumflex artery: A branch of the LCA (left coronary artery), this artery supplies the left atrium of the heart, the rear surfaces of the left ventricle, and the rear portion of the heart's dividing wall or septum.

occlusion: Blockage or obstruction by thrombus or plaque deposits within a blood vessel or passageway.

plaque: Soft deposits of fatty substances that harden with time and produce rocklike obstructions within vessels. Plaque production occurs due to high-fat dietary intake, sedentary lifestyles, and hereditary tendencies in patients with progressive atherosclerosis.

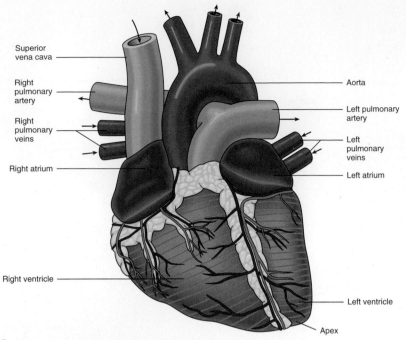

Figure 9-3 Major cardiac vessels of the heart

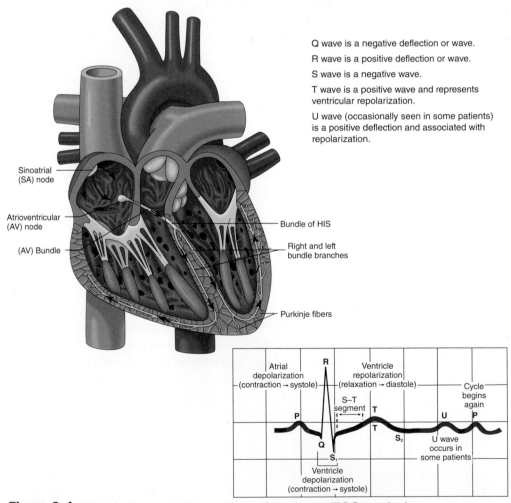

Q wave is a negative deflection or wave.

R wave is a positive deflection or wave.

S wave is a negative wave.

T wave is a positive wave and represents ventricular repolarization.

U wave (occasionally seen in some patients) is a positive deflection and associated with repolarization.

Figure 9-4 Electrical conduction system of the heart (ECG tracing)

Exercise 9.1

1. Name the two phases of the cardiac cycle: _____ and _____.

2. Name the three layers of heart muscle: _____, _____, and
_____.

3. Fill in the blanks with the correct term.

The _____ valve is located between the right atrium and right ventricle.

The _____ valve is located between the right ventricle and the pulmonary artery.

The _____ valve is located between the left atrium and the left ventricle.

The _____ valve is located between the left ventricle and the aorta.

ICD-10-CM Code Selection

This section presents guidelines for understanding the unique code selection for cardiology. Chapter 9 of ICD-10-CM, the Diseases of the Circulatory System (I10-I99) contains code sections for the following:

I00–I02 Acute rheumatic fever

I05–I09 Chronic rheumatic fever

I10–I15 Hypertensive diseases

I20–I25 Ischemic heart diseases

I26–I28 Pulmonary heart disease and diseases of pulmonary circulation

I30–I52 Other forms of heart disease

I60–I69 Cerebrovascular diseases

I70–I79 Diseases of arteries, arterioles, and capillaries

I80–I89 Diseases of veins, lymphatic vessels, and lymph nodes, not elsewhere classified

I95–I99 Other and unspecified disorders of the circulatory system

Additional codes are also used to identify the following conditions possibly related to the hypertensive state:

- Exposure to environmental tobacco smoke (Z77.22)

- History of tobacco use (Z87.89)

- Occupational exposure to environmental tobacco smoke (57.31)

- Tobacco dependence (F17 category)

- Tobacco use (Z72.0)

Hypertension

ICD-10-CM does not distinguish primary, benign, essential, systemic, or malignant into separate categories. I10 is assigned to indicate any of these forms of hypertension,

Coding Tip:

In ICD-10-CM, hypertension includes high blood pressure, hypertension documented as arterial, benign, essential, malignant, primary, land systemic.

including high blood pressure. When coding hypertension, there are extensive combination codes related to hypertension with heart disease, heart failure, and chronic kidney disease.

Hypertension with Heart Disease

The official ICD-10-CM Guidelines for Coding and Reporting Heart Conditions are assigned to a code from category I11 when a causal relationship is stated, such as due to hypertension or implied hypertensive.

When the documentation in the medical record:

- States "due to hypertension" *or* "hypertensive," the codes are selected from the I11 area.

- Does not state "due to hypertension" *or* "hypertensive," select both the Hypertension and the heart disease codes. Example: Malignant hypertension *and* cardiomegaly (or cardiac hypertrophy), codes I10 and I51.7. If the documentation states hypertensive cardiomegaly, then code I51.7.

- States "benign hypertension" *and* "congestive heart failure," select both the hypertension code and code for congestive heart failure. Example: Benign hypertension I10 *and* CHF I50.9.

Hypertensive with Chronic Kidney Disease

Early in the care, the physician may have a provisional diagnosis (rule out [R/O], chronic kidney failure versus acute kidney disease, etc.).

- This logic is different from the previous hypertension with heart disease concept. Here, the kidney failure with hypertension is coded as hypertensive chronic kidney disease.

- One code indicates both the hypertensive kidney disease and the chronic kidney failure.

Hypertensive Heart and Chronic Kidney Disease

When the documentation in the chart states any of the following, code selection is based on the combination code:

- Both hypertensive kidney disease and hypertensive heart disease

- Hypertension with kidney disease, it is coded as hypertensive heart and kidney disease

- Heart failure, select another code for the type from category I50

- CHF plus other systolic or diastolic failure, select additional codes

Hypertensive Cerebrovascular Disease (Sequencing and Prioritizing Concept)

Cerebrovascular disease should not be confused with cardiovascular disease. Cardiovascular disease describes diseases that affect the heart or blood vessels. Cerebrovascular disease is a condition that develops as a result of problems with the circulation of blood to the brain and the blood vessels in the brain that affect cognitive function. Some common types of cerebrovascular disease are stroke, transient ischemic attack (TIA), subarachnoid hemorrhage, and vascular dementia.

- In coding cerebrovascular disease, first assign a code from I60–I69, then an additional code for the appropriate hypertension documented.

    EXAMPLE: Cerebral atherosclerosis (or arteriosclerosis) due to malignant hypertension is sequenced I67.2, I10.

Hypertensive Retinopathy

Hypertensive retinopathy is damage to the retina due to hypertension.

    Two codes are necessary to identify this condition:

- Hypertensive retinopathy is first selected from H35.031–H35.039 category, with the sixth digit to describe right or left eye, both eyes, or unspecified eye; then the appropriate code from categories I10 to indicate the type of hypertension.

Hypertension, Secondary

- A code is assigned for the underlying cause or reason.

- An additional code for the hypertension is selected.

- Sequencing of codes is determined by the reason for the encounter or admission.

Hypertension, Transient

Transient means the hypertension comes and goes and is not consistently found. Often this is the diagnosis early in the treatment plan.

- Elevated blood pressure is coded as R03.0, Elevation of blood pressure reading (incidental, isolated, nonspecific), no diagnosis of hypertension, unless the patient has been diagnosed with hypertension previously. As long as the physician has not yet diagnosed the patient with hypertension, select R03.0 for as many encounters as documented. It is up to the physician to diagnose the patient with the illness/disease. This determination of the definitive diagnosis may occur over an extensive period, not necessarily during one encounter or visit.

- Pregnancy hypertension (also referred to as gestational hypertension) that is transient is coded from the O13 category with the fourth digit to indicate the trimester of the pregnancy.

- Review of the medical record is advised for correct coding.

Hypotension

Patients with low blood pressure are diagnosed with hypotension. Orthostatic hypotension, or postural hypotension, occurs when a person becomes dizzy when standing up from sitting or lying down. Symptoms may include dizziness and/or light-headedness, and serious cases may include fainting or syncope. An electrocardiogram (EKG or ECG) can measure heart rate and rhythm and an echocardiogram (ECHO) can be performed to visualize the heart via ultrasound. A Holter monitor can also check for heart problems that occur intermittently. Serious forms of hypotension may require a tilt table test to evaluate how the body reacts to changes in position. The patient is strapped to the table lying flat, and the table is raised from a horizontal position to an upright position with blood pressure, heart rate, and any changes in patient condition checked at frequent intervals. Conditions related to hypotension are coded from the I95 category. Nonspecific low blood pressure readings are coded R03.1 without a diagnosis of hypotension.

Injury and Poisoning

Code selection is a bit different for injuries with damage to blood vessels. First, the primary injury must be determined. Review the medical record to see if an injury to the blood vessels or other anatomy is documented. The code is selected based on this primary fact. Traumatic injury codes (S00–T14.9) include primary injuries with damage to nerves/blood vessels of the circulatory system (S15). The appropriate external cause code (V01–Y99) would be assigned as a secondary code.

Classification of Factors Influencing Health Status and Contact with Health Service (Z Codes)

ICD-10-CM codes Z00–Z99 lists codes used in any health care setting as either a first-listed or principal diagnosis, or as a secondary code depending on the reason for the encounter. Certain Z codes may only be used as first-listed or principal diagnosis. Categories of Z codes include contact/exposure, vaccinations, status, history of, screening, observation, counseling, and routine examinations.

History

Both the personal history of illness and the family history are commonly selected for cardiovascular disease. There are not specific codes for every possible type of medical history.

Personal history indicates the condition is past, the patient is no longer receiving treatment, there is a potential for recurrence, and continued monitoring of the care is required.

Family history codes are selected when documented, and the family history may cause a higher risk of illness for the patient.

Screening

Screening is the testing for disease or precursors to a disease in persons not demonstrating symptoms of a disease, many times for early detection or to determine a definitive diagnosis. Screening services may be performed to review specific diagnoses, or in members of a given age group that has a statistically higher risk, for example, of cardiovascular disease, and may include a lipid panel. Testing of a person to rule out or confirm a suspected diagnosis because the patient demonstrates a sign or symptom is a diagnostic exam, not a screening. In these cases, the sign or symptom would be coded to explain the reason for the test. When the patient is symptomatic, the codes are selected from the Ill-Defined Signs and Symptoms chapter, *not* from the screenings for the rule-out purpose. Select a code for the documented sign or symptom. Do not select a code as though the patient has the illness, disease, or condition.

When an office visit for other illness is performed, which includes a screening service, add the screening code in addition to the illness.

When a screening service is part of another screening, do not report two codes; for example, check of blood pressure is part of a routine physical examination.

When an illness is determined and treated during a screening visit, the screening is the first code and the finding is the second code.

Follow-Up

The follow-up codes are selected for ongoing care after the treatment has been completed and symptoms no longer exist. Code the follow-up as the first code, with the history of the condition as the second code. Chronic illness code selection does not utilize the follow-up concept.

Highlight:

If the illness recurs, the illness code rather than the follow-up code is used first

Misadventures and Complications of Surgical and Medical Care, Not Elsewhere Classified

ICD-10-CM codes T80–T88 are reported when the documentation indicates an incident occurred during the medical procedure. The following are examples of misadventures:

- Blood vessels are "nicked" during an operative session.

- Aspiration of fluid or tissue or a puncture occurs during heart catheterization.

- Sterile precautions fail during a procedure.

- A mechanical failure occurs in an instrument or apparatus during heart catheterization.

When the documentation reflects scenarios of an incident, add a T code to the other diagnosis codes. Additional codes (Y62–Y84) may be required to identify infection following a procedure, mechanical complication of heart valve graft, displacements of cardiac and vascular devices, implants, and catheters.

Highlight:

Have you ever heard "Never use 'rule out' code selection"? The proper code selection for physician services when the documentation states rule-out versus considering multiple possible diagnoses is the Signs and Symptoms ICD-10-CM codes. It is appropriate for the physician to chart rule out; however, it would be improper to select the ICD-10-CM code as though the patient has the disease prior to the definitive diagnosis.

ICD-10-CM Codes for the Diagnosis, Condition, Problem, or Other Reason for Encounter/Visit

First select a code for the chiefly responsible reason for the visit or encounter. The code is frequently a sign/symptom until it is confirmed by the physician.

Then, select additional codes for coexisting conditions that are being actively managed or affect current care. Remember to use the proper combination coding for cardiology when multiple organs or illnesses are present.

Chronic Diseases

The chronic illness code is selected for each date of service the physician has documented treatment for that illness. Otherwise, the chronic disease ICD-10-CM code is not selected and not reported on the claim, even if the illness continues.

> **Coding Tip:**
> The selection and the reporting of the chronic illness ICD-10-CM code might occur when the documentation reflects the treatment of the illness or that the illness is affecting the treatment plan, per specific date of the encounter. Just because a patient has a chronic illness does not justify reporting that ICD-10-CM code by every physician that cares for the patient.

Code All Documented Conditions That Coexist

Other illnesses that are present at the time of the visit, with documentation that treatment occurred, would have additional codes selected. If the illnesses are not treated or treatment is not documented, do not select additional codes. The "History of" codes are selected as additional codes whenever associated to the care for that particular date.

Patients Receiving Diagnostic Services Only

This coding rule commonly applies for cardiology services when the patient receives a diagnostic test and no additional professional care on the same date.

If the diagnostic test is immediately read (interpreted) with the written report, select the code for the definitive diagnosis located in the report. Additional pretest signs and symptoms are not selected. If the report does not indicate the definitive diagnosis and additional testing is ordered, then select the signs and symptoms.

Patients Receiving Therapeutic Services Only

Also common for cardiology is radiation therapy (nuclear cardiography) and cardiac rehabilitation encounters. These require the code selection to prioritize the sequence: first the Z code for therapeutic services, followed by the reason for the care today, or illness code.

Pre-Op Evaluations Only

When the patient has a preoperative ECG, the first code is Z13.6, and the second code is the reason for the surgery. Any abnormalities documented by the physician would be added as additional codes.

The preoperative ECG may be bundled into the admission services and not reimbursed by the insurance plan. Before performing the service, contact the insurance plan to determine the benefits and, if necessary, properly complete the ABN.

Exercise 9.2

1. Patient is scheduled for annual echocardiogram. As documented in her medical record, she was diagnosed with mitral valve regurgitation many years ago after taking fen-phen for weight loss. Patient will see the physician later in the week to review the results and discuss the treatment plan.

   Echocardiogram: Unchanged from previous test

   Select the proper ICD-10-CM codes: _____

(continues)

Exercise 9.2 (*continued*)

2. The patient is diagnosed with cardiac hypertrophy, largely due to hypertension. CHF. BP 155/85 sitting. Continued treatment plan, to be rechecked in three weeks.

     Select the proper ICD-10-CM codes: _____

3. Patient, age 41, is in the office for routine ECG for screening for family history of coronary artery disease. The ECG today is normal.

     Select the proper ICD-10-CM codes: _____

---

4. Code the following diagnosis and procedure using ICD-10-CM and CPT.

PATIENT: Williams, Betty

DOB: 01/20/35

HOSPITAL #: 4507789

PHYSICIAN: Alene Walker, MD

DATE: May 17, 20XX

CLINICAL INDICATIONS: Syncope

METHOD: The patient was brought to the Tilt lab and was placed supine for 5 minutes and was then tilted to 30 degrees for 5 minutes and finally to 60 degrees for 30 minutes.

   Next, the patient again was laid supine. IV Isuprel was administered at 0.04 mcg/kg/min. The patient was then tilted to 60 degrees for 22 minutes, again with continuous ergodynamic monitoring.

RESULTS: The baseline head-up tilt test revealed normal heart rate and blood pressure response following the administration of IV Isuprel. The patient's heart rate fell from 127 to 71/min and blood pressure fell from 123 to 105 mml Ig. The patient felt nauseated, but no syncope was elicited.

CONCLUSIONS: The patient probably does have a vasodepressor component to her syncope; however, the specificity of this test is impaired because the patient did not actually have a syncopal episode while on the table.

RECOMMENDATIONS: It would be reasonable to try a trial of low-dose beta blocker.

Alene Walker, MD

ICD-10-CM code(s) _____

CPT code(s) _____

---

5. Code the following office note.

PATIENT: Jack Jacks

DOB: 10/24/45

HOSPITAL #: 678910

PHYSICIAN: Davis Abercrombie, MD

DATE: October 11, 20XX

OFFICE VISIT: This new patient is in today complaining of SOA, wheezing, cough productive of clear-white sputum. He states he has difficulty breathing with exertion and just generally feels bad. He states he is a former smoker, smoking approximately two packs of cigarettes daily. He did quit this habit 3 years ago.

VITAL SIGNS: BP 186/108 right arm; 192/102 left arm. Pulse 92, slightly irregular. Respirations 22. Weight 202-1/2 lbs. Temp. 99.8°F.

(*continues*)

Exercise 9.2 (*continued*)

EXAMINATION: Exam reveals the blood pressure to be elevated. He states he currently takes Norvasc 5 mg each morning for blood pressure control. Lungs contain many crackling rales and rhonchi bilaterally. Wheezes are noted bilaterally. Heart has a normal sinus rhythm without murmurs or gallops. He has 2+ pitting edema in both lower legs and feet.

PROCEDURES TODAY IN THE OFFICE: ECG shows the NSR. Rate is normal. Chest x-ray, AP and lateral, shows pleural effusion increased in the right lung field. Blood is drawn for an electrolyte panel and sent to the lab for testing.

IMPRESSION:

1. Bronchial asthma with COPD
2. Early congestive heart failure
3. Benign essential hypertension

RECOMMENDATIONS:

1. Lasix 40 mg. one q.a.m. for edema
2. Increase Norvasc 5 mg to two q.a.m. for better control of blood pressure
3. Proventil Inhaler 2 puffs q.i.d.
4. Albuterol 2 mg p.o. b.i.d.
5. Patient is to return for check-up in one week.

Davis Abercrombie, MD

ICD-10-CM codes _____

CPT codes _____

---

6. Code the follow-up office progress note.

PATIENT: Jack Jacks

DOB: 10/24/45

HOSPITAL #: 678910

PHYSICIAN: Davis Abercrombie, MD

DATE: October 18, 20XX

OFFICE VISIT: This patient has returned today for check-up. He states he feels no better since his visit a week ago.

VITAL SIGNS: BP 162/92 right arm; 170/90 left arm. Pulse 88 and regular. Respirations 24. He does exhibit more difficulty breathing. Weight has increased to 208 lbs. Temp. 99°F.

EXAMINATION: Exam reveals the BP to be lower with the increase of the Norvasc on 10/11/XX. Lungs reveal congestion with crackling rales and rhonchi bilaterally. Heart has irregular rate and rhythm today as demonstrated on ECG done in the office. Repeat AP-PA and lateral chest x-ray in the office today continues to reveal the congestion bilaterally.

LABORATORY: Lab studies drawn a week ago and sent to the lab reveal a normal CBC. Electrolyte profile reveals potassium elevated at 9.2; otherwise normal study.

IMPRESSIONS:

1. Status asthmaticus bronchial asthma with COPD
2. Congestive heart failure
3. Benign essential hypertension

(continues)

Exercise 9.2 (*continued*)

RECOMMENDATIONS:

1. Continue Norvasc 10 mg q.a.m.
2. Increase Lasix to 80 mg q.a.m.
3. Continue Proventil 2 puffs q.i.d.
4. Increase Albuterol 2 mg t.i.d.
5. Schedule for a bronchoscopy at outpatient radiology center.

Mr. Jacks is to call on Friday to report on his condition, or sooner if he develops any additional problems.

Davis Abercrombie, MD

ICD-10-CM codes _____

CPT codes _____

---

7. Code the following report.

PATIENT: Jack Jacks

DOB: 10/24/45

HOSPITAL #: 678910

PHYSICIAN: Davis Abercrombie, MD

DATE: October 23, 20XX

HOUSE CALL: A house call was made at approximately 8:30 a.m. to patient's home after his wife called stating the patient felt worse, had more difficulty breathing and chest pain with exertion. He also complains of extreme nausea with vomiting.

Patient appears ill and in acute distress. His wife states he has been too ill to have the bronchoscopy done. Discussion is had with Dr. Jennings, thoracic-cardiovascular surgeon, and arrangements are made to transport the patient via ambulance to Dogood Hospital for further studies and treatment. In addition to the house call, one hour of prolonged service is documented at patient's home evaluating patient's condition and making necessary arrangements for transfer and admission to the hospital.

IMPRESSION:

1. Acute exacerbation of bronchial asthma with COPD.
2. Congestive heart failure
3. R/O myocardial infarction (etiology does not suggest MI and chest pain is probably related to CHF and COPD)
4. Nausea with vomiting

RECOMMENDATIONS:

1. He is given Phenergan 50 mg IM right gluteus medius.
2. Transfer to Dogood Hospital via ambulance for admission and evaluation by Dr. Jennings.

Davis Abercrombie, MD

ICD-10-CM codes _____

CPT codes _____

HCPCS code _____

Evaluation and Management of Cardiology Services

CPT codes are selected to describe and report the work performed in cardiology, using codes from the 30000, 70000, 90000, and Category III chapters of CPT. Many laboratory and additional diagnostic tests may be ordered, identifying the medical indication for the ordering of the study, all utilizing accurate code selection.

The Centers for Medicare & Medicaid Services (CMS) publishes updated information for the federally funded programs (Medicare retirement and disability, Railroad, Medicaid, TRICARE, and Federal employee plans). (See http://www.cms .gov.) The 1995 and 1997 *Documentation Guidelines for Evaluation and Management Services* were created in partnership between CMS and AMA for the documentation and code selection of encounters or visits. The rules state that per encounter the physician may choose to perform either the 1995 or the 1997 Evaluation and Management guidelines. Within each of the guideline sets is the option to provide the problem-focused to comprehensive level general multisystem examination (head-to-toe concept) or specialty examination (including cardiovascular), along with the history and medical decision-making components. It is necessary to review the E/M chapter for further guidance and clarification of the specific criteria required for the code selection. (See https://www.cms.gov for the E/M guidelines under the Medicare Learning Network link.)

Selection of the proper series of codes in the CPT code book starts according to place of service. For cardiology, place of service is very important and will affect the reimbursement dramatically. If services are provided at multiple locations within the same date (midnight to midnight) the guidelines for each code series will direct the coder regarding the code bundling. For example, when an E/M service is performed at the physician office location, and later on the same date the patient is admitted to the hospital, only one E/M code is selected, the hospital admit code 99221–99223, using the documentation from all locations.

Consultation encounters (whether provided at the physician office or other locations) have very detailed criteria for documentation and code selection. The criteria are:

- An opinion or advice *regarding a specific problem* is requested by another physician or professional. "Cardiology consult" is not satisfactory; the specific illness/disease or symptom needs to be documented in the request.

- A consultant may not initiate diagnostic treatment at the encounter. "I'll schedule the patient for PTCA" indicates the consultant has assumed the care without the treatment transition authorized by the sending/requesting physician, and is not correct according to the criteria.

- A consultant provides a written report to the requesting physician so that physician may manage the care for the specific problem. "For ___ (this illness/ disease) my recommendations for you are ___. Let me know if I can further assist you with the care of this patient" correctly describes a consultation service.

The Evaluation and Management chapter guidelines in CPT provide more details regarding the true definitions of consultation and the required documentation. It is important to note that effective January 2010, Medicare no longer accepts consultation codes. For Medicare claims, the coder/biller must assign the appropriate Evaluation/Management codes to indicate if the service was in the office or hospital. Chapter 15 discusses the use of E/M codes for Medicare for consultations.

Critical care services also have specific criteria for documentation. These codes may be selected for cardiology care.

Critical care is the direct care of the critically ill, managing vital organ system failure. High-complexity decision making must be documented, along with the "time in and time out" per episode. The total critical care time (unit/floor time) for the date, midnight to midnight, is then added for the selection of the code. Critical care codes are *not* selected based on the location of the service, and may be provided at any site. Management of noncritical care and no vital organ system deterioration are reported with the E/M codes, and not the critical care codes.

Critical care codes are selected based on time increments. Code 99291 includes the first 30 to 74 minutes, and 99292 covers additional 30-minute increments. For example, 105 minutes on one date is coded as:

99291 $\times$ 1 units

99292 $\times$ 2 units

If the diagnosis codes vary per line on the CMS-1500 claim form, link them appropriately for the actual services rendered.

When critical care codes are selected and reported on the claim in addition to any other E/M services provided by the same physician, modifier -25 may be required. Any additional surgical or other procedure codes may also be reported with the exception of this list of included services:

93561–93562 Interpretation of cardiac output measurements or blood gases results

71010, 71015, 71020 Chest x-rays

94760, 94761, 94762 Pulse oximetry

99090 Diagnostic data stored in computers (ECG, BP)

43752, 43753 naso-or oro-gastric tube placement, gastric intubation and aspiration

92953 Temporary transcutaneous pacing

94002–94004, 94660, 94662 Ventilatory management

36000, 36410, 36415, 36600 Vascular access procedures

> **Highlight:**
>
> Reminder: Medicare no longer reimburses consultation codes. These services are coded as new or established patient office visits or appropriate hospital service codes.

> **Highlight:**
>
> - For the emergency placement of endotracheal tube by laryngoscopy, select only the code for the ET tube placement. The reason for the placement must be documented.
> - Management and direction of CPR as a nonattending physician code selection is 92950. The time for this service is not included in the critical care time.
> - Routine monitoring is part of critical care services; do not select additional monitoring codes. If significant review and monitoring are required, document the time specifically required for the service.
> - Ventilation management and CPAP are included in critical care services.

Prolonged physician services with direct patient contact in the office or other outpatient setting may also be selected for cardiology services. These are selected when documentation reflects the additional time for management of the history, exam, or medical decision making beyond the usual care. This series of codes is not reported for the counseling or coordination of care concepts that may also present. Again, the time in and time out must be documented. The code selection process is similar to the critical care, in that all time provided for the date is added together to select the code. However, unlike critical care services, for prolonged services all additional services and procedures would also be coded and reported on the claim.

Prolonged services in the office or other outpatient setting with direct patient contact is coded as follows:

less than 30 minutes	Not reported separately
30–74 minutes (30 minutes–1 hr. 14 min.)	99354 × 1
75–104 minutes (1 hr. 15 min.–1 hr. 44 min.)	99354 × 1 and 99355 × 1
105 minutes or more (1 hr. 45 min. or more)	99354 × 1 and 99355 × 2 or more for each additional 30 minutes

The details of accurate coding will dramatically affect the reimbursement for cardiology services. The remainder of the CPT codes within the E/M chapter are also likely to be provided by the physician caring for cardiology patients.

93000 Series of CPT

Electrocardiography

Many diagnostic tools may be used to evaluate and assess various vessels; mitral, tricuspid, pulmonary, and aortic valves; electrical pathways; and the heart muscle. Furthermore, some diagnostic procedures naturally progress to therapeutic intervention, as explored later.

Electrocardiograms (ECG according to CPT, or EKG) are performed by physicians of various specialties to assess the heart's electrical activity patterns. Used for monitoring and evaluating many cardiovascular diseases, ECGs are especially helpful with congenital heart disease, congestive heart failure, arrhythmias, myocardial infarctions (MI), and valvular problems. In addition to 12-lead ECGs performed in the office and hospital setting, telephonic or computer transmission of rhythm strips may be performed.

> **Coding Tip:**
>
> Effective January 1, 2005, the Welcome to Medicare Initial Preventive Physical Exam (IPPE) was provided under the Medicare Prescription Drug, Improvement, and Modernization Act of 2003 under Medicare Part B. This is a once-in-a-lifetime benefit that must be performed within 12 months after effective date of Medicare Part B coverage. The codes for the IPPE (located in HCPCS) include the Physical Exam, HCPCS code G0402, and routine EKG, HCPCS Code G0403.
>
> CPT code 93000, Electrocardiogram, is not reported with the Welcome to Medicare exam.

The codes are selected based on the type of ECG and whether the physician has documented the interpretation and report or simply a *tracing*. A tracing is simply a strip that is generated out of the ECG machine. The ECG may be a 12-lead (wires) or less, attached to the patient with an electrode patch. Examples of ECG tracings are displayed in Figure 9–5.

ECGs are an inherent component of another commonly performed study, the treadmill or stress test. Exercise or medications may be used to "stress" the heart while monitoring the activity. The use of medications, such as adenosine, dipyridamole, and dobutamine, during the testing is known as pharmacological stress testing. The medications may be administered via various routes, commonly given orally or intravenously.

Highlight:

The CPT index does not reflect the abbreviations of EKG or ECG. The quickest use of the index is to look up the term electrocardiography.

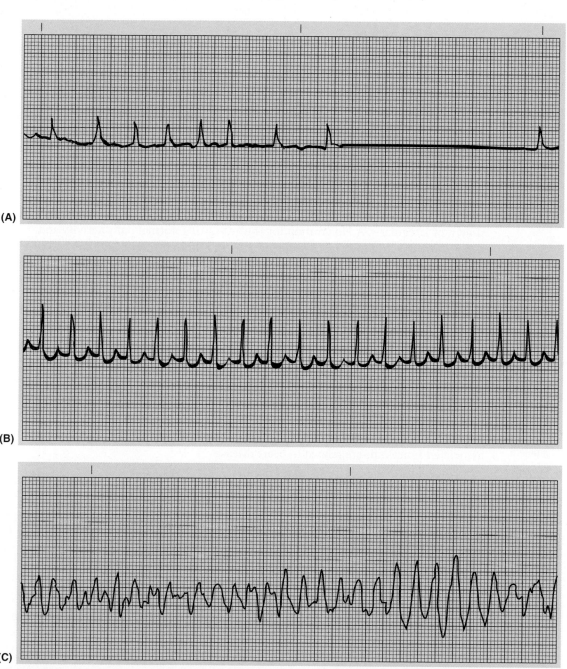

Figure 9-5 Examples of ECG tracings; (A) atrial fibrillation; (B) atrial tachycardia; (C) ventricular fibrillation

Drugs and/or radiopharmaceuticals or radiotracers may be administered either intravenously or by mouth to accumulate in the organ or area of the body being examined to provide diagnostic information for the physician. Thallium or technetium is commonly used.

Stress testing codes are also selected based on whether the physician provides the interpretation and report or simply the tracing.

> **Coding Tip:**
>
> Do not look up treadmill; you will not find it in the CPT index. The treadmill apparatus is used for the purpose of an exercise stress test.
>
> There are two index options:
>
> - Exercise stress test will guide you directly to Cardiac stress tests. This does not give you the option of combination with pulmonary function or other cardiac stress test options.
>
> or
>
> - Stress tests.

Highlight:

Stress tests include access for IV and infusion service and ECG strips. Additional HCPCSII codes are selected for the medications if purchased by the physician

Cardiac monitoring, such as a Holter monitor, is used to record the heart's electrical activity, particularly arrhythmias, in which the heart may beat too fast, too slowly, or irregularly. A Holter monitor is worn during normal daily activity and records any irregularities, usually during a 24- or 48-hour period, with various levels of analyses.

Echocardiography

Echocardiography (ECHO):
An ultrasound of the heart used to diagnose cardiovascular diseases and cardiac valve disorders.

Echocardiography (ECHO) is used to diagnose cardiovascular diseases. It can project the size and shape of the heart, pumping capacity, assessment of diseases of the heart valves, and any abnormalities in the pattern of blood flow, such as the backward flow of blood through partly closed heart valves, referred to as regurgitation. ECHO can help detect the presence and assess severity of ischemia that may be associated with coronary artery disease by assessing the motion of the heart wall. ECHO can also help detect any **cardiomyopathy** and determine whether any chest pain or associated symptoms are related to heart disease.

cardiomyopathy: A condition or general term describing a problem with the heart muscle.

Echocardiography is a sonogram or ultrasound of the heart that creates two-dimensional pictures of the cardiovascular system and also accurately assesses the velocity of blood and cardiac tissue using continuous wave Doppler ultrasound in order to assess cardiac valve areas and function. It detects any leaking of blood through the valves, abnormal communication between the left and right side of the heart, and calculation of cardiac output as well as the ejection fraction. New technology can use 3D real-time imaging. An ECHO is noninvasive and has no known side effects or risks.

Refer to Table 9–2 for common echocardiogram combination options involving multiple CPT codes.

Table 9-2 Echocardiography Diagnostics

Type of Echocardiogram	Description
TTE echocardiogram for congenital anomalies	Transthoracic Echocardiography, complete, for congenital anomalies 93303 Echocardiogram, limited, for congenital anomalies 93303
TTE echocardiogram with spectral Doppler and color-flow Doppler	Echocardiography, TTE, real-time with image documentation (2D), includes M-mode recording, complete with spectral Doppler ECHO and color-flow Doppler ECHO 93306
TTE echocardiogram for normal structures	Echocardiography, complete, real-time with image documentation (2D) with or without M-Mode recording, without spectral or color Doppler echocardiography 93307 Echocardiography, limited, real-time with image documentation (2D) with or without M-Mode recording, follow-up or limited study 93308
TEE for normal cardiac structures	Echocardiography, transesophageal, complete, real-time with image documentation (2D) (with or without M-Mode recording); including probe placement, image acquisition, interpretation, and report 93312 Placement of transesophageal probe only 93313 Image acquisition, interpretation, and report only 93314
TEE for congenital anomalies	Echocardiography, transesophageal, for congenital cardiac anomalies; including probe placement, image acquisition, interpretation, and report 93315 Placement of transesophageal probe only 93316 Image acquisition, interpretation, and report only 93317
Doppler ECHO	Doppler echocardiography, pulsed and/or continuous wave with spectral display, complete report +93320 Doppler echocardiography, pulsed and/or continuous wave with spectral display, limited report +93321
Color-flow mapping	Doppler color-flow velocity mapping +93325
TTE stress echocardiography	Echocardiography, real-time with image documentation (2D) with or without M-Mode recording, during rest and cardiovascular stress test using treadmill, bicycle exercise, and/or pharmacologically induced stress, with interpretation, and report 93350 Including performance of continuous electrocrdiographic monitoring with supervision by physician or other qualified healthcare provider +93351

A standard echocardiogram is known as a transthoracic echo (TTE), or cardiac ultrasound in which gel is applied to the chest and a probe or wandlike device is placed on the chest area to take images through the chest wall. The transesophageal echo (TEE) is a bit more complex, usually with an endoscopic instrument probe (or perhaps video camera) swallowed or intranasally introduced to evaluate the heart valves, chambers, and vessels. The codes are selected by the anatomical site and purpose, and then by the type of the ECHO (complete or limited).

Documentation for the 93306 or 93307 Transthoracic ECHO (TTE) will reflect 2D and M-mode examination requirements:

- All four chambers of the heart
- The aortic, mitral, and tricuspid valves
- The pericardium
- Adjacent portions of the aorta
- Complete functional and anatomical evaluation

- Measurements recorded or the reason not visualized

- Included as seen, pulmonary veins and arteries, pulmonic valve, and the inferior vena cava

If all of the previous components are not documented or provided, the *limited ECHO code* is selected. The permanent pertinent images, videotape, or digital data report and interpretation for the limited ECHO include relevant findings including quantitative measurements and any recognized abnormalities.

Documentation Requirements

If the permanent recordings are not available, the echocardiography codes are not selected at all. Documentation for echocardiograms includes the following:

- Thorough evaluation of organ or anatomical region

- Image documentation

- Final written report of interpretation

Echocardiography may progress to obtain a Doppler pulsed or continuous wave or color-flow mapping study using the same equipment, providing additional information for diagnosis. The Doppler color-flow mapping evaluates the valvular diameters, flow volumes, and pressure gradients.

A9700 for ECHO contrast or Q9957 for Perflutren lipid echo contrast material is the HCPCSII code to select when the supplies are purchased and provided by the physician.

Exercise 9.3

1. TEE is the acronym for _____. TTE stands for _____.
2. Holter monitors are worn to monitor the heart for _____ to _____ hours.
3. When coding for congenital cardiac anomalies, coders should take care that the _____ code matches and links to the appropriate CPT code category.
4. What are the correct codes to report to Medicare for the Welcome to Medicare Preventive Physical Exam (IPPE) and the routine ECG? _____ _____
5. Read the following medical report for an echocardiography study, then assign the correct ICD-10-CM and CPT codes.

Procedure Note

PATIENT: Adrian Babb

DOB: 06/11/1933

HOSPITAL #: 32116897

PHYSICIAN: Jason Finkle, DO

DATE: July 15, 20XX

CLINICAL INDICATION: This is an 82-year-old female recently presenting to Memorial Hospital with congestive heart failure and new onset atrial fibrillation. She is here for assessment of mitral regurgitation after treatment with Betapace and reversion to sinus rhythm. However, the patient is now back in atrial fibrillation with moderate to fast response and is still taking Betapace and Coumadin.

(continues)

Exercise 9.3 (*continued*)

STUDIES PERFORMED: Evaluation includes 2-D transthoracic echocardiography, color-flow imaging, and Doppler exam, and is technically adequate.

IMPRESSION:

1. Technically adequate study.

2. Overall left ventricular size is mildly dilated with normal wall thickness with diastolic function to assess because of atrial fibrillation. Overall systolic function appears to be at the lower limit of normal with an ejection fraction of 50 percent though evaluation is somewhat difficult because of the fast irregular rhythm. Segmental evaluation reveals no gross abnormality though the septum is difficult to assess in terms of its function and the posterior wall is not seen. However, other walls appear to contract normally.

3. Right ventricular size is normal with normal wall thickness and normal overall right ventricular function.

4. There is mild right atrial enlargement and moderate left atrial enlargement.

5. Valvular structures: The aortic valve is a normal structure without stenosis or regurgitation. The mitral valve is a normal structure without stenosis or prolapse and there is a mild mitral regurgitation. The tricuspid valve is a normal structure with stenosis with trace to mild tricuspid regurgitation.

6. There is no pericardial effusion. No gross intracardiac mass or thrombus is appreciated; however, left atrial appendage is never completely visualized.

7. Inferior vena cava collapsibility is normal, indicating normal right atrial pressure. Pulmonary artery pressure is normal.

CONCLUSION: Echocardiography reveals the patient to be back in atrial fibrillation with overall fairly well-preserved right and left ventricular systolic function though left ventricular function is somewhat difficult to assess and mild decrease in ejection fraction cannot be excluded. Diastolic function could not be assessed. There is only mild mitral regurgitation at this time. Right-sided pressures are normal.

Hard copy data are printed.

Jason Finkle, DO

ICD-10-CM code(s) _____

CPT code(s) _____

Invasive and Interventional Procedures

Sometimes, the ECG or echocardiography services do not provide the information for the diagnosis, or the physicians may choose to perform a more aggressive therapeutic procedure that is interventional. The therapy is selected based on the specific issue or illness. For example, the heart's electrical impulses may need electrical cardioversion, forcing the patient's electrical impulses back into a normal sinus rhythm, in a controlled pattern, for conditions such as tachycardia or atrial or ventricular fibrillation. This procedure may be referred to as cardioversion or defibrillation. **Cardioversion** can be performed using a cardioverter-defibrillator or medications. An **implantable cardioverter-defibrillator (ICD)** is a small battery-powered generator that is implanted in patients who are at risk for sudden cardiac death due to atrial and ventricular tachycardia as well as biventricular pacing in patients with congestive heart failure or bradycardia. The implantation of the ICD is similar

cardioversion: An electric shock to the heart muscle, which helps to convert an arrhythmia into a normal or sinus rhythm.

implantable cardioverter-defibrillator (ICD): A small battery-powered generator that is implanted in patients who are at risk for sudden cardiac death.

Cardiac catheterization: Is the insertion of a catheter into a chamber or vessel of the heart, performed for investigational and interventional purposes of the cardiac chambers and valves or coronary arteries.

angioplasty: A medical cardiology procedure in which a catheter with an inflatable balloon on the tip is passed through a vessel and inflated at the site of an obstruction within the vessel wall. As the balloon inflates, any soft plaque is flattened against the vessel wall to prevent obstruction of blood flow and to open up the vessel for blood passage.

stent: Following the dilation of an artery, usually by means of balloon angioplasty, the stent is loaded on a special catheter with an expandable balloon. Both devices are threaded into a guide catheter and threaded to the occlusion site. The cardiologist then positions and deploys the stent by expanding the balloon. The stent is composed of a meshlike material that assists in keeping the vessel open and clear of future occlusions.

to that of a pacemaker. The difference is pacemakers are more generally designed to consistently correct bradycardia while ICDs are more a permanent solution to safeguard against sudden abnormalities.

Cardiac Catheterization

When the physician is evaluating illness or disease within the coronary area (the heart), a **cardiac catheterization**, or angiogram, may be performed. Coronary artery disease (CAD) occurs when the arteries that supply blood to the myocardium become narrowed and may become blocked. This leads to ischemia of the heart muscle, causing angina. Congestive heart failure can also occur. A coronary artery **angioplasty** may be performed to keep the artery open. This procedure includes the insertion of a **stent** (a small mesh tube) in the artery to help keep it open (see Figure 9–8C later in the chapter).

Cardiac catheterization is a diagnostic medical procedure that includes introduction, positioning, and repositioning of a catheter (when needed) within the vascular system; recording of intracardiac and/or intravascular pressure; and final evaluation and report of the procedure. These procedures begin with an access or introduction of a specialized catheter through the skin, manipulating and feeding the catheter into the heart anatomy and conducting multiple professional services while the catheter is in place (Figure 9–6). The catheterization is typically visually reviewed on a screen, may be recorded using various processes of data storage, and captures anatomical measurements while in place. The catheter may also be used to obtain blood samples or measure blood gases.

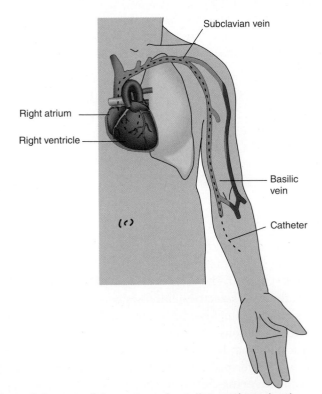

Figure 9-6 One of the possible routes of cardiac catheterization

The 93451–93572 series of CPT codes are for the heart (coronary, within or around the heart) catheterization procedures. The cardiac catheterization procedures often begin as a diagnostic procedure, while during the same session the care may progress to therapeutic or surgical care. There are two families of codes: one for congenital heart disease and one for other conditions.

The catheterization procedures include:

- Local anesthesia of the access site.

- If the CPT code has the conscious sedation symbol, then sedation is included.

- Access or introduction of the catheter by percutaneous (puncture of needle or catheter) or cutdown (small incision over the vessel) method (however, the injection services are not included; power injectors are additionally coded).

- Positioning and repositioning of the catheter within the postoperative time.

- Recording of intracardiac and intravascular pressure.

- Obtaining blood samples for gases or dilution.

- Measurements of cardiac outputs including electrode placement.

- Routine catheter removal, simple closure of the site or placement of a vascular closure device.

- Final interpretation and report.

The placement of the catheter is significant. CPT codes are based on whether the catheter placement is selective or nonselective. In selective catheterization, the catheter placement allows it to be moved, manipulated, or guided into a part of the venous or arterial system other than the aorta or vessel that has been punctured. Selective catheterization includes vessels of the same vascular family. The **vascular families** are defined as arterial, venous, pulmonary, portal, and lymphatic. In nonselective catheterization, the target vessel—a vein, an artery, or the aorta—is punctured and the catheter or needle is placed directly into it without any further manipulation. Codes are selected based on the final placement of the catheter tip. Catheter placement codes are selected for the physician placement of the catheter in each anatomical site.

vascular families: Arterial, venous, pulmonary, portal, lymphatic.

These services include any conscious sedation. Additional HCPCSII modifiers are applied for:

- LC left circumflex coronary artery

- LD left anterior descending coronary artery

- RC right coronary artery

- RT right (used to identify procedures performed on the right side of the body)

- LT left (used to identify procedures performed on the left side of the body)

- If the insurance plan does not accept the HCPCSII modifier codes of LC, LD, or RC to describe the anatomical sites, the modifier -59 with RT/LT may be required.

Figure 9–6 gives an example of the cardiac catheterization process.

Coding Tip:

The catheterization codes are selected by determining the access and the final destination of the tip of the placement of the catheter. As you read the report, make a note regarding each area and the specific services that are documented. This will guide you for the multiple code selection that is common. Watch to see if the tip is pulled back and inserted into another vessel of the exact same vascular family or another vascular family. If along the way the physician cuts, injects, or performs additional professional services, it is possible that more codes may be considered. After you have your notes, then compare them to the codes, the CPT guidelines, and finally the insurance bundling rules.

After you have selected the catheterization access code, then determine if the physician also provided an injection angiography service.

Highlight:

Coronary artery interventions include stent placement, atherectomy, and balloon angioplasty. Select one code for the most comprehensive service per coronary artery with the proper modifier. If additional services are provided in additional arteries/branches, select the add-on code. Do not indicate modifier -59 with the additional therapeutic services provided on the same artery.

Coronary artery angioplasty, atherectomy, or stenting includes the access procedure, infusion, fluoroscopy, and ECG.

Diagnostic right heart catheterization allows measurement of the pressure in the right side of the heart in conditions such as pulmonary hypertension and valvular heart disease. It is commonly performed with access inserted percutaneously into a large vessel, perhaps the femoral, internal jugular, or brachial or subclavian veins. The catheter is threaded over a guidewire and manipulated (positioned) into the right atrium, ventricle, pulmonary artery, and pulmonary capillary wedge. Swan-Ganz catheterization is the common method in which the catheter is passed into the right side of the heart and the arteries leading to the lungs to monitor function and blood flow of the heart. Left heart catheterization focuses on the pumping chamber of the heart. A ventriculogram shows the contractility of the left ventricle of the heart and is often used with cardiac catheterization and coronary angiography to look at the coronary arteries for blockages.

Coding Tip:

- If the patient has existing Swan-Ganz lines and a blood sample is collected, do not select an additional collection code. No additional professional service was necessary for the collection.

- Swan-Ganz catheters are often inserted for patients in order to carefully monitor their hemodynamic status. Table 9–3 lists types of cardiac catheters.

- Replacing a catheter may be performed to prevent further complications, infection, or illness. Although this is a common medical standard, it might not be an insurance-covered benefit for the patient. Prior to replacement of the catheter, an investigation of insurance benefits is required.

Table 9-3 Types of Cardiac Catheters

Angiographic catheter	One through which a contrast medium is injected for visualization of the vascular system of an organ
Balloon catheter	One whose tip has an inflatable balloon that holds the catheter in place or can dilate the lumen of a vessel, such as in angioplastic procedures
Cardiac catheter	A long, fine catheter designed for passage, usually through a peripheral blood vessel, into the chambers of the heart under radiographic control
Central venous catheter	A long, fine catheter introduced via a large vein into the superior vena cava or right atrium for administration of parenteral fluids or medications or for measurement of central venous pressure
Electrode catheter	Contains electrodes to pace the heart or to deliver high-energy shocks
Pacing catheter	Contains one or more electrodes on pacing wires that are used as a temporary cardiac pacing lead
Swan-Ganz catheter	A soft, flow-directed catheter with a balloon at the tip used to determine left ventricular function by measuring pulmonary arterial pressures

Balloon angioplasty of the coronary artery or percutaneous transluminal coronary angioplasty (PTCA) is a nonsurgical procedure that relieves narrowing and obstruction of the arteries to the muscle of the heart to allow more blood and oxygen to be delivered to the heart muscle. PTCA is also referred to as percutaneous coronary intervention (PCI), as this term includes the use of balloons, stents, and atherectomy devices. A small balloon catheter is inserted into an artery in the arm or groin and advanced to the narrowing in the coronary artery. The balloon is inflated to enlarge the lumen in the narrowed portion of the artery. PCI can relieve the chest pain of angina and improve the condition of a patient with unstable angina, and may lessen or stop a myocardial infarction without undergoing coronary artery bypass graft (CABG) surgery. The percutaneous codes are selected per vessel and per specific anatomical site. Additional procedures may be performed during the same session, and often additional codes with modifiers are selected. Figure 9–7 provides a diagram of the instrument within the vessel.

Injection Procedures

Cardiac catheterization codes (93451–93461), other than those for congenital heart disease, include contrast injections for imaging typically performed during these procedures. All injection procedures (codes 93561–93571) include radiological supervision, interpretation, and report.

Transcatheter Procedures

Transcatheter procedures are the therapeutic services that are provided through the catheter. The transcatheter procedure area of cardiology coding is rapidly growing, so watching for new codes and description changes is advised. The codes are for noncoronary services such as transcatheter closures of atrial septal defects under 2D and color Doppler echocardiographic guidance without fluoroscopy. Transcatheter aortic valve implantation is an alternative treatment to the conventional surgical valve replacement.

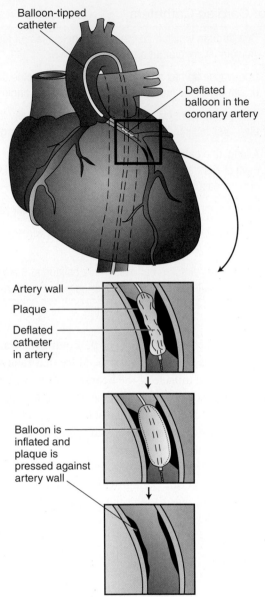

Figure 9-7 A percutaneous transluminal coronary angioplasty (PTCA); demonstrates the function of a balloon-tipped catheter during PTCA

For most of the codes, there are typically three components for the transcatheter procedures, and one should select a code for each component that is documented:

- Catheter placement/access
- Transcatheter therapeutic service
- Supervision and interpretation of the radiology imaging

Intracardiac Electrophysiological Procedures/Studies

Intracardiac electrophysiological studies are invasive diagnostic procedures that include the insertion and repositioning of electrode catheters, recording of electrograms before and during pacing or programmed stimulation of multiple sites in the heart, analysis of recorded information, and report of the procedure. In many cases, patients with arrhythmias are evaluated and treated at the same encounter. In this case, a diagnostic electrophysiological study is performed, induced tachycardia is mapped, and tissue is ablated depending on the diagnostic and mapping information. Codes for these procedures are obtained from the Medicine chapter of CPT. CPT codes indicate the therapeutic interventions, electrophysiology follow-up studies, cardioverter-defibrillator assessment, and intracardiac ablation of arrhythmias. Selection of CPT codes for the monitoring and analysis of **pacemaker** and/or AICD operations is based on documentation by the physician.

pacemaker: Electrical (battery-powered) device that helps maintain normal sinus heart rhythm by stimulating cardiac muscles to contract or pump. Pacemakers come in single or dual chamber models and are programmed to sense and correct low heart rates or abnormal rhythms. The devices can be set to a fixed number of beats per minute.

The 93600–93662 code series also includes the following services:

- Access or introduction of the electrode catheters
- Repositioning
- Recording of ECG prior to and during the test
- Analysis of information
- Report

Arrhythmia induction and mapping are typically diagnostic services; ablation is considered therapeutic, or for surgical correction of a problem. The physician determines the level of care to provide for each patient based on the reactions and findings.

Arrhythmia induction is an attempt to induce arrhythmias within the heart by performing pacing, programmed stimulation, and other techniques. Mapping is performed in addition to a diagnostic electrophysiological procedure and is not reported separately. Ablation is used to treat the tachycardia with the delivery of a radio frequency energy to the area to selectively destroy cardiac tissue. Atrial or ventricular arrhythmogenic pathway problems may be corrected by ablation during a surgical procedure, or with a pulmonary bypass procedure (using heart/lung perfusion equipment). CPT codes 33250–33261 are selected for these specialized services.

Select a code based on the exact procedure that is performed. Again, do not select a code for each repositioning and running test or ablation service.

Patient-Activated Event Recorder

CPT code 33282 is assigned for the implantation of a patient-activated cardiac event recorder, including programming and reprogramming. CPT code 33284 is used to code the removal of an implanted patient-activated event recorder.

The subsequent programming (not associated with the implantation service) is coded 93285. Follow-up evaluation of data is reported with codes 93291 or 93298.

Coding Tip:
When an electrophysiological study, mapping, and ablation are performed on the same date, each procedure should be reported separately.

Noninvasive Vascular Diagnostic Studies

CPT codes 93880–93893 are used to indicate various devices that analyze the flow of blood through arteries and vessels, by scanning or Doppler. The analysis may include the cranial, extremities, or abdominal areas. The criteria for selecting a CPT code require that:

- Hard copy output is created by the machine for all data.

- Bidirectional vascular flow is analyzed.

If the equipment does not provide these two criteria, the vascular study is included in the E/M visits codes and not additionally coded with the 93880 series of codes.

The equipment may progress from B-scan ultrasound to include Doppler mapping with color flow. The physician may require additional studies such as plethysmography or pulmonary studies.

> **Coding Tip:**
>
> Do not look up the test name by abbreviation, such as TCD.
>
>> For Doppler external studies, about the only index term referenced to it is Vascular studies.
>>
>> Next, look up Arterial or Venous, then the Anatomical site.
>
> Other approaches to the index for these tests may also work.

Visceral vascular is the anatomy of mesenteric, celiac, and renal vessels. When reporting 93975, a complete study per organ is required. With the duplex scan, a nonvascular abdominal ultrasound service may also be provided and an additional code would be selected.

30000 Series of CPT

Heart and Pericardium

The CPT codes for the 33010–33050 series are for surgical corrections of an illness/disease of the heart, such as removal of fluid from the pericardium, or removal of a foreign body or tumor. The operative report should clearly indicate the exact location of the surgical services that are rendered so that the codes can be specifically selected.

Pacemaker or Pacing Cardioverter-Defibrillator

Pacemakers have evolved, and often include the insertion of combination cardioverter-defibrillator pacemakers. A pacemaker may be required to regulate the heart rhythm either temporarily or permanently. The majority of pacemakers are implanted to treat bradycardia, a condition with symptoms of fainting, dizziness, fatigue, and shortness of air. A temporary pacemaker may be inserted transcutaneously, whereas the permanent pacemaker may require surgery to insert the leads and to create a "pocket" just beneath the skin for placement of the generator. The work for these services includes:

- Creation of the pocket for the system

- Attaching the electrodes/leads to the proper site for optimal response

- Programming the system (can be done intraoperatively or postoperatively)

The style of single chamber or dual chamber is determined based on medical necessity. The dual chamber electrodes/leads are placed with one in the atrium and one in the ventricle of the heart. If an additional electrode is placed in the coronary sinus vein for biventricular pacing, add-on code 33225 is also selected.

Formation of the pocket subcutaneously is included in the codes. If a thoracotomy is required for the placement of the epicardial electrodes, the 33202–33203 code series is considered.

Another procedure may either be repositioning the electrodes (33215 or 33226) or, more commonly, changing the electrodes (33206, 33208, 33210–33213, or 33224).

Biventricular pacing is also known as resynchronization therapy.

CPT code 33240 is selected for the insertion of an implantable defibrillator system, which includes the generator and leads. If the defibrillator is removed subcutaneously and the electrode system is removed via thoracotomy, select 33241 and 33243. If the physician progresses to insert a new system, select at least two codes plus the 93000 series codes. Select 33241 with 33243 *or* 33244 with 33249 as applicable.

> **Coding Tip:**
>
> The CPT descriptions call the removal or change of the battery "changing the pulse generator." Select one code for the removal and another code for the insertion of a new pulse generator. For example, 33234–33235 in addition to the 33212–33213 code may be selected.

Wounds of the Heart and Great Vessels

The codes in the 33300 series are usually for repairs due to trauma or other maloccurrence (procedural error) purposes. Examples are injuries related to gunshot wounds, stab wounds, or penetrating wounds related to automobile and other accidents. It is important to assign the external cause codes from ICD-10-CM to indicate the reason for the encounter.

Only if a separate incision were made into the heart (atrial or ventricular) for the removal of a coronary thrombus (blood clot) would an additional code be selected. Use of modifier -59 is required.

Cardiac Valves

These codes are selected based on the valve that is repaired and the type of the repair. The terminology for grafts is the same as with the integumentary system: homograft (porcine/pig) or allograft (synthetic). A cardiac bypass or devices such as a ring may be placed as well.

> **Coding Tip:**
>
> Look in the CPT index using these three steps:
>
> 1. Look under Valvuloplasty (this will guide you the most directly to the cardiac valves).
> 2. Select the specific valve: aortic, mitral, tricuspid, or pulmonary.
> 3. Select with or without bypass (use of the heart/lung machine).
>
> Select a code for each valve that is repaired or reconstructed.

Coronary Artery Anomalies

The codes in the 33500 series include endarterectomy and/or angioplasty related to coronary artery or malformation of coronary vessels. These anatomical abnormalities can be congenital and are not diagnosed until a cardiac event occurs later in life.

Endoscopy

33508 is selected to report when the harvest of the vein is obtained endoscopically. The code is a sister code to 33510–33523. Do not select 33508 if the procedure is performed without endoscope and is procured using an open surgical technique.

Venous Grafting Only for Coronary Artery Bypass

If the operative report states venous grafts only, select 33510–33516. The codes in this series include the harvest of the saphenous vein. The codes do not include the harvest of other vein segments.

Co-surgeons or assistant surgeons are likely to participate in these cases. Use modifiers to accurately report the proper person involved in the care.

Combination Arterial-Venous Grafting for Coronary Artery Bypass

Coronary artery bypass grafting (CABG) is a type of surgery that improves blood flow to the heart, typically to treat coronary artery disease (CAD), in which plaque builds up inside the coronary arteries and causes narrowing or blockage that reduces blood flow to the heart. During CABG, a healthy artery or vein is grafted to the blocked coronary artery to bypass the blocked portion of that artery. As many as four major blocked coronary arteries can be bypassed during one surgery.

Coronary artery bypass procedures are reported using either arterial grafts only with CPT codes 33533–33548 or a combination of arterial-venous grafts using add-on codes 33517–33530.

The harvest of the saphenous vein and artery for grafting is included, with the exception of the harvest of upper extremity artery (35600) or upper extremity vein (35500).

Arterial Grafting for Coronary Artery

Hints for the selection of these codes are the included vessels of:

- Internal mammary artery
- Gastroepiploic artery
- Epigastric artery
- Radial artery
- Arterial conduits procured from other sites

Repair of Heart and Anomalies

Services for the repair of the heart, such as septal defect, sinus of Valsalva, and total anomalous pulmonary venous drainage, are not specifically listed in the CPT index. They are found under:

- Heart
- Repair

Heart/Lung Transplantation

These procedures are not provided at every hospital; usually large centers have been designated for this particular service. There are three distinct components to describe physician work. If one physician provides all three components, three codes are reported, plus any additional therapeutic services that are performed during the case.

1. Harvest donor cadaver cardiectomy includes:

   - Pneumonectomy if indicated

   - Harvest of the heart

   - Preservation of the heart

   Additional CPT codes are selected if repair procedures are required for the donor heart. These are not included in the basic harvesting services.

2. Backbench work is the preparation of the donor heart for placement:

   - Dissection of the anatomy (two areas) that is to be placed

3. Recipient heart transplantation includes:

   - Lung transplantation

   - Recipient placement care

Arteries and Veins

The embolectomy and thrombectomy procedures include:

- The arteriogram

- Aortic procedures, including the sympathectomy

The codes are selected based on:

- Arterial or venous

- Procedure performed

- Anatomical site specifically

Endovascular Repair of Abdominal Aortic Aneurysm

Use modifier -50 when applicable for these codes. The codes in this series include:

- Open femoral or iliac artery exposure (access) 34812 or 34820

- Device manipulation and deployment (grafts) 34800–34805

- Closure of the arteriotomy site (access) (not reported separately)

- Balloon angioplasty within the target treatment zone (not reported separately)

- Stent deployment within the target treatment zone (not reported separately)

When providing endovascular repairs, additional codes are often selected for:

- Introduction of catheters

- 34825, 34826 for prosthesis placement and 75953 for the radiological supervision and interpretation (S&I)

- Extensive repair or replacement of arteries

- Fluoroscopic guidance 75952–75953

- Angiography

- Renal transluminal angioplasty

- Arterial embolization

- Intravascular ultrasound

- Balloon angioplasty of native arteries outside of the endoprosthesis target zone before or after the deployment of the graft

- Stent of native arteries outside of the endoprosthesis target zone before or after the deployment of the graft

These procedures often require the professional services of more than one physician, or two specialists. Modifier -62 is selected for each service code performed by multiple physicians.

> **Coding Tip:**
>
> Many cardiovascular procedures require the professional services of different specialists. Modifier -62 is selected for each procedure/service code performed by two surgeons working together as primary surgeons performing distinct portion(s) of a procedure.

Endovascular Repair of Iliac Aneurysm

Use modifier -50 when applicable for 34900. This code is selected for multiple purposes for repairing the iliac artery. The logic is similar to the previous endovascular includes/excludes. The fluoroscopic guidance partner code is 75954 for the angiography of the iliac arteries.

Direct Repair of Aneurysm or Excision and Graft Insertion for Aneurysm, Pseudoaneurysm, Ruptured Aneurysm, and Associated Occlusive Disease

If the patient has a diagnosis of an abdominal aortic aneurysm and occlusive disease, and an open aortobifemoral bypass to correct the aneurysm is performed, code only from this section of the CPT code book. The codes in this series are not selected if the procedure is performed via the vessel or endovascularly.

This series of codes (35001–35152) includes preparation of artery for anastamosis including endarterectomy. Select the codes based on the specific site and the type of aneurysm.

Bypass Graft Vein

A bypass graft by vein requires the harvesting of a vein or veins, which is coded as follows:

- For the saphenous vein, do not select an additional code.

- For an upper extremity vessel, an additional code is selected.

- For a femoropopliteal portion, an additional code is selected.

- For a graft from two distant (not connected) sites, also select the add-on code 35682; no modifier -51.

- For a graft from three-plus distant sites, also select the add-on code 35683; no modifier -51. The use of modifier -50 is reported when appropriate.

The bypass procedures often require multiple codes to report more than one bypass provided during one operative session. Read the entire operative report, making notes of each anatomical site of harvest, whether synthetic material is used, and where the connections are made for the bypass graft. When selecting the CPT code, read the guidelines and parenthetical tips carefully for additional codes to report.

Arteries may be harvested for the venous bypass, or composite grafts. Composite grafts are multiple veins connected together for use as an arterial bypass conduit. The codes are selected when two-plus segments are harvested from the opposite (contralateral) extremity from the bypass graft extremity.

Auxiliary procedures describe synthetic patches for additional services that are occasionally necessary. Transposition and reimplantation are performed to repair aneurysms or traumatic injuries.

Coding Tip:

1. An additional code for the thromboendarterectomy at the site of the aneurysm is not selected, per NCCI.

2. If the thromboendarterectomy due to vessel occlusion is at another site, select an additional code and add modifier -59 or RT/LT as applicable.

3. Also, if an endarterectomy is provided to place the graft, no additional code is selected; just the bypass code is reported.

4. When both aneurysm repair and bypass are at separate noncontiguous sites, select both codes and add modifier -59 or RT/LT as applicable.

5. Only one type of bypass per site is to be coded.

6. If different vessels are bypassed, separate codes may be reported.

7. If one vessel has multiple occlusions, with multiple bypasses at different sites, multiple codes are selected, and add modifier -59 or RT/LT.

8. The most comprehensive code is selected for each site of thrombectomy, embolectomy, or endarterectomy.

9. If a balloon thrombectomy fails, and converts to open thromboendarterectomy, select only the code for the open, more comprehensive procedure.

Repair Arteriovenous Fistula

Select for the surgical repair of congenital or acquired fistulas by vessel site.

Repair Blood Vessel Other Than for Fistula, With or Without Patch Angioplasty

Select from CPT codes 35201–35286 for direct repair of blood vessels, often for trauma purposes.

Thromboendarterectomy

These codes are not selected for coronary artery sites; select according to the vessel. Note that 35390 is an add-on code to use with 35301, should a return trip to surgery be required after one month. This logic is unique within this section of surgical codes.

Angioscopy

Angioscopy may be performed during another case, and if it is documented, select 35400, no modifier.

Transluminal Angioplasty, Atherectomy

Coronary artery disease (CAD) is the leading cause of death. CAD occurs when the arteries that supply blood to the myocardium or the heart muscle become narrowed and may become blocked. This leads to ischemia of the heart muscle and angina. Congestive heart failure can occur. A coronary artery angioplasty may be performed in an attempt to open the artery by passing a catheter to push the plaque against the wall of the artery to widen the lumen of the artery. Figure 9–8A shows a coronary artery angioplasty.

Atherectomy is the removal of an atheromatous deposit (an abnormal mass of fatty or lipid material) that is blocking the blood flow within a vessel. The blockage may be within the coronary artery itself or within any vessels. The fatty or plaque deposits impede blood flow and prohibit adequate circulation to a body organ,

(A) Conventional balloon angioplasty

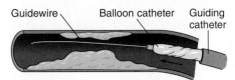

1. In conventional balloon angioplasty, a guiding catheter is positioned in the opening of the coronary artery. The physician then pushes a thin, flexible guidewire down the vessel and through the narrowing. The balloon catheter is then advanced over this guidewire.

2. The balloon catheter is positioned next to the atherosclerotic plaque.

3. The balloon is inflated, stretching and cracking the plaque.

4. When the balloon is withdrawn, blood flow is re-established through the widened vessel.

(B) Coronary atherectomy

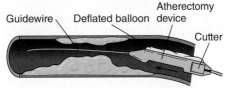

1. In coronary atherectomy procedures, a special cutting device with a deflated balloon on one side and an opening on the other is pushed over a wire down the coronary artery.

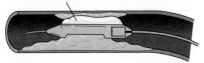

2. When the device is within a coronary artery narrowing, the balloon is inflated, so that part of the atherosclerotic plaque is "squeezed" into the opening of the device.

3. When the physician starts rotating the cutting blade, pieces of plaque are shaved off into the device.

4. The catheter is withdrawn, leaving a larger opening for blood flow.

(C) Coronary stent

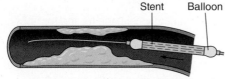

1. To place a coronary stent within a vessel narrowing, physicians use a special catheter with a deflated balloon and the stent at the tip.

2. The catheter is positioned so that the stent is within the narrowed region of the coronary artery.

3. The balloon is then inflated, causing the stent to expand and stretch the coronary artery.

4. The balloon catheter is then withdrawn, leaving the stent behind to keep the vessel open.

Figure 9-8 Procedures used to open clogged arteries; (A) balloon angioplasty; (B) coronary atherectomy; (C) coronary stent

thereby impeding proper function. The physician carefully cuts, or removes, the buildup either in total or in particles and pieces. If removed in one piece, it may be described as an extraction atherectomy. The procedure may be tedious, may advance to a more invasive procedure, or may be discontinued. Use modifier -53 to describe a procedure that is discontinued after it has been initiated. Figure 9–8B demonstrates the atherectomy procedure.

Select one code for the access, a second code for the angioplasty service, and another for the radiological supervision and interpretation.

The two components are often provided with another procedure; add the codes and modifiers as necessary.

If the physician provides the radiological supervision and interpretation, select a code from 75962–75968 or 75978. Select the code according to the access—either open or percutaneous—and then select a code by the vessel.

Coding Tip:

- When any percutaneous vascular procedure of the same site converts to a "similar" open procedure, select the code only for the open procedure.

- When a percutaneous vascular procedure is performed on one vessel at one site, and the open procedure is performed at another vessel and site, select multiple codes. Modifier -59 is added to the percutaneous vascular procedure.

- One access code per site is selected when both the interventional procedure and diagnostic angiography are performed at the same session.

- If the catheter is left in place and another is placed, do not report another access code.

- Do not select a second angiography code for verifying or checking the placement of the catheter.

- When diagnostic angiograms and percutaneous interventional procedures are performed on the same date, add modifier -59.

- If a complete angiogram is performed pre-op, and during the procedure a second angiogram is provided, do not select an additional code. If the previous angiogram was not complete, select modifiers -52 and -59 with documentation of the need to further define the anatomy.

When selecting codes for the percutaneous services, also code for the catheter placement and the supervision and interpretation radiology services performed by the same physician.

Venous Procedures

The codes in this series are selected for intravenous (IV) therapy (punctures through the skin). The infusion services are coded with additional codes if provided by the physician. The codes are selected based on the age of the patient and the type of venipuncture that is performed, whether a sample collection, transfusion, or cutdown.

In selecting the codes for the treatment of veins (e.g., telangiectasia versus varicose), watch the plural versus singular definition. For 36468, the code is selected one time, whether single or multiple injections of multiple veins were done; yet, for other than spider veins, the code 36470 is used per vein.

The code for endovenous ablation treatments automatically includes supervision and interpretation, and monitoring, without having to choose additional S & I codes.

The intravenous infusion service codes include the placement or access services. Do not select an additional code for the access service, whether IV or central venous pressure (CVP) line. Selective arterial catheterization access services are additionally coded.

Central Venous Access Procedures

Central venous lines are used for several medical conditions:

- To measure central venous pressure (CVP) that indicates the heart's ability to work as a pump

- To diagnose underlying cardiac pathology, such as heart failure

- To administer medications or fluids

- To obtain blood tests, particularly a venous oxygen saturation

- To obtain cardiovascular measures such as CVP

- To insert a pacing wire

Central venous access procedures or central line placement uses a central venous access catheter or device to access the major venous system. To qualify as a central venous access catheter or device, the tip of the catheter/device must end in the subclavian, brachiocephalic (innominate), or iliac veins, superior or inferior vena cava, or the right atrium. If it ends at a different site, then select from the other venous access codes and not the central venous access codes.

The access may be through various vessels—the jugular, subclavian, femoral, inferior vena cava, or peripherally (extremities or head). The physician may insert a subcutaneous catheter or place a subcutaneous port or pump or may directly insert it into a port or pump device. Read the report carefully for each possible service component. CPT codes 36555–36597 are selected for central venous access procedures. A complete table is located in CPT at the beginning of these codes to outline age factors, tunneled or nontunneled, and device/catheter:

- Insertion/access of the catheter or device through a new site may or may not be tunneled under the skin.

- Repair of the catheter or device without removal; the physician may use medications or instruments to clear the device and improve the function.

- Partial replacement of the central venous access device when only the catheter is replaced, keeping the port or pump in place.

- Complete replacement of the central venous access device through the same venous access site, exchanged out entirely.

- Removal of the device.

- Removal of obstructive material from the device.

- Repositioning of the catheter.

- If coding for multiple catheters from separate access sites, select the code with the quantity of two.

- When removing the old CVP line and placing a new one at a separate site, codes are selected for both procedures.

Supervision and interpretation imaging codes are selected in addition to the procedures. If the physician progresses to placing medications into the port/pump, additional codes are selected.

Arterial punctures are performed to obtain arterial blood gases and perhaps culture and sensitivity testing or for infusion therapy. The arterial puncture codes are selected for simple line placement.

Hemodialysis Access, Intervascular Cannulation for Extracorporeal Circulation, or Shunt Insertion

Hemodialysis cannulas have a tendency to clot and may require thrombectomy, medical injection, or revisions. Many of the codes have the description of a separate procedure, which indicates perhaps the procedure is being performed as part of another procedure. Review the report for each service, then whether modifier -59 is appropriate.

- The arteriovenous fistula serves as the connection port to the dialysis apparatus. If imaging services are provided, select additional codes.

Intravascular Ultrasound

Intravascular ultrasound is a medical imaging procedure using a specially designed catheter with a small ultrasound probe attached to the distal end of the catheter. The proximal end is attached to computerized ultrasound equipment. This allows the provider to see from inside blood vessels out through the surrounding blood column and the ability to visualize the inner wall of blood vessels in the patient.

The coronary arteries are the most frequent areas for imaging as the intravascular ultrasound can visualize plaque in the arteries that cannot be seen by angioplasty. In addition, intravascular ultrasound can be used to assess areas of stenosis and treatment for atheromatous plaque buildup, such as hydraulic angioplasty with or without stents, and the results of medical therapy.

The intravascular ultrasound services include:

- Vascular access

- All transducer manipulations and repositioning within the vessel

- Before and after the therapy

The intravascular ultrasound may be used during therapeutic procedures, and the procedure is sometimes included in the therapeutic procedure code. Investigate and research bundling issues for the specific insurance plan prior to selecting the additional intravascular ultrasound code. The Medicine section of CPT lists codes 92978 and 92979 for coding intravascular ultrasounds. These are both add-on codes that are reported in conjunction with the primary procedure, such as a percutaneous transluminal coronary balloon angioplasty (PTCA) of a single coronary artery. This would be coded 92982 for the PTCA with 92978 for the intravascular ultrasound.

The intravascular ultrasound procedures are different from many of the other CPT codes, as the access is included in the codes and not separately reported. However, the codes do not include other therapeutic services that may be performed via the catheter (transcatheter) or the supervision and interpretation imaging codes.

Stents

A stent is a small mesh tube used to treat narrowed or weakened arteries in the body and to prevent the artery from becoming blocked again. Stents are deployed to reinforce vessel walls, helping to prevent the obstruction of blood flow (see Figure 9–8C). The stent may be placed within the vessels leading toward the heart or other anatomical sites. If stents are placed within the heart (intracoronary), in addition to within the vessels, a separate code is selected for each. Stents are used in cardiovascular disorders such as coronary artery disease, in which plaque builds up within the coronary artery, narrowing the artery and reducing the flow of oxygen-rich blood to the heart muscle. Stents are also used for carotid artery disease, in which plaque can develop and limit flow of blood to the brain, putting the patient at risk for a stroke.

CPT codes 92928 and 92929 are used to report coronary artery stenting. When a coronary angioplasty or atherectomy is performed in the same artery, this is considered part of the stenting procedure and is not reported separately. The codes for the transcatheter placement into the carotid artery, including radiological supervision and interpretation, are located in the Category III codes of CPT: 0075T for the first vessel, and 0076T for each additional vessel. It is important to select the code based on the exact anatomical structure for these codes.

Ligation

Ligation, or *stripping,* of veins is less commonly performed today than in past years. Today, laser or radiofrequency ablation procedures are the methods of choice to care for large varicose veins. The codes are not selected for phlebitis or arteriography services. Ligation codes in CPT range from 37565 to 37785.

Exercise 9.4

1. Name the vascular families.
2. What is the name of the procedure performed for balloon angioplasty of the coronary artery?
3. What is the common method of catheterization performed on the right side of the heart and arteries leading to the lungs to monitor function and blood flow of the heart?
4. Code the following types of venipunctures from CPT.
   a. Finger stick for capillary blood by lancet to check blood glucose _____
   b. Venipuncture of venous blood for lipid panel _____
   c. Venipuncture of scalp vein of newborn in neonatal unit _____
5. What is the CPT code for direct repair and graft incision for a ruptured abdominal aortic aneurysm?

   _____

Radiology

Radiological supervision and interpretation are required for many procedures. The term *with contrast* is defined as material given intravascularly, intra-articularly (joint), or intrathecally. With cardiology, frequently contrast is used to visualize the vessels either before, during, or after various services. These services require separate codes from the radiology section of CPT.

Injection of intravascular contrast is part of the *with contrast* codes of CT, MRI, and MRA.

Highlight:

- If CPT does not describe the administration component, the administration of contrast code for access is not selected.

- For a risk prevention access line (in case of necessity during the procedure) or to administer the contrast, the access code is not selected.

- If other intravenous injections are performed on the same date, no additional code is selected for contrast administration on that date; they are considered bundled.

Highlight:

According to the NCCI, radiology services include:

- Limited historical inquiry regarding the reasons for the exam

- Allergies

- Informed consent

- Discussion of the follow-up

- Review of the medical record

If a separate, significantly identifiable E/M service is performed by the radiologist, an additional code may be selected, and may need a modifier.

Vascular Procedures
Aorta, Arteries, Veins, and Lymphatics

CPT code book guidelines describe transcatheter care with angiography services. When a diagnostic (when nothing is corrected) angiography is performed, do not select additional codes for the contrast injection, vessel measurement, or postangioplasty stent angiography. Read the description of the CPT codes carefully for accurate code selection.

When a diagnostic angiography is performed with an interventional procedure, additional codes are selected for the diagnostic study when:

No prior angiographic study is available for the surgeon

   and a full study is performed

   and decision to intervene is based on the study

or

Prior study is available

   and condition has changed

or inadequate visualization of the anatomy or pathology

or clinical change during the procedure that requires a new evaluation beyond the area of intervention

If the angiography is performed at a separate session, report all codes.

HCPCSII G0288 is selected for Reconstruction, CT angiography of aorta for the decision for surgery. G0288 is reported in addition to 74175 or 75635.

Transcatheter Procedures

The transcatheter procedures include the components of the contrast injection, vessel measurement, or completion angiography/venography unless the CPT description states otherwise.

Similar logic as in the previous section applies: If the need for the diagnostic test is documented, then both codes are selected. In the absence of documentation, additional codes are not selected.

Fluoroscopic Guidance

Fluoroscopic guidance codes are selected when the surgeon documents the fluoroscopy during the operative session, identifying the anatomy that is visualized. Physicians may describe the service as C-arm or retrograde.

Ultrasonic Guidance Procedures

These services may be performed in addition to the access or therapeutic services for various imaging.

Nuclear Medicine

Nuclear medicine is a specialty of medicine and medical imaging that uses a combination of radionuclides and pharmaceutical compounds to form radiopharmaceuticals, which are administered orally or intravenously. External detectors called gamma cameras capture and form images from the radiation emitted by the radiopharmaceuticals. Nuclear medicine studies are typically more organ or tissue specific, such as heart, lungs, bone, thyroid, whereas conventional radiological imaging focuses on a particular section of the body, such as chest x-ray or CT scan of abdomen/pelvis.

The nuclear medicine CPT codes are located in the Radiology chapter in the code range 78012–79999. Procedures related directly to the cardiovascular system range from 78414 to 78499. The elements or radiopharmaceuticals are also reported. Select an additional HCPCSII code (may or may not be a J code) when applicable.

Myocardial perfusion imaging evaluates the viability of the heart, how well the blood is circulating through the vessels, and the risks that may be present. Thallium chloride or other medications injected twice tag (mark) the red blood cells, allowing the physician to visualize the flow through the anatomical structures, via planar or spectral analysis.

Pharmacological stress may be injected during imaging procedures. Medications such as dipyridamole, dobutamine, and adenosine cause the heart to function as if it were operating under physical exercise. The cardiac stress testing codes are selected in addition to the imaging codes when these services are provided.

Multiple gated acquisition (MUGA) studies are provided to evaluate the cardiac phases of contraction and relaxation, identifying the right and left ventricular function. Gated exercise studies review the wall motion study and measurement of the blood ejection fraction or the assessment of the force of the blood passing through the ventricles.

Positron emission tomography (PET) evaluates the metabolic function of the heart. The medical necessity and the insurance benefits should be reviewed prior to providing the test, as this is a costly procedure and frequently is not a medical covered benefit. Select the CPT code 78459 for evaluation of the heart or 78491–78492 for imaging perfusion.

If the myocardial perfusion and imaging tests are provided with cardiac stress, also select the cardiac stress testing codes.

Highlight:

The access code is included in the procedure code, per NCCI. No additional code for the access service is selected.

multiple gated acquisition (MUGA): Cardiac blood pool imaging; nuclear and multigated ventriculogram is referred to as an MUGA. This diagnostic tool evaluates left ventricular function, ventricular aneurysms, intracardiac shunting, or other wall motion abnormalities. Technetium radioisotopes "tag" the blood's red cells or serum albumin. With the uptake of the radioactive isotope, a scintillation camera records the radioactivity on its primary left ventricular pass. The second pass includes an ECG and a gated camera used while the patient is manipulated to view all segments of the ventricle. Additional views may be obtained and observed after administration of sublingual (under the tongue) nitroglycerin or initiation of physical exercise.

Exercise 9.5

1. Define thrombolysis. _____
2. Define embolysis. _____
3. Pericardiocentesis withdraws fluid from what cardiac structure? _____
4. Cardiac tumors are known as _____.
5. Name the three types of atherectomy. _____, _____, _____
6. PTCA is an acronym for _____ _____ _____ _____.
7. The acronym AICD describes what device? _____
8. "EP" signifies _____.
9. What two main categories do pacemakers fall into? _____, _____
10. A pacemaker "battery" is also known as a _____.

Exercise 9.6

Assign the following diagnoses, symptoms, and disorders from ICD-10-CM.

1. Angina pectoris with benign hypertension _____
2. Atrial fibrillation _____
3. Mitral valve insufficiency, congenital _____
4. Acute ST elevation MI (STEMI) inferoposterior wall, initial _____
5. Abdominal aortic aneurysm _____
6. Anterior chest wall pain, R/O AMI _____
7. Family hx. of ischemic heart disease _____
8. Hypertensive heart disease _____
9. CHF with atrial fibrillation _____
10. Chronic rheumatic pericarditis _____
11. Patient is seen in the Urgent Care Center for atypical chest pain. Electrocardiogram is abnormal and the patient is referred to the hospital for cardiac evaluation and treatment. _____
12. A 72-year-old patient is diagnosed with ischemic cardiomyopathy and is referred to a cardiologist, with a 25-year history of cigarette smoking _____
13. Patient is seen in follow-up for recently diagnosed mitral valve stenosis _____
14. Medication refill was provided for an 86-year-old patient seen on follow-up for her hypertension. _____
15. The MRI results confirmed a recent cerebral infarction, which was determined to have been caused by a right cerebellar artery thrombosis. _____
16. A 68-year-old patient is admitted to CCU for evaluation of an acute myocardial infarction. _____
17. The patient is admitted for placement of a permanent pacemaker, AV sequential, for trifascicular heart block. _____
18. The patient, age 81 years, is seen in the ED for congestive heart failure. _____

Using Modifiers Effectively

Modifiers are selected to indicate special circumstances surrounding the specific encounter or procedure in order to allow the proper reporting on the claim. The procedure or encounter should be described as a "mirror image" of the services that were provided. This will entail use of the two-digit modifiers located in the CPT code book and also the HCPCSII national modifiers that are required by local carriers. Chapter 13 discusses modifiers and their use in detail.

Category III Codes in CPT

Category III codes contain a set of temporary codes for emerging technology procedures and services. The use of these codes allows physicians and other qualified health care professionals, insurers, health service researchers, and health policy experts to identify emerging technology, services, and procedures for clinical efficacy, utilization, and outcomes. According to CPT rules (and HIPAA), a coder must choose Category III codes in lieu of an unlisted CPT procedure code. The Category III codes are updated every January and July and can be accessed free of charge at http://www.ama-assn.org. Some examples:

0075T, Transcatheter placement of extracranial vertebral or intrathoracic carotid artery stent(s), including radiological supervision and interpretation, percutaneous; initial vessel

0076T, Each additional vessel (List with 0075T.)

Per CPT, when **ipsilateral** extracranial vertebral or intrathoracic carotid arteriogram (including imaging and selective catheterization) confirms the need for stenting, then codes 0075T and 0076T should be selected. These codes include all ipsilateral extracranial vertebral or intrathoracic carotid catheterization, all diagnostic imaging for ipsilateral extracranial vertebral or intrathoracic carotid artery stenting, and all related radiological supervision and interpretation. If stenting is not indicated, then the appropriate codes for selective catheterization and imaging should be reported in lieu of code 0075T.

ipsilateral: Same side.

Partner with 34800–34826

CPT codes 34841–34844 are used to code endovascular repair of visceral aorta (e.g., aneurysm, pseudoaneurysm or dissection, penetrating ulcer, intramural hematoma, or traumatic disruption) by deployment of a fenestrated visceral aortic endograft and all associated radiological supervision and interpretation, including target zone angioplasty, when performed, involving visceral branches (superior mesenteric, celiac and/or renal artery(ies)).

Code 34845–34848 for endovascular repair of visceral aorta and infrarenal abdominal aorta (e.g., aneurysm, pseudoaneurysm, dissection, penetrating ulcer, intramural hematoma, or traumatic disruption) with a fenestrated visceral aortic endograft and all associated radiological supervision and interpretation, including target zone angioplasty, when performed; including visceral artery endoprosthesis (superior mesenteric, celiac, or renal artery).

Category II Codes

Category II codes in CPT list supplemental tracking codes that can be used for performance measurement. The codes in this series are for tracking and data collection purposes, and are optional to report on the claim. They are intended to facilitate data collection about the quality of care rendered by coding certain services and test results that support established performance measures and that have an evidence base that can contribute to quality patient care and patient safety practices. Unlike the Category III codes, they may not be selected in lieu of a Category I (regular CPT) code. The Category II codes are also updated in January and July annually. These are the Category II codes that would likely present for cardiology services:

- 1000F, Tobacco use, smoking, assessed
- 1002F, Anginal symptoms and level of activity assessed
- 2000F, Blood pressure, measured
- 4000F, Tobacco use cessation intervention, counseling
- 4001F, Tobacco use cessation intervention, pharmacologic therapy

- 4003F, Patient education, written/oral, appropriate for patients with heart failure

- 4004F, Patient screened for tobacco use and received tobacco cessation intervention (counseling, pharmacotherapy, or both), if identified as a tobacco user

- 4008F, Beta-blocker therapy, prescribed

- 4010F, Angiotensin converting enzyme inhibitor therapy or angiotensin receptor blocker therapy, prescribed or currently being taken

- 4011F, Oral antiplatelet therapy, prescribed

- 4012F, Warfarin therapy, prescribed

- 4013F, Statin therapy, prescribed

Exercise 9.7

Code the following procedures and services from CPT.

1. Insertion of dual chamber pacemaker _____
2. Routine venipuncture _____
3. Electrocardiogram, 12 leads, with interpretation/report _____
4. Postop hemorrhage of chest, exploration _____
5. Pericardiotomy to remove blood clot _____
6. Pulmonary valve replacement _____
7. 2D transthoracic echocardiography with treadmill with Cardiolyte for stress induction, complete

    _____
8. Insertion and placement of Swan-Ganz catheter for monitoring _____
9. Heart-lung transplant with recipient cardiectomy/pneumonectomy _____
10. Transluminal balloon angioplasty, aortic vessel _____

Summary

Cardiology services progress from the early diagnostic stages, to the therapeutic stages, and to follow-up to check for correction of illness and disease.

Understanding of the anatomy and physiology terminology, the latest technology and devices, and the unique scenarios in cardiology service is required for accurate code selection. The professional coder will continually seek to learn as he or she gains experience in a practice.

References

AMA CPT Assistant. (2015). Chicago: American Medical Association.

AMA Current Procedural Terminology 2016 professional edition. (2015). Chicago: American Medical Association.

AMA HCPCS level II. (2015). Chicago: American Medical Association.

AMA Principles of CPT Coding. (2015). Chicago: American Medical Association.

Centers for Medicare & Medicaid Services (CMS) and National Center for Health Care Statistics (NCHS). (2014). *ICD-10-CM official guidelines for coding and reporting (FY 2015).* Retrieved from www.cms.gov.

Centers for Medicare and Medicaid Services. (2015). *National correct coding initiative policy manual for Medicare services.* Retrieved from http://cms.gov

Ehrlich, A., & Schroeder, C. (2013). *Medical terminology for health professions* (7th ed.). Clifton Park, NY: Cengage Learning.

ICD-10-CM expert for hospitals 2016 edition. (2015). Salt Lake City, UT: Optum360.

Neighbors, M., & Tannehill-Jones, R. (2010). *Human diseases.* Clifton Park, NY: Cengage Learning.

Scott, A., & Fong, E. (2008). *Body structures and functions* (11th ed.). Clifton Park, NY: Cengage Learning.

Texas Heart Institute. (2014). *Texas heart institute.* Retrieved from www.texasheart.org.

Learning Objectives

Upon successful completion of this chapter, you should be able to:

- Recognize and define female reproductive anatomy and physiology.
- Name the primary organs of the reproductive system.
- Define and illustrate proper usage of OB/GYN terminology.
- Accurately assign diagnosis and procedural codes for exercises.
- Sequence a series of codes with the most appropriate principal or primary diagnosis and procedure for claims.
- Explain the significance of global service in the practice of obstetrics and gynecology.
- State the differences between obstetric and gynecologic services.
- Name common diagnostics used in obstetrics and gynecology.

Key Terms

abortion	effacement	menopause	presentation
antepartum	gestation	ovulation	prolapse
anteverted	gravidity	parity	puerperium
copulation	lactation	parturition	retroverted
dilation	leiomyomas	pelvic relaxation	trimester
echography	menarche	postpartum	

Introduction

This chapter introduces the many facets of obstetrics and gynecology. Physicians working within this specialty care for the healthy obstetrical patient and treat diseases of the female reproductive organs such as benign or malignant tumors, hormonal disorders, infections, and disorders related to pregnancy. Basic terms, office and hospital procedures, and diseases related to this specialty are identified and described.

This chapter discusses how to accurately assign diagnosis codes for providers using ICD-10-CM. As a reminder, do not assign diagnostic codes for outpatient services where "suspected," "rule-out," "possible," or "probable" phrases precede the physician's impression. Instead, code the sign or symptom that prompted the visit.

This chapter also explores how to assign procedure codes relating to the specialty of obstetrics and gynecology using CPT.

Unique Aspects of Coding OB/GYN

A woman's reproductive organs are a very private part of her body, and many female patients discuss a variety of sensitive issues with their OB/GYN physician. Tactfulness in obtaining coding information and patient confidentiality must be observed by the coder. Female patients often feel close to their OB/GYN physicians and not only divulge delicate information but want the physician to act as their primary care physician (PCP). This is sometimes allowed by insurance companies and managed care plans, and occasionally the physician is listed as both a PCP and a specialist in the insurance directory. The coder needs to be aware whether the patient is seeking treatment from a PCP or a specialist because this affects the coding of evaluation and management services, especially for annual preventive services. Other physicians involved in the delivery of gynecologic and obstetric services include family practice physicians, general practitioners, doctors of osteopathic medicine, general surgeons, and internal medicine physicians.

Often, the physician's evaluation and management service turns into a counseling session, which may affect the E/M level. If this should occur and if the service is dominated by counseling, the time factor for the level selection should be utilized. Because of the close proximity of the urinary and genital systems, many OB/GYN physicians also diagnose and treat urinary problems. An understanding of urinary system CPT codes 50010 to 53899 and ICD-10-CM codes is necessary. Other unique aspects of coding OB/GYN are mentioned throughout this chapter.

Subspecialties of OB/GYN

Because of the complexities of the female reproductive system, several subspecialties exist to help deliver the best medical care. These include fetal diagnostics, gynecologic endoscopy, gynecologic oncology, clinical geneticist, perineonatologist, premenstrual syndrome medicine, reproductive endocrinology, and urogynecology. See Table 10–1 for a complete description of these subspecialties and Table 10–2 for abbreviations for various health care professionals.

Anatomy and Physiology of the Female Reproductive System

The primary function of the female reproductive system is to produce offspring. The ovaries are the sex organs that produce eggs to be fertilized by the male sperm. The ovaries also produce hormones that control the menstrual cycle and help maintain pregnancy. The sex hormones estrogen and progesterone play a vital role in the development and function of the reproductive organs and in sexual behavior and

Table 10-1 Subspecialties of OB/GYN

Subspecialty	Definition
Fetal diagnostics	Provides antepartum diagnostic and therapeutic services including antepartum fetal heart rate testing, high-resolution obstetrical ultrasound, fetal echocardiography, biophysical profile, fetal Doppler flow studies, chorionic villus sampling, amniocentesis, fetal umbilical vein blood sampling, and fetal surgery.
Gynecologic endoscopy	Specializes in the use of hysteroscopy, laparoscopy, and pelviscopy to diagnose and manage gynecologic conditions. Provides the service of laser therapy.
Gynecologic oncology	Provides comprehensive care for women with gynecologic neoplasms, including the surgical management of patients with cancer and preinvasive disease of the female genital tract. Provides the administration of chemotherapy, immunotherapy, and the coordination of radiation treatments.
Geneticist (clinical)	Specializes in the study of the causes and inheritance of genetic disorders including chromosomal aberrations and the transmission of genetic factors from generation to generation.
Perineonatologist	Specializes in maternal-fetal medicine and provides consultation on patients with complications of pregnancy. Services include genetic counseling, prematurity prevention, fetal echocardiography, and antenatal testing using the most current diagnostic and treatment modalities.
Premenstrual syndrome medicine	Provides patients with accurate diagnosis and individualized treatment for premenstrual syndrome.
Reproductive endocrinology	Provides medical care for women suffering from problems with menstruation, symptoms of masculinization, abnormal milk production of the breast, menopause, hormone replacement, and endometriosis. Specializes in the diagnosis and treatment of infertility including diagnostic laparoscopy, ovulation induction, intrauterine insemination, in vitro insemination, intrafallopian transfer, microsurgery, and donor oocyte transfer.
Urogynecology	Provides diagnosis and treatment for women with functional disorders of the lower urinary tract such as urinary stress incontinence and problems of anatomical support of the female pelvis.

Table 10-2 Abbreviations of Common OB/GYN Health Care Professionals

Abbreviation	Position
CCE	Certified Childbirth Educator
CMA	Certified Medical Assistant
CNM	Certified Nurse Midwife
FACOG	Fellow of the American College of Obstetricians and Gynecologists
IBCLC	International Board Certified Lactation Consultant
LPN	Licensed Practical Nurse
MD	Doctor of Medicine
PA-C	Physician's Assistant-Certified
RMA	Registered Medical Assistant
RN	Registered Nurse
NP	Nurse Practitioner

drive. They are also responsible for the development of secondary sex characteristics. Follicle-stimulating hormone (FSH) and luteinizing hormone (LH) are referred to as gonadotropins, which stimulate the production of other hormones and help produce the ovum (egg). The uterus houses the developing fetus and the vagina provides a route for delivery. The female breasts produce milk to feed the infant after birth.

External and Internal Structures

The female reproductive system consists of external and internal organs. The external organs are called the external genitalia and the internal organs consist of the vagina, the uterus, fallopian tubes, and ovaries.

External Genitalia

The external genitalia, also called the vulva, can be seen on physical examination and include the labia majora, labia minora, clitoris, urethral orifice, and mons pubis (Figure 10–1). The labia majora (large vaginal lips) are the outer folds of the vagina, and the labia minora (small vaginal lips) are the inner folds on either side of the orifice, the opening to the vagina. These serve as protective barriers. Bartholin's glands, located on either side of the vaginal orifice, and Skene's glands (Figure 10–1), located near the meatus, which is the external opening to the urethra, secrete lubricating fluids. Occasionally these glands get blocked and a cystic formation or abscess develops, which may become large and painful, needing incision and drainage. The clitoris, a very sensitive organ of erectile tissue, plays a role in sexual arousal and is the structure that corresponds to the male penis. The mons pubis is the hairy-covered, rounded area in the anterior part of the vulva. The perineum is the area located between the vaginal opening and the anus. This area is often cut during childbirth in a procedure called an episiotomy to prevent tissue from being torn.

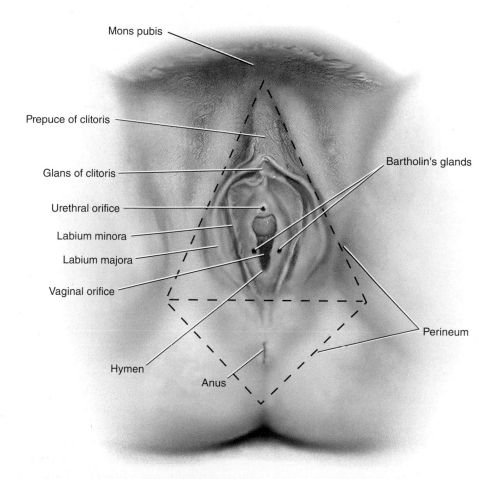

Figure 10-1 External female genitalia

Breasts

The breasts are two mammary glands that are considered accessory organs of the female reproductive system (Figure 10–2). Their primary function is to produce milk for the nourishment of the infant. After a woman gives birth, which is referred to as **parturition**, hormones stimulate **lactation**, which is the production of milk. These glands are divided into a number of lobes that are further subdivided and produce secretions that are channeled through ducts that culminate in the opening of the nipple. The pigmented area that surrounds each nipple is referred to as the areola.

parturition: Labor and delivery.

lactation: Process of secreting milk from the breasts.

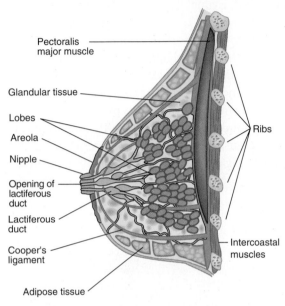

Figure 10-2 Sagittal view of female mammary glands

Labels: Pectoralis major muscle, Glandular tissue, Lobes, Areola, Nipple, Opening of lactiferous duct, Lactiferous duct, Cooper's ligament, Adipose tissue, Ribs, Intercoastal muscles

Internal Structures
Vagina

The vagina is a muscular tube that extends from the uterus to the exterior of the body (Figures 10–3 and 10–4). This thin, elastic canal provides an entrance from the outside to the internal organs. It receives the penis (and semen) during sexual intercourse, which is referred to as **copulation**, and serves as the birth canal that provides a passageway for the delivery of the infant.

copulation: Act of sexual intercourse.

Ovaries

The ovaries are the primary organs of the female reproductive system. They are two small, almond-shaped organs that are suspended by ligaments above and on either side of the uterus (Figure 10–4). They usually produce ova (eggs) about every 28 days during the reproductive years from **menarche** to **menopause**. Menarche is the beginning of the menstrual function. Menopause is the cessation, either naturally occurring or surgically caused. The ovaries also provide hormones that serve the needs of the reproductive cell and/or developing fetus. These hormones, estrogen and progesterone, are referred to as sex hormones and are responsible for the maturation of secondary sex characteristics such as axillary and pubic hair, onset of menses, widening of the pelvis, increased fat deposits, enlargement of accessory organs, and

menarche: Time when the first menstruation begins.

menopause: Time when menstruation ceases.

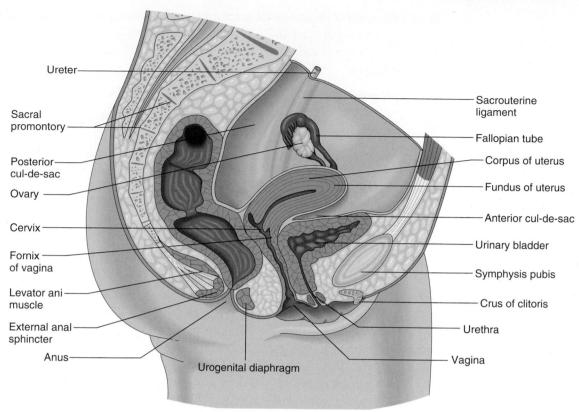

Figure 10-3 Female reproductive organs

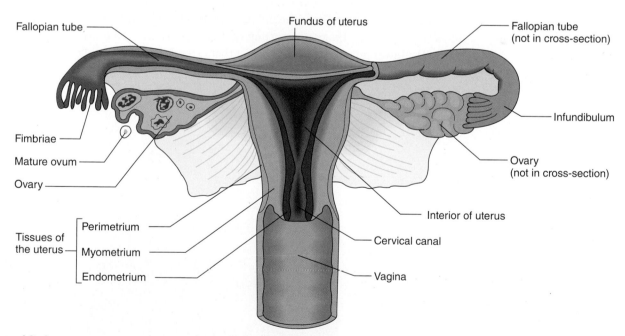

Figure 10-4 Anterior view of female reproductive organs

the development of breasts. Each ovum grows and develops within a small sac in the ovary, referred to as a follicle. The ovum matures under the influence of hormones and the follicle grows and finally bursts open to release the egg. This is referred to as **ovulation**.

ovulation: Release of the ovum from the ovary; usually occurs every 28 days.

Fallopian Tubes

The fallopian tubes, sometimes called oviducts or uterine tubes, originate just below the fundus of the uterus (Figure 10–4). The outer end of each tube curves over the top of each ovary and opens into the abdominal cavity. Although they are not connected to the ovary, the flared ends of the oviducts have fingerlike projections called *fimbriae* that sweep the ovum into the oviduct, where fertilization occurs. The fertilized egg then travels down the tube toward the uterus.

Uterus

The uterus is a pear-shaped structure situated between the urinary bladder and the rectum (Figure 10–3). It is a muscular organ that receives the fertilized ovum and provides an appropriate environment for the developing offspring (Figure 10–4). The wall of the uterus consists of three layers. The endometrium is the innermost glandular layer that is ever-changing with the menstrual cycle. The superficial portion of this mucous membrane pulls loose and sloughs off with menstruation each month. The myometrium is the bulky middle layer, which consists of smooth muscle. This muscle plays an important role during labor as it contracts and forces the fetus out of the womb. The perimetrium is the outer, membranous tissue layer, which is continuous with the broad ligaments that suspend the uterus.

The top, rounded portion of the uterus is called the *fundus*. As the uterus grows during pregnancy, the obstetrician palpitates the fundus and takes a measurement from the top of the fundus to the pubic bone to determine the size of the developing fetus (Figure 10–5). The major portion of the uterus is referred to as the corpus or body. The lower portion, a narrow outlet that extends into the vagina, is called the

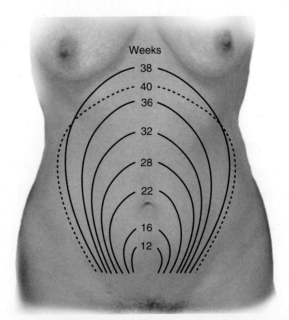

Figure 10-5 Approximate height of the fundus as the uterus enlarges during pregnancy

cervix. The cervix is the neck of the uterus and the area from which a Papanicolaou smear (Pap test) is taken. The opening in the cervix, referred to as the endocervical canal, dilates during labor to allow passage of the fetus. Four sets of ligaments hold the uterus in place and permit it to grow and move during pregnancy.

After the ovum implants in the rich blood supply offered by the endometrium, the placenta forms to serve as a transport system for blood and nutrients. The hormone human chorionic gonadotropin (hCG) begins to be secreted and is essential for the maturation and maintenance of pregnancy. This hormone can be measured in serum blood and urine and is detected in various forms of pregnancy testing.

Obstetrics and Gynecology (OB/GYN)

As the name implies, obstetrics and gynecology (OB/GYN) are two specialties in one. Unlike other specialties, OB/GYN almost exclusively cares for women. For details concerning specific coding challenges, the OB/GYN specialty is divided into separate areas dealing with the pregnant and the nonpregnant patient.

ICD-10-CM Coding for OB/GYN

The Chapter 15 codes in the ICD-10-CM guidelines associated with pregnancy have a sequencing priority. The official guidelines were current as of October 1, 2015, with specific information related to Complications of Pregnancy, Childbirth, and the Puerperium found in Chapter 15 of the guidelines. Chapter 15 codes are often placed first with other codes following from other chapters of ICD-10-CM for many encounters. Should the pregnancy be incidental to the encounter, code Z33.1 Pregnant state, incidental, should be used rather than Chapter 15 codes because no care or treatment of the pregnancy occurs during that particular encounter. The term "not affecting the pregnancy" statement is determined by the provider and should be documented.

Impending or threatened condition. Select the code with these standards:

- If the threatened condition did occur, code as confirmed diagnosis.

- If it did not occur, reference the Alphabetic Index to see if there is a code option for "impending or threatened."

If there are no subentry options under the main condition, code the existing underlying conditions that are present and *not* the condition that is impending or threatened.

HIV Infection in Pregnancy, Childbirth, and the Puerperium

Codes from Chapter 15 always take sequencing priority. If during pregnancy, childbirth or the puerperium, a patient is admitted because of an HIV-related illness, assign a principal diagnosis from subcategory O98.7-, Human immunodeficiency [HIV] disease complicating pregnancy, childbirth and the puerperium, followed by the code(s) for the HIV-related illness(es). If the encounter is for the purpose of asymptomatic HIV during pregnancy, select O98.7- and Z21.

For an asymptomatic patient encounter for HIV testing select Z11.4 for the HIV screening and additional codes for any high-risk behavior. Patients with inconclusive HIV serology, but no definitive diagnosis or manifestations of the illness, may be assigned code R75, Inconclusive laboratory evidence of human immunodeficiency virus [HIV]. HIV counseling (Z71.7) may be added to any of these encounters when performed and may also be the exclusive code for an encounter to discuss the results.

Coding examples for HIV encounters:

Asymptomatic patient normal risk, presenting for HIV testing	Z11.4 HIV screening
Asymptomatic patient with high-risk behavior presenting for testing	Z11.4 HIV screening and additional codes for associated high-risk behavior
Signs and symptoms of HIV of previously confirmed HIV-related disease	O98.7-, Human immunodeficiency [HIV] disease complicating pregnancy, childbirth, and the puerperium, followed by B20 and the code(s) for the HIV-related illness(es)
Counseling (additional code if documented)	Z71.7 HIV counseling

Primary Malignancy Previously Excised

If the primary malignancy has been excised from its site with no further treatment, Z85, Personal history of malignancy, is selected. If the diagnosed and treated malignancy metastasizes to another site, select the secondary malignancy code, followed with Z85 to indicate the former site of the primary malignancy.

Encounter for Current Treatment Chemotherapy and Radiation Therapy

If surgical removal is followed by chemotherapy or radiation therapy, select the neoplasm code. If the admission/encounter is for chemotherapy, immunotherapy or radiation therapy, assign Z51.0, Z51.11, or Z51.12 as appropriate. If the patient is receiving more than one treatment type, assign all applicable codes.

Complications of Chemo/Radiation Therapy

For complications of chemotherapy, immunotherapy or radiation therapy, assign Z51.0, Z51.11, or Z51.12 as appropriate, followed by the complication illness code(s).

Chapter 15 (O00–O9A)

Chapter 15 codes are placed on the mother's claim only, not the baby's. At the beginning of Chapter 15 in the tabular, the trimesters are listed as follows:

- 1st trimester: less than 14 weeks 0 days

- 2nd trimester: 14 weeks 0 days to less than 28 weeks 0 days

- 3rd trimester: 28 weeks 0 days until delivery

Most codes in Chapter 15 have a final character indicating the trimester of pregnancy. Guidelines state if a trimester is not a component of a code, it is because the condition always occurs in a specific trimester, or the concept of trimester of pregnancy is not applicable. The provider's documentation of the trimester or number of weeks may be used to assign the final character. Should the trimester not be documented, an unspecified trimester character is available for use.

Routine Antenatal/Prenatal Visits

If no complications are present, select Z34, Encounter for supervision of normal pregnancy. If other illness is treated at the encounter, do not list code Z34 in conjunction with other Chapter 15 codes.

Prenatal Outpatient Visits for High Risk

Select O09.-, Supervision of high-risk pregnancy prenatal visit as the first-listed diagnosis. Secondary codes from Chapter 15 may be used if appropriate.

Episode with No Delivery

For episodes when no delivery occurs, the principal diagnosis should correspond to the principal complication of the pregnancy that necessitated the encounter. Select as many codes as necessary to report all the complications addressed at the encounter.

Delivery

The principal diagnosis is the main circumstance for delivery. For C-sections, select a code describing the main reason the C-section is performed, unless it is unrelated to the condition resulting in the delivery (e.g., auto accident). For every delivery, an outcome of delivery code from category Z37 is required. Do not select the outcome of delivery codes on the newborn record or after the delivery; it is needed only on the mother's record at the time of the initial service.

Fetal Conditions Affecting the Mother

Codes from categories O35, Maternal care for known or suspected fetal abnormality and damage, and O36, Maternal care for other fetal problems, are assigned only when the fetal condition is actually responsible for modifying the management of the mother—that is, by requiring diagnostic studies, additional observation, special care, or termination of pregnancy.

In-Utero Surgery

If surgery is performed on the fetus during the prenatal time, a code from category O35 is selected. Do not select a code from Chapter 16 (perinatal codes) for the mother's record.

Diabetes in Pregnancy

For pregnant women with diabetes mellitus (DM), select a code from category O24 first, followed by a code from Chapter 4 diabetes code(s) (E08–E13), the type of DM and any associated complications. For Type 2 DM patients, add Z79.4 if current long-term use of insulin applies.

Gestational Diabetes

Gestational diabetes often presents in those who did not have diabetes mellitus (DM) previously. It raises the risk for DM after pregnancy. Select subcategory O24.4- for the gestational diabetes mellitus (DM). If treated with insulin, add Z79.4.

Normal Delivery O80

The O80 code is primary, and "solo." Do not select additional codes from Chapter 15; codes from other chapters may follow O80 only if not complicating the pregnancy. Add code Z37.0, Single live birth, is the only outcome of delivery code appropriate for use with code O80.

Peripartum and Postpartum Periods

The postpartum period begins immediately after delivery and continues for six weeks following delivery. The peripartum period is defined as the last month of pregnancy to five months postpartum.

Pregnancy-Related Complications after Six Weeks

The physician may diagnose a condition related to the pregnancy after the first six weeks. Select the code from Chapter 15 only if the documentation states that it is pregnancy related.

Admission for Routine Postpartum Care Following Delivery Outside the Hospital

When the mother delivers outside the hospital prior to admission and is admitted for routine postpartum care and no complications are noted, code Z39.0, Encounter for care and examination of mother immediately after delivery, should be assigned as the principal diagnosis.

Late Effect of Complication of Pregnancy

Code O94, Sequelae (Late Effect) of complication of pregnancy, childbirth, and the puerperium, is for use in those cases when an initial complication of a pregnancy develops a late effect requiring care or treatment at a future date.

Termination of Pregnancy and Spontaneous Abortions

In the circumstance where an attempted termination of pregnancy results in a liveborn fetus, assign code Z33.2, Encounter for elective termination of pregnancy and a code for the outcome of delivery from category Z37. Subsequent encounters for retained products of conception following a spontaneous abortion or elective termination of pregnancy are assigned the appropriate code from category O03, Spontaneous abortion, or codes O07.4, Failed attempted termination of pregnancy without complication, and Z33.2, Encounter for elective termination of pregnancy. This coding advice is appropriate even when the patient was discharged previously with a discharge diagnosis of complete abortion.

Alcohol and Tobacco Use

Codes under subcategory O99.31, Alcohol use complicating pregnancy, childbirth, and the puerperium, should be assigned for any pregnancy case when a mother uses alcohol during the pregnancy or postpartum, followed by a code from category F10 for Alcohol related disorders. Codes under subcategory O99.33, Smoking (tobacco) complicating pregnancy, childbirth, and the puerperium, should be assigned for any pregnancy case when a mother uses any type of tobacco product during the pregnancy or postpartum. A secondary code from category F17, Nicotine dependence, should also be assigned.

Screening

Screening is the testing for disease in well individuals. If a patient has a sign or symptom, and testing is performed to rule out or confirm a suspected diagnosis, this test is a "diagnostic examination" and not a screening. The sign or symptom is selected as the code. This fact is of utmost importance for Pap testing and mammography testing.

Screening may be the primary code if the purpose of the encounter is screening. If the encounter is for other reasons, list those first, followed by the screening. Do not list a screening code in addition to the routine pelvic examination, because it is inherent. Should a condition be discovered during the screening, follow the screening code with the condition codes.

Observation

If the encounter is for observation of a suspected condition that is not found, select a Z code. If any signs or symptoms are present, select those codes instead of the observation code. Observation diagnosis codes should be used in very limited circumstances.

Aftercare

Aftercare is defined as occurring after the initial treatment was completed, and the patient has continued current care during the healing and recovery phase. There is no time frame specified. If the care is for a current, acute disease, do not select an aftercare Z code. Exceptions to this rule are encounters for radiotherapy (Z51.0), immunotherapy (Z51.12), and chemotherapy (Z51.11). Aftercare for mastectomy procedures is common. Use aftercare code Z42.1 for breast reconstruction following a mastectomy.

Follow-Up

Follow-up differs from aftercare, in that follow-up care implies the condition has been fully treated and no longer exists. They should not be confused with aftercare codes, or injury codes with a 7th character for subsequent encounter, that explain ongoing care of a healing condition or its sequelae (late effect). If applicable, follow-up codes may be used in conjunction with personal history codes to assist in describing the full scenario.

Counseling

Counseling Z codes are not used in conjunction with a diagnosis code when the counseling component of care is considered integral to standard treatment.

Select codes from the Z30 or the Z31 series when the encounter is for family planning (contraceptive) or procreative management and counseling. More discussion regarding the selection of the Pap and pelvic ICD-10-CM codes will be found later in this chapter.

Obstetrics (OB)

Obstetrics is the branch of medical science that has to do with the pregnancy process from conception to childbirth and through the **puerperium**. The puerperium is the recovery time, after delivery, that it takes for the uterus to return to normal size—usually three to six weeks. The obstetrician provides maternity care, including the delivery of the child, and postpartum care for the healthy obstetrical patient as well as the patient experiencing complications brought on by the pregnancy and conditions that complicate the pregnancy such as anatomical defects or disease. Maternity CPT codes in the 59000 series are used for obstetrical care including abortion. This area of medicine is especially difficult to code because of the many intricacies that may stem from a complication, generating complex details that can affect a diagnosis. If the

puerperium: Time after delivery that it takes for the uterus to return to its normal size—usually three to six weeks.

patient were not pregnant, these conditions would be found in various chapters of ICD-10-CM; however, since the patient is pregnant, these conditions have been reclassified to the pregnancy chapter. The following main terms are used to locate various pregnancy complications in the Alphabetic Index of ICD-10-CM:

1. Childbirth

2. Delivery

3. Labor

4. Pregnancy

5. Puerperium

Newborn services are coded separately from the mother's services. Use a code from category Z37 to identify the outcome of delivery on the mother's chart.

Terms Common to OB

gravidity: Term used to indicate the number of pregnancies a woman has had; gravida is used with numerals (e.g., 0, I, II).

parity: Term used to indicate the number of pregnancies in which the fetus has reached viability; approximately 22 weeks of gestation. May also be used with a series of numbers to indicate the number of full-term infants, pre-term infants, abortions, and living children (e.g., para 0-1-0-1).

Gravidity and **parity** are terms used to describe a woman's history of pregnancy and childbirth. Gravidity refers to the number of pregnancies and parity refers to the number of pregnancies in which the fetus has reached viability, approximately 22 weeks of gestation. See Table 10-3 for a complete description of terms relating to reproductive history.

Table 10-3 Terms Relating to Reproductive History

Term	Meaning
Para	A term used with numerals to designate the number of pregnancies that have resulted in the birth of a viable offspring
Nullipara (0)	No live offspring
Unipara (i)	One live offspring
Bipara (ii)	Two live offspring
Tripara (iii)	Three live offspring
Quadripara (iv)	Four live offspring
Multipara	Two or more live offspring (also called pluripara)
Para 0-2-3-2	Series of numbers used to indicate the complete reproductive history. When a series of numbers are used:
Para 0	The first number represents full-term infants.
Para 0–2	The second number represents preterm infants.
Para 0-2-3	The third number represents abortions.
Para 0-2-3-2	The fourth number represents living children.
Gravida (g)	Pregnant woman
Primigravida	First pregnancy (also called unigravida)
Primipara	Delivery of one offspring regardless of whether it is alive or dead
Secundigravida	Second pregnancy
Multigravida	Many pregnancies (also called plurigravida)
G-2 para-1	Combination of gravidity and parity; two pregnancies with one live birth

The time while a woman is pregnant and fetal development takes place is referred to as **gestation**. The pregnancy is divided into three **trimesters**. The total gestation, from fertilization of the ovum to delivery of the baby, is approximately 266 days. However, the figure 280 days is used most often to calculate the estimated date of delivery (EDD) starting from the first day of the last menstrual period (LMP). The time from the LMP to less than 14 weeks and 0 days make up the first trimester. The fertilized ovum is referred to as an embryo during the first eight weeks of life. Starting from the 14th week of gestation to the end of the 27th week make up the second trimester. The third trimester starts at the 28th week of gestation and extends to the estimated date of confinement (EDC). When coding, it is important to understand what trimester a patient is in. In ICD-10-CM, the trimester is typically the sixth character in the code. The severity of a condition accompanying pregnancy can often be substantiated by the number of weeks of gestation in which it occurs. Instructional notes at the beginning of Chapter 15 require use of an additional code from Category ZA3 to indicate the weeks of gestation for all codes within the chapter.

Rhythmic contractions, dilation of the cervix, and a discharge of bloody mucus from the cervix and vagina, referred to as "show," mark the start of true labor. Labor is divided into three stages. Stage 1, the dilation stage, is the time from the onset of true labor to the complete dilation of the cervix, which usually reaches 10 cm in diameter. This may last from 6 to 24 hours and is the longest stage. Stage 2, the expulsion stage, is the period from full dilation to delivery of the infant. This stage usually takes about an hour for the first birth and approximately 20 minutes for subsequent births, but may take as long as two hours. Stage 3, the placental stage, is the final phase when the placenta, also called afterbirth, is delivered. This stage is usually accomplished in 15 minutes. See Figure 10–6. Failure to progress in any of the above stages of labor may constitute a complication and the possible need for a cesarean section to secure safe delivery of the fetus. Complications may include obstructed labor, abnormality of forces of labor, and long labor.

gestation: Time in which a woman is pregnant and fetal development takes place.

trimester: First, second, and third three-month period of which the pregnancy is divided.

Maternity Package of CPT

One of the unusual aspects of OB is the global fee that encompasses the **antepartum**, delivery, and **postpartum** period of a normal pregnancy. The initial and subsequent history; all physical examinations; recording of blood pressure, weight, fetal heart tones; routine urinalysis; and monthly visits up to 28 weeks' gestation are included in antepartum care. After 28 weeks, biweekly visits up to 36 weeks' gestation, and then weekly visits until delivery are also covered in antepartum care. All other visits or services should be coded separately.

Delivery services include the hospital admission with history and physical, the management of uncomplicated labor, and the vaginal or cesarean delivery. Episiotomy and use of forceps are also included. Any medical problems complicating the labor and delivery management should be coded separately utilizing codes in the Evaluation and Management section and Medicine section of the CPT manual.

Normal, uncomplicated hospital and office visits for six weeks following vaginal or cesarean section (C/S) delivery are included in postpartum care.

Because of the extended length of care of the OB patient, it is not unusual for more than one physician to provide complete obstetrical care. If a physician provides part or all of the antepartum and/or postpartum care but does not perform delivery due to referral to another physician or termination of pregnancy by abortion, the antepartum and postpartum care CPT codes 59409–59410 and 59414–59430 should be used.

antepartum: Time of pregnancy from conception to onset of delivery.

postpartum: Time after giving birth.

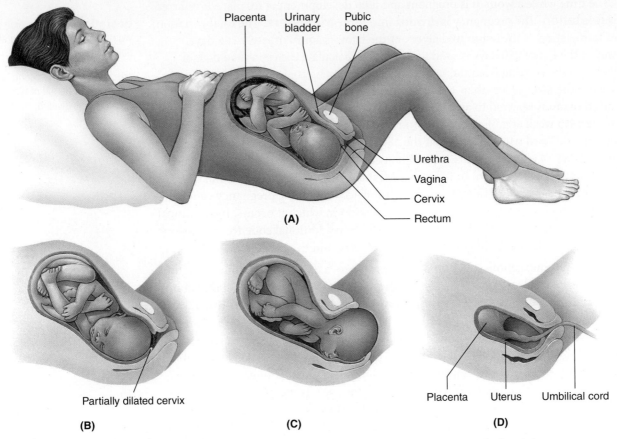

Figure 10-6 (A) Proper position of the fetus before labor and subsequent stages during labor;
(B) Stage 1: dilation; (C) Stage 2: expulsion; and (D) Stage 3: placental

Other E/M services used in OB include a new or established patient office visit to determine pregnancy, hospital observation services, office and hospital consultations, emergency department services, possible critical care services, and newborn care.

> **Coding Tip:**
>
> Trimesters at a glance:
>
> 1. First trimester—Conception to 14 weeks
> 2. Second trimester—14 weeks to 28 weeks
> 3. Third trimester—28 weeks to birth (typically 40 weeks)

Exercise 10.1

Use the ICD-10-CM and CPT manuals to code the following exercises.

1. At the physician's office, the obstetrician performs an ultrasound on a pregnant patient, 16 weeks' gestation, for complete fetal and maternal evaluation:

(continues)

Exercise 10.1 (continued)

One fetus, chorionic sac intact, measurement 20 grams, intracranial, spinal, abd, heart, cord, amniotic fluid, and placenta. The outcome proves a uterine-size date discrepancy.

What CPT and ICD-10-CM code(s) would be used to bill for this ultrasound service?

2. An obstetrical patient has just delivered twins. One is liveborn and one is stillborn. What ICD-10-CM code(s) would be used to show the outcome of delivery?

3. A woman was seeing her OB/GYN physician for part of her pregnancy until the physician moved to another city, necessitating her to establish care else where. What CPT code would this physician use to bill for the first five prenatal visits?

Maternity Care and Delivery of Normal Pregnancy

The vast majority of OB cases provided without complication and with a vaginal delivery, can be coded using CPT code 59400, Routine obstetric care including antepartum care, vaginal delivery (with or without episiotomy, and/or forceps), and postpartum care. ICD-10-CM code O80, Encounter for full-term uncomplicated delivery and Z37.0, indicating the outcome of delivery as a single liveborn infant, would be appropriate. For a cesarean delivery with routine obstetric care including antepartum and postpartum care, CPT code 59510 is used. Occasionally patients who have had a previous cesarean may successfully deliver vaginally. When this occurs, codes for VBAC (vaginal birth after cesarean), 59610–59614, are used.

Fetal monitoring during labor by the attending physician is considered a part of the obstetrical package. If a consulting obstetrician or perinatologist performs fetal monitoring during labor with written report, CPT codes 59050 or 59051 may be reported. Fetal nonstress tests and fetal contraction stress tests may be reported separately.

Complications In and Of Pregnancy

When a patient is admitted because of a condition that is complicating the pregnancy or is a complication of pregnancy, the code for the obstetric complication should be the principal diagnosis. Additional codes to add detail and specificity may be used where appropriate.

Some of the more common complications of pregnancy include anemia, gestational diabetes, and hydramnios. Anemia is a below-normal level of the number of erythrocytes (RBCs), the concentration of hemoglobin, or the volume of packed red blood cells (RBCs). These all affect the oxygen-carrying capacity of the blood and can be diagnosed by an abnormal complete blood count (CBC) or hematocrit (HCT), which is included in a routine prenatal laboratory test or obstetric panel. Gestational diabetes occurs when there is an onset of glucose intolerance during pregnancy. This can be determined from a fasting blood sugar (FBS) test to screen for diabetes. The patient may also have to undergo a postprandial (PP) blood test or glucose tolerance test (GTT) to better determine the level of intolerance. Hydramnios refers to an excess amount of amniotic fluid, which is seen on an ultrasound.

Toxemia is a rarer complication that may arise in pregnancy, as is toxoplasmosis. Toxemia, a potentially life-threatening condition for the patient and fetus, occurs most frequently in primiparas (see Table 10–4) who are 12 to 18 years old and women 35 years of age and older. It is rarely apparent before the twenty-fourth week of pregnancy. The toxemic patient presents with pregnancy-induced hypertension, proteinuria, and edema. This condition is also known as preeclampsia and if the patient's condition is not successfully treated, it may progress to eclampsia. As symptoms worsen, the patient may experience sudden weight gain, headaches, dizziness, spots before the eyes, nausea, and vomiting and ultimately have a seizure. If convulsions occur, they may result in abruptio placentae, which is a separation of the placenta from the uterus.

Toxoplasmosis is an acute or chronic widespread disease of animals and humans caused by the parasite *Toxoplasma gondii*. It is acquired by eating uncooked lamb, pork, or goat meat and by exposure to infected cat litter. It can infect a fetus transplacentally as a result of maternal infection. If the mother acquires toxoplasmosis, lesions may occur in the brain, heart, liver, lungs, and muscles. If the fetus contracts the congenital form, central nervous system lesions may occur, causing blindness, brain defects, and death.

The appropriate diagnosis code should be applied as the secondary diagnosis if a pregnant patient suffers an infection. A pregnancy complication code is to be coded first, as this would be a complication to the pregnancy. ICD-10-CM guidelines and the tabular for infections often reference to use an additional code from Chapter 1 (Infectious and Parasitic Diseases) to identify the infectious or parastic disease if known.

EXAMPLE:

O03.37	Sepsis following incomplete spontaneous abortion
A40.3	Sepsis due to Streptococcus pneumoniae
B95.0	Streptococcus, group A, as the cause of diseases classified elsewhere

Sepsis and septic shock associated with abortion, ectopic pregnancy, and molar pregnancy are typically classified to codes O03–O07 and O08 in Chapter 15.

Various medications may be used to rid complications of pregnancy, such as Braxton-Hicks contractions or premature **dilation**. Braxton-Hicks contractions are light, usually painless, irregular uterine contractions that gradually increase in intensity and frequency and become more rhythmic during the third trimester. They are often referred to as *false labor*. Although usually harmless, if they occur with great frequency during the first or second trimester, they occasionally cause premature **effacement** and/or dilation of the cervix. Effacement is the obliteration of the cervix as it shortens from 1 or 2 centimeters in length to paper thin, leaving only the external os. Dilation is the stretching and opening of the cervix during labor to facilitate the baby's passage through the pelvis. The stages of effacement and dilation usually let the health care staff determine how close a mother is to delivery. An oral or injectable medication, such as terbutaline sulfate, may be administered to "calm down" the Braxton-Hicks contractions and delay delivery of a premature infant. Appropriate injection codes from the Medicine section of the CPT and possible HCPCS Level II codes should be assigned to such situations.

dilation: Stretching and opening of the cervix during labor to facilitate the baby's passage through the pelvis; measured in centimeters.

effacement: Obliteration of the cervix during labor as it shortens from one or two centimeters in length to paper thin, leaving only the external os; expressed as a percentage.

Exercise 10.2

Use the ICD-10-CM manual to code the following exercises.

1. Hyperemesis gravidarum (mild), first trimester _____

2. Threatened labor (32 weeks gestation) _____

3. An expectant woman is on her way to a friend's house for lunch. While driving there she becomes very weak and takes herself to a nearby health care clinic. Her blood sugar is checked, and it is elevated. A diagnosis of gestational diabetes is made. _____

4. A 24-week pregnant woman with current edema of the joint areas and a history of high blood pressure suddenly began to have seizure like convulsions. Her husband called 911 and explained what was happening. An ambulance rushed her to the nearest hospital where she was diagnosed as having severe pre-eclampsia. _____

5. At her scheduled doctor's appointment, a 33-week primigravida mentions that she has been experiencing some bleeding on occasion. She states that it has not been painful; therefore, she only thought it to be normal for this stage of pregnancy. There is usually enough blood to cause her to wear undergarment protection. She also says this has been happening for the past three days. The physician sends her to the hospital for an ultrasound, and a diagnosis of antepartum hemorrhage is made. _____

Multiple Births and 7th Character for Fetus Identification

More than one fetus may or may not present a complication depending on the number, position, and week of gestation in which delivery occurs. With the use of fertility drugs, the number of multiple births has increased significantly. Where applicable, a 7th character is to be assigned for certain categories (O31, O32, O33.3–O33.6, O35, O36, O40, O41, O60.1, O60.2, O64, and O69) to identify the fetus for which the complication code applies.

Assign 7th character "0":

- For single gestations

- When the documentation in the record is insufficient to determine the fetus affected and it is not possible to obtain clarification

- When it is not possible to clinically determine which fetus is affected

When coding deliveries, always include a code for the status of the infant. These include codes from category Z37–Z38, which specify the "outcome of delivery." If a multiple pregnancy affects the fetus or newborn, use code P01.5. This code is from ICD-10-CM Chapter 16, and can only be used on the newborn record.

Ectopic Pregnancy

Ectopic pregnancy is a term used to indicate all forms of pregnancy in which implantation occurs outside the uterus. It is also called tubal pregnancy because 95 percent of ectopic pregnancies occur in the fallopian tube. See Figure 10–7 for potential sites of an ectopic pregnancy. If the embryo does not spontaneously abort, its growth may cause the tube to rupture. This becomes a life-threatening condition as hemorrhage occurs and may lead to peritonitis, an inflammation of the lining in the abdominal cavity, causing future infertility. Surgical intervention is needed; CPT codes 59120–59151 are to be used in conjunction with ICD-10-CM codes from category

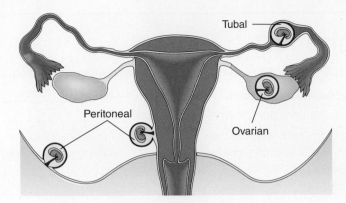

Figure 10-7 Potential sites of an ectopic pregnancy

O00 Ectopic Pregnancy. Any associated complications following the ectopic pregnancy should be captured through category O08.

Placental Anomalies

Abnormalities in the size, shape, or function of the placenta, placental membranes and cord, and the amniotic fluid make up placental anomalies. The most common occurrence is placenta accreta, in which the placenta grows deep into the muscle tissue of the uterus. The placenta does not release at the time of birth and bleeding may occur. Placenta previa occurs with implantation anywhere in the lower segment of the uterus. It may present a partial blockage of the cervix, called partial placenta previa, or full blockage, called full placenta previa. Refer to Figure 10–8. In either case, the patient is prone to bleeding and normally delivers by cesarean section to prevent hemorrhage and interruption of the fetal oxygen supply. Abruptio placenta, as mentioned earlier, is the premature separation of the placenta from the wall of the uterus. This usually happens after the twentieth week of gestation in women over 35 years of age who are multigravidas. This can be a life-threatening condition as hemorrhage may occur and interrupt the fetal blood supply. ICD-10-CM codes from category O43–O45 are used for these conditions.

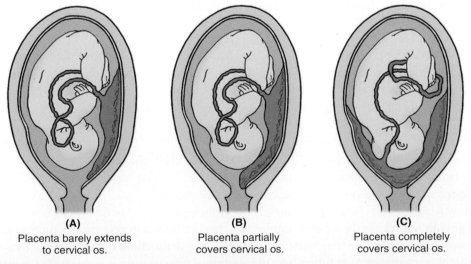

(A)	(B)	(C)
Placenta barely extends to cervical os.	Placenta partially covers cervical os.	Placenta completely covers cervical os.

Figure 10-8 Placenta previa: (A) low implantation (marginal); (B) partial placenta previa; (C) full placenta previa

Postpartum Disorders

Puerperal infections are those related to childbirth and occur during the postpartum period. Cleanliness and sterile techniques have improved the chances of avoiding such infections, and antibiotics have improved the chances of recovery. The treatment of most puerperal infections would fall under the global obstetrical package and not be coded separately. However, in the case of severe infection needing extended treatment, additional codes would be used and billed separately outside of the global obstetrical package.

EXAMPLES:

99254	Initial inpatient consultation
99183	Hyperbaric oxygen therapy
11000	Debridement of infected skin
O86.20	Urinary tract infection following delivery, unspecified

Exercise 10.3

Use the ICD-10-CM and CPT manuals to code the following exercises as if billing for the obstetrician.

1. Abruptio placentae, antepartum in the first trimester. _____
2. Transabdominal ultrasound is performed during a routine OB visit on a 24-week pregnant female showing multiple gestations. The physician informs her she is carrying triplets. _____
3. Laparoscopic surgical treatment of a tubal ectopic pregnancy requiring salpingectomy. _____

Diagnostics in OB

Several diagnostic procedures are used in the detection of pregnancy complications. Included is amniocentesis, a percutaneous transabdominal puncture of the uterus to obtain amniotic fluid. The fluid is examined in a laboratory to determine abnormalities in the fetus. An ultrasound, also called sonogram, may be used to visualize deep structures, such as the uterus, ovaries, and a baby in utero. The use of ultrasound can determine location, position, size, and some defects of the fetus, as well as placental localization and amount of amniotic fluid.

Chorionic villus sampling, a procedure usually performed during the end of the first trimester, can be used to diagnose certain genetic disorders. Fetal tissue is aspirated by catheter through the cervical canal from the villi area of the chorion under ultrasonic guidance. See Figure 10–9. The chorionic villi are branching projections on the outer layer of the developing embryo that provide exchange of oxygen and nutrients with carbon dioxide and waste products.

Abortion

The term **abortion** refers to the termination of a pregnancy before the fetus is viable regardless of whether it was elective or not. A spontaneous abortion (SAB) occurs naturally and is often referred to as a miscarriage. A therapeutic abortion (TAB) is an induced abortion, which is a deliberate interruption of the pregnancy. The term TAB originally referred to an abortion done for the physical and mental well-being of the

abortion: Termination of a pregnancy before the fetus is viable. Spontaneous abortion occurs naturally; also called miscarriage. Therapeutic abortion is induced and is a deliberate interruption of pregnancy.

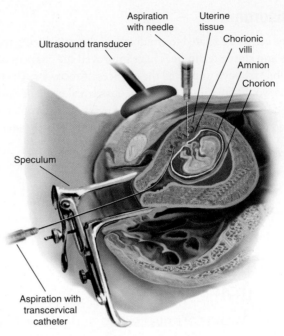

Figure 10-9 Chorionic villus sampling is used to help diagnose certain genetic disorders.

mother; however, today it is applied to all elective abortions. Although the term abortion is used to refer to both the SAB and the TAB, care should be exercised when speaking to a patient who has experienced a miscarriage. Various terms are used to better describe specific situations when an abortion occurs. Table 10–4 offers a complete listing of these terms with definitions. CPT codes 59812 to 59857, found under Maternity Care and Delivery in the Surgery section, are used for various types of abortion. Medical treatment of spontaneous complete abortion should be coded using Evaluation and Management codes 99201–99215 when seen in the office. Occasionally, a patient will be placed under observation in a hospital due to a spontaneous abortion. Evaluation and Management observation codes 99217–99226 or 99234–99236 would be commonly assigned, or hospital inpatient E/M codes 99221–99223, 99231–99233 would be assigned if the patient required admission to inpatient status.

Table 10-4 Types of Abortion

Type	Definition
Accidental	Abortion that occurs spontaneously
Ampullar	Tubal abortion
Artificial	Abortion surgically induced
Complete abortion	Abortion in which the complete products of conception are expelled
Criminal abortion	Illegal abortion
Early abortion	Abortion within the first 12 weeks of pregnancy
Elective abortion	Induced abortion done at the request of the mother for other than therapeutic reasons
Habitual abortion	Three or more consecutive spontaneous abortions occurring within the 20th week of gestation
Imminent abortion	Impending abortion

(continues)

Table 10-4 (continued)

Type	Definition
Incomplete abortion	Abortion in which parts of the products of conception are retained in the uterus
Inevitable abortion	Abortion that cannot be stopped
Infected abortion	Abortion associated with infection from retained material in the uterus
Missed abortion	Abortion in which the embryo or fetus has died prior to the 20th week of gestation and the products of conception have been retained for at least 8 weeks
Septic abortion	Abortion in which there is an infection of the products of conception and in the endometrial lining of the uterus
Spontaneous abortion (SAB)	Abortion occurring before the 20th week of gestation without apparent cause
Therapeutic abortion (TAB)	Abortion induced for the safeguard of the mother's mental or physical health; term also used for any legal abortion
Threatened abortion	Signs and symptoms of uterine bleeding and cramping before the 20th week of gestation that appear to threaten the continuation of pregnancy
Tubal abortion	Abortion where the embryo or fetus has been expelled through the distal portion of the fallopian tube

Anatomical Problems

The manner in which the fetus appears to the examiner during delivery is referred to as the fetal **presentation**. The correct fetal position is for the head to present first in a vertex presentation. Occasionally, the fetus may be stationed within the uterus in an inappropriate and incorrect position for birthing. It may become necessary for the health care provider to turn the baby to the correct delivery position. This is considered to be a type of pregnancy complication. Examples include breech presentation, brow presentation, face presentation, shoulder presentation, and transverse presentation. See Table 10–5 for a complete listing of presentations with definitions.

presentation: Manner in which the fetus appears to the examiner during delivery (e.g., breech, cephalic, transverse, vertex).

Table 10-5 Birthing Presentations

Presentation	Description
Breech presentation	Feet or buttocks present first.
Complete breech	Thighs of the fetus are flexed on the abdomen and the legs are flexed upon the thighs.
Frank breech	Legs of the fetus are extended over the anterior surface of the body.
Footling breech	Foot or feet present first.
Brow presentation	Baby's head is slightly bent forward so that the forehead (brow) presents first.
Cephalic presentation	Head of fetus presents in any position.
Compound presentation	Limb presents alongside the presenting part.
Face presentation	Head is sharply extended so that the face presents first.
Funic presentation	Umbilical cord appears during labor.
Longitudinal presentation	Long axis of fetus is parallel to long axis of mother.
Oblique presentation	Long axis of fetus is oblique (neither perpendicular nor parallel) to that of the mother.
Placental presentation	Placenta presents first.
Shoulder presentation	Shoulder presents first.
Transverse presentation	Side presents first; fetus is lying crosswise.
Vertex presentation	Upper and back parts of fetal head present first.

ICD-10-CM codes in category O64 are used for malposition and malpresentation of the fetus and require a 7th character to be assigned to identify the number and fetus that is affected. For example, code O64.1XX0 would be assigned for a single gestation in which the labor was obstructed labor due to breech presentation The 7th character 1–9 for category O64 all apply to multiple gestations. If there was no obstruction caused by the breech presentation, code O32.1XX0, Maternal care for breech presentation, single gestation, would be used in this scenario. The obstruction code for the breech and the breech presentation code would not be used together, as the guidelines provide a clear "Excludes" note reference.

A disproportionate relationship of the fetal head to the maternal pelvis is called cephalopelvic disproportion. Disproportions can be due to an unusually large fetus, an abnormally formed fetus, or an abnormality of the bony pelvis. ICD-10-CM codes found in category O33 are used for various disproportion problems, and O34 for abnormalities of the pelvis. Category O64 would also be used if the condition caused obstruction.

Fetal Problems

When a fetal condition affects the management of the mother (e.g., extra observation, in-depth diagnostic studies, or termination of pregnancy), ICD-10-CM codes from various categories would be assigned. For example, code O33.6XX0 is for maternal care for disproportion due to single hydrocephalic fetus.

Disease

Gestational trophoblastic disease (GTD) is a term used for abnormalities of the placenta that lead to tumorlike changes. Two of the more common types are hydatidiform mole and choriocarcinoma. Hydatidiform mole, also called molar pregnancy, appears as a mass of cysts resembling a bunch of grapes growing in the uterus and results from abnormal fertilization (Figure 10–10). The uterus enlarges and

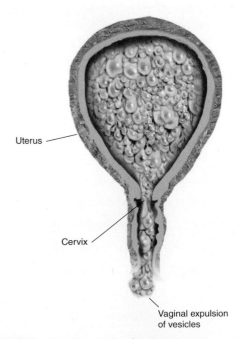

Uterus

Cervix

Vaginal expulsion of vesicles

Figure 10-10 Hydatidiform mole, or molar pregnancy

there are abnormally high levels of hCG, but there is no sign of fetal movement. Some moles are aborted spontaneously in midpregnancy; however, if the diagnosis is made early, abortion is usually performed to ensure complete removal of the abnormal cells, which could give rise to malignant tumors. Choriocarcinoma is a malignant tumor made up of placental tissue and often arises from a preexisting complete mole. The tumor cells are highly invasive and secrete abnormally high levels of hCG. This type of cancer metastasizes rapidly, but fortunately, it responds to chemotherapy if found early. A hydatidiform mole is classified using ICD-10-CM code O01.0, O01.1, or O01.9 unless it presents a malignancy; then it is classified using code D39.2. If a previous molar pregnancy affects the management of a current pregnancy, codes O09.10–O09.13 would be used.

Rh incompatibility occurs when a mother is Rh-negative, the father is Rh-positive, and the baby is Rh-positive. The mother's and baby's blood are incompatible, and, if mixed during delivery, can cause an immune response that results in a condition called erythroblastosis fetalis. In this condition, hemolysis occurs, which is the destruction of the fetal red blood cells. The medication RhoGAM, an Rh immune globulin, is given to the mother to suppress the immune reaction. This is usually administered halfway through the pregnancy and again within 72 hours of delivery. ABO blood typing can alert health care personnel to the possibility of this condition, and amniocentesis can aid both in the detection of erythroblastosis fetalis and in the intrauterine or fetal transfusion. RhoGAM is also recommended to Rh-negative patients who have had an abortion, miscarriage, or ectopic pregnancy to protect future Rh-negative infants. HCPCS code J2790 is the typical code used to bill for RhoGAM injections.

Lactation

Obstetricians are responsible for evaluating the female breast and diagnosing breast diseases and complications due to pregnancy. Disturbances in lactation may be due to a variety of reasons including abnormalities of parts of the mammary glands, anemia, emotional disturbances, malnutrition, and inflammation of the breast, referred to as mastitis. Most procedure codes relating to the breast would be found within the integumentary system of the Surgery section in the CPT manual.

Lactation consultants are persons trained in the art of breast-feeding. If certified, they hold the title International Board Certified Lactation Consultant (IBCLC). They may be independent or employed by an obstetrician, a clinic, or lactation institute.

Maternity Care and Delivery for Complications

There are codes to select for the combination of the antepartum, delivery, and the postpartum services for the *uncomplicated* case. See CPT 59400, 59510, 59610, and 59618. However, when care is provided for complications, select either the E/M codes for complication visits, or alternative procedure codes if the complication procedure is documented. The associated ICD-10-CM for the complication must be linked properly.

The services that are included in the combination codes are:

Antepartum

- Initial and subsequent history
- Physical examinations

- Recording of weight
- Blood pressures
- Fetal heart tones
- Routine chemical urinalysis
- Monthly visits to 28 weeks, biweekly visits to 36 weeks, and weekly to delivery

Delivery

- Admission including history and physical (H&P)
- Management of *uncomplicated* delivery (including delivery of normal placenta)
- Episiotomy
- Forceps delivery

Postpartum

- Visits for uncomplicated care at the hospital and physician office

Typically, besides caring for the pregnancy, more services are performed by the obstetrician. This is a partial listing of services.

- High-risk visits: Select E/M codes with the associated ICD-10-CM for the risk and treatment.
- Hyperemesis, preterm labor, premature rupture of membranes, cardiac problems, diabetes, hypertension, toxemia.
- Visits for primary care purposes: Select E/M with the associated ICD-10-CM code for the illness (cold, flu, etc.).
- Hospital visits during the pregnancy for complications

echography: Use of ultrasound to evaluate anatomy to aid in diagnosis.

- Maternal **echography**
- Fetal echography
- Fetal echocardiography
- Fetal biophysical profile
- Amniocentesis
- Chorionic villus sampling
- Fetal contraction stress test
- Fetal nonstress test
- Hospital and observation care visits for premature labor (prior to 36 weeks)
- Insertion of cervical dilator
- External cephalic version
- Standby for infant (select code 99360 if no procedures are performed, such as delivery)
- Insertion of transcervical or transvaginal fetal oximetry sensor
- Introduction of hypertonic solution and/or prostaglandins to initiate labor
- Tracheloplasty or hysterorrhaphy

Usually, the physician does not start the IV at the hospital; therefore, the physician does not select IV administration services.

> ## Highlight:
>
> Included in the maternity package per NCCI are:
>
> Fetal monitoring during labor
>
> Episiotomy
>
> Delivery of placenta
>
> Antepartum care
>
> Delivery
>
> Postpartum care
>
> Postoperative pain management provided by the same physician
>
> Venipuncture, venous intracath, IV for anesthetic agent by OB/GYN physician
>
> Services that are separately coded in addition to the maternity services are:
>
> Ultrasound
>
> Amniocentesis
>
> Special screening tests for genetic conditions
>
> Unrelated to the pregnancy conditions
>
> High-risk illness services

Depending on the circumstances, a physician or same group practice may provide only the first few visits, prior to transferring the care to another physician. If three or fewer antepartum visits are provided, select E/M codes. For four to six visits, select the 59425 code, whereas for seven or more visits, select the 52426 code.

The same concept may apply for the physician who provides only the delivery or the postpartum care. The CPT describes each of the service options for vaginal delivery or C-section.

During the C-section delivery, the physician may perform a tubal ligation. The code is an add-on code, 58611 to the C-section code. If the patient has benefits for this service, it should typically be reimbursed at 100 percent of the carrier's allowable amount.

Multiple Births and Twins

The coding for multiple births can be very complex. The births may not be equal; one may be successfully performed vaginally, whereas the second may require a C-section. Next, the diagnosis codes may vary between Baby A and Baby B. The insurance plan may further have special policies for reporting the services, so inquiry prior to submitting the claim should be accomplished. Submitting each service per line item is frequently required when coding for multiple births.

Highlight:

Patients who are followed by the same provider throughout the antepartum, delivery, and postpartum for twins or multiple births may utilize one of the global OB service codes if applicable. Consider the typical twin birth example:

Uneventful antepartum care up to 37 weeks was performed. Patient went into labor and delivered the first baby vaginally. The second required a C-section. Postpartum care was typical without complications.

This scenario would be coded as:

- 59510, Routine obstetric care including antepartum care, cesarean delivery, and postpartum care
- 59409, Vaginal delivery only

Note: Regardless of the order of the delivery, the global portion of the OB services is reportable based on the scenario above with a vaginal-delivery-only code for the additional delivery. Some carriers may require just one global OB care code with a modifier -22 to indicate a second delivery. Individual carriers vary for twin and multiple birth reporting and should be contacted prior to claim submission.

Postpartum Curettage

Postpartum curettage is rather commonly performed. This is the scraping of the uterine cavity to remove pieces of retained placenta or clots, using a curette, instrument, or suction. In reviewing the operative/procedure notes, watch for the possibility of the use of the hysteroscope rather than direct visualization and scraping.

Exercise 10.4

Use the ICD-10-CM and CPT manuals to code the following exercise.

1. Chorionic villus sampling, any method. _____
2. Breech presentation of fetus in womb. _____
3. Amniocentesis with ultrasonic guidance. _____

Gynecology (GYN)

The gynecologist treats females experiencing infertility, structural abnormalities of female organs, sexually transmitted diseases, sexual dysfunction, menstrual abnormalities, and other diseases. Female genital system CPT codes 56405–58999 and Laparoscopy/Hysteroscopy CPT codes 56300–56399 are used for most gynecological procedures including in vitro fertilization.

Evaluation and Management Services

As mentioned earlier, the OB/GYN physician can serve as a primary care physician and a specialist. The coder must be aware of when the physician is serving the patient in this capacity in order to code correctly.

When the physician's evaluation and management service turns into a counseling session, appropriate documentation and coding must be used. When counseling and/or coordination of care dominates more than 50 percent of the physician/patient face-to-face time spent in the office or other outpatient setting (or floor/unit time in a hospital or nursing facility), then time is considered the key factor to qualify for a particular level of E/M services.

> **EXAMPLE:** An established patient is seen for leukorrhea (white vaginal discharge). The physician performs a problem-focused history and examination with a straightforward medical decision, diagnosis *Trichomonas vaginalis* infection. When the physician prescribes medication and instructs the patient to have her sexual partner be treated, the patient reveals she has multiple sexual partners. A conversation evolves in which the patient asks several questions regarding other sexually transmitted diseases, contraceptive methods, and the effects of all of this on a possible future pregnancy. The face-to-face time the physician spends in counseling the patient ends up being 30 minutes.
>
> With this type of visit the physician typically spends 10 minutes face-to-face with the patient; however, because of the patient's questions, the extended time the physician spent was more than 50 percent, which now makes time the controlling factor to qualify for a higher level of E/M service. This office visit typically would be coded 99212; however, because of the extra time spent face-to-face with the patient (30 minutes instead of 10 minutes), the E/M service actually performed was a 99214. The physician must carefully document the nature of counseling in this case. The time factor cannot include any delays or interruptions not associated with patient counseling or coordination of care, even if the face-to-face time was not continuous.
>
> Preventive medicine counseling provided as a separate encounter, such as sexual practices or family problems, should be coded using individual counseling Evaluation and Management CPT codes 99401 to 99404. These codes cannot be used if the patient seeking counseling has symptoms or an established illness.

Special Service and Report Codes

Special service codes commonly used in the OB/GYN practice, found in the Medicine section of the CPT manual, are as follows:

99000	Handling of specimens for transfer from the physician's office to a laboratory
99024	Postoperative follow-up visit, normally included in the surgical package, to indicate that an evaluation and management service was performed during a postoperative period for a reason(s) related to the original procedure
99058	Service(s) provided on an emergency basis in the office, which disrupts other scheduled office services, in addition to basic service
99060	Service(s) provided on an emergency basis, out of the office, which disrupts other scheduled office services, in addition to basic service
99070	Supplies and materials provided by the physician over and above those usually included with the office visit or other services rendered
99071	Educational supplies, such as books, tapes, and pamphlets, for the patient's education at cost to physician or other qualified health care professional
99078	Physician educational services rendered to patients in a group setting

CPT Preventive Medicine Service

The preventive examination according to the CPT is age appropriate, comprehensive history and physical exam. The codes for new patients are: 99381–99387 and 99391–99397 for established patients. In the Chapter 5 discussion of E/M codes, the guidelines for selection of the preventive codes were discussed in detail. To encourage learning for this particular subject, these concepts will be repeated here, in a specialty-specific manner. The CPT refers to the well woman exam as a Preventive Medicine Service, and describes such services as follows:

1. The services depend on the age of the patient. In other words, the extent and topic of discussion, examination, and risk factor reduction for a 16-year-old female may vary from the extent and topic of discussion for a 36-year-old female or a 78-year-old female.

2. The comprehensive preventive services are not equal to the problem-oriented E/M services. In other words, the E/M guidelines describe how to determine the extent of the comprehensive illness examination: as a general multisystem exam or a complete single organ exam; the guidelines do *not* describe the examination requirements for the preventive examination.

3. The preventive services include counseling/anticipatory/risk factor reduction (e.g., contraceptive management counseling, preventive counseling on sexually transmitted diseases, age-specific screening recommendations, etc.).

4. All immunizations, ancillary studies, procedures, and additional screening tests are to be reported with a separate code. For instance, if a measles-mumps-rubella (MMR) immunization is rendered during the preventive medicine service, the MMR medication *plus* the administration code are reported; if a urinalysis dipstick is performed and documented, the additional urinalysis code is reported; if a surgical procedure is performed and documented, the additional surgical procedure code is reported. According to the CPT, the preventive medicine services are not part of the radiology, pathology, medicine, or other "package" (Table 10–6).

Table 10-6 Commonly Performed Services during a Preventive Medicine Service (Non-Medicare Patient)

CPT Code	Description
90471 also vaccine/toxoid code	Immunization administration; one vaccine
90472+ also vaccine/toxoid	Immunization administration; each additional vaccine
90473+ also vaccine/toxoid code	Immunization administration; by intranasal or oral route
90474+ also vaccine/toxoid code	Immunization administration; each additional vaccine
96372 and also the medication	Therapeutic injection
99173	Screening test of visual acuity, quantitative, bilateral (Snellen chart)
92567	Tympanometry (whisper test and tuning fork are part of the preventive exam and not separately coded)
81000–81003	Urinalysis dipstick services
81025	Urine pregnancy test
84830	Ovulation tests, by visual color comparison methods for HLH
99000	Collection and handling
93000	EKG, 12 lead with interpretation, for screening
86580	TB skin test, intradermal
86490	Coccidioidomycosis
86485	Candida skin test
36415	Collection of venous blood by venipuncture

5. The combination of a preventive and problem-oriented visit consideration.

   a. If during the preventive medicine service the physician provides care for an "insignificant or trivial problem/abnormality" that does *not* require additional history, examination, and medical decision making (MDM), then no additional E/M code is selected. For example, the physician performs a general medical preventive service, including a gyn pelvic exam with Pap collection, and progresses to order a TSH to check thyroid levels. If the physician does not perform an additional history, exam, and MDM at this encounter specifically regarding the labs ordered or other conditions addressed, then no additional E/M code is to be selected. Only the 9938X–9939X code would be reported. CPT provides code 99000 to report handling or conveyance of a specimen; however, coverage varies among insurance carriers and is often denied. If the blood was drawn at the same time, the blood draw code 36415 would also be reported (Figure 10–11).

As you can see, if the combination of preventive medicine services and the illness services are performed at the same encounter, on the same date, by the same physician, it is highly possible that the claim could be multiple pages.

   b. If during the preventive medicine service (described previously) the physician provides care for an illness or disease that is significant enough to require an *additional* history, examination, and medical decision making, then guidelines state to select the additional codes from the series 99201–99215 with modifier -25. For example, the physician cares for Hashimoto's disease during this encounter, with the performance of additional history, examination, and medical decision making that support level 99213. The annual exam with pelvic and Pap are completed. See claim example of reporting this combination encounter in Figure 10–12.

CMS and Preventive Services

CMS has gradually increased preventive and screening type services to Medicare beneficiaries, realizing the critical role prevention plays in overall health. Numerous services are now covered; however, they may be subject to limitations and requirements for eligibility. Annually, CMS updates and adds additional services to their coverage policies. The following are examples of screening services available to Medicare beneficiaries as of the date of this publication.

- Abdominal aortic aneurysm screening
- Adult immunizations
- Bone mass measurements
- Cancer screenings
- Cardiovascular screening
- Diabetes screening
- Diabetes supplies
- Diabetes self-management training

HEALTH INSURANCE CLAIM FORM

APPROVED BY NATIONAL UNIFORM CLAIM COMMITTEE (NUCC) 02/12

		PICA							PICA	

1. MEDICARE (Medicare#) ☐ MEDICAID (Medicaid#) ☐ TRICARE (ID#/DoD#) ☐ CHAMPVA (Member ID#) ☐ GROUP HEALTH PLAN (ID#) ☐ FECA BLK LUNG (ID#) ☐ OTHER (ID#) ☐

1a. INSURED'S I.D. NUMBER   (For Program in Item 1)

2. PATIENT'S NAME (Last Name, First Name, Middle Initial)

3. PATIENT'S BIRTH DATE MM DD YY   SEX M ☐ F ☐

4. INSURED'S NAME (Last Name, First Name, Middle Initial)

5. PATIENT'S ADDRESS (No., Street)

6. PATIENT RELATIONSHIP TO INSURED Self ☐ Spouse ☐ Child ☐ Other ☐

7. INSURED'S ADDRESS (No., Street)

CITY   STATE

8. RESERVED FOR NUCC USE

CITY   STATE

ZIP CODE   TELEPHONE (Include Area Code) ( )

ZIP CODE   TELEPHONE (Include Area Code) ( )

9. OTHER INSURED'S NAME (Last Name, First Name, Middle Initial)

10. IS PATIENT'S CONDITION RELATED TO:

11. INSURED'S POLICY GROUP OR FECA NUMBER

a. OTHER INSURED'S POLICY OR GROUP NUMBER

a. EMPLOYMENT? (Current or Previous) YES ☐ NO ☐

a. INSURED'S DATE OF BIRTH MM DD YY   SEX M ☐ F ☐

b. RESERVED FOR NUCC USE

b. AUTO ACCIDENT? YES ☐ NO ☐   PLACE (State)

b. OTHER CLAIM ID (Designated by NUCC)

c. RESERVED FOR NUCC USE

c. OTHER ACCIDENT? YES ☐ NO ☐

c. INSURANCE PLAN NAME OR PROGRAM NAME

d. INSURANCE PLAN NAME OR PROGRAM NAME

10d. CLAIM CODES (Designated by NUCC)

d. IS THERE ANOTHER HEALTH BENEFIT PLAN? YES ☐ NO ☐ *If yes*, complete items 9, 9a, and 9d.

READ BACK OF FORM BEFORE COMPLETING & SIGNING THIS FORM.
12. PATIENT'S OR AUTHORIZED PERSON'S SIGNATURE I authorize the release of any medical or other information necessary to process this claim. I also request payment of government benefits either to myself or to the party who accepts assignment below.

SIGNED   DATE

13. INSURED'S OR AUTHORIZED PERSON'S SIGNATURE I authorize payment of medical benefits to the undersigned physician or supplier for services described below.

SIGNED

14. DATE OF CURRENT ILLNESS, INJURY, or PREGNANCY (LMP) MM DD YY   QUAL.

15. OTHER DATE QUAL. MM DD YY

16. DATES PATIENT UNABLE TO WORK IN CURRENT OCCUPATION FROM MM DD YY TO MM DD YY

17. NAME OF REFERRING PROVIDER OR OTHER SOURCE

17a.

17b. NPI

18. HOSPITALIZATION DATES RELATED TO CURRENT SERVICES FROM MM DD YY TO MM DD YY

19. ADDITIONAL CLAIM INFORMATION (Designated by NUCC)

20. OUTSIDE LAB? YES ☐ NO ☐ $ CHARGES

21. DIAGNOSIS OR NATURE OF ILLNESS OR INJURY Relate A-L to service line below (24E)   ICD Ind.

A. Z01.419   B. _____   C. _____   D. _____
E. _____   F. _____   G. _____   H. _____
I. _____   J. _____   K. _____   L. _____

22. RESUBMISSION CODE   ORIGINAL REF. NO.

23. PRIOR AUTHORIZATION NUMBER

24. A. DATE(S) OF SERVICE						B. PLACE OF SERVICE	C. EMG	D. PROCEDURES, SERVICES, OR SUPPLIES (Explain Unusual Circumstances) CPT/HCPCS	MODIFIER	E. DIAGNOSIS POINTER	F. $ CHARGES	G. DAYS OR UNITS	H. EPSDT Family Plan	I. ID. QUAL.	J. RENDERING PROVIDER ID. #
From MM	DD	YY	To MM	DD	YY										
1	09	01	XX	09	01	XX	11		99386		A				NPI	
2	09	01	XX	09	01	XX	11		99000		A				NPI	
3															NPI	
4															NPI	
5															NPI	
6															NPI	

25. FEDERAL TAX I.D. NUMBER   SSN ☐ EIN ☐

26. PATIENT'S ACCOUNT NO.

27. ACCEPT ASSIGNMENT? (For govt. claims, see back) YES ☐ NO ☐

28. TOTAL CHARGE $

29. AMOUNT PAID $

30. Rsvd for NUCC Use

31. SIGNATURE OF PHYSICIAN OR SUPPLIER INCLUDING DEGREES OR CREDENTIALS (I certify that the statements on the reverse apply to this bill and are made a part thereof.)

SIGNED   DATE

32. SERVICE FACILITY LOCATION INFORMATION

a. NPI   b.

33. BILLING PROVIDER INFO & PH # ( )

a. NPI   b.

NUCC Instruction Manual available at: www.nucc.org   **PLEASE PRINT OR TYPE**   APPROVED OMB-0938-1197 FORM 1500 (02-12)

Figure 10-11 Claim example for preventive medicine visit, Pap smear, and specimen conveyance

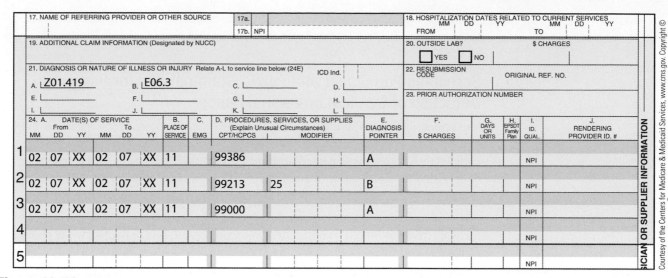

Figure 10-12 Claim example for preventive medicine visit, Pap smear, problem-oriented visit, and specimen conveyance

- Medical nutrition therapy (for Medicare beneficiaries with diabetes or renal disease)

- Glaucoma screening

- HIV screening

- Initial preventive physical exam (IPPE) aka "Welcome to Medicare" physical exam

- Annual wellness visit (AWV), with personalized protection plan

- Counseling to prevent tobacco use

- Smoking and tobacco-use-cessation counseling

Many of these services are statutorily exempt from deductible and/or coinsurance and may be limited to specific time allowances (e.g., annually, once every two years, etc.).

Diagnostic Pap Test

The diagnostic Pap tests are frequently covered by most insurance companies, including Medicare. Typically, the OB/GYN or primary care physician obtains the Pap smear and sends the specimen to the laboratory. Only certain illnesses are considered a covered benefit for the CMS patient:

- Previous cancer of the female genital tract

- Previous abnormal or suspicious Pap smear

- Abnormal or suspicious findings of female genital tract

- Neoplasm of the female genital tract

- Inflammatory disease of the female genital tract

- Abnormal bleeding

- Early onset of intercourse and multiple sexual partners are risk factors for cervical cancer, but this is probably related to exposure to STDs, especially human papillomavirus (HPV).

These indicators or conditions are to be documented in the medical record, and the correlative ICD-10-CM code is selected. The thin prep, Bethesda, or AutoPap may be used.

Screening Pap Smear and Pelvic Examinations for Early Detection of Cervical or Vaginal Cancer

The screening Pap smear is a national coverage decision. A screening Pap is covered by CMS and reported by the OB/GYN or primary care physician with HCPCSII code Q0091, Screening Papanicolaou smear; obtaining, preparing, and conveyance of cervical or vaginal smear to laboratory. Diagnosis codes Z12.4, Z01.411, Z01.419, Z12.72, and Z12.89 are to be used on the claim form.

This screening service is a covered service, allowed every 24 months (two years) for women not at high risk, or annually for women with one of the following risk factors:

1. A woman of childbearing age with an abnormal Pap test within the past three years.

2. Evidence of high risk of developing cervical cancer with qualified health care professional recommendation for more frequent testing than every three years. High risk is considered (ICD-10-CM code must be on the claim):

    Early onset of sexual activity under 16 years of age

    Multiple sexual partners (five or more per lifetime)

    History of STD (including HIV)

    Fewer than three negative or any Pap smear within the previous seven years

    DES-exposed daughters of women who took DES during pregnancy

Screening Pelvic Examination

There are specific coverage determinations for the screening pelvic exams for Medicare beneficiaries. A screening pelvic exam for non-Medicare patients is included in preventive codes 99381–99397. For Medicare beneficiaries, HCPCSII code G0101, Cervical or vaginal cancer screening; pelvic and clinical breast exam, is to be reported and is covered every two years for non–high-risk patients. With the use of code G0101, specific criteria *must* be performed and documented in order to report the service. CMS policy provides the following guidance for G0101:

1. The screening pelvic exam may be performed by a physician, certified nurse midwife, PA, NP, or CNS if authorized by state law.

2. Medicare allows for one exam every 24 months for asymptomatic patient: Z01.411, Z01.419, Z12.4-, or Z12.72.

3. Medicare allows for one exam every 12 months if high risk (Z77.9):

    Early onset of sexual activity under 16 years of age

    Multiple sexual partners (five or more per lifetime)

    History of STD (including HIV)

    Fewer than three negative or any Pap smear within the previous seven years

    DES-exposed daughters of women who took DES during pregnancy

4. Medicare allows for one exam every 12 months if woman of childbearing age (premenopausal), with abnormality present within the previous three years.

Use code G0101 for the pelvic examination, according to CMS (as listed in the 1997 E/M Genitourinary Examination Guidelines), which *must* include the examination of 7 of the following 11 elements:

1. Inspection and palpation of the breasts for masses, lumps, tenderness, symmetry, or nipple discharge

2. Digital rectal exam including sphincter tone, presence of hemorrhoids, rectal masses

3. External genitalia general appearance, hair distribution, or lesions

4. Urethral meatus size, location, lesions, or prolapse

5. Urethra masses, tenderness, scarring

6. Bladder fullness, masses, tenderness

7. Vagina general appearance, estrogen effect, discharge lesions, pelvic support, cystocele, or rectocele

8. Cervix general appearance, lesions, discharge

9. Uterus size contour, position, mobility, tenderness, consistency, descent, or support

10. Adnexa/parametria masses, tenderness, organomegaly, nodularity

11. Anus and perineum

If the G0101 is a covered benefit (once every 24 months, or 12 months for high risk), the patient is not obligated for a deductible for this particular service.

A combination E/M problem-oriented service provided on the same date by the same physician, may be submitted on the claim with modifier -25 if supported by the documentation.

When Q0091 for "Screening Pap smear; obtaining, preparing, and conveyance of cervical or vaginal smear to the lab" is selected in addition to the E/M service on the same date by the same physician, again modifier -25 is placed on the E/M. Table 10–7 is an example of common diagnoses used for these services.

Table 10-7 CMS Screening Pap Smear (Q0091) or Pelvic Exam (G0101) ICD-10-CM Chart

Low-Risk Codes	Every 24 Months
Z12.4	Special screening for malignant neoplasms, cervix
Z12.72	Special screening for malignant neoplasms, vagina. Use additional code from the category Z90.7- for acquired absence of cervix, uterus, ovaries, etc.
Z12.89	Special screening for malignant neoplasm, other site
Z01.419	Encounter for gynecological examination (general) (routine) without abnormal findings
Z01.411	Encounter for gynecological examination (general) (routine) with abnormal findings
Use High-Risk Codes as specified by CMS	*Once every 12 months*

Coding Tip:

Frequent visits to the CMS website are valuable as additional services are recommended by section 4104 of the ACA (American Care Act) to the USPSTF (United States Preventive Services Task Force), and adopted as eligible services for Medicare beneficiaries. Visit https://www.cms.gov and type in "preventive" in the search field to reach the CMS preventive page.

EXAMPLE: The patient requests a physical and is a newly enrolled Medicare beneficiary. All required elements for the Welcome to Medicare Physical (IPPE) are performed and documented with a care plan executed as required. Her last Pap smear and pelvic exam were three years ago. She has been asymptomatic during this time. The physician performs a pelvic examination to include 7 of 11 required anatomical sites, and obtains the Pap smear. During the examination, the physician discovers a breast lump and progresses to additional work up, documenting an additional expanded problem-focused history and exam, orders a breast ultrasound with possible biopsy and a diagnostic mammogram.

The codes shown on Figure 10–13 indicate how the claim should be submitted to Medicare. The ABN is not required in this instance; however, an ABN would be required if the patient had a frequency limitation situation for the HCPCSII G0101 or the Q0091. The handling/conveyance code 99000 is not recognized by CMS and is not reported.

Some state Medicaid programs have recently chosen to activate and to implement coding policies for the HCPCSII S0610 and S0612 codes, requiring the coder to research for the local Medicaid policies.

17b. NPI | FROM | TO

19. ADDITIONAL CLAIM INFORMATION (Designated by NUCC)

20. OUTSIDE LAB? ☐ YES ☐ NO | $ CHARGES

21. DIAGNOSIS OR NATURE OF ILLNESS OR INJURY Relate A-L to service line below (24E) ICD Ind.

A. Z01.419 B. E06.3 C. D.
E. F. G. H.
I. J. K. L.

22. RESUBMISSION CODE | ORIGINAL REF. NO.

23. PRIOR AUTHORIZATION NUMBER

	24. A. DATE(S) OF SERVICE From MM	DD	YY	To MM	DD	YY	B. PLACE OF SERVICE	C. EMG	D. PROCEDURES, SERVICES, OR SUPPLIES (Explain Unusual Circumstances) CPT/HCPCS	MODIFIER	E. DIAGNOSIS POINTER	F. $ CHARGES	G. DAYS OR UNITS	H. EPSDT Family Plan	I. ID. QUAL.	J. RENDERING PROVIDER ID. #
1	02	07	XX	02	07	XX	11		G0101		A				NPI	
2	02	07	XX	02	07	XX	11		99213	25	B				NPI	
3	02	07	XX	02	07	XX	11		Q0091		A				NPI	
4															NPI	
5															NPI	

PHYSICIAN OR SUPPLIER INFORMATION

Figure 10-13 Claim example for CMS pelvic exam and breast exam, Pap smear, problem-oriented visit, and specimen conveyance

Exercise 10.5

Use the ICD-10-CM and CPT manuals to code the following exercises.

1. A 25-year-old established patient presents to her gynecologist for her routine periodic comprehensive physical. _____

2. Office consultation for a 30-year-old with dysfunctional uterine bleeding; blood is drawn and sent to an outside laboratory for testing. She is diagnosed as having menometrorrhagia. _____

3. A 36-year-old patient calls in a panic because she has just found a large lump in her breast. She states "the skin looks funny around it and it hurts." The physician asks the staff to work her in on an emergency basis. _____

Contraception

One of the main reasons women see their gynecologists is for recommendations and prescriptions regarding contraception. Most methods of contraception are prescribed during an evaluation and management service. Birth control pills are the most commonly used contraceptive product in the United States. The patient requires a prescription from a physician and periodic monitoring of blood pressure and other risk factors. Other physician services regarding contraception that are not included in E/M services are injections of birth control medications, implantation of birth control capsules, insertion of birth control devices, and surgery. See Table 10–8 for a complete

Table 10-8 Female Contraceptive Methods

Method	Description
Abortion	Removal of embryo from the uterus
Abstinence	Voluntarily refraining from sexual intercourse
Birth control pill (BCP)	Synthetic hormones taken orally that interrupt normal hormone secretion and prevent ovulation
Cervical cap	A small, caplike device placed over the cervix prior to intercourse
Chemical barriers	Spermicidal creams, foams, and jellies placed deep in the vagina that create an unfavorable environment for sperm to survive
Coitus interruptus	Withdrawing the penis from the vagina before ejaculation
Diaphragm	A rubber or plastic dome-shaped mechanical barrier placed in the vagina near the cervix that prevents sperm from entering the uterus
Intrauterine device (IUD)	A small device placed in the uterus by the physician to prevent implantation of the fertilized egg
Morning-after pill (MAP)	Drug taken orally that contains estrogen and progesterone. When taken within 72 hours of unprotected intercourse, it interrupts the fertilization and/or implantation of the egg.
Progesterone implant	A synthetic implant, called Norplant, placed under the skin, that releases progestin over a five-year period to prevent ovulation
Progesterone injection	Synthetic progesterone, called Depo-Provera, administered every three months to prevent ovulation
Rhythm method	Abstaining from intercourse at the time of ovulation
Tubal ligation	Surgical procedure in which the uterine tubes are cut and ligated (tied) or cauterized (burned) or closed off with a small ring

listing of birth control methods. The procedure code for the insertion of implantable contraceptive capsules is found in the Surgery/Integumentary section of the CPT manual. Induced abortion is usually performed using the surgical procedure dilation and curettage. CPT codes 59840–59857 would apply to such services and are found in the Surgery/Maternity section.

Tubal ligation is a permanent method of birth control typically performed with a laparoscope. An incision is made in the abdomen, often in the umbilicus, and a small tube is inserted through which the ligation instrument is introduced. A cut, referred to as a transection, is made across the oviducts, and the uterine tubes are blocked so that a fertilized egg cannot pass into the uterus for implantation (Figure 10–14). Methods for blocking the tubes include fulguration

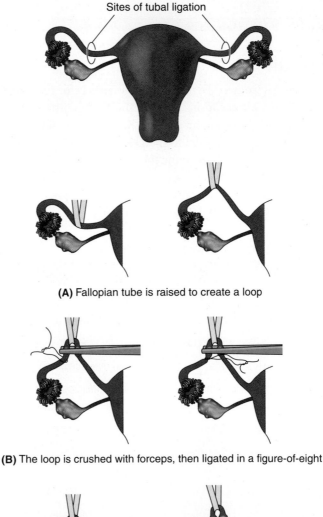

Sites of tubal ligation

(A) Fallopian tube is raised to create a loop

(B) The loop is crushed with forceps, then ligated in a figure-of-eight

(C) The loop is excised at the crushed zone

© Blamb/Shutterstock.com.

Figure 10-14 Procedure for tubal ligation as a permanent birth control method

(burning the ends of the tubes) or securing devices such as bands, clips, or Falope rings (which are put in place on the ends of the tubes). Various ligation procedure codes are found in the Laparoscopy/Hysteroscopy section of the CPT manual. If tubal ligation is performed at the same time as a cesarean section, add-on code 58611 would apply.

Office Procedures

A variety of office procedures are performed in a gynecologist's practice. During a routine gynecologic examination, a Pap smear is taken to evaluate cervical tissue for cancer. If the laboratory reports an abnormal Pap smear, a colposcopy may be performed. The colposcope is an instrument used to look into the vagina, opened with the use of a speculum, and to observe the cervix. The physician can see, under magnification provided by the colposcope, what areas of the cervix have abnormal cells. Often a sampling of cells is taken from the cervix and scrapings from the inner canal, referred to as a cervical biopsy with endocervical curettage. Procedure codes for colposcopy are found under the pertinent Endoscopy section within the Surgery/Female Genital System.

A common procedure performed to evaluate the endometrial lining of the uterus is an endometrial biopsy. This may be performed if the patient is experiencing dysfunctional uterine bleeding (DUB) or postmenopausal bleeding. A plastic tube is passed through the cervix into the uterine cavity and a sample of tissue is aspirated into the tube. A biopsy, using a metal instrument to collect a sample, may also be performed.

A more invasive procedure is dilation and curettage (D&C). The small cervical canal is opened or dilated to allow passage for a curette, an instrument used to scrape the lining of the endometrium (Figure 10–15). Both endometrial sampling and D&C allow for microscopic visualization of malignant cells for diagnostic purposes and are coded using CPT codes 58100–58120. When a D&C is performed with any other pelvic surgery, it may be viewed by some third-party payors as an integral part of the pelvic surgery and therefore not reimbursed.

Other office procedures include treatment for the destruction of genital warts and lesions in the vulvar area (56501 and 56515) or vagina (57061 and 57065). Cryosurgery is often performed on the cervix to freeze abnormal dysplastic tissue and allow normal tissue to grow in its place. Incision and drainage of a Bartholin's gland abscess are coded with 56420 whereas the excision and removal of the Bartholin's gland or cyst are found under the Excision subheading and are reported with code 56740. Important definitions describing a simple procedure, radical procedure, partial procedure, and complete for vulvectomy procedures are found at the very beginning of the Female Genital System surgery section.

Exploratory Laparotomy

When a patient presents with pelvic pain of unknown etiology, and the preliminary diagnostic tests do not review a specific finding, a common procedure is to perform a diagnostic laparoscopy. This simply describes the procedure in which scopes are inserted via small incisions to gain visual access to the abdomen to assess the anatomy. More often than not, while assessing the anatomy, the physician determines the cause of the pelvic pain and progresses to treating the problem. The problem may require an open procedure, referred to as a laparotomy if the

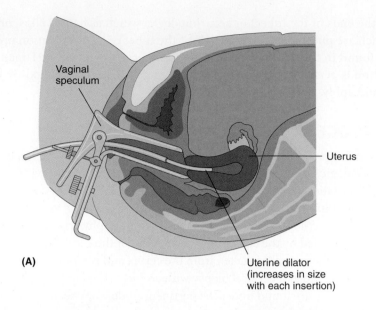

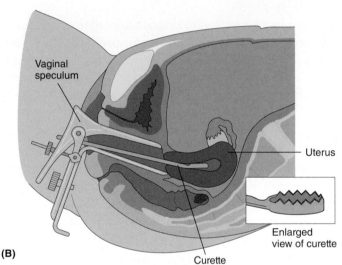

Figure 10-15 Dilation and curettage: (A) cervical dilation to open the cervical opening; (B) a curette is used to scrape the endometrial lining of the uterus.

problem cannot be corrected through the scope. Common problems include appendicitis, endometriosis, endometritis, ovarian cysts or tumors, leiomyomata (fibroid tumors), or other tumors. Laparoscopy procedures are specific to the condition being treated. Surgical laparoscopy always includes diagnostic laparoscopy and is a mainstay found throughout CPT within many laparoscopy procedural sections.

A rather common circumstance is removal of fibroid tumors (myomectomy) and hysterectomy (removal of uterus) at the same time. These procedures may be performed by an excisional or laparoscopic approach and are divided within their respective CPT categories. While both hysterectomy and myomectomy codes are based on the approach and weight, myomas also require consideration of the number of fibroids removed.

Highlight:

When a pelvic exam is performed in conjunction with a gyn procedure, as either a necessary or a confirmatory part of the procedure, the exam is not separately reported. A diagnostic pelvic exam may be performed for the purpose of deciding to perform a procedure. CPT guidelines provide the following in the Surgical Package Definition as not being separately reportable: "Subsequent to the decision for surgery, one related E/M encounter on the date immediately prior to or on the date of the procedure (including history and physical)." If, however, the decision for surgery was made during the E/M encounter, the service may be reported in addition. If the decision was for a major surgery (90 global days), modifier -57 would be reported. If the decision for a minor procedure was made, and if the procedure was performed on the same day, modifier -25 would be reported.

Laparoscopy

The laparoscopy describes the placement of the trocar and scope into the abdomen to assess various anatomical sites of the abdomen, the peritoneum, and the omentum (Figure 10–16). The first procedure is often for the purpose of diagnosing and evaluating the anatomical sites. If the procedure does not progress through this same site, select the code 49320 for the diagnostic laparoscopy. However, if the physician chooses to surgically treat a concern through the same scope, the surgical laparoscopic code is used instead. For laparoscopy with aspiration of a right ovarian cyst, select only the surgical laparoscopic code 49322-RT without the additional code for the diagnostic laparoscopy (49320).

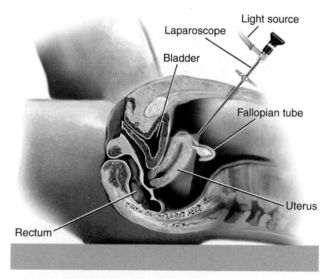

Figure 10-16 Laparoscopy

Exercise 10.6

Read the following operative report and select the CPT, ICD-10-CM, and any applicable modifiers.

PREOPERATIVE DIAGNOSIS: 1. Cyclic right lower quadrant pain, occurring at time of menses
2. Suspected endometriosis

POSTOPERATIVE DIAGNOSIS: 1. Stage II endometriosis   2. Pelvic adhesions   3. Left ovarian cyst

(continues)

Exercise 10.6 (*continued*)

PROCEDURES: 1. Operative laparoscopy with right salpino-oophorectomy

2. Lysis of adhesions

3. Ablation of endometriosis

4. Drainage left ovarian cyst

ANESTHESIA: General Anesthesia

IV FLUID: 800 mL of lactated Ringer's

ESTIMATED BLOOD LOSS: Minimal

COMPLICATIONS: None

INDICATIONS: The patient is a 49-year-old gravida vi, para 5, white female, who has noted severe pain in the right lower quadrant every time she has a period. The pain is sharp, constant, and remits when her menses end. This has been occurring every month and has been worsening over time. A pelvic ultrasound was normal with the exception of a 1.4 cm isoechoic lesion on the right ovary, questionably a complex cyst. Endometriosis was suspected and the patient wished definitive diagnosis and therapy with a laparoscopy.

FINDINGS: Diagnostic laparoscopy revealed a normal uterus with normal tubes bilaterally. There were endometriotic implants on both ovaries and peritoneal blebbing in the cul-de-sac. There were also foci of endometriosis in both ovarian fossae. The right ovary was densely adherent to the right pelvic sidewall. There was a filmy adhesion from the sigmoid colon to the left pelvic sidewall and another filmy adhesion of the right colon to the anterior abdominal wall. All adhesions were lysed and the right tube and ovary were removed.

PATHOLOGY: Right tube and ovary.

PROCEDURE: The patient was taken to the operative room and placed in the dorsal supine position. General endotracheal anesthesia was administered, and the patient placed in the modified dorsal lithotomy position via the Allen stirrups. An examination under anesthesia revealed a small, mobile, anteverted uterus without adnexal masses. The patient was then prepped, sterile draped, and her bladder emptied. A bivalve speculum was placed into the vagina and the anterior cervical lip grasped with a tenaculum. A Hulka clamp was gently placed into the uterus without difficulty for uterine manipulation and all other instruments were then removed from the vagina.

The infraumbilical and periumbilical areas were infiltrated with 0.25 percent Marcaine and the umbilicus was elevated with towel clips. A curvilinear incision was made in the inferior umbilicus and a Veress needle placed without difficulty. Correct positioning was confirmed with a hanging drop test. Four liters of carbon dioxide gas were insufflated until adequate pneumoperitoneum was obtained. The Veress was removed and a 7 mm trocar advanced. The video laparoscope was placed through the trocar sleeve and no trauma was noted at the insertion site.

The patient was placed in Trendelenburg and a 5 mm suprapubic port was placed under direct visualization. The pelvis was then inspected with the findings as noted above. Attention was paid to the right ovary, which had multiple endometriotic implants and was stuck down to the right pelvic sidewall. I felt this ovary was the cause of the pain, and she would benefit from removal. Another 5 mm trocar was placed in the left lower quadrant. The right tube was held on traction and the infundibulopelvic ligament cauterized and cut using the Everest bipolar forceps, which were set at 30 watts. Hemostasis was ensured.

(*continues*)

Exercise 10.6 (*continued*)

I had to mobilize the ovary off the pelvic sidewall and this was done by gently pulling the ovary upward. Using rather firm traction, the adhesions were bluntly lysed and the ovary was freed from the pelvic sidewall. The broad ligament beneath the utero-ovarian ligament was then cauterized and lysed. Next, the Everest forceps were used to cauterize the tube 1 cm lateral to the cornual area. This was cut. We were left with the utero-ovarian ligament, which was cauterized and cut, and in this way the tube and ovary were freed. Selected areas of bleeding on the uterus were made hemostatic and the operative site was inspected, hemostasis ensured.

The 7 mm umbilical trocar was removed and replaced with a 10 mm port. A 5 mm laparoscope was placed through the suprapubic site and the Endo Catch placed through the umbilical port. The tube and ovary were placed in the Endo Catch bag. The bag was cinched tightly and brought up to the umbilical incision. The trocar was removed and the tube and ovary within the bag were easily removed through the umbilical incision. This was handed off to pathology. The 10 mm trocar was then replaced and the 10 mm scope placed through the umbilical port.

The filmy adhesions from the sigmoid mesocolon were then held on traction and the adhesions easily taken down with the laparoscopic Endo Shears. Hemostasis was ensured. The filmy adhesions from the ascending colon to the anterior abdominal wall were taken down as well. We then turned our attention to the left ovary. The left tube was grasped and the underside of the ovary visualized. There were several foci of endometriosis as well as a 3 cm simple-appearing cyst on the lateral pole. Using a needle-tip Bovie, the endometriotic implants were all cauterized and the cyst opened. Serous fluid was drained. The cyst wall was then extensively cauterized using a combination of the Everest bipolar forceps, the laparoscopic Endo Shears, and finally Kleppinger bipolar forceps with ultimately excellent hemostasis achieved and the cyst wall completely cauterized to decrease the risk of future cyst formation. The ovarian capsule looked clean and no more endometriosis was noted.

The entire pelvis was then copiously irrigated and suctioned. Small foci of endometriosis in the cul-de-sac were all cauterized with the needle-tip Bovie. The site of the left ovarian cystectomy was inspected. Hemostasis ensured. The RSO operative site was inspected and hemostasis ensured. The procedure was terminated. All instruments removed from the abdomen, and pneumoperitomeum released. The umbilical fascia was reapproximated using a figure-of-eight suture of 0 Vicryl on the UR-6 needle. The umbilical incision was reapproximated using subcuticular suture of 4-0 Monocryl. Interrupted sutures of 4-0 Monocryl were place in the 5 mm ports. The Hulka clamp was removed from the uterus. She awoke from anesthesia and was taken to the recovery room in stable condition. The patient tolerated the procedure well. Sponge, lap, needle, and instrument counts were correct x2. One gram Ancef was given preoperatively.

CPT codes _____

ICD-10-CM codes _____

Vulva, Perineum, and Introitus

Incision and drainage (I&D) are anatomically described. If the anatomy is not documented clearly, consider selecting 10040, 1006X in lieu of the I&D for the vulva.

Destruction is the use of laser, cryo (portable or large), chemical, or electrosurgery to remove lesions. Select the code 56501 if the documentation states vulva or external genitalia and does not state complicated, or extensive. The extensive procedures would be reported with code 56515; however, coders should be aware that this term is not clarified by CPT and is based on the physician's judgment and documentation.

Biopsy of the vulva or perineum may be performed as part of another excision. Select 56605 for the first and 56606 for each additional lesion, if only biopsy or biopsies are performed. If the biopsy is not of the vulva or perineum, consider codes within the integumentary surgery section.

Vulvectomy codes are often described by the specific anatomical area of excision. The service coded 56633, Vulvectomy, radical, complete, is less often performed. The CPT code vulvectomy descriptions are very specific for the external genitalia area. In order to select the proper code, careful review of documentation with these descriptions is key. Physician documentation may vary from these terms; for example, extensive removal is often worded differently. Making accurate distinctions between the following terms is not difficult when the coder is aware of their separate, specific meanings:

- *Simple* is the removal of skin and superficial tissues.

- *Radical* is the removal of skin and deep superficial tissues.

- *Partial* is removal of less than 80 percent of the entire vulvar area.

- *Complete* is the removal of greater than 80 percent of the vulvar area.

Repair of the genitalia may use codes from various areas of the CPT code book. If coding for these services, it is necessary to review the parenthetical tips beneath code 56810. Whether or not the repair is due to obstetrical reasons will determine the code selection.

Exercise 10.7

Read the following operative report and select the CPT, ICD-10-CM, and any applicable modifiers.

PREOPERATIVE DIAGNOSIS: 1. Right Bartholin cyst 6 cm
2. Left labial cyst 4 cm

POSTOPERATIVE DIAGNOSIS: 1. Right Bartholin cyst 6 cm
2. Left labial cyst 4 cm

OPERATION PERFORMED: Marsupialization Bartholin right cyst, I&D left labial cyst

FINDINGS: Right labial Bartholin cyst about 6 cm, left labial cyst about 4 cm

PROCEDURE: The patient was taken to the OR. After general anesthetic was administered, sterilely cleaned and draped. First the right Bartholin site was identified and an incision made at the vaginal and vulvar junction for 3 cm. Purulent discharge was drained. Incision was exteriorized by a baseball stitch and marsupialization of the cyst wall was done without any complications.

Left labial cyst was identified again and drained on the inner side of the labia minora. Cyst wall was marsupialized. The patient tolerated the procedure well. Suture, sponge, instrument, and needle count was correct. Complete hemostasis achieved, triple antibiotic cream applied, and left the OR in stable condition.

CPT codes _____

ICD-10-CM codes _____

Vagina

Again, whether the procedure is obstetrical or nonobstetrical will affect the code selection, as will the terminology suffix describing the procedure: -*otomy* is cutting into; -*entesis* is aspiration. Vaginal lesions are internal; for external lesions, select the vulva codes.

Fitting and insertion of a tandem and/or vaginal ovoid for clinical brachytherapy is reported with code 57155. The actual insertion of radioelements for radiation therapy is listed within a parenthetical note below 57155, instructing the use of codes from the 77XXX series. Vaginal packing procedure code 57180 is sometimes required for spontaneous or traumatic hemorrhage for the nonobstetrical patient.

The repair of the vagina is usually performed in conjunction with another procedure, either urethral suspension work or other vaginal wall repair. Among common procedures performed is 57260, Anterior and posterior colporrhaphy, or the A&P repair. In reviewing operative notes, observe for the additional repair of the enterocele or other anatomical repairs. Also, determine if the approach for the repair is open, abdominal, or vaginal.

The paravaginal defect repairs the urethra, bladder, and the vaginal prolapse.

Colposcopy is the evaluation of the vagina using an endoscope. Frequently, the physician will obtain one biopsy or multiple tissue samples. 57421 is only to be reported once regardless of the number of biopsy tissue samples obtained. If the physician uses the colposcope to visualize the vulva or external genitalia, select codes 56820–56821; for visualizing the cervix, select 57452–57461. When reporting colposcopies of multiple sites, use modifier -51 as appropriate. A very common procedure is the colposcopy with loop electrode of the cervix (LEEP). However, if the physician also performs the colposcopy with endocervical curettage, this service is not coded additionally when the LEEP is performed.

> **Highlight:**
> If the colposcopy is performed as a scout for another procedure, the colposcopy is not coded.

Cervix

The cervical excision section (57500–57558) series of services is selected when the procedure performed is directly visualized, typically without the use of a colposcopy or other scope apparatus. The codes in this series are described by the type of the equipment that is used to treat the illness/disease. For example, the 57522 service LEEP is a common procedure.

The radical trachelectomy, with extensive removal of the pelvic anatomy, is often performed with multiple physicians. The -62 modifier is frequently selected with this service due to the complexity of the case. At the very least, the procedure usually requires a surgical assistant (modifier -80). Most of the additional procedures that are also performed during these extensive cases are the hysterectomy codes.

Uterus

The 58100 series contains commonly used codes, describing many cases. It will be necessary to read the descriptions carefully and to review the parenthetical tips in the CPT code book to accurately select the codes. Multiple coding is likely, with the common use of either the -51 or -59 modifier as appropriate.

Endometrial and endocervical biopsy is one code, if biopsies were obtained and sent for pathology. Not every case includes a biopsy. If the physician only excises (curettage), do not select the 58100 code.

Myomectomy, as previously discussed, is performed by open abdominal, vaginal, or laparoscopic approach. The services describe the number of tumors and the total weight of the tumors. This information is obtained in the operating room and is documented in the operative report by the surgeon and the pathology report.

Hysterectomy is the removal of the uterus. There are multiple codes for the open hysterectomy services, either through the abdomen or incision through the vagina. To code for the hysterectomy, the coder needs to read the operative report for these details:

- What is the approach? Abdomen is 58150–58240; vaginal open is 58260–58294.

- What tissue is removed: corpus uterus plus cervix, fallopian tube (salpingectomy) and/or ovary (oophorectomy) unilateral or bilateral? If more anatomy is removed, there may be a combination code that should be selected.

- Did the physician repair other anatomy during the case?

An intrauterine device is inserted into the uterus, using an instrument that guides it directly through the vagina into the cervix and places it in the uterus. There are various types of IUDs manufactured. A code is selected for the professional service to place the IUD into the uterus, and another HCPCSII code or 99070 is used for the IUD supply item if purchased by the physician for the patient.

The artificial insemination procedures are typically performed by infertility specialists but may be performed by any physician. The sperm-washing procedure is commonly performed by many OB/GYN physicians assisting in the early diagnosis.

Hysterosalpingography and chromatubation of the oviduct are usually performed using radiology procedures. The operative notes or radiology report for the additional 768XX procedures with the use of -26 modifier for the professional component must be reviewed. The physician may also guide a catheter to evaluate the patency of the fallopian tube (salping) from the uterine orifice to the ovary or fimbria area.

Endometrial cryoablation with endometrial curettage by use of ultrasound guidance is reported with code 58356.

Laparoscopy/Hysteroscopy

CPT frequently reminds us that surgical laparoscopy includes diagnostic laparoscopy when performed (see Figure 10–16).

Notice that two areas of the CPT code book may be involved in selecting the codes, depending on the anatomical sites that are entered. Both of these services are for *diagnostic* only care, and do not describe the surgical or therapeutic correction services.

> ### Coding Tip:
>
> Laparo = abdominal wall; a laparoscope inserted through abdominal wall directly visualizes the abdominal walls and anatomical structures within them.
>
> Hystero = uterus; a hysteroscope inserted through the vagina and cervix directly visualizes the canal and cavity of the uterus.

The 585XX series describe the scope entering through the abdomen, for the surgical removal of various areas. The weight of the uterus is again a necessary fact for selecting the code. According to the *CPT Assistant*, selecting 58550 indicates "most work is via the laparoscope, with a posterior cut into the vagina."

The 58558–58565 codes describe the scope entering through the canal and the cavity of the uterus, for surgical procedures done via the "hysteroscopy" route. The 58578 or 58579 unlisted codes should be used as a last resort when CPT Category I or Category III codes lack the procedural description. Category III codes should be reviewed semiannually in order to stay current with new and emerging procedures and services.

Exercise 10.8

Read the following operative report and select the CPT, ICD-10-CM, and any applicable modifiers.

PREOPERATIVE DIAGNOSIS(ES): 1. Dysfunctional uterine bleeding
2. Endometrial polyp

POSTOPERATIVE DIAGNOSIS(ES): 1. Normal appearing endometrial cavity
2. Small endometrial polyp arising from the posterior body of the uterus

PROCEDURE PERFORMED: 1. Endometrial ablation

ANESTHESIA: General

PROCEDURE: The patient was taken to the operating room after general anesthetic was administered. Sterilely cleaned and draped. Bladder was not catheterized. Bimanual exam revealed the uterus to be multiparous size, anteverted. Adnexa not palpable. Posterior vaginal wall retracted with a weighted speculum. Anterior lip of the cervix held with a tenaculum. Internal cervical os was dilated up to 7 mm without any complications. Hysteroscope was introduced along with light source. There was correct placement ascertained. Bilateral tubal ostia appeared normal. Endometrial cavity appeared normal. There was a small polyp posteriorly on the endometrial cavity. Hysteroscope was removed. Curettage was done and specimens sent for pathology. This was followed by further dilating the cervical canal to 8 mm, followed by introduction of a NovaSure instrument. After placing this NovaSure, ascertaining the position, the cavity assessment test was not passed in spite of two attempts. The procedure was abandoned. Instruments were removed. Hysteroscope reinserted. Cavity appears normal. There is no obvious pathology noted. Hysteroscope removed.

The patient tolerated the procedure well. There was a small tear on the anterior lip of the cervix, repaired with 2-0 Vicryl. Suture, sponge, instrument, and needle count correct. Left the operating room in stable condition.

CPT codes _____

ICD-10-CM codes _____

Oviduct

The first codes in the 58600 series describe the open approach. As with all areas of the CPT, it is improper to select open codes if the procedure approach is laparasopic. Other approaches are typically listed within their applicable section of CPT.

Laparoscopy of the Ovary and Tubes

It is not likely that the codes from the 493XX series would be used in combination with the 5866X series of codes, but, rather, in lieu of these codes. Read carefully to determine the exact anatomy and then compare to the description of the codes.

EXAMPLE:

58662 Laparoscopy, surgical; with fulguration or excision of lesions of the ovary (one), pelvic viscera or peritoneal surface by any method

versus

49222 Laparoscopy, surgical; with aspiration of cavity or cyst (ovarian cyst) single or multiple

Notice how similar the descriptions of these procedures are, both involving the ovary as the anatomical site. Code 58662 describes the ablation or the excision, whereas 49222 describes the aspiration.

Adhesions

Using codes for lysis of adhesions in CPT is clarified in the *CPT Assistant* with two examples. However, the operative note will need to describe the lysis of adhesions from the exact anatomical sites before a code can be selected. Were they removed from the intestine, adnexa, ovary, salping, uterus? Where the adhesions are connected and removed is key in selecting codes. Next, is lysis performed during an open approach or laparoscopically?

Past AMA *CPT Assistant* articles state that lysis of adhesions codes are selected when the adhesions are multiple in number, dense in nature, cover the primary field to preclude visualization, with "considerable" additional time and effort (documented) beyond the usual procedure, and increased risk to the patient. The operative note should clearly include these details when a code for lysis of adhesions is selected. The code may be a separate code if the anatomical area has a code describing lysis, or modifier -22 may be added to the primary procedure code describing the additional, unusual professional work effort. Additional reimbursement for this work is variable among payors.

> **Highlight:**
>
> Lysis of adhesions may be found within the description of certain CPT procedures and is not to be separately coded when performed with other surgical laparoscopic procedures.

Ovary

Ovarian cysts may be treated by aspiration with a laparoscope (49XXX) or with codes 58800 and 58820 for vaginal approach, 58805 and 58822 for abdominal approach, not using the scope, and describe drainage rather than simple aspiration procedure.

The excisional ovarian services describe either the open removal of the cyst or of the entire ovary. Most codes describe unilateral or bilateral within the description, so the use of the -50 modifier is not required. The 589XX series may be performed by more than one physician, typically with the second physician as a surgical assistant. Modifier -80 would be applicable to the second physician's claim.

Operating Microscope

Occasionally, the surgeon requires the use of the operating room microscope to aid in the visualization of the procedure. This code is not selected for small microscopic equipment, such as the loupes or glasses, nor is it selected for the listed codes. The code is selected in addition to most gynecologic services and most often would be used for either the perineonatologist services or the ovarian and salping work. Code 69990 is an add-on code, no modifier -51 is applied, and it should be paid without the multiple surgical payment reductions. Code 69990 provides an extensive listing of codes, which typically include the use of the operating microscope, which would preclude the use of the add-on code. Coders should review this code carefully.

Other Anatomical Sites

It is not uncommon for OB/GYN physicians to encounter additional illness or disease while performing their services, whether in conjunction with E/M visits or surgical procedures. It is therefore to be expected that the OB/GYN coder will have to become familiar with more than just the OB/GYN section of the code book. The surgeon may repair intestines, encounter vascular concerns or metastases, or perform an appendectomy, to name a few examples. Reading the operative note and asking the physician about details become necessities for the OB/GYN services.

Payment

For the OB/GYN services, investigating insurance benefits *prior* to the performance of the service is paramount. The benefits (or limitations) may vary, even during a nine-month pregnancy. Or, for the hysterectomy services, there is a high probability of certain quality indicators that must be provided before the case is scheduled for surgery, perhaps including a second opinion. Lacking these steps, the services are likely denied in full, with no payment to the physician for the excellent care that was rendered.

Exercise 10.9

Use the ICD-10-CM and CPT manuals to code the following exercises.

1. Laparoscopic tubal ligation using a Falope ring _____

2. Colposcopy with cervical biopsy and endocervical curettage for cervical dysplasia performed during a comprehensive initial consultation visit involving high complexity of medical decision making _____

3. Endometrial biopsy for postmenopausal bleeding on a new patient _____

4. Laser treatment for the destruction of 10 vaginal warts on an established patient _____

Hospital Procedures

The gynecologist is a specialized surgeon in the area of female reproductive organs. The CPT code 57410, Pelvic examination under anesthesia, is included in routine evaluation of the surgical field in all major and many minor gynecological procedures and is not to be reported separately. To report this code, medical necessity would need to be supported within the medical record documentation and most likely would require prior authorization.

Infertility

When a woman comes to the gynecologist for infertility, often the partner is included in the initial workup. Since most couples do not know where the problem lies, a simple semen analysis can rule out most male-related problems. Female problems are more plentiful and complicated to explore. Common problems include incompatible vaginal secretions or cervical mucus, anovulation, implantation problems, and blockage of the fallopian tubes.

Infertility is a very sensitive subject for patients and may be very difficult to manage. Tests such as a postcoital test (PCT) is an inspection of the mucus from the vagina after intercourse to detect the motility and viability of the sperm as it appears in the cervical mucus. Semen washing, using a chemical, is performed to produce better sperm motility. Hormone blood levels may be drawn at a specific time of the menstrual cycle to determine if the patient is ovulating. Hysteroscopy may be performed to visualize the lining of the uterus. Laparoscopy is used to visualize the outside of the uterus, the ovaries, and the fallopian tubes. In a procedure called hysterosalpingogram, frequently done with laparoscopy, dye is inserted via the cervix and forced up through the uterus and fallopian tubes. If it easily spills into the abdominal cavity, it is an indication that the uterine tubes are free from blockage. If it does not spill or requires much force to spill, it is an indication that there is a blockage. A catheter may also be inserted into the fallopian tube for diagnostic purposes or to help free the tube from obstruction.

Various forms of artificial insemination, intracervical or intrauterine, may be performed on the infertile woman. CPT codes 58321 and 58322 are used for such procedures. CPT codes 58970, 58974, and 58976 are used for in vitro fertilization procedures.

Exercise 10.10

Use the ICD-10-CM and CPT manuals to code the following exercises.

1. Sperm washing for artificial insemination. _____
2. A woman has tried to conceive for over a year. After a thorough physical examination and other diagnostic tests, she learns that her cervix is considered incompetent. _____
3. Repair of vaginal enterocele (vaginal approach) and rectocele with posterior colporrhaphy. _____
4. Hysterosalpingogram is done on an infertility patient for tubal occlusion. _____
5. Surgical assist for abdominal hysterectomy with bilateral salpingectomy, removal of right ovary, and lysis of adhesions. _____

---

anteverted: Tipped forward; in gynecology, this term is used to describe the normal position of the uterus.

retroverted: Tipped back; in gynecology, this term is used to describe the backward displacement of the uterus.

pelvic relaxation: Weakened condition of supporting ligaments of the uterus and bladder; caused by aging, trauma, or excessive stretching from the act of childbirth.

prolapse: Falling or dropping down of an organ from its normal position or location such as the uterus, bladder, vagina, or rectum.

Structural Abnormalities of the Female Organs

The normal position of the uterus is tipped slightly forward and referred to as **anteverted**. A **retroverted** uterus is tipped backward. With aging, trauma, or excessive stretching from the act of childbirth, the supporting ligaments of the uterus and bladder may become weakened and **pelvic relaxation** occurs. The displacement of the uterus, bladder, vagina, and rectum may cause significant discomfort and a variety of symptoms that may necessitate surgical correction.

Uterine **prolapse** occurs as pelvic muscles and ligaments become overstretched or weakened and allow the uterus to fall downward into the vaginal canal (Figure 10–17). A cystocele is the prolapse of the urinary bladder into the vagina causing pressure, urinary frequency, urgency, and incontinence with coughing, sneezing, laughing, or activity, referred to as urinary stress incontinence. A uterine suspension and anterior vaginal colporrhaphy may need to be performed to bring the bladder to its normal position and repair the stretched vagina. A vaginocele, also known as a colpocele, is a prolapse or falling of the vagina, or hernia protruding

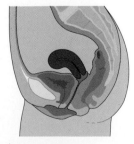
Normal uterus

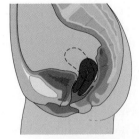
First-degree prolapse

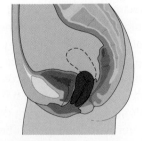
Second-degree prolapse

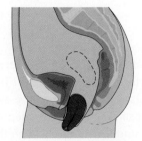
Third-degree prolapse

Figure 10-17 Varying degrees of uterine prolapse

into the vagina. A rectocele is the prolapse of the rectum into the vagina. This causes constipation, a bearing down feeling, and possibly incontinence of gas and feces.

Sexually Transmitted Diseases (STDs)

Sexually transmitted diseases (STDs), also called venereal diseases, are among the most common contagious diseases in the United States. Transmission occurs through body fluids such as blood, semen, and vaginal secretions passed to a partner during vaginal, anal, or oral sex. Occasionally they are spread by contact with infected skin. The physician is often able to make a diagnosis from visual examination. Serum blood tests and vaginal cultures are used to confirm the disease. Most treatment includes medication; often, it is the administration of oral or injectable antibiotics. Lesions are removed using chemical or surgical methods. Patient education and counseling are often involved to ensure patients do not spread the disease. See Table 10–9 for a listing and description of sexually transmitted diseases.

Table 10-9 Sexually Transmitted Diseases

Name	Definition
AIDS	Acquired immune deficiency syndrome is caused by human immunodeficiency virus (HIV). The virus attacks and destroys the immune system, leaving the body vulnerable to invasion by other microorganisms.
Chancroid	A bacterial infection, also called soft chancre, that causes ulceration and enlargement of the lymph glands (lymphadenopathy). It is usually contracted through sexual intercourse and can spread to other areas of the body.
Chlamydia	An infection that is caused by the bacterium *Chlamydia trachomatis*, which invades the vagina and cervix. It is the leading cause of infertility and pelvic inflammatory disease.
Condylomata acuminata	An infection that causes genital warts, which may itch or burn. It is spread by direct skin-to-skin contact during sexual intercourse.
Gonorrhea	A contagious inflammation of the genital mucous membrane transmitted chiefly by sexual intercourse and caused by the bacterium *Neisseria gonorrhoeae*. It is often spread unknowingly and can cause infertility, eye and throat infections, and pelvic inflammatory disease.
Hepatitis B	An inflammation of the liver, also called serum hepatitis, that results in liver cell destruction. As it travels throughout the body, the patient feels ill and may have fever, weight loss, jaundice, fatigue, abdominal pain, and digestive disturbances.
Herpes genitalis	Herpes simplex virus (HSV) type 2 is spread by direct skin-to-skin contact and causes a local infection that produces ulcerations on the skin and mucosa of the genitals.
Syphilis	The spirochete bacterium causes a chronic infection that sometimes appears as a chancre sore in the primary stage. In the second stage, as the organism spreads, it may involve any organ or tissue. During this time, numerous symptoms can be present as it becomes systemic. A latent period usually follows, which may last from 1 to 40 years when the patient is asymptomatic. Later, widespread invasion may take place, resulting in disabling or life-threatening conditions.
Trichomoniasis	Infection of the genitourinary tract caused by the protozoan *Trichomonas vaginalis*. It can cause urethritis (inflammation of the urethra) with dysuria (painful urination) and itching.

Cancer of the Female Reproductive Tract

Tumors of the reproductive tract are found in women of reproductive age and are most common in postmenopausal women. Various forms of benign and malignant neoplasms occur in all areas of the female reproductive tract. These malignant lesions account for 10 percent of all cancer deaths in women. See Table 10–10 for a listing and description of the most common forms of female reproductive tract cancer.

Table 10-10 Female Reproductive Tract Cancer

Type	Description
Cervical	One of the most common forms of gynecologic cancer. An ulceration of the cervix occurs, causing vaginal discharge and spotting. A Pap smear usually detects this slow-growing cancer in early stages. Cryotherapy, laser ablation, electrocautery, surgical resection (referred to as conization), and hysterectomy are all treatment options.
Endometrial	The most common cancer of the female reproductive tract, in which ulcerations of the endometrium develop and cause vaginal bleeding accompanied by a white or yellow vaginal discharge (leukorrhea). Most commonly occurs in postmenopausal women who have never had children. Diagnosis is made by endometrial biopsy or dilation and curettage. Complete hysterectomy with bilateral salpingo-oophorectomy is usually performed.
Ovarian	The leading cause of female reproductive cancer deaths in women. Abnormal tissue development occurs, leading to ovarian cancer, which is the most difficult of all female cancers to detect. A pelvic mass may be palpated on physical examination; however, this is usually at a later stage. The patient may experience lower abdominal pain, weight loss, and general poor health. A total abdominal hysterectomy with bilateral salpingo-oophorectomy is usually performed as well as excision of nearby lymph glands. If the cancer is found in later stages, a complete exenteration of the abdomen and pelvic organs may be necessary.
Uterine	Several types of endometrial carcinoma arise from the endometrial lining and may invade the uterine wall. Found most commonly in nullipara women between the ages of 50 and 60 years old, this form of cancer may metastasize to the ovaries, fallopian tubes, and other organs. Symptoms include menorrhagia; metrorrhagia; a watery or thick, foul-smelling discharge; and postmenopausal bleeding. Depending on the stage and the age of the woman, a hysterectomy and bilateral salpingo-oophorectomy may need to be performed.
Vaginal	A rare form of cancer exhibiting symptoms of leukorrhea and bloody vaginal discharge. Treatment usually involves surgical excision of the tumor.
Vulvar	Squamous cell carcinoma of the vulva accounts for 3% of all gynecologic cancers. It occurs mainly in postmenopausal women. A small, hard lump develops and grows into an ulcer. It may weep and bleed, and if not treated, it will metastasize to other areas.

Other Diseases of the Female Reproductive Tract

Endometriosis is a condition that occurs when endometrial tissue migrates outside of the uterus into the pelvic or abdominal cavity. This tissue implants on other organs and responds to hormonal signals as if it were within the uterus. The misplaced tissue fills with blood and sloughs off, causing severe pain. Although benign and self-limiting, it is a cause of infertility. Laparoscopy may confirm the diagnosis of endometriosis and is used to remove the endometrial implants.

Uterine fibroid tumors are the most common tumors of the female reproductive tract. They occur in 50 percent of all women who reach age 50. They are nonmalignant tumors, also called **leiomyomas**, which are made up of smooth muscle that grows within the myometrium of the uterus (Figure 10–18). The patient may be asymptomatic, or experience pelvic pain, constipation, urinary frequency, and heavy or prolonged periods. In younger women of childbearing age, myomectomy might be the recommended surgical treatment. In cases with multiple tumors or tumors large in size, or when the woman is not concerned with childbearing, a hysterectomy may be performed. Refer to Table 10–11 for a listing of hysterectomies.

leiomyomas: Myoma or tumor of muscular tissue involving the nonstriated muscle fibers, also known as fibroid tumors.

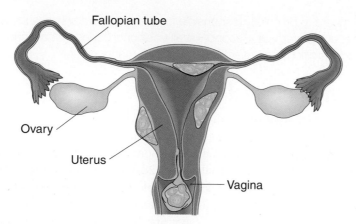

Figure 10-18 Example of fibroid tumors

Table 10-11 Types of Hysterectomies

Procedure	Definition
Hysterectomy	Surgical removal of the uterus
Supracervical hysterectomy	Surgical removal of the fundus and corpus portions of the uterus (leaving the cervix)
Total abdominal hysterectomy (TAH)	Complete surgical removal of the entire uterus using an abdominal approach
Vaginal hysterectomy (Vag Hyst)	Surgical removal of the uterus using a vaginal approach
Oophorectomy	Surgical removal of the ovary
Salpingectomy	Surgical removal of the fallopian tube
Salpingo-oophorectomy	Surgical removal of both the fallopian tube and the ovary (unilateral for one; bilateral for two)
Hysterosalpingo-oophorectomy	Surgical removal of the uterus, fallopian tube, and ovary
Total abdominal hysterectomy with bilateral salpingo-oophorectomy	Surgical removal of uterus, both tubes, and both ovaries

Ovarian cancers continue to be ranked fifth as one of the leading causes of cancer death in women according to the Centers for Disease Control and Prevention (CDC), United States Cancer Statistics.

ICD-10-CM Coding for Hysterectomies

Establishing medical necessity for a hysterectomy is crucial. A simple sign and symptom code such as "abdominal pain" would not justify removal.

Be sure to locate the main term(s) in the Alphabetic Index, of ICD-10-CM, first. Review any subterms under the main term and follow any cross-reference instructions. Always verify the code that has been selected from the index by using the Tabular List. Refer to any instructional notations and assign the code to the highest level of specificity. Code the diagnosis until all elements are completely identified.

EXAMPLE: A patient has a hysterectomy for intramural leiomyoma of uterus.

ICD-10-CM code D25.1

Always sequence the primary diagnosis first. The primary diagnosis is listed by the use of the ICD-10-CM code that represents the diagnosis, condition, problem, or other reason for the encounter/visit shown in the medical record to be chiefly responsible for the outpatient services provided during the encounter/visit. Second, list all additional codes that describe any coexisting conditions that affect patient care or management.

Menstrual Abnormalities

The beginning of menstruation is called menarche. As mentioned earlier, this occurs at puberty with the secretion of the female sex hormones estrogen and progesterone. Menstrual disorders are often triggered by hormonal abnormalities that control the menstrual cycle. The normal menstrual cycle is 28 days with an average length of blood flow lasting five days. The first day of any blood loss is considered the first day of the menstrual cycle whether it is spotting or a regular flow. This day is important in the calculation and determination of what may be happening to cause an abnormal cycle. A woman typically menstruates throughout her reproductive years until the onset of menopause, which is the cessation of menses. If a patient does not have a menstrual flow, it is called amenorrhea. Painful or difficult menstruation is referred to as dysmenorrhea. Excessive menstrual flow or too frequent menstruation is called abnormal uterine bleeding. See Table 10–12 for a list of common terms relating to the menstrual cycle.

Table 10-12 Terms Relating to Menstruation

Term	Definition
Amenorrhea	Without menses
Dysmenorrhea	Painful menstruation
Menarche	Beginning of menstrual function at time of puberty
Menometrorrhagia	Excessive uterine bleeding at and between menstrual periods
Menopause	Cessation of hormone production and menstruation
Menorrhalgia	Painful menses
Menorrhagia	Excessive uterine bleeding at time of menstruation
Menorrhea	Discharge at time of menses
Menostaxis	Prolonged menstrual period
Menses	The regular recurring uterine bleeding from the shedding of the endometrium
Metrorrhagia	Uterine bleeding occurring at irregular intervals
Oligomenorrhea	Scanty or infrequent menstruation
Postmenopause	The period of life after menopause
Premenstrual	Occurring before regular menstruation

Inflammatory Conditions

Inflammatory conditions of the female genital tract may be localized or involve other genital organs and adjacent structures. The suffix -itis on the end of a word indicates an inflammation. The beginning of the term indicates the organ involved. Some conditions are cervicitis (cervix), endometritis (endometrium), oophoritis (ovaries), salpingitis (uterine tubes), vaginitis (vagina), vulvitis (vulva), and vulvovaginitis (vulva and vagina). There are many reasons for female genital inflammation. A spermicide, tampon, or the act of intercourse could cause a local inflammation. The fungal infection *Candida albicans,* also known as *Monilia* or yeast infection, can cause vulvovaginitis. Bacterial and viral infections, such as those found in venereal disease, are common causes of inflammation, genital tract infections, and pelvic inflammatory disease (PID).

PID is an inflammation of the entire female reproductive tract, the most common cause of which is an STD. As these organisms travel up the fallopian tubes into the abdominal cavity, the body fights to get rid of them. PID symptoms include fever, chills, backache, a foul-smelling vaginal discharge, and a painful, tender abdomen. During this process adhesions may form, attaching organs to other organs and blocking the lumen (opening) of the fallopian tube. This is the most common cause of infertility. In severe cases, the peritoneum, a membrane that covers the abdominal wall, becomes inflamed and a condition called peritonitis may result. If the infection gets into the bloodstream, septicemia and even death may occur.

The Female Breast

Gynecologists evaluate the female breast and diagnose breast disease. Most procedure codes for these services would be found within the integumentary system of the surgery section in the CPT manual. A common benign condition of the breast in which small sacs of tissue and fluid develop is fibrocystic breast disease. In this disease cystic lumps or nodules are noticed in the breast and may be accompanied by premenstrual tenderness. A mammogram confirms this diagnosis.

A fibroadenoma is a common benign neoplasm of the breast derived from glandular tissue. Following the instructions in ICD-10-CM Chapter 2 for coding a neoplasm, first research the main term "fibroadenoma" in the Alphabetic Index. Refer to the Neoplasm table to assign the correct code, always confirming in the tabular index.

A majority of breast lumps are discovered by women on self-examination. Others are found by the gynecologist, who performs a breast examination as part of the routine gynecologic examination, or by mammography, a radiographic examination of the breasts for the detection of cancer. Some signals include skin changes, puckering, or leakage from the nipple. Most women needing lumpectomy or mastectomy for the removal of malignant tumors and breast tissue are referred to general surgeons. See Chapter 7 of this book for additional information regarding breast procedures.

> **Highlight:**
>
> While breast cancer occurs mostly in women, it does occur in men. ICD-10-CM contains several specific codes for male breast as well as female breast.

Exercise 10.11

Use the ICD-10-CM manual to code the following exercises.

1. Endometriosis of the broad ligament _____
2. Chlamydial vulvovaginitis _____
3. Fibrocystic breast disease _____
4. Mittelschmerz _____
5. Carcinoma in situ of the cervical canal _____

Use the ICD-10-CM and CPT manuals to code the following exercises.

6. Uterine suspension with anterior colporrhaphy for uterine prolapse with cystocele _____

(continues)

Exercise 10.11 (continued)

7. I&D of Bartholin's gland abscess complicating pregnancy _____

8. Resection for ovarian malignancy with bilateral salpingo-oophorectomy and omentectomy _____

9. A healthy seven-pound baby boy delivered naturally and without any complications

   _____

10. Patient presented with persistent anal and vaginal irritation. A pinworm exam and test were positive. Pelvic exam findings revealed associated vulvovaginitis. _____

Summary

The practice of obstetrics and gynecology are two specialties in one that serve the needs of pregnant and nonpregnant women.

The reproductive organs consist of the external genitalia, vagina, uterus, fallopian tubes, and ovaries. The primary purpose of the reproductive organs is to produce offspring.

Obstetrics is the branch of medical science that has to do with the pregnancy process from conception to childbirth and through the puerperium. A global package concept is used to code and bill for obstetrical services, which include normal uncomplicated antepartum, delivery, and postpartum care.

A pregnancy is divided into three trimesters and labor is divided into three stages. Complications in and of pregnancy are numerous and include abortion, anatomical problems, anemia, ectopic pregnancy, fetal problems, gestational diabetes, hydramnios, placental anomalies, malpresentations, multiple births, postpartum disorders, and Rh incompatibility.

A gynecologist is a physician and surgeon who treats females experiencing infertility, structural abnormalities of female organs, sexually transmitted diseases, sexual dysfunction, menstrual abnormalities, inflammatory conditions, breast disease, female cancer, and other diseases. OB/GYN physicians perform preventive services including contraceptive counseling, screening Pap smears, breast examinations, and complete physical examinations. Unique aspects of coding OB/GYN include the dual role of the physician serving the pregnant and nonpregnant patient, and acting as primary care physician and specialist. Many sensitive issues surrounding OB/GYN services and the complexities of the complications of and in pregnancy add to the difficulty in coding this specialty.

References

AMA Current Procedural Terminology 2016 professional edition. (2015). Chicago: American Medical Association.

Centers for Medicare & Medicaid Services (CMS) and National Center for Health Care Statistics (NCHS). (2015). ICD-10-CM official guidelines for coding and reporting (FY 2016). Retrieved from www.cms.gov.

Centers for Medicare and Medicaid Services. (2015). *National correct coding initiative policy manual for Medicare services.* Retrieved from https://cms.gov.

Chabner, D-E. (2014). *The language of medicine* (10th ed.). St. Louis, MO: Elsevier.

Dorland. (2012). *Dorland's illustrated medical dictionary* (32nd ed.). Philadelphia, PA: Elsevier.

ICD-10-CM expert for hospitals 2016 edition (2015). Salt Lake City, UT: Optum360.

Miller-Keane & O'Toole, M. T. (2005). *Encyclopedia & dictionary of medicine, nursing, & allied health* (7th ed.). Philadelphia, PA: Elsevier.

Venes, D. (Ed.). (2013). *Taber's cyclopedic medical dictionary* (22nd ed.). Philadelphia, PA: F. A. Davis Company.

Radiology, Pathology, and Laboratory

Learning Objectives

Upon successful completion of this chapter, you should be able to:

- Identify subsections of the radiologic section.
- Code the various types of radiologic procedures.
- Identify the different types of laboratory procedures.
- Explain the difference between qualitative and quantitative.
- Code the different procedures related to the radiology and laboratory sections.

Key Terms

automated

brachytherapy

computerized
  tomography (CT)
  scan

hyperthermia

intracavitary

magnetic resonance
  imaging (MRI)

mammography

manual

qualitative

quantitative

radiation absorbed
  dose (rad)

ribbons

sources

Introduction

This chapter introduces specialty coding in the areas of radiology and laboratory and pathology. The focus is mainly on CPT coding, with relevant examples from ICD-10-CM integrated where appropriate. The first half of this chapter covers the specialty of radiology and includes nuclear medicine and diagnostic ultrasound. The second half of the chapter discusses pathology and laboratory guidelines. Keep the CPT code book handy while studying this chapter.

Radiology

Radiology is a medical specialty that involves the use of radioactive substances such as x-rays and radioactive isotopes in the prevention, detection, diagnosis, and treatment of disease. The field of radiology includes many specialty areas, including radiation therapy, nuclear medicine, ultrasound, computed tomography, magnetic resonance imaging, and special procedures such as angiography. A radiographer is a specialist who produces images (or radiographs) of parts of the human body. Depending on their level of training and experience, radiographers may also perform more complicated tests such as preparing contrast media for patients to drink and operating special equipment used for computerized tomography, magnetic resonance imaging, and ultrasound. Radiation therapists prepare cancer patients for treatment and administer prescribed radiation doses to parts of the body. A radiologist is a physician who interprets the images prepared by the radiographer and makes patient treatment recommendations.

CPT—Radiology

The radiology section of the CPT code book includes seven subsections:

1. Diagnostic Radiology (Diagnostic Imaging)
2. Diagnostic Ultrasound
3. Radiologic Guidance
4. Breast, Mammography
5. Bone/Joint Studies
6. Radiation Oncology
7. Nuclear Medicine

The coder should become familiar with the differences between these subsections and not code based on the area of the body being treated because each subsection covers details of the area of the anatomy being treated. For example, diagnostic procedures on the spine and pelvis, such as a radiologic examination of the spine, are included within the Diagnostic Radiology subsection. Ultrasound procedures such as echography of the spinal canal are included within the Diagnostic Ultrasound subsection. "Notes" are provided at the beginning of the subsections, as well as within other parts of the subsections that explain terminology, such as A-mode, M-mode, B-scan, or real-time scan modes of diagnostic ultrasound.

Physician Billing

Most physician offices do not have radiologic equipment in their offices and, therefore, refer patients to hospitals or radiologic outpatient facilities. In these cases, the coders for these physicians would not be assigning radiology codes unless the physician provides radiologic supervision and interpretation.

Radiologic Guidance

The Radiology section of CPT contains codes for Radiologic Guidance divided into the headings of fluoroscopic, computed tomography, and magnetic resonance. Note must be taken that many CPT surgical procedures already include the statement, "including radiologic supervision and interpretation," and a code from this section cannot be added to the surgical code, as the example below indicates correct coding of the procedure.

> **EXAMPLE:** Transcatheter retrieval, percutaneous, of intravascular foreign body (e.g., fractured venous or arterial catheter), includes radiologic supervision and interpretation, and imaging guidance (ultrasound or fluoroscopy), when performed. The physician submits code 37197.

Highlight:
The radiologic supervision and interpretation codes do not apply to the radiation oncology subsection.

Radiology Modifiers

It is often necessary to modify procedures or services codes. This section introduces the common radiology modifiers and provides examples of how each might be used.

-22: Unusual Procedural Services

This modifier is intended for use when the service provided is greater than that usually required for the listed procedure. Modifier -22 may be used with **computerized tomography (CT) scan** codes when additional slices are required or more detailed examination is necessary.

> **computerized tomography (CT) scan:** This type of radiologic procedure is used to scan any part of the body; most useful in scanning brain, lung, mediastinum, retroperitoneum, and liver.

-26: Professional Component

The professional component includes supervision of the procedure, reading and interpreting the results, and documenting the interpretation in a report. This service can be done by the physician who ordered the radiologic procedure or by the radiologist on staff at the hospital or outpatient center. The physician would report a professional component by attaching the modifier -26 to the appropriate radiologic procedure.

-TC: Technical Component

The technical component "TC" is added to the CPT radiology code for the facility that owns the equipment. This includes the use of equipment, supplies and processing, and the technician at a hospital or an outpatient or diagnostic imaging facility. Modifier -TC is an HCPCS Level II modifier.

> **Coding Tip:**
>
> When reporting a code describing "radiologic supervision and interpretation," do not report modifier -26 along with the procedure. The "radiologic supervision and interpretation" code already describes the professional component.

> **EXAMPLE:** 73550 Radiologic examination of femur. The physician should report the following: 73550-26. The clinic should report the following: 73550-TC.

> **EXAMPLE:** Peritoneogram with the physician providing only the supervision and interpretation of this procedure. The physician should report the following:
>
> 74190 Peritoneogram, (after injection of air or contrast), radiologic supervision and interpretation.
>
> In this example, modifier -26 would not be appropriate because the descriptor code 74190 already indicated that the physician provided only the supervision and interpretation for the procedure. Adding the modifier would cause the claim to be denied.

> **EXAMPLE:**
>
> 74329 Endoscopic catheterization of the pancreatic ductal system, radiologic supervision and interpretation.

-51: Multiple Procedures

Modifier -51 may be reported to identify that multiple radiologic procedures were performed on the same day or during the same episode.

-52: Reduced Services

Modifier -52 may be reported to identify that a radiologic procedure is partially reduced or eliminated at the discretion of the physician.

-53: Discontinued Procedure

Modifier -53 is used when the physician elected to discontinue or terminate a diagnostic procedure, usually because of risk to the patient.

-59: Distinct Procedural Service

Modifier -59 may be used to identify that a procedure or service was distinct or independent from other services provided on the same day.

-RT and -LT Modifiers

Modifiers -RT and -LT are HCPCS Level II modifiers that should be used when unilateral procedures are performed. When bilateral procedures are performed, Report these modifiers to reflect a bilateral radiologic procedure, code the procedure twice and attach -RT to one of the codes and -LT to the other, or CPT modifier 50 to indicate both sides. The use of the RT/LT or 50 modifiers is determined by the insurance carrier.

> **Highlight:**
>
> Modifiers -RT and -LT apply to Medicare claims, and their use varies according to reporting requirements of medical programs and other third-party payors.

EXAMPLE:

73510-RT and 73510-LT Radiologic examination, hips, minimum two views each hip, bilateral.

Exercise 11.1

Assign the appropriate CPT codes for the following procedure(s); include modifiers and HCPCS Level II modifiers when applicable.

1. Radiologic examination, temporomandibular joint, open and closed mouth; unilateral
   _____

2. Radiologic examination, chest, two views, frontal and lateral; professional component only
   _____

3. Radiologic examination, knee, arthrography, radiologic supervision and interpretation
   _____

4. Barium enema with KUB _____

5. Hysterosalpingography, radiologic supervision and interpretation _____

6. Radiologic exam of the chest using Bucky studies _____

7. X-ray of pelvis and hips, age 10 _____

8. X-ray of tibia and fibula, left leg, two views _____

9. Abdominal x-ray, single anteroposterior view _____

10. Intravenous pyelogram with KUB _____

Diagnostic Radiology (Diagnostic Imaging)

The production of a picture, image, or shadow that represents the object being investigated is diagnostic radiology. The classic technique for imaging is the x-ray. (Figure 11–1 indicates the radiographic projection positions for a chest x-ray.)

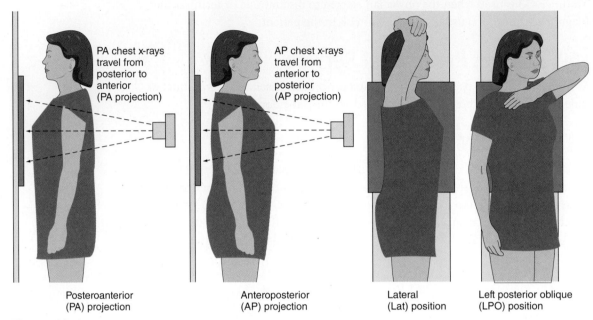

PA chest x-rays travel from posterior to anterior (PA projection)

AP chest x-rays travel from anterior to posterior (AP projection)

Posteroanterior (PA) projection

Anteroposterior (AP) projection

Lateral (Lat) position

Left posterior oblique (LPO) position

Figure 11-1   Different radiographic positions used to obtain various views of chest x-rays

magnetic resonance imaging (MRI): This type of radiologic procedure is used to scan brain, spinal cord, soft tissues, and adrenal and renal masses. More superior scan than the CT.

Codes 70010–76499 describe diagnostic radiology services. They are further subdivided by anatomical site and then by specific type of procedure performed: CT scan, MRI, x-ray, and MRA scan. These radiology procedures may be found in the Alphabetic Index of the CPT manual by referring to the main terms *x-ray, CT scan,* **magnetic resonance imaging (MRI)**, and *magnetic resonance angiography (MRA).*

CPT provides separate codes for radiologic procedures using contrast media. *Contrast media* is a term used to describe chemical substances that are introduced into the body to enable the soft tissue vessels and organs (e.g., the liver) to be seen with x-rays. The contrast medium is administered either orally or intravenously. Examples of some contrast media are barium, iohexol, and Renografin. Common x-ray procedures using contrast material include barium enema, endoscopic retrograde cholangiopancreatogram, fistulogram, intravenous pyelogram, and hysterosalpingogram.

CT scans may also be performed with or without contrast material (Figure 11–2). This radiologic procedure is helpful in evaluating the brain, lung, mediastinum, retroperitoneum, and the liver.

In most instances, MRI scans are almost equal to CT scans, but MRIs are superior in evaluating the brain, spinal cord, soft tissues, and adrenal and renal masses (Figure 11–3). For patients who have metallic objects, such as pacemakers, metallic fragments, and vascular clips in the central nervous system, this procedure is contraindicated. Contrast material may also be used when performing MRI scans; the most common is gadolinium (gadopentetate dimeglumine). Figure 11–4 shows a typical MRI setting.

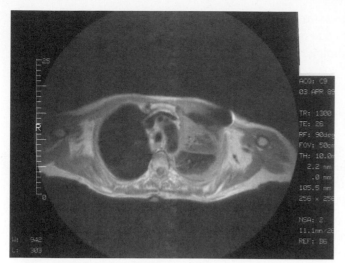

Figure 11-2 An example of computerized tomography: a CT scan of a chest showing pleural effusion

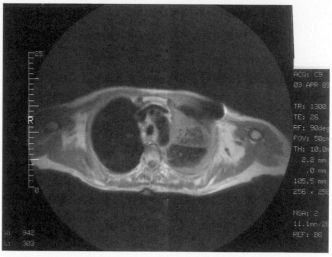

Figure 11-3 An example of magnetic resonance imaging: an MRI of a chest

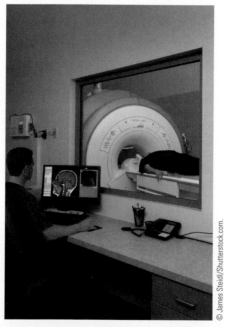

Figure 11-4 A patient lies completely still while receiving an MRI. Medical professionals review the images recorded by the MRI scan.

Interventional Radiology

Interventional radiology is a specialty of radiology where image-guided procedures are used to diagnose and treat many diseases in all anatomical systems. Interventional procedures are less invasive, and many conditions that once required surgery can now be treated nonsurgically by interventional radiologists. Interventional radiology employs the use of x-rays, CT, ultrasound, MRI, and other imaging modalities to advance a catheter or probe into the body to treat at the source of the disease

Coding Tip:

Transluminal balloon angioplasty of the peripheral artery is performed with radiologic supervision and interpretation. Code 75962 would be assigned.

nonsurgically. These treatments are less painful, have less risk to the patient, and less recovery time when compared to open surgery. Angioplasty and stents are examples of the use of interventional radiologic procedures used in the lower extremities to treat peripheral arterial disease.

Diagnostic Ultrasound

Diagnostic ultrasound is considered a subsection that lists codes 76506–76999. Similar to diagnostic radiology, it is also further subdivided by anatomical sites. These codes may be found in the index by referring to *ultrasound* or *echography*. Diagnostic ultrasound involves the use of high-frequency waves to visualize internal structures of the body. Ultrasounds are commonly performed for evaluation of the abdomen, pelvis, and ear, and for gynecologic and obstetrical diagnoses. Figure 11–5A and 11–5B illustrate some examples of diagnostic ultrasound equipment.

Four types of diagnostic ultrasound are recognized:

A-mode   A one-dimensional ultrasonic measurement procedure.

M-mode   A one-dimensional ultrasonic measurement procedure with movement of the trace (delayed time for the sound to hit the specimen being scanned and then be reflected back to the probe) to record amplitude and velocity of moving echo-producing structures. This mode is used for the heart and vessels using color flow.

B-scan   A two-dimensional ultrasonic scanning procedure with a two-dimensional display. This scan is the same as A-mode, except with two-dimensional display.

Real-time scan   A two-dimensional ultrasonic scanning procedure with display of both two-dimensional structure and motion with time. *Real time* means that the image can be visualized as it is being produced.

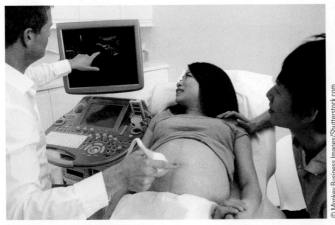

(A)

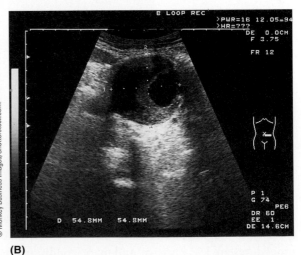

(B)

Figure 11-5 (A) Ultrasonic equipment; (B) a diagnostic ultrasound

Highlight:

The medicine chapter in the CPT manual also includes ultrasound involving the following areas:

Arterial Studies of the Extremities (93922–93931)

Venous Studies of the Extremities (93965–93971)

Cerebrovascular Arterial Studies (93880–93895)

Visceral and Penile Vascular Studies (93975–93982)

Ultrasound of the Heart—Echocardiography (93303–93355)

Exercise 11.2

Assign the appropriate CPT codes for the following procedure(s); include CPT modifiers and HCPCS Level II modifiers, when applicable.

1. Echography, pregnant uterus, B-scan and/or real-time scan with image documentation; complete _____

2. Echography, transvaginal _____

3. Ultrasonic guidance for pericardiocentesis, radiologic supervision and interpretation _____

4. Ultrasonic guidance for interstitial radioelement application _____

5. Gastrointestinal endoscopic ultrasound, radiologic supervision and interpretation _____

6. CT scan of pelvis, with contrast material _____

7. Ultrasound, transabdominal, 22 weeks, real-time _____

8. MRI of the cervical spine, no contrast _____

9. Ultrasound of the pelvis, nonobstetric, real time, complete _____

10. CT scan of maxillofacial area without contrast material _____

Breast Mammography

A radiographic examination of the breasts is referred to as **mammography**. Mammography uses low-energy x-rays to examine the human breast and is used to screen the breast to detect the presence of tumors or precancerous cells or in a diagnostic follow-up. The annual routine screening mammography is usually a bilateral (two-view film) study of each breast. In the event of an abnormal mammogram of one or both breasts resulting in a more diagnostic procedure, CPT contains specific codes for the unilateral mammography or bilateral mammography used to follow up the screening mammogram. It is important to code mammography correctly as insurance plans that cover routine preventive procedures allow one screening mammogram annually. Incorrectly coding a diagnostic follow-up mammogram as a screening mammogram will result in a denial for reimbursement by the insurance carrier.

mammography: The process of using low-energy x-rays to examine the human breast as both a screening and diagnostic tool.

EXAMPLE: A patient is referred to the diagnostic center for her annual routine mammogram (77057). The mammography report shows a small nodule in the left outer quadrant of the left breast. The right breast is a normal study. The patient returns to the diagnostic center for a repeat mammogram of the left breast (77055-LT).

Coding Tip:

Since mammography procedures in CPT are indicated by unilateral or bilateral code selections, modifier -50 is not assigned with these procedures.

CPT also provides codes for computer-aided detection analysis, in which film radiographic images are digitized to allow the radiologist a more enhanced digital image of the breast(s). These are indicated in CPT as add-on codes that are assigned in conjunction with the mammography code.

The magnetic resonance imaging (MRI) codes, unilateral and bilateral, for the breast are also included in the mammography section.

Figure 11–6 demonstrates a mammography.

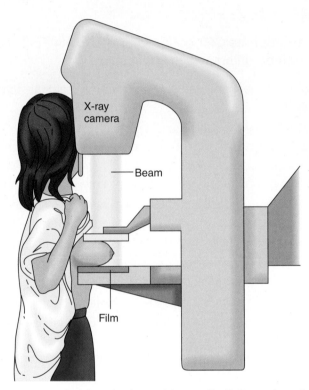

X-ray camera

Beam

Film

Figure 11-6 In mammography, the breast is gently flattened and radiographed from various angles to detect any abnormalities.

Radiation Oncology

The radiation oncology codes (77261–77799) describe therapeutic use of radiation to treat diseases, especially neoplastic tumors. Radiation therapy is used as a primary therapy to treat certain types of malignancies, such as leukemia. The most common type of radiation used in treatment is electromagnetic radiation with x-rays and gamma rays.

radiation absorbed dose (rad): A unit of measure in radiation.

X-rays are photons generated inside a machine, while gamma rays are photons emitted from a radioactive source. Radiation is measured in units known as the **rad (radiation absorbed doses)** or the gray, which is equal to 100 rad.

The delivery of radiation may be external or internal. External radiation therapy involves the delivery of a beam of ionizing radiation from an external source through the patient's skin toward the tumor region. Internal radiation therapy, also known as brachytherapy, involves applying a radioactive material inside the patient or in close proximity. This material may be contained in various types of devices such as tubes, needles, wires, seeds, and other small containers (Figure 11–7). Common radioactive materials used in brachytherapy include radium-226, cobalt-60, cesium-137, and iodine-125. The three types of brachytherapy are interstitial (into the tissues), **intracavitary** (implanted into body cavities), and surface applications. Interstitial brachytherapy involves the use of radiation sources placed in special devices and then implanted in body cavities. Surface application brachytherapy uses radioactive material that is contained on the surface of a plaque or mold and applied directly or close to the surface of the patient.

intracavitary: Within a body cavity.

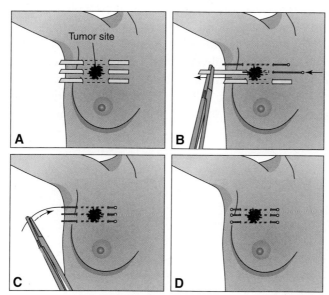

Figure 11-7 Brachytherapy, used in the treatment of breast cancer: (A) hollow metal needles are placed on the tumor site; (B) hollow metal catheters replace needles; (C) radioactive material is placed in catheters; (D) radioactive implants remain in place during treatment.

Radiation Treatment Delivery

The series of codes 77401–77425 indicate the technical component of delivering the radiation treatment, as well as the various energy levels administered. To assign these codes, the appropriate information is needed:

1. The number of treatment areas involved

2. The number of ports, parts, or devices that are surgically implanted (e.g., for easy removal of blood)

3. The number of shielding blocks, or shields, used to protect parts of the body from radiation

4. The total million electron volts (MEV) administered

Hyperthermia

hyperthermia: This procedure uses heat to raise the temperature of a specific area of the body to try to increase cell metabolism and increase the destruction of cancer cells.

Hyperthermia involves using heat to raise the temperature of a specific area of the body to try to increase cell metabolism and, consequently, increase the destruction of cancer cells. Hyperthermia is usually performed as an adjunct to radiation therapy or chemotherapy. The hyperthermia codes (77600–77620) in the CPT book include external, interstitial, and intracavitary treatment. If administered at the same time, radiation therapy should be reported separately.

Clinical Brachytherapy

brachytherapy: A natural or manmade radioactive element that is applied in or around a particular treatment field.

sources: Intracavitary placement or permanent interstitial placement in clinical brachytherapy.

ribbons: Temporary interstitial placement in clinical brachytherapy.

Clinical **brachytherapy** uses natural or manmade radioactive elements that are applied in or around a particular treatment field. A therapeutic radiologist provides supervision of radioactive elements and interpretation of appropriate dosages. When the services of a surgeon are needed, a modifier -66 (surgical team) or -62 (two surgeons) may be reported to ensure that both physicians are reimbursed. Codes 77750–77799 include the admission to the hospital and daily visits provided by the physician. The codes differentiate between interstitial and intracavitary brachytherapy and are further subdivided to identify the number of **sources** or **ribbons** applied: simple (1–4 sources/ribbons), intermediate (5–10 sources/ribbons), or complex (>10 sources/ribbons). CPT defines sources as intracavity placement or permanent interstitial placement. Ribbons refer to temporary interstitial placement.

Highlight:

Surgeons are required for this type of therapy because this procedure is done internally on a patient. If any type of complication occurs internally, a surgeon might need to assist the radiologist.

Exercise 11.3

Assign the appropriate CPT codes for the following procedure(s). Include modifiers and HCPCS Level II modifiers when applicable.

1. Teletherapy isodose plan (hand); simple (one or two) unmodified ports directed to a single area of interest _____

2. Radiation treatment delivery, two separate treatment areas, three or more ports on a single treatment area, use of multiple blocks, 15 MEV _____

3. Hyperthermia, externally generated; superficial heating degree is 3 cm _____

4. Intracavitary radiation application; complex _____

5. Supervision, handling, loading of radiation _____

6. Screening mammogram, annual, routine _____

7. Mammogram, right breast, computer-aided _____

8. MRI, both breasts _____

9. Infusion of radiation solution to include follow-up care for three months _____

10. DXA for bone density of hips, pelvis, and spine _____

Nuclear Medicine

Nuclear medicine involves the administration of radioisotopes (radioactive elements that assist in the diagnosis of disease). The radioactive isotope deteriorates spontaneously and emits gamma rays from inside the body that enable the physician to view internal abnormalities. Some radioisotopes are selectively absorbed by tumors or by specific organs in the body and thus make them visible on the scan. This subsection (78012–79999) includes nuclear medicine procedures according to body systems, such as cardiovascular. Some of the more common diagnostic nuclear medicine scans include bone, cardiac, lung, renal, and thyroid scans, as well as thallium-201, technetium-99m pyrophosphate, technetium-99m ventriculogram, and the multigated acquisition scans.

Bone Scans

Bone scans are performed as part of metastatic workups, to identify infections such as osteomyelitis; to evaluate the hip with a prosthetic device; to distinguish pathologic fractures from traumatic fractures; and to evaluate delayed union of fractures.

Cardiac Scans

Cardiac scans are performed for diagnosis of myocardial infarction, stress testing, measurement of cardiac output, and diagnosis of ventricular aneurysms.

Thallium-201 Scan

The thallium-201 scan examines myocardial perfusion, with normal myocardium appearing as "hot," and ischemic or infarcted areas appearing as "cold."

Technetium-99m Pyrophosphate Scan

The technetium-99m pyrophosphate scan identifies recently damaged myocardial tissue, and it is most sensitive 24 to 72 hours after an acute myocardial infarction.

Technetium-99m Ventriculogram Scan

The technetium-99m ventriculogram scan identifies abnormal wall motion, cardiac shunts, size and function of heart chambers, cardiac output, and ejection fraction.

Multigated Acquisition Scan

The multigated acquisition scan (MUGA) is another form of this type of study.

Lung Scans

Ventilation-perfusion (V/Q) lung scans can reveal pulmonary disease, chronic obstructive pulmonary disease, and emphysema. When performed along with chest x-rays, these scans are important tools in evaluating pulmonary emboli.

Renal and Thyroid Scans

Renal scans are performed to evaluate the overall functions of the kidneys. Thyroid scans are most commonly performed with technetium-99m pertechnetate, and they are useful in detecting nodules.

> **Coding Tip:**
>
> When these tests are performed during exercise and/or pharmacologic stress, the appropriate stress testing code from the 93015–93018 range should be reported in addition to the appropriate code from the nuclear medicine subsection.

Exercise 11.4

Assign the appropriate CPT code for the following procedure(s). Include modifiers and HCPCS Level II modifiers when applicable.

1. Thyroid imaging, with uptake; single determination _____
2. Liver and spleen imaging; static only _____
3. Cardiac shunt detection _____
4. PET scan, whole body _____
5. Renal scan with vascular flow and function study _____
6. Gastric emptying study _____
7. Ureteral reflux study/voiding cystogram with urinary bladder residual study _____
8. Brain imaging, two views _____
9. PET myocardial imaging, metabolic evaluation _____
10. Bone marrow imaging, multiple areas _____

Exercise 11.5

1. Read the following report, then assign the correct ICD-10-CM and CPT codes for physician billing.

RADIOLOGY REPORT

Patient Name: Jan Clure   Admitting Physician: Ken Shallow, M.D.

Hospital No.: 11049   Procedure: Intraoperative cholangiogram

X-ray No.: 15-1504   Date: 03/12/XX

FINDINGS: Intraoperative cholangiogram was performed. Contrast was injected through the cystic duct remnant. There was mild dilatation of the common duct with free flow of contrast into the duodenum. However, there was a 6 mm filling defect in the proximal common duct that probably represents a stone.

IMPRESSION: Evidence of a common duct stone. Mild dilatation of the common bile duct.

_____

Ann Jones, M.D.

AJ: xx

D: 03/13/XX

T: 03/13/XX

C: Bernard Kester, M.D.

ICD-10-CM code(s) _____   CPT code(s) _____

(continues)

Exercise 11.5 (*continued*)

2. Read the following report, then assign the correct ICD-10-CM and CPT codes for physician billing.

RADIOLOGY REPORT

Patient Name: Sam Chandler

Hospital No.: 11503

X-ray No.: 15-29050

Admitting Physician: Lisa Andrews, M.D.

Procedure: Chest, PA only

Date: 12/13/XX

When films are compared to previous radiographs, there is interval increase of the right subcutaneous emphysema. There is interval demonstration of very small pneumothorax along the right lower chest. There is some interval change in the position of the right lower chest catheter, the tip of which is seen at a lower level than in the previous exam. There is no interval change in the position of the second catheter. Heart and lungs appear unremarkable without any active process; unchanged since previous exam.

IMPRESSION: Increase in right subcutaneous emphysema, nontraumatic. Chronic right pneumothorax, small.

_____

Larry Erwin, M.D.

LE: xx

D: 12/13/XX

T: 12/13/XX

ICD-10-CM code(s) _____   CPT code(s) _____

3. Read the following report, then assign the correct ICD-10-CM and CPT codes for physician billing.

RADIOLOGY REPORT

Patient Name: Ellen Parker

Hospital No.: 11259

X-ray No.: 15-2823

Admitting Physician: Sara Loyola, M.D.

Procedure: Right hip and pelvis

Date: 09/25/XX

Right Hip

There is a fracture through the right femoral neck. There is also evidence of intertrochanteric fracture of the right hip. No other joint or soft tissue abnormalities.

IMPRESSION: Intertrochanteric fracture of the right hip. There also appears to be a fracture of the right femoral neck.

Pelvis

A bipolar left hip prosthesis is noted in place. There is an intertrochanteric fracture of the right hip. There also appears to be a nondisplaced fracture through the right femoral neck. No other joint or soft tissue abnormalities.

IMPRESSION: Intertrochanteric fracture of the right hip. There is also evidence of a nondisplaced fracture through the right femoral neck.

_____

Paula Robins, M.D.

PR: xx

D: 09/25/XX

T: 09/25/XX

ICD-10-CM code(s) _____   CPT code(s) _____

(*continues*)

Exercise 11.5 *(continued)*

4. Read the following chart notes and radiology report and assign the correct ICD-10-CM and CPT codes for physician billing.

Patient Name: Sala, Roberto   Date: 6/28/XX

This is a new patient in the office today complaining of an injury to the right foot. This morning he accidentally smashed his right foot into a kitchen cabinet and has noticed pain and swelling on ambulation since then.

EXAMINATION: V.S.: W-191.5, BP-110/80 (sitting), P-64 & reg, R-16, T-96. His LT FOOT is quiescent. His right foot has an enlarging hematoma on the dorsum with warmth and flexion deformities of the proximal interphalangeal joints as before with tenderness over the entire forefoot region.

IMPRESSION: Trauma right foot

PLAN: We will check an x-ray of the right foot to rule out fracture. If there is none, he will treat with rest, ice, and mild compression from a sock and elevation and after a day or two if he feels well may then proceed to prn heat.

ADDENDUM: Because of the results of the x-ray the 2nd and 3rd toe were taped with paper tape to help in immobilization.

_____

Lowery Johnson, M.D.

ICD-10-CM code(s) _____   CPT code(s) _____

RADIOLOGY REPORT

Patient Name: Roberto Sala   Physician: Lowery Johnson, M.D.
Hospital No.: 11259989-998   Procedure: AP & lateral of RT foot
x-Ray No.: 15-7784511   Date: 06/28/XX

Two views of the right foot reveal a faint line of translucency in the proximal shaft in the 2nd toe about 1/3 proximal to PIP. There is also soft tissue swelling.

IMPRESSION: 1. A small nondisplaced fracture of the shaft of the 2nd proximal phalanx.

_____

Carole Kincaid, M.D.
Radiologist

ICD-10-CM code(s) _____   CPT code(s) _____

5. Read the following chart notes and radiology report and assign the correct ICD-10-CM and CPT codes for physician billing.

Patient Name: Highgrove, Lynn   Date: 10/18/XX

She is again about the same as on her last visit. She has had no stomatitis, dermatitis, pruritis, GI upset, or increase in bruising.

EXAMINATION: V.S.: W-178.5, BP-130/80 (sitting), P-64 & reg, R-16, T-96.4 Skin, mouth, and nose are clear (she has a rather chronic malar flush). I believe that there is more synovial thickening of

---

(continues)

Exercise 11.5 (*continued*)

the fifth proximal interphalangeal joint and especially the fourth one on the right, which is becoming more cystic. Thickening of the second and third metacarpophalangeal joints, the right is greater than the left, which remains a problem. Her wrists, elbows, and shoulders are unremarkable. Hips and trochanters are essentially normal. Knees demonstrate soft tissue hypertrophy with crepitation. Her ankles are puffy. Her feet are quintessence with bony hypertrophy.

IMPRESSION: Rheumatoid arthritis

PLAN: Call in Rx for methotrexate 2.5 mg #16 with no refills. Continue 10 mg q week. Continue prednisone 7.5 mg q.o.d., calcium and vitamin D and the folic acid. I will monitor her CBC and because of the meds a liver profile and SMA. We will now evaluate x-rays of her hands to compare with those taken in 2011 to see the extent of joint damage and/or progression. We will also arrange for a DEXA bone density over the next month or two because of the chronic Prednisone dosage. She will return for follow-up in four weeks but call sooner if needed.

_____

Lowery Johnson, M.D.

ICD-10-CM code(s) _____ CPT code(s) _____

RADIOLOGY REPORT

Patient Name: Lynn Highgrove
Hospital No.: 225987
X-ray No.: 15-55894778

Physician: Lowery Johnson, M.D.
Procedure: Bilateral Hands, AP and lateral
Date: 10/18/XX

Multiple views of the hands reveal juxta-articular osteoporosis. There is some degenerative change at each 2nd and 3rd distal interphalangeal joint and each 1st interphalangeal joint in the left first metacarpophalange. There is significant erosive and cystic change in the 3rd left proximal interphalangeal joint with joint space narrowing, soft tissue swelling and ulnar deviation of the middle phalange. There is loss of cartilage space in the second left, second and third right metacarpophalange with erosive change at in the second metacarpophalangeal joint on the right and possibly the third joint. These films were compared to ones taken on June 5th, 2011. They show definite progression of erosive change and cartilage loss at the third left proximal interphalangeal joint and some increase in cartilage loss at the second left metacarpophalangeal joint On the right there is no significant change and degenerative change with spur formation is also noted from both sets of films at the second right proximal interphalangeal joint.

IMPRESSION: 1. Rheumatoid arthritis of the hands with erosions and some progression particularly in the left third proximal interphalangeal joint since 2011.

_____

Carole Kincaid, M.D
Radiologist

ICD-10-CM code(s) _____ CPT code(s) _____

(*continues*)

Exercise 11.5 (*continued*)

6. Read the following chart notes and radiology report and assign the correct ICD-10-CM and CPT codes for physician billing.

Patient Name: Thomas, Daniel   Date: 11/12/XX

He was doing well until four to five weeks ago when he noted the onset of pain again in his LT shoulder and upper arm. It is often worse after bed and definitely worse on motion of the LT shoulder. This happened after he began gardening but he does not particularly remember traumatizing it. He also had pain and swelling in his right second proximal interphalangeal joint, which is starting to feel slightly better. He has had no stomatitis, dermatitis, GI upset, chest pain or increase in fatigue.

EXAMINATION: V.S.: W-170, BP-166/76 (sitting), P-68 & reg, R-16, T-96.4 He is in some distress from left shoulder pain with motion. His hands show bony hypertrophy but there is definite thickening, slight erythema, warmth, tenderness and pain on flexion of the right second proximal interphalangeal joint with some restriction of flexion due to a rather chronic tenosynovitis. His metacarpophalangeal and distal interphalangeal joints are otherwise unremarkable. There is decrease in extension of the left elbow, which is not tender or inflamed. The right elbow and each wrist are normal. There is significant limitation of abduction of the left shoulder by almost 60 degrees with pain on abduction, external and internal rotation; rotation is also limited. His right shoulder shows restriction of abduction by about 30 degrees with some stiffness on rotation. There is limitation of rotation and lateral tilt of the cervical spine. Thoracic spine is unremarkable. He has straightening of the lumbosacral spine with decrease in extension and flexion but denies pain or tenderness. There is decrease in external rotation of each hip by 40 degrees on the right, 60 on the left with some ache in the left. His knees and ankles are unremarkable. His feet show some bony hypertrophy.

IMPRESSION: Arthritis, SLE versus RA. He also has LT shoulder capsulitis.

PLAN: I will continue to monitor his UA, metabolic functions and liver profile because of the NSAID and also check a sed rate again to R/O traumatic arthropathy. We will check an x-ray of his LT shoulder today. In addition he will receive 80 mg of Depo-Medrol IM and begin the use of Darvocet-N-100 q 6 h prn pain. Given Rx for #60 with 3 refills. He may increase the Naprelan to 500 mg t.i.d., p.c. for 10 days. He was then reminded again about ROM exercises for his left shoulder including wall, crawl, pendulum exercises and isometric rotator cuff strengthening. If he is not better over the next 10 days he will call and injection may be warranted. Otherwise return for follow-up in about six months but call sooner if needed.

_____

Lowery Johnson, M.D.

ICD-10-CM code(s) _____   CPT code(s) _____

RADIOLOGY REPORT

Patient Name: Daniel Thomas   Physician: Lowery Johnson, M.D.

Hospital No.: 11503   Procedure: Left Shoulder, AP and Lateral

x-ray No.: 15-2922560   Date: 11/12/XX

Views of the left shoulder reveal large cystic areas in the humeral head. There is a considerable amount of calcification around the bicipital groove and in the subacromial space with corticated erosions on the superior surface of the humeral head near the bicipital groove and another erosive

(*continues*)

Exercise 11.5 (*continued*)

lesion on the inferomedial aspect of the humerus. A small spur is also seen near the superior border of the glenoid fossa and at the medial inferior border of the head of humerus at the medial aspect of the erosion. The acromioclavicular joint is well maintained. The glenohumeral articulation appears normal.

IMPRESSION: Erosive arthropathy of the left humeral head with degenerative osteoarthritis. Calcific subacromial bursitis

_____

Carole Kincaid, M.D.
Radiologist

10-CM code(s) _____   CPT code(s) _____

CPT—Pathology and Laboratory

Similar to radiology, clinical laboratory testing is critical to the detection, diagnosis, and treatment of disease. Under physicians' orders, medical technologists, technicians, or other qualified laboratory personnel perform a range of specialized tests by examining body fluids, such as urine, blood, feces, sputum, tissues, and cells. Laboratory personnel prepare patient specimens for examination and interpret tests, looking for microorganisms such as parasites, analyzing the chemical contents of body fluids, and matching blood types. All test results are then reported to the physician who initially ordered the test.

The pathology and laboratory section of CPT includes services by a physician or by technologists under the responsible supervision of a physician. This section includes codes for such services and procedures as organ or disease panel tests, urinalysis, hematologic and immunologic studies, and surgical and anatomical pathologic examinations.

These are the specific subsections in this chapter of the CPT code book:

Organ- or Disease-Oriented Panels	80047–80076
Drug Assay	80300–80377
Therapeutic Drug Assays	80150–80377
Evocative/Suppression Testing	80400–80439
Consultations (Clinical Pathology)	80500–80502
Urinalysis	81000–81099
Molecular Pathology	81161–81479
Genomic Sequencing Procedures (GSPs) and Other Molecular Multianalyte Assays	81410-81471
Multianalyte Assays with Algorithmic Analyses	81500–81599
Chemistry	82009–84999
Hematology and Coagulation	85002–85999
Immunology	86000–86849
Tissue Typing	86805–86849

Transfusion Medicine	86850–86999
Microbiology	87003–87999
Anatomic Pathology	88000–88099
Cytopathology	88104–88199
Cytogenetic Studies	88230–88299
Surgical Pathology	88300–88399
In Vivo (e.g., Transcutaneous) Laboratory Procedures	88720–88749
Other Procedures	89049–89240
Reproductive Medicine Procedures	89250–89398

Physician Billing

Highlight:

Reminder: When blood is drawn in the physician's office and is sent out for testing, the physician's office can bill only for the venipuncture. The laboratory or source performing the requested tests will bill the patient for services rendered.

When reporting laboratory services provided by the physician, the coder must determine whether the physician performed the complete procedure or only a component of it. Some physician offices maintain sophisticated laboratory equipment on their premises so they are able to provide complete lab testing. A complete test would include obtaining the sample/specimen (blood or urine), handling the specimen, performing the actual procedure/test, and analyzing and interpreting the results. In these physician office labs (POLs), the laboratory technician must be credentialed to perform the test at the moderate or above complexity level, and many times, this individual is responsible for posting those charges for the coders to bill. (See the Clinical Laboratory Improvement Amendments section later in this chapter.) Most physicians send blood samples to an outside lab or a hospital lab for testing. In these cases the physician may only report the collection and handling of the specimen.

> **EXAMPLE:** Dr. Smith performed a biopsy of the ovary, and the specimen was sent to a pathologist for review and interpretation. Dr. Smith uses the code 58900 for the actual biopsy of the ovary. The pathologist reports 88305 for the review and interpretation of the specimen.

Highlight:

Venous blood may be collected in a variety of ways. These procedures are located in the Surgery/Cardiovascular section of CPT. Of note, 36415 is a routine collection of venous blood by venipuncture, and 36416 is the collection of capillary blood specimen by finger, heel, or ear stick. Both of these collection methods are common in the physician office. Figure 11–8A shows the collection of capillary blood by puncture of the fingertip. Figure 11–8B demonstrates a routine venipuncture.

> **EXAMPLE:** A patient is seen in the office for his annual examination for hypertension and hypercholesterolemia. The patient is currently prescribed medication for hypercholesterolemia. Blood is drawn in the office today for a lipid panel and hepatic or liver function panel and will be sent to a local laboratory for testing. The physician codes for the annual examination and the venipuncture. The laboratory will code and submit charges for the lipid and hepatic panels.

The Medicine Section of CPT contains codes used for handling and transferring specimens when the specimen is obtained/collected in an office or other setting and sent off-site for testing. These codes are addressed in Chapter 12 of this textbook and do not include collection of venous or capillary blood.

Clinical Laboratory Improvement Amendments

The Clinical Laboratory Improvement Amendments (CLIA 1988) were passed by Congress in 1988 and enacted in 1992 to improve the quality of laboratory tests performed on specimens taken from the human body and used in diagnosis, prevention, and treatment of disease. All laboratories must register with CLIA and comply with its requirements to be certified by the U.S. Department of Health and Human Services (DHHS). CLIA regulates laboratory testing and requires clinical laboratories to be certified by individual states as well as the Center for Medicare and Medicaid Services (CMS) before they can accept human samples for diagnostic testing.

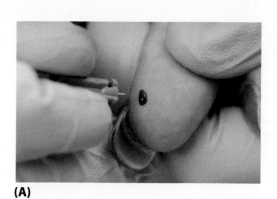

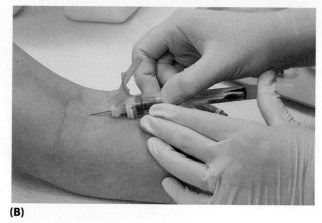

(A)   **(B)**

Figure 11-8 Blood-collection methods: (A) capillary puncture of fingertip; (B) routine venipuncture using a vacuum tube

Three federal agencies are responsible for CLIA: The Food and Drug Administration (FDA), Center for Medicare and Medicaid Services, and the Center for Disease Control (CDC). Each agency has a unique role in assuring quality laboratory testing:

FDA

- Categorizes tests based on complexity.
- Reviews requests for Waiver by Application.
- Develops rules/guidance for CLIA complexity categorization.

CMS

- Issues laboratory certificates.
- Collects user fees.
- Conducts inspections and enforces regulatory compliance.
- Approves private accreditation organizations for performing inspections and approves state exemptions.
- Monitors laboratory performances on Proficiency Testing and approves these programs.
- Publishes CLIA rules and regulations.

CDC

- Provides analysis, research, and technical assistance.
- Develops technical standards and laboratory practice guidelines, including standards and guidelines for cytology.
- Conducts laboratory quality improvement studies.
- Monitors proficiency testing practices.
- Develops and distributes professional information and educational resources.
- Manages the CLIA committee.

A few laboratories, such as those that perform only forensic tests, those certified by the National Institute on Drug Abuse to perform urine testing, those that perform research unrelated to patient treatment, and those that are with licensure are exempt from CLIA regulations.

CLIA designated four levels of testing based on complexity: waived tests, physician-performed microscopy tests (also waived tests), moderate-complexity tests, and high-complexity tests. Waived tests and physician-performed microscopy tests are of low complexity (Table 11–1). To perform these tests, a laboratory must obtain a certificate of waiver. Approximately 75 percent of all tests performed in the United States are of moderate complexity and include tests such as throat cultures, white blood counts, gram staining, and urine cultures. High-complexity tests involve specialized procedures in cytogenetics,

Table 11-1 Waived Tests

Dipstick or tablet reagent urinalysis for the following: • Bilirubin   • Glucose   • Hemoglobin   • Ketone   • Leukocytes   • Nitrite   • pH   • Protein   • Specific gravity   • Urobilinogen
Fecal occult blood
Spun microhematocrit
Microscopic examination of the following: • Urine sediment   • Pinworm preparation   • Vaginal wet mount preparation
Ovulation tests: visual color tests for human luteinizing hormone
Whole blood clotting time
Urine pregnancy tests
Slide card agglutination tests to screen for the following: • Antistreptolysin O (ASO)   • C reactive protein (CRP)   • Rheumatoid factor   • Infectious mononucleosis
Gram stain (on discharges and exudates)
Potassium hydroxide (KOH) preparation on cutaneous scrapings
Erythrocyte sedimentation rate
Sickle cell screening: methods other than electrophoresis
Glucose screen whole blood dipstick method: visual color comparison determination
Semen analysis
Automated hemoglobin by single analyte instruments

histocompatability, histopathology, and cytology. Laboratories performing moderate- and high-complexity tests go through a series of CMS certifications and are inspected by the DHHS every two years. A complete list of waived and other levels of testing as well as criteria for certification, rules, and guidelines are available at www.cms.gov.

Quantitative and Qualitative Studies

The laboratory and pathology section includes codes that will state whether the procedure is **quantitative** or **qualitative** in nature. Qualitative screening refers to tests that detect the presence of a particular analyte (substance), constituent, or condition. Typically, qualitative studies are performed first to determine if a particular substance is present in the sample being evaluated. In contrast, quantitative studies provide results expressing specific numerical amounts of an analyte in a sample. These tests are usually performed after a qualitative study and identify the specific amount of a particular substance in the sample.

quantitative: Expresses specific numerical amounts of an analyte.

qualitative: Tests that detect a particular analyte.

> **EXAMPLE:** Human chorionic gonadotropin (hCG) quantitative code 84702 represents a pregnancy test. When this test comes back from the lab, it will have a titer or number that represents how many weeks the patient is pregnant. Human chorionic gonadotropin (hCG) qualitative code 84703 represents a pregnancy test with a negative or positive reading.

Pathology and Laboratory Modifiers

These are some of the most commonly used modifiers in the pathology and laboratory section.

-22: Unusual Procedural Services

This modifier is intended for use when the service provided is greater than the one usually required for the listed procedure.

-26: Professional Component

In circumstances where a laboratory or pathologic procedure includes both a physician (professional) component and a technical component, modifier -26 can be reported to identify the physician (professional) component.

-32: Mandated Services

Modifier -32 may be reported when groups such as a third party payor or peer review organization mandates a service.

-52: Reduced Services

Modifier -52 may be reported to indicate that a laboratory or pathologic procedure is partially reduced or eliminated at the discretion of the physician.

-53: Discontinued Procedure

Modifier -53 may be reported to indicate that the physician elected to terminate a procedure due to circumstances that put the patient at risk.

-59: Distinct Procedural Service

Modifier -59 may be used to identify a procedure or service that was distinct or independent from other services provided on the same day. This modifier may be used when procedures are performed together because of a specific circumstance, though they usually are not.

-90: Reference (Outside) Laboratory

Modifier -90 may be reported to indicate that another party besides the reporting physician performed the actual laboratory procedure.

> **EXAMPLE:** Dr. Smith performed a venipuncture to obtain a blood sample for an obstetrical panel. He prepared the sample for transport and it was sent to an outside lab for testing. Dr. Smith should report 80055-90 to describe the laboratory test with the interpretation and analysis being performed at an off-site lab, along with a code for the venipuncture, 36415.

-91: Repeat Clinical Diagnostic Laboratory Test

Modifier -91 may be reported when it is necessary to repeat the same laboratory test on the same day on the same patient to obtain subsequent (multiple) results. This modifier is not to be used when a test is rerun for confirmation, if there are testing problems with the specimen or equipment, or for any reason when one reportable result is all that is required.

-92: Alternative Laboratory Platform Testing

Modifier -92 is used when all or part of a kit or transportable instrument consists of a single-use, disposable analytical chamber that does not require dedicated laboratory space.

> **Coding Tip:**
>
> HCPCS modifier QW is used on Medicare claims to indicate a laboratory test is a low-complexity test that is classified as waived according to CLIA. Examples:
>
> Urine pregnancy test 81025-QW
>
> Acon *H. pylori* test device 86318-QW
>
> HemoCue Hemoglobin 85018-QW

Organ- or Disease-Oriented Panels

Codes 80047–80076 are used to code laboratory procedures known as panels or profiles in which more than one procedure is typically performed from one blood sample, and the procedures are commonly performed together to diagnose an organ dysfunction or to monitor a disease. Some of the panels in this series include the basic metabolic panel, the general health panel, and the electrolyte panel. For example, the basic metabolic panel includes all of the following and is described in two different code sets based on testing for ionized calcium or total calcium.

- Calcium (ionized or total)
- Carbon dioxide
- Chloride
- Creatinine
- Glucose
- Potassium

- Sodium

- Urea nitrogen (BUN)

These panel components are not intended to limit the performance of other tests. If one performs tests specifically indicated for a particular panel, those tests should be reported separately in addition to the panel.

> **EXAMPLE:** Lipid panel to check total serum cholesterol, HDL, LDL, and triglycerides—can be diagnostic or to monitor hypercholesterolemia.

> **EXAMPLE:** Hepatic function panel to check/monitor liver enzyme function. Commonly used in conjunction with the lipid panel to check liver function for patient on statin medication.

Drug Assay

Drug procedures are divided into three subsections: therapeutic drug assay, drug assay, and chemistry. Code selection is based on the reason, purpose, and type of patient results obtained. Drug testing in the drug assay subsection has two major categories:

1. Presumptive drug class—Procedures used to identify possible use or nonuse of a drug or drug class. This testing may be followed by a definitive test in order to specifically identify drugs or metabolites.

2. Definitive drug class—Qualitative or quantitative tests to identify possible use or nonuse of a drug. These tests identify specific drugs and associated metabolites, and are not required prior to a definitive drug test.

Drug classifications are listed in CPT as Drug Class List A and Drug Class List B. Drug Class List A contains drugs or classes of drugs that are commonly assayed by presumptive procedures. The methodology is typically used when the results are capable of being read by direct optical observation, including instrument assisted (dipsticks, cups, cards, cartridges), or by instrumented test systems, such as discrete multichannel chemistry analyzers utilizing immunoassay or enzyme assay.

Drug Class List B contains drugs or classes of drugs that may be assayed by presumptive procedures. This typically requires more resources than the drugs listed in Drug Class List A, and may include drug class specific preanalytical sample preparation in a manual process such as ELISA (Enzyme linked immunosorbent assay).

Definitive drug identification methods are able to identify individual drugs and distinguish between structural isomers but not necessarily stereoisomers. Isomers are compounds with the same chemical formula but different structures. Stereoisomers are two substances that have the same atoms, and same structure but atoms are positioned differently. Definitive methods include, but are not limited to, gas chromoatography with mass spectrometry and liquid chromatography mass spectrometry and exclude immunoassays (e.g., IA, EIA, ELISA, RIA, EIMT, FPIA) and enzymatic methods (e.g., alcohol dehydrogenase). CPT does contain a Table of Definitions and Acronym Conversions listing the drug testing term or acronym and the definition.

As mentioned previously in this chapter, qualitative testing detects the presence of a particular chemical or substance being measured or analyzed. If there is presence of a substance, quantitative testing may be performed to provide specific numerical amounts or quantities of the chemical or substance in the patient's system.

Highlight:

When two identical tests are performed in the therapeutic drug assay testing on the same day at different times, modifier -91 can be used for multiple tests.

Therapeutic Drug Assays

This examination is quantitative and used to monitor medications prescribed for a patient. Examples of types of medications are antibiotics, antidepressants, sedatives, anticonvulsants, immunosuppressants, tranquilizers, and antiarrhythmics.

Evocative/Suppression Testing

Coding Tip:

Attendance and monitoring by the physician during the test should be reported with the appropriate code as well as the prolonged physician care codes if they apply.

These tests (code range 80400–80439) allow the physician to determine a baseline of the chemical and the effects on the body after agents are administered that are evocative (materials that a patient must take because the body does not produce them naturally) or suppressive. In reviewing the codes in this series, note that the description for each panel identifies the type of test included in that panel, as well as the number of times a specific test must be performed.

> **EXAMPLE:** 80422 Glucagon tolerance panel, for insulinoma. This panel must include the following:
>
> Glucose (82947 × 3)
> Insulin (83525 × 3)

Urinalysis

Urinalysis is a diagnostic test that can be conducted in many ways. It can serve as a qualitative or quantitative test. A basic urinalysis involves the dipstick or tablet reagent testing for bilirubin, glucose, hemoglobin, ketones, leukocytes, nitrite, pH, protein, specific gravity, urobilinogen, or any number of these constituents. A urinalysis may be automated or nonautomated, with or without microscopic examination, depending on the type of testing done within the facility. Figure 11–9 demonstrates a reagent strip immersed into urine for testing.

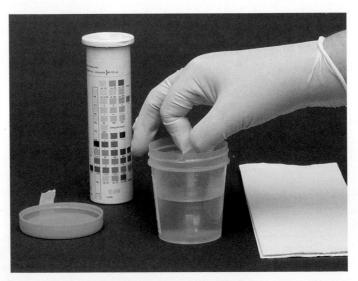

Figure 11-9 A reagent strip is used as a urine test.

Molecular Pathology

Molecular pathology is an emerging discipline within pathology that focuses on the study and diagnosis of disease through the examination of molecules within organs, tissues, or body fluids by studying DNA, RNA, and proteins, especially in the area of inherited diseases. Some examples of gene testing are BRCA and HER2 testing for breast cancer and APOE for Alzheimer's disease. CPT contains a detailed Molecular Pathology Gene Table listing the claim designation, abbreviated and full gene name, an example of commonly associated proteins/diseases, and the CPT code assigned for the pathology procedure (81161–81479), divided into two tiers. Codes 82009–84999 are used to report individual chemistry tests. Examination of these specimens is quantitative unless specified. Clinical information derived from the results of laboratory data that is mathematically calculated (final calculations after all specimens have been analyzed through a machine) is considered part of the test procedure and therefore is not a separately reportable service. Figure 11–10 is an example of a Clinitek 50 urine chemistry analyzer.

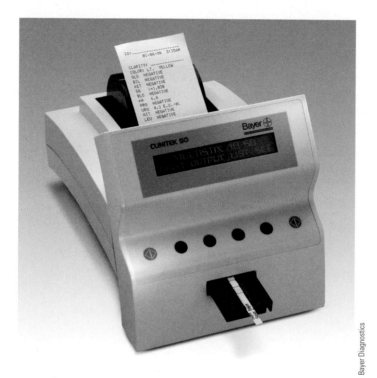

Figure 11-10   Clinitek 50 urine chemistry analyzer

In coding glucose procedures, be aware of different methods of testing:

- 82945 Glucose, body fluid, other than blood (joint fluid, urine, cerebrospinal fluid).

- 82947 Glucose, quantitative blood except reagent strip.

- 82948 Glucose, quantitative blood using a reagent strip, usually performed with a finger stick.

- 82950 Glucose, post glucose dose, also referred to as post-prandial test, or two hours after a meal or ingestion of glucola. This is common in testing pregnant women for gestational diabetes.

- 82951 Glucose tolerance testing (GTT) includes glucose dose. Blood is obtained as fasting specimen, after consumption of glucola, and every hour afterward as indicated by the physician. The codes for the GTT can be three specimens (82951) or each additional beyond three specimens (82952). This testing is normally performed to diagnose diabetes mellitus or hypoglycemia.

- 82962 Glucose monitoring device for blood for home use (referred to as glucometer testing). HCPCS modifier QW may be appended for waived testing for Medicare.

Glycohemoglobin or glycated hemoglobin, referred to as HbA1c, is a blood test to determine how well a patient's diabetes is being controlled beyond the normal fasting blood sugar or glucose. HbA1c can be used in conjunction with home glucose monitoring to provide an average of glucose readings to make adjustments in diabetic medications. CPT code 83036 is used for in-office use and 83037 for home use.

> **Coding Tip:**
> Watch codes for glucose versus glucagon testing. Glucose is a simple sugar; glucagon is a hormone secreted by the pancreas.

Hematology and Coagulation

Hematology is the study of blood cells and blood-forming tissues. Coagulation relates to the clotting process of blood. Codes 85002–85999 are used to report such procedures as complete blood counts (CBC) and bone marrow aspiration and biopsy, and coagulation procedures such as a partial thromboplastin time (PTT). A complete blood count includes:

- White blood cell count (WBC)
- Red blood cell count (RBC)
- Hemoglobin (HGB)
- Hematocrit (HCT)
- Mean corpuscular hemoglobin concentration (MCHC)
- Mean corpuscular volume (MCV)
- Differential screen (WBC)
- Platelet count
- Mean corpuscular hemoglobin (MCH)

Figure 11–11 shows a blood-filled microhematocrit tube after centrifugation.

automated: Laboratories that assay large numbers of samples mechanically.

manual: Performing something by hand or with the hands.

> **Coding Tip:**
> When coding the different types of procedures in the hematology and coagulation section, the coder should understand the difference between automated and manual testing. **Automated** testing is the use of clinical laboratory instruments that assay large numbers of samples (blood, urine, etc.) mechanically, and **manual** testing is performed by a technician who counts the cells present on a slide under the microscope.

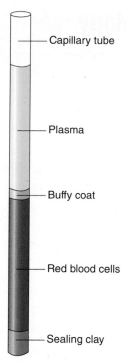

— Capillary tube

— Plasma

— Buffy coat

— Red blood cells

— Sealing clay

Figure 11-11 Microhematocrit filled with blood following centrifugation

Immunology

Codes 86000–86849 are used to report components of the immune system and their functions. Different procedures that are done in this section are HIV testing and testing for infectious agents and antigens. Included in this section is Tissue Typing, including assay and crossmatch.

> **EXAMPLE:**
>
> 86592 Syphilis test qualitative
> 86803 Hepatitis C antibody

Transfusion Medicine

Codes 86850–86999 are used to report blood typing, transfusion, and antibody identification.

Microbiology

Codes 87003–87999 are used to report identification and classification of different types of bacteria by various identification methods. For example, separate codes exist for different types of cultures, such as stool, throat, or urine. This section also covers mycology, parasitology, and virology.

Anatomical Pathology

Codes 88000–88099 are used to report autopsies (postmortem examination). These codes represent physician services only. Use modifier -90 for outside laboratory services.

Cytopathology

Codes 88104–88199 are used to report Pap smears (Figure 11–12), needle aspirations, chromosomal testing, and other cytology screenings.

> **EXAMPLE:** A patient is seen in the office for a routine annual Pap smear and pelvic examination. The cervical smear obtained at the time of the visit is sent to a cytopathology laboratory for screening and interpretation. The physician uses the preventive medicine service code from the Evaluation and Management section of the CPT to bill for the encounter with the patient and the collection of the specimen. The cytopathologist reports from codes 88141–88155, 88164–88167, or 88174–88175 for the screening and interpretation, depending on the type of screening/evaluation performed.

Cytogenic studies, 88230-88299, includes tissue cultures and chromosome analysis.

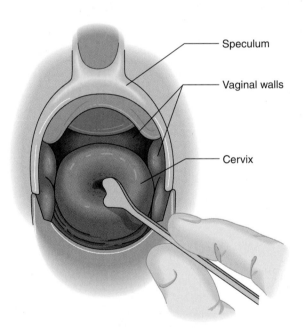

Speculum

Vaginal walls

Cervix

Figure 11-12 A Pap smear consists of swabbing the cervix to obtain cells for microscopic examination.

Surgical Pathology

Codes 88300–88399 are used to report specimens removed during surgical procedures known as a unit of service. CPT defines a specimen as "tissue or tissues that is/are submitted for individual and separate attention, requiring examination and pathologic diagnosis."

Services 88300–88309 include accession, examination, and reporting of the specimen. Service codes 88304–88309 describe all other specimens requiring gross and microscopic examination, and represent additional ascending levels of physician work.

Level I	88300	Surgical pathology diagnosed by gross examination only, without microscopic examination
		Example: Gross examination of renal calculi
Level II	88302	Gross and microscopic to confirm identification and the absence of disease
		Example: Foreskin, newborn
Level III	88304	Gross and microscopic examination for other specimens
		Example: Abortion, cystic lesions, appendix, gallbladder, polyps, tonsils, etc.
Level IV	88305	Gross and microscopic examination
		Example: Biopsies, polyps, fractures, etc.
Level V	88307	Gross and microscopic examination
		Example: Non-traumatic extremity amputation
Level VI	88309	Gross and microscopic examination
		Example: Total resection of colon

When submitting two or more specimens, separate codes should be used to identify the appropriate level for each.

EXAMPLE:

Gross and microscopic examination of two separate fallopian tube biopsies.

The pathologist reports the codes 88305 and 88305 to identify the examination of two separate specimens. Additional codes are used to identify special stains, histochemistry, cytochemistry, immunohistochemistry components, or antibodies and other analysis.

> **Highlight:**
> Codes 88300–88309 include the accession, examination, and reporting of a specimen. When performed by the pathologist, services identified in codes 88311–88365 and 88399 may be reported.

Exercise 11.6

Assign CPT codes to the pathology and laboratory procedures; use two-digit modifiers when applicable.

1. Sedimentation rate, nonautomated _____

2. Urine pregnancy test, by visual color comparisons _____

3. General health panel _____

4. Semen analysis for volume, count, motility, and differential _____

5. Vitamin K _____

6. Confirmatory test for HIV-1 antibody _____

7. Folic acid; serum _____

8. Chlamydia, IgM _____

(continues)

Exercise 11.6 (*continued*)

9. Ova and parasites, direct smears concentration and identification _____

10. Complete blood count (CBC), automated and differential WBC, automated _____

11. Urinalysis nonautomated without the microscope _____

12. Histamine _____

13. Basic metabolic panel with total calcium _____

14. Prothrombin time _____

15. Syphilis test qualitative _____

16. Lee and White coagulation study _____

17. Throat culture, bacterial, disk method _____

18. Annual Pap smear, thin layer prep, automated screening with physician supervision

    _____

19. Stool test for *Helicobacter (H.) pylori* _____

20. hCG pregnancy test, quantitative _____

Exercise 11.7

Assign ICD-10-CM codes for the following scenarios.

1. A patient on long-term use of Lipitor for hypercholesterolemia has a six-month check of his lipid panel. _____

2. A 36-year-old female has routine bilateral screening mammography for fibrocystic disease of the right breast. _____

3. A patient diagnosed with hemophilia A has routine bleeding and clotting tests. _____

4. Pathology results from a kidney biopsy on a one-month-old infant were conclusive for autosomal recessive polycystic kidney disease a genetic disorder typically fatal in children. _____

5. After the patient questioned the accuracy of an at-home pregnancy kit, a urine pregnancy test performed in the clinic confirmed conclusively that the patient was indeed pregnant. _____

6. Patient sent from ER for x-ray of clavicle. X-ray demonstrates nondisplaced fracture of lateral end of the left clavicle. _____

Summary

As doctors and scientists learn about the causes of various types of diseases, coders will continue to learn each and every year more and more codes with higher levels of specificity. The American Medical Association looks at the changes annually in the health care field to review new and better technology.

Technology is always advancing in medicine, particularly in radiology, pathology, and the laboratory, and will change the dynamics of coding these areas.

References

AMA Current Procedural Terminology 2016 professional edition. (2015). Chicago, IL: American Medical Association.

Centers for Medicare and Medicaid Services. (2015, March 5). *Clinical laboratory improvement amendments.* Retrieved from http://www.cms.gov/clia.

Greathouse, J.S. (2006). *Radiographic positioning and procedures: A comprehensive approach.* Clifton Park, NY: Cengage Learning.

Ehrlich, A., & Schroeder, C. (2013). *Medical terminology for health professions* (7th ed.). Clifton Park, NY: Cengage Learning.

Keir, L., Wise, B., Krebs, C., & Kelley-Arney, C. (2012). *Medical assisting, administrative and clinical competencies* (7th ed.). Clifton Park, NY: Cengage Learning.

Lindh, W.Q., Pooler, M., Tamparo, C.D., Dahl, B.M., & Morris, J. (2014). *Delmar's comprehensive medical assisting: Administrative and clinical competencies.* Clifton Park, NY: Cengage Learning.

Stepp, C., & Woods, M. A. (1998). *Laboratory procedures for medical office personnel.* Philadelphia, PA: Saunders.

White, L., Duncan, G., & Baumle, W. (2011). *Foundations of nursing* (3rd ed.). Clifton Park, NY: Cengage Learning.

Medicine

Learning Objectives

Upon successful completion of this chapter, you should be able to:

- Identify the variety of service categories in the CPT Medicine chapter.
- Select codes for both a vaccine and its administration.
- Explain the rules and appropriate use of modifiers in this section.

Key Terms

administration

end-stage renal
   disease (ESRD)

immune globulin

infusion

injection

modality

osteopathic
   manipulative
   treatment (OMT)

psychiatry

toxoids

vaccine

Introduction

The Medicine chapter is an unusual chapter of CPT. Coders frequently refer to this coding area as the "melting pot" section. Specifically, it includes a wide array of services and procedures for various anatomical sites and diagnostic and therapeutic purposes.

Medicine Guidelines

Since most codes within the Medicine section are truly unique, specific guidelines immediately prior to each section of codes are critical to review. It is common in this chapter for multiple codes to be selected when performed on the same date by the same physician. The use of modifiers varies and may not be necessary for certain categories, as many of the codes are modifier exempt, designated as an add-on code, or have special instructional guidelines. Read very carefully all section guidelines prior to selecting the code.

The categories contained in the CPT Medicine chapter are shown in Table 12–1.

Table 12-1 Medicine Chapter Categories in CPT

Category	Code Range
Immune Globulins (the medication supply)	(90281–90399)
Immunization (vaccine/toxoid) Administration	(90460–90474)
Vaccines and Toxoids (the supply component)	(90476–90479)
Psychiatry Services	(90785–90899)
Biofeedback	(90901–90911)
Dialysis	(90935–90999)
Gastroenterology	(91010–91299)
Ophthalmology	(92002–92499)
Otorhinolaryngologic	(92502–92700)
Cardiovascular	(92920–93799)
Noninvasive Vascular	(93880–93998)
Pulmonary	(94002–94799)
Allergy and Clinical Immunology	(95004–95199)
Endocrinology	(95250–95251)
Neurology and Neuromuscular Procedures	(95803–96020)
Medical Genetics and Genetic Counseling Services	(96040)
Central Nervous System Assessments/Tests	(96101–96127)
Health and Behavior Assessment/Intervention	(96150–96155)
Hydration, Therapeutic, Prophylactic, Diagnostic Injections and Infusions, and Chemotherapy and other Highly Complex Drug/Agent Administration	(96360–96549)
Photodynamic Therapy	(96567–96571)
Special Dermatological Procedures	(96900–96999)
Physical Medicine and Rehabilitation	(97001–97799)
Medical Nutrition Therapy	(97802–97804)
Acupuncture	(97810–97814)
Osteopathic Manipulative Treatment	(98925–98929)
Chiropractic Treatment	(98940–98943)
Education and Training for Patient Self-Management	(98960–98962)
Non-Face-to-Face Nonphysician Services	(98966–98969)
Special Services, Procedures and Reports	(99000–99091)
Qualifying Circumstances for Anesthesia	(99100–99140)
Moderate (Conscious) Sedation	(99143–99150)
Other Services and Procedures	(99170–99199)
Home Health Procedures/Services	(99500–99602)
Medication Therapy Management Services	(99605–99607)

Coding Tip:
Many services within the Medicine section are provided in combination with other services throughout CPT. Insurance plans may have specific requirements for the use of modifier -25, modifier -51, or modifier -59, all common for many of these procedures and services. This area of CPT also houses numerous services frequently performed and reported by qualified, nonphysician personnel.

Immune Globulins (90281–90399)

immune globulin: Animal protein with activity similar to that of a human antibody.

The Medicine chapter begins with a listing of medications known as **immune globulins**. These medications are commonly rendered to prevent illness, often after the patient has been exposed to the illness. The CPT guides the selection of an *additional* code as appropriate (96365–96368, 96372, 96374, 96375) for the administration as this section represents the immune globulin product only. Also, as we discussed earlier, all of the codes in this series are modifier -51 exempt. Figure 12–1 reflects a typical claim for the administration of hepatitis IG IM during a follow-up encounter on a patient being seen with hypertension.

Immunization Administration (90460–90474)

administration: The professional service of giving or rendering, often associated with medications or solutions.

injection: A parenteral route of administration during which a needle penetrates the skin or muscle; e.g., subcutaneous injection, intramuscular injection.

The codes in this series are reported for any route of **administration.** Codes 90460–90461are selected when the physician or other qualified health care professional performs counseling with a patient through 18 years of age and family at the time of the encounter. The **injections** and other routes of administration are reported for *each* vaccine/toxoid component given. It is important to understand that some immunizations are considered to be a "combination"; that is, multiple medications are within one vial or bottle and are administered by one method (for example, intramuscularly). To report these new codes, it necessary to know "how many" components are within the combination vaccine/toxoid.

> **EXAMPLE:** A young patient presents to her pediatrician for an MMR immunization. The physician counsels the mother regarding the vaccine and administers the immunization from one syringe. The service would be coded as:
>
> | | |
> |---|---|
> | 90707 | Measles, Mumps, and Rubella virus vaccine (MMR) |
> | 90460 | Immunization administration, first vaccine component |
> | 90641 × 2 | Each additional vaccine component |
>
> *This scenario represents the product (MMR) and the administration of each of the three components of the MMR since it is a combination vaccine.*

See Figure 12–2 for proper reporting on the claim form.

If the physician does not provide counseling at the encounter or if the patient is over 18 years of age, the administration of the vaccine is reported with a code from the series 90471–90474. These codes are separated by the type of administration *regardless* of whether the vaccine or toxoid is a combination or a single component. An additional code from the vaccines and toxoids series is also selected. Any applicable preventative service or well-child visit would also be reported. See Figure 12–3 for reporting of this scenario on the claim form.

Vaccines and Toxoids (90476–90749)

vaccine: A suspension of microorganisms that is administered to prevent illness.

toxoids: Toxins that are treated and revised, given to stimulate antibody production.

The **vaccine** and **toxoid** codes represent the actual supply and are found in the CPT book. Outside of immune globulins and the vaccine and toxoid codes, all other substances and medications will be found in the J code section of the HCPCSII code book. All of the codes in this series are modifier -51 exempt. It is common upon review of the medical record to find multiple vaccines during one encounter or

HEALTH INSURANCE CLAIM FORM

APPROVED BY NATIONAL UNIFORM CLAIM COMMITTEE (NUCC) 02/12

↑ CARRIER

PICA ☐☐   PICA ☐☐

1. MEDICARE ☐ (Medicare#)   MEDICAID ☐ (Medicaid#)   TRICARE ☐ (ID#/DoD#)   CHAMPVA ☐ (Member ID#)   GROUP HEALTH PLAN ☐ (ID#)   FECA BLK LUNG ☐ (ID#)   OTHER ☐ (ID#)   1a. INSURED'S I.D. NUMBER (For Program in Item 1)

2. PATIENT'S NAME (Last Name, First Name, Middle Initial)

3. PATIENT'S BIRTH DATE MM | DD | YY   SEX   M ☐ F ☐

4. INSURED'S NAME (Last Name, First Name, Middle Initial)

5. PATIENT'S ADDRESS (No., Street)

6. PATIENT RELATIONSHIP TO INSURED   Self ☐ Spouse ☐ Child ☐ Other ☐

7. INSURED'S ADDRESS (No., Street)

CITY   STATE

8. RESERVED FOR NUCC USE

CITY   STATE

ZIP CODE   TELEPHONE (Include Area Code) ( )

ZIP CODE   TELEPHONE (Include Area Code) ( )

9. OTHER INSURED'S NAME (Last Name, First Name, Middle Initial)

10. IS PATIENT'S CONDITION RELATED TO:

11. INSURED'S POLICY GROUP OR FECA NUMBER

a. OTHER INSURED'S POLICY OR GROUP NUMBER

a. EMPLOYMENT? (Current or Previous) ☐ YES ☐ NO

a. INSURED'S DATE OF BIRTH MM | DD | YY   SEX   M ☐ F ☐

b. RESERVED FOR NUCC USE

b. AUTO ACCIDENT? ☐ YES ☐ NO   PLACE (State)

b. OTHER CLAIM ID (Designated by NUCC)

c. RESERVED FOR NUCC USE

c. OTHER ACCIDENT? ☐ YES ☐ NO

c. INSURANCE PLAN NAME OR PROGRAM NAME

d. INSURANCE PLAN NAME OR PROGRAM NAME

10d. CLAIM CODES (Designated by NUCC)

d. IS THERE ANOTHER HEALTH BENEFIT PLAN? ☐ YES ☐ NO *If yes*, complete items 9, 9a, and 9d.

READ BACK OF FORM BEFORE COMPLETING & SIGNING THIS FORM.

12. PATIENT'S OR AUTHORIZED PERSON'S SIGNATURE I authorize the release of any medical or other information necessary to process this claim. I also request payment of government benefits either to myself or to the party who accepts assignment below.

SIGNED _____ DATE _____

13. INSURED'S OR AUTHORIZED PERSON'S SIGNATURE I authorize payment of medical benefits to the undersigned physician or supplier for services described below.

SIGNED _____

↑ PATIENT AND INSURED INFORMATION

14. DATE OF CURRENT ILLNESS, INJURY, or PREGNANCY (LMP) MM | DD | YY   QUAL.

15. OTHER DATE QUAL. MM | DD | YY

16. DATES PATIENT UNABLE TO WORK IN CURRENT OCCUPATION FROM MM | DD | YY TO MM | DD | YY

17. NAME OF REFERRING PROVIDER OR OTHER SOURCE

17a.   17b. NPI

18. HOSPITALIZATION DATES RELATED TO CURRENT SERVICES FROM MM | DD | YY TO MM | DD | YY

19. ADDITIONAL CLAIM INFORMATION (Designated by NUCC)

20. OUTSIDE LAB? ☐ YES ☐ NO $ CHARGES

21. DIAGNOSIS OR NATURE OF ILLNESS OR INJURY Relate A-L to service line below (24E)   ICD Ind.

A. Z20.5   B. Z70.1   C. ____   D. ____
E. ____   F. ____   G. ____   H. ____
I. ____   J. ____   K. ____   L. ____

22. RESUBMISSION CODE   ORIGINAL REF. NO.

23. PRIOR AUTHORIZATION NUMBER

24. A. DATE(S) OF SERVICE From MM DD YY	To MM DD YY	B. PLACE OF SERVICE	C. EMG	D. PROCEDURES, SERVICES, OR SUPPLIES (Explain Unusual Circumstances) CPT/HCPCS	MODIFIER	E. DIAGNOSIS POINTER	F. $ CHARGES	G. DAYS OR UNITS	H. EPSDT Family Plan	I. ID. QUAL.	J. RENDERING PROVIDER ID. #
1	07 01 XX	07 01 XX	11		99213	25	A,B		1		NPI	
2	07 01 XX	07 01 XX	11		90371		A,B		1		NPI	
3	07 01 XX	07 01 XX	11		96372		A,B		1		NPI	
4											NPI	
5											NPI	
6											NPI	

25. FEDERAL TAX I.D. NUMBER   SSN ☐ EIN ☐

26. PATIENT'S ACCOUNT NO.

27. ACCEPT ASSIGNMENT? (For govt. claims, see back) ☐ YES ☐ NO

28. TOTAL CHARGE $

29. AMOUNT PAID $

30. Rsvd for NUCC Use

31. SIGNATURE OF PHYSICIAN OR SUPPLIER INCLUDING DEGREES OR CREDENTIALS (I certify that the statements on the reverse apply to this bill and are made a part thereof.)

SIGNED _____ DATE _____

32. SERVICE FACILITY LOCATION INFORMATION

a. NPI   b.

33. BILLING PROVIDER INFO & PH # ( )

a. NPI   b.

↑ PHYSICIAN OR SUPPLIER INFORMATION

NUCC Instruction Manual available at: www.nucc.org   **PLEASE PRINT OR TYPE**   APPROVED OMB-0938-1197 FORM 1500 (02-12)

Figure 12-1 CMS-1500 claim form for the administration of hepatitis IG IM with an E/M service

Figure 12-2 CMS-1500 claim form for preventive visit, MMR, and flu shot with provider vaccine counseling

Figure 12-3 CMS-1500 claim form for preventive visit, MMR, and flu shot without provider vaccine counseling

session. An additional code for the administration of each of the vaccine and toxoid codes will need to be reported with codes 90460–90474.

Psychiatry (90785–90899)

psychiatry: The branch of medicine that focuses on mental disorder study, treatment, and prevention.

The guidelines for the **psychiatry** series of codes describe services performed in all care settings. The diagnostic psychiatric services such as evaluations and psychotherapy may be provided to individuals, the family, or group. Interactive complexity may warrant additional resource and is separately reportable with add-on code 90785 when performed at the same time as certain services. Interactive complexity refers to the use of specific communication factors other than the usual verbal type, such as play equipment typically furnished to children or the use of language interpreters. It may also be used for impaired patients, emotional or discordant family members. Specific examples are provided in CPT to assist with qualification of code 90785. Psychiatrists have the option of using E/M services or the psychiatric services for evaluation of the patient. Should psychotherapy services be performed by the psychiatrist during the E/M service, three, time-based add-on codes (90833, 90836, 90838) are to be reported along with E/M. No modifier is required as these are specific add-on codes for use with the E/M service only. Psychologists and licensed clinical social workers (LCSWs) may not use E/M codes or services that contain an E/M component. Psychotherapy services for the nonphysician therapist may be reported with codes 90832, 90834, and 90837.

The psychiatric diagnostic evaluation (90791 and 90792) services are separated by a selection of a diagnostic evaluation only or evaluation "with medical services." The psychiatric evaluation with the medical component may only be performed by the physician. Both of these services, are for assessments or reassessments and do not include psychotherapeutic services. Guidelines specifically state, "Psychotherapy services, including for crisis, may not be reported on the same day."

Psychotherapy Services

Psychotherapy is the treatment of mental illness and behavioral disturbances by the professional through definitive communication, attempts to alleviate emotional disturbances, reverse or change patterns of behavior, and encourage growth. Psychotherapy services are represented by established times and are selected by the exact description for the type of therapy, the location for the care, and the total face-to-face time documented. Psychiatrists have the option of selecting a psychotherapy code with or without an E/M component. This E/M component is not distinguished by leveling criteria as required elsewhere within the evaluation and management coding section.

Interactive therapy often involves the use of toys or items encouraging the patient to demonstrate actions and may be reported separately with add-on code 90785.

If the psychiatric care includes procedures or additional treatment such as electroconvulsive therapy or hypnotherapy, additional codes are selected.

> **Coding Tip:**
> Psychiatric services are usually considered mental health benefits by most insurance plans. Patient coverage for these services has opened up since the ACA mandated health coverage. Contacting the insurance plan prior to rendering the care is recommended. For patients who have coverage, it is not uncommon for carriers to pay mental health benefits at a different rate in comparison to other health care benefits.

Biofeedback (90901–90911)

The codes in this series require specialized training. Code 90901 identifies all methods of biofeedback provided with the exception of anorectal biofeedback, which is reported with code 90911. If more than one modality is used during the training, code 90901 is still reported only once for the total service provided.

Dialysis (90935–90999)

The kidney functions to remove wastes and urea from the body. The buildup of waste in the bloodstream results in additional medical concerns by causing the heart and other organs to function inefficiently also. When the kidney fails to perform partially or entirely, physicians may order the use of mechanical equipment to remove the urea. The equipment is connected to the patient by introducing a vascular access device or catheters (Figure 12–4).

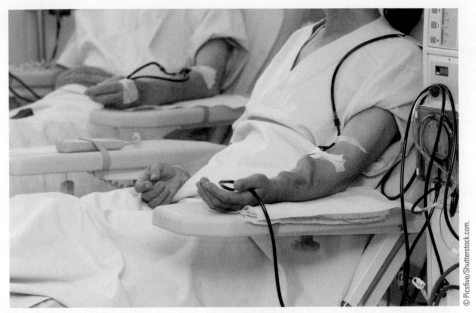

Figure 12-4 Dialysis equipment is used in patients whose kidney function has been compromised. The procedure needs to be repeated often to remove waste and urea from the body.

end-stage renal disease (ESRD): Commonly used term for irreversible kidney failure.

End-stage renal disease (ESRD) describes the chronic illness. The CPT codes are divided into two categories for the care of ESRD and other dialysis patient care. The ESRD dialysis codes 90951–90962 are selected one time for the entire month (30 days) when a patient has received a complete assessment. The codes are selected based on the number of face-to-face visits. The ESRD code includes:

- Establishment of the dialysis cycle

- Evaluation and management outpatient care for dialysis

- Telephone calls and patient management during the dialysis

Inpatient hemodialysis and related E/M services are reported with codes 90935 and 90937. When significant additional E/M services *not* related to dialysis are documented with appropriate history, exam, and medical decision making, an additional E/M code and modifier -25 may be reported.

If an ESRD patient has not had a complete assessment during the month for various reasons stated in the guidelines, age-specific codes 90967–90970 are to be reported per day for the services provided.

Gastroenterology (91010–91299)

The majority of the codes in the gastroenterology section are selected when diagnostic services are performed on the esophagus or gastric (stomach) area to assist in making a diagnosis or evaluating functions or disease. After a small amount of topical anesthetic gel is applied to the area of insertion, the patient assists by swallowing upon command, while the tube is inserted to the site. Measurements may be obtained during the procedure, providing the results to assist the physician in determining a definitive diagnosis. Washings and other specimens are often obtained and submitted to the laboratory.

Commonly performed procedures include an esophageal acid reflux test (91034) and code 91105 for gastric lavage in the event of a poisoning or hemorrhage.

Anorectal manometry, a rectal compliance test, and fecal irrigation codes are also listed within this section.

Ophthalmology (92002–92499)

The ophthalmologic service codes, 92002–92014, represent a combined E/M and ophthalmoscopy service. Depending on the level of documentation and the care that was actually provided, providers will select between two levels, intermediate and comprehensive. These CPT codes also specify new patient or established patient, using the standard AMA/CPT definitions. The routine ophthalmoscopy is part of the general and special ophthalmologic services.

The intermediate service includes:

- The evaluation of a new or existing illness *with* a new diagnostic or management problem that is not related to the primary diagnosis

- History, general medical observation

- External ocular and adnexal examination

- Other diagnostic procedures as indicated

- Use of mydriatic (pupil-dilating) drugs

- Slit lamp examination, keratometry, *routine* ophthalmoscopy, retinoscopy, tonometry, or motor evaluation

- Routine ophthalmoscopy

The comprehensive service includes the following descriptors:

- A general medical evaluation of the complete visual system

- May be at more than one session

- History, general medical observation

- External and ophthalmoscopic examinations

- Gross visual fields

- Basic sensorimotor examination

- Biomicroscopy

- Exam with cycloplegic or mydrisis

- Tonometry

- Initiation of diagnostic and treatment programs such as prescription of medication, arranging for diagnostic services, consultations, or radiology and laboratory procedures

- Slit lamp examination, keratometry, *routine* ophthalmoscopy, retinoscopy, tonometry, or motor evaluation

- Routine ophthalmoscopy

When special ophthalmologic services are performed, an additional code is selected. Special ophthalmologic service is an evaluation beyond that of the general ophthalmologic service, or is reported when special treatment is rendered.

Carefully review the descriptions surrounding these CPT codes to determine whether to apply modifier -50 (bilateral procedure) to the code when performing the services on both eyes and the potential of modifier -52 (reduced services) when the service is performed on only one eye. Typically, this information is within a parenthetical statement below the code description.

> **Coding Tip:**
> Insurance plans may vary in their policies for the use of modifier -50 and modifier -52 within the eye section. The Medicare Fee Schedule published annually by CMS further depicts multiple concepts for bilateral indicators. HCPCSII codes may describe eye services such as glaucoma screening or S codes for BCBS patients. Some carriers prefer HCPCSII codes for some of these services in lieu of the CPT codes. Contacting the carrier first may assist in clean claims processing.

Contact Lens Services

Physicians may also provide care for contact lens patients, such as fitting, instructions, training, and incidental revisions. Additional codes (92310–92326) are selected for the prescription of the optical and physical characteristics as this is not part of the general ophthalmologic service. Occasionally, patients will have a follow-up appointment with no need for additional fitting. This contact lens service is included in the general ophthalmologic service; no additional code is selected for the contact lens care in this scenario.

Ocular Prosthetics

Artificial eye codes are unilaterally described, and typically only one is fitted. The use of modifiers -RT and -LT are required to properly report the eye.

Spectacle Services

The CPT codes in the 92340 series are selected when the physician fits the patient for eyeglasses (spectacles), with the measurement of anatomical facial characteristics, lab specification order, and final fitting. The codes do not include the actual eyeglasses that are typically purchased by the patient. The mere writing of the prescription for the spectacle is included with the refraction code.

Otorhinolaryngologic Services (92502–92700)

The codes in this series are selected when otorhinolaryngologic diagnostic and treatment services beyond the usual are provided, or when no E/M services are performed. The codes are categorized by the type of testing that is performed, often depicting the function testing.

It is very important with each of these services to investigate the insurance coverage prior to performing the service. It is possible the patient may not have coverage, or may have limited coverage due to the diagnosis, indication, or limited frequency of the testing. For Medicare patients, provide a completed advance beneficiary notice prior to the service being performed.

Cochlear implants and device analysis and programming are reported with codes 92601–92604. The actual placement of the cochlear implant is reported with code 69930 in the surgical (nervous system) section of CPT.

Cardiology (92950–93799)

Refer to Chapter 9, Cardiology and the Cardiovascular System, for an in-depth discussion of this area of the CPT code book. Several code changes have been made over the past few years for both diagnostic and therapeutic procedures. The AMA has a designated committee that continues to revise the codes for improved accuracy of cardiology services reporting. To use these codes, carefully review the numerous definitions of each section, as they are helpful and quite detailed.

Pulmonary (94002–94799)

Unlike other CPT codes, the pulmonary codes *include* the laboratory procedure, with the interpretation and the results. The codes do not include medications that are used during the procedures, so the medications should be reported using the appropriate HCPCSII code. Commonly performed services are pulse oximetry to determine patient oxygen saturation levels and services that measure pulmonary function and lung capacity. Code 94640 is used for both treatment and diagnostic purposes. It states "inhalation treatment," which is often documented in the medical record as a "nebulizer treatment." Medications administered through the nebulizer may be separately reported with the appropriate J code. This same code can also be used for diagnostic purposes that might require sputum induction to obtain a specimen.

When the documentation reflects a significant separately identifiable E/M service, the additional E/M code with modifier -25 is selected.

CPT parenthetical tips are abundant for this series of codes, often describing details for the specific components or if additional services are performed on the same date.

Allergy and Clinical Immunology (95004–95199)

This section of CPT is most often used by the allergist. Administration of allergens for therapy may be given by other providers. Typically during the first encounter, an E/M service is provided. Allergy testing (e.g., the scratch tests, Figure 12–5) is

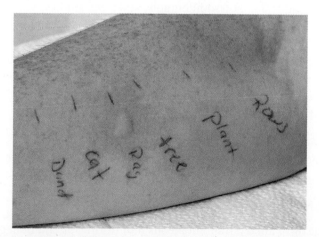

Figure 12-5 Allergens are placed on the skin in scratch tests to determine specific allergies. The individual pictured shows an allergic reaction to ragweed.

reported separately and includes the interpretation and report. Once the tests have been interpreted, immunotherapy may be started to desensitize the patient to the allergen.

Immunotherapy treatments (allergy injections) using extracts are given at intervals determined by the physician's clinical judgment. These injections may be administered by the allergy specialist physician or other physicians.

Allergy therapy is expanding, based on clinical trials and improvements. There are a few codes for the environmental concepts.

Creating or mixing allergens is listed as "provision of allergen extracts." The administration of the allergen may occur at the same office/practice where the allergen extract is prepared, or the bottle may be given to another physician office for the administration services. Code 95180, Rapid desensitization, is reported per hour for the patient having a serious reaction.

> **Coding Tip:**
> CPT describes the allergen dose as the amount of antigen administered in a single injection from a multiple-dose vial. A single-dose vial contains a single dose of antigen administered in one injection.

Endocrinology (95250–95251)

There are two ambulatory glucose monitoring codes for interstitial tissue fluid, which requires a minimum of 72 hours of continuous monitoring. This includes patient training, printout of the recording, and sensor removal. Code 95251 is for the interpretation and report.

Neurology and Neuromuscular Procedures (95803–96020)

Sleep Testing

The CPT guidelines state that polysomnography and sleep studies require continuous and simultaneous monitoring and recording of parameters of sleep for six hours or more of testing. This is with physician review, interpretation, and report. If less than six hours is recorded, modifier -52 is attached to the code. Most procedures require an attendant technologist. Polysomnography must record sleep and staging, including an electroencephalogram (EEG) for brain activity, electrooculogram (EOG) for eye activity, and electromyogram (EMG) for skeletal muscle activity.

Extra parameters include the following and may include others:

- ECG (electrocardiogram for heart activity)
- Airflow
- Ventilation and respiratory effort
- Gas exchange by oximetry, transcutaneous monitoring, or end tidal gas analysis

- Extremity muscle activity, motor activity/movement

- Extended EEG monitoring

- Penile tumescence

- Gastroesophageal reflux

- Continuous blood pressure monitoring

- Snoring

- Body positions

The EEG, muscle range-of-motion testing, and EMG tests are rather straightforward procedures. Recording of 20–40 minutes is included in routine EEG codes 95816–95822. The extended EEG codes, 95812–95813, are for reporting beyond 40 minutes.

Intraoperative Neurophysiology

Code 95940 for intraoperative neurophysiological monitoring is an add-on code, typically reported as one code per hour, during neurosurgical procedures. It depicts the activities of the brain while the surgery is under way and is very helpful for treatment and optimal therapeutic results.

Neurostimulators, Analysis-Programming

The neurostimulators are inserted using surgical codes, from the 60000 series of the CPT. The codes in the 95970–95982 series are selected for the professional service to program the devices and/or analyze the responses. The devices may also be filled with medications, either chemotherapy or other medications, for continuous internal drug delivery.

Motion Analysis

Performing the services represented by codes in the 96000 series requires a laboratory facility capable of performing videotaping from both sides, front, and back, and 3-D kinetics.

Medical Genetics and Genetic Counseling Services (96040)

This face-to-face service is for use by qualified, nonphysician genetic counselors, reported in 30-minute increments. These services are somewhat difficult to get reimbursed as the counselors usually are not credentialed by the payor. Special requests and letters are commonly submitted to the carrier for prior approval. Genetic counseling provided by a physician is to be reported with the appropriate E/M codes.

Central Nervous System Assessments/Tests (96101–96127)

Central nervous system (CNS) testing includes visual motor responses and abstractive abilities that will be formulated into a written report. Many are developmental tests or neurobehavioral examination. To report any "per hour" code, a minimum of 31 minutes must be provided.

> **Highlight:**
> Code 95940 is reported per 15 minutes of service. Code 95940 requires reporting only the portion of time the monitoring professional was physically present in the operating room providing one-on-one patient monitoring. No other cases may be monitored at the same time.

> **Coding Tip:**
> A common service is the Mini-Mental State Exam. This service does not justify the selection of the CNS testing. The exam would be captured as part of the exam of an E/M service and is not additionally coded.

Health and Behavior Assessment (96150–96155)

> **Coding Tip:**
>
> The codes in the health and behavior assessment series are selected when a provider other than a physician performs the service. If a physician performs these services, guidelines direct to the Evaluation and Management section, where a problem-oriented E/M code, and not the Health Assessment codes, would be selected.

The codes in the 96150 series are specifically selected for the health care depicted in the guidelines just prior to the code. The codes are very similar to either the psychiatric service or counseling rule for E/M. The codes are not preventive services.

The assessment is for the intervention of biopsychosocial factors for physical health, designed to correct specific disease. An illness or disease has been diagnosed, but not a mental health problem. If the patient has both psychiatric, E/M, preventive, individual counseling or group counseling, *and* health assessment, only one code is selected for the predominant service. Both codes are not selected for the same date of service, even if one is earlier in the day and the other service later the same day.

Hydration, Therapeutic, Prophylactic, and Diagnostic Injections and Infusions (96360–96379)

infusion: Introduction of a solution into tissue or an organ via intravenous therapy.

Infusions are intravenous therapy in which a bag or bottle of solution infuses into the patient over a course of time, often referred to as a drip line. An IV push is administered continuously by a manual process in which the nurse, most typically, pushes the ordered substance directly into the IV line. Guidelines in CPT clearly state the inclusion of certain supplies and services necessary to facilitate the infusion or injection. The following are not reported separately:

- Local anesthesia

- IV start

- Access to an indwelling IV, subcutaneous catheter, or port

- Flushing the IV line at the conclusion of the infusion

- Standard tubing, syringes, and supplies

For declotting of a port or catheter, code 36593 would be reported.

Hierarchies have been created within this section when more than one type of injection, infusion, or combinations are being performed. Only one "initial" service code may be reported unless a separate IV site is used. This "initial" service is selected based on the physician's knowledge of the patient's clinical condition(s) and treatment(s) regardless of the order. If, for example, the patient presented for IV therapeutic treatment of an infection, but hydration is required prior to the treatment, the IV therapeutic infusion "initial" code would be used first, even though the hydration service occurred first. Guidelines state that the hydration in this instance would be considered incidental. Coders should note that this differs from the hierarchy rules for the facility.

> ## Coding Tip:
>
> Time is always a factor for infusion reporting. Noting the definition of a "push" is critical for some infusion reporting. Guidelines state that an intravenous or intra-arterial "push" is defined as one of the following:
>
> - An injection in which the health care professional who administers the substance/drug is continuously present to administer the injection and observe the patient
>
> - An infusion of 15 minutes or less

Hydration Infusion Only

Select 96360–96361 specifically for hydration IV infusions. Hydration includes prepackaged fluid and electrolytes and other examples provided within this CPT section. Typically these types of infusions require minimal special handling and preparation; however, they do require direct physician supervision. Often, hydration infusions do not require advanced practice training.

Highlight:
If hydration services are performed concurrently, code 96360 should not be reported.

The rule for reporting hydration infusion services is that the infusion must last at least 31 minutes to report the first hour code, 96360. A second unit may be reported using add-on code 96361 if the infusion lasts at least 31 minutes beyond the first hour (91 minutes).

Therapeutic, Prophylactic, and Diagnostic Infusions and Injections (Non-Chemotherapeutic) (96365–96379)

Unlike the hydration infusion services, therapeutic, prophylactic, or diagnostic infusions and injections require special consideration and training of staff. Physician direct supervision is also required. These codes are not intended to be reported by the physician when the services are performed in the facility setting. The initial hour for IV infusion, code 96365, requires at least 16 minutes of infusion time; otherwise, it would be reported as a push. (See the Coding Tip on reporting time of infusions.) The add-on code 96366 is for each additional hour, which requires at least 30 minutes beyond the first hour, or 91 minutes, to be reported. The prolonged service codes and modifiers are not used in addition to the codes in this series; however, an additional physician encounter may occur. If the additional history, exam, and medical decision making or critical care services are documented, select additional E/M codes and use modifier -25. Code 96372 is a common drug injection administration code often listed on the encounter form/superbill. This administration code would be used, for example, for a subcutaneous or intramuscular injection of an antibiotic, vitamin B_{12}, and steroids, for example. This code would not be used for vaccine and toxoid administrations. Those services are reported with 96365, 96366, 90471, and 90472. Several parenthetical notes beneath code 96372 should be reviewed for additional guidance when administering antineoplastic hormonal and nonhormonal substances. Further, since these services require direct physician supervision, if the provider is not available for supervision and the service is rendered, the administration code 96372 might not be reported, but rather, the minimal E/M service code 99211.

These codes represent administration service only and not the actual drug/ substance or supply. Report the HCPCSII J code for the medications or solutions that are given. The administration codes within this section are also used to report the administration of immune globulin codes 90281–90399.

> **EXAMPLE:** A 25-year-old patient was administered 1000 mg of vancomyacin HCl intravenously. The start time of the infusion was 10:05 a.m. with the infusion end time documented as 12:33 p.m. The total time of the actual IV administration was 2 hours and 28 minutes.
>
> Correct coding for this scenario: 96365, 96366, J3370× 2.
>
> Rationale: Code 96365 for the first hour of infusion would be reported, and add-on code 96366 would be used for the second. The remaining 28 minutes are not captured, as the guidelines state greater than 30 minutes beyond 1 hour increments are required to report another unit of 96366. The appropriate HCPCSII J-code, J3370 for the vancomyacin, would be reported with "2" in the units field, as this code is per 500 mg.

Chemotherapy and Other Highly Complex Drug Administration (96401–96549)

Highlight:

The HCPCSII "J" codes are most frequently used to report chemotherapy drugs and other highly complex biological agents.

Chemotherapy codes 96401–96549 are selected for the parenteral administration of nonradionuclide antineoplastic drugs and antineoplastic agents. The term includes other highly complex drugs or highly complex biological agents that require direct physician supervision and intraservice supervision of staff. Chemotherapy administration services require advanced practice training and additional staff instruction and competency, as these agents are very risky and require special consideration of patient monitoring, preparation, dosage, disposal, and so forth. Typical infusion supplies and services are included as listed above; however, the access or catheterization services are additionally coded.

If a significant, separately identifiable E/M service is also performed and documented in addition to the description of the chemotherapy services, a code is selected for both, and modifier -25 is added to the E/M. Preparation of the chemotherapy is included in the administration. If preparation is extensive, modifiers should be selected.

A separate code is selected for each method of administration and each medication, paying special attention to time if it is stated within the code descriptor.

Photodynamic Therapy and Dermatological Procedures (96567–96999)

Photodynamic therapy and dermatological procedures are often performed by dermatology practices, correcting skin illnesses. Use of laser therapy for inflammatory skin disease is also included within this section. Additional E/M services are often documented, and codes are selected in addition for these services when applicable.

Physical Medicine and Rehabilitation (97001–97546)

The codes in the 97001 series are selected for physical therapist and occupational therapist services. A code is selected for each service performed and documented. The codes are not flagged with a modifier -51 exemption; however, the guidelines within this section instruct coders not to append modifier -51 to codes 97001–97755.

Modalities

A **modality** is considered to be any physical agent applied to produce a therapeutic change to the patient's biological tissue. Modalities are to be applied by qualified health care professionals. The scope of practice in each state may designate who can or cannot perform the services. Investigation is required prior to selecting the codes if they are provided outside of the typical physical or occupational therapy setting.

modality: Application of any therapeutic or physical agent.

> **Highlight:**
>
> Common modalities such as hot and cold packs, traction, electrical stimulation, infared, ultraviolet, diathermy, and whirlpool are frequent modalities used in physical therapy.

There are two categories, supervised and constant attendance, for modality reporting. For the supervised services, the provider direct contact is not required, whereas for the constant attendance services the provider performs the care directly. The modalities requiring constant attendance by the therapist are reported in 15-minute increments.

Therapeutic Procedures

These are services for the application of skills or services to improve function, directly performed by the physician or therapist. The services are at various locations and describe a variety of specific techniques or training. Many of the descriptions state each 15 minutes of time; therefore, the medical record documentation should also describe the time in increments of 15 minutes. The quantity documented in the medical record is counted for each 15-minute segment and reported on the claim. For example, 45 minutes of massage therapy would be reported with code 97124 × 3.

Active Wound Care Management (97597–97610)

The CPT active wound management code descriptions are detailed within the code descriptor. The services include the removal of tissue, assessment of the wound, and instructions. Nonselective removal of tissue is defined as the use of wet-to-dry dressing removal, enzyme removal, or abrasion. Selective removal is the use of scissors or sharps, scalpel, forceps, or other instruments. The active wound care service is directly performed by providers practicing within the scope of their professional state licensure. Active wound care is to:

- Remove devitalized and/or necrotic tissue

- Promote healing

An instructional note in CPT states debridement codes 11042–11047 are not to be reported with the active wound care codes.

The codes are selected based on each session and the total square centimeters of surface area.

Medical Nutrition Therapy (97802–97804)

The codes in the 97802 series describe specific medical nutrition therapy and intervention provided by a professional *other than the physician*. When a physician provides medical nutrition therapy, the E/M code or other specific treatment service (e.g., tube placement) is selected. The medical nutrition therapy codes are reported in 15-minute increments for either individual care or group sessions. This area of coding is very subject to variations in coverage by commercial carriers and is frequently performed by registered dietitians.

Acupuncture (97810–97814)

Highlight:

Reinsertion of needles is frequent during acupuncture treatment and is reported in the total time calculation.

A code from the 97810–97814 series is selected for an acupuncture service performed with or without electrical stimulation. These professional services are reported in 15-minute increments of personal (face-to-face) contact time with the patient, not the duration of acupuncture needle(s) placement (Figure 12–6). Only one initial code can be reported for the first 15-minute increment followed by the respective add-on code for each additional 15 minutes.

When the documentation shows an additional E/M service, the service may be reported separately with modifier -25 appended.

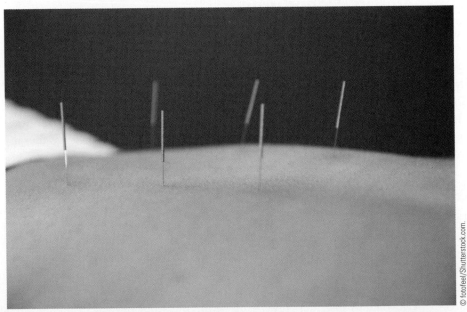

Figure 12-6 Acupuncture is becoming an increasingly popular form of alternative medicine for management of a variety of diseases and conditions.

Osteopathic Manipulation (98925–98929)

Osteopathic manipulative treatment (OMT) is a manual treatment performed by the physician for the care of somatic dysfunction and other disorders. The service is abbreviated as OMT, and the codes are reported by the number of body areas treated. The following body regions are described in the subsection guidelines:

- Head
- Cervical
- Thoracic
- Lumbar
- Sacral
- Pelvic
- Lower extremities
- Upper extremities
- Rib cage
- Abdomen and viscera region

osteopathic manipulative treatment (OMT): Manual treatment performed by the physician for the care of somatic dysfunction and other disorders.

Note these regions are not described the same as the body areas in the E/M chapter and guidelines.

When an E/M history, exam, and medical decision-making service is documented in addition to the OMT service, select an additional E/M code and add modifier -25. Different diagnoses are not required; however, additional charting is required to support the E/M service separately.

Chiropractic Manipulative Treatment (98940–98943)

The chiropractic manipulative treatment (CMT) is defined as manual treatment to influence joint function. The codes are selected based on documentation of medical necessity and whether the spinal or extraspinal regions are treated (Table 12–2). CMT services are typically performed and reported by chiropractors.

Table 12-2 CMT Regions

CMT Spinal Regions (98940, 98941, or 98942)	CMT Extraspinal Regions (98943)
Cervical region including the atlanto-occipital joint	Head region including temporomandibular joint, excluding the atlanto-occipital joint
Thoracic region including the costovertebral and costotransverse joint	Lower extremities
Lumbar region	Upper extremities
Sacral region	Rib cage excluding costotransverse and costovertebral joints
Pelvic region	Abdomen

This section allows for additional E/M coding when warranted, again with the use of modifier -25. The advance beneficiary notice is frequently required for these services. Investigation to determine the coverage policies and provider participation with a plan is suggested prior to providing services to the patient.

Education and Training for Patient Self-Management (98960–98962)

This series of codes is for qualified, nonphysician health care professionals to report educational and training services prescribed by a physician. The primary focus is to teach the patient, caregiver, or both how to effectively manage the patient's condition. The standardized curriculum and nonphysician health care professional qualifications must be consistent with guidelines established and recognized by physician societies, nonphysician associations and societies, or other appropriate sources. An example of standardized curriculum can be found at the American Diabetes Association or the Endocrine Society for patient assistance with diabetes. State scope and licensure are frequently reviewed by carriers, and careful consideration is highly recommended prior to reporting these services. This is particularly true when determining how the claim is to be submitted. Some carriers require the service to be reported by the qualified nonphysician professional while others require the supervising physician to report it.

Non-Face-to-Face Nonphysician Services (98966–98969)

Telephone services provided by a physician are to be reported with codes 99441–99443 found within the E/M section, and the physician online evaluation is reported with code 98969. The section 98966–98968 is specifically for qualified nonphysician professionals assessing an established patient when the service is initiated by the patient, parent, or guardian. Other stipulations in the CPT guidelines state the service may not be reported separately if it is related to a previous assessment service or procedure provided within the past seven days, or related to a visit within the next 24 hours or soonest available appointment. The telephone codes are broken down by time increments, requiring the provider to document the total time of the non-face-to-face nonphysician service. The online medical evaluation service requires permanent storage (electronic or hard copy) of the encounter and is reported only once for the same episode of care during the seven-day period. Guidelines state the sum of communication includes related telephone calls, provision of prescriptions, lab orders, results, and so forth pertaining to the online patient encounter.

Special Services, Procedures, and Reports (99000–99091)

This unique section is utilized by both physicians and other qualified health care professionals. Medicare does not cover the services in this section, as they are felt to be included in other services performed. Codes such as handling and conveyance (99000) vary in coverage by commercial payors. Code 99058 is for providing a service on an emergency basis in the office that disrupts other scheduled office services, and is reported in addition to the basic service. Analysis of clinical data stored in a computer such as blood pressures, ECGs, and hematologic data is captured with code 99090. A host of unique services that clearly represent additional work provided by the physician, other provider, and staff can be captured by some of these special services and procedure codes.

Coding Tip:

Several times throughout this book we have said, "Just because there is a CPT code does not mean the service will be paid." This concept is of utmost importance for the codes in the 99000 series. There are CPT codes and descriptions for many services that the insurance plan may have determined to be bundled into another CPT code. Investigation with each insurance plan is required prior to selecting the codes and reporting on the claims.

Qualifying Circumstances for Anesthesia (99100–99140)

All of the 99100 series of codes are add-on codes and are duplicated in the Medicine section from the Anesthesia section. They may be selected in addition to a variety of anesthesia codes, located in the Anesthesia chapter of CPT; however, documentation must state the qualifying circumstance. Not all insurance plans accept the qualifying circumstances codes; therefore, it is necessary to investigate prior to selecting the codes. See Chapter 6 for additional information on coding anesthesia services.

Moderate (Conscious) Sedation (99143–99150)

This is commonly known as *conscious sedation,* and correlates to the bull's-eye CPT symbol ⊙. Whenever the bull's-eye symbol is in front of the CPT code, the code includes the moderate sedation. If the code lacks the symbol and the moderate sedation is performed according to the guidelines, these codes may be used in addition to the procedure being performed. CPT codes 99143–99145 require the service to be performed by the same physician who does the procedure, and the codes are differentiated for patients younger than age five and those five years and older. This type of sedation is to achieve a medically controlled state of depressed consciousness while maintaining the patient's airway, protective reflexes, and ability to respond to stimulation or verbal commands. An independently trained observer is also required to monitor the patient.

If another physician performs the conscious sedation on behalf of the physician doing the procedure, and if that service is done in the facility setting, the second physician may report codes 99148–99150.

Other Services and Procedures (99170–99199)

The codes in the Other Services area of the CPT code book are often overlooked. When the service is documented, the code should be selected and the insurance plan should be contacted to determine the coverage prior to submitting the claim. For example, code 99173 is the screening eye test frequently performed with preventive examinations for all ages of patients. Many insurance plans do cover this CPT service in addition to the preventive medicine services even though CPT preventive guidelines clearly state the service is to be reported separately when performed.

Code 99175 is for administration of ipecac for individual emesis and monitoring/observation until the stomach is emptied adequately of all poison. Additional codes such as therapeutic phlebotomy services and hyperbaric oxygen therapy with physician attendance and supervision are included in this section.

Home Health Procedures/Services (99500–99600)

The home health procedures/services series of codes is *not* for physician services. These are selected when nonphysician professionals provide home health care described by the therapeutic codes or other services rendered. Physicians providing home health services are instructed to utilize home visit codes 99341–99350.

Right after these are the home infusing services, selected for the administration of drugs by infusion at the home setting. Code 99601 is for the first two hours of home infusion drug administration and code 99602 for each additional hour.

Medical Therapy Management Services (99605–99607)

Referred to as *MTMS*, this interesting set of codes is for the pharmacist to report when face-to-face patient assessment and intervention is provided upon patient request. It is not to be used to describe the provision of product-specific information or routine dispensing. Often, physicians have patients ask the pharmacist certain questions or ask patients to take their vitamins and other medications to the pharmacist to check for any potential interactions. Pharmacists may also be asked to help the patient gain a thorough understanding of the drug, or to give special counseling on a substance (Figure 12–7).

Figure 12-7 Medical therapy management service codes are specific for the pharmacist to use when face-to-face patient assessment and counseling are requested.

At the time of this publication, pharmacists continue to struggle with reimbursement of MTMSs as carriers often do not cover them or deny claims on the basis that the pharmacist would not typically be credentialed in this arena.

The AMA has clarified the definition of a new patient for MTMS as a patient who has received pharmaceuticals within a particular pharmacy chain. If a patient goes from one pharmacy to another of the same chain, that patient is considered an established patient for MTMS reporting purposes.

Exercise 12.1

Find the CPT and ICD-10-CM code(s) for the following exercises.

1. A 64-year-old patient with no prior history of hearing difficulties was seen for a pure tone air, auditometry threshold test, immediately after experiencing an acute onset of significant bilateral hearing loss.

   CPT: _____ ICD-10-CM: _____

2. The patient underwent a transtelephonic rhythm strip pacemaker evaluation on his pacemaker. The cardiologist checked the pulse generator the week previously and has now determined it to be faulty. The battery will be replaced over the weekend in the outpatient surgery department.

   CPT: _____ ICD-10-CM: _____ ICD-10-CM: _____

3. A four-year-old is brought in by her mother to have the pediatrician pierce her ears.

   CPT: _____ ICD-10-CM: _____

4. An Olympic runner required a physical therapy reevaluation for proper training and performance improvement while he continues to heal from his right Achilles' tendon strain. The PT assistant placed hot wraps around the foot for 10 minutes. The physical therapist then provided 15 minutes of iontophoresis and electrical stimulation to the area.

   CPT(s): _____

   ICD-10-CM: _____

Summary

The Medicine chapter includes a wide array of services and procedures. Multiple CPT codes are likely to be selected in reporting the services that are performed in this section, and often these services will accompany many other codes listed in other areas of CPT.

References

AMA CPT assistant. (2013). Chicago: American Medical Association.

AMA Current Procedural Terminology 2016 professional edition. (2015). Chicago: American Medical Association.

CHAPTER 13

Modifiers: A Practical Understanding

Learning Objectives

Upon successful completion of this chapter, you should be able to:

- Describe the purpose and general use of modifiers.
- Recognize the difference in CPT and HCPCSII modifiers.
- Determine correct selection and function of modifiers to procedures and services.
- Append modifier(s) appropriately on the CMS-1500 claim form.
- Identify compliance issues and modifier audit triggers.

Key Terms

CPT modifiers

HCPCS level II modifiers

modifiers

NCCI associated
modifier

PATH

Introduction

The CPT codes and descriptors cannot possibly account for every situation or scenario that may deviate from typical reporting purposes. **Modifiers** provide a way to change or alter the service without compromising the procedural code foundation and intent. In short, modifiers are two-digit numeric or alphanumeric characters that are appended to CPT and HCPCS level II (HCPCSII) codes. CPT is maintained by the CPT Editorial Panel, which meets three times a year to discuss issues associated with new and emerging technologies, and to review and discuss current procedures and services relative to corresponding CPT codes. The panel also forms various committees to further address issues such as modifiers when questions or concerns pertaining to change or revisions are necessary. A slight change to a CPT modifier may have an enormous impact on one specialty or affect providers as a whole from a reimbursement perspective. For this reason, careful consideration to precise language and use of each of the modifiers is critical. This author appreciated the process from attending some of these modifier committee meetings in years past and cautions providers and coders to proceed judiciously when determining correct modifier appendage.

The CPT and HCPCSII code set includes the listing of modifiers and their descriptions and applications. With the implementation of HIPAA, the insurance plans must recognize CPT and HCPCSII modifiers within the code set. Interpretation for intended use, however, may vary by payor.

CPT Modifiers

CPT modifiers are two-digit modifiers (except for Genetic Testing Code Modifiers; see CPT Appendix I) that are placed directly after the base code and used more commonly on Category I codes. They assist in further describing the procedures or services and are selected to indicate special circumstances. Modifiers are necessary to signal a variance from the description of the base code. At the time of this publication, there were approximately 35 CPT modifiers listed in CPT Appendix A. When appropriate and if applicable, a CPT modifier may be appended to a HCPCSII code and a **HCPCS level II modifier** to a CPT code (e.g., 20611-LT, G0101-25). CPT provides the following examples of variations that modifiers may be used to indicate to the recipient of a report or service:

- A service or procedure had both a professional and a technical component.

- A service or procedure was performed by more than one physician and/or in more than one location.

- A service or procedure was increased or reduced.

- Only part of a service was performed.

- An adjunctive service was performed.

- A bilateral procedure was performed.

- A service or procedure was provided more than once.

- Unusual events occurred.

modifiers: A two-digit number placed after the usual procedural code, which represents a particular explanation to further describe the procedure/service or circumstances involved with the procedure.

CPT modifiers: A two-digit number in CPT created to indicate that a service or procedure performed has been altered by some specific circumstance but not changed in its definition or code.

HCPCS level II modifiers: Two alpha-numeric indicators created and maintained by CMS to provide additional information regarding a procedure, service, or supply.

Modifier Placement

With the revision of the CMS-1500 claim form in 2012, carriers can accept up to 12 diagnoses and four modifiers on a line (Figures 13–1 and 13–2).

Figure 13-1 CMS-1500 modifier field

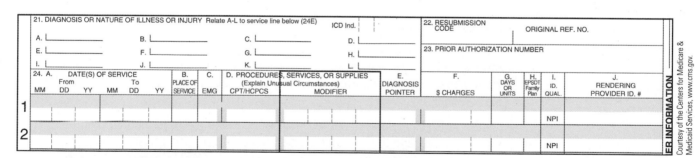

Courtesy of the Centers for Medicare & Medicaid Services, www.cms.gov. Copyright © 2017 Cengage Learning®.

Figure 13-2 Placement of five-digit CPT codes and modifier on claim form

Current Procedural Terminology © 2015 American Medical Association. All Rights Reserved.

Coding Tip:

This modifier should not be appended to an E/M service.

22: Increased Procedural Services

When the work required to provide a service is substantially greater than typically required, it may be identified by adding modifier 22 to the usual procedure code. Documentation must support the substantial additional work and the reason for the additional work (e.g., increased intensity, time, technical difficulty of procedure, severity of patient's condition, physical and mental effort required).

Modifier 22 is typically used when an increase in reimbursement should be considered. As stated in the description, the documentation must support the *substantial* additional work.

Additional significant time, excessive blood loss, and grossly obstructed surgical field are a few of the reasons to use modifier 22. Often a request for documentation to support the claim will need to be sent. Some carriers may require the use of a modifier 22 form that allows the provider to indicate specific information explaining the additional work increasing the service.

> **EXAMPLE:** Physician performed a procedure in which the patient's weight was in excess of 370 pounds. Due to the difficulty in maneuvering the patient and persistent obstruction limiting the provider from gaining clear access to the surgical field, the procedure took two and a half times longer than usual.

Inappropriate Use: Do not append modifier 22 to an E/M service. Do not use for reporting additional minimal work or time.

23: Unusual Anesthesia

Occasionally, a procedure that usually requires either no anesthesia or local anesthesia must be done under general anesthesia because of unusual circumstances. This circumstance may be reported by adding modifier 23 to the procedure code of the basic service.

> **EXAMPLE:** A patient suffered lacerations to her arm and face from an assault. Due to the mental condition of the patient, the physician finds it necessary to have the patient generally anesthetized to complete the repairs. The unusual Anesthesia modifier 23 would be appended to the repair codes.

Inappropriate Use: Modifier 23 is not for use with anesthesia codes or when using local or topical anesthesia.

24: Unrelated Evaluation and Management Service by the Same Physician or Other Qualified Health Care Professional During a Postoperative Period

The physician may need to indicate that an evaluation and management service was performed during a postoperative period for a reason unrelated to the original procedure. This circumstance may be reported by adding modifier 24 to the appropriate level of E/M service.

Modifier 24 has been a target of the past Office of Inspector General (OIG) audits because of excessive reporting during the postoperative period. This modifier prevents the E/M service from denying when a provider is seeing the patient for an unrelated condition during a 10- to 90-day postoperative period.

> **EXAMPLE:** Patient presented to her primary care provider (PCP) after having an I & D procedure of a pilonidal cyst. The I & D code used was associated with 10 follow-up days. Three days later, the patient presented again to her PCP for treatment of a sinus infection. The E/M service with modifier 24 (i.e., 99212-24) would be appropriate for the sinus-related visit and is necessary for claims payment. The appropriate diagnosis for the sinus infection further supports the significantly separately identifiable service that is being provided during the postoperative period.

Inappropriate Use: It is not necessary to use modifier 24 on the E/M service when the procedure period assigned to the code is 0 global days. Do not use if the provider or a provider in the same group practice was not the provider of the procedure in the postoperative period. For example, a patient receives laceration repair services by the emergency department physician at the hospital. Three days later, she visits her PCP for an unrelated illness. As a different provider/group, the PCP would not use modifier 24.

25: Significant, Separately Identifiable Evaluation and Management Service by the Same Physician or Other Qualified Health Care Professional on the Same Day of the Procedure or Other Service

It may be necessary to indicate that on the day a procedure or service identified by a CPT code was performed, the patient's condition required a significant, separately identifiable E/M service above and beyond the other service provided or beyond the usual preoperative and postoperative care associated with the procedure that was performed. A significant, separately identifiable E/M service is defined or substantiated by documentation that satisfies the relevant criteria for the respective E/M service to be reported (see Evaluation and Management Services Guidelines for instructions on determining level of E/M service). The E/M service may be prompted by the symptom or condition for which the procedure and/or service was provided. This is key for claims payment and appeals, as CPT states different diagnoses are not required for reporting the E/M services on the same date. The modifier 25 may only be appended to the appropriate E/M service.

> **Coding Tip:**
> This modifier is not used to report an E/M service that resulted in a decision to perform surgery according to CPT. It references the user to see modifier 57.

Modifier 25 is frequently abused or used incorrectly. CMS noted that modifier 25 was used inappropriately over 35 percent of the time in a 2002 review. This modifier may only be used on an E/M service and must be justified as significantly separate and identifiable to the other procedure or services being performed. The OIG continues to watch this modifier closely for misuse. Again, a separate diagnosis is not required as a stipulation in using modifier 25. The documentation must substantiate the separate E/M service.

> **Coding Tip:**
> Medicare allows modifier 25 with the following codes:
>
> 99201–99499
>
> 92002–92014
>
> G0101–G0175
>
> Additional information regarding modifier 25 can be found in the NCCI Modifiers section later in this chapter.

EXAMPLE: Patient presents with shortness of breath and wheezing. Upon taking an expanded problem-focused history and exam, the physician determines the patient is having an acute asthmatic attack and administers a nebulizer treatment. The diagnosis is the same for both the E/M encounter and the treatment. The E/M service should reflect modifier 25 to prevent the carrier from bundling the treatment and evaluation service together. The codes to report for this scenario are 99213-25, 94640.

Inappropriate Use: It is not necessary to report modifier 25 with an E/M service every time an additional service such as an immunization or blood draw is performed. CPT notes throughout the manual when to use modifier 25 with the E/M service. Many insurance companies post their own policy regarding modifier 25 use as their policy may differ from CPT intent.

26: Professional Component

There are certain procedures that may include a combination of a physician component and a technical component. When the physician component is reported separately, the service may be identified by adding modifier 26 to the usual procedure number.

Heavy use of modifier 26 is found within the radiology section of CPT but is also used on certain codes in surgery, pathology, and the medicine section. Often the facility will report the technical component of the same radiology 7xxxx code with modifier TC modifier.

EXAMPLE: The patient fell off a horse injuring his shoulder, and was taken to the ER for potential fracture treatment. Two View x-rays were taken and read by the contracting hospital radiologist for final interpretation and report. The radiologist would use modifier 26, as the equipment and technician are owned by the facility. The services would be submitted as follows:

Radiologist would report: 73030-26

Facility would report: 73030-TC

Inappropriate Use: Do not split the technical and professional component of an allowed service simply to gain additional reimbursement. If a provider owns the x-ray equipment and performs all components (provides technician, film, and equipment and does the interpretation and report) of the service, no modifier is necessary.

32: Mandated Services

Services related to *mandated* consultation or related services such as a governmental, regulatory agency, or a third-party payor may be identified by adding modifier 32 to the basic procedure.

Modifier 32 is not only informational but is often linked to a service reimbursable by someone other than the typical health plan. This modifier is frequently used to code for second and third opinions and basically says to the requester, "You asked for it and you are responsible for payment." Sometimes payment is requested prior to mandated services being delivered. Special guidance in mandated situations warrant checking first with the responsible payor for appropriate claims reporting.

EXAMPLE: The patient recently completed final therapy for a work-related injury and is now being considered for final disability rating. The carrier is requiring a second opinion by a different physician regarding the impairment rating before making its final determination. The service provided was coded as 99456-32.

Inappropriate Use: Do not use on patient-initiated services.

> **Coding Tip:**
> Modifier 47 would not be used as a modifier for anesthesia procedures.

47: Anesthesia by Surgeon

Regional or general anesthesia provided by the surgeon may be reported by adding modifier 47 to the basic service. (This does not include local anesthesia.)

Periodically, the operating surgeon may need to provide regional anesthesia, or on rare occasions, general anesthesia. The surgeon would report modifier 47 on the same surgical code on a second line. This modifier is typically allowed by payors for selected procedures only.

EXAMPLE: A 30-year-old male suffering multiple foreskin infections and ulcerations underwent excision of penile post-circumcision adhesions. The same surgeon performed a regional penile block prior to performing the procedure. The codes to report the anesthesia by the surgeon are 54162-47 and 64450.

Inappropriate Use: Not appropriate to use this modifier on anesthesia procedure codes 00100–01999 or for local anesthetic according to CPT. Do not report modifier 47 for moderate conscious sedation.

50: Bilateral Procedure

Unless otherwise identified in the listings, bilateral procedures that are performed at the same session should be identified by adding modifier 50 to the appropriate five-digit code.

If the same procedure is performed on both the right and the left side, the modifier 50 is appended (if applicable) to the procedure/service code on a single line. Listing "1" or "2" in the units field will depend on the payor when using modifier 50. Modifier LT and RT are also allowed by many carriers. CMS allows either the 50 modifier to be used, or the LT and RT (Figure 13-3) and typically reimburses 150 percent of the allowable for bilateral procedures.

EXAMPLE: Patient underwent bilateral thoracic, paravertebral facet injections at the T3 level to assist with pain management. The code is 64490-50.

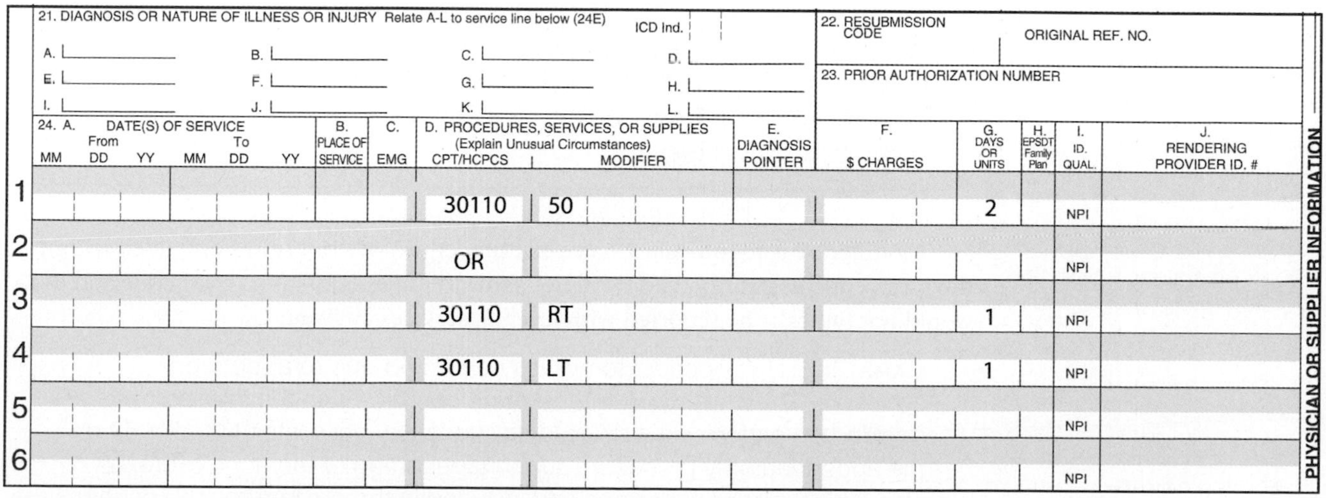
21. DIAGNOSIS OR NATURE OF ILLNESS OR INJURY Relate A-L to service line below (24E) ICD Ind.
A. B. C. D.
E. F. G. H.
I. J. K. L.
22. RESUBMISSION CODE ORIGINAL REF. NO.
23. PRIOR AUTHORIZATION NUMBER

	24. A. DATE(S) OF SERVICE From MM DD YY To MM DD YY	B. PLACE OF SERVICE	C. EMG	D. PROCEDURES, SERVICES, OR SUPPLIES (Explain Unusual Circumstances) CPT/HCPCS	MODIFIER	E. DIAGNOSIS POINTER	F. $ CHARGES	G. DAYS OR UNITS	H. EPSDT Family Plan	I. ID. QUAL.	J. RENDERING PROVIDER ID. #
1				30110	50			2		NPI	
2				OR						NPI	
3				30110	RT			1		NPI	
4				30110	LT			1		NPI	
5										NPI	
6										NPI	

PHYSICIAN OR SUPPLIER INFORMATION

Figure 13-3 Examples for reporting bilateral procedures on the claim

Inappropriate Use: Do not use with codes that are inherently bilateral or contain the phrase of "unilateral or bilateral" within the code description.

51: Multiple Procedures

When multiple procedures, *other than* E/M services, physical medicine and rehabilitation services, or supplies (e.g., vaccines), are performed at the same session by the same provider, the primary service or procedure may be reported first. The additional procedure(s) or service(s) may be identified by appending modifier 51 to the additional procedure or service code(s).

> **Coding Tip:**
>
> This modifier should not be appended to designated add-on codes (see Appendix D of the CPT manual) or to codes where guidelines preclude use.

Modifier 51 indicates a multiple procedure concept; however, add-on codes are modifier 51 exempt. Multiple procedure reductions and rules vary by payor but often favor a 25 percent to 50 percent reduction in secondary and tertiary procedures reported with modifier 51. Medicare will pay 100 percent of the fee schedule for the first allowed amount and 50 percent for the second through fifth procedures. Codes with the modifier 51 exempt ⊘ symbol are also listed in Appendix E of the CPT manual. Medicare does not recommend modifier 51 submission as it has hard-coded the logic into its processing system to automatically append the modifier to the correct procedure code(s) submitted on the claim.

> **EXAMPLE:** A 3 cm intermediate laceration repair to the right hand and a simple 1 cm repair to the right arm were performed at the same session. The codes are 12042 and 12001-51.

Inappropriate Use: Do not use with E/M, physical medicine and rehab, or provision of supplies or with add-on codes.

52: Reduced Services

Under certain circumstances, a service or procedure is partially reduced or eliminated at the physician's discretion. The service provided can be identified by its usual procedure number and the addition of modifier 52, signifying that the service (not a fee) is reduced. This provides a means of reporting reduced services without disturbing the identification of the basic service.

> **Coding Tip:**
>
> For hospital outpatient reporting of a previously scheduled procedure/service that is partially reduced or canceled as a result of extenuating circumstances or those that threaten the well-being of the patient prior to or after administration of anesthesia, see modifiers 73 and 74 (see modifiers approved for ambulatory surgery center (ASC) and hospital outpatient use).

Modifier 52 is to indicate a service or procedure was not fully completed within the given code descriptor. CMS will not allow modifier 52 with an E/M code and it would not typically be reported with leveling services anyway.

> **EXAMPLE:** An appendectomy was performed due to a ruptured appendix. The physician left the wound open to drain the infection and decided on performing a delayed closure a few days later. Modifier 52 on the appendectomy procedure supports reporting of the nonclosure, as closure is typically performed and included in the procedure. The code is 44960-52.

Inappropriate Use: Not intended for cancellations of services nor is it to be used to reduce a patient financial responsibility. It is for reporting reduction of a procedure or service.

53: Discontinued Procedure

Under certain circumstances, the physician may elect to terminate a surgical or diagnostic procedure. Due to extenuating circumstances or those that threaten the well-being of the patient, it may be necessary to indicate that a surgical or diagnostic procedure was started but discontinued. This circumstance may be reported by adding modifier 53 to the code reported by the physician for the discontinued procedure.

Key phrases within this modifier description are "extenuating circumstances" and "those that threaten the well-being of the patient." The notes in modifier 53 direct outpatient hospital and ambulatory surgical center reporting of modifiers 73 and 74.

EXAMPLE: A 61-year-old patient was prepped for a total colonoscopy due to ongoing abdominal pain. During the procedure, the physician was able to get beyond the splenic flexure. However, the physician was unable to advance the colonoscope to the cecum due to an obstruction. The code is 45378-53.

Inappropriate Use: This modifier is not used to report the elective cancellation of a procedure prior to the patient's anesthesia induction and/or surgical preparation in the operating suite.

54: Surgical Care Only

When one physician performs a surgical procedure and another provides preoperative and/or postoperative management, surgical services may be identified by adding modifier 54 to the usual procedure number.

55: Postoperative Management Only

When one physician performed the postoperative management and another physician performed the surgical procedure, the postoperative component may be identified by adding modifier 55 to the usual procedure number.

56: Preoperative Management Only

When one physician performed the preoperative care and evaluation and another physician performed the surgical procedure, the preoperative component may be identified by adding modifier 56 to the usual procedure number.

Splitting a bill for claims submission is often very difficult and requires coordination between the providers when possible. Carriers vary regarding reporting, but many have adopted the Medicare standard.

EXAMPLE: Dr. Jones performed an extracapsular cataract removal with insertion of intraocular lens prosthesis by manual technique to a patient's right eye on March 2, 2015. Dr. Jones would bill the surgery with the 54 modifier. Dr. Smith assumed the postoperative care for the entire 90 days beginning March 3, 2015 (the day after surgery is when the 90-day postoperative period begins). Dr. Smith then relinquished care May 31, 2015. Both providers are due their portion of reimbursement for the patient care. See Figures 13–4 and 13–5 for the codes used by each physician.

Modifier 56 is rarely used independently, as the surgical procedure often includes the preoperative portion of the service. If preoperative "clearance" is being provided,

21. DIAGNOSIS OR NATURE OF ILLNESS OR INJURY Relate A-L to service line below (24E)					ICD Ind.			22. RESUMBISSION CODE		ORIGINAL REF. NO.	
A. _____		B. _____		C. _____	D. _____						
E. _____		F. _____		G. _____	H. _____			23. PRIOR AUTHORIZATION NUMBER			
I. _____		J. _____		K. _____	L. _____						

24. A. DATE(S) OF SERVICE From / To						B. PLACE OF SERVICE	C. EMG	D. PROCEDURES, SERVICES, OR SUPPLIES (Explain Unusual Circumstances) CPT/HCPCS | MODIFIER		E. DIAGNOSIS POINTER	F. $ CHARGES	G. DAYS OR UNITS	H. EPSDT Family Plan	I. ID. QUAL.	J. RENDERING PROVIDER ID. #
MM	DD	YY	MM	DD	YY										
1 03	02	XX						66984	54 RT				1		NPI
2															NPI

Courtesy of the Centers for Medicare & Medicaid Services, www.cms.gov. Copyright © 2017 Cengage Learning®.

Figure 13-4 Split-bill example: Dr. Jones

21. DIAGNOSIS OR NATURE OF ILLNESS OR INJURY Relate A-L to service line below (24E)					ICD Ind.			22. RESUMBISSION CODE		ORIGINAL REF. NO.	
A. _____		B. _____		C. _____	D. _____						
E. _____		F. _____		G. _____	H. _____			23. PRIOR AUTHORIZATION NUMBER			
I. _____		J. _____		K. _____	L. _____						

24. A. DATE(S) OF SERVICE From / To						B. PLACE OF SERVICE	C. EMG	D. PROCEDURES, SERVICES, OR SUPPLIES (Explain Unusual Circumstances) CPT/HCPCS | MODIFIER		E. DIAGNOSIS POINTER	F. $ CHARGES	G. DAYS OR UNITS	H. EPSDT Family Plan	I. ID. QUAL.	J. RENDERING PROVIDER ID. #
MM	DD	YY	MM	DD	YY										
1 03	02	XX						66984	55 RT				90		NPI
2															NPI

Courtesy of the Centers for Medicare & Medicaid Services, www.cms.gov. Copyright © 2017 Cengage Learning®.

Figure 13-5 Split-bill example: Dr. Smith

modifier 56 is *not* to be used, as the use of this modifier would require the provider to discuss the risks and benefits, gather consent for the procedure, and so forth. Typically, preoperative clearance is provided by a physician other than the surgeon and is reported with the appropriate level of E/M service.

57: Decision for Surgery

An evaluation and management service that resulted in the initial decision to perform the surgery may be identified by adding modifier 57 to the appropriate level of E/M service.

Modifier 57 continues to be scrutinized by CMS and other payors. This modifier provides separate E/M payment as it indicates that the E/M encounter determined the surgical decision.

EXAMPLE: A new patient presented to the ENT with difficulty swallowing and worsening symptoms over the course of the past month. The physician evaluated the patient, performing a comprehensive history and detailed exam with findings of a large obstructive laryngeal mass. The decision for immediate surgery the same day was necessary to remove the tumor. The code is 99203-57.

Inappropriate Use: Do not use modifier 57 for the decision to perform a minor procedure (0–10 follow-up days).

58: Staged or Related Procedure or Service by the Same Physician During the Postoperative Period

It may be necessary to indicate that the performance of a procedure or service during the postoperative period was (a) planned or anticipated (staged); (b) more extensive than the original procedure; or (c) for therapy following a surgical procedure. This circumstance may be reported by adding modifier 58 to the staged or related procedure.

Current Procedural Terminology © 2015 American Medical Association. All Rights Reserved.

Modifier 58 is typically paid at 100 percent of the allowable by Medicare and most payors. Understanding the difference between 78 and 58 is important. Modifier 58 has three potential options for use in the descriptor. Following is an example of an anticipated return for further services.

> **CPT EXAMPLE:** A suspicious hyperkeratotic lesion measuring 2.5 cm on the back was removed. The pathology report came back indicating grossly inadequate margins. The patient underwent a successful re-excision five days later of approximately 1.5 cm of skin to clear the lesion margins. The first procedure would be coded as 11403, indicating an excised diameter of 2.1 to 3.0 cm. The re-excision, performed 5 days later, would be reported with code 11402-58.

Inappropriate Use: Not to be used for complications or unanticipated return back to the operating or procedure room.

> **Note:**
> For treatment of a problem that requires a return to the operating or procedure room (e.g., unanticipated clinical condition), see modifier 78.

59: Distinct Procedural Service

Under certain circumstances, it may be necessary to indicate that a procedure or service was distinct or independent from other non-E/M services performed on the same day. Modifier 59 is used to identify procedures or services, other than E/M services, that are not normally reported together but are appropriate under the circumstances. Documentation must support a different session, different procedure or surgery, different site or organ system, separate incision or excision, separate lesion, or separate injury (or area of injury in extensive injuries) not ordinarily encountered or performed on the same day by the same individual. Only when there is not a more descriptive modifier available, and the use of modifier 59 best explains the circumstances, should it be used.

In 2015, Medicare introduced four new HCPCSII modifiers, which are considered subsets to modifier 59, as they explain the procedural distinction.

XE	Separate Encounter
XS	Separate Structure
XP	Separate Practitioner
XU	Unusual Nonoverlapping Service

Modifier 59 is another highly scrutinized modifier that has been used inappropriately based on past audits and OIG reports. It is used to identify procedures and services that are not normally reported together but are appropriate under the circumstances. It is known as the *unbundling* modifier.

> **EXAMPLE:** Bone debridement from a 4-sq-cm heel ulcer and from a 10-sq-cm ischial ulcer was performed. At the same session, a different wound totaling 26-sq-cm is dehisced subcutaneously from the abdomen. The codes are 11044, 11042-59, 11045-59.

Inappropriate Use: Modifier 59 is to be used only as a last resort unless otherwise specified in CPT. It is not to be used with E/M services, nor should it be used to simply bypass bundling edits inappropriately. See additional information regarding modifier 59 in the NCCI Modifiers section of this chapter.

> **Note:**
> Modifier 59 should not be appended to an E/M service. To report a separate and distinct E/M service with a non-E/M service performed on the same date, see modifier 25.

62: Two Surgeons

When two surgeons work together as primary surgeons performing distinct part(s) of a procedure, each surgeon should report his or her distinct operative work by adding modifier 62 to the procedure code and any associated add-on code(s) for that procedure as long as both surgeons continue to work together as primary surgeons. Each surgeon should report the co-surgery once using the same procedure code. If additional procedure(s) (including add-on procedures) are performed during the same surgical session, separate codes may also be reported with modifier 62 added.

Reimbursement is typically divided between co-surgeons at 150 percent of the allowable. Certain procedures will frequently require two surgeons in concert to successfully complete the task. Insurance carriers should be contacted prior to performing a procedure as a co-surgery to verify coverage allowance.

> **Note:**
>
> If a co-surgeon acts as an assistant in the performance of additional procedures during the same surgical session, those services may be reported using separate procedure codes with modifier 80 or modifier 82, as appropriate.

EXAMPLE: A 58-year-old male required a pituitary tumor excision. The procedure was performed nonstereotactically and with a transnasal approach. The procedure required the skills of both the neurosurgeon and the otolaryngologist. They would report the following:

- Neurosurgeon: 61548-62
- Otolaryngologist: 61548-62

Inappropriate Use: Do not confuse co-surgery modifier 62 with assistant surgery modifiers 80 and 82.

63: Procedure Performed on Infants Less than 4 kg

Procedures performed on neonates and infants up to a present body weight of 4 kg may involve significantly increased complexity and physician work commonly associated with these patients. This circumstance may be reported by adding modifier 63 to the procedure number.

Modifier 63 may *only* be appended (unless otherwise designated) to a surgical CPT code within the range of 20000–69990. Procedures on infants less than 4 kg is technically more difficult with regard to maintenance of homeostasis and complexity of work. When a provider reports an eligible procedure or service with modifier 63, typical reimbursement reflects approximately 120 to 125 percent of the allowable service. Appendix F of CPT lists all codes exempt from modifier 63 use.

Examples of Procedures. The American Academy of Pediatrics recommends using this modifier for services that are *not* specific to neonates such as:

Lumbar puncture	Peritoneocentesis
Bladder catheterization	Thoracentesis
Thoracostomy	Pericardiocentesis

Inappropriate Use: Modifier 63 should not be appended to any CPT codes listed in the Evaluation and Management Services, Anesthesia, Radiology, Pathology/Laboratory, or Medicine sections.

66: Surgical Team

Under some circumstances, highly complex procedures (requiring the concomitant services of several physicians, often of different specialties, plus other highly skilled, specially trained personnel, and various types of complex equipment) are carried out under the "surgical team" concept. Such circumstances may be identified by each participating physician with the addition of modifier 66 to the basic procedure number used for reporting services.

EXAMPLE: Three surgeons perform a unilateral renal allotransplantation with a recipient nephrectomy on a 58-year-old patient. Surgeon A reports 50365-66, Surgeon B reports 50365-66, and Surgeon C reports 50365-66.

> **Coding Tip:**
> The CMS guidelines for surgical teams are found in Chapter 12 of the Medicare Carriers' Manual. A report must be submitted with each claim to show the portion of the procedure in which the submitting physician was involved. Pricing and reimbursement are reviewed for each provider individually.

76: Repeat Procedure or Service by Same Physician or Other Qualified Health Care Professional

It may be necessary to indicate that a procedure or service was repeated by the same physician or other qualified health care professional subsequent to the original procedure or service. This circumstance may be reported by adding modifier 76 to the repeated procedure or service.

Modifier 76 is used when the exact procedure requires subsequent reporting by the same provider.

> **EXAMPLE:** An asthmatic patient required an additional nebulizer treatment during an office visit as persistent wheezing and tightness were still present. Both nebulizer treatments would be reported. The first code, 94640, would be listed without the modifier and the second, 94640-76, on a separate line.

Inappropriate Use: This modifier should not be appended to an E/M service.

77: Repeat Procedure by Another Physician or Other Qualified Health Care Professional

It may be necessary to indicate that a basic procedure or service was repeated by another physician or other qualified health care professional subsequent to the original procedure or service. This circumstance may be reported by adding modifier 77 to the repeated procedure or service.

Modifiers 76 and 77 may be reported for services requiring comparatives. It may also be necessary to repeat a service as a follow-up after treatment. If the same provider performs the service, use modifier 76. If a different provider repeats the service, modifier 77 should be utilized.

Insurance carriers may require a description of the service on the claim form or may request a copy of the documentation to see the medical necessity for the repeat procedure.

Inappropriate Use: This modifier should not be appended to an E/M service.

78: Unplanned Return to the Operating/Procedure Room by the Same Physician or Qualified Health Care Professional following Initial Procedure for a Related Procedure During the Postoperative Period

It may be necessary to indicate that another procedure was performed during the postoperative period of the initial procedure (unplanned procedure following initial procedure). When this procedure is related to the first and requires the use of an operating/procedure room, it may be reported by adding modifier 78 to the related procedure. (For repeat procedures, see modifier 76.)

An unplanned return trip to the OR or procedure room by the same physician may be caused by complications (i.e., hemorrhage), following an initial procedure within the postoperative period. If the return to the OR was planned, modifier 58 should be used.

> **Coding Tip:**
>
> For modifier 78, Medicare will reduce the total allowed amount by the postoperative care percentage assigned by CMS for that procedure. Typical CMS payment for the postoperative period for the first procedure includes the follow-up from both procedures. Payment for the modifier 78 procedure will only include the intraoperative portion of the surgery, which is usually between 80 percent and 90 percent of the total global allowance listed in the Medicare Physician Fee Schedule. The procedure reported with modifier 78 does not begin a new global period or provide additional time. The current global period simply continues.

79: Unrelated Procedure or Service by the Same Physician or Other Qualified Health Care Professional During the Postoperative Period

The physician may need to indicate that the performance of a procedure or service during the postoperative period was unrelated to the original procedure by the same physician. This circumstance should be reported by using modifier 79. (For repeat procedures on the same day, see modifier 76.)

Unlike modifier 78, modifier 79 takes on a new global period.

80: Assistant Surgeon

Surgical assistant services may be identified by adding modifier 80 to the usual procedure number(s). This modifier may also be used by other qualified health care professionals as defined by state scope of practice and licensure. Use of the assistant surgeon modifier 80 is not to be confused with the co-surgeon modifier 62 in which two providers work in concert on their distinct parts to complete a surgery. An assistant surgeon is often referred to as "another set of needed hands."

81: Minimum Assistant Surgeon

Minimum surgical assistant services are identified by adding modifier 81 to the usual procedure number.

82: Assistant Surgeon (When Qualified Resident Surgeon Not Available)

The unavailability of a qualified resident surgeon is a prerequisite for use of modifier 82 appended to the usual procedure code number(s).

Assistant surgeon modifiers will vary for use based on individual payors. Typically a physician assisting another physician would report modifier 80. Carrier preauthorization for surgical assists is recommended, as the procedure approval for surgical assists is vastly different among carriers.

> **Coding Tip:**
> CMS will reimburse at either the lower of the actual charge or 16 percent of the approved global surgery fee schedule amount for modifier 80 and 82. Other carriers typically reimburse approximately 18 percent to 22 percent of the procedure allowable.

Minimal assists are reported with modifier 81 and are for "minimal surgical assisting," not for reporting a specific provider type. HCPCSII modifier AS is to report physician assistant (PA), clinical nurse specialist (CNS), or nurse practitioner (NP) services for assistant-at-surgery. In a **PATH** situation (physicians at teaching hospitals), it is expected that residents will assist with most surgical procedures to gain experience. However, when a qualified resident is not available to assist, another physician may need to step in. This assistance is reported with modifier 82.

PATH: Medicare rules governing payment for physicians at teaching hospitals (PATH) to ensure that claims accurately reflect the level of service provided to patients.

90: Reference (Outside) Laboratory

When laboratory procedures are performed by a party other than the treating or reporting physician, the procedure may be identified by adding modifier 90 to the usual procedure number.

Modifier 90 is used to reference an outside lab only. Typically, there are not fees attached to these codes, as they are often required by the insurance company when ordering labs, and so on.

91: Repeat Clinical Diagnostic Laboratory Test

In the course of treatment of the patient, it may be necessary to repeat the same laboratory test on the same day to obtain subsequent (multiple) test results. Under these circumstances, the laboratory test performed can be identified by its usual procedure number and the addition of modifier 91.

Modifier 91 may only be used for laboratory test(s) performed more than once on the same day on the same patient.

Inappropriate Use: Modifier 91 may not be used when tests are rerun to confirm initial results; due to testing problems with specimens or equipment; or for any other reason when a normal, one-time, reportable result is all that is required.

92: Alternative Laboratory Platform Testing

When laboratory testing is being performed using a kit or transportable instrument that wholly or in part consists of a single-use, disposable analytical chamber, the service may be identified by adding modifier 92 to the usual laboratory procedure code (HIV testing 86701–86703). The test does not require permanent dedicated space; hence, by its design it may be hand-carried or transported to the vicinity of the patient for immediate testing at that site, although location of the testing is not in itself determinative of the use of this modifier.

This modifier may only be used on HIV testing codes 86701–86703.

99: Multiple Modifiers

Multiple modifier 99 is rarely used or required. The use of this modifier was intended to be listed in the first modifier position, alerting the carrier that additional modifiers were following the code. The problem with modifier 99 is that many carriers only recognize the first and second modifier positions even though there are four available positions on the CMS 1500 claim form. If one of those positions is taken up by the multiple modifier 99, the tertiary and fourth position may not be picked up.

Exercise 13.1

Indicate whether each statement is true or false.

1. CPT and HCPCSII modifiers may be used between code sets when appropriate.

2. Modifier 58 is to be used when a complication occurs and the patient requires a return trip to the operating room.

3. Add-on codes should not be used with modifier 51 when reporting multiple procedures.

4. Modifiers are for optional use only by physicians and coders.

Modifiers Approved for Ambulatory Surgery Center (ASC) and Hospital Outpatient Use

Coding for the ambulatory surgery center (ASC) and outpatient hospital services is somewhat different than coding for physician services. Two distinct differences are that only certain modifiers allowed in other settings may be used for these settings, and that the modifiers 27, 73, and 74 can only be used in these settings. The following modifiers are approved for use in this setting and are listed in CPT Appendix A.

25	Significant, Separately Identifiable Evaluation and Management Service by the Same Physician on the Same Day of the Procedure or Other Service
27	Multiple Outpatient Hospital E/M Encounters on the Same Date
50	Bilateral Procedure
52	Reduced Services
58	Staged or Related Procedure or Service by the Same Physician During the Postoperative Period
59	Distinct Procedural Service
73	Discontinued Out-Patient Hospital/Ambulatory Surgery Center (ASC) Procedure Prior to the Administration of Anesthesia
74	Discontinued Out-Patient Hospital/Ambulatory Surgery Center (ASC) Procedure after Administration of Anesthesia
76	Repeat Procedure or Service by Same Physician or Other Qualified Health Care Professional
77	Repeat Procedure by Another Physician or Other Qualified Health Care Professional
78	Unplanned Return to the Operating/Procedure Room by the Same Physician or Other Qualified Health Care Professional Following Initial Procedure for a Related Procedure During the Postoperative Period
79	Unrelated Procedure or Service by the Same Physician or Other Qualified Health Care Professional During the Postoperative Period
91	Repeat Clinical Diagnostic Laboratory Test

Exercise 13.2

Assign the appropriate modifier(s) to the following scenarios.

1. The surgical procedure required an additional 40 minutes because of excessive blood loss and hemorrhage. _____

2. During an established patient's annual physical, two additional E/M key components were performed related to an ongoing chronic illness. _____

3. Due to the severe pain the patient was suffering from multiple injuries, it was necessary to perform the laceration repairs under general anesthesia. _____

4. The test was repeated since the first sample was inadequate. _____

5. Although the procedure for the left arm lipoma was distinct from the other lipoma on the same arm, it was still necessary to excise them both today. _____

6. The mother was frustrated that her child would need to have the procedure repeated. This time, she chose to have a different provider perform the surgery. _____

HCPCS Level II Modifiers

CMS began developing national HCPCSII codes and modifiers in the early 1980s. HCPCSII was selected as one of the HIPAA standardized code sets because of its wide acceptance nationally among both public and private insurers. The CPT book includes a small section of frequently used HCPCSII modifiers that CMS and the AMA agreed to include in CPT. Table 13-1 gives examples.

HCPCSII includes the "build a modifier" concept when coding for ambulance services. See the A code section of the HCPCS Level II code book.

Table 13-1 HCPCS Level II Modifier Examples

Anatomical Modifiers	
E1 Upper left eyelid	TA Left foot, great toe
E2 Lower left eyelid	T1 Left foot, second digit
E3 Upper right eyelid	T2 Left foot, third digit
E4 Lower right eyelid	T3 Left foot, fourth digit
LS FDA-monitored intraocular lens implant	T4 Left foot, fifth digit
LC Left circumflex coronary artery	T5 Right foot, great toe
LD Left anterior descending coronary artery	T6 Right foot, second digit
RC Right coronary artery	T7 Right foot, third digit
	T8 Right foot, fourth digit
	T9 Right foot, fifth digit
Administrative and Miscellaneous Modifiers	
AI Principal physician of record	JW Drug amount discarded/not administered to any patient
AH Clinical psychologist	KX Requirements specified in the medical policy have been met
GA Medicare ABN-waiver of liability statement issued	LT Left side

(continues)

Table 13-1 (*continued*)

Administrative and Miscellaneous Modifiers	
GC Service performed by a resident under the direction of a teaching physician	QW CLIA waived test
GE Service performed by a resident without the presence of a teaching physician under the primary care exception	Q6 Services furnished by a locum tenens physician
	RT Right side
	TC Technical component

Exercise 13.3

Fill in the blanks.

1. Medicare will not allow modifier _____ to be used with an E/M code to show the level criteria have not been met.
2. HCPCSII modifiers LT and RT may be used in place of modifier _____ for some payors.
3. To report a procedure performed on the right lower eyelid, the physician should report modifier _____ .
4. Modifier _____ should be used to report a service performed by a nurse midwife.

NCCI Modifiers

The National Correct Coding Initiative, or NCCI, includes specific information pertaining to modifier use within the bundling edits. Only if clinical circumstances justify should modifiers be appended to the CPT or HCPCSII code. Health care providers and entities may find themselves in a penalty situation for appending modifiers to simply bypass an NCCI edit. The clinical circumstance must be documented and supported in the medical record to justify use. Not all CPT and HCPCSII modifiers are included in the NCCI as approved or allowed.

The active NCCI modifiers include:

- Anatomical modifiers: E1–E4, FA, F1–F9, TA, T1–T9, LT, RT, LC, LD, RC, LM, RI
- Global surgery modifiers: 24, 25, 57, 58, 78, 79
- Other modifiers: 27, 59, 91, XE, XS, XP, XU

> **Coding Tip:**
>
> Modifier 22 is not a modifier that bypasses an NCCI edit; however, its use is occasionally relevant to an NCCI edit. The NCCI states: "If the edit allows use of NCCI-associated modifiers to bypass it and the clinical circumstances justify use of one of these modifiers, both services may be reported with the NCCI-associated modifier. However, if the NCCI edit does not allow use of NCCI-associated modifiers to bypass it and the procedure qualifies as an unusual procedural service, the physician may report the column one HCPCS/CPT code of the NCCI edit with modifier 22."

Highlight:

As a result of scrutiny by government payors, modifier 25 remains at the top of items checked in an audit. NCCI guidelines state that modifier 25 may be appended to E/M services reported with minor surgical procedures (global period of 000 or 010 days) or procedures not covered by global surgery rules (global indicator of XXX).

Further, NCCI reasoning clarifies the use of minor surgical procedures and XXX procedures. Since both of these procedure types include pre-procedure, intra-procedure, and post-procedure work inherent in the procedure, the provider should not report an E/M service for this work. Final comments from NCCI include, "Medicare Global Surgery rules prevent the reporting of a separate E/M service for the work associated with the decision to perform a minor surgical procedure whether the patient is a new or established patient."

When coders first review the NCCI code pairs, they will see a column with indicators of 0, 1, or 9. The CMS website provides the following Table 13–2 regarding **NCCI associated modifiers** used in determining bypass of a pair edit.

NCCI associated modifier: Indicates modifiers associated with NCCI that may or may not be allowed to be used with a specified code pair.

Table 13-2 Modifier Indicator Table

0 (Not Allowed)	There are no modifiers associated with NCCI that are allowed to be used with this code pair; there are no circumstances in which both procedures of the code pair should be paid for the same beneficiary on the same day by the same provider.
1 (Allowed)	The modifiers associated with NCCI are allowed with this code pair when appropriate.
9 (Not Applicable)	This indicator means that an NCCI edit does not apply to this code pair. The edit for this code pair was deleted retroactively.

NCCI EXAMPLE: In reviewing Table 13–3, be sure to read the column headers. The code pair edit with column 1 CPT code 38221 (bone marrow biopsy) and column 2 CPT code 38220 (bone marrow, aspiration only) includes two distinct procedures when performed at separate anatomical sites or separate patient encounters. In these circumstances, it would be acceptable to use modifier 59.

Table 13-3 Example from NCCI Table of Column 1/Column 2 Edits

Column 1/Column 2 Edits				
Column 1·	**Column 2**	**Effective Date**	**Deletion Date** (* = no data)	**Modifier** 0 = not allowed 1 = allowed 9 = not applicable
38221	J0670	20100701	*	1
38221	01112	20020101	*	0
38221	38220	20020101	*	1

If, however, both 38221 and 38220 are performed through the same skin incision at the same patient encounter, which is the usual practice, modifier 59 should *not* be used. Although CMS does not allow separate payment for code 38220 with 38221 when bone marrow aspiration and biopsy are performed through the same skin incision at a single patient encounter, code G0364, Bone marrow aspiration performed with bone marrow biopsy through the same incision on the same date of service is allowed with code 38221 in this scenario. Code 01112 (anesthesia for bone marrow aspiration/biopsy) would not be eligible for a modifier to bypass the edit when reported with code 38220.

Anesthesia Physical Status Modifiers

The physical status modifiers are HCPCSII modifiers that are listed in both the Anesthesia guideline section of CPT and in Appendix A of the CPT modifiers. They are to be placed only with the anesthesia codes, in the 00100 series. The American Society of Anesthesiology (ASA) assists in policies clarifying each description and the use of the P modifiers. The use of these unique P modifiers and their descriptions (Figure 6–2) are found in Chapter 6 of this book.

Exercise 13.4

Match the modifier type with the correct modifier.

1. _____ CPT I modifier   a. 52
2. _____ HCPCSII modifier for ABN use   b. 1
3. _____ HCPCS II modifier, anatomical   c. GA
4. _____ Outpatient/ASC modifier   d. R
5. _____ CPT I reduced modifier   e. T1
6. _____ NCCI modifier indicator   f. 27
7. _____ Ambulance origin   g. 25

Complete the following coding scenarios by selecting the CPT/HCPCSII code and any applicable modifiers.

8. A very difficult vaginal delivery only, utilizing forceps, was performed. The physician has documented the complex nature of the delivery, the additional time, and the outcome. _____

9. The physician performed the interpretation and report of an unattended sleep study that included simultaneous recording of heart rate, oxygen saturation, respiratory airflow, and thoracoabdominal movement. _____

10. A specialist provided a comprehensive history, detailed exam, and moderate-complexity decision making during the patient's first office visit. This was after receiving a request from the patient's insurance company for a second opinion regarding possible lap band surgery. The specialist submitted his written report, which included his findings and opinion on the medical necessity to proceed with the surgery. _____

Summary

Familiarity with the CPT and HCPCSII modifiers and concepts will assist with accurate reporting. Some modifiers are unique to their code set while others may be used across different code sets. National Correct Coding Initiative–approved modifiers are essential to Medicare billing. These modifiers are closely monitored by CMS and other state and federal programs. The descriptions within Appendix A of the CPT may lend assistance with determining the specific nature of use for individual modifiers and often will provide additional direction. Listing multiple modifiers in correct order on the claim form will ensure accurate interpretation. Using modifiers is not an option in today's coding environment but a true fundamental ingredient to proper claims submission.

References

AMA Current Procedural Terminology 2016 professional edition. (2015). Chicago: American Medical Association.

Centers for Medicare & Medicaid Services. (2015). *National correct coding initiative policy manual for Medicare services.* Retrieved from https://www.cms.gov.

CPT and HCPCS Modifier Quick Finder Tool (16th ed.). (2015). Aurora, CO: Robin Linker & Associates, Inc.

Understanding Medicare's NCCI: Logic and interpretation of the edits (2009). Chicago: American Medical Association.

CHAPTER 1

Billing and Collections

Learning Objectives

Upon successful completion of this chapter, you should be able to:

- Explain the importance of billing and collection practices in the outpatient setting.
- Demonstrate the patient registration process.
- Compare the advantages and disadvantages between cycle billing and monthly billing.
- List the advantages and disadvantages of a computerized billing system.
- Explain the accounts receivable process.
- Explain account aging and the purpose of an age analysis.

Key Terms

accept assignment

account aging

accounts receivable (A/R)

Affordable Care Act (ACA)

bankruptcy

birthday rule

charge slip, superbill, fee ticket, or encounter form

cycle billing

electronic medical record (EMR)

emancipated minor

Fair Debt Collection Practices Act

HIPAA transaction and code sets

limiting charge

Medicare physician fee schedule (MPFS)

monthly billing

nonparticipating provider (nonPAR)

participating provider (PAR)

professional courtesy

relative value unit (RVU)

Resource-Based Relative Value Scale (RBRVS)

skip

Truth in Lending Act

usual, customary, and reasonable (UCR) fees

Introduction

Previous chapters have discussed coding rules, including specialty area guidelines. This chapter gives instruction in proper billing techniques and the collection of payment in the ambulatory care setting.

The United States Census Bureau reported in 2010 the following statistics for health insurance coverage:

- Approximately 83.7 percent are covered by health insurance.
- Approximately 55.3 percent are covered by employer-sponsored plans.

- Approximately 9.8 percent direct-purchase plans.

- Approximately 31 percent are covered by government funded plans (Medicaid, Medicare, and Military).

- Approximately 2.5 million young adults have gained health insurance as a result of the provision in the Affordable Care Act that allows them to remain on their parents' insurance plans until age 26.

The Patient Protection and Affordable Care Act (PPACA), referred to as the **Affordable Care Act (ACA)**, is a national law that reforms both the health care and health insurance industries in America. The ACA was passed by Congress and then signed into law by President Barack Obama on March 23, 2010. On June 28, 2012, the Supreme Court rendered a final decision to uphold the health care law. This law increases the quality, availability, and affordability of private and public health insurance to over 44 million uninsured Americans and works to reduce the growth in health care spending. A brief outline of the ACA follows:

Affordable Care Act: A national law that reforms both the health care and health insurance industries to increase the quality, availability, and affordability of private and public health insurance to all Americans.

- Ends preexisting condition exclusions for children under the age of 19 years

- Keeps young adults covered under a parent's health insurance plan until the age of 26 years

- Ends arbitrary withdrawals of insurance covered

- Guarantees the right to appeal a denial of payment

- Expands preventive care, many with no copayment or deductible

- Creates new incentives on workplace wellness programs

The Billing Process

The billing process begins when the patient calls the office for an appointment. Front office personnel must be trained in the following:

- New patient registration and established patient recheck

- Interpretation of insurance contracts

- Verification of current demographic information

- Verification of insurance benefits

- Collecting copayments/coinsurance and deductibles

- Preparation of the encounter form

- Posting financial transactions to the patient account

A major objective of accurately coding diagnoses and procedures and submitting claims with correct information is to receive reimbursement for services rendered. This leads to another vital function in any facility—the billing and collections process. Obtaining information for billing occurs the first time the patient comes into the office, clinic, or hospital and completes the registration form. This information is then checked with the patient on each return to the facility in order to maintain updated patient records, both medical and financial.

In assigning codes for diagnoses and procedures and linking these codes accurately to indicate the medical necessity, accuracy and completeness are important in the billing, reimbursement, and collections for services rendered in any health care facility.

Exercise 14.1

Match the diagnosis with the procedure to show a valid linkage for medical necessity.

Diagnosis

1. Migraine headache
2. Chronic otitis media
3. Substernal chest discomfort
4. Nocturia
5. Family history of prostate cancer
6. Prostatic hypertrophy
7. Epilepsy
8. Liver dysfunction due to statin use
9. Coagulation disorder/on blood thinner

10. Cholecystitis
11. GERD
12. Tuberculosis
13. R/O diabetes mellitus
14. Fracture of tibia/fibula
15. Family hx. of breast cancer
16. Cystic lesion of breast
17. Pernicious anemia
18. Herniated L4–L5
19. Bursitis of shoulder
20. COPD
21. Family hx. of colon cancer
22. Epistaxis
23. Breast abscess
24. Anemia
25. Burn of forearm, partial thickness

Procedure

A. Mammogram
B. Upper GI/EGD
C. ORIF
D. MRI of lumbar vertebrae
E. Injection of Demerol and Phenergen
F. Complete blood count
G. Debridement with dressing
H. Ultrasound of gallbladder/HIDA scan
I. Steroid injection into bursas
J. Colonoscopy
K. TURP
L. Nasal packing
M. Incision and drainage
N. Urinalysis
O. Pulmonary function study
P. Puncture aspiration
Q. PSA
R. Chest x-ray
S. Vitamin B_{12} injection
T. Hepatic function panel
U. GTT
V. EKG
W. EEG
X. Pro time
Y. Myringotomy

Patient Registration

Patient registration forms vary from practice to practice but all should contain the following information (Figure 14–1):

- Patient's full name, address, birth date, Social Security number, marital status
- Telephone numbers where patient can be reached: home, work, and cell phone, as well as e-mail address

Lowery B. Johnson, M.D.
Hwy 311 Suite A31
Sellersburg, IN 47172
812-555-1234

Please complete this form.

NAME: _____

STREET ADDRESS: _____ APT: _____

CITY: _____ STATE: _____ ZIP: _____

HOME PHONE (& area code): _____

WORK PHONE (& area code): _____

CELL PHONE (& area code): _____

E-MAIL ADDRESS: _____

SOCIAL SECURITY NUMBER: _____

SEX: Male _____ Female _____ Age _____ Date of Birth _____

MARITAL STATUS: Married _____ Single _____ Separated _____ Divorced _____ Widowed _____

PERSON TO CONTACT IN EMERGENCY: _____ PHONE: _____

EMPLOYED: Full Time _____ Part Time _____ Retired _____ Not Employed _____

EMPLOYER: Company Name: _____ Phone:_____

       Address: _____

       Location/Department Where You Work: _____

STUDENT STATUS: Full-time Student _____ School _____

       Part-time Student _____ School _____

INSURANCE COMPANY: _____

    Policy Number: _____ Group Number: _____

    Name of Insured: _____ Relationship to You: _____

    Address: _____

    Deductible: _____ Percent of Coverage: _____

OTHER INSURANCE COMPANY: _____

    Policy Number: _____ Group Number: _____

    Name of Insured: _____ Relationship to You: _____

    Address: _____

    Deductible: _____ Percent of Coverage: _____

WHAT BRINGS YOU TO SEE THE DOCTOR? _____

_____

IS YOUR CONDITION RELATED TO:

    AUTO ACCIDENT: _____ DATE: _____ STATE WHERE OCCURRED: _____

    OTHER ACCIDENT: _____ DATE: _____ STATE WHERE OCCURRED: _____

    YOUR EMPLOYMENT: _____

NAME OF REFERRING PHYSICIAN: _____

Figure 14-1 Patient registration form

- Health insurance information—carrier's name, name of insured, plan name/ identification number, group and/or policy numbers

- Name of responsible party (spouse, parent, guardian) and contact information

- Address, phone number, and Social Security number of responsible party and the relationship to the patient

- Emergency contact information

- A photocopy of the patient's driver's license or other photo identification

Additional information may be requested, such as if the visit or encounter is related to an accident or injury, particularly a work-related incident.

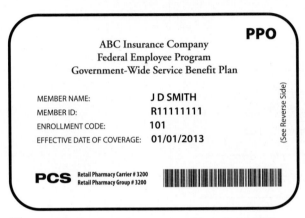

Figure 14-2 Insurance card (front and back)

At the time the patient completes necessary paperwork, an Authorization for Release of Information may be obtained. This form goes beyond the treatment, payment, or other health care operations for disclosure of other requested information. Also signed at this encounter is the acknowledgment of receipt of HIPAA Privacy Notice. Examples of the authorization and the HIPAA Privacy Notice appear in Figures 14–3A and 14–3B.

Fee Schedules

Before studying the processes of billing and collection of payment, it is essential to understand that patient fees are based on three commodities the physician provides: time, judgment, and services.

Individual medical practices determine fees that will be charged for those services and procedures performed in the office. This fee schedule may be based on several factors:

- The economic level of the community

- The physician's experience

- The medical specialty of the practice

- Charges of other physicians in the area

- The cost of the service or supply

JOHNSON MEDICAL CLINIC
Authorization for Release of Information

Name: _____   Date of Birth: _____

Address: _____   City, State, Zip: _____

Patient ID#: _____   Phone Number: _____

☐ I authorize Johnson Medical Clinic
    to release information to:

AND/OR

☐ I authorize Johnson Medical Clinic
    to obtain information from:

Name of Provider or Facility

Name of Provider or Facility

Address

Address

City, State, Zip Code

City, State, Zip Code

Phone #Fax # (Include area code)

Phone #Fax # (Include area code)

PURPOSE OF THIS REQUEST: (check one) ☐ Health Care ☐ Insurance Coverage ☐ Personal ☐ Other

TYPE OF RECORDS AUTHORIZED: ☐ Psychiatric/Psychological Evaluation and/or Treatment
    ☐ Drug/Alcohol Evaluation and/or Treatment

SPECIFIC INFORMATION AUTHORIZED (select one or more as appropriate):

☐ Assessments   ☐ Progress Notes   Laboratory Test Results: _____

☐ Diagnostic impression   ☐ Discharge Summary   Treatment Plans

☐ Treatment Summary

☐ Other (please describe): _____

One-time Use/Disclosure: I authorize the one-time use or disclosure of the information described above to the person/provider/organization/facility/program(s) identified. **My authorization will expire:**
    ☐ When the requested information has been sent/received.
    ☐ 90 days from this date.   ☐ Other: _____

Periodic Use/Disclosure: I authorize the periodic use/disclosure of the information described above to the person/provider/organization/facility/program(s) identified as often as necessary to fulfill the purpose identified in this document.
    My authorization will expire:
    ☐ When I am no longer receiving services from the Johnson Medical Clinic.
    ☐ One year from this date.   ☐ Other: _____

I understand that:
    I do not have to sign this authorization and that my refusal to sign will not affect my abilities to obtain treatment.
    I may cancel this authorization at any time by submitting a *written* request to the Johnson Medical Clinic, except where a disclosure has already been made in reliance on my prior authorization.
    If the person or facility receiving this information is not a health care or medical insurance provider covered by privacy regulations, the information stated above could be redisclosed.
    If the authorized information is protected by Federal Confidentiality Rules 42CFR, Part 2, it may not be disclosed without my written consent unless otherwise provided for in the regulations.
    Release of HIV-related information requires additional information.
    If the medical record information is not sent to another care provider, there may be a charge for the requested records.

Signature of Patient or Legal Representative: _____   Date: _____

Relationship to Patient *(if requester is not the student):* ☐ Parent ☐ Legal Guardian ☐ Other _____

Patient or Representative has been provided a copy of this authorization: _____
                                              Staff member providing copy

Figure 14-3A Example of Authorization for Release of Information

JOHNSON MEDICAL CLINIC
HIPAA PATIENT'S PRIVACY NOTICE

1. We will inform patients of how we may use their medical information, including:

   a. sharing treatment information among doctors, technicians, and other persons in our practice who need to know;
   b. insurance companies and all billing and collection procedures, methods, and policies;
   c. all clerical reasons including chart audits, research, and appointment reminders;
   d. for any reason required by law;
   e. upon request of the Veteran's Administration or the military if the patient is on active duty or is a reservist;
   f. to protect the safety of our own staff;
   g. as required for public health issues.

2. The patient has the right to privacy, including:

   a. the right to receive a copy of his or her medical records and have his or her medical information interpreted if the patient does not understand the information in the record. HIPAA regulations recommend a time frame for responding to requests for patient medical records of 30–60 days;
   b. The ability to require us to amend medical information if the patient feels it is inaccurate or incomplete;
   c. The right to restrict which legitimate sources we can share the patient's medical information.

3. Our medical practice has the responsibility to:

   a. change this notice as laws are revised or interpreted;
   b. inform patients of this Privacy Notice.

4. The patient has a right to complain regarding alleged privacy violations. These complaints may be submitted in writing to our Privacy Officer or with the Secretary of Health and Human Services in Washington, D.C.

5. Our medical practice has designated as its Privacy Officer, T. L. Smith, Privacy Officer/Administrator, Johnson Medical Clinic, Hwy 311, Suite A31, Sellersburg, IN 47172. Phone 812-555-1234; fax 812-555-1235.

6. This Privacy Notice may be updated for future changes/revisions.

Patient Signature _____   Date _____

Clinic Representative _____   Date _____

I, _____ ,hereby authorize Johnson Medical Clinic to release medical or billing information on my behalf to the following person(s):

_____   _____
_____   _____
_____   _____

_____   _____
Patient Signature   Date

Figure 14-3B Example of HIPAA Patient's Privacy Notice

Exercise 14.2

1. List the three commodities a physician has to sell when setting fees for the medical office.

   a. _____

   b. _____

   c. _____

2. What is the purpose of copying the patient's insurance card and retaining it in the patient's medical chart?
3. Why is it important to have an emergency contact in the patient's information?
4. List three conditions included in the Affordable Care Act.

The maximum amount the insurance carrier or government program will cover for specified services is called the *allowable charge* or *allowed amount*. The difference between the physician charge and the allowable charge is called a *nonallowed charge*. Allowable charges are often based on **usual, customary, and reasonable (UCR) fees**.

Usual—The physician's average fee for a service or procedure

Customary—The average fee for that service or procedure within an area, based on national trends rather than regional or local customs

Reasonable—A fee that is generally accepted for a service or procedure that is extraordinarily difficult or complicated, requiring more time or effort for the physician to perform

EXAMPLE: Dr. Johnson charges $150 for a new patient office visit, including a complete history and physical examination. The usual fee charged for this same service of other physicians in the same community with similar training and experience ranges from $125 to $200. Dr. Johnson's fee of $150 is within the customary range and would be paid under an insurance plan's usual and customary basis.

usual, customary, and reasonable (UCR) fees: A method used to average fee profiles to determine what is allowable for reimbursement.

Resource-Based Relative Value Scale (RBRVS): A method of predetermining values for physician services for Medicare established in 1992, calculating units based on services performed, practice expenses, and professional liability insurance.

Exercise 14.3

1. Dr. Dogood, a gastroenterologist, performs flexible diagnostic sigmoidoscopies in the office. His charge for this procedure is $195. The usual fee charged for this procedure by other gastroenterologists in this city is from $190 to $210.

   Is Dr. Dogood's fee within the usual and customary range for insurance payment?

The **Resource-Based Relative Value Scale (RBRVS)** is the payment system for reimbursement of physician services, procedures, outpatient physical and occupational therapy, radiology services, and diagnostic tests based on the **Medicare physician fee schedule (MPFS)**. CMS reviews and revises this fee schedule annually. All services and/or procedures are standardized to measure their value as

Medicare physician fee schedule (MPFS): A listing of allowable charges for services rendered to Medicare patients.

relative value unit (RVU):
Payment component based on physician work, practice expense, and malpractice expense.

compared with other services provided. For each CPT-coded service or procedure, a **relative value unit (RVU)** is assigned to each of three components:

1. Physician work—based on the time and intensity in providing the service (judgment, technical skill, and physical effort)

2. Practice expense—overhead costs involved in providing a service (rent, equipment, utilities, and salaries)

3. Malpractice expense or liability insurance

The geographic area is also considered in the formula to calculate payment. The total RVU is multiplied by the conversion factor to obtain the reimbursement for the CPT code. A conversion factor is the dollar amount by which each CPT code's total RVU value is multiplied to obtain reimbursement for a service. In addition, a geographic adjustment factor (GAF) known as the GPCI (geographic practice cost index) is applied to account for different costs for different services nationwide. This conversion factor is updated annually by CMS and is calculated by estimating the sustainable growth rate (SGR), which is the target rate of growth in spending for physician services. The conversion factor is then calculated based on legislation and the need to align actual spending with the target provided by the SGR.

Figure 14–4 shows an example of the formula for determining physician fee schedule payments.

EXAMPLE: A level IV office service in 2011:

(Work RVUs × Work GPCI) + (Practice expense RVUs × Practice expense GPCI) + (Liability insurance RVUs × Professional liability insurance GPCI) = Total RVUs × Conversion factor = Medicare payment

(2.56) (1.009) + (0.62) (1.001) + (0.22) (1.110) = 3.44

(Total RVUs) (Conversion factor) = Medicare payment

(3.44) ($33.9764) = $116.88

limiting charge: A percentage limitation on fees that nonparticipating physicians are allowed to bill Medicare patients above the fee schedule amount.

nonparticipating provider (nonPAR): A health care provider who has not signed a contract with an insurance company (also known as an out-of-network provider).

participating provider (PAR): A health care provider who has signed a contract with an insurance company to provide medical services to subscribers in the contract plan (also known as an in-network provider).

A **limiting charge** is the percentage limitation on fees that **nonparticipating provider (nonPAR)** are allowed to bill Medicare patients above the fee schedule amount. The limiting charge applies to every service listed in the Medicare physician's fee schedule that is performed by a nonparticipating (nonPAR) physician, including global, professional, and technical services. Different prices are listed for each CPT code. The fee schedule amount is determined by multiplying the relative value unit (RVU) weight by the geographic index and the conversion factor. The **participating provider (PAR)** receives the fee schedule amount. For the nonparticipating physician, the fee schedule amount of the allowable payment is slightly less than the participating physician's payment. Chapter 15 further explains nonPAR versus PAR requirements.

The limiting charge is important because that is the maximum amount a Medicare patient can be billed for a service. Medicare usually pays 80 percent of the allowable amount for covered services. The patient can then be billed the difference between the Medicare payment and the limiting charge. The patient is notified of the limiting charge for each service on the Medicare Summary Notice.

The Medicare website (https://www. cms.gov) provides an overview of the MPFS as well as a Physician Fee Schedule Lookup tool to assist in determining fee payments.

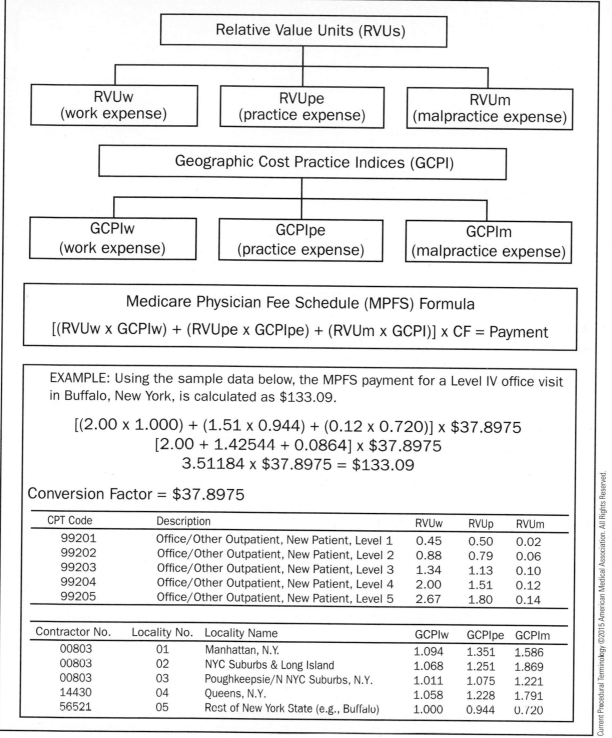

Figure 14-4 showing:

Relative Value Units (RVUs)
- RVUw (work expense)
- RVUpe (practice expense)
- RVUm (malpractice expense)

Geographic Cost Practice Indices (GCPI)
- GCPIw (work expense)
- GCPIpe (practice expense)
- GCPIm (malpractice expense)

Medicare Physician Fee Schedule (MPFS) Formula

[(RVUw x GCPIw) + (RVUpe x GCPIpe) + (RVUm x GCPI)] x CF = Payment

EXAMPLE: Using the sample data below, the MPFS payment for a Level IV office visit in Buffalo, New York, is calculated as $133.09.

$$[(2.00 \times 1.000) + (1.51 \times 0.944) + (0.12 \times 0.720)] \times \$37.8975$$
$$[2.00 + 1.42544 + 0.0864] \times \$37.8975$$
$$3.51184 \times \$37.8975 = \$133.09$$

Conversion Factor = $37.8975

CPT Code	Description	RVUw	RVUp	RVUm
99201	Office/Other Outpatient, New Patient, Level 1	0.45	0.50	0.02
99202	Office/Other Outpatient, New Patient, Level 2	0.88	0.79	0.06
99203	Office/Other Outpatient, New Patient, Level 3	1.34	1.13	0.10
99204	Office/Other Outpatient, New Patient, Level 4	2.00	1.51	0.12
99205	Office/Other Outpatient, New Patient, Level 5	2.67	1.80	0.14

Contractor No.	Locality No.	Locality Name	GCPIw	GCPIpe	GCPIm
00803	01	Manhattan, N.Y.	1.094	1.351	1.586
00803	02	NYC Suburbs & Long Island	1.068	1.251	1.869
00803	03	Poughkeepsie/N NYC Suburbs, N.Y.	1.011	1.075	1.221
14430	04	Queens, N.Y.	1.058	1.228	1.791
56521	05	Rest of New York State (e.g., Buffalo)	1.000	0.944	0.720

Figure 14-4 Formula for determining physician fee schedule payments

Exercise 14.4

1. What do each of the following acronyms represent?
    a. GAF
    b. RBRVS
    c. RVU
    d. GPCI
    e. MPFS
    f. SGR
    g. PAR
    h. nonPAR

Payment and Billing Processes

Payment at Time of Service

Communication lines must be open between the patient and the medical office to maintain effective collection practices. Patients should know up-front the provider's billing policies and collection procedures. Use the patient's initial contact with the office as the first point of control for collections. When making the appointment for the new patient, take a few minutes to discuss payment policies. Get insurance information at this time to check provider participation agreement and verify if your physician(s) participates with the patient's insurance plan. This saves both the staff and the patient valuable time. When appointments are scheduled for established patients, they can be reminded of an outstanding balance and asked to make a payment when they come in.

A patient brochure is an effective method to explain the office's payment and collection policies established by the physician employers and managers of the practice as indicated in Figure 14–5. The brochure can be mailed to the new patient prior to

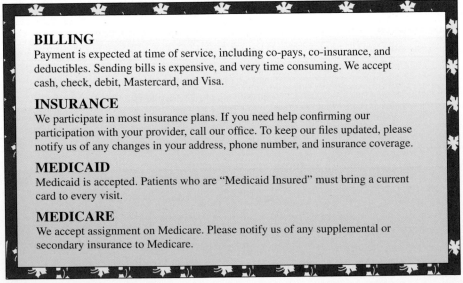

BILLING
Payment is expected at time of service, including co-pays, co-insurance, and deductibles. Sending bills is expensive, and very time consuming. We accept cash, check, debit, Mastercard, and Visa.

INSURANCE
We participate in most insurance plans. If you need help confirming our participation with your provider, call our office. To keep our files updated, please notify us of any changes in your address, phone number, and insurance coverage.

MEDICAID
Medicaid is accepted. Patients who are "Medicaid Insured" must bring a current card to every visit.

MEDICARE
We accept assignment on Medicare. Please notify us of any supplemental or secondary insurance to Medicare.

Figure 14-5 Billing and insurance excerpts from a patient brochure

the first appointment. Patients appreciate knowing their payment responsibilities. If the patient anticipates a problem in meeting the outlined payment policy, a payment schedule can be worked out that is agreeable to both the patient and the office.

Displaying a notice in the office stating that payment at time of service is required has the following advantages:

- It ensures prompt collection of fees.
- It eliminates further bookkeeping work.
- It reduces the cost of preparing and mailing a statement to the patient.
- It increases cash flow for the practice.

Many offices encourage payment at time of service by accepting cash, personal checks, and major credit and debit cards. It is important as part of the contractual agreement with participating insurance companies that copayments and coinsurance be collected at the time of service.

When a patient pays in cash, carefully count the cash before placing it in the cash drawer. Always prepare a receipt to give to the patient as a record of cash payment as shown in Figure 14–6.

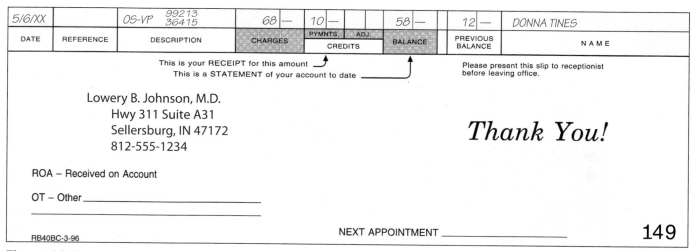

Figure 14-6 Receipt for payment given to a patient, especially for cash payments

When a patient pays by check, review the check to see that it is properly written:

- The date is current.
- The amount of the check is the correct amount.
- The name of the physician or practice is spelled properly.
- The person whose name is imprinted on the check signs the check.
- Never accept a check for more than the amount due.
- If a patient is new or unfamiliar, identification can be requested.

An example is shown in Figure 14–7.

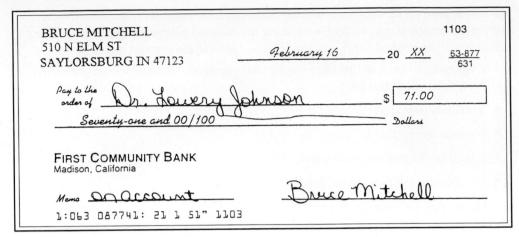

Figure 14-7 Payment by check

Immediately endorse the check and place in the cash drawer for the bank deposit to be made that day.

Credit and debit cards are a popular method of payment in the medical office. Patients find these cards convenient, especially when the bill is large. To accept debit and credit cards in the medical office, the bank or financial institution must be contacted to establish the account. There is a service charge or fee to accept debit and credit cards that is deducted from payment issued to the office. For example, if a patient charges services totaling $50 on a credit card, the office will receive between $45 and $49.

The American Medical Association (AMA) condones the acceptance of these cards in the medical office but advises not to use this as an advertising lure for the practice. Also, patients paying by debit and credit card should not be charged higher fees to recover the service charge by the bank or financial institution to the practice.

Credit and Payment Policy

Payment at time of service is not always possible for all patients and for many practices. Therefore, it is important to have a formal credit and collection policy established. Following are some questions to address in setting up this policy:

- When will payment be due from the patient?
- What kind of payment arrangements can be made?
- How and when will patients be reminded of overdue accounts?
- When is the bill considered delinquent?
- When exceptions are made to the policy, who makes them?
- Will a collection agency be utilized?

A written, straightforward credit and collection policy will eliminate confusion and serve as a guide to both the patient and the billing personnel.

In some situations, a payment schedule is arranged with determination of a down payment, whether interest is to be charged, and scheduling of installment payments scheduled. When there is a bilateral agreement between the physician and the patient to pay for a procedure in more than four installments, the physician must disclose finance charges in writing. The **Truth in Lending Act** (also known as Regulation Z of the Consumer Protection Act) protects consumers by requiring creditors to disclose certain

Truth in Lending Act: A consumer protection act requiring a written statement when there is a bilateral agreement between the physician and patient to pay for a procedure in more than four installments, disclosing finance charges, if any.

information about finance charges, annual percentage rates, payment amount, and fees that may be charged to the consumer. It requires providers of installment credit to clearly state the charge in writing and express the interest as an annual rate. Even if no finance charges are made, a disclosure statement must be completed and contain the following conditions:

- Fees for services

- Amount of any down payment

- The date each payment is due

- The date of the final payment

- The amount of each payment

- Any interest charges to be made

The agreement must be discussed with the patient or guarantor, and both the physician and the patient or guarantor must agree on the terms and sign the agreement.

The AMA rules that it is appropriate to assess finance or late charges on past-due accounts, if the patient is given advance notice. This can be done by:

- Displaying a notice at the reception desk

- Publishing the notice in the patient brochure

- Including the notice on the patient statement

Figure 14–8 gives an example of notice of late charges on the patient registration form.

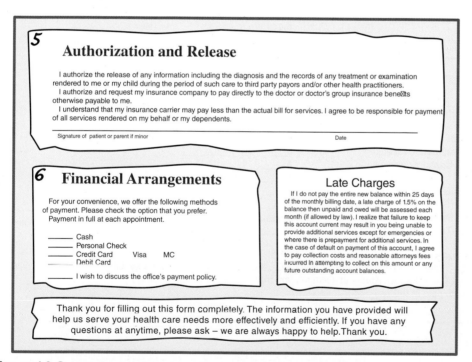

Figure 14-8 A patient registration form explaining late charges

The patient signs the agreement and is given a copy. A copy is retained with the patient's record. If a patient decides to pay a certain amount on a bill monthly, with the office billing monthly for the full amount, and there are no interest charges applied, the Truth in Lending Act does not apply. Figure 14–9 gives an example of this agreement.

Lowery B. Johnson, M.D.
Hwy 311 Suite A31
Sellersburg, IN 47172
812-555-1234

TRUTH IN LENDING PAYMENT AGREEMENT

Patient ___Autumn Leaf___

Address ___10586 Payment Place #2 E___

___Sellersburg, IN 47178___

I agree to pay $ 200.00 per ~~week~~/month on my account balance of $ 1000.00 .

Payments are due by the ___5th___ of each Month and will begin ___May 5, 20XX___
                                (week/month)   (date)

Interest will/will not be charged on the outstanding balance (see Truth-In-Lending form below for rate of interest).

I agree that if payments are not made in the full amount stated above or if payments are not received on time, the entire account balance will be considered delinquent and will be due and payable immediately.

I agree to be responsible for any reasonable collection costs or attorney fees incurred in collecting a delinquent account.

_____
Date

_____
Signature

_____

This disclosure is in compliance with the Truth In Lending Act.

_____
Responsible Party if other than Patient

City, State Zip Code

1. Cash Price (Medical and/or Surgical Fee)	$ 1200.00
Less Cash Down Payment (Advance)	$ 200.00
2. Unpaid Balance of Cash Price	$ 1000.00
3. Amount Financed	$ 1000.00
4. FINANCE CHARGE	$ – 0 –
5. Total of Payments (3+4)	$ 1000.00
6. Deferred Payment Price (1+4)	$ 1200.00
7. ANNUAL PERCENTAGE RATE	– 0 –

The "Total of Payments" shown above is payable to Lowery B. Johnson, M.D., at the address shown above in ___5___ monthly installments of $ 200.00 , the first installment being payable ___May 5th___ , 20XX, and all subsequent installments are due on the same day of each consecutive month until paid in full.

_____
Date

_____
Signature

Figure 14-9 Truth in Lending Agreement

Another important agreement is the Surgical Disclosure Notice (see an example in Figure 14–10). Physicians and other health care providers, particularly surgeons and assistant surgeons, must notify beneficiaries in writing of projected out-of-pocket expenses for elective surgery and noncovered procedures when charges exceed $500 or more. Elective surgery is defined by CMS as a nonemergency surgery or procedure

Goodmedicine Clinic ■ 1 Provider St ■ Anywhere US 12345 ■ (101) 111-2222

Name of Medicare Benificiary _____   Date _____

As previously discussed, I am not accepting Medicare assignment for reimbursement of your surgery. Medicare regulations require that I provide the following information to patients who are considering surgery that will cost $500 or more.

Type of surgery: _____

Name of provider: _____

Estimated actual charge: $ _____

Estimated Medicare payment: $ _____

Patient's estimated payment (includes coinsurance): $ _____

ACKNOWLEDGED AND AGREED BY:

_____   _____
Signature of Medicare Beneficiary   Date   Signature of Provider   Date
or Legal Representative

Figure 14-10 Example of a Surgical Disclosure Notice

that can be scheduled in advance, is not considered life-threatening, and would not result in death or permanent impairment of health if delayed.

The Omnibus Budget Reconciliation Act (OBRA) of 1987 requires the following information be provided to the patient in writing as a disclosure of surgical charges:

- Estimated actual charge for surgery
- Excess of the provider's actual charge as compared with the approved charge
- Applicable coinsurance amount
- Estimated Medicare payment
- Beneficiary's out-of-pocket expense

Exercise 14.5

1. What conditions must be outlined in the Truth in Lending disclosure statement?
2. What is CMS's definition of elective surgery?
3. What must be disclosed in the Surgical Disclosure Notice?
4. An 8-year-old patient is scheduled for a tonsillectomy to be performed in the ambulatory surgical center. Since the patient has no insurance coverage, the parents arrange a payment plan with the surgeon's office with payments to be made monthly for six months. What financial form is completed for this procedure?

Billing

Patient billing can range from a simple process to a more complicated procedure. It must be done efficiently and accurately and in an organized manner. Receiving payment for services rendered is the income of the practice and necessary for it to succeed. Billing can be handled internally by the medical office staff, or, for a fee, by an outside billing agency. The type of billing done within the medical facility depends on the size of the practice, the patient load, and financial goals.

Payment at time of service is the expected norm in today's medical offices and is the best opportunity to collect fees, especially copayments, coinsurance, and deductibles, as well as existing balances. In addition, most insurance companies require a copayment that contractually should be collected at the time of the encounter or service. The **charge slip, superbill, fee ticket, or encounter form**, as indicated in Figure 14–11, is given to the patient at the checkout desk, serving as the first statement.

charge slip, superbill, fee ticket, or encounter form: A three-part form with a record of account information for services performed including charges and payment; can also serve as an insurance reporting form.

The Complete Statement

Statements to patients must be professional looking, legible, and accurate and include all services and charges. They should contain not only the information for the patient but information needed to process medical insurance claims:

- Patient's name and address
- Patient's or member's insurance identification number
- Member's or insured's address if different from the patient
- Insurance carrier
- Date of service
- Description of service
- Accurate procedure (CPT), diagnosis (ICD-10-CM), and HCPCS codes for insurance processing
- Itemization of fees for services performed with charges totaled
- Provider's name, address, and telephone number

> **Highlight:**
>
> In mailing any statement, always enclose a self-addressed return envelope to make payment convenient for the patient.
>
> Use return envelopes of another color to assist in prompting patients to pay. A green envelope attracts more attention than a white envelope. It may prompt a patient to take a second look at what it is and who it is from.

Figures 14–12A and 14–12B are examples of a complete statement.

Not all patients are able to pay at the time of service and not all practices can accommodate payment at time of service. Sending a statement in the mail can be accomplished by:

- Mailing a special statement form or copy of the ledger card, which can be typed or printed
- Mailing an electronic statement, resulting in a more professional-looking statement

Lowery B. Johnson, M.D.
Hwy 311 Suite A31
Sellersburg, IN 47172
812-555-1234

ID.# 237485319
Provider # 19368

ABN ☐   GC ☐

OFFICE VISITS	CPT	FEE	OFF. PROC. CONT'D	CPT	FEE	LABS CONT'D	CPT	FEE	INJECTIONS	CPT	FEE
NEW PATIENT			Biopsy Lesion 1st Lesion	11100		PSA Total	84153		Allergy Shot X1	95115	
Level 1	99201		Each add'l Lesion	11101		Rapid Strep Test	87880		Allergy Shot X2	95117	
Level 2	99202		Skin Tag Removal up to 15	11200		Sed Rate, Nonauto	85651		B-12 Injection	J3420	
Level 3	99203		Destruction 1 Lesion	17000		SGOT (AST)	84450		Demerol 100 MG	J2175	
Level 4	99204		Destruction 2-14 Lesions, each	17003		Special Handling	99000		Demerol & Phenergan Combined	J2180	
Level 5	99205		Ear Lavage	69210		SGPT (ALT)	84460		Depomedrol 80 MG	J1040	
ESTABLISHED PATIENT			EKG	93000		T4	84436		Depoprovera 150	J1050	
Level 1	99211		Foreign Body Removal-Ear	69200		TSH	84443		Depo-estradiol to 5 MG	J1000	
Level 2	99212		Foreign Body Removal-Eye	65205		Uric Acid	84550		Depo-testadiol to 1 ML	J1060	
Level 3	99213		Holter Monitor	93225		Urine Pregnancy Test	81025		Kenalog Per 10 MG	J3301	
Level 4	99214		Medicare Prostate Exam	G0102		Urinalysis/dipstick w/ micro	81000		Phenergan	J2550	
Level 5	99215		Nebulizer Treatment	94640		Urinalysis/dipstick w/o micro	81002				
PREVENTIVE MEDICINE NEW PATIENT			Pap Smear	Q0091		Urinalysis, auto w/ micro	81001				
Age 1-4 Yrs	99382		PELVIC/BREAST	G0101		Urinalysis, auto w/o micro	81003				
Age 5-11 Yrs	99383		Spirometry	94010		Wet Mount	87210				
Age 12-17 Yrs	99384		Spirometry/Pre & Post	94060							
Age 18-39 Yrs	99385		Vision Screen	99173							
Age 40-64 Yrs	99386		Vision, Auto	99172		**IMMUNIZATIONS**			**X-RAYS**		
Age 65 & Older	99387					ADMIN. FEE	96372		Abdomen (AP)	74000	
						ADMIN FEE-ATB (antibiotic)	96372		Ankle 2V/3V	73600/73610	
PREVENTIVE MEDICINE ESTABLISHED PT			**LABS**			ADMIN. FEE - IMMUN	90471		Cervical 2V/3V	72040	
Age 1-4 Yrs	99392		Fingerstick Medicare	36416		ADMIN. FEE IMMUN - EACH ADD	90472		Chest 1V/ Chest 2V	71010/71020	
Age 5-11 Yrs	99393		Venipuncture	G0001/36415		Tdap	90715		DEXA scan (Spine)	77080	
Age 12-17 Yrs	99394		Bun	84520		DtaP	90700		Finger(s) Min. 2V	73140	
Age 18-39 Yrs	99395		CBC	85025		Polio	90712		Foot 2V	73620	
Age 40-64 Yrs	99396		Creatinine Blood	82565		MMR	90707		Lumbar Spins 2V/3V	72100	
Age 65 & Older	99397		DNA Probe-Chlamydia	87490		HIB	90645		Mammogram-Diagnostic Bilat.	77056-TC	
			DNA Probe-Gonorrhea	87590		Hepatitis B - 0-17 Yrs/18 & Up	90744/90746		Mammogram-Screening	77057-TC	
PROLONGED SERVICES			Glucose, Serum	82947		18 & Up / Medicare	90746/G0010		Mammogram-Unilateral Diag.	77055-TC	
One Hour	99354		Glucose Finger	82948		Influenza/Medicare	90658/G0008		Wrist 2V	73100	
Add'l 30 Min	99355		Hemoglobin Gly (A1C)	83036		Varicella	90716				
CONSULTATION			Hepatic Function Panel	80076		Pneumovax/Medicare	90732/G0009				
Level 1, Problem Focused	99241		KOH	87220		Hepatitis A - 2 Dose 0-17 Yrs/18 & Up	90633/90632				
Level 2, Expanded	99242		LDL, Direct	83721		TD	90718				
Level 3, Detailed Low,	99243		Lipid Panel	80061		Tetanus	90703				
Level 4, Compre/Mod	99244		Metabolic Panel, Basic	80048		Rocephin Per 250 MG	J0696				
Level 5, Compre/High	99245		Metabolic Panel, Comp	80053		LA Bicillin 1,000,000 U	J0561				
OFFICE PROCEDURES			Occult Blood	82270							
Aspiration, Puncture Hematoma	10160		PPD	86580							
Audiometry (Air Only)	92552		Protime	85610							

Diagnosis: (1) _____
(2) _____
(3) _____
(4) _____

DATE   TIME   PATIENT   REASON   PRIOR BALANCE

TICKET NO.   DR.#   DOCTOR   LOCATION   D.O.B.   TODAY'S CHARGE

PATIENT NO.   RESPONSIBLE PARTY   PH #   REFERRING DR.   ADJUSTMENTS

Return Appointment: _____

SEX M F   ADDRESS   CITY/STATE   ZIP CODE

RECAP   OVER 90   OVER 60   OVER 30   CURRENT   TOTAL DUE   PT BC CS PAY CHOICE   TODAY'S PAYMENTS

Other: _____

INSURANCE COMPANY   BA SCT POLICY I.D.   RELATIONSHIP TO INSURED   BALANCE DUE
SELF SPOUSE CHILD OTHER

Figure 14-11 Charge slip, superbill, fee ticket, or encounter form

DATE	TRANSACTION TYPE	AMOUNT	TRANSACTION DESCRIPTION	RESPONSIBLE PARTY	ITEM BALANCE
03/11/20XX	Charg	80.00	OFFICE VISIT, NEW PATIENT - LEVEL 3 Insur Filed on 03/30/XX to Payer-A	Patient	46.95
04/03/20XX	Charg	1157.79	FISTULECTOMY SUBMUSCULAR Insur Filed on 04/21/XX to Payer-A	Payer-A	1157.79
04/13/20XX	Paymt	−26.55	From Payer-A, for 03/11/20XX		
04/13/20XX	Adjmt	−6.50	From Payer-A, for 03/11/20XX PER EOB PT RESP DEDUCT/COPAY 4-13-XX		

ACCOUNT NO.	0–30 DAYS	31–60 DAYS	61–90 DAYS	91–120 DAYS	OVER 120 DAYS	PATIENT DUE
17665	46.95	0.00	0.00	0.00	0.00	$46.95

ACORDIA OF CENTRAL IND (461)   ID: XPN406761759   PRI   <-- Payer-A

INS. PENDING
$1157.79

4723

Figure 14-12A Patient statements show procedure, charge, payment, and adjustment. This patient statement includes an aging of the bill, the amount currently due, and the amount pending insurance.

The statement should include an area to indicate credit or debit card information as a method of payment, or the website where electronic payment can be made.

Ledger Card or Special Statement Form

A special statement form is another way to bill the patient. It is typed or printed and also mailed in a window envelope. The statement lists the date of service, description of service, charges, payments, and balance since the last statement mailed.

Electronic Medical Record

electronic medical record (EMR): Computer-based medical record or patient chart.

The **electronic medical record (EMR)** is defined as the patient record created for a single medical practice or facility using a computer, tablet, voice recognition system, or scanner. Figure 14–13 illustrates the EMR data flow.

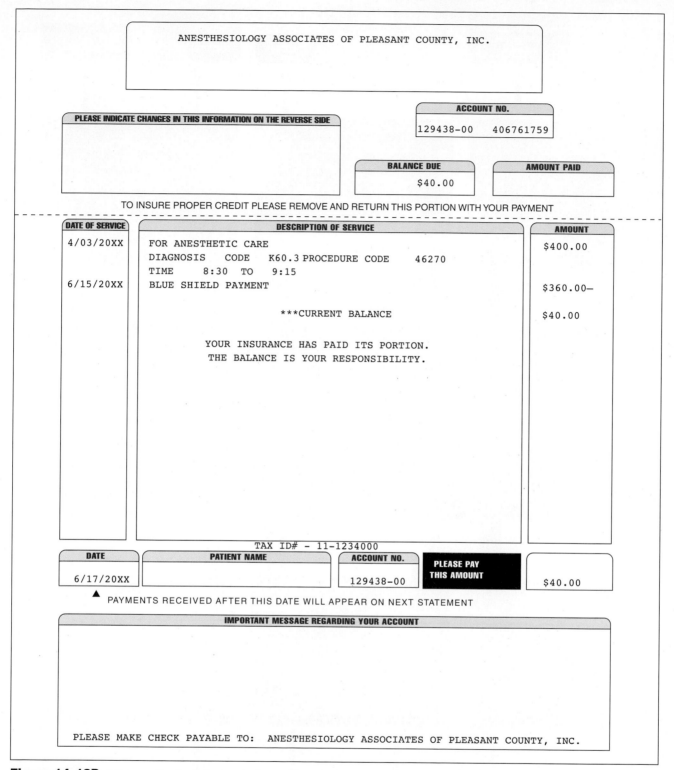

ANESTHESIOLOGY ASSOCIATES OF PLEASANT COUNTY, INC.

PLEASE INDICATE CHANGES IN THIS INFORMATION ON THE REVERSE SIDE

ACCOUNT NO.

129438-00   406761759

BALANCE DUE

$40.00

AMOUNT PAID

TO INSURE PROPER CREDIT PLEASE REMOVE AND RETURN THIS PORTION WITH YOUR PAYMENT

DATE OF SERVICE	DESCRIPTION OF SERVICE	AMOUNT
4/03/20XX	FOR ANESTHETIC CARE	$400.00
	DIAGNOSIS CODE K60.3 PROCEDURE CODE 46270	
	TIME 8:30 TO 9:15	
6/15/20XX	BLUE SHIELD PAYMENT	$360.00—
	***CURRENT BALANCE	$40.00
	YOUR INSURANCE HAS PAID ITS PORTION.	
	THE BALANCE IS YOUR RESPONSIBILITY.	

TAX ID# – 11-1234000

DATE	PATIENT NAME	ACCOUNT NO.	PLEASE PAY THIS AMOUNT	
6/17/20XX		129438-00		$40.00

▲ PAYMENTS RECEIVED AFTER THIS DATE WILL APPEAR ON NEXT STATEMENT

IMPORTANT MESSAGE REGARDING YOUR ACCOUNT

PLEASE MAKE CHECK PAYABLE TO: ANESTHESIOLOGY ASSOCIATES OF PLEASANT COUNTY, INC.

Figure 14-12B   This patient statement shows the amount due after the insurance carrier has paid the practice.

Introduced in Chapter 1, HITECH has allowed physicians' practices to invest in (EMR) systems to enter and document patient office and hospital notes, test results, and medications, as well as the integration of patient billing and the accounts receivable process in the office.

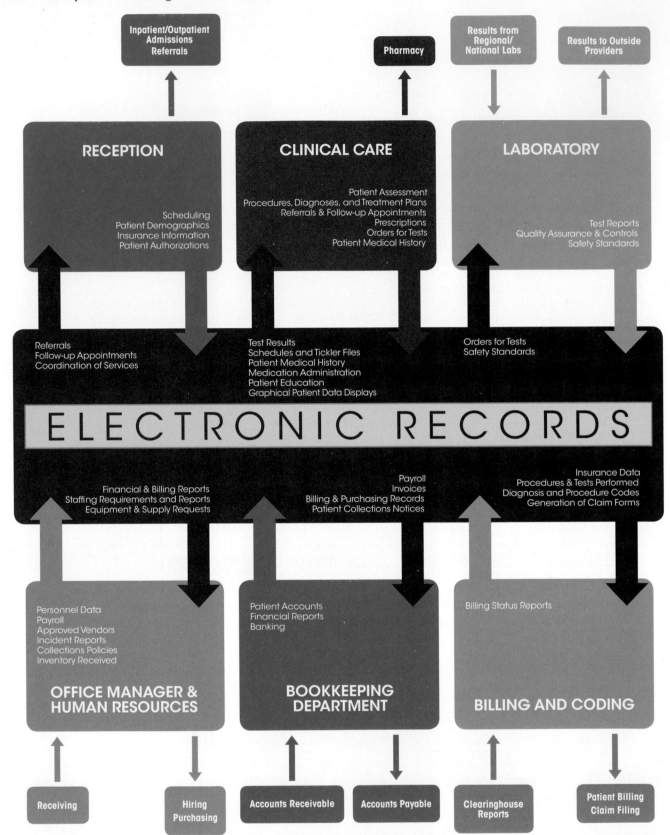

Figure 14-13 Total practice management software (TPMS) data flow

Federal requirements to mandate national use of the EMR is outlined in three stages referred to as *Meaningful Use,* which is using certified electronic health record (EHR) technology to:

- Improve quality, safety, efficiency, and reduce health disparities.

- Engage patients and families in their health care.

- Improve quality of care coordination and communication among other health care providers.

- Maintain privacy and security of patient health information.

To meet these objectives, three stages of Meaningful Use were outlined:

Stage 1, 2011–2015: Data capture and sharing—the purchase of a certified EMR system and use within the medical record to demonstrate patient care

Stage 2, 2014: Advanced clinical processes—patient portals and health care–related online applications for patient interaction and communication with health care providers

Stage 3, 2016: Improved outcomes—improving quality, safety, and efficiency with improving population health

Electronic medical records call for not only the confidentiality and privacy of a patient's record but security of that record. HIPAA Security Rule mandates regulations to protect electronic information and provide safeguards pertaining to storage, transmission, and access to protected health care information.

One security measure is the use of passwords for individuals to access various computer files. A computer program can also track individual access to files. Annual in-service training for employees in privacy and security standards should be performed. Many facilities now require employees to sign a confidentiality statement that outlines consequences of not maintaining patient confidentiality.

HIPAA transaction and code sets standards have been implemented to provide a standardized electronic format for providers and payors to send and receive transactions. These include:

HIPAA transaction and code sets: Any set of codes used for encoding data elements, such as tables of terms, medical concepts, diagnosis and procedure codes.

- Health Care Eligibility Benefit Inquiry and Response—Information about a patient's health plan, covered treatments and procedures, and any coordination of benefits (Figures 14–14A and 14–14B)

- Health Care Claim or Encounter Information—For billing, diagnosis and procedure codes, and payment requests a provider sends to a payor

- Health Care Claim Status Request—To check status of a claim submitted for reimbursement

- Health Care Services Review—Request for precertification and referral

- Claims Payment and Remittance Advice—Payment and remittance advice via electronic funds transfer (EFT) to the provider's designated bank account

Prior to implementing a computerized system, consideration must be given to changes in the way administrative procedures are performed.

The implementation of an electronic medical record system has challenges as well as advantages. It is important to recognize these and to make adequate preparation for any disruption to the efficiency of office functions during the transition to the electronic medical record. Training in basic computer functions and terminology is essential.

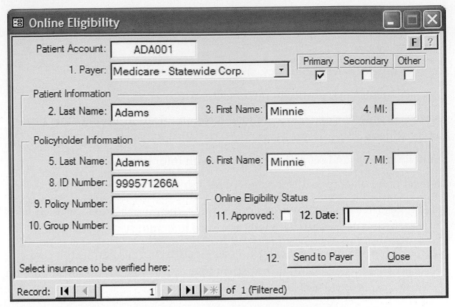

Figure 14-14A Online eligibility window prior to transaction

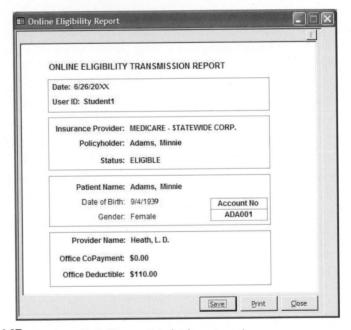

Figure 14-14B Online eligibility transmission report

The advantages of electronic functions in the medical office include:

- *Efficiency.* Repetitive tasks can be performed in a variety of formats. Patient data, once initially entered into the computer, can be used in different formats without reentering the same information, such as insurance forms, patient statements, superbills, and mailing labels. Office computers can be networked to allow multiple users access to files in the computer database at various workstations.

- *Accessibility.* Information entered into the computer is much easier to retrieve when needed. Patient information, once entered, can be retrieved and displayed on the monitor (screen) with a few simple functions, without having to search manually through filing systems to locate information needed.

- *Updates and corrections.* Updating and/or correcting patient files can be performed much more quickly and easily than in a manual system where changes/updates would need to be made in several different areas. Changing a patient's address can be performed in the patient information menu; once changes are made, they are automatically transferred to other data fields existing in the program.

- *Production.* Computers can process a large amount of information much faster than using manual methods. Compiling information for statistical or research purposes can be performed with very few keystrokes using an electronic system. Patient files can be searched to generate reports requesting information such as past-due accounts.

- *Reduced costs.* After the initial cost of purchasing the electronic system and software, operating costs are decreased due to the reduction of time required in performing administrative procedures.

Many offices will attest that the advantages of an electronic system outweigh the disadvantages. Some of the challenges are:

- *Initial cost.* There is an initial investment for the purchase of the computer and peripherals such as a printer and the programs (software) the office has selected for setting up an electronic system. Medical management software costs will vary from vendor to vendor. Hardware expense will depend on the number of computer terminals and the type and number of printers required for the practice. Determining the computer requirements that meet the needs of the medical office is important before purchasing the computer system. It is also financially beneficial to shop around and negotiate the best deal that meets the specific needs of the practice. As mentioned in Chapter 1, the American Recovery and Reinvestment Act (ARRA) and the creation of HITECH made financial funding and incentives available through CMS to assist physician offices and hospitals to adopt and use certified electronic medical records.

- *Initial investment of time.* It takes considerable time to learn how to operate an electronic program. Many software vendors will provide staff training as well as technical support when problems are encountered. Converting from a manual to an electronic system can take six months to a year and frustration can occur in the conversion process. Once the conversion process is completed, the outcome is positive. Proper training of all personnel will help overcome some of the frustration that may occur.

- *Transition process.* Much data must be entered before complete conversion to an electronic system can occur. For example, patient registration records must be set up by entering demographic information on each patient. Diagnosis and procedure codes most frequently used in the medical office will also need to be entered. There are software programs available with codes already included so that only a few codes may need to be entered. Coding software is also available for purchase. While the data are being entered, front office procedures are still being performed manually. Once all information is entered and the electronic system is operational, entering additional information is not a time-consuming task.

- *Malfunctions.* Even the best electronic system and software can and will occasionally fail due to operator error, malfunction of the hardware, or a "bug" in the system. Making a regular backup copy of the information and keeping it secure are essential.

It is important when purchasing a medical management program to look closely at the administrative needs of the office and what type of features or options will allow the office to perform tasks easily and efficiently. These programs are available through software vendors.

Systems of specialization in a medical management computer program are:

1. File maintenance

2. Appointment scheduling

3. Patient registration

4. Posting transactions

5. Insurance billing

6. Reports

- *File maintenance.* Before the office can perform administrative procedures, a number of tasks must be performed in the file maintenance system so that the program will operate properly. These tasks include entering the practice and provider information, diagnosis and procedure codes, insurance carriers, and referring physicians into the database and assigning passwords. In addition, any standard unique employer identifiers assigned to the participating physician or medical practice by the insurance carrier should be entered.

- *Scheduling appointments.* Electronic appointment scheduling allows front office staff to schedule, cancel, reschedule, and locate an appointment rapidly. In addition, a daily appointment list can be printed, as well as a cancellation log and patient reminder card.

- *Patient registration.* Once the patient has completed the patient registration form, an account can be established. This is done by entering the demographic and insurance data into the database (Figures 14–15A and 14–15B). The patient's chart can also be prepared at this time.

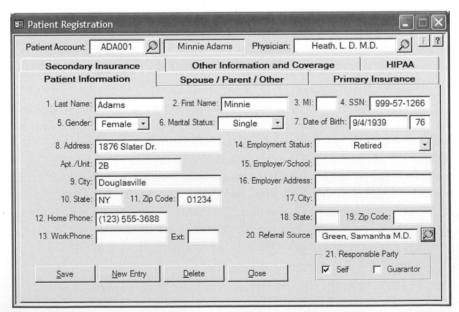

Figure 14-15A Patient demographic information in the patient registration record

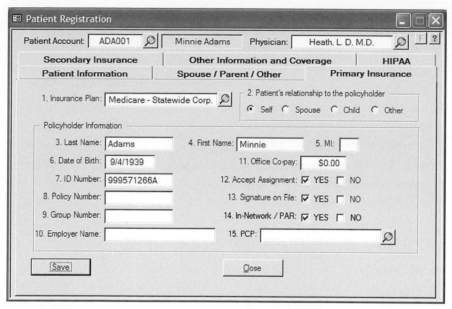

Figure 14-15B Primary insurance information in the patient registration record

- *Posting transactions.* Charges for procedures and services performed by the provider can be entered as well as payments made by the patient or third-party payor to generate a current balance. Transactions should be posted daily. A hard copy can be printed for the patient as a receipt, patient statement, or insurance claim (Figure 14–16).

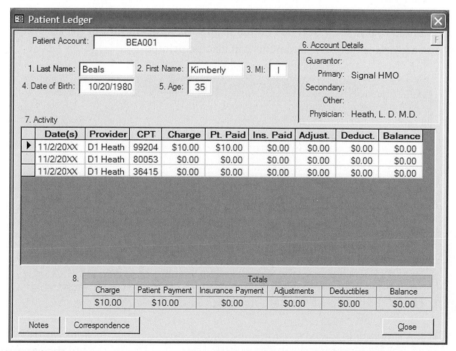

Figure 14-16 Patient's ledger open on the computer screen shows transactions posted with patient copayment.

- *Patient billing.* When charges and payments are posted to the patient's account, the information is stored in the database and is available for patient billing. The management program can search the database to retrieve information necessary to generate statements for patients with outstanding balances. After the statements are printed, they are folded and mailed in window envelopes, or a self-mailer can be used.

- *Insurance billing.* When posting charges to a patient account, procedure and diagnosis codes are also entered. This information is stored in the database and is later used to complete the insurance claim form.

- *Reports.* This system can generate a variety of reports to allow the physician to review practice and business activities. For example, information can be obtained to track volume and type of procedures performed in the office.

Generating the Electronic Statement

To generate statements, the correct software application will need to be selected. All financial accounts in the practice database with a balance due will be processed. In preparing the bills, the computer will select the accounts that meet the criteria that have been selected for processing, such as accounts that are 30 days past due with a finance charge applied. Another example for this process is to omit statement preparation for Medicaid patients. When this preparation process is complete, the statement will be printed. The order in which statements are printed can also be selected to meet the needs of the office and/or postal regulations for presort rates. This could be by alphabetic order for office needs or by zip code for lower presort rates.

Medical office management software can be purchased with options that include messages to be placed on the statement such as overdue payment reminders and status of insurance filing or even the patient's next appointment date (Figure 14–17). Other options include mailing labels for statements generated and a summary report listing patients billed that include account numbers and the total amount of the statement. In addition, a grand total of all statements can also be printed.

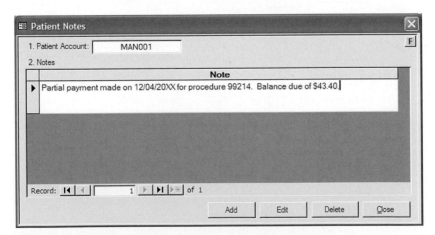

Figure 14-17 Example of notation made for patient billing

Patient statements are now ready to be mailed, and there are options for this process. Standard envelopes may be used with printed labels attached to the envelopes. Window envelopes can be used with statements inserted along with a return envelope for payment. A time-saving method is the mailer statement, also called a self-mailer, which prints the patient statement and a return envelope in continuous form with perforation for separation, as seen in Figure 14–18.

STATEMENT

Account
No.

Amount
Due

AMOUNT PAID $ _____

Please Return This Portion With Your Remittance

Statement
Date

Retain This Portion Of Statement For Your Records

DATE	PROFESSIONAL SERVICE	CHARGE	PAID	BALANCE

CURRENT AMOUNT	AMOUNT 31-60 DAYS PAST DUE	AMOUNT 61-90 DAYS PAST DUE	AMOUNT 90 DAYS OR MORE PAST DUE	TOTAL AMOUNT DUE

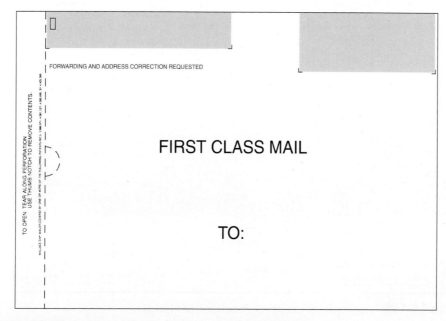

FORWARDING AND ADDRESS CORRECTION REQUESTED

TO OPEN TEAR ALONG PERFORATION
USE THUMB NOTCH TO REMOVE CONTENTS.

FIRST CLASS MAIL

TO:

Figure 14-18 Computerized statement with self-mailer

Many payments are received daily in the mail, particularly insurance payments. These payments are posted in the electronic system in the same manner (Figures 14–19A and 14–19B). No receipt is required unless specifically requested by the patient. Physician charges for visits, surgeries, and other services performed in a hospital, nursing home, or other facility are also posted.

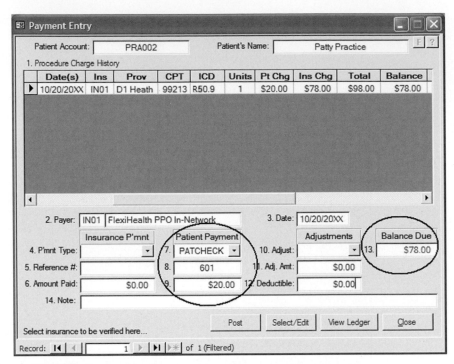

Figure 14-19A Example of payment entry transaction

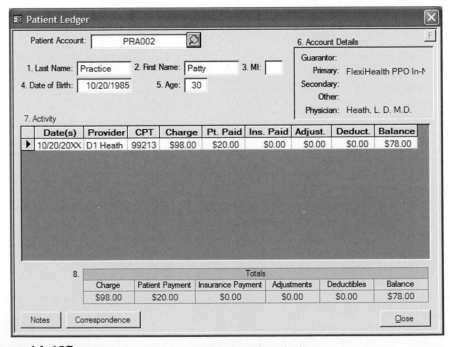

Figure 14-19B Example of computerized patient ledger

In addition to charges added to an account and payments credited to an account, adjustments can also be applied to an account (Figure 14–20).

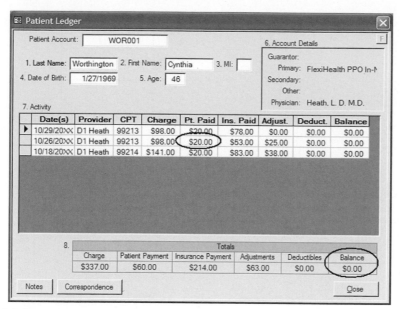

Figure 14-20 Example of patient payment, insurance payment, and adjustments

Adjustments, also known as "write-offs," are changes made in a patient's account not related to charges incurred or payments received. Some examples of adjustments are adding a late charge or a bank fee for a returned check, or a participating provider's deduction per contract agreement. Figure 14–21 shows a Blue Cross Blue Shield discount on a hospital charge.

Adjusting the account keeps the account current and the accounts receivable figure up to date.

Electronic Billing

Within the electronic medical record software, selected CPT, ICD-10-CM, and HCPCS codes can be electronically transferred to a billing statement. Fees for services and procedures performed can be abstracted from the fee schedule component of the practice management system. Patient demographic information, payor information, place of service location, and national provider identifiers (NPIs) for the physician or other provider are entered. Scrubber software may be used to review for discrepancies or errors and compare submitted information to general billing and coding guidelines as well as specific payor information and guidelines. Newer advanced features may recognize medical necessity mandates, National Correct Coding Initiative (NCCI) edits, and modifier specifications to identify specific payor requirements. Any problems, errors, or omissions may be flagged by the software and returned to the medical practice for corrections and the ability to submit clean claims the first time.

Electronic bills can be processed and sent to insurance companies and/or patients more quickly. Payments from third-party payors are often made as an electronic transfer, and questions may also be processed electronically to expedite the process.

+H Hospital

P.O. Box 4187
Riverside, IN 13290
812-555-2422

STATEMENT

STATEMENT DATE	PAY THIS AMOUNT	ACCOUNT NUMBER
5/16/20XX	243.27	1025411

DATE OF SERVICE	SHOW AMOUNT PAID HERE
4/03/20XX	$

PATIENT NAME

PLEASE DETACH AND RETURN TOP PORTION WITH YOUR PAYMENT

DATE	DESCRIPTION	PAYMENTS	BALANCE
4/23/20XX	FINAL BILL AMOUNT		4,025.75
05/11/20XX	BLUE CROSS OF IN DISCOUNT	1,520.52CR	
05/11/20XX	PAYMENT—BLUE CROSS 13	2,261.96CR	

TOTAL AMOUNT DUE****	243.27

━━━ PLEASE NOTE ━━━

YOUR INSURANCE COMPANY HAS PAID ITS SHARE OF YOUR BILL.
THE ABOVE BALANCE IS NOW DUE FROM YOU.
**QUESTIONS CONCERNING YOUR ACCOUNT CALL

Your Insurance has been billed. This copy of your bill is for your records.

Figure 14-21 Insurance payment and adjustment of a hospital statement

A practice management system can be implemented to incorporate the patient's account and the daily log and to submit patient statements.

As in manual patient billing, it is important to monitor the claims process and follow up on delinquent claims. Using electronic medical records, the claims process can be monitored more closely. The system can provide lists of patients receiving medical services, procedures, and treatment and their status in the billing process: Has the bill been generated? Has the bill been paid or denied by an insurance company or third-party payor?

Bookkeeping Tips

The electronic medical record can also assist in the bookkeeping process by utilizing the same practice management function.

Bookkeeping is the recording of daily business transactions. The physician's office is a business, and complete, correct, and current financial records are important for:

- Prompt billing and collection procedures
- Accurate reporting of income to federal and state agencies
- Financial planning of the practice

Bookkeeping functions include:

- Patient account information—obtained from the patient registration form.

- Daily log or journal—typically recorded or entered from charge slips/fee tickets/ superbills, so that all charges are entered. Do not forget outside charges— hospital rounds, nursing home rounds, house calls, or other unscheduled visits.

- Accounts receivable—the total amount owed to the medical practice based on outstanding balances of patient accounts.

- Accounts payable—the amounts the medical practice owes to vendors or suppliers.

- Office or business disbursements—amounts paid for medical supplies, salaries, equipment, and other daily expenditures necessary to run and maintain the operation of the medical practice.

- Summary of charges, receipts, and disbursements—reflects charges, payments received, and disbursements summarized each month, quarter, and annually. This is important information that the practice manager or accountant needs to monitor collection of payments and expenditures on a daily, monthly, quarterly, and/or yearly basis in order to determine the financial standing of the practice.

External Billing

An outside or external billing service can be contracted to manage patient accounts. The service maintains the ledger cards and posts charges and payments from copies of superbills, charge slips, fee tickets, or computerized listings provided by the medical office. The service prepares monthly statements with instructions that payments be returned to them. It deposits payments directly to the medical office's bank account and submits a report of all transactions.

This billing method works well in practices with limited clerical staff or those with a large patient load. There should be one employee responsible for coordinating activities between the office and the billing service.

Exercise 14.6

1. What legislative act created funding and financial incentives to assist medical providers and facilities in the adoption and use of the EMR?
2. What is an example of making an adjustment to a patient's account?
3. What is the importance of collecting payment at time of service?

(continues)

Exercise 14.6 *(continued)*

4. What are some of the challenges in the implementation of the electronic medical record system?

5. Place an X in the space provided to indicate information to include on a patient statement.

_____ Patient's name and address

_____ Patient's date of birth/age

_____ Date of service/procedure

_____ Description of service/procedure

_____ Patient's next of kin

_____ Patient's telephone number

_____ Provider's name, address, telephone number

_____ Patient's chief complaint for service/procedure

_____ Patient's social security number

_____ Charges, payments, adjustments

The Billing Process

When to mail out statements to patients is often determined by the size of the medical practice and the economic status of the community. Smaller offices may find the monthly billing cycle to be the most efficient. Large practices may prefer cycle billing as it allows flexibility in the billing schedule.

Monthly Billing

monthly billing: Billing patients at one designated time of the month.

Monthly billing is just what the name states: billing all patients at a designated time of the month. Typically, statements should leave the office on the 25th of the month to be received by the first day of the following month. A major disadvantage of monthly billing is other duties may be neglected during this time-consuming period.

Cycle Billing

cycle billing: Accounts divided alphabetically into groups with each group billed at a different time.

In **cycle billing**, all accounts are divided alphabetically into groups, with each group billed at a different time. Statements are prepared in the same schedule each month. In a large practice with numerous statements to process monthly, this is a more efficient method of billing. The statements can be mailed as they are completed or mailed at one time. A typical cycle billing schedule is shown in Table 14–1. This can be varied to accommodate the needs of the individual practice. The major advantage of cycle billing is that it provides a steady flow of funds throughout the month.

Table 14-1 Typical Schedule for Cycle Billing System

To Cycle Bill Patient Accounts:
1. Divide the alphabet into four sections: A–F, G–L, M–R, S–Z.
2. Prepare statements for patients whose last names begin with A through F on Wednesday and mail them on Thursday of the first week of the month.
3. Prepare statements for patients whose last names begin with G through L on Wednesday and mail them on Thursday of the second week of the month.
4. Prepare statements for patients whose last names begin with M through R on Wednesday and mail them on Thursday of the third week of the month.
5. Prepare statements for patients whose last names begin with S through Z on Wednesday and mail them on Thursday of the fourth week of the month.

Past-Due Accounts

No matter how efficient and effective the billing process may be, there will still be collections on some accounts. The most common reasons for a past-due account are:

- Inability to pay—simply not having the money to pay the bill. Medical bills have last priority.

- Negligence or forgetfulness, or misplacing the statement.

- Unwillingness to pay. When a patient complains about a charge or refuses to pay, it may have nothing to do with finances. There could be dissatisfaction with the care or treatment received. The physician or office manager should be made aware of those situations for immediate attention.

Exercise 14.7

1. Name the three most common reasons an account may become past due.

a. _____

b. _____

c. _____

2. Name the two types of billing processes.

The Collections Process

Collection of delinquent accounts begins with determining how much has been owed for what length of time.

Accounts receivable (A/R) is the amount of money owed to the medical practice by its patients. **Account aging** or age analysis is a method of identifying how long an account is overdue by the length of time it has been unpaid. The accounts are aged into the following categories:

Current—0 to 30 days

31 to 60 days

accounts receivable (A/R): The amount of money owed to the medical practice by its patients.

account aging: A method of identifying how long an account is overdue by the length of time it has been unpaid.

61 to 90 days

91 to 120 days

120 days and over

Aging of an account determines how long charges have remained unpaid from one billing date to another. Aging can begin the date the statement is sent to a patient or based on the aging parameters within a billing system. Any unpaid amount ages by 30 days each time another statement is sent.

Electronic programs for medical office management can automatically calculate and age the balance due on individual overdue accounts to indicate the length of time the account has been overdue.

The classification of past-due accounts and the account aging process is necessary to review and determine which accounts need follow-up. An age analysis is a summary that lists all patient account balances, when the charges were made, the most recent payment received, and any special notes concerning the account, as shown in Figure 14–22.

04/04/20XX									Page 1
SUMMARY AGING REPORT BY ACCOUNT BASED ON DATE PATIENT BILLED (Pat. Only)									
All Accounts									
Aging Category: 1–5 DOL Pay <= 04/04/20XX									
Acc #	*Name*	*Phone No.*	*DOL Pay*	*Unapplied*	*Current*	*31–60*	*61–90*	*120+*	*Total*
114	Rawles, Deb	812-555-1256	03/20/20XX		102.50				102.50
25	Leaf, Autumn	812-555-7789	12/02/20XX					250.00	250.00
110	Martin, Kathy	502-555-1134	02/14/20XX			115.00			115.00
214	Burton, Craig	502-555-1459	03/15/20XX		53.75				53.75
REPORT TOTALS					156.25	115.00		250.00	521.25

Figure 14-22 Summary of account aging

Management consultants recommend collecting fees at the time of service, and a collection ratio of at least 90 percent should be maintained. A collection ratio is a method used to gauge the effectiveness of the ambulatory care setting's billing practices. This is calculated by dividing the total collections by the net charges (gross charges minus adjustments). This yields a percentage, which is the collection ratio, as explained in Table 14–2.

Table 14-2 Collection Ratio

Total receipts	= $40,000
Managed care adjustments	= $ 3,000
Medicare adjustments	+ $ 2,000
Total received	= $45,000
Total charges	÷ $52,000
Collection ratio after adjustments	= 86.5 percent

Another important factor is the accounts receivable ratio, which measures the speed with which outstanding accounts are paid, which is generally two months. The accounts receivable ratio is figured by dividing the current A/R balance by the average monthly gross charges. The A/R ratio provides a picture of the state of collections and probable loss within the practice. The longer an account is past due, the less the likelihood of successfully collecting the account.

Collection Techniques

An effective approach to the collection of past-due accounts in the medical office is a combination of letters and telephone calls. It is preferable to first call the patient concerning the delinquent account. The patient may have misplaced or forgotten the bill, and a telephone call can often resolve the situation quickly and inexpensively. When making telephone collection calls, there are ethical issues to remember:

- Be tactful, courteous, and diplomatic.

- Treat patients respectfully.

- Do not threaten or antagonize.

The **Fair Debt Collection Practices Act** is designed to protect consumers against abusive practices by debt collectors. This act sets the following rules for making collection calls:

Fair Debt Collection Practices Act: A consumer protection policy against abusive collection practices by debt collectors.

- Do not call before 8 a.m. or after 9 p.m. or make excessive calls. Calling before or after these time frames may be considered harassment.

- Do not use abusive language or make threats to coerce a consumer into making a payment.

- Do not post or publish a list of consumers who allegedly refuse to pay debts, except to report to a credit reporting agency.

- Do not threaten to notify an employer that a consumer has not paid bills.

- Do not advertise or publicize the debt to embarrass a consumer into paying.

- Do not discuss the patient's debt with anyone other than the person responsible for payment.

- Do not send misleading letters that appear to be from a government agency or court.

- Do not try to collect more than is owed.

- A debtor may be contacted at work unless the collector knows or has reason to know that the employer prohibits an employee from receiving such calls or that it is inconvenient for the debtor to receive debt collection calls at work.

- If a debtor is represented by an attorney, a collector cannot communicate with the debtor unless the attorney grants permission or fails to respond to the collector's communications within a reasonable time.

Highlight:

Check state laws regarding guidelines for times to make collection calls. Be aware of the different time zones within state boundaries and nationwide to avoid an abusive telephone collection practice.

In addition to the Fair Debt Collection Practices Act and the Truth in Lending Act discussed earlier, other laws governing collection practices that health care employees must be familiar with are:

- *Fair Credit Reporting Act.* Provides guidelines for the reporting and collecting of credit background information to businesses to use in evaluation of an individual's application for credit, insurance, or employment. It allows consumers to learn the nature and substance of information collected about them by credit reporting agencies, and to correct and update information as it is used in evaluating a person's application for credit, insurance, or employment.

- *Guide Against Debt Collection Deception (Federal Trade Commission).* Provides guidelines for creditors in their collection efforts, and provides the consumer with protection from fraudulent and deceptive tactics.

- *Telephone Consumer Protection Act of 1991.* Protects against unwanted telephone solicitations, most commonly referred to as telemarketing. Charities or other tax-exempt nonprofit organizations are exempt from this act as well as those who have previously had business with the company or agency.

- *Equal Credit Opportunity Act.* Prohibits discrimination in the granting of credit on the basis of sex, race, age, marital status, religion, or nationality. This also prevents discrimination against an applicant who receives public assistance income or has exercised rights under the Consumer Credit Protection Act, such as disputing a credit card bill or credit bureau report. Under this act, the individual has a right to know the reason credit was denied, such as having too little income or employment less than a certain amount of time.

- *Fair Credit Billing Act.* This act applies to disputes related to billing errors. For example:

  ○ Unauthorized charges

  ○ Charges that list the wrong date or amount

  ○ Failure to post payments and other credits

  ○ Failure to send statements to the current address (provided the creditor receives the change of address in writing at least 20 days before the billing period ends)

  ○ States a 60-day time limit for patients who have a complaint with a bill to inquire about the error. The complaint must be acknowledged and documented within 30 days of receipt of the complaint. The provider has a maximum of 90 days or two billing cycles to correct the error. In the event no error is detected, an explanation of the bill and its accuracy must be given to the patient.

Highlight:

Keep accurate records in telephone collections. Document what was said, any amount of a promised payment, and date of the promised payment. If nothing is received at that time, follow-up will be necessary.

Collection Letters

The most effective approach to collections combines telephone calls and letters on past-due accounts. Collection letters are sent to encourage patients to pay past-due balances after regular statements have been mailed. Lack of payment is usually not considered serious until after 60 days. When there has been no response to telephone calls and statements, a series of collection letters begins. Collection experts recommend the steps shown in Table 14–3.

Table 14-3 Collection Timeline

Payment at time of service	Payment is received at time of the service or visit; payment and insurance information is obtained and discussed.
30 days after service rendered	First billing statement is sent.
60 days past due	Second billing statement is sent with reminder of past-due balance; Letter or telephone call is initiated to discuss payment arrangements and document the commitment in writing (Figure 14–23).
90 days past due	Third billing statement is sent with strong reminder of past-due balance. No payment or other contact will result in collection action (Figure 14–24).
120 days past due	Final notice is sent requesting payment. Specify time frame for payment; no payment will result in turnover to collection agency (Figure 14–25).
Final action	No payment or other correspondence results in turnover to collection agency. Notice of termination letter is sent certified mail, return receipt requested (Figure 14–26).

Lowery B. Johnson, M.D.
Hwy 311 Suite A31
Sellersburg, IN 47172
812-555-1234

May 3, 20XX

Autumn Leaf
10586 Payment Place #2E
Sellersburg, IN 47178

Dear Ms Leaf:

As we discussed in our telephone conversation today, we will expect a payment from you in the amount of $125.00 on May 15 and the balance of $125 on June 15, 20XX.

Please notify our billing office immediately if any problem should occur to prevent payment of this past due account.

Sincerely,

Susan B. Dunn
Office Manager

Figure 14-23 Letter to follow up a telephone call

The final notice letter should be exactly that: a final demand for payment. If letters continue to be sent after the final notice, the patient will doubt attempts at collecting the account. The final notice letter should be sent certified mail, return receipt requested. This provides documentation the letter was mailed and received by the patient. If the letter is undeliverable, it will be returned to the billing office marked accordingly.

Lowery B. Johnson, M.D.
Hwy 311 Suite A31
Sellersburg, IN 47172
812-555-1234

July 5, 20XX

Autumn Leaf
10586 Payment Place #2E
Sellersburg, IN 47178

Dear Ms. Leaf:

We have not received payments from you as promised in the telephone call with you on May 3, 20XX.

Your account remains unpaid with a balance of $250.00, which is 90 days past due. Mastercard and Visa are accepted for your convenience in paying this bill, as well as cash and checks.

Please call me at 555-2244 if you have a question about your account. Otherwise, we expect your payment immediately.

Sincerely,

Susan B. Dunn
Office Manager

Figure 14-24 Collection letter at 90 days

When all collection attempts by the medical office have been unsuccessful, many practices seek the assistance of an outside collection agency. At this point, many practices will terminate medical services to the patient. An example of this Notice of Termination of Medical Services Letter is seen in Figure 14–26. This letter is also mailed to the patient by certified mail, return receipt requested for legal purposes for documentation of delivery and receipt. If undeliverable, it will be returned to the billing office, marked accordingly.

Highlight:
Never place a past-due notice on the mailing envelope of the statement, or use a postcard to communicate financial or collection information. This is an invasion of privacy.

Collection Agencies

When choosing a collection agency, ask for referrals from other physicians, ambulatory care centers, and hospitals. Many agencies deal specifically with health

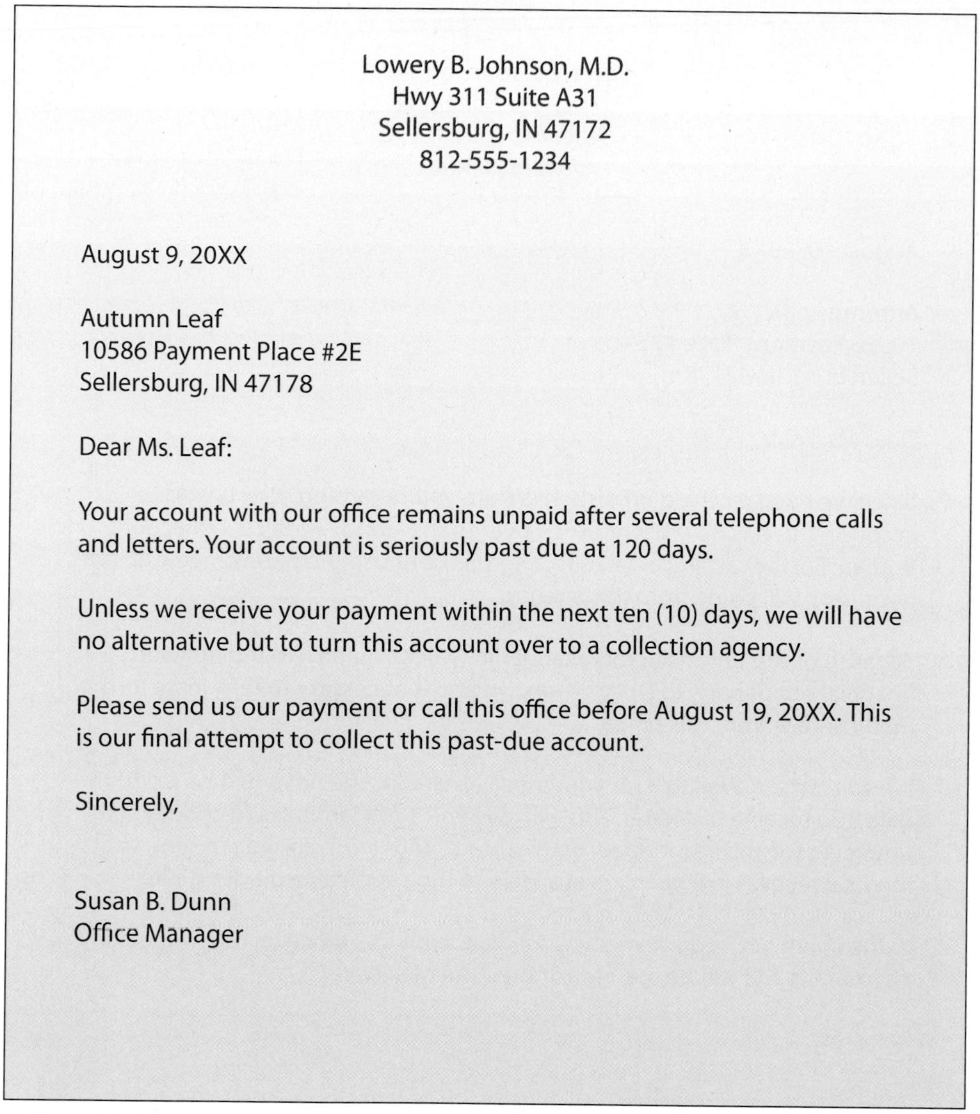

Lowery B. Johnson, M.D.
Hwy 311 Suite A31
Sellersburg, IN 47172
812-555-1234

August 9, 20XX

Autumn Leaf
10586 Payment Place #2E
Sellersburg, IN 47178

Dear Ms. Leaf:

Your account with our office remains unpaid after several telephone calls and letters. Your account is seriously past due at 120 days.

Unless we receive your payment within the next ten (10) days, we will have no alternative but to turn this account over to a collection agency.

Please send us our payment or call this office before August 19, 20XX. This is our final attempt to collect this past-due account.

Sincerely,

Susan B. Dunn
Office Manager

Figure 14-25 Collection at 120 days—final notice requesting payment

care facilities and will work compatibly with the medical office's philosophy of ethics in patient care. Ask what the agency's approach is for collection methods and request sample letters and notices.

When a collection agency has been selected, the following patient information must be supplied:

- Full name and last known address
- Name of employer and business address
- Name of spouse, if applicable
- Total owed
- Date of last payment or charge on the account
- Method taken by the office to collect the debt
- Any response to collection attempts

Lowery B. Johnson, M.D.
Hwy 311 Suite A31
Sellersburg, IN 47172
812-555-1234

August 19, 20XX

Autumn Leaf
10586 Payment Place #2E
Sellersburg, IN 47178

Dear Ms. Leaf:

Since we have received no response from you regarding your past-due account, this has now been turned over to the Goody Medical Collections Bureau. Further attempts at collecting this debt using whatever legal action necessary will come from this agency.

Because of the unsatisfactory manner in which you have handled your financial obligations to Dr. Johnson, we find it necessary to terminate further medical care from this office.

We will remain available for your medical care for the next 30 days from the date you receive this letter. This will give you sufficient time to choose a physician for your continued medical care. With your signed consent, your medical records will be made available to the physician you designate.

In the event you require medical services from this office in the next 30 days, payment in full will be required at the time of service.

Sincerely,

Susan B. Dunn
Office Manager

Figure 14-26 Notice of termination letter

Once the account has been turned over to the collection agency, the medical office should follow these guidelines:

1. Note on the patient's account that it has been given to the collection agency.

2. Discontinue sending statements.

3. Refer the patient to the collection agency if he or she contacts the office about the account.

4. Promptly report any payments received by the office to the agency, as a percentage of this payment is due them.

5. Contact the agency if new information is obtained that could help in collecting the debt.

The collection agency will retain a portion of payment recovered, usually 40 to 60 percent.

Small Claims Court

In certain circumstances, consideration may be given to bringing a delinquent case to small claims court. Small claims courts typically:

- Handle cases that involve only a limited amount of debt (which varies from state to state)

- Do not permit representation by an attorney or collection agency but do allow another person, such as the bookkeeper or office manager, to represent the office

- Are efficient in their proceedings and less expensive to utilize (no attorney fee)

A key factor when using small claims court is that the court only determines if the charge or account is valid. If the court rules in favor of the medical office, the office still must collect the money from the defendant.

Special Collection Situations

Bankruptcy

Bankruptcy is defined as a legal declaration of an individual's inability to pay debts owed. The number of individual bankruptcies filed in the United States continues to rise. This is especially true as the elderly population increases and as lost jobs and decreased benefits mean a growing number of individuals and families in need of medical procedures and services are uninsured.

This increase has a significant impact on health care providers, whose bills often make up a large portion of the debts discharged in the bankruptcy court. Because the physician's fee is an unsecured debt, it is one of the last to be paid, according to the U.S. Bankruptcy Court website.

Bankruptcy is governed under the Bankruptcy Act of 1978 and the Bankruptcy Amendment Acts of 1984, 1986, and 1994. There are different types or chapters of bankruptcy, usually determined by legal advice that can be voluntary or involuntary. The main objectives of a bankruptcy proceeding are the collection and distribution of a debtor's assets and the discharge of the debtor from obligations. The decree terminating the bankruptcy proceeding is called a *discharge*, which releases the debtor from the debt. The most common types of bankruptcy involving patients are:

bankruptcy: A legal declaration of an individual's inability to pay debts.

- Chapter 7: A "straight" bankruptcy under which assets are liquidated in order to pay creditors.

- Chapter 13: Bankruptcy for consumers with a regular income when plans are developed to pay all or part of their debts to their creditors over a specified period of time.

What should a medical office do when a patient files bankruptcy? When verbal or written notice is received that a debtor has filed bankruptcy, immediately discontinue all collection attempts, as an Automatic Stay provided for by the Bankruptcy Code requires creditors to immediately discontinue all efforts to collect a debt, take possession of collateral, enforce a lien, or collect receivables of a debtor. The U.S. Bankruptcy Court is now involved, and it will make the decision about who will receive any assets that are available. Any further contact with the debtor may constitute a violation of the protection of the bankruptcy court. For questions, contact the medical practice's attorney or the debtor's attorney. On receiving notice of a bankruptcy proceeding for an account that has been turned over to a collection agency, contact the agency immediately. Copies of any bankruptcy notices received from the bankruptcy court should be sent to the agency so that appropriate action may be taken on the account.

Figures 14–27, 14–28, and 14–29 are examples of notices from bankruptcy court.

Billing Minors

Statements for services performed for minors must be addressed to a parent or guardian.

A statement addressed to a child, or patient under the legal age declared in that state, may prove difficult to collect if the parents take the attitude that they are not responsible because the statement is not addressed directly to them. If the parents are separated or divorced, the parent who brings the child to the office for medical services may be responsible for payment. Financial agreements in these circumstances exist between the parents and should not involve the medical staff.

birthday rule: Guideline for determination of the primary insurance policy when dependents are covered on two or more policies.

In some circumstances, a child may be covered under two insurance policies. The **birthday rule** determines which policy is primary and which is secondary. The birthday rule states that the primary policy is the one taken out by the policyholder with the earliest birthday occurring in the calendar year.

> **EXAMPLE:** Tom Brown is a dependent child carried on both parents' policies. His father's policy is through his employment at General Motors. His mother's policy is a group policy through her employer, Good Samaritan Hospital.
>
> > The father's birth date is June 6, 1983.
> >
> > The mother's birth date is February 1, 1985.
> >
> > February 1 is the earlier birth date in the year and would be the primary policy for Tom, with his father's policy secondary.

If both policyholders have the same birth dates, the primary policy is the policy in effect the longest. The *year* of birth is not considered in the birthday rule.

Emancipated Minors

Minors cannot be held responsible for payment of a bill unless they are emancipated.

emancipated minor: A person under the age of majority, usually 18 to 21 years of age as defined by state statute, who is self-supporting, married, serving in the armed forces, and/or living separate from parents.

An **emancipated minor** is a person under the age of majority, usually 18 or 21 years old as defined by state statute, who is one of the following:

- Married
- Self-supporting
- Serving in the armed forces
- Living separate from parents or a legal guardian

An emancipated minor who comes to the medical facility requesting treatment is responsible for the charges incurred.

B9A (Official Form 9A) (Chapter 7 Individual or Joint Debtor No Asset Case) (12/12)

UNITED STATES BANKRUPTCY COURT_____District of_____

Notice of
Chapter 7 Bankruptcy Case, Meeting of Creditors, & Deadlines

[A chapter 7 bankruptcy case concerning the debtor(s) listed below was filed on _____(date).]
or [A bankruptcy case concerning the debtor(s) listed below was originally filed under chapter_____on
_____(date) and was converted to a case under chapter 7 on_____(date).]

You may be a creditor of the debtor. **This notice lists important deadlines.** You may want to consult an attorney to protect your rights. All documents filed in the case may be inspected at the bankruptcy clerk's office at the address listed below. NOTE: The staff of the bankruptcy clerk's office cannot give legal advice.

Creditors -- Do not file this notice in connection with any proof of claim you submit to the court.
See Reverse Side for Important Explanations.

Debtor(s) (name(s) and address):	Case Number:
	Last four digits of Social-Security or Individual Taxpayer-ID (ITIN) No(s)./Complete EIN:
All other names used by the Debtor(s) in the last 8 years (include married, maiden, and trade names):	Bankruptcy Trustee (name and address):
Attorney for Debtor(s) (name and address):	
Telephone number:	Telephone number:

Meeting of Creditors

Date: / /   Time: ( ) A. M.   Location:
                                  ( ) P. M.

Presumption of Abuse under 11 U.S.C. § 707(b)
See "Presumption of Abuse" on the reverse side.

Depending on the documents filed with the petition, one of the following statements will appear.

      The presumption of abuse does not arise.
            Or
      The presumption of abuse arises.
            Or
      Insufficient information has been filed to date to permit the clerk to make any determination concerning the presumption of abuse. If more complete information, when filed, shows that the presumption has arisen, creditors will be notified.

Deadlines:
Papers must be *received* by the bankruptcy clerk's office by the following deadlines:
Deadline to Object to Debtor's Discharge or to Challenge Dischargeability of Certain Debts:

Deadline to Object to Exemptions:
Thirty (30) days after the *conclusion* of the meeting of creditors.
Creditors May Not Take Certain Actions:

In most instances, the filing of the bankruptcy case automatically stays certain collection and other actions against the debtor and the debtor's property. Under certain circumstances, the stay may be limited to 30 days or not exist at all, although the debtor can request the court to extend or impose a stay. If you attempt to collect a debt or take other action in violation of the Bankruptcy Code, you may be penalized. Consult a lawyer to determine your rights in this case.

Please Do Not File a Proof of Claim Unless You Receive a Notice To Do So.

Creditor with a Foreign Address:

A creditor to whom this notice is sent at a foreign address should read the information under "Do Not File a Proof of Claim at This Time" on the reverse side.

Address of the Bankruptcy Clerk's Office:	For the Court:
	Clerk of the Bankruptcy Court:
Telephone number:	
Hours Open:	Date:

Figure 14-27 Chapter 7 Notice of bankruptcy

Source: www.uscourts.gov.

B9E (Official Form 9E) (Chapter 11 Individual or Joint Debtor Case) (12/12)

UNITED STATES BANKRUPTCY COURT_____**District of**_____	

Notice of
Chapter 11 Bankruptcy Case, Meeting of Creditors, & Deadlines

[A chapter 11 bankruptcy case concerning the debtor(s) listed below was filed on _____ (date).]
or [A bankruptcy case concerning the debtor(s) listed below was originally filed under chapter_____on
_____ (date) and was converted to a case under chapter 11 on_____(date).]

You may be a creditor of the debtor. **This notice lists important deadlines.** You may want to consult an attorney to protect your rights. All documents filed in the case may be inspected at the bankruptcy clerk's office at the address listed below.
NOTE: The staff of the bankruptcy clerk's office cannot give legal advice

Creditors -- Do not file this notice in connection with any proof of claim you submit to the court.
See Reverse Side for Important Explanations.

Debtor(s) (name(s) and address):	Case Number:
	Last four digits of Social-Security or Individual Taxpayer-ID (ITIN) No(s)./Complete EIN:
All other names used by the Debtor(s) in the last 8 years (include married, maiden, and trade names):	Attorney for Debtor(s) (name and address): Telephone number:

Meeting of Creditors

Date: / /   Time: (   ) A. M.   Location:
                                       (   ) P. M.

Deadlines:
Papers must be *received* by the bankruptcy clerk's office by the following deadlines:

Deadline to File a Proof of Claim:
Notice of deadline will be sent at a later time.

Creditor with a Foreign Address:
A creditor to whom this notice is sent at a foreign address should read the information under "Claims" on the reverse side.

Deadline to File a Complaint to Determine Dischargeability of Certain Debts:

Deadline to File a Complaint Objecting to Discharge of the Debtor:

First date set for hearing on confirmation of plan
Notice of that date will be sent at a later time.

Deadline to Object to Exemptions:

Thirty (30) days after the *conclusion* of the meeting of creditors.

Creditors May Not Take Certain Actions:
In most instances, the filing of the bankruptcy case automatically stays certain collection and other actions against the debtor and the debtor's property. Under certain circumstances, the stay may be limited to 30 days or not exist at all, although the debtor can request the court to extend or impose a stay. If you attempt to collect a debt or take other action in violation of the Bankruptcy Code, you may be penalized. Consult a lawyer to determine your rights in this case.

Address of the Bankruptcy Clerk's Office:	For the Court:
	Clerk of the Bankruptcy Court:
Telephone number:	
Hours Open:	Date:

Source: www.uscourts.gov.

Figure 14-28 Chapter 11 Notice of bankruptcy

B10 (Official Form 10) (04/13)

UNITED STATES BANKRUPTCY COURT _____	PROOF OF CLAIM

Name of Debtor: Case Number:

NOTE: *Do not use this form to make a claim for an administrative expense that arises after the bankruptcy filing. You may file a request for payment of an administrative expense according to 11 U.S.C. § 503.*

Name of Creditor (the person or other entity to whom the debtor owes money or property):

Name and address where notices should be sent:

COURT USE ONLY

❏ Check this box if this claim amends a previously filed claim.

Court Claim Number:_____
  (*If known*)

Telephone number: email:

Filed on:_____

Name and address where payment should be sent (if different from above):

❏ Check this box if you are aware that anyone else has filed a proof of claim relating to this claim. Attach copy of statement giving particulars.

Telephone number: email:

1. Amount of Claim as of Date Case Filed: $_____

If all or part of the claim is secured, complete item 4.

If all or part of the claim is entitled to priority, complete item 5.

❏ Check this box if the claim includes interest or other charges in addition to the principal amount of the claim. Attach a statement that itemizes interest or charges.

2. Basis for Claim: _____
  (See instruction #2)

3. Last four digits of any number by which creditor identifies debtor: __ __ __ __	**3a. Debtor may have scheduled account as:** _____ (See instruction #3a)	**3b. Uniform Claim Identifier (optional):** __ (See instruction #3b)

4. Secured Claim (See instruction #4)
Check the appropriate box if the claim is secured by a lien on property or a right of setoff, attach required redacted documents, and provide the requested information.

Nature of property or right of setoff: ❏Real Estate ❏Motor Vehicle ❏Other
Describe:

Value of Property: $_____

Annual Interest Rate_____% ❏Fixed or ❏Variable
(when case was filed)

Amount of arrearage and other charges, as of the time case was filed, included in secured claim, if any:
$_____

Basis for perfection: _____

Amount of Secured Claim: $_____

Amount Unsecured: $_____

5. Amount of Claim Entitled to Priority under 11 U.S.C. § 507 (a). If any part of the claim falls into one of the following categories, check the box specifying the priority and state the amount.

❏ Domestic support obligations under 11 U.S.C. § 507 (a)(1)(A) or (a)(1)(B).

❏ Wages, salaries, or commissions (up to $12,475*) earned within 180 days before the case was filed or the debtor's business ceased, whichever is earlier – 11 U.S.C. § 507 (a)(4).

❏ Contributions to an employee benefit plan – 11 U.S.C. § 507 (a)(5).

❏ Up to $2,775* of deposits toward purchase, lease, or rental of property or services for personal, family, or household use – 11 U.S.C. § 507 (a)(7).

❏ Taxes or penalties owed to governmental units – 11 U.S.C. § 507 (a)(8).

❏ Other – Specify applicable paragraph of 11 U.S.C. § 507 (a)(__).

Amount entitled to priority:

$_____

Amounts are subject to adjustment on 4/01/16 and every 3 years thereafter with respect to cases commenced on or after the date of adjustment.

6. Credits. The amount of all payments on this claim has been credited for the purpose of making this proof of claim. (See instruction #6)

Figure 14-29 Bankruptcy court notice of discharge of debtor(s)

(*continues*)

B10 (Official Form 10) (04/13)   2

7. Documents: Attached are **redacted** copies of any documents that support the claim, such as promissory notes, purchase orders, invoices, itemized statements of running accounts, contracts, judgments, mortgages, security agreements, or, in the case of a claim based on an open-end or revolving consumer credit agreement, a statement providing the information required by FRBP 3001(c)(3)(A). If the claim is secured, box 4 has been completed, and **redacted** copies of documents providing evidence of perfection of a security interest are attached. If the claim is secured by the debtor's principal residence, the Mortgage Proof of Claim Attachment is being filed with this claim. *(See instruction #7, and the definition of "redacted".)*

DO NOT SEND ORIGINAL DOCUMENTS. ATTACHED DOCUMENTS MAY BE DESTROYED AFTER SCANNING.

If the documents are not available, please explain:

8. Signature: (See instruction #8)

Check the appropriate box.

❒ I am the creditor.   ❒ I am the creditor's authorized agent.   ❒ I am the trustee, or the debtor,   ❒ I am a guarantor, surety, indorser, or other codebtor.
                                                                          or their authorized agent.   (See Bankruptcy Rule 3005.)
                                                                          (See Bankruptcy Rule 3004.)

I declare under penalty of perjury that the information provided in this claim is true and correct to the best of my knowledge, information, and reasonable belief.

Print Name: _____
Title: _____
Company: _____
Address and telephone number (if different from notice address above): _____   _____   _____
                                                                      (Signature)   (Date)
_____
_____
_____
Telephone number: _____   email: _____

Penalty for presenting fraudulent claim: Fine of up to $500,000 or imprisonment for up to 5 years, or both. 18 U.S.C. §§ 152 and 3571.

INSTRUCTIONS FOR PROOF OF CLAIM FORM
The instructions and definitions below are general explanations of the law. In certain circumstances, such as bankruptcy cases not filed voluntarily by the debtor, exceptions to these general rules may apply.
Items to be completed in Proof of Claim form

Court, Name of Debtor, and Case Number:
Fill in the federal judicial district in which the bankruptcy case was filed (for example, Central District of California), the debtor's full name, and the case number. If the creditor received a notice of the case from the bankruptcy court, all of this information is at the top of the notice.

Creditor's Name and Address:
Fill in the name of the person or entity asserting a claim and the name and address of the person who should receive notices issued during the bankruptcy case. A separate space is provided for the payment address if it differs from the notice address. The creditor has a continuing obligation to keep the court informed of its current address. See Federal Rule of Bankruptcy Procedure (FRBP) 2002(g).

1. Amount of Claim as of Date Case Filed:
State the total amount owed to the creditor on the date of the bankruptcy filing. Follow the instructions concerning whether to complete items 4 and 5. Check the box if interest or other charges are included in the claim.

2. Basis for Claim:
State the type of debt or how it was incurred. Examples include goods sold, money loaned, services performed, personal injury/wrongful death, car loan, mortgage note, and credit card. If the claim is based on delivering health care goods or services, limit the disclosure of the goods or services so as to avoid embarrassment or the disclosure of confidential health care information. You may be required to provide additional disclosure if an interested party objects to the claim.

3. Last Four Digits of Any Number by Which Creditor Identifies Debtor:
State only the last four digits of the debtor's account or other number used by the creditor to identify the debtor.

3a. Debtor May Have Scheduled Account As:
Report a change in the creditor's name, a transferred claim, or any other information that clarifies a difference between this proof of claim and the claim as scheduled by the debtor.

3b. Uniform Claim Identifier:
If you use a uniform claim identifier, you may report it here. A uniform claim identifier is an optional 24-character identifier that certain large creditors use to facilitate electronic payment in chapter 13 cases.

4. Secured Claim:
Check whether the claim is fully or partially secured. Skip this section if the

claim is entirely unsecured. (See Definitions.) If the claim is secured, check the box for the nature and value of property that secures the claim, attach copies of lien documentation, and state, as of the date of the bankruptcy filing, the annual interest rate (and whether it is fixed or variable), and the amount past due on the claim.

5. Amount of Claim Entitled to Priority Under 11 U.S.C. § 507 (a).
If any portion of the claim falls into any category shown, check the appropriate box(es) and state the amount entitled to priority. (See Definitions.) A claim may be partly priority and partly non-priority. For example, in some of the categories, the law limits the amount entitled to priority.

6. Credits:
An authorized signature on this proof of claim serves as an acknowledgment that when calculating the amount of the claim, the creditor gave the debtor credit for any payments received toward the debt.

7. Documents:
Attach redacted copies of any documents that show the debt exists and a lien secures the debt. You must also attach copies of documents that evidence perfection of any security interest and documents required by FRBP 3001(c) for claims based on an open-end or revolving consumer credit agreement or secured by a security interest in the debtor's principal residence. You may also attach a summary in addition to the documents themselves. FRBP 3001(c) and (d). If the claim is based on delivering health care goods or services, limit disclosing confidential health care information. Do not send original documents, as attachments may be destroyed after scanning.

8. Date and Signature:
The individual completing this proof of claim must sign and date it. FRBP 9011. If the claim is filed electronically, FRBP 5005(a)(2) authorizes courts to establish local rules specifying what constitutes a signature. If you sign this form, you declare under penalty of perjury that the information provided is true and correct to the best of your knowledge, information, and reasonable belief. Your signature is also a certification that the claim meets the requirements of FRBP 9011(b). Whether the claim is filed electronically or in person, if your name is on the signature line, you are responsible for the declaration. Print the name and title, if any, of the creditor or other person authorized to file this claim. State the filer's address and telephone number if it differs from the address given on the top of the form for purposes of receiving notices. If the claim is filed by an authorized agent, provide both the name of the individual filing the claim and the name of the agent. If the authorized agent is a servicer, identify the corporate servicer as the company. Criminal penalties apply for making a false statement on a proof of claim.

Figure 14-29 (Continued)

Exercise 14.8

1. Explain the correct procedure to follow in billing a minor.
2. Define emancipated minor.
3. Applying the birthday rule to the following scenario, which policy is primary?

   Jennifer Catz is a nine-year-old child carried on both her parents' health care policies. Her father's policy is through his employment at General Foods.

   Jennifer's mother is employed at National American Life Insurance Company with medical insurance coverage through her employer.

   Jennifer's father's birth date is September 2, 1960.

   Jennifer's mother's birth date is September 28, 1956.

The purpose of the Fair Debt Collection Practices Act is to protect consumers against abusive practices by debt collectors. In the space provided for questions 4–8, put "T" for each statement that is true and "F" for each statement that is false as it relates to this act.

4. _____ One cannot threaten to notify an employer that a consumer has not paid bills.
5. _____ Calls are to be made between 8 a.m. and 9 p.m. (Note: Be sure to check time differences to adhere to this law.)
6. _____ The time difference in a region does not matter when calling for debt-collection purposes.
7. _____ Embarrassing a consumer by advertising or publishing debt information is acceptable.
8. _____ A special collection fee can be added to the amount that is owed.

Tracing Skips

A **skip** is a person who has apparently moved without leaving a forwarding address. If a statement is returned to your office "No Forwarding Address," or "Undeliverable," determine first if there were any errors made in addressing the envelope. Compare the address on the envelope with the one on the patient registration form in the chart. If the address is correct, the billing office may try to call the patient. The copy of the driver's license obtained during the patient registration process can be used as a tracking device to locate the patient. If all these efforts fail, a decision should be made on whether to pursue the debt. This usually depends on office policy and the amount that is owed. The unpaid account could be turned over to a collection agency at this time.

skip: A person who has apparently moved without leaving a forwarding address.

Exercise 14.9

1. Explain the *first* thing to do when a statement is returned to the office, "Moved—No Forwarding Address."

Billing for a Deceased Patient

Health care providers sometimes write off accounts of deceased patients simply due to lack of information on whom to bill and how to bill. Not charging for services to a patient who dies or reducing the fee could be misinterpreted as physician failure in treatment and result in a malpractice case.

When the patient has Medicare, submit the claim with the physician accepting assignment by marking X in "Yes" box in Block 27. **Accept assignment** means the physician or provider will accept what Medicare pays and not bill the difference between the cost of the service and the Medicare payment. For example, Medicare is billed for a service that cost $150. The Medicare payment is in the amount of $98. When the provider accepts assignment, the payment of $98 is accepted as payment in full. The remaining balance or difference of $52 is adjusted or written off. No signature is required by a family member. In Block 12 where the patient's signature is required, type in "Patient Died (date)."

If the physician does not accept assignment on a Medicare patient, the balance on the account will remain unpaid until the estate is settled. Individuals filing to receive benefits on behalf of a deceased beneficiary are encouraged to submit documentation to establish their entitlement, such as a letter of appointment, proof of executorship, and copies of receipted funeral bills.

When notification is received that a patient has died, show courtesy by not sending a statement in the first week or so after the death. Address the statement to "Estate of (name of patient)" and mail to the patient's last known address. If the office had a long-term relationship with the deceased, the surviving spouse or family member usually will notify the billing office if there is an estate and who is the executor or administrator.

A call to the probate court in the county clerk's office where the estate was entered can verify that the estate has been or will be probated. If there is a special form for the billing provider to complete, such as proof of claim, the clerk of the probate court, the executor, or the administrator will assist you in filing your claim.

accept assignment: To accept payment received for a claim as full payment after copayment and/or coinsurance amounts have been collected.

Professional Courtesy

professional courtesy: Medical treatment free of charge or at a reduced rate, or accepting what insurance pays as full payment to physicians and their families, office employees and their families, and other health care professionals, such as dentists, pharmacists, and clergy, as determined by office policy.

The Centers for Medicare & Medicaid Services (CMS) defines **professional courtesy** as providing health care services on a free or discount basis to a physician, his or her immediate family members, and office staff. The Stark II/Phase II regulations of CMS have set criteria for allowing this practice: Professional courtesy is offered to all physicians on the providing entity's bona fide medical staff or in the local community without regard to the volume or value of referrals or other business generated between the parties.

Health care services provided as a professional courtesy must be services typically provided by the entity. The professional courtesy policy must be in a written format and meet approval of the governing body of the health care provider. Extending professional courtesy should not violate the CMS Anti-Kickback Statute, the Stark Law, or any federal or state law or regulation governing billing or submission of claims.

Financial Hardship

Many times a patient simply cannot pay due to limited income or no insurance. The Code of Medical Ethics requires physicians to provide medical care to those who need it, regardless of ability to pay. Free treatment for hardship cases is at the physician's discretion; however, the physician must be aware that under the Equal Credit Opportunity Act, if one patient receives free or reduced-fee treatment based on inability to pay, other patients under similar circumstances must be extended the same financial consideration, or a charge of discrimination could be brought against the physician. In the event of an acute problem or emergency, the physician could provide free or reduced fee-treatment or services, then refer the patient to local clinics that may provide free or reduced-fee services based on government funding.

Waiver of Copayment

Under the False Claim Act, the government position is that physicians who waive fees by providing free or discounted services submit false claims because of misrepresentation of actual charges. The Special Fraud Alert of the Office of Inspector General (OIG) emphasizes that "routine" waiver of co-pay or deductibles is equivalent to misstating the actual charge.

Stark II, Phase III, allows the following exceptions for professional courtesy discounts as follows:

1. Discounts must be offered to all physicians in the local community or service area without regard to whether they are referral sources.

2. The professional courtesy policy must be in writing.

3. The policy may not be available to anyone who is a beneficiary of Medicare or Medicaid or any other federal healthcare program (i.e., retired physicians on Medicare).

4. If the courtesy involves any reduction of co-pay or deductible, the insurer must be notified in writing of the reduction. (This could be interpreted in breach of contract by commercial carriers.)

Exercise 14.10

Place an X in the space provided to indicate the correct procedures for billing for a deceased patient.

_____ Address the statement to the deceased at his or her last known address.

_____ Address the statement to the estate of (patient's name) mailed to last known address.

_____ Accept assignment when billing a third-party payor.

_____ Send the statement as soon as the patient expires.

_____ Contact probate court to check the status of the estate/will.

Exercise 14.11

Match the term with its definition, placing the correct letter in the space provided.

_____ **1.** Bankruptcy   **a.** the patient's financial record

_____ **2.** Birthday rule   **b.** a record of payment received

(continues)

Exercise 14.11 (continued)

_____	3. Receipt	c. the amount of money owed to a business
_____	4. Charge slip/ encounter form	d. legal declaration of inability to pay debts
_____	5. Posting	e. accounts grouped to bill at different times throughout the month
_____	6. Transaction	f. transferring information from one record to another
_____	7. Account	g. form providing account information, charges, payments, and CPT and ICD-10-CM codes
_____	8. Accounts receivable	h. the occurrence of a financial activity to be recorded
_____	9. Cycle billing	i. determination of primary and secondary policy of a child
_____	10. Skip	j. one who avoids paying bills

Summary

Initial patient contact usually starts with a telephone call inquiring about the practice and scheduling the appointment. The initial face-to-face contact starts at the reception window with patient registration for preparation of the patient record. There must be an understanding of the patient registration process for both new and established patients. There must be a working knowledge of insurance regulations, especially those contracts with which the physician participates such as HMOs and federal programs.

Billing procedures, including deductibles, copayments, and referrals, as well as the actual billing process, must be accurately performed. The collection policy and how to handle various collection problems must be managed by understanding federal and state regulations mandating this process.

Continuing education is required to keep up to date and current in changes relative to administrative skills. This is accomplished by attending seminars and reading newsletters, manuals, and bulletins. Today's technology allows patients to communicate and interact with health care providers through e-mail and websites. Many physicians can answer basic questions or concerns by e-mail. As this communication mode increases, insurance carriers will need to consider a reimbursement format for services rendered using these nontraditional methods. The Evaluation/Management section of CPT now contains codes for Non-Face-to-Face Services, including telephone services, online medical evaluations, and interprofessional telephone/internet consultations. The guidelines for assigning codes from this section should be reviewed carefully for criteria and date/time limitations.

References

Centers for Medicare & Medicaid (CMS). Retrieved from https://www.cms.gov.

Correa, C. (2011). *Getting started in the computerized medical office* (2nd ed.). Clifton Park, NY: Cengage Learning.

Fordney, M. (2013). *Insurance handbook for the medical office* (13th ed.). St. Louis, MO: Elsevier, Saunders.

Fordney, M., French, L., & Follis, J. (2008). *Administrative medical assisting* (6th ed.). Clifton Park, NY: Cengage Learning.

Green, M., & Rowell, J. (2015). *Understanding health insurance: A guide to billing and reimbursement* (12th ed.). Clifton Park, NY: Cengage Learning.

Health IT. Retrieved from www.healthit.gov.

United States Bankruptcy Court. Retrieved from http://www.uscourts.gov /bankruptcycourts.html.

United States Census Bureau. 2010 statistics. Retrieved from http://www.census.gov.

Filing the Claim Form

Learning Objectives

Upon successful completion of this chapter, you should be able to:

- Abstract information from the patient medical record to complete the CMS-1500 claim form.
- Complete the CMS-1500 for commercial and government carriers.
- Recognize common guidelines to complete the CMS-1500 claim form.
- Differentiate between a participating (PAR) provider and a nonparticipating (nonPAR) provider.
- Explain the four parts of Medicare.
- Define Medicaid and the regulations mandated for provider participation.
- Define the regulations mandated for workers' compensation coverage.
- Explain the functions of the health maintenance organization (HMO).
- Define TRICARE and CHAMPVA.
- Identify various Blue Cross Blue Shield policies and their benefits.
- Explain the basic components of the Affordable Care Act (ACA).

Key Terms

advance beneficiary notice (ABN)	Reconciliation Act (COBRA)	explanation of benefits (EOB)	National Provider Identifier (NPI)
Blue Cross Blue Shield (BCBS)	coordination of benefits (COB)	Medicaid	preexisting condition
CHAMPVA	copayment	Medicare	remittance advice (RA)
coinsurance	crossover claim	Medicare Summary Notice (MSN)	signature on file
Consolidated Omnibus Budget	deductible	Medigap	TRICARE

Introduction

As discussed in Chapter 14, the majority of patients seeking health care have some type of insurance coverage. This means completion of a claim form, an intricate part of the billing process, is necessary. Chapter 14 also introduced the Patient Protection and Affordable Care Act (PPACA), or The Affordable Care Act (ACA) designed to make health care accessible to everyone. A Health Insurance Marketplace is available to offer consumers options to subscribe for health care coverage at www.healthcare.gov. Several states have created their own state Marketplace to purchase health care coverage at the state's website. This act created Accountable Care Organizations (ACOs) that are a group of health care providers working together with the goal of coordinating patient care and communicating health care with other health care providers.

Each insurance program such as Medicare and Medicaid has terms pertinent to its particular program. The terminology that is common to all programs is discussed before each program is introduced.

What is really meant when the question is asked, "What kind of insurance do you have?" In the medical office, we are referring to health insurance. Health insurance is defined as a contract between the insured and an insurance company or government program designed to reimburse a portion of the cost of medically necessary treatment to those who are sick or injured, or preventive services as a means of preventing illness or injury, or for early diagnosis and treatment. Medical care and treatment can be rendered in many settings: physician's offices, clinics, hospitals, ambulatory care centers, and nursing homes, just to name a few. More and more medical care today is performed in the outpatient setting as a means of reducing medical costs.

Medical practices today see patients with a variety of health insurance plans:

- Commercial plans
- Group health plans
- Health maintenance organizations (HMOs)
- High-deductible health plans (HDHP)
- Catastrophic plans
- Medicare
- Medigap
- Medicaid
- Individual policies
- TRICARE/CHAMPVA
- Workers' compensation

Third-party payors involved in the reimbursement proceedings in the medical practice may be insurance companies and employers. A third-party payor is an individual or company that makes a payment on a debt but is not a party involved in the creation of the debt, or it serves as a payor for an insurance company through which the patient is insured. In the physician–patient contract, the first party is the patient who is seeking medical care; the second party is the physician or provider of the service or supply.

Many of the plans just listed will be covered later in this chapter. Other plans are outlined as follows.

As mentioned earlier, the Affordable Care Act (ACA) is a law that reforms both the U.S. health care and health insurance industries. The law increases the quality, availability, and affordability of private and public health insurance to Americans without insurance coverage, as well as working to curb the rising costs of health care spending and give more control to consumers and physicians in health care decisions. Government health plans were created under this Act in many states, which are referred to as the Health Insurance Marketplace. These plans provide coverage for essential medical services such as emergency care, hospitalization, preventive care, maternity/pediatric care, mental health services, lab procedures, and prescription drugs. The difference in various plans offered through the Marketplace is the cost. As mandated by the ACA, coverage cannot be denied for preexisting medical conditions, and cannot be canceled in the event of a major illness and become too costly to insure. This act also expands Medicaid to help "cover the gap" between those who qualify for cost assistance through the Marketplace and those who qualified for Medicaid under previous Medicaid guidelines.

Consolidated Omnibus Budget Reconciliation Act (COBRA): A law to assist employees in continuing health care coverage in the event of termination of employment, reduction of work hours, divorce, separation, or death of an employee.

The **Consolidated Omnibus Budget Reconciliation Act (COBRA)** was enacted in 1986 to assist workers and their families keep their group health coverage in the event of the following:

- Voluntary or involuntary termination of the covered employee's employment for reasons other than "gross misconduct"

- Reduced hours of work for the covered employee

- Covered employee becoming entitled to Medicare

- Divorce or legal separation of a covered employee

- Death of a covered employee

- Loss of status as a "dependent child" under plan rules

Under COBRA, the employee or family member may qualify to keep the group health plan benefits for a set period of time, depending on the reason for losing the health coverage, by paying the premium of the plan.

A high-deductible health plan (HDHP) allows a member to select a plan with a lower monthly premium but a higher deductible. The monthly payment is less, but when health care is needed, the beneficiary pays more out of pocket before the insurance company covers medical costs. Many employer-sponsored health plans offer the HDHP with a health reimbursement arrangement (HRA) or with a health savings account (HSA). The member contributes money from the paycheck before taxes to pay for health costs not covered by insurance, such as copays, coinsurance, dental or eye care.

A catastrophic plan is a low-cost health plan that generally offers a lower monthly premium but a high annual deductible that could equal the maximum out-of-pocket limits allowed under the Affordable Care Act. Catastrophic plans cover the essential health benefits that all policies sold through individual states' Marketplace must include, but the full deductible must be paid before the plan pays any for the care. These plans also cover the first three primary care visits and preventive care for free, even if the deductible has not yet been met.

Due to the variety of health insurance plans, there will be various methods of reimbursement:

- *Fee-for-service* reimbursement is the traditional method of reimbursement. Each service performed has a price that is charged to the patient's account.

- *Capitation* is the reimbursement method used by some HMOs and other managed care plans. This method pays the health care provider a fixed amount per person enrolled for a period of time regardless of whether expenses are incurred or not, rather than by the type or number of services performed.

- *Episode-of-care* reimbursement is a payment method of issuing one lump sum for services rendered to a patient for a specific illness. Global surgical fee payment is an example of this reimbursement method for physicians who perform major surgeries. The global surgical fee payment includes the preoperative visit, the surgery, and the postoperative visit. Any surgical complications are usually paid on a fee-for-service basis.

When a policyholder has two or more medical insurance policies, **coordination of benefits** determines the plan of payment. Coordination of benefits (COB) is a ruling in an insurance policy or state law requiring insurance companies to coordinate reimbursement of benefits when a policyholder has two or more medical insurance policies. This is a legal requirement so that the benefits from the combined policies do not exceed 100 percent of the covered benefits of the combined policies for all medical expenses submitted.

coordination of benefits: Coordination of payment of services submitted on the claim form when a patient is covered by two or more primary medical insurance policies.

Exercise 15.1

1. Define health insurance.
2. Name four types of health insurance plans presented to the health care facility.

    1. _____ 2. _____ 3. _____ 4. _____

3. Name four health care settings in which medical treatment can be given.

    1. _____ 2. _____ 3. _____ 4. _____

4. What is outlined in the Affordable Care Act?
5. What is the purpose of COBRA?
6. What do the following abbreviations mean?

    a. COBRA

    b. ACA

    c. COB

    d. HMO

    e. HDHP

    f. CMS

    g. AMA

The Health Insurance Claim Form

Claim forms can be submitted to the carrier electronically or on paper. In April 1975, the American Medical Association (AMA) approved a universal claim form called the health insurance claim form, or HCFA-1500. This was a standardized form that could be used to submit both group and individual claims for physician services. In 1990, the HCFA-1500 was revised and renamed CMS-1500. This is printed in red so insurance companies can optically scan claims using optical character recognition (OCR).

The National Uniform Claim Committee (NUCC), American Medical Association, and Centers for Medicare & Medicaid Services have worked together to revise the CMS-1500 form (referred to as the 02/12 version) to include the listing of ICD-10-CM codes for diagnosis or nature of illness or injury required in filing claim forms today. Up to 12 ICD-10-CM codes may be listed. Examples of the 02/12 version of the CMS-1500 form will be provided later in this chapter.

The UB-04 form is used to bill institutional services, such as services performed in hospitals.

The CMS-1500 is the standardized claim form accepted by Medicare, Medicaid, TRICARE, and private companies, although electronic claims submission is preferred to reduce the costs and expedite reimbursement. An example is shown in Figure 15–1.

The following guidelines are recommended in the preparation of claims for OCR:

- Claim forms should be typed if not submitted electronically. Any handwritten data, with the exception of items or fields requiring signatures, will have to be manually processed, resulting in a delay in payment of the claim.

- Recommended font for computer-generated claims is Courier New. Do not use italics, bold, or script.

- Claim forms must be typed on the original red printed form. Photocopies of claims cannot be optically scanned.

- Do not interchange a zero with the alpha character O or alpha character I with number 1, especially with ICD-10-CM codes.

- Use pica type (10 characters per inch) and type all alpha characters in uppercase or capital letters.

- Leave one blank space between the patient/policyholder's last name, first name, and middle initial.

- Do not use punctuation to separate the patient's last name and first name.

- Do not use titles such as Mr., Ms., or Dr. It is necessary to indicate the titles of Sr. or Jr. as they appear on the patient's insurance ID card.

- Do not add dollar signs, decimals, or commas in any dollar field.

- List only one procedure per line.

- Do not add a dash in front of a procedure code modifier.

- Do not add parentheses when designating the area code of the telephone number, as they are imprinted on the form.

- *Do* use two zeros in the cents column when the fee is listed in whole dollars.

- All dates should be typed using eight-digit dates representing month, day, and year, taking care to remain within the vertical dividers within the item or field.

  EXAMPLE: 01/01/2016

Completing the CMS-1500

The patient information required to complete the top portion of the CMS-1500 is retrieved from the patient's registration form found in the chart. Verify the patient has signed the release of medical information statement either by signing the claim form or a special form unique to the practice and retained in the patient's chart to indicate

HEALTH INSURANCE CLAIM FORM

APPROVED BY NATIONAL UNIFORM CLAIM COMMITTEE (NUCC) 02/12

□□ PICA | PICA □□□

1. MEDICARE MEDICAID TRICARE CHAMPVA GROUP HEALTH PLAN FECA BLK LUNG OTHER **1a. INSURED'S I.D. NUMBER** (For Program in Item 1)
□ (Medicare#) □ (Medicaid#) □ (ID#/DoD#) □ (Member ID#) □ (ID#) □ (ID#) □

2. PATIENT'S NAME (Last Name, First Name, Middle Initial) **3. PATIENT'S BIRTH DATE** MM DD YY SEX M □ F □ **4. INSURED'S NAME** (Last Name, First Name, Middle Initial)

5. PATIENT'S ADDRESS (No., Street) **6. PATIENT RELATIONSHIP TO INSURED** Self □ Spouse □ Child □ Other □ **7. INSURED'S ADDRESS** (No., Street)

CITY | STATE **8. RESERVED FOR NUCC USE** CITY | STATE

ZIP CODE | TELEPHONE (Include Area Code) ( ) ZIP CODE | TELEPHONE (Include Area Code) ( )

9. OTHER INSURED'S NAME (Last Name, First Name, Middle Initial) **10. IS PATIENT'S CONDITION RELATED TO:** **11. INSURED'S POLICY GROUP OR FECA NUMBER**

a. OTHER INSURED'S POLICY OR GROUP NUMBER **a. EMPLOYMENT?** (Current or Previous) □ YES □ NO **a. INSURED'S DATE OF BIRTH** MM DD YY SEX M □ F □

b. RESERVED FOR NUCC USE **b. AUTO ACCIDENT?** □ YES □ NO PLACE (State) **b. OTHER CLAIM ID** (Designated by NUCC)

c. RESERVED FOR NUCC USE **c. OTHER ACCIDENT?** □ YES □ NO **c. INSURANCE PLAN NAME OR PROGRAM NAME**

d. INSURANCE PLAN NAME OR PROGRAM NAME **10d. CLAIM CODES** (Designated by NUCC) **d. IS THERE ANOTHER HEALTH BENEFIT PLAN?** □ YES □ NO *If yes,* complete items 9, 9a, and 9d.

READ BACK OF FORM BEFORE COMPLETING & SIGNING THIS FORM.
12. PATIENT'S OR AUTHORIZED PERSON'S SIGNATURE I authorize the release of any medical or other information necessary to process this claim. I also request payment of government benefits either to myself or to the party who accepts assignment below.

SIGNED _____ DATE _____

13. INSURED'S OR AUTHORIZED PERSON'S SIGNATURE I authorize payment of medical benefits to the undersigned physician or supplier for services described below.

SIGNED _____

14. DATE OF CURRENT ILLNESS, INJURY, or PREGNANCY (LMP) MM DD YY QUAL. **15. OTHER DATE** QUAL. MM DD YY **16. DATES PATIENT UNABLE TO WORK IN CURRENT OCCUPATION** FROM MM DD YY TO MM DD YY

17. NAME OF REFERRING PROVIDER OR OTHER SOURCE 17a. 17b. NPI **18. HOSPITALIZATION DATES RELATED TO CURRENT SERVICES** FROM MM DD YY TO MM DD YY

19. ADDITIONAL CLAIM INFORMATION (Designated by NUCC) **20. OUTSIDE LAB?** □ YES □ NO $ CHARGES

21. DIAGNOSIS OR NATURE OF ILLNESS OR INJURY Relate A-L to service line below (24E) ICD Ind.
A. |___ B. |___ C. |___ D. |___
E. |___ F. |___ G. |___ H. |___
I. |___ J. |___ K. |___ L. |___

22. RESUBMISSION CODE | ORIGINAL REF. NO.

23. PRIOR AUTHORIZATION NUMBER

24. A. DATE(S) OF SERVICE From MM DD YY To MM DD YY | **B. PLACE OF SERVICE** | **C. EMG** | **D. PROCEDURES, SERVICES, OR SUPPLIES** (Explain Unusual Circumstances) CPT/HCPCS MODIFIER | **E. DIAGNOSIS POINTER** | **F. $ CHARGES** | **G. DAYS OR UNITS** | **H. EPSDT Family Plan** | **I. ID. QUAL.** | **J. RENDERING PROVIDER ID. #**

1 | | | | | | | | | NPI |
2 | | | | | | | | | NPI |
3 | | | | | | | | | NPI |
4 | | | | | | | | | NPI |
5 | | | | | | | | | NPI |
6 | | | | | | | | | NPI |

25. FEDERAL TAX I.D. NUMBER SSN EIN □ □ **26. PATIENT'S ACCOUNT NO.** **27. ACCEPT ASSIGNMENT?** (For govt. claims, see back) □ YES □ NO **28. TOTAL CHARGE** $ **29. AMOUNT PAID** $ **30. Rsvd for NUCC Use**

31. SIGNATURE OF PHYSICIAN OR SUPPLIER INCLUDING DEGREES OR CREDENTIALS (I certify that the statements on the reverse apply to this bill and are made a part thereof.)

SIGNED _____ DATE _____

32. SERVICE FACILITY LOCATION INFORMATION
a. NPI b.

33. BILLING PROVIDER INFO & PH # ( )
a. NPI b.

NUCC Instruction Manual available at: www.nucc.org **PLEASE PRINT OR TYPE** APPROVED OMB-0938-1197 FORM 1500 (02-12)

Figure 15-1 CMS-1500 claim form

signature on file. This special form authorizes the processing of the claim form without the patient's signature on each form submitted. In Item 12 of each claim form filed for that patient, "signature on file" may be entered, as in Figure 15–2.

READ BACK OF FORM BEFORE COMPLETING & SIGNING THIS FORM.	
12. PATIENT'S OR AUTHORIZED PERSON'S SIGNATURE I authorize the release of any medical or other information necessary to process this claim. I also request payment of government benefits either to myself or to the party who accepts assignment below.	13. INSURED'S OR AUTHORIZED PERSON'S SIGNATURE I authorize payment of medical benefits to the undersigned physician or supplier for services described below.
SIGNED ___SIGNATURE ON FILE___ DATE_____	SIGNED ___SIGNATURE ON FILE___

Courtesy of the Centers for Medicare & Medicaid Services, www.cms.gov. Copyright © 2017 Cengage Learning®.

Figure 15-2 "Signature on file"

signature on file: A statement entered on the claim form for authorization purposes, indicating the patient has signed a release of medical information retained in the patient's chart.

This dated, signed statement to release information is generally considered to be valid for one year from the signature date. However, most offices update medical records yearly, including the statement to release medical information. Undated signed forms are assumed to be valid until revoked by the patient or guardian. CMS allows government programs to accept both dated and undated authorizations.

There are exceptions to the need for a signed authorization for release of information. These exceptions are patients covered by Medicaid and those covered by workers' compensation. The federal government has mandated in these programs that the patient is a third-party beneficiary in a contract between the health care provider and the governmental agency that sponsors these programs. When the provider agrees to treat Medicaid patients or a workers' compensation patient, it agrees to accept the program's payment as payment in full for covered procedures performed to those patients. The patient can only be billed for services that are not covered, or when the insurance carrier determines the patient was ineligible for benefits on the dates of services reported.

If the patient is physically or mentally unable to sign, the person representing the patient may sign for the patient. This is accomplished by indicating the patient's name on the signature line, followed by the representative's name, address, relationship to the patient, and the reason the patient cannot sign. Medicare and Medigap carriers accept this authorization indefinitely unless the patient or the patient's representative revokes this arrangement.

If the patient is illiterate or physically handicapped and unable to sign the authorization, an X can be made on the signature line. A witness must sign his or her name and address next to the X.

Another exception to the signed authorization is when filing claims for medical services provided by a physician to patients seen at a hospital that are not expected to be seen in that physician's office for follow-up care. These patients are required to sign an authorization for treatment and release of medical information at the hospital before being seen by the health care provider. If the hospital's release form is written to include the release of information from the hospital and the physician's service in treating the patient, claims submitted by the physician's office for his or her charges do not require a separate release of medical information form from the patient. "Signature on file" can be entered in Item 12. The hospital can provide a copy of the signed authorization if it is needed at a later date for verification purposes.

Item 13 of the CMS-1500 is the assignment of benefits authorization. The patient's signature here allows the insurance company to pay claim benefits directly to the physician or provider rather than to the patient. Obtaining this authorization can also be accomplished by a statement assigning benefits to the physician, as demonstrated in Figure 15–3.

The lower portion of the CMS-1500 contains information abstracted from the patient's medical record.

Lowery B. Johnson, M.D.
Hwy 311 Suite A31
Sellersburg, IN 47172
812-555-1234

ASSIGNMENT OF BENEFITS

I instruct my insurance company to pay benefits directly to Dr. Lowery Johnson for services rendered and that such payment should be mailed to this physician's office. A photocopy of this assignment shall be as valid as the original.

I also authorize this office to release such medical information as may be required to process my claim with the insurance company.

_____

Signature

_____

Date

Figure 15-3 Special form for authorization and assignment of benefits

Exercise 15.2

1. What is the purpose of obtaining a signature on file form?
2. What are the two exceptions to the need for release of information?
3. What is the recommended procedure to obtain the signature for release of medical information when the patient is treated in the hospital and not expected to be seen for follow-up in the office?

The following instructions are generally recognized for filing commercial and health maintenance organization (HMO) fee-for-service claims. Some regional carriers may require information in special blocks based on local requirements; typically, those blocks are marked "Reserved for NUCC Use."

Program-specific instructions for Medicare, Medicaid, and other health care insurers follow later in this chapter.

Patient and Policy Identification

Item 1—Program Destination Boxes

Check the appropriate box of program for which you are submitting the claim form: Medicare, Medicaid, TRICARE, CHAMPVA, Group Health Plan, FECA Black Lung, or Other (Figure 15–4). ("Other" indicates HMOs, commercial insurance, automobile accident, liability, or workers' compensation.)

1. MEDICARE	MEDICAID	TRICARE	CHAMPVA	GROUP HEALTH PLAN	FECA BLK LUNG	OTHER	1a. INSURED'S I.D. NUMBER	(For Program in Item 1)
☐ (Medicare#)	☐ (Medicaid#)	☐ (ID#/DoD#)	☐ (Member ID#)	☐ (ID#)	☐ (ID#)	☐ (ID#)		

Courtesy of the Centers for Medicare & Medicaid Services, www.cms.gov.

Figure 15-4 CMS-1500 Blocks 1 and 1A

Item 1a—Insured's Identification Number

Enter the insurance identification number as it appears on the policyholder insurance card. Do not use hyphens or other punctuation.

Item 2—Patient's Name

Enter the full name, last name first, followed by first name and middle initial, of the patient (Figure 15–5). Incorrect format of name or nicknames could cause rejection of the claim. Commas can be used to separate last name, first name, but no periods.

> **EXAMPLE:** SMITH, JOHN, T

2. PATIENT'S NAME (Last Name, First Name, Middle Initial)	3. PATIENT'S BIRTH DATE MM DD YY SEX M ☐ F ☐	4. INSURED'S NAME (Last Name, First Name, Middle Initial)

Courtesy of the Centers for Medicare & Medicaid Services, www.cms.gov.

Figure 15-5 CMS-1500 Blocks 2, 3, and 4

Item 3—Patient's Birth Date

Enter birth month, date, and year, using eight-digit dates. Place dates in between parallel lines. Check the appropriate box to indicate patient's gender.

> **EXAMPLE:** 01/01/1950

Item 4—Insured's Name

Enter last name first, followed by first name, then middle initial, with no commas to separate as it appears on the insurance card.

Item 5—Patient's Address

Enter patient's complete mailing address on line 1, city and two-letter initials of state on line 2, zip code, area code, and telephone number on line 3 (Figure 15–6).

5. PATIENT'S ADDRESS (No., Street)	6. PATIENT RELATIONSHIP TO INSURED Self ☐ Spouse ☐ Child ☐ Other ☐	7. INSURED'S ADDRESS (No., Street)	
CITY STATE	8. RESERVED FOR NUCC USE	CITY	STATE
ZIP CODE TELEPHONE (Include Area Code) ( )		ZIP CODE TELEPHONE (Include Area Code) ( )	

Courtesy of the Centers for Medicare & Medicaid Services, www.cms.gov.

Figure 15-6 CMS-1500 Blocks 5, 6, 7, and 8

Item 6—Patient Relationship to Insured

Check the appropriate box for patient's relationship to insured when Item 4 is completed. If the patient is an unmarried domestic partner, check the "Other" box.

Item 7—Insured's Address

Enter the insured's mailing address and telephone number. When the address is the same as the patient's, enter the word SAME. Complete this item only when items 4, 6, and 11 are completed.

Item 8—Reserved for NUCC use.

This field was previously used to report "Patient Status," which has been eliminated and reserved for NUCC use. The NUCC will provide instructions for any use of this field. (None are specific at the time of this publication.)

Item 9—Other Insured's Name

If none, *leave blank.* If there is secondary or supplemental health care coverage, the insured's name of the secondary policy is entered: last name, first name, middle initial of the enrollee in the secondary plan to allow for coordination of benefits. (Figure 15–7). In 9a, enter the policy number and/or group number of the secondary policy. Items 9b and 9c were previously used to report "Other Insured's Date of Birth, Sex" and "Employer's Name or School Name." These items are currently reserved for NUCC use and will provide instructions for any use of this field. Item 9d, "Insurance Plan Name of Program Name," identifies the name of the plan or program of the other insured as indicated in Item 9 for coordination of benefits.

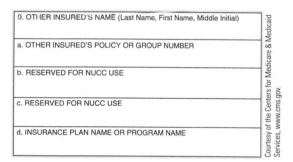

Figure 15-7 CMS-1500 Block 9

Item 10—Is Patient's Condition Related To

See Figure 15–8 and the following details.

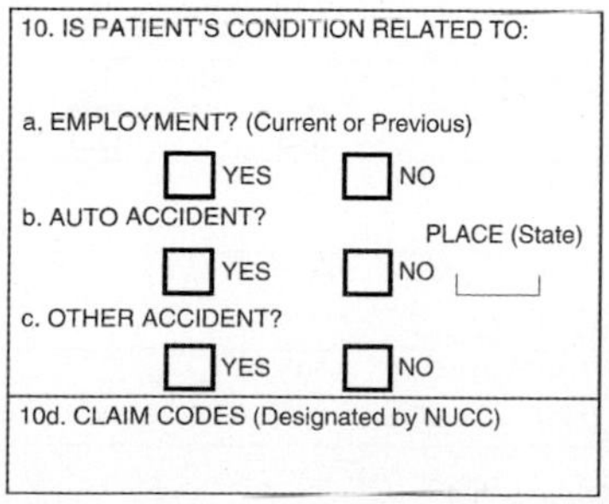

Figure 15-8 CMS-1500 Block 10

Item 10a—Employment (Current or Previous)

In most cases, mark the NO box. YES indicates the services reported in Item 24D are related to an on-the-job injury and the previously filed workers' compensation claim has been rejected. To file a claim with a commercial carrier in these circumstances, a copy of the Workers' Compensation Explanation of Benefits and/or letter indicating rejection of the claim must be attached to the commercial claim. Make sure the "Other" box is marked in Item Number 1 of the claim form.

Item 10b—Auto Accident

Enter in the appropriate box. YES indicates possible third-party liability. The commercial health insurance claim carrier will return the claim until the issue of third-party liability coverage is settled. Make sure the "Other" box is marked in Item 1 of the claim form and the insured information from the auto insurance company is entered in Items 11–11d.

Item 10c—Other Injury

Enter in the appropriate box. YES indicates possible third-party liability and requires the two-character abbreviation of the state of the patient's residence. Enter appropriate ICD-10-CM codes in Item 21 in addition to the code(s) for the type of injury to indicate cause of injury and its place of occurrence. Make sure the "Other" box is marked in Item 1 of the claim form, and the insured information from the auto insurance company is entered in Items 11–11d. Relationship to insured is also marked "Other."

Item 10d—Claims Codes (Designated by NUCC)

Applicable claim codes designated by the NUCC are reported here. It is necessary to refer to the most current instructions from public or private payors regarding the need to report claim codes, if applicable.

Item 11—Insured's Policy Group or FECA Number

See Figure 15–9. Enter the insured's policy or group number as it appears on the insured's health care identification card. Do not use hyphens or spaces to separate within the number. If Item 4 is completed, then this item should also be completed. Item 11a. Item 11b "Other Claim ID (Designated by NUCC)" will contain applicable claim identifiers for claims submitted to property and casualty payors, such as automobile, homeowners, or workers' compensation insurers. For example, a homeowner's claim may be identified with claim identifier Y4, followed by the claim number.

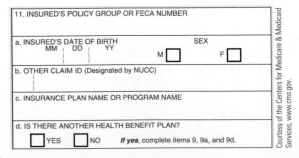

Figure 15-9 CMS-1500 Block 11

Not all workers' compensation policies have FECA numbers. FECA (Federal Employees' Compensation Act) provides workers' compensation coverage to federal and postal workers, including wage replacement and medical and vocational rehabilitation benefits for work-related injury and occupational illness. For example, coal miners afflicted with black lung disease and the federal workers injured in the 1995 Oklahoma City bombing tragedy are covered under FECA.

Item 11c—Insurance Plan Name or Program Name

Enter the primary payor's program or plan name or the nine-digit PAYERID of the primary insurer, if available.

Item 11d—Is There Another Health Benefit Plan?

Enter in the NO box if patient is covered by only one insurance. If YES is marked, complete Items 9, 9a, and 9d to indicate a secondary policy.

Item 12—Authorization for Release of Information

See Figure 15–10. Patient's signature is entered here, or "Signature on file" (SOF), to indicate that an electronic signature is on file. This signature authorizes release of medical information necessary to process the claim.

READ BACK OF FORM BEFORE COMPLETING & SIGNING THIS FORM. 12. PATIENT'S OR AUTHORIZED PERSON'S SIGNATURE I authorize the release of any medical or other information necessary to process this claim. I also request payment of government benefits either to myself or to the party who accepts assignment below. SIGNED ________ DATE ________	13. INSURED'S OR AUTHORIZED PERSON'S SIGNATURE I authorize payment of medical benefits to the undersigned physician or supplier for services described below. SIGNED ________

Courtesy of the Centers for Medicare & Medicaid Services, www.cms.gov.

Figure 15-10 CMS-1500 Blocks 12 and 13

Item 13—Authorization for Payment of Benefits to the Provider

The patient's signature authorizes direct payment to the physician or supplier for the benefits due the patient (Figure 15–10). "Signature on file" (SOF) is acceptable if an assignment statement has been previously signed by the patient or his/her authorized representative and is on file.

Diagnostic and Treatment Data

Item 14—Date of Current Illness, Injury, or Pregnancy (LMP)

See Figure 15–11. Enter date from the patient's medical record, if it is available. In cases where the history does not give the first date but does give an approximation, count back to the approximated date and enter it on the claim form. For pregnancy, the date given is for the last menstrual period (LMP). For injuries or accidents, it is important to enter the date of that accident and/or injury. Dates entered in this Item 14 can be the six-digit or eight-digit date. In addition to the date, there is a field for applicable qualifier: Onset of Current Symptoms or Illness 431; Last Menstrual Period 484.

14. DATE OF CURRENT ILLNESS, INJURY, or PREGNANCY (LMP) MM | DD | YY QUAL.	15. OTHER DATE QUAL. | MM | DD | YY	16. DATES PATIENT UNABLE TO WORK IN CURRENT OCCUPATION FROM MM | DD | YY TO MM | DD | YY

Courtesy of the Centers for Medicare & Medicaid Services, www.cms.gov.

Figure 15-11 CMS-1500 Blocks 14, 15, and 16

EXAMPLE: If today's date is 01/9/2016, and the medical record states "injured 2 months ago," the date entered would be 11/09/2015.

Item 15—Other Date

Other Date identifies additional date information about the patient's condition or treatment, specifically related to the date of the encounter. Enter another date related to the patient's condition or treatment and the applicable qualifier to identify which date is being reported if required by the insurance carrier.

454	Initial Treatment
304	Latest Visit or Consultation
453	Accident
455	Last x-ray
471	Prescription
090	Report Start (Assumed Care Date)
091	Report End (Relinquished Care Date)
444	First Visit or Consultation

Item 16—Dates Patient Unable to Work in Current Occupation

Enter data to indicate the period of time the patient was unable to work, if applicable. An entry in this field may indicate employment-related insurance coverage. Otherwise, leave blank.

Item 17—Name of Referring Provider or Other Source

See Figure 15–12. Enter the name of the referring/ordering physician(s) or other health care provider, if any of the following services are listed in Item 24D:

consultation, surgery, diagnostic testing, physical or occupational therapy, home health care, or durable medical equipment

Courtesy of the Centers for Medicare & Medicaid Services, www.cms.gov.

Figure 15-12 CMS-1500 Blocks 17, 17a, 18, 19, and 20

A referring or ordering provider is a physician or nonphysician practitioner who requests an item or service for the beneficiary, including those listed above or pharmaceutical services. For assistant surgeon claims, enter the name of the attending surgeon. Otherwise, leave blank.

Additional instructions to CMS-1500 form version 02/12: Enter one of the following qualifiers as appropriate to identify the role that this physician (or nonphysician practitioner) is performing:

Qualifier	Provider Role
DN	Referring Provider
DK	Ordering Provider
DQ	Supervising Provider

Enter the qualifier to the left of the dotted vertical line on Item 17.

Item 17a

Leave blank.

Item 17b—NPI of Referring Physician

Enter the referring, ordering, or supervising physician or nonphysician practitioner's named in Item 17, National Provider Identifier (NPI) number. If there is no referring provider, leave blank.

The NPI is a 10-digit unique identification number for covered health care providers required by HIPAA. Covered providers must share their NPI with other providers, health plans, clearinghouses, and any entity that may need it for billing purposes.

Item 18—Hospitalization Dates Related to Current Services

Enter the admission date and the discharge date using six-digit or eight-digit , if any procedure/service is provided to a patient who is admitted for inpatient services (e.g., to a hospital or skilled nursing facility). Otherwise, leave blank.

Item 19—Additional Claim Information (Designated by NUCC)

Information to be entered is determined by public or private payors regarding the use of this field. Consult the appropriate billing manual or payor to determine if any information is required for this item. This area is usually reserved for physical or occupational therapists, chiropractor services, or an unlisted procedure code or a claim for a drug or supplies that are not otherwise classified.

Item 20—Outside Lab

Enter X in the NO box if all laboratory procedures included on this claim form were performed in the provider's office.

Enter X in the YES box if laboratory procedures listed on the claim form were performed by an outside laboratory or entity other than the billing provider and billed to the referring health care provider. If YES is entered, enter the total amount charged (purchase price) for all tests performed by the outside laboratory. The physician's charge to the patient for each test should be entered as a separate line in Item 24F and the name and address of the outside laboratory included in Item 32.

> **Highlight:**
>
> Some local carriers may have other specific instructions for completing Block 20.

Item 21—Diagnosis or Nature of Illness or Injury (Relate A–L to service line below (24E))

Enter the applicable ICD indicator to identify which version of ICD codes is being reported.

9 ICD-9-CM (Used for services rendered until 10/1/15)

0 ICD-10-CM

Enter the ICD-10-CM code(s) for the diagnoses or conditions treated on this claim in this space (Figure 15–13). Twelve codes can be submitted per claim form, listing the primary diagnosis code first, followed by any secondary diagnostic codes. To link the correct ICD-10-CM code with the CPT code in Item 24D, use the diagnosis pointer in Item 24E to indicate the letter of the line. All diagnoses and procedures must be supported by documentation in the medical record. If the patient's encounter at the medical facility has no formal diagnosis, enter the code for the patient's complaints or symptoms.

21. DIAGNOSIS OR NATURE OF ILLNESS OR INJURY Relate A-L to service line below (24E) ICD Ind.	22. RESUBMISSION CODE ORIGINAL REF. NO.
A. |____ B. |____ C. |____ D. |____	
E. |____ F. |____ G. |____ H. |____	23. PRIOR AUTHORIZATION NUMBER
I. |____ J. |____ K. |____ L. |____	

Figure 15-13 CMS-1500 Blocks 21, 22, and 23

The number of indicators in Item 24E can vary by insurance carrier. Many accept only one indicator per service or procedure. Unless there are concurrent conditions related to the encounter, it is recommended to list only one indicator for an illness or injury, procedure, or treatment per claim.

Item 22—Resubmission and/or Original Reference Number

List the original reference number for resubmitted claims. Refer to the most current instructions from the public or private payor regarding the use of this field and any number to indicate a replacement or void/cancel of prior claim. This item is used only for claim resubmissions and not used for original claim submissions.

Item 23—Prior Authorization Number

Enter the assigned prior authorization number, referral number, or Clinical Laboratory Improvement Amendments (CLIA) number when the patient's insurance plan requires specific services to be authorized by the patient's primary physician or the carrier's managed care department before the procedure is performed.

Item 24A—Date(s) of Service

Enter the date the procedure was performed in the "From" and "To" columns (Figure 15–14). If there is only one date of service, enter that date under "From" and leave "To" blank. To list similar procedures with same procedure codes and charges performed on consecutive dates, indicate the last day the procedure was performed in the "To" column. Grouping is allowed only for services on consecutive days. The number of days must correspond to the number of units in 24G. In Item 24G, enter the number of consecutive days or units in the "days/units column." The number of days must correspond to the number of units in 24G. Do not submit charges for services or procedures performed in different years on the same claim form. Doing so may result in deductible and eligibility factors that could result in a pending or rejected claim, therefore delaying payment.

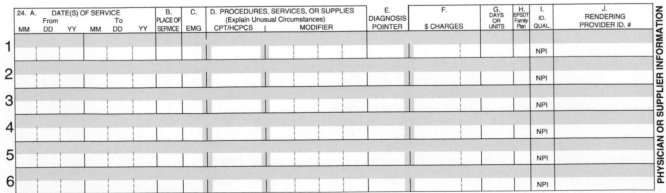

Figure 15-14 CMS-1500 Block 24

Item 24B—Place of Service (POS)

Enter the correct two-digit POS code number from the following list of codes.

Pharmacy	01
Unassigned	02
School (primary purpose is education)	03
Homeless Shelter	04
Indian Health Service Freestanding Facility	05
Indian Health Provider-Based Facility	06
Tribal 638 Freestanding Facility	07
Tribal 638 Provider-Based Facility	08
Prison/Correctional Facility	09
Unassigned	10
Office	11
Home	12
Assisted Living Facility	13
Group Home	14
Mobile Unit	15
Temporary Lodging (hotel, campground, cruise ship, resort)	16
Walk-In Retail Health Clinic	17
Place of Employment/Worksite	18
Unassigned	19
Urgent Care Facility	20
Inpatient Hospital (other than psychiatric)	21
Outpatient Hospital	22
Emergency Room—Hospital	23
Ambulatory Surgical Center	24
Birthing Center	25
Military Treatment Facility	26
Unassigned	27–30
Skilled Nursing Facility	31
Nursing Facility	32
Custodial Care Facility	33
Hospice	34
Unassigned	35–40
Ambulance—Land	41
Ambulance—Air or Water	42
Unassigned	43–48
Independent Clinic	49
Federally Qualified Health Center	50
Inpatient Psychiatric Facility	51
Psychiatric Facility—Partial Hospitalization	52
Community Mental Health Center	53
Intermediate Care Facility/Mentally Retarded	54
Residential Substance Abuse Treatment Facility	55

Psychiatric Residential Treatment Center	56
Nonresidential Substance Abuse Treatment Facility	57
Unassigned	58–59
Mass Immunization Center (roster billing method)	60
Comprehensive Inpatient Rehabilitation Facility	61
Comprehensive Outpatient Rehabilitation Facility	62
Unassigned	63–64
End-Stage Renal Disease Treatment Facility	65
Unassigned	66–70
State or Local Public Health Center	71
Rural Health Center	72
Unassigned	73–80
Independent Laboratory	81
Unassigned	82–98
Other place of service not identified above	99

CMS has updated this list to accommodate new facilities available to render patient care. Go to the Centers for Medicare & Medicaid Services' website https://www.cms.gov, then click on Medicare and Place of Service Codes. This gives a description for each Place of Service Code. Any codes not listed are classified as "unassigned" codes reserved for future use. The CPT manual also contains a complete list of POS codes in the front of the book.

Item 24C—EMG (Emergency Treatment)

Enter X in this box when the health care provider determines that a medical emergency existed and a delay in treatment would be injurious to the patient. This is especially important in a managed care situation if no prior authorization was obtained before the start of emergency treatment.

Item 24D—Procedures, Services, or Supply Codes

Enter the correct five-digit CPT code or HCPCS Level II/III code number and up to four 2-digit modifiers for the procedure being reported in this item. No more than six procedures/services can be listed per claim.

Item 24E—Diagnosis Pointer

Enter the reference number (A through L) for the ICD-10-CM code listed in Item 21 that most closely justifies the medical necessity for each procedure listed in Item 24D. Do not enter ICD-10-CM codes in 24E.

> ### Highlight:
> Some carriers will accept more than one reference number on Item 24e (diagnosis indicator). If more than one reference number is used, the first number stated must represent the primary diagnosis that justifies the medical necessity for performing the procedures on that line. Do not use commas, dashes, or slashes to separate multiple reference numbers.

Item 24F—Charges

Enter the charge for the procedure charged to the patient's account. If identical, consecutive procedures are reported on one line, enter the *total* fee charged for the combined procedures.

Item 24G—Days or Units

Enter the number of days or units of the service reported on each line. This item is most commonly used for multiple visits, such as inpatient hospital visits, units of medications or supplies, anesthesia minutes, or oxygen volume. If only one service is performed, the number 1 should be entered.

Item 24H—EPSDT (Early and Periodic Screening for Diagnosis and Treatment)

Leave blank except for Medicaid claims for services that are provided under the special Medicaid EPSDT program. See the section for Medicaid CMS-1500 instructions later in this chapter.

Item 24I

Enter in the shaded area of 24I the qualifier identifying if the number is a provider who does not have an NPI number. The NUCC defines the following qualifiers used:

0B	State License Number
1G	Provider UPIN Number
G2	Provider Commercial Number
LU	Location Number
ZZ	Provider Taxonomy

The rendering provider is the person or company (laboratory or other facility) who rendered or supervised the care. In the case where a substitute provider (locum tenens) was used, enter that provider's information here. Report the identification number in Items 24I and 24J only when different from information recorded in Items 33a and 33b.

Item 24J

The individual rendering the service is reported in Item 24J. The rendering provider is the person or company (laboratory or other facility) who rendered or supervised the care. In the case where a substitute provider (*locum tenens*) was used, enter that provider's information here. Enter the rendering provider's NPI number in the lower unshaded area. In the case of a service provided incident to the service of a physician or nonphysician practitioner, when the person who ordered the service is not supervising, enter the NPI of the supervisor in the lower unshaded portion.

Provider/Billing Entity Identification

Item 25—Federal Tax ID Number

See Figure 15–15. Every physician, whether in a solo practice or group practice, is issued an individual federal tax identification number referred to as an employer identification number (EIN). The Internal Revenue Service issues this number for income tax purposes. Every physician also has a social security number (SSN) for personal use. Enter the appropriate number and check the appropriate box. Enter the provider's employer identification number (EIN) and mark the appropriate box.

25. FEDERAL TAX I.D. NUMBER	SSN EIN	26. PATIENT'S ACCOUNT NO.	27. ACCEPT ASSIGNMENT? (For govt. claims, see back) ☐ YES ☐ NO	28. TOTAL CHARGE $	29. AMOUNT PAID $	30. Rsvd for NUCC Use
	☐☐					

Courtesy of the Centers for Medicare & Medicaid Services, www.cms.gov.

Figure 15-15 CMS-1500 Blocks 25, 26, 27, 28, 29, and 30

Item 26—Patient Account Number

If a numerical identification is assigned by the provider to identify the patient's account or ledger card, enter that number here. Leave blank if the practice files patient accounts by patient name rather than number.

Item 27—Accept Assignment

Enter an X in the appropriate box. Participating physicians *must* accept assignment. Nonparticipating physicians may accept on a case-by-case basis. When a patient has both Medicare and Medicaid, assignment must be accepted on these claims as defined by participation in the Medicaid program. Accepting assignment means the physician or provider will accept what Medicare pays and not bill the difference between the cost of the service and the Medicare payment. The difference is adjusted or written off.

The following providers or suppliers must file claims accepting assignment:

- Clinical diagnostic laboratory services
- Physician services to Medicare/Medicaid beneficiaries
- Participating physician/supplier services
- Services of physician assistants, nurse practitioners, clinical nurse specialists, nurse midwives, certified registered nurse anesthetists, clinical psychologists, and clinical social workers
- Ambulatory surgical center services for covered procedures
- Home dialysis supplies and equipment
- Ambulance services

Item 28—Total Charge

Add all charges on this claim form and enter the total billed amount in this item. If multiple claims for one patient are completed because more than six services/procedures are reported, the total charge recorded on each claim form must represent the total of the items on the claim form submitted.

Item 29—Amount Paid

Enter the amount the patient has paid toward the required annual deductible, or any copayments collected from the patient for the procedures listed on this claim form, or payment received by other payors.

Item 30—Reserved for NUCC Use

This item was previously used to report the *balance due*. This item has been eliminated in the 02/12 version. NUCC will provide instructions for any future use of this field.

Item 31—Signature of Physician or Supplier

See Figure 15–16. Enter the legal signature of the practitioner or supplier, including degrees or credentials, "Signature on file" or "SOF," and the date signed. More often than not, this will be indicated as an electronic signature on file.

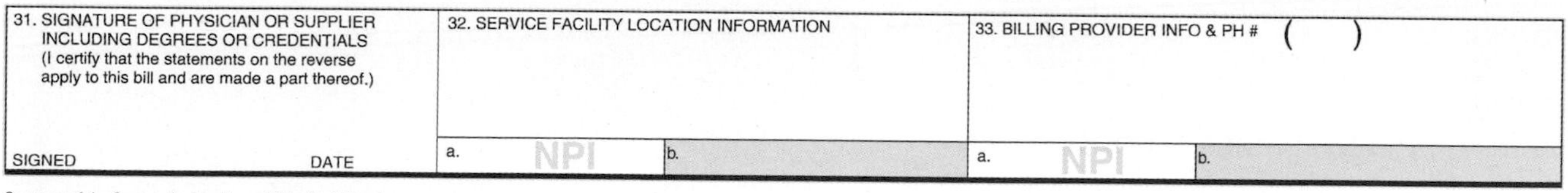

Figure 15-16 CMS-1500 Blocks 31, 32, and 33

Item 32—Service Facility Location Information

Give the name and address of the location where the service was provided—the office, hospital, nursing facility, patient's home, and so forth. If the YES box in Item 20 is checked, enter the name and address of the laboratory that performed the laboratory procedures.

When filing claims for durable medical equipment, orthotic, and prosthetics, enter the name, address, or location where the order was accepted.

When billing for purchased diagnostic tests performed outside the physician's office but billed by the physician, enter the name, address, and NPI of the facility where the test was performed.

Item 32a—NPI Number

Enter the 10-digit NPI number of the provider, facility, or supplier entered in Item 32a.

Item 32b—Service Facility Location Information

Leave blank.

Item 33—Billing Provider Info & Phone

Enter as follows: 1st Line—Name of the practice/clinic

                       2nd Line—Street or physical location

                       3rd Line—City, state, and zip code

Item 33a—NPI Number

Enter the 10-digit NPI of the billing provider in 33a.

Item 33b—Other ID Number

This field is generally not reported unless instructed by payor.

Figure 15–17 is an example of a completed CMS-1500 form.

Common Errors That Delay Claims Processing

After checking the claim form for errors, retain a copy of the claim for office files, post the date of the claim filing on the patient's account/ledger, and mail to the insurance carrier. Some common errors that delay processing of the claim, or result in rejection of the claim, are:

- Incorrect patient insurance identification number

- Incorrect CPT code with failure to use modifier when valid

- Incorrect ICD-10-CM code with failure to use a fourth through seventh character when required

Highlight:

When filing insurance claims for a medical practice, it is critical to obtain and read updated billing manuals, newsletters, and brochures that contain changes as they become effective.

HEALTH INSURANCE CLAIM FORM

APPROVED BY NATIONAL UNIFORM CLAIM COMMITTEE (NUCC) 02/12

PICA			PICA

1. MEDICARE ☐ (Medicare#) MEDICAID ☐ (Medicaid#) TRICARE ☐ (ID#/DoD#) CHAMPVA ☐ (Member ID#) GROUP HEALTH PLAN ☒ (ID#) FECA BLK LUNG ☐ (ID#) OTHER ☐ (ID#)   **1a. INSURED'S I.D. NUMBER** (For Program in Item 1)
RGA403082214

2. PATIENT'S NAME (Last Name, First Name, Middle Initial)
PEARL OPAL J

3. PATIENT'S BIRTH DATE MM 12 DD 24 YY 1968 SEX M ☐ F ☒

4. INSURED'S NAME (Last Name, First Name, Middle Initial)
PEARL BRUCE J

5. PATIENT'S ADDRESS (No., Street)
7775 SMITH RD

6. PATIENT RELATIONSHIP TO INSURED
Self ☐ Spouse ☒ Child ☐ Other ☐

7. INSURED'S ADDRESS (No., Street)
SAME AS PATIENT

CITY SMITHFIELD   STATE IN

8. RESERVED FOR NUCC USE

CITY   STATE

ZIP CODE 47222   TELEPHONE (Include Area Code) (555) 5554773

ZIP CODE   TELEPHONE (Include Area Code) ( )

9. OTHER INSURED'S NAME (Last Name, First Name, Middle Initial)

10. IS PATIENT'S CONDITION RELATED TO:

11. INSURED'S POLICY GROUP OR FECA NUMBER
12390

a. OTHER INSURED'S POLICY OR GROUP NUMBER

a. EMPLOYMENT? (Current or Previous) ☐ YES ☒ NO

a. INSURED'S DATE OF BIRTH MM 07 DD 07 YY 1967 SEX M ☒ F ☐

b. RESERVED FOR NUCC USE

b. AUTO ACCIDENT? ☐ YES ☒ NO PLACE (State)

b. OTHER CLAIM ID (Designated by NUCC)

c. RESERVED FOR NUCC USE

c. OTHER ACCIDENT? ☐ YES ☒ NO

c. INSURANCE PLAN NAME OR PROGRAM NAME
CIGNA

d. INSURANCE PLAN NAME OR PROGRAM NAME

10d. CLAIM CODES (Designated by NUCC)

d. IS THERE ANOTHER HEALTH BENEFIT PLAN? ☐ YES ☒ NO *If yes*, complete items 9, 9a, and 9d.

READ BACK OF FORM BEFORE COMPLETING & SIGNING THIS FORM.
12. PATIENT'S OR AUTHORIZED PERSON'S SIGNATURE I authorize the release of any medical or other information necessary to process this claim. I also request payment of government benefits either to myself or to the party who accepts assignment below.
SIGNED SOF   DATE

13. INSURED'S OR AUTHORIZED PERSON'S SIGNATURE I authorize payment of medical benefits to the undersigned physician or supplier for services described below.
SIGNED SOF

14. DATE OF CURRENT ILLNESS, INJURY, or PREGNANCY (LMP) MM 05 DD 01 YY 20xx QUAL. 431

15. OTHER DATE QUAL. 454 MM 05 DD 01 YY 20XX

16. DATES PATIENT UNABLE TO WORK IN CURRENT OCCUPATION FROM MM DD YY TO MM DD YY

17. NAME OF REFERRING PROVIDER OR OTHER SOURCE
17a.
17b. NPI

18. HOSPITALIZATION DATES RELATED TO CURRENT SERVICES FROM MM DD YY TO MM DD YY

19. ADDITIONAL CLAIM INFORMATION (Designated by NUCC)

20. OUTSIDE LAB? ☐ YES ☐ NO $ CHARGES

21. DIAGNOSIS OR NATURE OF ILLNESS OR INJURY Relate A-L to service line below (24E)   ICD Ind.
A. N39.0   B.   C.   D.
E.   F.   G.   H.
I.   J.   K.   L.

22. RESUBMISSION CODE   ORIGINAL REF. NO.

23. PRIOR AUTHORIZATION NUMBER

24. A. DATE(S) OF SERVICE From MM DD YY	To MM DD YY	B. PLACE OF SERVICE	C. EMG	D. PROCEDURES, SERVICES, OR SUPPLIES (Explain Unusual Circumstances) CPT/HCPCS	MODIFIER	E. DIAGNOSIS POINTER	F. $ CHARGES	G. DAYS OR UNITS	H. EPSDT Family Plan	I. ID. QUAL.	J. RENDERING PROVIDER ID. #
1 05 01 XX		11		99213		1	65 00	1		NPI	0213456789
2 05 01 XX		11		81000		1	32 00	1		NPI	0213456789
3										NPI	
4										NPI	
5										NPI	
6										NPI	

25. FEDERAL TAX I.D. NUMBER 752166173 SSN ☐ EIN ☒

26. PATIENT'S ACCOUNT NO. 9876541

27. ACCEPT ASSIGNMENT? (For govt. claims, see back) ☒ YES ☐ NO

28. TOTAL CHARGE $ 97 00

29. AMOUNT PAID $

30. Rsvd for NUCC Use

31. SIGNATURE OF PHYSICIAN OR SUPPLIER INCLUDING DEGREES OR CREDENTIALS (I certify that the statements on the reverse apply to this bill and are made a part thereof.)
SIGNED SOF   DATE 05/0

32. SERVICE FACILITY LOCATION INFORMATION
HWY 311 STE A31
SELLERSBURG IN 47172
a. 0213456789   b.

33. BILLING PROVIDER INFO & PH # ( )
LOWERY JOHNSON MD
HWY 311 STE A31
SELLERSBURG IN 47172
a. 0213456789   b.

NUCC Instruction Manual available at: www.nucc.org   **PLEASE PRINT OR TYPE**   APPROVED OMB-0938-1197 FORM 1500 (02-12)

Figure 15-17 CMS-1500 completed for a commercial insurance carrier

- ICD-10-CM code does not correspond with the CPT code to validate that the service performed or treatment provided by the physician was medically necessary

- Failure to identify referring physician and NPI

- Incorrect charges or total amounts that do not equal total charges

- Missing Place of Service code; the POS code is required for Medicare, Medicaid, CHAMPVA, TRICARE, and most commercial carriers

- Incorrect, missing, or duplicate dates of service

- Incomplete provider information such as name, address, identification numbers

When the insurance company receives the claim form, the computer first scans the claim form for patient and policy identification to match with subscriber name. CPT codes are checked with services determined to be covered procedures for that policy. CPT codes are crossmatched with ICD-10-CM codes to verify the medical necessity of the claim.

The insurance carrier also checks its common data file to determine if the patient is receiving concurrent care for the same condition by more than one physician.

Charges submitted on the claim form are verified with the allowed charges of the policy. Determination is made of the patient's annual deductible obligation. The **deductible** is the total amount the patient must pay for covered services before insurance benefits are payable. Copayment requirement is then determined. **Copayment** is a specified dollar amount the patient must pay the provider for each visit or service, usually paid at the time the service is rendered. **Coinsurance** is paid by the patient to the health care provider and is a specified percentage of the insurance-determined allowed fee for each service.

Submitted claims can be classified as clean, dirty, pending, rejected, or incomplete. A clean claim is one that contains all information necessary for processing, patient information is complete and current, and the claim is submitted in a timely fashion. A clean claim has no deficiencies and passes all electronic requirements for submission.

A dirty claim is one that is submitted with errors and requires manual processing. Many of these claims result in payment delay and/or rejection. A claim that is pending means it is being reviewed, or additional information is required. A rejected claim is one that has questions and needs additional information, requiring resubmission of the claim by the provider. An incomplete claim is one with missing information and requires correction and resubmission by the provider.

Computer-aided programs are now available to assist providers in the coding and billing process. Claim scrubber software reviews the claim for errors in the claim format as well as coding problems or inconsistencies. Encoder software is primarily used to assign appropriate codes for services and procedures, but it also aids in eliminating unbundling of services and in recognizing appropriate modifiers and CPT/ICD-10-CM agreement for services. Many billing software packages contain a prebilling process that reviews claims electronically or by paper before submission to allow for immediate correction and clean claim submission.

deductible: A specified amount of covered medical expense that must be paid by the insured to a health care provider before benefits will be reimbursed by the insurance company.

copayment: A specified dollar amount a patient or policyholder must pay to the health care provider for each medical service or procedure received, as determined in the insurance contract.

coinsurance: A specified amount of insurance determined for each service the patient must pay the health care provider.

explanation of benefits (EOB): A summary explaining an insurance company's determination for reimbursements of benefits; for Medicare claims, this is referred to as a remittance advice (RA).

The **explanation of benefits (EOB)** is a summary explaining how the insurance company determines its reimbursement, containing the following information:

- A list of all procedures and charges submitted on the claim form
- A list of procedures submitted on the claim form but not covered by the policy
- A list of all allowed charges for each covered procedure
- The amount of the deductible, if any, subtracted from the total allowed charges
- The patient's financial responsibility for the claim, such as the copayment
- The total amount payable on this claim by the insurance company
- Direct payment means the physician receives the insurance check and the EOB Direct payment occurs when:

1. The physician participates with an insurance carrier in a contract agreement.

remittance advice (RA): A summary explaining the insurance company's determination for reimbursement of benefits; also referred to as explanation of benefits.

2. The patient signs the Item 13 authorization of benefits statement on the CMS-1500 claim form to have benefits paid directly to the physician.

3. Item 27 on the CMS-1500 form is marked YES to accept assignment.

An example of a carrier's EOB is shown in Figure 15–18.

Medicare Summary Notice (MSN): A summary explaining Medicare's determination for reimbursement of benefits and other actions on claims (previously called Explanation of Medicare Benefits (EOMB)).

Highlight:

An explanation of benefits (EOB) may also be referred to as a **remittance advice (RA)** by carriers. The Medicare explanation or summary is called a **Medicare Summary Notice (MSN)**. Individual carriers may refer to the EOB as a health care claim summary or other similar terms.

Exercise 15.3

Answer the following questions related to the CMS-1500 claim form.

_____ 1. How many CPT codes can be entered on the claim form?

_____ 2. How many ICD-10-CM codes can be entered on the claim form?

_____ 3. What does POS represent?

_____ 4. Where can a complete list of POS codes be found?

_____ 5. What does the EIN represent?

_____ 6. What does SOF represent?

_____ 7. What is the purpose of Item 10 a–c on the CMS form?

_____ 8. Where are modifiers entered on the CMS form?

_____ 9. Where is the referring provider's NPI entered?

_____ 10. What does EPSDT mean in Item 24H?

HEALTH CARE CLAIM SUMMARY

This summary shows claims processed for the insured of   ALICE BROWN   ID NUMBER   406-7
Any payments shown were made during the period of   JUN 01, 20XX   through JUN 08, 20XX

TOTAL CHARGES PROCESSED	$400.00

TOTAL PAID TO YOU	$.00	TOTAL PAID TO PROVIDER	$360.00

TOTAL AMOUNT NOT PAID	$40.00

This amount is the sum of the LESS DEDUCTIBLE column plus the AMOUNT NOT PAID column

PLEASE REFER TO THE CODES IN THE EXPL COLUMN AND THEIR EXPLANATIONS.

CLAIM NUMBER	PATIENT	PROVIDER (PROV)	TYPE OF SERVICE	SERVICE DATES FROM	TO	TOTAL CHARGES	BASIC PAYS YOU OR PROVIDER	ELIGIBLE CHARGES	MAJOR MEDICAL LESS DEDUCT-IBLE	PAYS YOU OR PROVIDER	AMOUNT NOT PAID
8138064538	SANDRA	GINGER Q MAGUIRE	ANESTHESIA	0403XX	0403XX	400.00		400.00		360.00PROV	40.00
						400.00	.00PROV	400.00	.00	360.00PROV	40.00

IF YOUR BENEFIT SUMMARY INCLUDES CHARGES YOU DON'T RECOGNIZE, IT COULD BE THE RESULT OF A MISHANDLED OR FRAUDULENT CLAIM. PLEASE NOTIFY YOUR CUSTOMER SERVICE REPRESENTATIVE.

EXPLANATION:
872 THIS AMOUNT IS THE COINSURANCE (SHARE) THAT IS YOUR RESPONSIBILITY UNDER YOUR POLICY

THIS IS NOT A BILL

FOR CUSTOMER ASSISTANCE CALL TOLL FREE 1-800-555-1234
SEND WRITTEN INQUIRIES TO: JOHNSON INSURANCE COMPANIES, INC, PO BOX 111 JOHNSONVILLE IN 11111-2345

DEAR INSURED: This summary of claims received on behalf of you and any other persons covered under your policy. We are providing it to you to help you better understand how your coverage is working to protect you.

CONTACT US AT THE PHONE OR ADDRESS SHOWN ABOVE:
IF YOU HAVE MOVED; we will correct your address.
IF YOUR IDENTIFICATION CARD HAS BEEN LOST OR STOLEN; we will replace it.
IF YOU HAVE ANY QUESTIONS ABOUT THIS CLAIM SUMMARY OR YOUR COVERAGE; we will be glad to answer them.

ADDITIONAL REMINDERS:
- WE CANNOT RETURN ANY PAPERS YOU SEND US. If you need to send us this summary or any other papers, please make photocopies beforehand. You may need them for income tax purposes.
- YOU HAVE THE RIGHT TO APPEAL ANY CLAIM WE DON'T PAY OR PAY ONLY IN PART. Mail us a request to review your claim within sixty (60) days of the date you received this summary.

Figure 15-18 Sample of an insurance carrier's explanation of benefits; "The amount not paid is the coinsurance (share) that is your responsibility under your policy."

Medicaid

In 1965, Congress passed Title 19 of the Social Security Act establishing a jointly sponsored federal and state government medical assistance program to provide medical care for persons with incomes below the national poverty level. This assistance program is known as **Medicaid**. Each state administers its own Medicaid program while the Centers for Medicare & Medicaid monitor the state-run programs and establish requirements for service delivery, quality, funding, and eligibility standards. Individual states may have local names for their program, such as Medi-Cal in California and TennCare in Tennessee. Coverage and benefits vary greatly from state

Medicaid: A jointly sponsored federal and state government medical assistance program to provide medical care for persons with incomes below the national poverty level.

to state since each state mandates its own program following federal guidelines. The current qualifications for Medicaid eligibility are as follows:

- Medically indigent low-income individuals and families.

- Aged and disabled persons covered by Supplemental Security Income (SSI) and Qualified Medicare Beneficiaries (QMBs).

- Persons covered by Aid to Families with Dependent Children (AFDC) funds. AFDC covers:

  - Children and qualified family members who meet specific income eligibility requirements

  - Pregnant women who meet the income requirements and would qualify if their babies were already born

  - Other pregnant women not covered by AFDC

  - Persons receiving institutional or other long-term care in nursing and intermediate care facilities

Other programs and benefits sponsored by Medicaid are as follows:

- Early and Periodic Screening, Diagnostic, and Treatment (EPSDT) provides preventive services such as physical examinations, immunizations, dental, vision, and hearing examinations to children under the age of 21 years.

- The State Children's Health Insurance Program (SCHIP) is a federal program that allows states to create or expand existing insurance programs to provide additional federal funding for uninsured children under the age of 19 years that may not otherwise qualify for Medicaid coverage.

- Programs of All-Inclusive Care for the Elderly (PACE) is part of the Medicare program but is an optional service for state Medicaid plans that choose to include this option. It is a capitated payment system to provide a comprehensive package of community-based services as an alternative to institutional care for persons age 55 or older who require a nursing facility level of care. Physicians and other health care providers contract to participate with PACE programs to offer health, medical, and social services to provide preventive, rehabilitative, curative, and supportive care in hospitals, homes, and nursing facilities to assist the patient to maintain independence and improve the quality of life. Patients must be enrolled in PACE to receive benefits offered by the program.

- Medicaid also works with Medicare to serve beneficiaries with low income who qualify for financial assistance. One of these programs is the Qualified Medicare Beneficiary (QMB). Under the QMB program, Medicaid pays the monthly Medicare Part A and Part B premiums, Medicare deductibles, and coinsurances or copayments for the enrolled individual. These recipients must be aged or disabled, qualify for Medicare benefits, have limited financial resources, and have incomes below the federal poverty level.

- Some states now have managed care plans in their Medicaid program. This works much the same way as other managed care plans in which the patient has a primary care physician and must utilize physicians, clinics, and hospitals that participate in the plan.

Many of these plans have a copayment requirement or a share of the cost paid each month for Medicaid eligibility. In some states, this is referred to as spend down or liability.

Typical Medicaid-covered services to those patients classified as medically needy are:

- Inpatient hospital services deemed medically necessary

- Laboratory and x-ray services

- Nursing facility services and home health services for patient entitled to nursing facility services under the individual state's Medicaid plan

- Early and Periodic Screening, Diagnosis, and Treatment (EPSDT) services for children under age 21

- Family planning services and supplies

- Physician services

- Home health aides

- Medical supplies and appliances for home use

- Pregnancy-related services and services for conditions that might complicate pregnancy

- Sixty (60) days postpartum pregnancy-related services

- Medical and surgical services performed by a dentist

- Certified pediatric and family nurse practitioners (allowed to practice under state law)

The patient must present a valid Medicaid identification card on each visit. Eligibility should be confirmed for each visit, since eligibility could fluctuate from month to month. Failure to check eligibility could result in a denial of payment. Preauthorization is required for inpatient hospitalizations and certain other procedures and services as mandated by state and federal law.

Any provider who accepts a Medicaid patient must accept the Medicaid-determined payment as payment in full. It is against the law for a provider to bill a Medicaid patient for Medicaid-covered services. Some states require providers to sign formal Medicaid participation contracts; other states do not require contracts. However, because most Medicaid patients have income below the poverty level, collection of fees for uncovered services is difficult.

Payment to providers from Medicaid is received on several claims at one time. A Medicaid remittance advice is included with payment outlining the current status of claims submitted and payment received, denied, or other payment issues. It is important to review and compare the remittance advice information with claims submitted to properly apply payment and any adjustments necessary to the account and any additional action on the claim.

CMS-1500 is the claim form used in most states to submit a provider's fees. Some states do use a state-developed special optical scanning form. The local Medicaid office can supply this information if there is uncertainty about what claim form to use.

The following instructions are for filing Medicaid claims using the CMS-1500 form only.

> **Highlight:**
> Medicaid is the payor of last resort. If there is other medical coverage or liability, this must be billed first.

Item 1	Enter an X in the Medicaid box.
Item 1a	Enter patient's Medicaid ID number. Do not use hyphens or spaces.
Item 2	Enter patient's name: last name, first name, middle initial with no punctuation as it appears on the Medicaid card.

Item 3	Patient's date of birth (entering eight-digit dates). Enter an X in the correct space to indicate patient's gender.
Item 4	Enter patient's name or leave blank.
Item 5	Enter patient's address and telephone number.
Item 6	Enter an X for "self" or leave blank.
Item 7	Enter address or leave blank.
Item 8	Reserve for NUCC use.
Item 9–9d	Leave blank unless there is additional insurance coverage, such as commercial insurance.
Item 10a–10c	Enter X in the NO boxes. If an X is entered in the YES box for auto accident, enter the two-character state abbreviation of the patient's residence.
Item 10D	Leave blank. If the state administrator contractor requires for Medicaid managed care programs, enter E for emergency or U or urgent care.
Item 11a–d	Leave blank.
Item 12	Leave blank. Patient's signature is not required on Medicaid claims.
Item 13–16	Leave blank.
Item 17	Enter the complete name and credentials of health care professional referring, requesting, ordering, or prescribing, if appropriate. Otherwise, leave blank.
Item 17a	Leave blank.
Item 17b	Enter the 10-digit National Provider Identifier (NPI) of the professional listed in Item 17. Otherwise, leave blank.
Item 18	Enter dates, if appropriate.
Item 19	Leave blank. Reserved for local use as determined by the individual state Medicaid program.
Item 20	Enter an X in the NO box if all laboratory services reported on the claim were performed in the provider's office. An X may be entered in the YES box if services were provided by an outside laboratory. The total amount charged by the outside laboratory must be entered in the charges box.
Item 21	Enter up to 12 ICD-10-CM codes for diagnoses or conditions treated or medically managed related to the encounter.
Item 22	Enter the original claim reference number plus Medicaid code if applicable only if the claim is being resubmitted. Otherwise, leave blank.
Item 23	Enter the Medicaid prior authorization number if applicable. If written authorization was obtained, attach a copy to the claim. Otherwise, leave blank.
Item 24A	Enter the date the service or procedure was rendered in the "To" column. The "From" column is only used if services or procedures of the same CPT code were performed on consecutive days during a range of dates. The number of consecutive dates is entered in Item 24G.
Item 24B	Enter the appropriate Place of Service (POS) code to identify the location where the procedure, service, or encounter was performed.
Item 24C	Enter E if the service or procedure was provided for a medical emergency, regardless of where it was provided. Otherwise, leave blank.
Item 24D	Enter CPT code(s) or HCPCS code(s) and modifiers as appropriate. Up to four modifiers can be listed.

Item 24E	Enter the diagnosis pointer number from Item 21 that relates to the medical necessity for this service on this line.
Item 24F	Enter the charge for each reported procedure or service rendered. When multiple procedures or services are reported on the same line, enter the total fee charged for them.
Item 24G	Enter the number of days or units for procedures or services reported in Item 24D.
Item 24H	Enter E if the service is rendered under the Early and Periodic Screening, Diagnosis, and Treatment program. Enter F if the service is for family planning. Enter B if the service can be both EPSDT and family planning. Otherwise, leave blank, unless indicated by an individual state's Medicaid program.
Item 24I	Leave blank unless specific instructions are provided by the individual state's Medicaid program.
Item 24J	The individual rendering the service or procedure is reported in Item 24J. The rendering provider is the person or company (laboratory or other facility) who rendered or supervised the care. In the case where a substitute provider (locum tenens) was used, enter that provider's information here. Enter the rendering provider's NPI number in the lower unshaded area. In the case of a service provided incident to the service of a physician or nonphysician practitioner, when the person who ordered the service is not supervising, enter the NPI number of the supervisor in the lower unshaded area.
Item 25	Enter provider's social security number (SSN) or employer identification number (EIN). Enter X for the appropriate box for number entered.
Item 26	If applicable, enter the patient account number.
Item 27	Enter X in the YES box to indicate the provider agrees to accept assignment.
Item 28	Enter total charges for services or procedures entered in Item 24.
Item 29	Leave blank.
Item 30	Enter total charges.
Item 31	Enter the provider's name and credential, and date the claim was completed and submitted, or indicate if electronic signature is on file.
Item 32	Enter the name and address, where procedures or services were provided.
Item 32a	Enter the 10-digit NPI of the provider entered in Item 32.
Item 32b	Leave blank.
Item 33	Enter the provider's billing name, address, and phone number.
Item 33a	Enter the 10-digit NPI of the billing provider or group practice.
Item 33b	Leave blank.

Figure 15–19 is an example of a completed CMS-1500 for a Medicaid patient.

The deadline for submitting Medicaid claims varies from state to state. Claims should be filed as soon as possible. With Medicare/Medicaid crossover claims, Medicare guidelines set a deadline of December 31 of the year following the date of service. A **crossover claim** occurs when the Medicare carrier will electronically transfer the information submitted on the Medicare claim form to Medicaid or a Medigap carrier. Medicare will also process the patient's Medicare deductible and coinsurance responsibilities and any information regarding a noncovered service or procedure by Medicare.

crossover claim: An electronic transfer of information submitted on a Medicare claim to Medicaid or the patient's Medigap carrier.

HEALTH INSURANCE CLAIM FORM

APPROVED BY NATIONAL UNIFORM CLAIM COMMITTEE (NUCC) 02/12

PICA								PICA

1. MEDICARE ☐ (Medicare#) MEDICAID ☒ (Medicaid#) TRICARE ☐ (ID#/DoD#) CHAMPVA ☐ (Member ID#) GROUP HEALTH PLAN ☐ (ID#) FECA BLK LUNG ☐ (ID#) OTHER ☐ (ID#)

1a. INSURED'S I.D. NUMBER (For Program in Item 1)
25788530123

2. PATIENT'S NAME (Last Name, First Name, Middle Initial)
JONES BONNIE

3. PATIENT'S BIRTH DATE MM 10 DD 10 YY 1990 SEX M ☐ F ☒

4. INSURED'S NAME (Last Name, First Name, Middle Initial)
SAME AS PATIENT

5. PATIENT'S ADDRESS (No., Street)
7611 MORTON ST

6. PATIENT RELATIONSHIP TO INSURED Self ☐ Spouse ☐ Child ☐ Other ☐

7. INSURED'S ADDRESS (No., Street)
SAME AS PATIENT

CITY TEMPLE STATE IN

8. RESERVED FOR NUCC USE

CITY STATE

ZIP CODE 47555 TELEPHONE (Include Area Code) (555) 5555678

ZIP CODE TELEPHONE (Include Area Code) ( )

9. OTHER INSURED'S NAME (Last Name, First Name, Middle Initial)

10. IS PATIENT'S CONDITION RELATED TO:

11. INSURED'S POLICY GROUP OR FECA NUMBER

a. OTHER INSURED'S POLICY OR GROUP NUMBER

a. EMPLOYMENT? (Current or Previous) ☐ YES ☒ NO

a. INSURED'S DATE OF BIRTH MM DD YY SEX M ☐ F ☐

b. RESERVED FOR NUCC USE

b. AUTO ACCIDENT? ☐ YES ☒ NO PLACE (State)

b. OTHER CLAIM ID (Designated by NUCC)

c. RESERVED FOR NUCC USE

c. OTHER ACCIDENT? ☐ YES ☒ NO

c. INSURANCE PLAN NAME OR PROGRAM NAME

d. INSURANCE PLAN NAME OR PROGRAM NAME

10d. CLAIM CODES (Designated by NUCC)

d. IS THERE ANOTHER HEALTH BENEFIT PLAN? ☐ YES ☒ NO *If yes*, complete items 9, 9a, and 9d.

READ BACK OF FORM BEFORE COMPLETING & SIGNING THIS FORM.
12. PATIENT'S OR AUTHORIZED PERSON'S SIGNATURE I authorize the release of any medical or other information necessary to process this claim. I also request payment of government benefits either to myself or to the party who accepts assignment below.

SIGNED _____ DATE _____

13. INSURED'S OR AUTHORIZED PERSON'S SIGNATURE I authorize payment of medical benefits to the undersigned physician or supplier for services described below.

SIGNED _____

14. DATE OF CURRENT ILLNESS, INJURY, or PREGNANCY (LMP) MM 06 DD 25 YY 20XX QUAL.

15. OTHER DATE QUAL. 454 MM DD YY

16. DATES PATIENT UNABLE TO WORK IN CURRENT OCCUPATION FROM MM DD YY TO MM DD YY

17. NAME OF REFERRING PROVIDER OR OTHER SOURCE 17a. 17b. NPI

18. HOSPITALIZATION DATES RELATED TO CURRENT SERVICES FROM MM DD YY TO MM DD YY

19. ADDITIONAL CLAIM INFORMATION (Designated by NUCC)

20. OUTSIDE LAB? ☐ YES ☐ NO $ CHARGES

21. DIAGNOSIS OR NATURE OF ILLNESS OR INJURY Relate A-L to service line below (24E) ICD Ind.

A. R11.2 B. C. D.
E. F. G. H.
I. J. K. L.

22. RESUBMISSION CODE ORIGINAL REF. NO.

23. PRIOR AUTHORIZATION NUMBER

24. A. DATE(S) OF SERVICE From MM DD YY	To MM DD YY	B. PLACE OF SERVICE	C. EMG	D. PROCEDURES, SERVICES, OR SUPPLIES (Explain Unusual Circumstances) CPT/HCPCS | MODIFIER	E. DIAGNOSIS POINTER	F. $ CHARGES	G. DAYS OR UNITS	H. EPSDT Family Plan	I. ID. QUAL.	J. RENDERING PROVIDER ID. #
1	06 25 XX		11		99212	1	56 00	1		NPI	0213456789
2	06 25 XX		11		96372	1	20 00	1		NPI	0213456789
3	06 25 XX		11		J2550	1	30 00	1		NPI	0213456789
4										NPI	
5										NPI	
6										NPI	

25. FEDERAL TAX I.D. NUMBER 752166173 SSN ☐ EIN ☒

26. PATIENT'S ACCOUNT NO. 15890325

27. ACCEPT ASSIGNMENT? (For govt. claims, see back) ☒ YES ☐ NO

28. TOTAL CHARGE $ 106 00

29. AMOUNT PAID $

30. Rsvd for NUCC Use

31. SIGNATURE OF PHYSICIAN OR SUPPLIER INCLUDING DEGREES OR CREDENTIALS (I certify that the statements on the reverse apply to this bill and are made a part thereof.)

SIGNED _____ DATE _____

32. SERVICE FACILITY LOCATION INFORMATION
HWY 311 STE A31
SELLERSBURG IN 47172
a. 0213456789 b.

33. BILLING PROVIDER INFO & PH # ( )
LOWERY JOHNSON MD
HWY 311 STE A31
SELLERSBURG IN 47172
a. 0213456789 b.

NUCC Instruction Manual available at: www.nucc.org **PLEASE PRINT OR TYPE** APPROVED OMB-0938-1197 FORM 1500 (02-12)

Figure 15-19 Completed CMS-1500 for Medicaid

Medicare

Medicare is a federal health insurance program authorized by Congress and administered by the Centers for Medicare & Medicaid Services (CMS), which select Medicare administrative contractors (MACs) to process Medicare Part A and Part B programs. Created in 1965 as Title 18 of the Social Security Act, it is the largest single medical program in the United States and offers benefits in all 50 states. The Medicare program consists of four parts:

- Medicare Part A: Hospital insurance, which pays for inpatient hospital care, skilled nursing facility stays, hospice care, and some home health care services. Claim form UB-04 is used to report services for reimbursement to Medicare.

- Medicare Part B: Medical insurance, which pays for physician services, outpatient hospital care, durable medical equipment, clinical lab services, and other services not covered by Medicare Part A. Claim form CMS-1500 is used to report services for reimbursement to Medicare.

- Medicare Part C: Medicare Advantage (formerly named Medicare + Choice), which includes managed care and private fee-for-service plans that provide contracted care to Medicare patients. This is an alternative to the original Medicare plan reimbursement under Medicare Part A. CMS-1500 or UB-04 is submitted depending on type of services provided.

- Medicare Part D: Prescription drug plans, which provide prescription drug coverage for a variety of Medicare plans. Medicare beneficiaries must present a Medicare prescription drug card to pharmacies.

Persons eligible for Medicare benefits include:

- People age 65 and over, retired, on Social Security Administration (SSA) benefits, railroad retirement, or civil service retirement

- People who have received Social Security Disability Insurance (SSDI) benefits for two years

- People with end-stage renal disease (ESRD)

Local Social Security Administration offices as well as the online website are available to assist in applying for Medicare benefits. All persons who meet the eligibility requirements receive Medicare Part A benefits (hospital insurance). Medicare Part A covers inpatient, institutional services, hospice, and home health care.

Those persons eligible for full medical benefits may choose to take Medicare Part B (medical insurance) by paying an annual premium to the Social Security Administration or having the premium automatically deducted from the monthly social security check.

As previously discussed in Chapter 14, it is important to always check the patient's insurance card or cards and retain a photocopy in the patient's medical record. This is especially important with a Medicare patient as the card indicates whether the patient has both Medicare Parts A and B, and the effective dates. It will also verify the correct Medicare claim or identification number. A replica of a Medicare card is shown in Figure 15–20.

Medicare: A federal health insurance program for persons over 65 years of age, retired, on social security benefits, receiving social security disability benefits, or end-stage renal disease coverage.

This is the patient's health insurance claim number. It must be shown on all Medicare claims exactly as it is shown on the card—*including the letter at the end.*

This shows hospital insurance coverage.

This shows medical insurance coverage.

The date the insurance starts is shown here.

Figure 15-20 Example of Medicare card, showing patient has Parts A and B

When a husband and wife both have Medicare, they receive separate cards and claim numbers. A patient whose Medicare claim number ends in "A" will have the same social security number and claim number. A patient whose Medicare claim number ends in "B" or "D" will have different social security and Medicare claim numbers.

Table 15–1 designates what some of the letters following a Medicare claim number represent.

Table 15-1 Explanation of Some of the Common Letters Following a Medicare Claim Number

Code	Description
A	Primary claimant (wage earner)
B	Husband's number when wife is 62 years or older
D	Widow, age 60 or older
HA	Disabled claimant (wage earner)
HB	Wife of disabled claimant, age 62 or over
C1–C9	Child, includes minor, student, or disabled child
M	Uninsured—Premium health benefits (Part A)
M1	Uninsured—Qualified for but refused health insurance benefits (Part A)
TA	Medicare Qualified Government Employment (MQGE)
TB	MQGE aged spouse
W	Disabled widow

A distinction from this Medicare format is Railroad Retirement Medicare. This Medicare claim number has one to three letters before the numbers, as shown in Figure 15–21. Railroad retirement beneficiaries have the same benefits and deductibles under Parts A and B as other Medicare recipients.

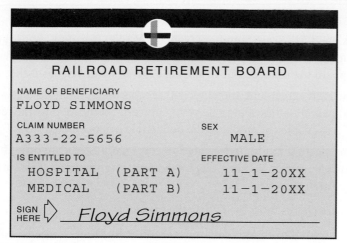

RAILROAD RETIREMENT BOARD

NAME OF BENEFICIARY
FLOYD SIMMONS

CLAIM NUMBER   SEX
A333-22-5656   MALE

IS ENTITLED TO   EFFECTIVE DATE
 HOSPITAL   (PART A)   11-1-20XX
 MEDICAL   (PART B)   11-1-20XX

SIGN
HERE ▷   *Floyd Simmons*

Figure 15-21 Example of a Railroad Medicare card, showing patient
has Parts A and B

Medicare Part A

Medicare Part A is the portion of the Medicare program that reimburses institutional providers for inpatient hospital care, hospice, and some home health services.

Medicare Part B

This chapter will focus on Medicare Part B and the filing of the CMS-1500, which is the part designed to cover such outpatient services as:

- Physician office services
- Physical therapy
- Diagnostic lab testing
- Radiology
- Preventive medical services
- Influenza, pneumonococcal, and hepatitis B vaccines
- Drugs that are not self-administered
- Ambulance services
- Durable medical equipment and supplies used in the home certified by a physician

Today the majority of physicians contract to be a Medicare participating (PAR) provider. Medicare participating providers must accept assignment, meaning they agree to accept Medicare's approved amount for a particular service in full. Incentives to increase the number of health care providers signing PAR agreements include:

- Direct payment of all claims
- Faster processing of claims resulting in quicker reimbursement
- A 5 percent higher fee schedule than nonparticipating providers
- Bonuses provided to Medicare administrative contractors for recruitment and enrollment of PARs

- Publication of an annual directory listing participating providers
- All unassigned Medicare Summary Notices (MSNs) (formerly known as explanation of benefits [EOB] forms) to patients include a message making them aware of the reduced out-of-pocket expenses and savings if they use a PAR

Under the PAR agreement, the physician accepts assignment on all claims, agreeing to 80 percent of the allowable payment from Medicare plus the remaining 20 percent of reasonable charges after the deductible has been met.

Physicians electing not to participate as a contracted Medicare provider (nonparticipating provider or nonPAR) can accept assignment on a claim-by-claim basis, but there are restrictions.

- All Medicare claims must be filed by the provider.
- Fees are restricted to charging no more than the limiting charge on nonassigned claims.
- The beneficiary can be billed up to 15 percent above the Medicare approved amount.
- Collections are restricted to only the deductible and coinsurance due at the time of service on assigned claims.
- NonPARs *must* accept assignment on clinical laboratory charges.
- Patients must sign a Surgical Disclosure Notice for all nonassigned surgical fees over $500.
- Balance *billing* by a nonPAR is forbidden.

Table 15–2 gives an example of a nonPAR fee and payment rate. Table 15–3 is an example of a PAR fee and payment rate.

Table 15-2 Example of NonPAR Fee and Payment Rate

NonPAR limiting fee or charge	$85.00
NonPAR approved rate	$70.00
The difference between limiting fee or charge and nonPAR rate	$15.00
Plus (+) 20% of nonPAR approved rate of $70.00	$14.00
Patient Owes	$29.00

Table 15-3 Example of PAR Fee and Payment Rate

PAR charges usual fee	$100.00
PAR Medicare-allowed rate	$75.00
PAR adjusted difference between the usual charge and approved rate	$25.00
Patient pays PAR 20% of approved rate	$15.00

NonPARs who accept assignment will be reimbursed the Medicare-allowed fee. However, the Medicare payment will only be at the nonPAR approved rate. NonPARs submitting an assigned claim may collect any unpaid deductible and the 20 percent coinsurance determined from the Medicare Physician Fee Schedule (MPFS). If the full fee is collected at the time of service, the assigned status of the claim becomes void and the nonPAR limiting fee is then in effect, and the provider may also be fined for violation of MPFS requirements.

Federal law requires all physicians and suppliers to submit claims to Medicare if they provide a Medicare-covered service to a patient enrolled in Medicare Part B. The CMS-1500 is the form used to submit those claims.

Federal law also mandates accepting assignment on all clinical laboratory charges when the patient has lab services and other medical or surgical services. The nonPAR physician accepts assignment on only the lab services. In such a case, two claim forms will need to be submitted, one for the lab procedures with Item 27 checked YES to accept assignment, and one for other services.

Assignment must be accepted on all services performed by the following providers/practitioners:

- Nurse practitioners
- Certified nurse midwives
- Certified nurse anesthetists
- Anesthesiologist assistants
- Physician assistants
- Clinical psychologists
- Clinical social workers
- Clinical nurse specialists
- Registered dietitians
- Mass immunization roster billers
- Physician lab services
- Ambulance services
- Ambulatory surgical center services
- Clinical diagnostic laboratory services
- Home dialysis supplies and equipment

Medicare is only required to pay for services and supplies that are considered to be reasonable and medically necessary for the diagnosis stated on the claim form. Medicare will not cover procedures considered experimental or still under investigation or being tested. To be considered medically reasonable and necessary, the supply or service must:

- Be consistent with the symptoms or diagnosis of the illness or injury under treatment
- Be necessary and consistent with generally accepted professional medical standards
- Not be furnished primarily for the convenience of the patient, attending physician, or other physician or supplier

Welcome to Medicare Visit

The Medicare Prescription Drug, Improvement, and Modernization Act of 2003 (MMA) expanded Medicare's preventive benefits by offering an initial preventive physical examination (IPPE). This is a once-in-a-lifetime benefit that must be performed within 12 months after the effective date of Medicare Part B coverage for a new beneficiary. The "Welcome to Medicare Visit" is intended to introduce new beneficiaries to important screenings and vaccinations. The health care provider can perform a comprehensive examination consisting of seven components:

1. A review of the patient's medical and social history with attention to risk factors for modification

2. A review of the patient's potential risk factors for depression

3. A review of the patient's functional ability and level of safety

4. A physical examination to include the patient's height, weight, blood pressure, visual acuity, and measurement of body mass index (An electrocardiogram may also be performed and interpreted if deemed appropriate by the provider, based on the individual's medical and social history.)

5. End-of-life planning

6. Education, counseling, and referral based on the results of the review and evaluation services described in the previous five components

7. Education, counseling, and referral, including a brief written plan such as a checklist for obtaining the appropriate screening and/or other Medicare Part B preventive services

HCPCS codes are assigned to bill for the IPPE:

- G0402   Initial preventive physical exam (IPPE), face-to-face visit, services limited to a new beneficiary during the first 12 months of Medicare enrollment

- G0403   Electrocardiogram, routine ECG with 12 leads; performed as a component of the IPPE with interpretation and report

- G0404   Tracing only, without interpretation and report, performed as a component of the IPPE

- G0405   Interpretation and report only, performed as a component of the IPPE

As a provision of the Affordable Care Act, Medicare can now cover an Annual Wellness Visit (AWV), providing Personalized Prevention Plan Services (PPPS) at no cost to the beneficiary. This new benefit provides an ongoing focus on prevention that can be adapted as individual health needs change over time. This service is provided as an initial visit with annual subsequent visits. The Initial AWV (HCPCS code G0438) includes the following key elements to a beneficiary by a health professional:

- Establishment of the beneficiary's medical family history.

- Measurement of height, weight, body mass index, blood pressure, and other routine measurements as deemed appropriate, based on the beneficiary's medical and family history.

- Establishment of a list of current providers and suppliers that are regularly involved in providing medical care to the beneficiary.

- Detection of any cognitive impairment that the beneficiary may have.

- Review of a beneficiary's potential risk factors for depression.

Highlight:

The performance of a screening electrocardiogram (EKG) is determined by the primary care physician as a necessary procedure as part of the IPPE and requires a "G" code from HCPCS, not the CPT code.

Coding Tip:

The appropriate code to submit to Medicare for the IPPE is G0402.

- Review of the beneficiary's functional ability and level of safety, based on direct observation of the beneficiary.

- Establishment of a written screening schedule for the beneficiary, such as a checklist for the next 5 to 10 years.

- Establishment of a list of risk factors and conditions of which primary, secondary, or tertiary interventions are recommended or underway for the beneficiary, including any mental health conditions or any such risk factors or conditions that have been identified through an IPPE, and a list of treatment options and their associated risks and benefits.

- Provision of personalized health advice to the beneficiary and a referral, as appropriate, to health education or preventive counseling services or program aimed at reducing identified risk factors and improving self-management or community-based lifestyle interventions to reduce health risks, and promote self-management and wellness.

The subsequent AWV service performed annually (HCPCS code G0439) includes the following key elements furnished to an eligible beneficiary by a health professional:

- Update the beneficiary's medical/family history.

- Measurement of weight, blood pressure, and other routine measurements as deemed appropriate, based on medical and family history.

- Update the list of current medical providers and suppliers that are regularly involved in providing medical care to the beneficiary, as was developed at the initial AWV.

- Detection of any cognitive impairment that the beneficiary may have.

- Update the written screening schedule, as developed at the initial AWV.

- Update the list of risk factors and conditions for which primary, secondary, or tertiary interventions are recommended or are underway for the beneficiary, as was developed at the initial AWV.

- Furnish appropriate personalized health advice to the beneficiary and a referral, as appropriate, to health education or preventive counseling service or programs.

The Annual Wellness Visit is a preventive wellness visit and not a routine physical checkup. Medicare Part B does not provide coverage for routine physical examinations. Medicare provides coverage for the AWV as a Medicare Part B benefit. There is no coinsurance or copayment and no Medicare Part B deductible for this benefit.

The CMS website (https://www.cms.gov) contains quick-reference information on Medicare's preventive services with a complete listing of the services and appropriate HCPCS/CPT codes to assign as well as specific ICD-10-CM codes if required, especially for screening purposes. This reference list also includes who is covered, the frequency of the service for Medicare coverage, and any copayment/coinsurance or deductible for the beneficiary to pay. There is also a reference sheet outlining the seven IPPE components and what is required in each one, including the recommended preventive screenings.

Advance Beneficiary Notice

An **advance beneficiary notice (ABN)** is a written notice provided to a Medicare beneficiary by a physician, provider, or supplier prior to a medical service or procedure being performed. The ABN indicates that the service or procedure may

advance beneficiary notice (ABN): Notice to health insurance beneficiaries that the program will probably not pay for a service. The patient assumes financial responsibility for paying the provider directly for the service.

not be reimbursed by Medicare, states the reason Medicare denial is anticipated, and requests that the beneficiary sign the form to guarantee personal payment for those services or procedures. When a medical service or procedure is governed by frequency limitations or may possibly be considered not medically necessary, the ABN allows the patient to be financially responsible if Medicare denies payment.

In cases where the provider feels the treatments or services are justified, the options are explained to the patient with an agreement in writing to pay the full cost of the uncovered procedure. This advance beneficiary notice (ABN) agreement is signed by the patient prior to receiving the medical service. This advance notice must state a reason why the physician believes Medicare is likely to deny the claim. The notice must contain accurate information so the patient can make an informed decision on whether or not to receive the service and pay for it without Medicare reimbursement.

An acceptable advance notice as determined by CMS must include the following:

- Date of service

- A narrative of the particular service

- A statement that the physician/supplier believes Medicare is likely to deny payment for the particular service

- An accurate reason why the physician/supplier believes Medicare is likely to deny payment

- The beneficiary's signed and dated agreement to pay, obtained *before* the service is performed

Failure to obtain this advance beneficiary notice for services that Medicare finds are not reasonable and necessary will result in the following:

- Nonparticipating physicians who do not accept assignment must refund to the patient any amounts collected that have been denied by Medicare as not reasonable and necessary.

- The participating physician or nonparticipating physician accepting assignment may be held liable for services considered by Medicare to be not reasonable and necessary. If payment has been collected from the beneficiary for such services, the provider is required to refund the amount collected from the patient within 30 days of receiving Medicare's notice.

An example of a CMS-approved ABN appears in Figure 15–22.

When a service or procedure is never covered by Medicare, the patient can sign a Notice of Exclusion of Medicare Benefits (NEMB) to clearly state to the patient before the service or procedure is provided that the patient will have to pay for it.

Medicare as Primary or Secondary Coverage

Medicare can be primary insurance coverage, a secondary payor, or supplemental policy. It is important to know the Medicare status in order to correctly submit the claim form.

Circumstances under which Medicare may be secondary to other insurance include:

- Group health plan coverage such as the person who continues working after the age of 65

Highlight:

The ABN is signed when the service or procedure is sometimes covered by Medicare, but may not be covered in a particular situation and/or not deemed medically necessary for that patient. It is a required form for billing the patient.

Providers are not required to have a patient sign the Notice of Exclusion of Medicare Benefits (NEMB) for payment for services never covered by Medicare.

A. Notifier:

B. Patient Name: **C. Identification Number:**

Advance Beneficiary Notice of Noncoverage (ABN)

<u>**NOTE:**</u> If Medicare doesn't pay for **D.** _____ below, you may have to pay.

Medicare does not pay for everything, even some care that you or your health care provider have good reason to think you need. We expect Medicare may not pay for the **D.** _____ below.

D.	E. Reason Medicare May Not Pay:	F. Estimated Cost

WHAT YOU NEED TO DO NOW:

- Read this notice, so you can make an informed decision about your care.
- Ask us any questions that you may have after you finish reading.
- Choose an option below about whether to receive the **D.** _____ listed above.
  Note: If you choose Option 1 or 2, we may help you to use any other insurance that you might have, but Medicare cannot require us to do this.

G. OPTIONS: Check only one box. We cannot choose a box for you.

☐ **OPTION 1.** I want the **D.** _____ listed above. You may ask to be paid now, but I also want Medicare billed for an official decision on payment, which is sent to me on a Medicare Summary Notice (MSN). I understand that if Medicare doesn't pay, I am responsible for payment, but **I can appeal to Medicare** by following the directions on the MSN. If Medicare does pay, you will refund any payments I made to you, less co-pays or deductibles.

☐ **OPTION 2.** I want the **D.** _____ listed above, but do not bill Medicare. You may ask to be paid now as I am responsible for payment. **I cannot appeal if Medicare is not billed**.

☐ **OPTION 3.** I don't want the **D.** _____ listed above. I understand with this choice I am **not** responsible for payment, and **I cannot appeal to see if Medicare would pay.**

H. Additional Information:

This notice gives our opinion, not an official Medicare decision. If you have other questions on this notice or Medicare billing, call **1-800-MEDICARE** (1-800-633-4227/**TTY:** 1-877-486-2048).

Signing below means that you have received and understand this notice. You also receive a copy.

I. Signature:	**J. Date:**

According to the Paperwork Reduction Act of 1995, no persons are required to respond to a collection of information unless it displays a valid OMB control number. The valid OMB control number for this information collection is 0938-0566. The time required to complete this information collection is estimated to average 7 minutes per response, including the time to review instructions, search existing data resources, gather the data needed, and complete and review the information collection. If you have comments concerning the accuracy of the time estimate or suggestions for improving this form, please write to: CMS, 7500 Security Boulevard, Attn: PRA Reports Clearance Officer, Baltimore, Maryland 21244-1850.

Form CMS-R-131 (03/11)   Form Approved OMB No. 0938-0566

Courtesy of the Centers for Medicare & Medicaid Services, www.cms.gov.

Figure 15-22 Advance beneficiary notice

- Third-party liability coverage such as automobile accidents

- Work-related illness and injury that falls under workers' compensation, veterans' benefits, or black lung disease

- Disability coverage through an employer-sponsored group health plan

When Medicare is primary, additional insurance is often purchased to supplement the Medicare program by covering the patient's deductible and coinsurance obligations. This additional coverage can be Medigap or Employer Sponsored Medicare Supplemental Plan. A **Medigap** policy is a private, commercial insurance plan with the premiums paid directly by the patient, which is offered to persons entitled to Medicare benefits to supplement those benefits. It is designed to "fill in the gaps" in Medicare coverage by providing payment for some of the charges for which Medicare does not have responsibility due to deductibles, coinsurance amounts, or other Medicare-imposed limitations. These policies must meet federal government standards for Medigap coverage. These claims are handled in one of two ways:

> **Medigap:** A private, commercial insurance plan purchased by a patient as a supplementary plan to Medicare coverage.

1. PAR—Medicare is filed first, then the Medicare carrier can electronically transfer claim information completed in Items 9 and 9D to the Medigap carrier.

2. NonPAR providers are not required to include Medigap information on the claim form, although many offices will file the Medigap claim for the patient. To do this, the patient must provide a copy of the Medicare Summary Notice (MSN) with the Medigap claim.

An employer-sponsored plan is a plan available to employees at the time of their retirement from the company. These plans are not regulated by the federal government but follow the guidelines established in the employer's regular health insurance plan. Premiums are paid to the insurance carrier via the employer. Health care providers are not required to file claims through employer-sponsored retirement plans, although many do, or the patient can file for benefits after the Medicare MSN is received.

The following list outlines step by step how to complete the CMS-1500 for a primary Medicare claim, with a Medigap supplemental policy:

Item 1	Enter X in Medicare box.
Item 1a	Enter Medicare ID number as it appears on the card including alpha suffix for traditional Medicare, alpha prefix for Railroad Medicare.
Item 2	Enter last name, first name, and middle initial as they appear on the Medicare card. Use no punctuation.
Item 3	Enter patient's date of birth using eight-digit dates (e.g., 01/01/1939). Mark appropriate gender of the patient.
Item 4	Enter "Same" or leave blank.
Item 5	Enter patient's address and telephone number.
Item 6	Enter "Self" or leave blank.
Item 7	Enter "Same" or leave blank.
Item 8	Leave blank.
Item 9	Enter last name, first name, middle initial to indicate Medigap or any secondary or supplemental insurance plan *if different* from patient's name in Item 2. If patient and insured are the same, enter "Same," if appropriate.
Item 9a	Enter "Medigap," followed by the policy and/or group number, if appropriate.

Item 9b	Leave blank.
Item 9c	Leave blank.
Item 9d	Enter Medigap plan information if Item 9a is completed for coordination of benefits or a secondary insurance plan.
Items 10a–10c	Enter YES in the appropriate boxes to indicate whether the patient's condition is related to employment, auto, or other accident. If any are checked YES, the third-party liability or workers' compensation would be primary and filed first; Medicare would not process the claim until the provider submits a remittance advice from the liable party.
Item 11	Enter the primary policyholder's group number if the patient is covered by a group health plan.
Item 11a	Enter the primary insurance policyholder's date of birth and gender.
Item 11b	Leave blank.
Item 11c	Enter the name of the primary policyholder's insurance plan. (Be sure to attach or submit a copy of the remittance advice to the claim if the primary insurance is not Medicare.)
Item 11d	Mark YES to indicate a supplemental or Medigap plan.
Item 12	Patient signature required or patient can sign a separate authorization for release of medical information retained in the patient's chart. If authorization is on file, enter "Signature on File," or SOF.
Item 13	Enter "Patient Signature on File" if the patient has a signed Medicare authorization on file. The signature in this field also authorizes payment of mandated Medigap benefits to the participating provider or supplier if required Medigap information is included in Item 9 and its subdivisions. The patient's or authorized representative's signature must be on file as a separate Medigap authorization. The Medigap assignment on file must be insurer specific. It may state that the authorization applies to all occasions of service until it is revoked. The signature on file may be an actual signature or an electronically generated signature.
Item 14	Enter six- or eight-digit date of the beginning of the illness reported on this claim, or date accident or injury occurred, or last menstrual period (LMP) of obstetric patients. Medicare does not require a qualifier in Item 14.
Item 15	Leave blank.
Item 16	If the patient is employed and unable to work in current occupation, enter the six- or eight-digit dates. This entry may indicate employment-related insurance coverage.
Item 17&17b	Enter name of referring, requesting, ordering, or supervising physician, and the National Provider Identifier (NPI) number of this physician. Leave blank if physician provides or performs all services listed. (Item 17a is left blank.)

Enter also one of the following qualifiers as appropriate to identify the role this physician is performing:

Qualifier	Provider Role
DN	Referring Provider
DK	Ordering Provider
DQ	Supervising Provider

The qualifier is entered to the left of the name of the referring provider.

Highlight:

If the secondary insurance information in Items 9, 9a, and 9d is a Medigap policy, these items must be complete and accurate in order to transfer or cross over claim information to the Medigap insurer.

The following list groups provider services, differentiating referring, requesting, ordering, and supervising physician:

Group 1—Physician Services

- Consultation
- Surgery
- Independent diagnostic radiology provider
- Independent diagnostic laboratory provider

All claims for Group 1 providers need the name and NPI number for the referring provider. Both the referring and the ordering physician's name must be included if the consultant personally orders and performs diagnostic testing on a patient.

Group 2—Nonphysician Services

- Physical therapy
- Audiology
- Occupational therapy
- Durable medical equipment (DME)
- Prosthesis
- Orthotic devices
- Parenteral and enteral nutrition
- Immunosuppressive drug claims
- Portable x-ray services

All claims for Group 2 providers need the name and NPI number of the ordering physician.

Group 3—Physician Extender/Limited License Practitioners

- Physician assistants
- Nurse practitioners
- Other limited license practitioners referring patients for consultation services

All claims for Group 3 providers need the name and NPI number for the supervising physician.

Item 18	Enter six- or eight-digit Dates of Admission and Discharge when services relate to hospitalization.
Item 19	Completed as required based on Medicare guidelines. Some examples are: • Enter "Attachment" when a pathology report, operative report, or other attachment is required. • An explanation about an unusual or unlisted service. • Enter a six- or eight-digit date for x-rays taken for chiropractor claims. • CPT code for "Not Otherwise Classified Drug" in Item 24D enter name of the drug.
Item 20	Complete this item when billing for diagnostic tests subject to the anti-markup payment limitation. Enter the acquisition price under charges

if the YES field is checked to indicate that an entity other than the entity billing for the service performed a diagnostic test listed on this claim form. Enter the total amount charged by the outside entity and the outside entity's name, mailing address, and NPI in Item 32.

Enter X in the NO box if all laboratory procedures reported on the claim were performed in the provider's office and did not involve an outside entity.

Item 21	Enter ICD-10-CM codes with primary reason for the encounter as the first-listed code. Up to 12 codes may be entered. The ICD Indicator identifies the ICD code being reported. Enter the applicable ICD indicator according to the following:

Indicator	Code Set
9	ICD-9-CM diagnosis (services provided before October 1, 2015)
0	ICD-10-CM diagnosis (services provided October 1, 2015)

Item 22	Leave blank.
Item 23	Enter Quality Improvement Organization (QIO) prior authorization number if required for procedure requiring QIO prior approval.
Item 24A	Enter six- or eight-digit date of service in "From" column. "To" column is used only if billing for same service, same CPT code, on consecutive days. For consecutive dates, first date of service is in "From" field, last date of service is in "To" field.
Item 24B	Enter appropriate Place of Service (POS) code. (See the list of POS codes in the Item 24 discussion earlier in this chapter or refer to CPT manual.)
Item 24C	Leave blank.
Item 24D	Enter CPT or HCPCS code for the service performed and any appropriate modifier.
Item 24E	Enter the reference number (1 through 12) as the diagnosis pointer for the ICD-10-CM code from Item 21 that best proves medical necessity for this service.
Item 24F	Enter the amount charged for service or procedure reported. For consecutive services reported on one line, enter the charge for a single service, and indicate the number of units in 24G.
Item 24G	Enter number of units reported on this line. If only one procedure or service is reported, enter 1. This field is most commonly used for multiple visits, units of supplies, anesthesia minutes, or oxygen volume.
Item 24H	Leave blank (reserved for Medicaid claims).
Item 24I	Enter the ID Qualifier in the shaded portion.
Item 24J	Enter the 10-digit NPI number in the lower unshaded portion.
Item 25	Enter physician's federal tax employer ID number, marking the "EIN" box, or social security number (no hyphens or spaces).
Item 26	Enter the patient's account number assigned by the provider.
Item 27	Mark YES to indicate the provider agrees to accept assignment. Otherwise, mark NO.

YES must be marked for all PAR claims. NonPARs may mark either box. Assignment *must* be accepted on the following claims:

- Medicare/Medicaid crossover claims

- All clinical diagnostic laboratory services
- Services performed by physician assistants, nurse practitioners, midwives, nurse anesthesiologists, clinical psychologists, and social workers
- Ambulatory surgical center services for covered ASC procedures
- Home dialysis supplies and equipment
- Ambulance services
- Drugs and biologicals

Item 28	Enter total charges submitted on this claim.
Item 29	Enter payments made by patient or another payor for covered services reported on this claim. Otherwise, leave blank.
Item 30	Leave blank.
Item 31	Enter provider's name and credentials, either signature or signature stamp, and date claim was prepared.
Item 32	Enter the name and address of the facility where services were performed. This could be the patient's home, a physician's office, a hospital, an outside laboratory facility, a skilled nursing facility, or a DMEPOS supplier.
Item 32b	Enter the 10-digit NPI of the provider entered in Item 32.
Item 33	Enter the provider's billing name, address, and phone number.
Block 33a	Enter the 10-digit NPI of the billing provider or supplier.

Clarification of EIN, NPI, and PAYERID

An employer identification number (EIN) is assigned by the Internal Revenue Services to each individual physician for income tax purposes (Item 25 of CMS-1500).

A social security number (SSN) is issued to each physician and is entered in Item 25 if the physician is new to the practice/facility and has not yet received the tax identification number.

National Provider Identifier (NPI): A 10-digit number assigned by CMS to identify the provider of service on the CMS-1500 claim form. This number is used to standardize and simplify the use of provider identification to detect and trace fraudulent and abusive submission of claim forms.

NPI is the **National Provider Identifier**, assigned by CMS as an identification number for Medicare claim forms, bills, and correspondence. The NPI is a 10-digit number to identify the provider with a two-digit location identifier. The objective of the NPI number is to develop a uniform system to standardize and simplify the use of provider identification. It assists in detecting and tracing fraudulent and abusive submission of claim forms. When using the NPI, it is entered in Items 17b, 24J, 32a, and 33a.

PAYERID is the payor identification number assigned to identify all third-party payors of health care claims.

Figure 15–23 shows a completed claim form for a patient with Medicare Part B and Medigap coverage.

Medicare/Medicaid (Medi-Medi)

Medicare patients whose incomes are below the federal poverty level are also eligible for Medicaid, referred to as Medi-Medi. When a patient has both Medicare and Medicaid, the claim can be filed by "crossover" method. This means once the billing office has submitted the claim to Medicare, Medicare will automatically electronically

HEALTH INSURANCE CLAIM FORM

APPROVED BY NATIONAL UNIFORM CLAIM COMMITTEE (NUCC) 02/12

CARRIER →

| 2 | PICA | | | | | | | | | PICA | |

| 1. MEDICARE ☒ (Medicare#) | MEDICAID ☐ (Medicaid#) | TRICARE ☐ (ID#/DoD#) | CHAMPVA ☐ (Member ID#) | GROUP HEALTH PLAN ☐ (ID#) | FECA BLK LUNG ☐ (ID#) | OTHER ☐ (ID#) | 1a. INSURED'S I.D. NUMBER (For Program in Item 1) 322758721B |

2. PATIENT'S NAME (Last Name, First Name, Middle Initial)	3. PATIENT'S BIRTH DATE	SEX	4. INSURED'S NAME (Last Name, First Name, Middle Initial)
SANDERS ELIZABETH D	MM DD YY	M ☐ F ☒	SAME AS PATIENT

5. PATIENT'S ADDRESS (No., Street)	6. PATIENT RELATIONSHIP TO INSURED	7. INSURED'S ADDRESS (No., Street)
8900 TIN ROOF CT	Self ☐ Spouse ☐ Child ☐ Other ☐	SAME AS PATIENT

CITY	STATE	8. RESERVED FOR NUCC USE	CITY	STATE
SELLERSBURG	IN			

ZIP CODE	TELEPHONE (Include Area Code)	ZIP CODE	TELEPHONE (Include Area Code)
47172	(555) 7521111		( )

9. OTHER INSURED'S NAME (Last Name, First Name, Middle Initial)	10. IS PATIENT'S CONDITION RELATED TO:	11. INSURED'S POLICY GROUP OR FECA NUMBER

| a. OTHER INSURED'S POLICY OR GROUP NUMBER MEDIGAP 23110 | a. EMPLOYMENT? (Current or Previous) ☐ YES ☒ NO | a. INSURED'S DATE OF BIRTH MM DD YY SEX M ☐ F ☐ |

| b. RESERVED FOR NUCC USE | b. AUTO ACCIDENT? ☐ YES ☒ NO PLACE (State) | b. OTHER CLAIM ID (Designated by NUCC) |

| c. RESERVED FOR NUCC USE | c. OTHER ACCIDENT? ☐ YES ☒ NO | c. INSURANCE PLAN NAME OR PROGRAM NAME |

| d. INSURANCE PLAN NAME OR PROGRAM NAME UNITED HEALTHCARE | 10d. CLAIM CODES (Designated by NUCC) | d. IS THERE ANOTHER HEALTH BENEFIT PLAN? ☒ YES ☐ NO If yes, complete items 9, 9a, and 9d. |

READ BACK OF FORM BEFORE COMPLETING & SIGNING THIS FORM.

12. PATIENT'S OR AUTHORIZED PERSON'S SIGNATURE I authorize the release of any medical or other information necessary to process this claim. I also request payment of government benefits either to myself or to the party who accepts assignment below.

SIGNED **SOF** DATE _____

13. INSURED'S OR AUTHORIZED PERSON'S SIGNATURE I authorize payment of medical benefits to the undersigned physician or supplier for services described below.

SIGNED **SOF**

PATIENT AND INSURED INFORMATION →

14. DATE OF CURRENT ILLNESS, INJURY, or PREGNANCY (LMP) MM DD YY 06 18 20XX QUAL. 304	15. OTHER DATE QUAL. MM DD YY	16. DATES PATIENT UNABLE TO WORK IN CURRENT OCCUPATION MM DD YY MM DD YY FROM TO

| 17. NAME OF REFERRING PROVIDER OR OTHER SOURCE THOMAS DUDLEY MD | 17a. 17b. NPI 5662090100 | 18. HOSPITALIZATION DATES RELATED TO CURRENT SERVICES MM DD YY MM DD YY FROM TO |

| 19. ADDITIONAL CLAIM INFORMATION (Designated by NUCC) | 20. OUTSIDE LAB? ☐ YES ☐ NO $ CHARGES |

| 21. DIAGNOSIS OR NATURE OF ILLNESS OR INJURY Relate A-L to service line below (24E) ICD Ind. A. M75.51 B. C. D. E. F. G. H. I. J. K. L. | 22. RESUBMISSION CODE ORIGINAL REF. NO. 23. PRIOR AUTHORIZATION NUMBER |

24. A. DATE(S) OF SERVICE		B. PLACE OF SERVICE	C. EMG	D. PROCEDURES, SERVICES, OR SUPPLIES (Explain Unusual Circumstances)		E. DIAGNOSIS POINTER	F. $ CHARGES	G. DAYS OR UNITS	H. EPSDT Family Plan	I. ID. QUAL.	J. RENDERING PROVIDER ID. #
From MM DD YY	To MM DD YY			CPT/HCPCS	MODIFIER						
1 06 18 XX		11		99212		1	160 00	1		NPI	0112566213
2										NPI	
3										NPI	
4										NPI	
5										NPI	
6										NPI	

25. FEDERAL TAX I.D. NUMBER SSN EIN 752166173 ☐ ☒	26. PATIENT'S ACCOUNT NO. 52809203	27. ACCEPT ASSIGNMENT? (For govt. claims, see back) ☒ YES ☐ NO	28. TOTAL CHARGE $ 380 00	29. AMOUNT PAID $	30. Rsvd for NUCC Use

| 31. SIGNATURE OF PHYSICIAN OR SUPPLIER INCLUDING DEGREES OR CREDENTIALS (I certify that the statements on the reverse apply to this bill and are made a part thereof.) SIGNED DATE | 32. SERVICE FACILITY LOCATION INFORMATION 40111 S FIFTH ST SMITHFIELD IN 47222 a. 0112566213 b. | 33. BILLING PROVIDER INFO & PH # ( ) DANTE CARROLL MD 40111 S FIFTH ST SMITHFIELD IN 47222 a. 0112566213 b. |

NUCC Instruction Manual available at: www.nucc.org   **PLEASE PRINT OR TYPE**   APPROVED OMB-0938-1197 FORM 1500 (02-12)

PHYSICIAN OR SUPPLIER INFORMATION →

Figure 15-23 Completed CMS-1500 for Medicare-Medigap claim

transfer the Medicare claim and payment information to Medicaid for payment of any service that is covered by Medicaid but not Medicare.

It is important to remember that assignment must be accepted on Medi-Medi claims. Medicare payment should be received by the billing office two to four weeks after the Medicare payment has been received with Medicaid payment to follow. If assignment is not taken, both Medicare and Medicaid payments may be sent to the patient, and a collection problem could exist due to state policy of not billing the patient for covered services.

A completed CMS-1500 for Medicare-Medicaid services is shown in Figure 15–24. Note in Item 27, assignment *must* be accepted by marking the YES box.

Extra-coverage plans are insurance plans that cover a specific disease or special hospital indemnity policies. The specified disease plans pay only upon documentation and physician certification of the disease, such as cancer or AIDS. Special hospital indemnity plans are advertised as policies paying a specified amount for every day the patient is hospitalized. Payment for these claims is made directly to the patient and is not reportable to Medicare or any other primary health insurance plan.

Medicare as Secondary Payor

Medicare is a secondary payor when the patient is eligible for Medicare and also covered by one or more of the following plans:

- An employer-sponsored group health plan with more than 20 covered employees

- Disability coverage through an employer-sponsored group health plan with more than 100 covered employees

- A third-party liability policy if treatment is for an injury covered by automobile insurance and self-insured liability plans

- Workers' compensation injury or illness

- End-stage renal disease covered by an employer-sponsored group health plan of any size during the first 18 months of the patient's eligibility for Medicare

- A Veterans Affairs (VA) preauthorized service for a beneficiary eligible for both VA benefits and Medicare

- Black lung disease

All primary plans are filed first. Medicare is filed after the explanation of benefits from the primary plan has been received. A copy of the EOB or remittance advice must be copied or scanned to attach to the Medicare claim when submitted. Providers are not required to file Medicare secondary claims unless the patient specifically requests it.

For clarification purposes of primary and secondary plans, when a Medicare patient is seen in the medical office, a Medicare secondary payor form can also be completed by the Medicare beneficiary. An example of this form is shown in Figure 15–25.

The deadline for filing Medicare claims is December 31 of the year following the date of service. However, all claims should be filed promptly to avoid potential problems with billing and collections.

HEALTH INSURANCE CLAIM FORM

APPROVED BY NATIONAL UNIFORM CLAIM COMMITTEE (NUCC) 02/12

| 2 | PICA | | | | | | | | PICA |

1. MEDICARE	MEDICAID	TRICARE	CHAMPVA	GROUP HEALTH PLAN	FECA BLK LUNG	OTHER	1a. INSURED'S I.D. NUMBER	(For Program in Item 1)
☒ (Medicare#)	☐ (Medicaid#)	☐ (ID#/DoD#)	☐ (Member ID#)	☐ (ID#)	☐ (ID#)	☐ (ID#)	234052713A	

2. PATIENT'S NAME (Last Name, First Name, Middle Initial)
DOMAIN PETER R

3. PATIENT'S BIRTH DATE MM 03 DD 05 YY 1930   SEX M ☒   F ☐

4. INSURED'S NAME (Last Name, First Name, Middle Initial)
SAME AS PATIENT

5. PATIENT'S ADDRESS (No., Street)
75 LINCOLN TR

6. PATIENT RELATIONSHIP TO INSURED
Self ☒   Spouse ☐   Child ☐   Other ☐

7. INSURED'S ADDRESS (No., Street)
SAME AS PATIENT

CITY SMITHFIELD   STATE IN

8. RESERVED FOR NUCC USE

CITY   STATE

ZIP CODE 47222   TELEPHONE (Include Area Code) (555) 7361856

ZIP CODE   TELEPHONE (Include Area Code) ( )

9. OTHER INSURED'S NAME (Last Name, First Name, Middle Initial)
SAME AS PATIENT

10. IS PATIENT'S CONDITION RELATED TO:

11. INSURED'S POLICY GROUP OR FECA NUMBER

a. OTHER INSURED'S POLICY OR GROUP NUMBER
10234052713

a. EMPLOYMENT? (Current or Previous)
☐ YES   ☒ NO

a. INSURED'S DATE OF BIRTH MM DD YY   SEX M ☐   F ☐

b. RESERVED FOR NUCC USE

b. AUTO ACCIDENT?   PLACE (State)
☐ YES   ☒ NO

b. OTHER CLAIM ID (Designated by NUCC)

c. RESERVED FOR NUCC USE

c. OTHER ACCIDENT?
☐ YES   ☒ NO

c. INSURANCE PLAN NAME OR PROGRAM NAME

d. INSURANCE PLAN NAME OR PROGRAM NAME
MEDICAID

10d. CLAIM CODES (Designated by NUCC)

d. IS THERE ANOTHER HEALTH BENEFIT PLAN?
☒ YES   ☐ NO   *If yes*, complete items 9, 9a, and 9d.

READ BACK OF FORM BEFORE COMPLETING & SIGNING THIS FORM.

12. PATIENT'S OR AUTHORIZED PERSON'S SIGNATURE I authorize the release of any medical or other information necessary to process this claim. I also request payment of government benefits either to myself or to the party who accepts assignment below.

SIGNED SOF   DATE

13. INSURED'S OR AUTHORIZED PERSON'S SIGNATURE I authorize payment of medical benefits to the undersigned physician or supplier for services described below.

SIGNED SOF

14. DATE OF CURRENT ILLNESS, INJURY, or PREGNANCY (LMP) MM 03 DD 11 YY 20XX QUAL. 434	15. OTHER DATE QUAL. MM DD YY	16. DATES PATIENT UNABLE TO WORK IN CURRENT OCCUPATION FROM MM DD YY TO MM DD YY

17. NAME OF REFERRING PROVIDER OR OTHER SOURCE
17a.
17b. NPI

18. HOSPITALIZATION DATES RELATED TO CURRENT SERVICES
FROM MM 03 DD 11 YY 20XX   TO MM 03 DD 15 YY 20XX

19. ADDITIONAL CLAIM INFORMATION (Designated by NUCC)

20. OUTSIDE LAB?   ☐ YES   ☐ NO $ CHARGES

21. DIAGNOSIS OR NATURE OF ILLNESS OR INJURY Relate A-L to service line below (24E)   ICD Ind.
A. I48.91   B. I50.9   C.   D.
E.   F.   G.   H.
I.   J.   K.   L.

22. RESUBMISSION CODE   ORIGINAL REF. NO.

23. PRIOR AUTHORIZATION NUMBER

24. A. DATE(S) OF SERVICE From MM DD YY	To MM DD YY	B. PLACE OF SERVICE	C. EMG	D. PROCEDURES, SERVICES, OR SUPPLIES (Explain Unusual Circumstances) CPT/HCPCS	MODIFIER	E. DIAGNOSIS POINTER	F. $ CHARGES	G. DAYS OR UNITS	H. EPSDT Family Plan	I. ID. QUAL.	J. RENDERING PROVIDER ID. #
1	03 11 XX		21		99222		1	210 00	1		NPI	0213456789
2	03 12 XX	03 14 XX	21		99232		12	196 00	2		NPI	0213456789
3	03 15 XX				99238		12	185 00	1		NPI	0213456789
4											NPI	
5											NPI	
6											NPI	

25. FEDERAL TAX I.D. NUMBER   SSN ☐ EIN ☒
752166173

26. PATIENT'S ACCOUNT NO.

27. ACCEPT ASSIGNMENT? (For govt. claims, see back)   ☒ YES   ☐ NO

28. TOTAL CHARGE $ 591 00

29. AMOUNT PAID $

30. Rsvd for NUCC Use

31. SIGNATURE OF PHYSICIAN OR SUPPLIER INCLUDING DEGREES OR CREDENTIALS (I certify that the statements on the reverse apply to this bill and are made a part thereof.)

SIGNED   DATE

32. SERVICE FACILITY LOCATION INFORMATION
DOGWOOD COMMUNITY HOSPITAL
8080 FIFTH AVE
TEMPLE IN 47555

a. 9246803690   b.

33. BILLING PROVIDER INFO & PH # ( )
LOWERY JOHNSON MD
HWY 311 STE A31
SELLERSBURG IN 47172

a. 0213456789   b.

NUCC Instruction Manual available at: www.nucc.org   **PLEASE PRINT OR TYPE**   APPROVED OMB-0938-1197 FORM 1500 (02-12)

Figure 15-24 Completed CMS-1500 for Medicare-Medicaid (Medi-Medi) claim

Current Procedural Terminology © 2015 American Medical Association. All Rights Reserved.

Practon Medical Group, Inc.
4567 Broad Avenue
Woodland Hills, IN 12345
Telephone 013-486-9002

LIFETIME BENEFICIARY CLAIM AUTHORIZATION AND INFORMATION RELEASE

Patient's
Name___Busaba McDermott___Medicare I.D. Number_329-98-6745_

I request that payment of authorized Medicare benefits be made either to me or on my behalf to (name of physician/supplier) for any services furnished me by that physician/supplier. I authorize any holder of medical information about me to release to the Centers for Medicare and Medicaid Services and its agents any information needed to determine these benefits or the benefits payable to related services.

I understand my signature requests that payment be made and authorizes release of medical information necessary to pay the claim. If other health insurance is indicated in Item 9 of the CMS-1500 claim form or elsewhere on other approved claim forms or electronically submitted claims, my signature authorizes releasing of the information to the insurer or agency shown. In Medicare assigned cases, the physician or supplier agrees to accept the charge determination of the Medicare carrier as the full charge, and the patient is responsible only for the deductible, coinsurance, and noncovered services. Coinsurance and the deductible are based upon the charge determination of the Medicare carrier.

Busaba McDermott   May 15, 20XX
Patient's Signature   Date

Figure 15-25 Medicare special authorization and assignment form

Submitting a Claim for a Deceased Patient

To submit a claim for a patient who has died, the following rules apply:

1. Participating physician—Assignment is accepted in Item 27 of the CMS-1500. In Item 12, any previous signature on file is now invalid. Enter the statement "Patient died on (date)."

2. Nonparticipating physician—Assignment may be accepted as above. If the physician does not accept assignment, the following must be submitted:

   a. The person representing the estate of the deceased or the person responsible for the bill signs Item 12 of the CMS-1500.

   b. Include the name and address of the responsible party or the person representing the estate.

   c. Item 27 of the CMS-1500 is marked NO.

A facility or provider not familiar with the deceased patient or unsure of the responsible party or a representative of the estate can contact the probate court in the county clerk's office for verification of an estate to be probated.

Any balance remaining on the account of the deceased patient will remain open until the estate is settled. If any portion of the bill has previously been paid by the patient's family, this person must complete a CMS-1660 form for reimbursement. This form can be obtained from the CMS website.

Health Maintenance Organizations (HMOs)

Many physicians today are enrolled as participating physicians in health maintenance organizations, more commonly referred to as HMOs.

The term *managed care* is derived from the HMO concept of medical care. They manage, negotiate, and contract for health care at the same time, keeping health care costs down. The goal of HMOs is to promote wellness and preventive medical care, covering the cost of annual examinations, routine x-rays, laboratory procedures, Pap smears, and mammograms. This encourages patients to undergo routine annual checkups, which can save costs by diagnosing medical problems before they become critical, therefore helping to lower medical costs.

To participate in an HMO plan, members and dependents must enroll in the plan. Most HMOs charge their members a copayment (specified dollar amount) for office visits, emergency room visits, and other services. Most insurance cards for HMO patients indicate these copay amounts on the card. The patient is responsible for this fee and it should be collected at the time of the visit. If it is not paid, the patient is billed directly for the copay amount. Physicians participating in an HMO are listed in a directory published by the HMO that is available to its members. The member chooses a physician from the list as a primary care physician (PCP), also referred to as a gatekeeper, to manage the health care of the member. This management requires the patient to contact the PCP for referrals to hospitals, emergency rooms, and specialists.

The following example illustrates how the PCP manages the health care of an HMO patient.

> **EXAMPLE:** A patient makes an appointment with the primary care physician to discuss symptoms possibly related to allergies: headaches, nasal drainage, cough. Oral medications alleviate the symptoms but side effects from the medications occur: daytime drowsiness, insomnia at night, and dry mouth. The PCP refers the patient to an allergist for consultation and allergy testing. The referral form states how many visits may be required (consultation, allergy testing, and allergy vaccine if indicated).

Prior authorization or preapproval is required by HMOs for hospital admissions and surgeries.

TRICARE and CHAMPVA

TRICARE and **CHAMPVA** are federal government programs that provide health care benefits to families of personnel currently serving in the uniformed services, retired military personnel, and veterans of the armed forces. A veteran is defined as a person who has served in the armed forces and is no longer in the service after receiving an honorable discharge.

TRICARE: Health care program for active duty members of the military and their dependents (previously known as CHAMPUS).

CHAMPVA: Health care program for dependents of disabled veterans or those who died as a result of conditions related to their armed service.

TRICARE (formerly named CHAMPUS) is a health benefits program for active duty members (referred to as sponsors) of the uniformed services and their families, retirees and their families, and survivors of all uniformed services who are not eligible for Medicare. Active duty and retired members include Army, Marine Corps, Air Force, Navy, Coast Guard, National Oceanic and Atmospheric Administration (NOAA), and Public Health Service.

- Spouse and unmarried children up to age 21 (age 23 if a full-time student) of military members who are on active duty in the uniformed services as noted above

- Disabled children over age 21

- Military retirees and eligible family members

- Spouse and unmarried children of deceased, active, or retired service members as long as the spouse has not remarried

- Former spouses of military personnel who meet length-of-marriage criteria and other requirements

- Outpatient services for spouse and children of North Atlantic Treaty Organization (NATO) nation representative

- Beneficiaries that are disabled and less than 65 years of age who have Medicare Parts A and B

- Spouses, former spouses, or dependent children of military personnel if the family member has been physically or emotionally abused and the former military member has been found guilty and discharged for the offense

Individuals not eligible for TRICARE are:

- CHAMPVA beneficiaries

- Those eligible for Medicare age 65 and over not enrolled in Medicare Part B

- Military personnel parents

- Those eligible for medical care and treatment at a military facility or from a civilian provider

Those serving in active duty in the military services and those dependents eligible for TRICARE mainly receive health care services from a military treatment facility or hospital. When the service is not available at such a facility, a nonavailability statement (NAS) is required for the following:

- Nonemergency inpatient services

- Transfer of a beneficiary to another hospital

- Maternity care (valid from entry into the prenatal program until 42 days postpartum)

- Referral to a civilian provider for care not available at a military facility

An NAS certification is valid for 30 days and could result in nonpayment for medical services if not obtained. No advance authorization is required in an emergency.

TRICARE defines a medical emergency as a "sudden and unexpected onset of a medical condition, or the acute worsening of a chronic condition, that is treating of life, limb or sight, and which required immediate medical treatment or which required treatment to relieve suffering from painful symptoms. Pregnancy-related medical emergencies must involve a sudden and unexpected medical complication that puts the mother, the baby, or both at risk." Emergency care is usually obtained at a hospital emergency department.

TRICARE's definition of an urgent medical problem is "an immediate illness or injury for which treatment is medically necessary but which would not result in disability or death if left untreated." Preauthorization is required for treatment by a civilian medical facility or provider for urgent medical problems.

The Defense Enrollment Eligibility Reporting System (DEERS) is a computerized database that providers can use to check eligibility of a TRICARE patient. TRICARE provides three choices of health care benefits:

1. TRICARE Prime operates as a managed care program of a full-service health maintenance organization (HMO) with a point-of-service option. Benefits go beyond the Extra and Standard plans to provide additional coverage for preventive and primary care services, such as immunizations and physical examinations. Military treatment facilities are the principal source of health care under this option.

2. TRICARE Extra is a network of physicians operating as a preferred provider organization (PPO).

3. TRICARE Standard is the fee-for-service cost-sharing option available to all beneficiaries seeking care from a military treatment facility or civilian provider or facility.

TRICARE does utilize a network of physicians and participating physicians. These providers file claims and are reimbursed directly from TRICARE. Some plans require copays, coinsurance, and deductibles.

An authorized provider is a physician, hospital, or other health care provider approved by TRICARE to provide medical care and supplies. These providers can be medical doctors, dentists, podiatrists, psychologists, doctors of osteopathic medicine, or optometrists. Nonphysician providers approved are nurses, audiologists, speech and physical therapists, physician assistants, nurse practitioners, social workers, and certified nurse midwives.

A nonparticipating physician may provide medical services to a patient with TRICARE. These physicians may charge TRICARE patients no more than 115 percent of the TRICARE allowable charge, or limiting charge. The nonparticipating provider may accept assignment on a case-by-case basis.

CHAMPVA is the acronym for Civilian Health and Medical Program of the Veterans Administration, or the Department of Veterans Affairs. CHAMPVA is not an insurance program but rather a service benefit program with no contracts and no premiums. CHAMPVA covers the expenses of dependent spouses and children of veterans with total, permanent, service-connected disabilities. It also covers surviving spouses and dependent children of veterans who have died in the line of duty or as a result of disabilities connected to the uniformed service.

CHAMPVA beneficiaries are allowed to choose civilian health care providers.

In the civilian medical facility treating the TRICARE or CHAMPVA patient, follow these guidelines to process a CMS-1500 claim for services rendered:

1. Check the patient's identification card for name, ID number, issue date, effective date, and expiration date. Scan or a copy of the front and back of the card.

Highlight:
TRICARE/CHAMPVA uses the term sponsor instead of insured or subscriber. The sponsor is the service person—active duty, retired, deceased— whose relationship to the patient provides eligibility for the program.

Filing the CMS-1500 for TRICARE/CHAMPVA

Follow the same instructions for all boxes of the CMS-1500 with the exception of the following:

Item 1	Enter an X in the TRICARE or CHAMPVA box.
Item 1a	Enter the appropriate information for the patient:
	TRICARE: Sponsor's social security number.
	CHAMPVA: Patient's Veterans Affairs file number.
	NOAA/NATO: Type "NOAA" or "NATO" and sponsor's ID number.
Item 4	Enter the sponsor's last name, first name, and middle initial.
Item 7	Enter the sponsor's mailing address and telephone number.
Items 9, 9a–d	Complete when there is secondary insurance.
Items 17a–17b	Name and NPI of referring physician. If patient is referred from a military treatment facility, enter name of facility and attach form DD 2161 "Referral for Civilian Medical Care."
Item 27	Enter X in the YES box to accept assignment. NonPARs may elect to accept assignment on a case-by-case basis. If assignment is not accepted by a nonparticipating provider, mark NO.

If a patient has other insurance, including workers' compensation and liability policies, TRICARE and CHAMPVA are secondary payors.

TRICARE is primary when the other insurance is Medicaid or a supplemental policy to TRICARE.

The deadline for filing TRICARE and CHAMPVA claims is one year from date of service.

Figure 15–26 is an example of a completed CMS-1500 claim form for a TRICARE patient.

Workers' Compensation

Workers' compensation is a program covering on-the-job accidents and injuries or illness related to employment. This program is mandated by federal and state governments. Premiums are paid by employers to a statewide fund to cover medical expenses and a portion of lost wages directly related to the employee's injury or illness. This premium is determined by the number of employees and the degree of risk posed by the job. Workers' compensation benefits are not awarded if the worker/patient was found negligent in performing the duties of his or her job.

> **EXAMPLE:** A worker is a house painter and has a few beers at lunch. He returns to work and, while painting the exterior of a house, falls from the ladder to the ground, suffering a severe sprain to his back. Alcohol testing may reveal the drinks at lunch preceding the fall and injury at work. In this case, the employer would not be liable for the worker's injuries.

Workers' compensation benefits vary from state to state. Five principal types of benefits may be available:

1. Medical treatment—Hospitals, physician and medical services, medications, and supplies are covered for treatment that is reasonable and medically necessary for the injured or ill worker.

HEALTH INSURANCE CLAIM FORM

APPROVED BY NATIONAL UNIFORM CLAIM COMMITTEE (NUCC) 02/12

| 2 | PICA | | | | | | PICA | |

1. MEDICARE ☐ (Medicare#) **MEDICAID** ☐ (Medicaid#) **TRICARE** ☒ (ID#/DoD#) **CHAMPVA** ☐ (Member ID#) **GROUP HEALTH PLAN** ☐ (ID#) **FECA BLK LUNG** ☐ (ID#) **OTHER** ☐ (ID#)

1a. INSURED'S I.D. NUMBER (For Program in Item 1)
300543030

2. PATIENT'S NAME (Last Name, First Name, Middle Initial)
DUCHANE PATRICIA S

3. PATIENT'S BIRTH DATE MM 07 DD 01 YY 2009 **SEX** M ☐ F ☒

4. INSURED'S NAME (Last Name, First Name, Middle Initial)
DUCHANE WILLIAM T

5. PATIENT'S ADDRESS (No., Street)
2510 NORTH ST APT 21B

6. PATIENT RELATIONSHIP TO INSURED
Self ☐ Spouse ☐ Child ☒ Other ☐

7. INSURED'S ADDRESS (No., Street)
ZION AIR FORCE BASE

CITY DUVALL **STATE** IN

8. RESERVED FOR NUCC USE

CITY APPLACHIA **STATE** NY

ZIP CODE 47232 **TELEPHONE (Include Area Code)** (555) 2932190

ZIP CODE 22330 **TELEPHONE (Include Area Code)** ( )

9. OTHER INSURED'S NAME (Last Name, First Name, Middle Initial)

10. IS PATIENT'S CONDITION RELATED TO:

11. INSURED'S POLICY GROUP OR FECA NUMBER

a. OTHER INSURED'S POLICY OR GROUP NUMBER

a. EMPLOYMENT? (Current or Previous) ☐ YES ☒ NO

a. INSURED'S DATE OF BIRTH MM 01 DD 25 YY 1985 **SEX** M ☒ F ☐

b. RESERVED FOR NUCC USE

b. AUTO ACCIDENT? ☐ YES ☒ NO **PLACE (State)**

b. OTHER CLAIM ID (Designated by NUCC)

c. RESERVED FOR NUCC USE

c. OTHER ACCIDENT? ☐ YES ☒ NO

c. INSURANCE PLAN NAME OR PROGRAM NAME
TRICARE

d. INSURANCE PLAN NAME OR PROGRAM NAME

10d. CLAIM CODES (Designated by NUCC)

d. IS THERE ANOTHER HEALTH BENEFIT PLAN? ☐ YES ☒ NO *If yes,* complete items 9, 9a, and 9d.

READ BACK OF FORM BEFORE COMPLETING & SIGNING THIS FORM.
12. PATIENT'S OR AUTHORIZED PERSON'S SIGNATURE I authorize the release of any medical or other information necessary to process this claim. I also request payment of government benefits either to myself or to the party who accepts assignment below.

SIGNED **SOF** DATE

13. INSURED'S OR AUTHORIZED PERSON'S SIGNATURE I authorize payment of medical benefits to the undersigned physician or supplier for services described below.

SIGNED **SOF**

14. DATE OF CURRENT ILLNESS, INJURY, or PREGNANCY (LMP) MM 06 DD 25 YY 20XX QUAL. **434**

15. OTHER DATE QUAL. MM DD YY

16. DATES PATIENT UNABLE TO WORK IN CURRENT OCCUPATION FROM MM DD YY TO MM DD YY

17. NAME OF REFERRING PROVIDER OR OTHER SOURCE

17a.
17b. NPI

18. HOSPITALIZATION DATES RELATED TO CURRENT SERVICES FROM MM DD YY TO MM DD YY

19. ADDITIONAL CLAIM INFORMATION (Designated by NUCC)

20. OUTSIDE LAB? ☐ YES ☐ NO **$ CHARGES**

21. DIAGNOSIS OR NATURE OF ILLNESS OR INJURY Relate A-L to service line below (24E) **ICD Ind.**

A. SO8.112 B. W09.2XXA C. D.
E. F. G. H.
I. J. K. L.

22. RESUBMISSION CODE **ORIGINAL REF. NO.**

23. PRIOR AUTHORIZATION NUMBER

24. A. DATE(S) OF SERVICE From To						B. PLACE OF SERVICE	C. EMG	D. PROCEDURES, SERVICES, OR SUPPLIES (Explain Unusual Circumstances) CPT/HCPCS	MODIFIER	E. DIAGNOSIS POINTER	F. $ CHARGES		G. DAYS OR UNITS	H. EPSDT Family Plan	I. ID. QUAL.	J. RENDERING PROVIDER ID. #
MM	DD	YY	MM	DD	YY											
1	06	25	XX				23		99282		12	185	00	1		NPI	1789023451
2	06	25	XX				23		12051	E1	12	110	00	1		NPI	1789023451
3																NPI	
4																NPI	
5																NPI	
6																NPI	

25. FEDERAL TAX I.D. NUMBER 753467120 **SSN** ☐ **EIN** ☒

26. PATIENT'S ACCOUNT NO.

27. ACCEPT ASSIGNMENT? (For govt. claims, see back) ☒ YES ☐ NO

28. TOTAL CHARGE $ 295 00

29. AMOUNT PAID $

30. Rsvd for NUCC Use

31. SIGNATURE OF PHYSICIAN OR SUPPLIER INCLUDING DEGREES OR CREDENTIALS (I certify that the statements on the reverse apply to this bill and are made a part thereof.)

SIGNED DATE

32. SERVICE FACILITY LOCATION INFORMATION
DOGOOD COMMUNITY HOSPITAL
8080 FIFTH AVE
TEMPLE IN 47555

a. 1246803690 b.

33. BILLING PROVIDER INFO & PH # ( )
DONALD KING MD
2805 NAPOLEON BLVD
TEMPLE IN 47555

a. 1789023451 b.

NUCC Instruction Manual available at: www.nucc.org **PLEASE PRINT OR TYPE** APPROVED OMB-0938-1197 FORM 1500 (02-12)

Figure 15-26 Completed CMS-1500 for TRICARE claim

2. Temporary disability indemnity—The ill or injured person receives wage compensation benefits.

3. Permanent disability indemnity—This can be permanent total disability, in which the employee's ability to work and earn wages is permanently and totally lost, or permanent partial disability, in which part of the employee's capacity to work and earn wages is lost.

4. Vocational rehabilitation benefits—Many times an injured worker may not be able to return to the job previously held at time of injury but is a candidate for education and/or training for other employment to allow a return to the workforce.

5. Death benefits—The dependents/survivors of a worker who has died because of an accident or illness may receive compensation for their loss based on the employee's earning capacity at the time of the injury or illness.

Three types of workers' compensation claims may be submitted:

1. Nondisability claim—This is when an employee who receives a minor injury is seen and treated by a physician but does not require time missed from work for recovery.

2. Temporary disability claim—This is a total or partial disability that occurs when an employee cannot perform work duties from the date of the injury until the employee returns to full work duties or limited duty, or is medically determined to be permanently disabled.

3. Permanent disability—This is when an employee's injury results in impairment of normal function of a body part, such as loss of a body part, that is expected to continue through the lifetime. A case manager will evaluate the severity of the injury, the age of the injured person, and the occupation of the injured. Most often, temporary disability is granted to see if the person can improve or be eligible for rehabilitation before reaching the final determination of permanent disability.

Most states have an Employer's Report of Occupational Injury or Illness that must be completed for documentation and reporting of a work-related injury or illness. The physician rendering treatment to an injured employee must also complete a report of occupational injury or illness form. This form documents details of the accident or illness in the patient's own words with the patient's complaints and symptoms. The physician enters objective findings from the examination and all x-ray and laboratory results and a full description of the treatment and the treatment plan. Information must be submitted as to the patient's ability to return to work and an estimated date to return to regular or limited duty and any job restrictions. This form must be signed and dated in ink by the physician. This report is not a form submitted for reimbursement. This may be a CMS-1500 form or other form as required by the state workers' compensation fund. The injured worker receives no bills, pays no deductible or coinsurance, and is covered 100 percent for medical expenses related specifically to that injury or illness.

In most states, information in the patient's medical record is accessible to the injured patient's employer and the insurance claims adjuster. Understand that the only information accessible is what has been provided for the workers' compensation case only. It does not include other information in the medical record unrelated to the injury or illness currently being treated. All other information in the record is confidential and requires an authorization to be released to a third party.

Figure 15–27 is one example of a First Report of Injury or Illness form that would be completed by a provider for workers' compensation.

Highlight:

Workers' compensation has no deductible and no copayments, and the employer pays all premiums. All providers treating a workers' compensation patient must accept assignment and accept the compensation payment as payment in full. The patient is not billed for services for any work-related injury or illness.

STATE OF CALIFORNIA

DOCTOR'S FIRST REPORT OF OCCUPATIONAL INJURY OR ILLNESS

Within 5 days of your initial examination, for every occupational injury or illness, send two copies of this report to the employer's workers' compensation insurance carrier or the insured employer. Failure to file a timely doctor's report may result in assessment of a civil penalty. In the case of diagnosed or suspected pesticide poisoning, send a copy of the report to Division of Labor Statistics and Research, P.O. Box 420603, San Francisco, CA 94142-0603, and notify your local health officer by telephone within 24 hours.

	PLEASE DO NOT USE THIS COLUMN
1. INSURER NAME AND ADDRESS	
2. EMPLOYER NAME	Case No.
3. Address No. and Street City Zip	Industry
4. Nature of business (e.g., food manufacturing, building construction, retailer of women's clothes.)	County
5. PATIENT NAME (first name, middle initial, last name) 6. Sex ☐ Male ☐ Female 7. Date of Birth Mo. Day Yr.	Age
8. Address: No. and Street City Zip 9. Telephone number ( )	Hazard
10. Occupation (Specific job title) 11. Social Security Number - -	Disease
12. Injured at: No. and Street City County	Hospitalization
13. Date and hour of injury or onset of illness Mo. Day Yr. Hour _____ a.m. _____ p.m. 14. Date last worked Mo. Day Yr.	Occupation
15. Date and hour of first examination or treatment Mo. Day Yr. Hour _____ a.m. _____ p.m. 16. Have you (or your office) previously treated patient? ☐ Yes ☐ No	Return Date/Code

Patient please complete this portion, if able to do so. Otherwise, doctor please complete immediately, inability or failure of a patient to complete this portion shall not affect his/her rights to workers' compensation under the California Labor Code.

17. DESCRIBE HOW THE ACCIDENT OR EXPOSURE HAPPENED. (Give specific object, machinery or chemical. Use reverse side if more space is required.)

18. SUBJECTIVE COMPLAINTS (Describe fully. Use reverse side if more space is required.)

19. OBJECTIVE FINDINGS (Use reverse side if more space is required.)
A. Physical examination

B. X-ray and laboratory results (State if non or pending.)

20. DIAGNOSIS (if occupational illness specify etiologic agent and duration of exposure.) Chemical or toxic compounds involved? ☐ Yes ☐ No
ICD-9 Code ___ ___ ___ - ___ ___

21. Are your findings and diagnosis consistent with patient's account of injury or onset of illness? ☐ Yes ☐ No If "no", please explain.

22. Is there any other current condition that will impede or delay patient's recovery? ☐ Yes ☐ No If "yes", please explain.

23. TREATMENT RENDERED (Use reverse side if more space is required.)

24. If further treatment required, specify treatment plan/estimated duration.

25. If hospitalized as inpatient, give hospital name and location   Date   Mo. Day Yr.   Estimated stay
admitted

26. WORK STATUS -- Is patient able to perform usual work? ☐ Yes ☐ No
If "no", date when patient can return to: Regular work ____/____/____
Modified work ____/____/____   Specify restrictions _____

Doctor's Signature _____   CA License Number _____

Doctor Name and Degree (please type) _____   IRS Number _____

Address _____   Telephone Number (_____)_____

FORM 5021 (Rev. 4) 1992

Any person who makes or causes to be made any knowingly false or fraudulent material statement or material representation for the purpose of obtaining or denying workers' compensation benefits or payments is guilty of a felony.

Figure 15-27 An example of a workers' compensation form for report of injury or illness

Filing the CMS-1500 for Workers' Compensation

Follow the same instructions for all boxes of the CMS-1500 with the exception of the following:

Item 1	Enter an X in the FECA/Black Lung box. (FECA is the abbreviation for the Federal Employee Compensation Act.)
Item 1a	Enter patient's social security number.
Item 4	Enter the name of the patient's employer.
Item 6	Enter an X in the "Other" box.
Item 7	Enter the employer's mailing address and telephone number.
Item 8	Enter an X in the Employed box.
Item 9, 9a–d	Leave blank.
Item 10a	Enter X in the YES box.
Item 10b–c	Enter appropriate boxes as to automobile or other accident. If YES is marked to indicate auto accident, enter the two-character state abbreviation of the patient's residence.
Item 11	Enter the nine-digit FECA number assigned to the claim when work-related incident.
Item 11b	Enter the claim number assigned by the workers' compensation third-party payor.
Item 11c	Enter the name of the workers' compensation payor.
Item 14	Enter date of accident, injury, or illness.
Item 15	If a prior episode of the same or similar illness began, enter the date of occurrence.
Item 16	Enter dates patient was unable to work in current occupation.
Item 23	Enter any preauthorization number assigned by the workers' compensation payor.
Item 27	Mark the YES box to accept assignment.

Blue Cross Blue Shield

Blue Cross Blue Shield (BCBS): One of the oldest and largest insurance providers providing health benefits nationwide.

Blue Cross Blue Shield (BCBS) is a nationwide corporation providing health care benefits such as hospital expenses, outpatient care, dental and vision benefits, and home care to its members. Typically Blue Cross covers hospital expenses; Blue Shield covers physician services.

Coverage plans vary under BCBS coverage. Basic types of policies offered are traditional or fee-for-service plans, indemnity plans that offer choices and flexibility to subscribers, and managed care plans. Blue Cross Blue Shield also offers a Federal Employee Health Benefits Program, which covers federal employees and dependents, and Medicare supplemental plans, or Medigap plans. A traditional or fee-for-service plan may have higher premiums but lower out-of-pocket expenses for the patient. An indemnity benefit policy may feature lower premiums with a deductible and coinsurance amount payable by the subscriber. Providers may include those participating with the various plans by signing contract agreements, preferred providers who contract in the plan's preferred provider network (PPN), or nonparticipating providers.

Many Blue Cross Blue Shield plans have converted to a for-profit status operating as any other private insurance carrier. This allows a variety of plans with deductibles, copayments, and specific coverage benefits differing from patient to patient. Reimbursement will depend on the specific plan. For example, the patient may pay the physician directly and ask the physician office to file a Blue Shield claim that would reimburse the patient. A physician's office may file a claim and bill the patient for the difference between the payment and fee charged. The payment is usually sent to the insured for services provided by nonparticipating physicians. Participating physicians are paid directly. Various methods are used by BCBS to determine payment:

- Primary method of payment is usual, customary, and reasonable (UCR) fees.

- Many BCBS plans use the physician fee schedule to determine the allowed fees for each procedure for reimbursement.

As with many other health insurance companies, Blue Shield negotiates participating contracts with providers. A Blue Shield participating (PAR) provider must submit claims for its patients and adjust the difference between the amount charged and the approved fee on all covered services included in a policy written by the local corporation with payments made directly to the PAR.

Providers who have not signed a participating contract (nonPARs) can bill the entire amount of the fee charged for services performed. The billing office or patient can file the claim. In either case, the payment will be sent directly to the patient.

BCBS plans have unique features that set them apart from other commercial health insurance groups:

- A patient's policy cannot be canceled by BCBS due to poor health or greater-than-average benefit payments.

- Any rate increase and/or benefit changes must get approval from the state insurance commissioner.

- BCBS plans can be converted from group to individual coverage and can be transferred from state to state.

- In negotiating contracts with health care providers, Blue Shield agrees to make prompt, direct payment of claims; provide assistance with claim filing; and provide training seminars, manuals, and newsletters to keep personnel current and up-to-date in billing and claim filing.

In some states, BCBS assists in the administration of government programs such as Medicaid, Medicare, and TRICARE. Many patients have BCBS as supplemental coverage to Medicare. One of the largest national plans is the Federal Employee Program (FEP) serving federal government employees. Cards in this plan have the words "Government-Wide Service Benefit Plan," and the identification number begins with an R, followed by eight digits. On the front of the card is a three-digit enrollment code. There are four enrollment options the government employee can select when applying for the program:

101	Individual, high option plan
102	Family, high option plan
104	Individual, standard (low) option plan
105	Family, standard (low) option plan

The FEP is primary when a patient also has TRICARE or MEDICAID. It coordinates benefits with Medicare Parts A and B, and any other employer group policy.

The deadline for filing Blue Shield claims is one year from the date of service.

Exercise 15.4

Match the term with its definition, placing the letter of the correct answer in the space provided.

_____	1. Workers' Compensation
_____	2. Medicaid
_____	3. Blue Cross Blue Shield
_____	4. Medicare Part A
_____	5. Medicare Part B
_____	6. Medicare Part C
_____	7. Medicare Part D
_____	8. TRICARE/CHAMPVA

1. A nationwide federation of local for-profit organizations providing health care to all its subscribers

2. Managed care and private fee-for-service plans for Medicare patients

3. Hospital insurance for persons age 65 and over, disabled, or with end-stage renal disease

4. Federal program providing health care benefits to families of armed forces and retired military personnel and veterans

5. Prescription drug coverage for Medicare patients

6. An assistance program to provide medical care for persons with incomes below the national poverty level

7. Medical coverage optional for persons age 65 and over, disabled, or with end-stage renal disease for outpatient services

8. Coverage for work-related illness or injury

Filing the CMS-1500 for Blue Cross Blue Shield

Follow the same instructions for all boxes of the CMS-1500 with the exception of the following:

Item 1   Enter X in the Group Health Plan box if the patient is covered by such a plan. Otherwise, enter the X in Other.

Item 1a   Enter the BCBS identification number as it appears on the card.

Item 6   Enter an X in the appropriate box to indicate patient's relationship to the policyholder. If the patient is an unmarried domestic partner, enter an X in the "Other" box.

Item 11   Enter the subscriber's BCBS group number if covered by a group health plan.

Box 11c   Enter the name of the subscriber's BCBS health insurance plan.

Figure 15–28 is an example of a Blue Shield claim form.

Figure 15-28 Completed CMS-1500 for Blue Shield claim

Electronic Claim Processing

One function of a computerized office system is the preparation and generation of insurance claims. An electronic claim is filed using electronic data interchange (EDI) to submit claims. This can reduce costs and expedite reimbursement, as payment may be processed within approximately 7 to 14 days after the insurance carrier has received the claim. The billing program scans the medical practice database to obtain the information necessary to complete each block on the claim form. Claim forms can then be transmitted electronically directly to the insurance carrier. A paper claim can be printed if needed to send to an insurance carrier or retain in the office files. Electronic claims are easier to track and form an audit trail and proof of receipt of claims processed. It is less costly in time and money as it eliminates postage and mailing of claims, and reduces the amount of paper to file and store. EDI also improves communication between a provider and the insurance carrier by exchanging information in real time. This includes eligibility verification, claim inquiries, and claim status. Electronic funds transfer (EFT) provides quicker payment to the provider.

The Health Insurance Portability and Accountability Act (HIPAA) of 1996 legislated health insurance reform and administrative simplification. One provision of the administrative simplification directs the federal government to provide electronic standards for electronic transfer of health care data between health care providers and payors. This standardizes the format for electronic claim submission. The HIPAA code set standards allow a health care provider to check patient eligibility and deductibles, request prior authorization, submit claims electronically, send attachments, check status of claims, and receive remittance advice or explanation of benefits summaries. Fee schedules, limiting charges, and codes can be accessed. Carrier manuals and other information can be obtained from individual websites such as the Centers for Medicare & Medicaid Services.

As discussed in Chapter 14, the billing process begins with making the patient appointment and gathering basic patient information at that time. Detailed demographic information on the patient registration form can be completed by the patient before the appointment and brought to the facility at the time of the visit or completed at the first office encounter. Information from the registration form is entered into the computer to generate both the patient's medical record and financial record. With computerized practice management systems, many encounter forms are scanned to input services and procedures with charges and diagnoses into the patient's record and financial account. This information is stored in the database to be retrieved at a later time to file the insurance claim. Figure 15–29 gives an example of primary insurance information in the patient registration record.

Electronic claims can be submitted using a carrier-direct system. This requires entering the claim form data and transmits via the modem over the telephone line directly to an insurance carrier. A distinct advantage of the carrier-direct system is the error-edit process. If an error is made during the electronic filing process, the error is identified and can be corrected immediately.

Physicians can also use electronic data interchange to receive, process, edit, sort, and transmit claims by using software systems. A *clearinghouse*, also known as a *third-party administrator*, can be used to receive insurance claims, separate

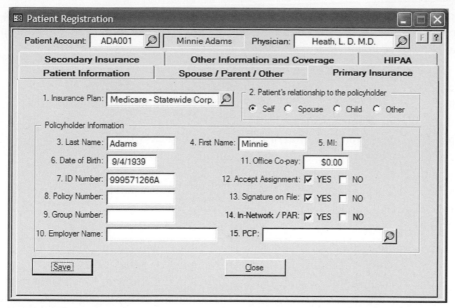

Figure 15-29 Primary insurance information in the patient registration record

by carrier, edit each claim for errors, and forward claims electronically to the designated carrier. A clearinghouse can also process manual claims to carriers that do not have electronic claim file systems in place. All claims are checked for completeness and accuracy before being processed for reimbursement. Claims that are incorrect are manually reviewed. Rejected claims are returned to the medical practice.

The submission of electronic claims has many advantages when compared to the manual process. One of the biggest advantages is improved cash flow, as payment from electronically submitted claims is received or deposited electronically in two weeks or less, compared to four to eight weeks when completed manually. Electronic claim submission leaves an audit trail of chronologically submitted data. A software program can be installed to edit claims to ensure correct coding and billing practices. An error can be corrected immediately to avoid further delay in the submission of a claim.

It is important to update billing and claim submission software as ICD-10-CM and CPT codes are added, deleted, or changed annually. Failure to do so can result in rejected claims.

Insurance Claims Follow-Up

A system must be developed in order to follow up insurance claims. A tickler file can be set up as a manual system or in the electronic system as a reminder to telephone or send inquiries to insurance carriers about unpaid claims. A copy of the claim form can be filed in the tickler file, then retrieved when the remittance advice (RA), explanation of benefits (EOB), Medicare Summary Notice (MSN), and/or check is received. Review the RA, EOB, or MSN and compare with the claim form. A copy of the RA, EOB, or MSN can be attached to the claim form copy and filed in a folder for paid claims.

Copies of claim forms remaining in the tickler file past the time limit for processing of payment denial can be resubmitted to the insurance carrier, indicating on the copy that this is a second request.

Medicare's *Conditions of Participation* requires providers to retain copies of insurance claims and copies of all attachments for at least a period of five years, unless state law specifies a longer period of time. HIPAA mandates the retention of health insurance claims and accounting records for a minimum of six years, unless state law specifies a longer period of time. Claims filed electronically comply with this regulation by retaining the source documents generating the claim, such as superbills, charge slips, encounter forms, and the daily summary of claims transmitted and received during that time frame. Although commercial carriers have no specific rulings on retention of claims submitted, it is good business practice to retain claims until all transactions have been completed.

An insurance claims register can also be used to follow status of claim forms. This can be a three-ring binder using indexes identifying various insurance companies. A copy of the claim form can be filed under the index of the insurance carrier, and the submission information is recorded in the insurance claims register. The register, as demonstrated in Figure 15–30, contains columns to note the date the claim was submitted, the amount of the claim, and the date payment was received. When payment is received and posted to the patient's account, the copy of the claim is removed from the binder and placed in the patient's chart or a separate file maintained for audit purposes. A line is drawn through the information on the register to indicate the claim status is complete. An electronic record can also be established for this purpose.

INSURANCE CLAIM REGISTRY						
Date Filed	Patient Name	ID Number	Insurance Company	Amount Filed	Amount Paid	Follow-up Date
05/11/20XX	Opal Pearl	403-08-2214	CIGNA	$ 54.00		06/30/20XX
06/25/20XX	Patricia Duchane	300-54-3030	CHAMPUS	$ 295.00	$ 236.00	

Figure 15-30 An insurance claim registry can be used to follow status of claim forms.

Problem Claims

No matter how accurate, complete, and efficient the medical office may be, there will still be problem claims that require some type of action. Some of these problems are claims that are denied, rejected, or lost; incorrect payment; down coding; and pending claims.

When claims are delinquent or pending, this means payment is overdue because the claim is being reviewed, additional information is required, or an error has been made. An insurance tracer form can be used to follow up these problem claims, as indicated in Figure 15–31.

State laws require insurance companies to notify the insured when a claim is denied and the reason for the denial. Federal laws require Medicare to issue an explanation for each denied service.

Claim forms are date-stamped when received by the insurance carrier. A claim number is assigned and logged into the payor system. If the claim has not

INSURANCE COMPANY_____ DATE _____

ADDRESS:_ _____

PATIENT NAME_____ NAME OF INSURED_____

IDENTIFICATION NUMBER_____

EMPLOYER NAME & ADDRESS_____

DATE CLAIM FILED_____ CLAIM AMOUNT_____

Attached is a copy of the original claim submitted to you on _____. We have not yet received a request for additional information and still await payment of this claim. Please review the attached duplicate and process for payment.

If there are any questions regarding this claim, please answer the following and return this letter to our office.

IF CLAIM HAS BEEN PAID:

        Date of payment: _____

        Amount of payment: _____

        Payment made to: _____

IF CLAIM HAS BEEN DENIED:

        Reason for denial: _____

                    _____

        Has the patient been notified? ☐ Yes   ☐ No

IF CLAIM IS STILL PENDING:

        Please state reason why:

                _____

                _____

Please return this insurance claim tracer in the enclosed envelope or you may fax to (222) 663-2211.

Thank you in this request.

Sincerely,

Judy Jolly, CMA
Insurance Specialist

Figure 15-31 An example of an insurance claim tracer used to follow up on delinquent claims

been received and logged in or has been lost, a copy of the original claim can be resubmitted, indicating this is a copy of the original claim submitted on (date).

Earlier in this chapter, the most common reasons why claim forms are rejected were listed. When claim forms are rejected, make the necessary corrections or provide additional information, and resubmit the claim for regular processing. Do not send a corrected claim for review or appeal.

When a claim is denied, it is usually denied due to medical coverage policy or program issues. These issues may be:

- The procedure was not a covered service in the policy.

- Treatment submitted was for a **preexisting condition**.

- Patient was no longer covered by policy when service was rendered, or service was performed before coverage was in effect.

- Service was not medically necessary.

When a claim is denied because of an error such as failure to code a diagnosis or procedure, or not including the NPI, a Medicare Redetermination Request Form, CMS-20027 (Figure 15–32), can be completed to resubmit a corrected claim. The statement "resubmission, corrected claim" must be entered in Item 19 of the CMS-1500 claim form to indicate the correction of a previously submitted claim form.

When a review may be requested for a denied claim, a Medicare Reconsideration Request Form, CMS-20033, may be completed (Figure 15–33). It is necessary to explain on this form justification for the service or procedure denied and the reason for reimbursement. The following documents must be attached to this form:

- Copy of the original insurance claim form

- Copy of the RA, EOB, or MSN showing the denial

- Copy of any documents to support the claim, such as pathology or operative report

Occasionally claims are processed by an insurance carrier with the result of lowered reimbursement due to down coding. Down coding occurs in the following situations:

- Insufficient diagnostic information submitted on the claim form

- Conversion of a CPT or ICD-10-CM code submitted on a claim form by the insurance carrier

- Routine use of unspecified ICD-10-CM codes

The impact of down coding is lowered reimbursement. Review the RA, EOB, or MSN to identify reasons a claim may be down coded. Use appropriate codes, indicate the medical necessity of the ICD-10-CM and CPT codes, and code to the highest level of specificity. Chapter 16 gives detailed steps in the review and appeals process.

Figure 15–34 is a summary linking the cycle that occurs from the patient visit to payment.

preexisting condition: A medical condition under active treatment at the time application is made for an insurance policy, possibly resulting in an exclusion of that disease or illness.

DEPARTMENT OF HEALTH AND HUMAN SERVICES
CENTERS FOR MEDICARE & MEDICAID SERVICES

MEDICARE REDETERMINATION REQUEST FORM — 1ST LEVEL OF APPEAL

1. Beneficiary's name:_____

2. Medicare number: _____

3. Item or service you wish to appeal: _____

4. Date the service or item was received: _____

5. Date of the initial determination notice (please include a copy of the notice with this request):
(If you received your initial determination notice more than 120 days ago, include your reason for the late filing.)

_____

_____

_____

5a. Name of the Medicare contractor that made the determination (not required):

_____

5b. Does this appeal involve an overpayment? ☐ Yes ☐ No
(for providers and suppliers only)

6. I do not agree with the determination decision on my claim because:

_____

_____

_____

7. Additional information Medicare should consider:

_____

_____

_____

8. ☐ I have evidence to submit. Please attach the evidence to this form or attach a statement explaining what you intend to submit and when you intend to submit it. You may also submit additional evidence at a later time, but all evidence must be received prior to the issuance of the redetermination.

☐ I do not have evidence to submit.

9. Person appealing: ☐ Beneficiary ☐ Provider/Supplier ☐ Representative

10. Name, address, and telephone number of person appealing: _____

_____

11. Signature of person appealing: _____

12. Date signed:_____

Form CMS-20027 (12/10)

Courtesy of the Centers for Medicare & Medicaid Services, www.cms.gov.

Figure 15-32 Medicare Redetermination Request Form

DEPARTMENT OF HEALTH AND HUMAN SERVICES
CENTERS FOR MEDICARE & MEDICAID SERVICES

MEDICARE RECONSIDERATION REQUEST FORM — 2ND LEVEL OF APPEAL

1. Beneficiary's name: _____

2. Medicare number: _____

3. Item or service you wish to appeal: _____

4. Date the service or item was received: _____

5. Date of the redetermination notice (please include a copy of the notice with this request):
   (If you received your redetermination notice more than 180 days ago, include your reason for the late filing.)

   _____

   _____

   5a. Name of the Medicare contractor that made the redetermination (not required if copy of notice attached):

   _____

   5b. Does this appeal involve an overpayment? ☐ Yes   ☐ No
   (for providers and suppliers only)

6. I do not agree with the redetermination decision on my claim because:

   _____

   _____

   _____

7. Additional information Medicare should consider:

   _____

   _____

8. ☐ I have evidence to submit. Please attach the evidence to this form or attach a statement explaining what you intend to submit and when you intend to submit it. You may also submit additional evidence at a later time, but all evidence must be received prior to the issuance of the reconsideration.

   ☐ I do not have evidence to submit.

9. Person appealing: ☐ Beneficiary   ☐ Provider/Supplier   ☐ Representative

10. Name, address, and telephone number of person appealing: _____

    _____

11. Signature of person appealing: _____

12. Date signed: _____

PRIVACY ACT STATEMENT: The legal authority for the collection of information on this form is authorized by section 1869 (a)(3) of the Social Security Act. The information provided will be used to further document your appeal. Submission of the information requested on this form is voluntary, but failure to provide all or any part of the requested information may affect the determination of your appeal. Information you furnish on this form may be disclosed by the Centers for Medicare and Medicaid Services to another person or government agency only with respect to the Medicare Program and to comply with Federal laws requiring or permitting the disclosure of information or the exchange of information between the Department of Health and Human Services and other agencies. Additional information about these disclosures can be found in the system of records notice for system no. 09-70-0566, as amended, available at 71 Fed. Reg. 54489 (2006) or at http://www.cms.gov/PrivacyActSystemofRecords/downloads/0566.pdf

Form CMS-20033 (12/10)

Figure 15-33 Medicare Reconsideration Request Form

INSURANCE CLAIM FORM SUMMARY

| Charge Slip/Superbill |

1. Charge slip or superbill is attached to the outside of the patient's chart.

2. Physician sees patient, completes charge slip/superbill by marking service and diagnosis, signs charge slip/superbill, and indicates if patient needs an appointment to return.

3. Patient "checks out" at reception desk, makes return appointment if indicated by physician, and pays copay or other charges.

| Ledger Card/Account |

4. Charge slip/superbill is used to post services, charges, and payments to the patient's account.

| Insurance Claim Form |

5. Claim form is completed and submitted to insurance carrier.

| Insurance Claims Register |

6. Copy of claim form is filed in pending file. Date of submission is posted on ledger card/account and recorded in the insurance claims register.

| Payment |

7. Payment is received and posted to patient's ledger card/account. Check is endorsed and recorded on bank deposit slip.

| Patient Statement |

8. Bill the patient for any balance due.

| Patient or Paid File |

9. Claim form copy is retrieved from the pending file and attached to the EOB and filed in patient's chart or paid file for audit.

Figure 15-34 A summary of the billing and claim form cycle from the time the patient is first seen in the office until the claim is paid

Exercise 15.5

Match the term with its definition, placing the letter of the correct answer in the space provided.

_____	1. Capitation	a.	Authorization to pay benefits directly to the physician
_____	2. Coinsurance	b.	A summary of explanation of reimbursement of benefits by an insurance carrier
_____	3. Crossover claim	c.	An individual or company making a payment on a debt
_____	4. Medigap	d.	A reimbursement method that pays a fixed amount per person
_____	5. EOB, RA, MSN	e.	An electronic transfer of information submitted on a Medicare claim to Medicaid or the patient's Medigap carrier
_____	6. Copayment	f.	A private, commercial insurance plan to supplement Medicare coverage
_____	7. Deductible	g.	The total amount the patient must pay for covered services before benefits are payable
_____	8. Third-party payor	h.	A specified percentage a patient must pay for each service or procedure after the deductible has been met
_____	9. Assignment of benefits	i.	A specified amount determined for each service the patient must pay the health care provider, usually when the service is rendered
_____	10. Coordination of benefits	j.	Coordination of payment of services submitted on the claim form when a patient is covered by two or more primary medical insurance policies

Exercise 15.6

1. A patient has a blepharoplasty of both upper eyelids performed by a well-known plastic surgeon. What is the coding error on the following CMS-1500 form that would result in lower payment of the procedure?

19. ADDITIONAL CLAIM INFORMATION (Designated by NUCC)								20. OUTSIDE LAB? ☐ YES ☐ NO	$ CHARGES		
21. DIAGNOSIS OR NATURE OF ILLNESS OR INJURY Relate A-L to service line below (24E) ICD Ind.								22. RESUBMISSION CODE ORIGINAL REF. NO.			
A. H01.004 B. H01.001 C. D.								23. PRIOR AUTHORIZATION NUMBER			
E. F. G. H.											
I. J. K. L.											
24. A. DATE(S) OF SERVICE From MM DD YY	To MM DD YY	B. PLACE OF SERVICE	C. EMG	D. PROCEDURES, SERVICES, OR SUPPLIES (Explain Unusual Circumstances) CPT/HCPCS	MODIFIER	E. DIAGNOSIS POINTER	F. $ CHARGES	G. DAYS OR UNITS	H. EPSDT Family Plan	I. ID. QUAL.	J. RENDERING PROVIDER ID. #
1				15822			850 | 00			NPI	
2										NPI	
3										NPI	
4										NPI	
5										NPI	
6										NPI	

PHYSICIAN OR SUPPLIER INFORMATION

Courtesy of the Centers for Medicare & Medicaid Services, www.cms.gov. Copyright © 2017 Cengage Learning®.

(continues)

Exercise 15.6 (*continued*)

2. A 74-year-old patient is referred by Dr. Dogood to Dr. Bones, an orthopedic surgeon, for evaluation of pain in the left knee joint after slipping on a wet floor at home. The patient states she did not actually fall. An x-ray of the left knee reveals a peripheral tear of the medial meniscus. A CMS-1500 form is completed by Dr. Bones's office for the office visit and x-ray of the left knee, then sent to Medicare. What is missing on the following CMS-1500 form?

17. NAME OF REFERRING PROVIDER OR OTHER SOURCE	17a.		18. HOSPITALIZATION DATES RELATED TO CURRENT SERVICES
Robert Bones MD	17b. NPI		FROM MM DD YY TO MM DD YY
19. ADDITIONAL CLAIM INFORMATION (Designated by NUCC)			20. OUTSIDE LAB? ☐YES ☐NO $ CHARGES

Courtesy of the Centers for Medicare & Medicaid Services, www.cms.gov. Copyright © 2017 Cengage Learning®.

3. A patient diagnosed with anemia is sent to the lab for a CBC with differential, iron and iron binding capacity, and a stool for occult blood. What is the coding error submitted on the following CMS-1500 form submitted by the lab?

21. DIAGNOSIS: A. D50.0

Line	CPT/HCPCS
1	85025
2	83540
3	83550
4	82270

Courtesy of the Centers for Medicare & Medicaid Services, www.cms.gov. Copyright © 2017 Cengage Learning®.

4. A patient is seen in the office complaining of rectal burning and discomfort, especially with bowel movements. Examination today reveals a perianal abscess. This is incised and drained and the patient will return in five days for recheck. What is the coding error on the following CMS-1500 form?

21. DIAGNOSIS: A. L02.91

Line	CPT/HCPCS
1	46060

Courtesy of the Centers for Medicare & Medicaid Services, www.cms.gov. Copyright © 2017 Cengage Learning®.

(continues)

Exercise 15.6 (*continued*)

5. A 66-year-old patient comes in to see his PCP for his Welcome to Medicare Preventive Visit. The physician performs the IPPE as well as a complete EKG as part of the IPPE. What is the coding error on the CMS-1500 form?

19. ADDITIONAL CLAIM INFORMATION (Designated by NUCC)				20. OUTSIDE LAB? ☐ YES ☐ NO	$ CHARGES

21. DIAGNOSIS OR NATURE OF ILLNESS OR INJURY Relate A-L to service line below (24E)   ICD Ind. |
A. Z00.00   B. _____   C. _____   D. _____
E. _____   F. _____   G. _____   H. _____
I. _____   J. _____   K. _____   L. _____

22. RESUBMISSION CODE   ORIGINAL REF. NO.

23. PRIOR AUTHORIZATION NUMBER

24. A. DATE(S) OF SERVICE From MM DD YY — To MM DD YY	B. PLACE OF SERVICE	C. EMG	D. PROCEDURES, SERVICES, OR SUPPLIES (Explain Unusual Circumstances) CPT/HCPCS | MODIFIER	E. DIAGNOSIS POINTER	F. $ CHARGES	G. DAYS OR UNITS	H. EPSDT Family Plan	I. ID. QUAL.	J. RENDERING PROVIDER ID. #
1			G0402	1					NPI
2			93000	1					NPI
3									NPI
4									NPI
5									NPI
6									NPI

PHYSICIAN OR SUPPLIER INFORMATION

Summary

Today's insurance specialists, medical billers and coders, and medical assistants must have current knowledge of deductibles, copayments, and referrals. Skill is required for CPT, HCPCS, and ICD-10-CM coding and the medical necessity documented for reimbursement. There must be an understanding of the CMS-1500 claim form and the filing process in the practice, whether it is paper or electronic. There must be a working knowledge of Medicaid, Medicare and its secondary payors, as well as all participating provider agreements, and what information is required to submit claim forms.

In addition to understanding what amounts can be billed to the patient, coders must also know when amounts are to be adjusted. When claims are rejected or denied or payment is not received, it is important to know how to request a review of the claim or pursue an appeal. Chapter 16 will continue with the audit and appeals process.

It is essential to remain current in the profession by attending training and continuing education seminars and reading newsletters and bulletins published by the insurance carriers as proposed changes become implemented.

References

Centers for Medicare & Medicaid Services (CMS). Retrieved from https://www.cms.gov.

Fordney, M. (2013). *Insurance handbook for the medical office* (13th ed.). Philadelphia, PA: Elsevier.

Green, M., & Rowell, J. (2015). *Understanding health insurance: A guide to billing and reimbursement* (12th ed.). Clifton Park, NY: Cengage Learning.

HIPAA standard code set. U.S. Department of Health and Human Services. Retrieved from http://dhhs.gov

Lindh, W., Pooler, M., Tamparo, C., & Dahl, B. (2014). *Comprehensive medical assisting: Administrative and clinical competencies* (5th ed.). Clifton Park, NY: Cengage Learning.

State Department of California, Department of Industrial Relations. *Doctor's first report of occupational injury or illness.* Retrieved from http://www.dir.ca.gov/

CHAPTER 6

Payment for Professional Health Care Services, Auditing, and Appeals

Learning Objectives

Upon successful completion of this chapter, you should be able to:

- Recognize the payment cycle steps.
- Explain the components for payment, calculation, and payment strategy.
- Describe participating, nonparticipating, and deactivation status with Medicare.
- Recognize internal and external obstacles to accurate and timely payment.
- Pinpoint discrepancies in billing and documentation.
- Identify audit flags, targets, and compliance concepts.

Key Terms

advance beneficiary notice (ABN)

Association of Health Care Auditors and Educators (AHCAE)

audit

Balanced Budget Act (BBA)

capitation

covered service

downcoding

False Claims Act

medical necessity

Medicare Modernization Act

nonparticipating (nonPAR) provider

Office of Inspector General (OIG)

overpayment

participating (PAR) provider

point of service (POS)

preferred provider organization (PPO)

reimbursement

unbundling

upcoding

withhold

Introduction

This chapter discusses the typical payment cycle for physician office services, defining the multiple processes that affect the financial results. The payment cycle components will be reviewed in detail, from the initial phase through the appeal and potential **audit** phase. Most health insurance companies use ID cards with alphanumeric numbers. Typically, the first three letters (alpha prefix) identify the plan, followed by the assigned patient identification number. Table 16–1 introduces a few of the common acronyms and abbreviations that may be referred to by the insurance world.

Table 16-1 Example of Health Insurance Prefixes

A	Annuitant
MA	Spouse
WA	Widow of retired husband
WCA	With dependent children (husband retired)
WD	Widow (husband died prior to retirement)
WCD	Widow with dependent children (husband died prior to retirement)
PA	Parent of annuitant
PD	Parent (annuitant died prior to retirement)
JA	Joint annuitant
H	Retired husband
MH	Spouse
WH	Widow
WCH	Widow and child

audit: An evaluation of the billing practices within a medical office. Medical billing and insurance records are abstracted and compared to investigate proper billing, coding, and documentation technique and practices.

Payment Cycle

Every cog in the wheel must turn properly in order for the payment cycle to efficiently produce revenue and cash flow. The importance of these steps—and the potential sanctions for those who choose to purposefully bypass the rules—are presented in this chapter.

The health care system has suffered many changes in the payment cycle throughout the years. In years past, a service was rendered and the patient might have made payment directly to the medical professionals, handling his own billing and waited to get reimbursed. With contractual obligations and HIPAA guidance, that old model is rarely used today. Now, much more commonly, the professionals and facilities are paid long after the care was provided and the claim was submitted. This retroactive payment concept is termed **reimbursement**. Unfortunately, it is becoming increasingly difficult for physicians and the health care organizations to obtain payment for their services in a timely manner. Battling of inappropriate insurance tactics often results in several resubmissions or phone calls before payments get released. Reimbursement issues might also stem from errors created on the billing side for various reasons. These behaviors have created needless costs to the health care system and further support the industry need for certified coders and billers.

reimbursement: The act of being paid back or payment in exchange for goods or services.

The majority of patients expect their insurance plan will cover the health care services entirely. In reality, most patients' insurance plan coverage has limitations, whether established by the employer when setting up the benefit package or if patients are paying on their own. Employers make difficult decisions when selecting the health insurance benefit plans for their employees, and rising costs of health insurance premiums and stringent rules due to the Affordable Care Act continue to cause employers to reconsider benefit packages. Very few insurance plans (other than a "celebrity style" Lloyds of London policy) cover any and all health care situations.

Many patients expect that their insurance plan will pay for any and all health care services the physician and/or hospital deems appropriate. Unfortunately, the patient often does not understand the limitations of his or her insurance benefits prior to accessing the health care system. For example, many patients may not realize the financial obligation for the copayment and/or the deductible amount upon using emergency room care. Nor are most patients knowledgeable regarding the definition of emergency versus urgent care, or other definitions that apply to their particular insurance. The first time many patients learn of their insurance plan's limitations and of their financial obligations for services rendered is upon their arrival for care at the emergency room.

This same learning curve is common for many types of patient care, including diagnostic testing (e.g., PET scans), mental health care, physical and occupational therapy, preventive services, and, increasingly, drug coverage benefits. Patients begin to understand their insurance benefits and limitations only when they access the care.

More commonly the patient presents his or her insurance card at the time of receiving health care, and the patient only pays the applicable copayment and deductible at the time of the service. The claim is sent to the insurance plan to obtain the remainder of the payment (or partial payment). Each state legislates rules for the timely payment of claims. Typical insurance payments may occur as early as 10 days or as long as two years after the treatment. States often publish specific rules as to the claim submission requirements and processing time lines for providers and insurance companies. Appeal processes and specified time frames are often published on the state websites.

Regardless of insurance guidelines or state-specific rules, simply understanding the concept that "reimbursement is a process" will make the sometimes-daunting tasks more manageable.

Appointment

For most physician offices and hospital outpatient planned care, the payment cycle begins when the appointment is scheduled for the patient. For hospital inpatient care, commonly the patient will arrive at the emergency room for care, without a scheduled appointment.

Excellent verbal and customer service skills demonstrated by staff members while setting up the appointments are perhaps the most valuable marketing and patient retention asset that a practice or organization has. The public often selects providers based on plan participation and secondly, on their first and important impression.

Obtaining Patient Demographic Information

Obtaining patient demographic information is one of the most important aspects affecting the payment for health care services today. *Accuracy is paramount, and verification of eligibility and benefit coverage for each encounter and service is required.* This is essential to the cash flow of the organization. Every detail that is captured at this early stage will dramatically affect the financial processes for the physician practice or hospital system.

Details of importance are:

- *Patient's last name*—Names can change due to marriage or other legal reasons. Be sure to verify the last name on file with the insurance company.

- *Social security number*—It is now required for the newborn child very soon after the birth.

- *Date of birth for both the patient and the spouse*—This determines which insurance plan has the primary obligation for the payment. The primary policy is the one taken out by the policyholder with the earliest birthday occurring in the calendar year.

- *Intent to file insurance claim*—Does the patient intend to submit an insurance claim for the services today? Sometimes the patient may choose to personally pay for care, and not submit a claim to the insurance plan.

- *Insurance card information*—A copy of the front and back of the insurance card is required and should be inspected at *each encounter.*

  - The insurance ID or group numbers, where to send the claim, whom to call to determine if the patient is insured, and the benefits listed in the card often change.

  - The copayment and deductible amounts may or may not be stated on the card.

- *Employer information*—The employer information frequently changes.

- *Patient status of single, married, divorced, custody, student*—Obtain a copy of the decree or other document as soon as possible to assist in determining financial responsibility.

- *Accident or work-related injury information*—Is the care related to employment or an accident?

  - Obtain the exact workers' compensation or accident information immediately.

  - Be sure to get the information for the claims adjuster assigned to the accident or injury claim and any visit/treatment approval in writing prior to rendering services when possible.

- *Claims submission information*—Get the information such as address and phone number as to where you need to send the claim. Since medical record notes will often be requested prior to processing, providers will typically drop the claims to paper and attach the medical record documentation at the time of the original claims submission.

Medicare refers to Health Insurance Claim Numbers as HICN numbers. These numbers are assigned by the Social Security Administration and identify the patient as a Medicare beneficiary. The HICN format requirement for Medicare is nine digits followed by at least one letter in the tenth position referred to as a BIC, or beneficiary identification code. The A, for example, signifies the patient is a retired worker over age 65 or disabled. The B indicates the "wife" of a retired worker over age 65 or disabled. This letter is then followed by numbers 1–9 or letters. For example, an HICN ending in D1 stands for a widower. Table 16–2 is a partial list of these suffixes.

Table 16-2 Partial List of Medicare HICN Suffix Descriptions

Suffix	Beneficiary Identification Information (excerpts only, not a complete list—visit https://www.cms.gov)
A	Primary claimant
B	Aged wife, age 62 or over (1st claimant)
B1	Aged husband, age 62 or over (1st claimant)
B2	Young wife, with a child in her care (1st claimant)
C1–C9, CA–CK	Child (includes minor, student or disabled child)
D	Aged widow, 60 or over (1st claimant)
D1	Aged widower, age 60 or over (1st claimant)
D6	Surviving divorced wife, age 60 or over (1st claimant)
E	Mother (widow) (1st claimant)
E1	Surviving divorced mother (1st claimant)
E4	Father (widower) (1st claimant)
E5	Surviving divorced father (widower) (1st claimant)
F1	Father
F2	Mother
F3	Stepfather
F4	Stepmother
F5	Adopting father
F6	Adopting mother
W	Disabled widow, age 50 or over (1st claimant)
W1	Disabled widower, age 50 or over (1st claimant)
W8	Disabled surviving divorced wife (3rd claimant)
WR	Disabled surviving divorced husband (1st claimant)
W2	Disabled surviving divorced husband (2nd claimant)

Contacting the Insurance Plan

The patient's insurance plan may require that many policies and procedures be followed prior to providing the care. The first step required for each encounter or visit is to verify the patient is insured with that particular insurance plan. The process for verifying eligibility may be to call or check electronically. This may sound like a simple requirement but in reality may be very challenging. Examples include determining if a patient is insured soon after he or she is hired by a new employer, determining if a child patient is insured after a divorce is final, and determining if an underage patient who is pregnant and not dependent on her parents is insured. This is known as checking the eligibility of the insured.

The next step is to check the insurance benefits coverage and policies for the planned care, services, or items. Depending on the type of insurance, checking on coverage may require a separate telephone call or electronic site, which may vary from the previous encounter verification for eligibility (e.g., diagnostic testing versus surgical procedure).

Determining the policies and procedures for the claim submission for the planned service is recommended. In many cases, the insurance plan may require that certain quality steps be taken prior to payment for the care. Knowing the current policies prior to the care will increase the potential for payment and will certainly improve the time required for payment. Because of the Affordable Care Act, or ACA, many plans provide certain benefits as required by law. The payment responsibility, however, will vary as to coverage /deductible differences. This is especially true for new technology, new scientific items, expensive medical care, and cosmetic or other radical surgical cases.

If the insurance plan describes the planned care as not a covered benefit, the patient should be informed prior to delivering the service, if known. If the patient is Medicare, the patient must be informed and presented with an **advance beneficiary notice (ABN)** to sign, indicating whether the patient authorizes the service to be performed. A patient who authorizes a service is then aware that Medicare will most likely deny the service (along with the reason why) and is given an estimated cost of what his or her financial responsibility will be (Figure 16–1). Even though the ABN procedure is required only for Medicare patients, the principles are helpful for all patients regardless of the health insurance plans that the physician (or facility) is contracted with as a **participating (PAR) provider**. More information regarding the ABN procedure is discussed later in the chapter; at this point, it is sufficient to understand that obtaining the ABN will dramatically affect the payment cycle.

advance beneficiary notice (ABN): Notice to health insurance beneficiaries that the program will probably not pay for a service. The patient assumes financial responsibility for paying the provider directly for the service.

participating (PAR) provider: Physician who contracts to accept assignment (receives payment directly) from the health insurance program.

Care Begins

During the time the care is being rendered, very often the patient will ask for additional care or the physician will deem it necessary to provide more services than planned. The key is to provide the information accurately, discuss any questions, and properly complete any necessary consent forms prior to rendering the additional services.

Encounter Forms, Superbills, Fee Slips, or Charge Tickets

Upon audit, it is frequently discovered that if a separate encounter form, superbill, fee slip, or charge ticket is used, the information on the form might not accurately correlate to the information within the medical record. Upon interviewing staff members, it is not uncommon to hear something such as, "the form didn't have that as an option." This seems to be particularly true for accurately linking ICD-10-CM codes to each and every service that is performed and also for the specific dose and route of medications given. Updating the encounter form at least annually will assist with coding updates and efficiency. Most offices print fewer forms, allowing for more frequent form updates. With the continual migration to the electronic medical record (EMR), practices may discontinue altogether the use of a separate form for capturing services and rely solely on the EMR for this data.

The style of the physician encounter form is very important. Table 16–3 depicts excerpts that are common concepts for a physician encounter form used in the office setting. Obvious patient demographic information is required and typically printed

(A) Notifier(s):
(B) Patient Name: *(C)* Identification Number:

ADVANCE BENEFICIARY NOTICE OF NONCOVERAGE (ABN)

<u>NOTE:</u> If Medicare doesn't pay for *(D)*_____ below, you may have to pay.

Medicare does not pay for everything, even some care that you or your health care provider have good reason to think you need. We expect Medicare may not pay for the *(D)*_____ below.

(D)	*(E)* Reason Medicare May Not Pay:	Cost:

WHAT YOU NEED TO DO NOW:

- Read this notice, so you can make an informed decision about your care.
- Ask us any questions that you may have after you finish reading.
- Choose an option below about whether to receive the *(D)*_____ listed above.
  Note: If you choose Option 1 or 2, we may help you to use any other insurance that you might have, but Medicare cannot require us to do this.

(G) OPTIONS: **Check only one box. We cannot choose a box for you.**

☐ **OPTION 1.** I want the *(D)*_____ listed above. You may ask to be paid now, but I also want Medicare billed for an official decision on payment, which is sent to me on a Medicare Summary Notice (MSN). I understand that if Medicare doesn't pay, I am responsible for payment, but **I can appeal to Medicare** by following the directions on the MSN. If Medicare does pay, you will refund any payments I made to you, less copays or deductibles.

☐ **OPTION 2.** I want the *(D)*_____ listed above, but do not bill Medicare. You may ask to be paid now as I am responsible for payment. **I cannot appeal if Medicare is not billed**.

☐ **OPTION 3.** I don't want the *(D)*_____ listed above. I understand with this choice I am **not** responsible for payment, and **I cannot appeal to see if Medicare would pay.**

(H) Additional Information:

This notice gives our opinion, not an official Medicare decision. If you have other questions on this notice or Medicare billing, call **1-800-MEDICARE** (1-800-633-4227/**TTY**: 1-877-486-2048).

Signing below means that you have received and understand this notice. You also receive a copy.

(I) Signature:	*(J)* Date:

According to the Paperwork Reduction Act of 1995, no persons are required to respond to a collection of information unless it displays a valid OMB control number. The valid OMB control number for this information collection is 0938-0566. The time required to complete this information collection is estimated to average 7 minutes per response, including the time to review instructions, search existing data resources, gather the data needed, and complete and review the information collection. If you have comments concerning the accuracy of the time estimate or suggestions for improving this form, please write to: CMS, 7500 Security Boulevard, Attn: PRA Reports Clearance Officer, Baltimore, Maryland 21244-1850.

Form CMS-R-131 (03/11)   Form Approved OMB No. 0938-0566

Courtesy of the Centers for Medicare & Medicaid Services, www.cms.gov.

Figure 16-1 Advance Beneficiary Notice

with additional information such as patient account balances. Additional forms may be beneficial for procedures or hospital inpatient physician services. Encounter form descriptions need to match CPT codes, guiding toward accurate selection. An area for ranking diagnosis is critical. Renaming the visits (Level 4, for example for a 99214) can be risky. Each checked or circled CPT service needs to clearly indicate the ICD-10-CM codes that correlate to each service clearly documented in the medical record. All too often, the encounter formats do not provide a simple approach to this valuable data.

Table 16-3 Snapshot Example of Part of an Encounter Form

Date of service:				Waiver? yes / no		
Patient name:				Insurance:		
Address:				Subscriber name:		
				Group #:		
				Account #:		
Phone:				Copay:		
DOB:	Age:		Sex:	Physician name:		

Office visit	New	Est	Dx	Office procedures	Code	Dx
HX, EX, MDM Mod: 24, 25, 32, 57				Anoscopy	46600	
Minimal		99211		Audiometry	92551	
PF, PF, SF	99201	99212		Cerumen removal	69210	
EPF, EPF, LC	99202	99213		Colposcopy	57452	
D, D, LC–MC	99203	99214		Colposcopy w/biopsy	57455	
C, C, MC	99204	99215		ECG, w/interpretation	93000	
C, C, HC	99205			ECG, rhythm strip	93040	
				Endometrial biopsy	58100	
Preventive Care	**New**	**Est**		Flexible sigmoidoscopy	45330	
Under age 1 year	99381	99391		Flexible sigmoidoscopy w/biopsy	45331	
Age 1–4 years	99382	99392		Fracture care, cast/splint	29___	
Age 5–11 years	99383	99393		Site: _____		
Age 12–17 years	99384	99394		Nebulizer	94640	
Age 18–39 years	99385	99395		Nebulizer demo	94664	
Age 40–64 years	99386	99396		Spirometry	94010	
Age 65 years & older	99387	99397		Spirometry, pre and post	94060	
Medicare Preventive Services				Tympanometry	92567	
Pap		Q0091		Vasectomy	55250	
Pelvic & breast		G0101		**Skin procedures**	**Code**	**Units**
Prostate/PSA		G0103		Burn care, initial	16000	
Welcome to Medicare exam		G0402		Foreign body, skin, simple	10120	
Flu shot Admin		G0008		Foreign body, skin, complex	10121	
Pneumonia shot Admin		G0009		I&D, abscess	10060	
				I&D, hematoma/seroma	10140	
				Laceration repair, simple	120___	
				Site: ___ Size: ___		

Encounters and services that are performed by the physician at facilities outside of the physician office are also key to submitting accurate claims.

Often referred to as *rounding cards,* these encounter cards are kept in the lab coat pocket of physicians rounding on patients in the facility setting. The physician transfers service information onto the card to give to the coding/billing department.

A common finding upon audit is a claim submission for a discharge from the hospital, lacking a description of the minutes if over 30 minutes; or the time in and time out for certain procedures while performing critical care services; or the care of a patient in multiple settings during one date, midnight to midnight. Depending on the specialty, the hospital services may describe 100 percent of the practice, certainly requiring frequent and detailed information to be transmitted or shared with the coder. Some physicians carry tools such as a laptop, personal digital assistant (PDA), or other electronic wireless apparatus to assist in tracking the services provided. Additionally, some hospitals allow direct access to the medical record system from the physician office locations electronically. The physician office can then print if needed, the necessary operative reports, pathology or radiology results, inpatient progress notes, and so forth.

While the move to a completely electronic medical record system is being pushed forward, within the physician office location, there may be providers who have not yet embraced this mechanism of practice support. They may use separate encounter forms for various individuals or diagnostic testing services. Some common forms are an encounter form for the x-ray technician within an orthopedic practice setting, and a laboratory form for the lab technician within an internal medicine practice. As automation is implemented, all of these details need to be considered very carefully, encouraging accurate selection of the codes for the exact services that are rendered.

Coding Tip:

The term "incident to" refers to a service provided "incidental to" a physician's service (i.e., a nurse practitioner following up on a patient's diabetes where the physician previously saw the patient). Coding "incident to" would allow billing of the service for 100 percent of the allowable fee, to be submitted under the physician. Otherwise, the nurse practitioner could report the service and Medicare would reimburse at an 85 percent rate.

The physician does not have to be physically present in the treatment room while the service is being provided, but must be present in the immediate office suite to render assistance if needed. When this is done, it is highly recommended to obtain the written policies and procedures from the insurance plan, as the rules vary per insurance plan.

For CMS, the incident-to policies are strictly enforced; therefore, one should follow exactly every detail of the policies. For example, physicians must be present on-site at the time of the encounter. The service must be an integral part of a service previously performed by the physician. A new Medicare patient being seen by the NP would have to be billed under the NP's number: The NP is providing initial care, so the service would not be incidental to the physician. The incident-to policies have limitations (e.g., they do not apply for all services, at all locations, performed by all staff levels of licensure). Each insurance plan tends to have policies, not necessarily equal to the strict CMS policy. The scope of practice of health care professionals does not necessarily correlate to the insurance payment policies. This typically causes many questions and confusion in the field, necessitating detailed investigation and education for the coder. Incident-to policies are easily violated, and violations are prevalent within the Medicare system. These rules warrant additional review by the providers before determining incident-to billing.

As electronic medical records become more available and utilized in the industry, it is anticipated that fewer encounter/charge tickets will be in use. The capture will be automated by following the patient through the practice electronically rather than with paper.

Hospital facilities also meet with challenges of documentation and capturing data for the chargemaster. The working diagnosis is often not documented, since the ICD-10-CM codes are selected with a different set of guidelines than the outpatient guidelines. For the hospital, it is advantageous for the physician to list the symptoms or preliminary diagnoses leading to the diagnosis-related group (DRG). Another challenging area is the documentation of complications or comorbidities that may arise during care. This is a huge revenue factor for hospital facilities. Focused education for this alone would dramatically affect reimbursements for hospitals. The chargemaster encounter format should be frequently reviewed and will affect financial reimbursements to the hospital.

Cheat Sheets and Reference Guides

Cheat sheets (the common term for quick-reference sheets that help in adhering to policy, *not* in cheating on them) tend to be either the documentation format for the E/M encounter (the AMA/CPT codes and the 1995 and/or 1997 Guidelines) or the listing of commonly used ICD-10-CM and procedure codes. Cheat sheets may be helpful, but they are not all-inclusive by any means. Relying only on a cheat sheet can lead to errors resulting in extensive sanctions. If one is utilized, the resulting coding should be closely monitored for accuracy.

Template forms and electronic health record issues continue to grow. Of great concern acknowledged by CMS and medical record auditors is the issue of record cloning when using an electronic health record (EHR) or electronic medical record (EMR). A cloned record includes material copied and pasted from the patient's record or generic profile into the history and physical exam sections and may or may not provide a unique assessment and plan. Each patient encounter needs to be unique and individualized based on the patient's presenting problem.

A template simply lists certain components or items that might need to be filled in or completed. A CMS task force reviewed EHR issues for purposes of *Meaningful Use.* For example, if providers selected and used an EHR system that is certified by Meaningful Use criteria as outlined in the *Federal Register,* July 10, 2010, they may have been eligible for an incentive payment.

As the industry continues with advancements to electronic medical record systems, the risk of abuse or fraud escalates if the formats for collecting information are not properly implemented to accurately capture the actual services performed.

The second common cheat sheet is a specialty ICD-10-CM listing. Shortcomings of these quick references include the lack of specificity, or, more importantly, a nonspecific or an incomplete description. Unfortunately, an alarming number of staff members utilize specialty "cheat sheets" because they believe these are the only codes available for selection, perhaps in the absence of ever seeing an ICD-10-CM code book or ability to navigate easily through cumbersome electronic data files. Clearly, there are many more coding options and requirements than a typical cheat sheet could accommodate. When updating cheat sheets or reference guides, keep an audit trail by placing the date of the revision on the form. ICD-10-CM guidelines are essential and helpful in determining the multiple codes that may be required to accurately describe the patient's condition for the encounter. Finding the accurate code to indicate the reason for ordering a test, for example, is nearly impossible without referring to the full ICD-10-CM resource.

Finally, it is wise to begin training personnel in the basics of using the ICD-10-CM index—locating, sequencing, recognizing common abbreviations and indicators. With the inception of ICD-10-CM, cheat sheets have become lengthy and abbreviated with cross-reference to the tabular for additional character selection.

Collection of Payment at the Time of Service

If the patient chose to personally pay for the service, simply collect the entire amount for all care at the cashier window. Most practices have set up mechanisms to accept many forms of payment such as cash or checks, debit or credit cards.

If the patient owes for previous care, collect this fee as well, according to financial policies in place. Give careful consideration to contractual obligations, as the physician who participates with one or more plans may still be required to file a claim for noncovered services to the plan.

Charge Entry and Immediate Payment

Once the encounter form or charges have been entered by the practice or the billing department/company, the claims are submitted for processing. These functions may be performed off- or on-site, but regardless, need to be carefully reviewed for accuracy. It is import to make sure all appropriate CPT, ICD-10-CM, and HCPCSII codes are complete and linked, assigning any necessary modifiers, and checking patient and provider information. When payment has been given to the practice (e.g., copayments, payment on an account, private pay), it should be accounted for with a receipt to the patient and an entry in the accounting or billing system. If posting is performed off-site, a tracking log for payments is critical to protect both the patient and the practice. Most physician offices use automated billing or practice management systems that allow both the bills to be generated and payment information to be entered into the patient's account. Reconciliation procedures with the practice's accounting system are often in a separate module but may have a mechanism of connecting to the billing software, gathering the charge and payment data to assist with balancing the accounts receivable. Hospital facilities may handle payments by various methods, due to the volume of patients and personnel. The cash and daily balancing should be managed effectively to avoid embezzlement risks. Again, depending on the size of the organization, this process may vary; however, incorporating strong security and efficiency principles in overseeing the financial processes is recommended for all organizations. Policies and procedures for handling charges and payments, whether in a physician practice, a billing company, or a facility, protect both the entity and the employee.

Submit the Claim

Depending on the practice management system, the claim preparation may begin at the cashier desk or may actually be submitted at this point. Smaller practices tend to implement streamlined processes, actually completing the coding and remaining details concurrently with the cashiering process. Other organizations may use a worksheet (encounter capture form) and enter partial details at the time of the visit, and then another person/department verifies the details of the information prior to submitting the claim. Verification at this point may include review of pathology or radiology reports, surgical operative notes, hospital visit or critical care notes, and so forth.

Whatever the method, it is imperative and required by law that the claim be transmitted with accurate information in each field, including the applicable CPT, ICD-10-CM, and HCPCSII codes and modifiers if needed.

Most providers send the CMS-1500 claim form electronically. If submitting a paper claim rather than an electronic transmitted claim, most insurance plans, including the majority of the CMS carriers, require the use of the standard CMS-1500 claim form. The form is printed in red ink, allowing optical scanning upon receipt. See Chapter 15 in this book for detailed information.

Payor Receipt of the Claim

Some practice management systems provide an alert system or front-end claims scrubbing software, indicating aspects of the claim that may be erroneous and require immediate attention prior to transmitting directly to the insurance plan.

The insurance carrier will typically receive the claim through a clearinghouse, or hub, which forwards the claim to the insurance carrier. Fields for electronic transmission have been updated from the CMS-1500 paper claim process to newer, streamlined HIPAA transaction and data sets with electronic field capability. Some insurance plans allow tracking of the claim upon receipt by the insurance plan through the various departments. When available, resubmission or sending of corrected information may expedite the claim payment. Otherwise, the claim may be rejected with a standard notice.

Resubmission of claims has limitations based on the insurance plan, especially the time limit from the date of the service to the initial claim date. This time limit is likely to vary from insurance plan to insurance plan and also from state to state, depending on the timely payment rules per state or contract. It is recommended that billing take place on a daily basis as most insurance contracts specify timely filing limits and requirements. If the contract does not state a limit, check the state law. Typical claims filing is required within 90 days of the services being rendered, but as stated above, this varies by carrier. Most state laws require carriers to acknowledge receipt of the claim within a specified time and outline time limit instructions when providers need to appeal.

Follow-Up

The beginning of this chapter stressed that the collection of accurate information from the patient is a key factor for payment. The next most important factor is claim follow-up. Many coders/billers spend 50 percent or more of their time researching on nonpayments, resubmittals, sending additional information upon request, or sending in an appeal for the claim. In general, the actual transmission of the claim is a very small portion of the payment cycle. These duties may be outsourced, provided by a different department, or combined with other coding and billing functions. When claims grow older than 90 days, providers and facilities may consider contracting with companies that specifically work on claims follow-up. Often, private pay accounts are referred for payment arrangements and collection activities when necessary.

Accuracy of Payment on Arrival

The payment may be sent to the organization in an electronic format, with a separate report to review, or by a check. There are systems that provide optional features such as allowing for automatic posting of the payment to the patient account. Many practices and facilities continue to post payments manually. In either case, reconciliation of the payment to the accounting system must be accurate.

When the payment arrives, each line item (service or supply) must be reconciled for the patient service and for the insurance plan agreement. When payment is not received, the cause must be investigated. Did the practice overlook a process of the payment cycle? Were improper codes selected? Was a modifier inappropriately indicated for this insurance plan or omitted? Is it the responsibility of the patient?

If the payment is received, is the payment amount correct according to the contract with the insurance plan? Next, evaluate the patient's financial obligation according to the explanation of benefits (EOB). Perhaps the deductible was not collected at the time of the service, or the copayment or coinsurance was not as described during the verification procedure or was not known at the time of the encounter. Enter the patient's obligation into the system, and flag the system to send an invoice to the patient for the portion that is due. Do not waive the copayments and deductibles for the patient obligation, including for professional courtesy purposes. This will often create a breach of contract situation for the provider or facility and may cause a potential discrimination situation among patients.

The CMS website (https://www.cms.gov) includes resources on HIPAA and provides the following information regarding submission and processing of claims:

> The Health Insurance Portability & Accountability Act of 1996 (HIPAA) named certain types of organizations as covered entities, including health plans, health care clearinghouses, and certain health care providers. HIPAA also adopted certain standard transactions for Electronic Data Interchange (EDI) of health care data. These transactions are: claims and encounter information, payment and remittance advice, claims status, eligibility, enrollment and disenrollment, referrals and authorizations, and premium payment. Under HIPAA, if a covered entity conducts one of the adopted transactions electronically, they must use the adopted standard. This means that they must adhere to the content and format requirements of each standard. HIPAA also adopted specific code sets for diagnosis and procedures to be used in all transactions. The HCPCS (Ancillary Services/Procedures), CPT-4 (Physicians Procedures), CDT (Dental Terminology), ICD-9 (Diagnosis and Hospital Inpatient Procedures), ICD-10 (As of October 1, 2015), and NDC (National Drug Codes) codes with which providers and health plan are familiar, are the adopted code sets for procedures, diagnoses, and drugs.

CMS has published on its website the standard listing of rejection codes and their definitions.

Appealing the Claim

The claim may have been partially paid per line item, or paid fully on selective line items, or unfortunately, not paid at all.

It is important to identify the root cause for the issue, the extent of the problem, and who is accountable. The decision tree for claim denials may include many people.

Upon investigation, communication with the state medical society, the specialty societies, or the AMA may be required. Insurance legislative actions are more and more often required to resolve issues of nonpayment. Timely payment rules vary tremendously and are frequently updated by state legislation.

Upon receiving the rejection, two steps are recommended prior to submitting an appeal. First, depending on the reason for the rejection, you may want to obtain a second opinion, preferably in writing. Review these findings with the physician, and determine the proper coding for all services, including CPT, HCPCSII, ICD-10-CM, and all potential modifier use. Second, obtain the written policies and procedures for the services from the insurance plan. Most insurance plans allow access to their policies on the Internet for their participating (contracted) physicians/organizations. If a physician is nonparticipating, it might be more difficult to obtain the information. On occasion, the patient can request the policy. The policies may guide toward various coding edits (either bundling codes or using specific diagnosis codes showing the **medical necessity** of a service) to correspond with the insurance benefits.

> **medical necessity:** The justification for an action or service based on the patient's condition, problem, or illness.

Some claims may simply be resubmitted, with the corrections entered on the claim. Particularly if a specific piece of data is missing such as a modifier, enter the omitted information and resend. Claims that are unpaid should not simply be resent without researching them first. If the rejection is for "truncated ICD-10-CM, lacking specificity," for example, the claim would need to be corrected. The physician is required to submit the claim with the ICD-10-CM code at the highest level of specificity for the date of service reflecting the services rendered. Telephone appeals may sometimes correct the issue, without the need for resubmission or a formal appeal procedure. Contact the provider hotline or other appeal line first to attempt to correct the issue verbally. For repeated issues or a trend in rejections, ask kindly to speak with a supervisor. The supervisor may have the ability to override the system and pay the claim, or may provide solution for future claims submission.

The formal appeal process should be outlined in the participating insurance contract or policies of the insurance plan. For nonparticipating physicians, the process is much the same, starting with a phone call. It is not unusual to submit an appeal letter from the physician explaining the specific reason the physician believes the care should be paid, including any special report components or additional information of support. In this correspondence, describe the issue or need for coverage, or the circumstances beyond the routine or normal that occurred for this particular patient, and ensure that these circumstances are documented in the medical record. Scientific data, presentations, or other documents for accepted community standard of care may assist in the acceptance.

If the claim appeal is rejected, the next step may be a hearing. Some insurance plans allow only the physician to attend the hearing. If possible, a certified coder, the administrator, and possibly an attorney should attend the hearing with the physician, depending on the circumstances and the level of revenue.

Figure 16–2 shows a sample appeal letter, which would need to be revised based on the specific care and procedure. Some dictation tips are to list the additional work to perform the procedure, patient safety, quality of care indicators, complications and comorbidity, unique scenario for this particular patient, and impossibility to provide alternative medical care and why. Avoid descriptions that simply request an increased payment amount, unless the contract clearly indicates the fee schedule was inappropriately paid. The appeal process is not typically the venue used to request an increase in the contractual allowances or fee schedule.

August 30, 20XX

(physician name)
(physician address)

Dear Dr._____:

RE: *(Enter the reason for the appeal, medical policy, edit, computer issue, new scientific procedure, etc.)*

        Beneficiary/Patient Name:
        Insured ID#_____Group ID#_____
        Authorization#_____*(if applicable)*
        Claim#_____
        Date of Service_____

I am writing to respectfully request medical review for the care that was provided for *(patient name).* The professional services performed for this case were: *(state the complications, beyond the usual, unique requirements, exceptional professional care, etc.)*
        (1)
        (2)
        (3)

The HIPAA transaction and data set standards for CPT, HCPCSII, ICD9-CM, and modifiers were selected according to: *(reference specifically)*

- AMA/CPT page _____, CPT Assisant Article _____, CPT Changes _____ year, CPT Principles
- HCPCSII page _____, Coding Policy # _____ per our carrier, Coding Policy newsletter from _____
- ICD-10-CM Guidelines: Section: _____, of Coding Clinic article _____
- Modifier use per (CCI, or insurance policy edits)

Attached please find the written response from (CPC or professional coding resource) regarding the accuracy of the code selection with a copy of the medical documentation including the radiology, pathology, and other reports. Also, attached please find the professional publications for the scientific value (e.g., articles from *JAMA, New England Journal of Medicine,* etc.) describing the standard of care.

Thank you for your prompt response.

Sincerely,

(physician name)

Figure 16-2 Sample appeal letter

Medicare Fee-for-Service Original Appeals Process

Medicare beneficiaries, providers, and suppliers have the right to appeal claims decisions once the Medicare Contractor makes an initial decision. This pertains to amounts paid and whether or not the service is covered. By law, Medicare offers five levels in the Part A and Part B appeals process. The levels, listed in order, are:

- **Level 1: Redetermination:** by the Medicare payment processor—fiscal intermediary (FI), carrier, or MAC (Medicare Appeals Council)
- **Level 2: Reconsideration:** by a Qualified Independent Contractor (QIC)
- **Level 3: Hearing:** by an Administrative Law Judge (ALJ)
- **Level 4: Review by the Medicare Appeals Council**
- **Level 5: Judicial Review in U.S. District Court:** An individual has 60 days to file for judicial review, with the AIC (as of 2015) threshold being at least $1,460 in dispute

Medicare Redetermination Request

CMS has a form for some of the appeals processes that are helpful. The form for redetermination is CMS-20027, and it must be submitted with any correspondence. An individual, provider, or supplier must file an appeal within 120 days of the initial decision on a claim, and the FI, carrier, or MAC, must issue its decision within 60 days (Figure 16–3).

Appeals for reconsideration must be filed within 180 days of the redetermination and the QIC must issue its decision within 60 days. The CMS website provides form CMS-20033 for filing for a reconsideration. Redetermination and reconsiderations are the most commonly used levels of Medicare appeals.

Medicare Request for Hearing by an Administrative Law Judge (ALJ)

If the carrier determination is not satisfactory or if greater issues need to be addressed, the next step is to submit the CMS-20034 A/B, which is usually completed by an attorney, attaching all previous correspondence. At this level, an individual, provider, or supplier must file an appeal within 60 days of the QIC's reconsideration, provided that the case involves the threshold, which is adjusted annually. The ALJ must issue a decision within 90 days. This form is two pages (Figure 16–4).

Exercise 16.1

1. When is the advance beneficiary notice completed and signed?
2. List the steps for the payment cycle in the correct order.
3. What are two very important factors for the payment cycle?

DEPARTMENT OF HEALTH AND HUMAN SERVICES
CENTERS FOR MEDICARE & MEDICAID SERVICES

MEDICARE REDETERMINATION REQUEST FORM — 1ST LEVEL OF APPEAL

1. Beneficiary's name:_____

2. Medicare number: _____

3. Item or service you wish to appeal: _____

4. Date the service or item was received: _____

5. Date of the initial determination notice (please include a copy of the notice with this request):
   (If you received your initial determination notice more than 120 days ago, include your reason for the late filing.)

   _____

   _____

   _____

   5a. Name of the Medicare contractor that made the determination (not required):

   _____

   5b. Does this appeal involve an overpayment? ☐ Yes ☐ No
   (for providers and suppliers only)

6. I do not agree with the determination decision on my claim because:

   _____

   _____

   _____

7. Additional information Medicare should consider:

   _____

   _____

   _____

8. ☐ I have evidence to submit. Please attach the evidence to this form or attach a statement explaining what you intend to submit and when you intend to submit it. You may also submit additional evidence at a later time, but all evidence must be received prior to the issuance of the redetermination.

   ☐ I do not have evidence to submit.

9. Person appealing: ☐ Beneficiary ☐ Provider/Supplier ☐ Representative

10. Name, address, and telephone number of person appealing: _____

    _____

11. Signature of person appealing: _____

12. Date signed:_____

PRIVACY ACT STATEMENT: The legal authority for the collection of information on this form is authorized by section 1869 (a)(3) of the Social Security Act. The information provided will be used to further document your appeal. Submission of the information requested on this form is voluntary, but failure to provide all or any part of the requested information may affect the determination of your appeal. Information you furnish on this form may be disclosed by the Centers for Medicare and Medicaid Services to another person or government agency only with respect to the Medicare Program and to comply with Federal laws requiring or permitting the disclosure of information or the exchange of information between the Department of Health and Human Services and other agencies. Additional information about these disclosures can be found in the system of records notice for system no. 09-70-0566, as amended, available at 71 Fed. Reg. 54489 (2006) or at http://www.cms.gov/PrivacyActSystemofRecords/downloads/0566.pdf

Form CMS-20027 (12/10)

Figure 16-3 CMS-20027 form for formal redetermination

DEPARTMENT OF HEALTH AND HUMAN SERVICES
OFFICE OF MEDICARE HEARINGS AND APPEALS

REQUEST FOR MEDICARE HEARING BY AN ADMINISTRATIVE LAW JUDGE ❑ **Part A**

Effective July 1, 2005. For use by party to a reconsideration determination issued by a Qualified Independent Contractor (QIC) ❑ **Part B**
(Amount in controversy must be $100 or more.)

Send copies of this completed form to:
Original — *Office of Medicare Hearings and Appeals Field Office specified in the QIC Reconsideration Notice*
  Copy — *Appellant* *Copy* — *All other parties*
Failure to send a copy of this completed request to the other parties to the appeal will delay the start date of your appeal.
Did you send all required copies? ❑ Yes ❑ No

Appellant *(The party appealing the reconsideration determination)*

Beneficiary *(Leave blank if same as the appellant.)*	Provider or Supplier *(Leave blank if same as the appellant.)*
Address	Address
City State Zip Code	City State Zip Code
Area Code/Telephone Number	E-mail Address	Area Code/Telephone Number	E-mail Address
Health Insurance (Medicare) Claim Number	Document control number assigned by the QIC

QIC that made the reconsideration determination	Dates of Service From To

I DISAGREE WITH THE DETERMINATION MADE ON MY APPEAL BECAUSE:

_____

_____

_____

You have a right to be represented at the hearing. If you are not represented but would like to be, your Office of Medicare Hearings and Appeals Field Office will give you a list of legal referral and service organizations. *(If you are represented and have not already done so, complete form CMS-1696.)*

Check **Only One** Statement:	❑ I **wish** to have a hearing.	Check **Only One** Statement:	❑ I **have** additional evidence to submit.
	❑ I **do not wish** to have a hearing and I request that a decision be made on the basis of the evidence in my case. *(Complete form HHS-723, "Waiver of Right to an ALJ Hearing.")*		❑ I **have no** additional evidence to submit.

If you have additional evidence to submit, please attach the evidence or attach a statement explaining what you intend to submit and when you intend to submit it. If you are a provider, supplier, or beneficiary represented by a provider or supplier, the evidence must be accompanied by a good cause statement explaining why the evidence is being submitted for the first time at the ALJ level.

The appellant should complete No. 1 and the representative, if any, should complete No. 2. If a representative is not present to sign, print his or her name in No. 2. Where applicable, check to indicate if appellant will accompany the representative at the hearing. ❑ Yes ❑ No

1. (Appellant's Signature)	Date	2. (Representative's Signature/Name)	Date
Address		Address	❑ Attorney ❑ Non-Attorney
City State Zip Code		City State Zip Code	
Area Code/Telephone Number	E-mail Address	Area Code/Telephone Number	E-mail Address

Answer the following questions that apply:
  A) Does request involve multiple claims? (If yes, a list of all the claims must be attached.) ❑ Yes ❑ No
  B) Does request involve multiple beneficiaries? (If yes, a list of beneficiaries, their HICNs and the dates of service.) ❑ Yes ❑ No
  C) Did the beneficiary assign his or her appeal rights to you as the provider/supplier? ❑ Yes ❑ No
     (If yes, you must complete and attach form CMS-20031. Failure to do so will prevent approval of the assignment.)

Must be completed by the provider/supplier if representing the beneficiary:

I waive my rights to charge and collect a fee for representing _____ before the Office of
Medicare Hearings and Appeals.   *(Beneficiary name)*

Signature of provider/supplier representing beneficiary	Date

CMS-20034 A/B U3 (08/05) EF 08/2005   ATTACH A COPY OF THE RECONSIDERATION DETERMINATION
                                              (IF AVAILABLE) TO THIS COPY.

Figure 16-4 CMS-20034 A/B U3 to request a Medicare hearing   *(continues)*

Must be completed by the provider/supplier if representing the beneficiary, they furnished the item(s) or services(s) at issue, and the appeal involves a question of liability under section 1879(a)(2) of the Social Security Act:

I waive my right to collect payment from the beneficiary for the furnished items or services at issue involving 1879(a)(2) of the Social Security Act.

Signature of provider/supplier representing beneficiary	Date

TO BE COMPLETED BY THE OFFICE OF MEDICARE HEARINGS AND APPEALS

Is this request filed timely? ❏ Yes ❏ No

If no, attach appellant's explanation for delay. If there is no explanation, send a Notice of Late Filing of Request for ALJ Hearing to the appellant and representative, if applicable, to request such an explanation.

Request received on	Field Office	Employee
Assigned on	Assigned by	Assigned to

Special response case? ❏ Yes ❏ No

If yes, explain why and state the targeted adjudication deadline.

_____

_____

Interpreter/translator needed (including sign language) ❏ Yes ❏ No

If yes, type needed:

_____

_____

If appellant not represented, has a list of legal referral and service organizations been provided. ❏ Yes ❏ No

PRIVACY ACT STATEMENT

The legal authority for the collection of information on this form is authorized by the Social Security Act (section 1155 of Title XI and sections 1852(g)(5), 1860D-4(h)(1), 1869(b)(1), and 1876 of Title XVIII). The information provided will be used to further document your appeal. Submission of the information requested on this form is voluntary, but failure to provide all or any part of the requested information may affect the determination of your appeal. Information you furnish on this form may be disclosed by the Office of Medicare Hearings and Appeals to another person or governmental agency only with respect to the Medicare Program and to comply with Federal laws requiring the disclosure of information or the exchange of information between the Department of Health and Human Services and other agencies.

CMS-20034 A/B U3 (08/05) EF 08/2005

Figure 16-4 (Continued)

Insurance Participation Agreements (Contracts)

Health Insurance Agreements

In reality, the practice of medicine is also a business, requiring effective business skills that are not typically part of medical school training. For the purpose of providing health care services, physicians and health care organizations choose to review and potentially execute (sign) insurance participation agreements (contracts). When the employers in the community select insurance for their employees, they will need various physicians and health care providers (participating providers) to select from. If the patients choose to see a participating physician or facility, they are motivated in some manner, typically including the financial motivation of greater coverage and less out-of-pocket expense. Patients may have limited or no coverage unless they see a participating provider. The participating physician anticipates a more productive schedule and more patient volume as a result of being included in the list of participating providers published by the patient's insurance plan. In return, the physician typically agrees to a decreased payment amount from the insurance plan and other limitations. Within the contract language, many additional terms are likely, binding the physician to many other policies and procedures created by the insurance plan. Every participation agreement contract should be negotiated in detail with a corporate attorney prior to signing and should be renegotiated as necessary. Any potential carve-outs, which are specific items or services specially priced by the plan, or physician expenses for particularly costly supplies necessary to perform certain procedures should be carefully reviewed.

The contracts may include these structured plans or modifications of them:

- HMO—Health maintenance organization
- POS—**Point of service (POS)**
- PPO—**Preferred provider organization (PPO)**

When a physician or health care organization decides not to participate with the health insurance plans, alternative means of advertising, marketing, and business development are usually required. One new term for this concept of practicing is *boutique*. The practice may have a contractual relationship with patients, describing a package of services or items.

Workers' Compensation and Auto Insurance Agreements

Unlike health insurance plans, workers' compensation and automobile insurance medical coverage are offered by only a few insurance networks. These agreements are likely governed by state laws; hence, the use of an attorney to negotiate is even more important. HIPAA rules and regulations do not bind these, however.

Government Payment

The government is by far the largest purchaser of health care services in the United States, well into billions of dollars annually. Since it is the largest, as with any business, the purchaser outlines certain expectations. The complexity is

point of service (POS): The insurance plan encourages the patient to seek health care at a specific location or facility, typically where a contract for less cost has been negotiated.

preferred provider organization (PPO): The health care provider signs a contract to join a group, usually an insurance plan. The physician name is then published in a listing, the listing may be resold, or the patients may receive incentives and discounts when choosing to have the care with a PPO.

increased with bureaucracy and politics, and the system becomes convoluted and challenging for everyone. Reform of the system is needed in order to adequately provide health care for beneficiaries in the future. The process of reform has begun, with the implementation of the **Medicare Modernization Act**, and continues today.

Medicare Modernization Act: Federal law upgrading, streamlining, and revising the Centers for Medicare and Medicaid Services.

As stated in previous chapters, government payors include:

- Medicare
- Medicare for Disabilities (any age)
- Railroad Retirement
- Medicaid
- Federal employees (e.g., U.S. postal workers)
- TRICARE/CHAMPVA
- Indian Health Services, which may choose to adopt CMS policies

Therefore, a choice to provide or not to provide care for government patients may dramatically affect the volume of patients and the potential income of a physician or facility.

History of Medicare

Medicare began under President Lyndon B. Johnson in 1965, as a portion of the Social Security Act. The basic intention was to provide a level of health care for every senior citizen. Over the course of time, Congress has recommended various services and has created guidelines for the budget and spending. In 1991, the resource-based relative value system (RBRVS) set the physician fee schedule at a specific rate, determined by a complex calculation. Today, the RBRVS continues to be used as one of the major payor systems in determining procedural and service valuation.

The RBRVS system, under the COBRA/OBRA rules, requires a balanced budget annually. In simplistic terms, as more CPT codes for services and items are approved for covered benefits, additional funds are not available from Congress. The total money pool is to be divided between all of the **covered services**, determined by CMS. The **Balanced Budget Act (BBA)** of 1997 also added a few screening and prevention services to the covered benefits for the first time, a segment of services that has grown tremendously as of the date of this publication.

covered service: A contracted benefit from the insurer to the provider and patient. For example, while infertility treatment may not be a covered service, testing and treatment until infertility is diagnosed may be a covered service with the insurer.

Balanced Budget Act: Legislation designed to balance the federal budget enacted during the Clinton administration.

Each year, the planned fee schedule is introduced as proposed rules in the *Federal Register*. The Physician Fee Schedule, Outpatient Prospective Payment System, and Hospital Payment Schedule are the most popular CMS documents obtained by most health organizations. The proposed rules allow formal comments, usually for 60 days; then they are republished in the *Federal Register* as law, indicating the effective dates. If Congress is inclined, the final rules may be revised, again with publication of a proposed set of rules and the final rules. In general, many details of the government system are found in the *Federal Register* documents.

Also annually, the patient's deductible amount and the contribution amount per CPT or HCPCSII code are published in the *Federal Register*. The patient obligation fees have slowly increased over the years.

The Department of Health and Human Services oversees the Centers for Medicare & Medicaid Services. The secretary of HHS serves on the presidential cabinet.

Enrollment with Medicare

In 2007, the National Provider Identifier (NPI) numbers for providers began to be assigned. The application form to enroll for this number began in the spring of 2005 and is now an online, automated process. The NPI numbers replace the multiple provider numbers that were required by various insurance contracts.

When planning to care for Medicare patients, the physician is expected to enroll *prior* to caring for Medicare patients. The CMS system has three major forms to complete when enrolling to provide Medicare services. The forms are the CMS-855B, CMS-855I, and CMS-855R. Providers applying for enrollment in Medicare must furnish their National Provider Identifier (NPI) number on the enrollment applications. The NPI is required for HIPAA compliance and standard transactions. Enrollment applications without the NPI will be rejected.

Upon careful completion, the lengthy forms are sent to the CMS carrier. The processing of the enrollment forms is typically three to six months but may be longer, depending on certain issues. Early enrollment is recommended. Upon completion of the enrollment, the provider number is assigned, whether to an individual or a group of physicians.

Participating Providers

The participating providers agree to abide by the CMS policies and procedures, medical coverage determinations, and claim submission processes. In return, the payment as published in the physician fee schedule is made to the physician; therefore, the physician collects the deductible and coinsurance amount from the patient. Remember that the physician will not be paid the usual and customary fee of the practice; the CMS portion of the payment will be based on the CMS participation fee schedule. The patient is obligated for 20 percent of each service plus the deductible amount, and this portion may be paid either by the patient personally or by a secondary Medicare supplemental insurance plan.

Nonparticipating Providers

The **nonparticipating (nonPAR) provider** may choose for each Medicare patient whether to submit the claim as accepting assignment, which is to agree to the CMS policies and procedures, medical coverage determinations, and claim submission processes, or not. However, the claim and the fee charged to the patient are completely fixed, as the limiting charge listed in the fee schedule. In other words, the amount charged per CPT code is limited, and it is improper to collect more than that amount from the patient at any time, whether participating or nonparticipating. The CMS will pay nonparticipating claims at a 5 percent lower rate and the payment will be sent directly to the patient. The physician then collects the CMS payment from the patient, the 20 percent for each service plus the deductible amount at the time of the care.

For participating and nonparticipating providers, the patient is obligated to pay his or her portion of the fee, and the physician or health care organization is obligated to collect the fee. Waiving any deductibles or coinsurance amounts due is illegal and creates a high risk of investigation. In the past, this was referred to as a professional courtesy. Once the patient has chosen to have the claim submitted, the patient has a financial obligation for the care. The only exception to this concept is

nonparticipating (nonPAR) provider: Providers not contracting (participating) with the insurance plan. Medicare nonPAR provider must not exceed the limiting charge when billing beneficiaries.

if the patient is indigent, in which case the provider may choose to waive the fees. For the physician office, proof of indigence is not required and no forms are necessary. It is recommended, however, that any write-offs for these purposes be done after the claim has been processed. For the hospital setting, a form is completed, stating financial need.

The physician, whether participating or nonparticipating, is obligated to submit the claim for the patient to the CMS carrier. Beneficiaries do not submit claims for the care.

Opt-Out

The opt-out concept is the final CMS category. Section 1802 of the Act, as amended by §4507 of the BBA of 1997, permits a physician/practitioner to opt out of Medicare and enter into private contracts with Medicare beneficiaries if specific requirements of this instruction are met. This is the private contracting concept. The physician chooses to notify the CMS carrier of the decision to opt out of CMS for two years. If the physician changes his or her mind within the first 90 days, a written affidavit may reverse the choice; otherwise, the two-year period is implemented. If at the end of the two years the physician chooses to reactivate as PAR or nonPAR, the enrollment system is implemented, which again could take time. The opt-out invitation is sent on a specific date each year, allowing the physician to reenter the CMS system at a specific time. Therefore, the total time out of the system may be a bit longer than the two years.

While an opt-out physician, the physician agrees with the patient on the service and the payment amount. The published Medicare fee schedule, rules, and policies do not apply, and usual claims are not submitted to CMS at all. The financial processes are between the patient and the physician directly. Chapter 15 of the Medicare Benefit Policy Manual, Section 40, should be carefully reviewed for specific guidelines for the Medicare opt-out option.

A physician who has opted out may provide emergency care and submit claims for the emergency services.

Medicare Resources

Each state is assigned to various carriers who have contracted to manage the Medicare beneficiaries. The carriers have multiple responsibilities surrounding the coverage, claims process, and appeals management, each with at least one or more physicians serving as a medical director. The carriers also implement the rules and regulations as disseminated by CMS nationally, and now policies are based on national coverage determinations rather than local carrier determinations.

The carriers allow anyone to access information and coverage policies on the Web—no log-in process is required. There is also an index on the website of all the carriers by provider type and topic. The CMS website is https://www.cms.gov.

In this book, we do not have the ability to publish the multiple rules and regulations that surround the care for Medicare patients. Prior to rendering the care and submitting the claim, the physician is required to implement all policies and procedures according to the CMS concepts. This may entail many laws, such as fraud and abuse, antitrust, Stark Amendments, and the **False Claims Act**, which carry immensely expensive fines, potential recoupment or forfeiture of future claim payments, or jail.

False Claims Act: Federal legislation that prohibits submission of claims for services not rendered or for any services considered fraudulent upon investigation.

Another important topic briefly discussed earlier in this chapter is the Incident to Physician Service rules, which are very detailed. It is advisable to review the policies for this rule in detail and implement carefully.

Advance Beneficiary Notice

One of the most important documents created for Medicare beneficiaries is the advance beneficiary notice (ABN) form.

The forms and procedures for completing the ABN are slightly different between physician/outpatient facilities and inpatient facilities. The physician and outpatient facility procedures will be described first.

Effective March 2011, the CMS-R-131 forms were revamped. These forms standardized the language, the size of the print font, and the procedure for obtaining the signatures. Refer back to Figure 16–1 for the CMS-R-131 (March 2011) form. These are the general steps for providing an ABN:

1. Notification is given to the patient if the physician believes charges may not be paid by Medicare because the service is considered nonmedically necessary according to Medicare (because of either local carrier or national policy).

2. A written ABN is given to the patient *before* the service is rendered.

3. The patient is notified of the CPT code(s) for the services and an estimated total financial obligation the patient will be responsible for. Determining this financial obligation fact may entail detailed investigation by contacting the secondary insurance Medicare supplement plan, and investigating the deductible payment amounts to date, prevention coverage carveouts, medication payment options, and perhaps other information.

4. The ABN is offered if there is a genuine doubt of payment, as evidenced by stated reasons. Reasons for the denial are required on the form.

5. The ABN is not required for statutorily excluded services or items. Unfortunately, most Medicare patients and many providers do not have any awareness of the statutory limitations; hence, effective communication and education are often required.

6. The beneficiary agrees to pay for the service by signing the form requesting the service regardless of coverage.

7. Minimal alterations to the format are considered acceptable by CMS; however, the official ABN form instructions should be reviewed first. The ABN must give the patient the reason CMS will deny the charges, in detail. Terms such as "medically unnecessary" and "Medicare will not pay" are not acceptable. The physician must provide an informed reason to the patient. Terms such as the following should be used:

   • Medicare Part B usually does not pay for this many visits or treatments (frequency limitations).

   • Medicare Part B usually does not pay for this service.

   • Medicare Part B usually does not pay for such an extensive service.

   • Medicare Part B usually does not pay for this equipment.

   • Medicare Part B usually does not pay for this lab test.

8. Two criteria must be met: (1) the patient must receive the notice with the details previously described, and (2) the patient must comprehend the information. For this reason, simple terminology is necessary on the ABN forms.

9. For any Medicare patient encounter, the ABN must be personally offered, face to face.

10. Timely response to questions regarding the form is required, further explaining the reason for anticipated CMS nonpayment.

11. The ABN must be given in advance of the procedure, with time for the patient to rationally decide.

12. If the patient or authorized representative refuses to sign after being clearly educated, the circumstances must be charted and these details added to the ABN form. The physician then determines whether to provide the care free of charge, accept partial payment, or refuse care entirely for the patient.

When the ABN is properly completed, the patient is financially obligated for the total fee amount charged by the physician for that CPT code, and the amount is not associated with the Medicare Physician Fee Schedule Limiting Charges. This service should be reported on claim submission with modifier GA appended to the CPT/HCPCSII code, which denotes the signed ABN on file.

Managed Care Payments

For managed care, health maintenance organization (HMO), point of service (POS), and preferred provider organization (PPO) agreements are the various payment methodologies. The payment structure may include payments other than those for the specific line item of service listed on the claim. The entire payment or a portion of the payment may be an incentive payment, based on criteria developed by the insurance plan. The criteria may be either profit based or quality based. A profit-based incentive is often described with the term **withhold**. For each CPT code submitted, an amount is put aside by the insurance plan. One example of the criteria for the withhold would be: If the entire network of physicians in the community area provides cost-effective care, a portion of the withhold amount may be distributed to the participating physicians the following year. The parties that share in the withhold and the percentage of withholding and distribution vary per contract.

Another common method of payment is **capitation**. The physician is paid a flat fee, usually monthly, to manage the health care for a group of assigned patients, whether or not a particular patient receives any encounter or visits during the month. The capitation payments are usually distributed to the primary care physicians and certain specialists of the network. The capitation payment may also include certain other frequently used services, such as a venipuncture for lab tests. The capitation payments are entered into the practice management system, according to the policies of the practice. Capitation payments often describe risk pools. Risk pool criteria are established by the insurance plan, usually associated with the network providing the health care, the health of the patients within the network, and other details. The risk pool may or may not have incentive payout distributions to the health care providers.

Modifications of the HMO agreements are evolving. Common examples include limiting the location for the care (the patient must use a certain hospital or emergency room), limiting the medications allowed on the formulary used by the physician

withhold: A percentage held out by the managed care organization as an incentive to keep costs, admissions, and referrals low each year. If the provider follows the plan strategy, the withhold percentage is returned with interest at a predetermined time.

capitation: Represents a common managed care payment strategy by which providers are paid according to the number of patients choosing a physician as primary caregiver. The capitation payment is made for a predetermined amount at a predetermined time each quarter or year.

(or only covering generic medications), requiring the patient to get a second opinion prior to a surgical procedure, or requiring the patient to have specific medical procedures before surgical options can be covered.

Payments are expected to correlate to the agreements in the contract. The contract is likely to state the period of time after the care within which the claim is to be submitted, the terms for selection of codes and their definitions, the appeal process, and so on. The contract may dramatically affect the profit for the practice, depending on the volume of patients covered by that insurance plan. Understanding the policies prior to signing the agreement is wise and will affect the bottom line.

In most of the agreements, the patient is obligated only for the copayment or coinsurance and the deductible for any covered service.

Traditional Indemnity Plans

Traditional indemnity plans are commonly referred to as 80 percent/20 percent commercial insurance plans. The physician is paid 80 percent of the physician practice usual, customary, and reasonable (UCR) fee schedule (which is often disputed as being inaccurate), and the patient is obligated for 20 percent. A physician fee schedule is randomly developed, or chosen based on a percentage of another methodology such as a percentage of RBRVS. When the individual physician determines the price for a particular service, basically creating his or her own charges for the services, the insurance company is not obligated to pay that rate for reimbursement. By agreeing to participate, the physician agrees to accept the discounted fee schedule presented by the insurance plan rather than the UCR rate, and then accept 80 percent of that new insurance plan fee schedule. The patient is obligated to pay 20 percent. If the patient chooses to visit a nonparticipating physician with a nonassigned claim, the patient may have 100 percent financial obligation or may be responsible for 80 percent of the physician's UCR fees. Contracts today often bundle various insurance programs into one master agreement. In other words, if the physician agrees to the HMO contract, the physician might also agree to the traditional indemnity plan contract at the same fee schedule rate and other rules and policies for that carrier. Selecting to participate in certain plans and not others within one company is becoming less available as an option for the physician.

Third-Party Administrator

Some insurance plans choose to have the claims processed by an outside organization, rather than performing the task within their organization. These outside firms are known as third-party administrators (TPAs). Claims are processed according to the policies of the insurance plan, implementing the edits as instructed. Appeals may or may not be managed by the TPA organization.

Exercise 16.2

1. What are the three physician options for CMS?
2. What is the name of the ABN form that is required to be used for CMS patients?
3. The ABN is necessary for only CMS patients. True or false?

Denials and Rejections

Frequently, upon receipt of the claim at the insurance plan, the claim is reviewed using an edit software system. When the factors and details for the edit are published, this is considered an open system, similar to the National Correct Coding Initiative (NCCI). The NCCI consists of three parts: (1) a manual of text describing rules and expectations for the code selections, (2) a list of mutually exclusive CPT code pairs, and (3) a list of CPT bundling matches. The ICD-10-CM edits for CMS are published within the policies of either the National Coverage Determinations (NCDs) or the Local Coverage Determinations (LCDs) and are not listed within the NCCI. NCDs are created by CMS for use by Medicare carriers in the United States. Local carriers create LCDs with various coverage and payment policies by state. More NCDs are anticipated in the future. The CPT manual is updated each October, whereas the listings for Column 1 and Column 2 and the mutually exclusive pair listings (see Table 13–3, for example), are updated at midnight each quarter.

> **Coding Tip:**
>
> The NCCI is a free download from the CMS website https://www.cms.gov, available on the date of implementation. For accuracy and ease, download it on the first business date of each quarter, directly to your desktop. That way it will be at your fingertips for the claims that are transmitted or reviewed each quarter.
>
> Not all insurance plans ascribe to sharing this type of information. NCCI code pair edits are automated prepayment edits that prevent improper payment when certain codes are submitted together for Part B-covered services. In addition to code pair edits, the NCCI includes a set of edits known as Medically Unlikely Edits (MUEs). An MUE is a maximum number of Units of Service (UOS) allowable under most circumstances for a single HCPCS/CPT code billed by a provider on a date of service for a single beneficiary.

The importance of the key factors of the payment cycle covered at the beginning of the chapter should now be evident. Receipt of payment of the claim is dependent on accurate data. Other causes for denials for the submission of paper or electronic claims are:

- Patient demographic data are incorrect.

- Spouse data are incorrect.

- ID numbers are wrong.

- Patient is not eligible for the insurance plan.

- CPT codes are incorrect.

- Modifier use is incorrect.

- ICD-10-CM linkage is incorrect.

- Gender for the service listed is incorrect.

- Claim is a duplicate of a service already submitted.

- Service is not covered by this insurance plan.

- Additional information is requested (e.g., operative note, pathology report, etc.).

Practices and organizations often miss charges for services that are rendered; this is known as lost charges, or noncaptured charges. Most often, this occurs due to inadequate communication from the physician to the coding personnel. However, other factors such as assumptions, hearsay, or prior rules may also affect the charge entry process. Effective preventive action includes managing all of the worksheets or tickets to make certain every patient that was seen for the date of service has been charged. Another step is to double-check that all care that is rendered has been accurately indicated, as well as the exact medical necessity for the specific care. Updating the worksheets at least quarterly and encouraging discussion of all services that are rendered at the physician office will improve the likelihood of charge capture.

Medications that are administered at the physician office are to be entered on the worksheet/ticket encounter form. When a different medication brand, dose, or item is purchased, as discussed in Chapter 3, the code will likely be different and may affect reimbursement dramatically.

Electronic medical record systems are expanding quickly within the medical profession and may include an automated charge capture component. The accuracy of the code selection remains paramount, and the risk of fraud for erroneous code selection lies with the person entering the data. For the practices that continue using paper charting, the typical form for capturing charges may be called the encounter form, ticket, or worksheet. Whether electronic or paper capture forms are used, the information for options and the updating of the processes should be done at least quarterly. New codes, new policies, and new concepts are evolving and need to be implemented effectively.

Staying on top of the rejections and getting to the bottom of what caused them will best improve the processes to yield dramatic financial improvements.

Another frequent cause for rejections is upgrade or revision of the practice management system. The system upgrade may not correlate to the clearinghouse properly, and again the data sets may be erroneous.

Additionally, rejections and denials are typically abundant annually at the time the code sets are updated. ICD-10-CM codes are implemented for health insurance plans every October 1, while the HCPCSII and CPT codes are activated every January 1. Workers' compensation and automobile insurers may not activate new codes on these same dates. For financial and legal reasons, each practice *must* purchase all of the code books and implement the new codes in a timely manner or face potential loss.

HIPAA requires health insurance plans and clearinghouses to use standard rejection codes and descriptions.

Appeals

It is becoming increasingly difficult to transmit a claim indicating fully the services performed and documented with the correct coding. This is frequently due to the edit systems that are implemented by the insurance plans. Although HIPAA requires use of certain code sets, the definition and intent for interpretation for use of those codes are not mandates. When multiple services are reported on a claim for non-Medicare patients, the probability for a rejection of at least one service or inappropriate bundling of vastly different services is unfortunately high.

Compliant Documentation

The term *compliant documentation* refers to the documentation that is necessary to justify the codes selected and information reported on the health insurance claim. Remember, the rules are not exclusively enforced for government payors only, and since the inception of HIPAA, the rules apply for all electronic health insurance claims. Medical necessity is justified by the medical record documentation in which the physician has indicated the reasons for the care and service(s) provided. When the ICD-10-CM code is listed on the claim, the reason for it must be clearly documented within the medical record. The same expectations apply to CPT and HCPCSII coding.

In the absence of compliant documentation, the risk for investigation and potential fraud and abuse sanctions is high. The sanctions and penalty fines are given to the individual who knowingly performed the error. Sanctions are not exclusive to the physician or owner of the organization. It is illegal to submit claims for payment to Medicare or Medicaid that you know or should know are false or fraudulent according to the Office of Inspector General (OIG). All persons who are involved with the transmission of the claim or capturing medical record information share in the risk of investigation and fines, if they intentionally choose not to abide by the laws.

The primary emphasis throughout this book has been on accurate documentation of the care provided. A related emphasis on adhering to the law is equally important. A final review of each claim should be made to ensure the following:

- Are the codes selected on the claim accurately documented in the chart?
- Are the records legible and consistent?
- Do all entries include the date, health care professional name, and signature?
- Are test recordings properly depicted?
- Are the abbreviations standard and clear?

Health care professionals can augment the medical record, adding a note after the date/time of the initial date if the entry or information is necessary. It is improper to alter the medical record or revise previous information without justification. Great steps should be taken, keeping in mind the revision must be kept visible with the avoidance of tampering. If tampering is evident, it is sure to be detected during an investigation and may be grounds for a felony. Do not purposely alter the medical record for unjust reasons and certainly, never for false or fraudulent reasons. Providers should contact their malpractice carriers for instructions on making appropriate amendments and late entries to the medical record and include these instructions in office policies and procedures. This is important information to include in annual compliance training for the entire office staff.

Risky Behavior

Downcoding

downcoding: The selection of a lower-level code (CPT or HCPCSII) than the supporting documentation.

For some reason, many physicians and their staff have the misguided understanding that if a lower-level code is always selected, it is "safer." The term for this is **downcoding**. It is certainly not safer and may in fact trigger an investigation of a different sort. Sometimes undercoding is a flag for substandard care or perhaps overutilization. The selection of the CPT, HCPCSII, and ICD-10-CM codes are required to be accurately reported based on the services rendered and documented. Data on codes in claims are compared by geographic area and by specialty. For E/M services, this is commonly known as bell-curve data. If one physician consistently submits claims with lower level E/M codes, the data might signal the need for a review. Accurately and correctly reporting the service as it was provided will always assist with compliant practices.

Upcoding

Upcoding is the selection of a code that contains higher criteria than supported by the documentation. Areas of particular caution, as discussed in Chapter 5, Evaluation and Management, are services that require higher criteria, such as levels 4 and 5 on an E/M outpatient service. Upcoding is also an issue when surgical procedures are reported with greater procedural descriptors and/or components than what was actually performed. Again, this borders on a potential false claim.

> **upcoding:** The action of selecting a higher level of service or procedure code than the documentation or diagnoses support for the purpose of receiving higher reimbursement.

Unbundling

Unbundling refers to reporting multiple codes rather than one specific code that describes the entire service. Medicare and some commercial carriers often publish a list or policies outlining certain services that may be bundled. Obvious code bundles in CPT are those services in which a code descriptor is listed separately and is also contained within another greater service or combination procedure code. Specifically unbundling the service(s) to gain higher financial reimbursement is prohibited.

> **unbundling:** Practice of billing multiple procedure codes for a group of procedures that are covered by a single comprehensive CPT code.

Frequency

Services may have a frequency limitation. Seeking alternative means to report frequency is not acceptable. Services should be provided at a frequency rate based on medical necessity and normal industry standards.

Professional Courtesy

Professional courtesy is often problematic for the following reasons:

- It creates a potential breach in the contract between the physician and insurance company, whether the waivers are for a partial or full fee.

- If the recipient of professional courtesy has made past or future referrals, this may be deemed a kickback.

- The waiving of copayment, coinsurance, or deductible may be perceived as an inducement.

- Waiving fees for some patients may cause a discrimination situation.

Exercise 16.3

1. List five common risky behaviors that are considered fraudulent activity.
2. Is down coding safer than upcoding?
3. What is the name of the edit system that is used by CMS?
4. When is the CMS edit system updated?
5. What does the term *compliant documentation* refer to?

Auditing Essentials

Auditing is often looked upon as a negative factor in compliance, but in fact it often provides "proof" that a service was appropriately coded and reported. Developing auditing skills was a challenge in years past because a support mechanism similar to those in the clinical and coding arena has been absent. As for coding, a credential in auditing is recommended and required by many health care entities. With the use of proper auditing and monitoring, heavy paybacks, fines, and penalties can be averted. Compliance plans without an auditing component are comparable to making a cake without the batter. A key ingredient is missing.

Association of Health Care Auditors and Educators (AHCAE): Association for auditors, educators, clinicians and compliance professionals dedicated to high-level education and training, auditing certification, recognition, and support in both the professional and facility settings.

The **Association of Health Care Auditors and Educators (AHCAE)** is an organization that provides national certifications and intensive training for medical record chart auditors to measure and validate a skill set in the following three areas:

- Certified Healthcare Chart Auditor (CHCA). This certification is designated for medical record chart auditors designated as having expertise in professional (physician) based auditing.

- Certified Healthcare Chart Auditor—Facility (CHCAF). This certification is for medical record chart auditors designated as having expertise in facility (outpatient and inpatient) auditing.

- Certified Healthcare Chart Auditor—Surgical (CHCAS). This certification is for medical record chart auditors designated as having expertise in surgical based (professional) auditing.

The AHCAE can be contacted at http://www.ahcae.org.

Audit Process

The first step prior to implementing an audit may be to contact the attorney. If an audit is sought by the attorney in preparation for professional advice or guidance, the audit and the findings are confidential. The confidentiality may become extremely valuable should an investigation ensue, because the information derived by the audit would now be considered protected under attorney-client privilege, and the auditor would not likely be called to testify against the practice. Alternatively, if a practice hires an auditor directly and then contacts an attorney, the information derived at the audit may be used against the practice and the auditor called to testify against the practice. Practical wisdom includes knowing that there are times when the attorney should be the very first call for compliance and audit processes. Establishing policies and procedures for consulting and auditing services is a true safeguard.

overpayment: Excess amount paid in error by the insurer for codes or documentation used to support the claim for payment.

Another important aspect of initiating the audit by contacting the attorney is that if the auditor should discover a major **overpayment**, the attorney will provide guidance as to the process of negotiating and/or refunding any money that may be due to the health plan. Regardless, policies and procedures must be followed in accordance with participation agreements.

If underpayments are discovered, depending on the claim filing limits of the insurance plan or state law, it is possible that a revised claim or an appeal may be submitted.

Audit Types

Internal auditing is becoming more prevalent among large facilities and payors where the practice or organization evaluates its own policies, procedures, documentation, and claims information. The audit may be for compliance or for financial purposes and should be a basis for improving quality. Conducting an internal or external audit after implementation of a compliance plan is essential. Physicians, practices, and plans need to be sure that whoever is conducting the audit has ample expertise in the subject matter being reviewed. Specific auditing associations and specialized training are becoming more important to health care compliance since auditing and monitoring was listed in the *Federal Register* as one of the OIG's seven criteria for compliance programs. There are multiple forms available and a few software options to assist in certain auditing processes. It is important to define the auditing scope and keep track of the progress (or lack of progress) for each audit. Figure 16–5 shows one example only, as not all audits are performed this way. Taking guidelines and turning them to questions is a great way to start an audit plan.

External audits are when an outside consultant or nonemployee of the organization evaluates the documentation, claims, and/or data. If possible, at the conclusion of the audit, the auditor should be scheduled for an educational review meeting. This meeting can prove invaluable because specific examples aid rapid learning of coding concepts. Providers find it helpful to see their own documentation used in the practical application.

Planning for an external audit performed for compliance purposes should at the very least include the following:

- It should be requested by the corporate attorney.

- Services to be reviewed should be defined within the scope of the audit request.

- Findings should be presented in a formal report with recommendations.

- An educational post-audit review session should be provided by the auditor(s) when possible.

Payor Audits

Payor audits are on the rise nationwide. These audits are performed by the insurance plan for various purposes. They may be requested as outlined in the participation agreement and may be prospective or retrospective audits, for quality or for financial purposes. Usually, the payor audits also allow for an appeal process, although the process could be very time consuming for physicians. Payor audits may also hire outside consultants and corporations to perform the services, as demonstrated by the CMS Comprehensive Error Rate Testing (CERT). CERT recommends improvements of the CMS system after reviewing claims and claims processing.

An audit may be triggered by specific physician data, such as that depicting outliers from the "bell curve" in comparison to other, similar physicians; or the review might be completely random, generated by a computer to simply fill an internal auditing and monitoring quota. A physician submitting a higher volume of a specific CPT code may alert the audit department at the insurance plan. Sometimes audits are triggered by a goal of the organization, such as reviewing all of one service or diagnosis; this especially applies to the most-reported diagnosis-related groups (DRGs) at inpatient facilities. Regardless, many payor audits result in a cost to the physician or organization, from audit expenses in general all the way to fines, sanctions, jail, or recoupment of future claim payments. Overpayment requests have become more common. A letter of request for an overpayment is received at the practice and an overpayment is identified for a particular patient refund.

1. Randomly select five evaluation and management encounters (both inpatient and outpatient) for review of each physician audited.

2. Is the medical record complete and legible?

3. Attempt to locate the following:
   A. Reason for encounter (medical necessity issues)
   B. Relevant history
   C. Examination findings
   D. Prior diagnostic findings (if applicable)
   E. Assessment of the patient
   F. Clinical impression or diagnosis(es)
   G. Plan of care, treatment or further disposition of the patient
   H. Date and legible identity of performing provider
   I. Signature

4. If not documented, is the rationale for ordering further diagnostics or workup implied?

5. Are past and present diagnoses accessible to the treating or consulting physician?

6. Are appropriate health risk factors identified/stated?

7. Is there documentation regarding the patient's progress, response to and/or changes in treatment, and/or revision of diagnosis(es)?

8. Are billing services/procedures and diagnoses supported within the medical record?

9. Compare billed procedures to performed date of service. Are these dates consistent?

10. Compare billed diagnosis(es) to documented diagnosis(es). Are these consistent?

11. Are the billing and performing provider the same?

12. Analyze and evaluate documentation by reviewing required components for each billed service.

13. Score documentation according to audit tools provided.

14. Complete audit analysis sheet on each service level reviewed:
    A. Tally points scored and compare to billed services.
    B. Show discrepancies, insufficiencies, omissions, etc.
    C. Make needed recommendations.
    D. Make constructive suggestions and appropriate comments.
    E. Illustrate missing components for satisfaction of service level requirements.

15. Sign and date each analysis sheet with name and title of reviewer/auditor as well as the date of the review.

16. Analyze level-of-service patterns billed by each physician.

17. Compare/contrast individual physician billing patterns within the practice.

18. Consult with the managing partner before presenting findings to determine whether results should be presented to the group or individually to the specific physician.

19. Furnish each physician with his or her individual results.

20. Prepare a summary of findings both on an individual and group basis. Furnish this summary to each physician reviewed along with individual findings and results.

21. Retain complete copy of the report, which should include the date of review and reviewer's name, title, and contact information.

Figure 16-5 Performing an on-site audit: a 21-step work plan

Once validated, the money is refunded. If there are multiple patients, the issue of recoupment on future services for many patients poses additional posting frustration. Prior to returning overpayments, state law must be reviewed, as there are specialized time factors to be considered.

While the majority of practices perform many E/M services, the audit of a practice should review services beyond strictly E/M codes for effective compliance.

Many hospitals and other facilities conduct financial audits, which may be performed for a variety of purposes. The financial audit may review the chargemaster efficiency, correlation to the UB-04 claim, average length of stay days, DRG assessment, taxation, or for other investigational purposes.

Hospitals tend to analyze the total days in accounts receivable (A/R), whereas physicians typically view total income or revenue as the main factor. A more complete monthly financial review may better guide to the specific areas that need improvement. The revenue/payment cycle may have indicators that suggest additional evaluation for the organization such as:

- What is the ratio of A/R days to the total outstanding amount?

- What is the collection ratio? Is there a decrease in the cash collection (a cashier issue or a change in the practice/services), a particular insurance plan (possible bankruptcy or other tactics), billing, or practice?

- Is there a management system revision (biller not posting, electronic payments not transmitting, etc.), or a change in turning over to collection company process?

- Are the patients complaining?

- Is there an increased volume of rejections? (Did something change on the insurance plan side, or in the process?)

Refer to Figure 16–6 for compliance terminology.

The Office of Inspector General

The **Office of Inspector General (OIG)** works with FBI staff members and assists CMS with support and enforcement. The website http://www.oig.hhs.gov offers critically important information for compliance and issues guidance in numerous areas, advisory opinions, and information regarding many specific situations faced by physicians and other health care providers.

Office of Inspector General (OIG): The office that enforces the rules of CMS and federal agencies.

Typically, evidence is collected over a course of time, commonly on claims that have been previously adjudicated. The collection of evidence may extend over a long or short period of time. One of the greatest fallacies is that "if the claim is paid, it must be OK and not considered fraudulent activity." Quite to the contrary, the claim may be paid purposefully by CMS and the activity reported to the Benefit Integrity Unit, Office of Inspector General (OIG), for further review. Other agencies may refer problems or engage the OIG's assistance.

Steps to Take When an Investigator Arrives

Compliance plans should include information such as the handling of an investigation or cold call by government authorities. Usually, an investigation begins after evidence is gathered. Correspondence requesting copies of medical records, claims, and/or refund

BBA—Balanced Budget Act of 1997. A bipartisan agreement adding new penalties for fraud while providing budget-neutral modifications to the RBRVS for subsequent years. This act added preventive screening to the Social Security Act for the first time.

Corporate integrity agreement—A governmentally mandated compliance program between a health care corporation and the government in the settlement of a fraud and abuse investigation.

DHHS/HHS—The Department of Health and Human Services or HHS. CMS is part of this department of the federal government.

FCA—False Claims Act. This act prohibits "knowingly" submitting false or fraudulent claims to government payors and/or submission of false records or statements to conceal, avoid, or decrease an obligation to pay money or property to the government. "Knowingly" is defined by this act as having actual knowledge of false information, acting in deliberate ignorance of the truth and/or falsity of information, and/or acting in reckless disregard of the truth or falsity of information.

Health care compliance—Ensuring that a health care provider or facility is providing and billing for services according to the laws, regulations, and guidelines governing that organization.

HIPAA—Health Insurance Portability and Accountability Act. Legislation designed to fight health care fraud by a broader expansion of HHS-OIG jurisdiction for all health insurance payors along with substantial increases in the investigative resources available to the OIG and FBI for health care enforcement. This law also clarifies and increases the number of health care fraud and abuse offenses while significantly increasing administrative and criminal penalties.

OIG—Office of the Inspector General. An enforcement division for the DHHS, responsible for investigation and enforcement of fraud and abuse cases and legislation.

Qui tam action—A lawsuit, usually brought by an employee (often referred to as a "whistleblower"), in regard to specific employer activities that the employee believes to be fraudulent or abusive.

Figure 16-6 Glossary of compliance terminology

requests may preface a site investigation. Alternatively, depending on the issue, no previous notice and an immediate visit are possible. The visit may be quiet and discreet, or it may entail the local sheriff and other criminal enforcement staff—sometimes with guns drawn.

When an investigation occurs, it is based on federal law, with federal investigation processes. Upon arrival, the investigator must show his or her credentials, and the practice should verify the accuracy of the credentials prior to releasing information. Next, the practice should immediately contact its attorney and share information only if advised by the attorney. During the entire time of the investigation, staff should remain professional, courteous, and kind.

Depending on the level of concern for the specific organization and issues involved, an investigation is likely to entail some or all of the following:

- Interviewing of current and past staff members

- Possible private interviews with beneficiaries regarding the exact care that was rendered

- Request for copies of medical records or a search and seize warrant for the entire removal of medical records (investigators may have hired a contractor to remove records immediately from the site)

- Confiscation of computers, servers, laptops, and any other equipment

- Copies of billing records, encounter forms, or other worksheets

The individuals who are found guilty of committing an act of fraud will be prosecuted. Criminal, civil monetary penalty, or administrative sanctions are possible. Here are some examples of fines that have been imposed and related negative consequences:

- Full-page advertisement in the local newspaper describing what the practice or organization or person did

- Fines and sanctions by provider, CPT codes, and number of claims with time period identified (could be years)

- Exclusion from all federally funded programs

- Licensure impact (may be reviewed by licensing board)

- Additional health plans cease contracts

- Being placed under a mandated corporate integrity agreement (CIA) for ongoing auditing and monitoring with the assistance of an independent review organization (IRO), typically for five years

- Hospital staff privileges cease

- Monetary penalties

- Jail time

OIG Work Plan

The OIG annually publishes its Work Plan stating the areas that will be reviewed for accuracy. This document guides all compliance officers and auditors to the specific areas to evaluate for potential risk. If a practice implements the procedures properly, it is highly unlikely an investigation would occur.

The OIG has also published Compliance Plan Guidelines for various organizations, outlining the steps that must be included to create an effective compliance plan. There is a straightforward outline for the creation of a Physician Practice Compliance Plan in Figure 16–7. Every practice should be able to answer the following questions:

- What is your code of conduct for the organization? What are the compliance monitoring efforts? Who is responsible?

- What is the training and education for practice ethics, policies and procedures, coding, and documentation?

- What is the internal auditing process?

- What are the lines of communication?

- What is the disciplinary action plan?

- What is the response to violations detected through the investigation or disclosure of incidents?

If an effective compliance plan is in place, it may be considered during the investigation and *may* decrease the potential sanctions. A compliance plan, however, is not likely to fully negate the risk for fines, sanctions, or recoupments. It is expected only that the plan will guide toward good policies and procedures in the management of the claims processes.

It is wise to conduct an audit, initiated by an attorney, prior to implementing the compliance plan. This baseline audit will serve as the benchmark, demonstrating the improvements that have been achieved upon implementation of the compliance plan. Figure 16–7 identifies compliance essentials that should be implemented.

- Conduct internal monitoring and auditing.
- Implement compliance and practice standards.
- Designate a compliance officer or contact.
- Conduct appropriate training and education.
- Respond appropriately to detected offenses and develop corrective action.
- Develop open lines of communication.
- Enforce disciplinary standards through well-publicized guidelines.
- Involve outside legal counsel as needed or appropriate.

Figure 16-7 Effective compliance plan guidance

All facilities and types of claims are subject to review for accuracy. The OIG Work Plan identifies annually a broad range of main topics such as:

- Medicare and Medicaid Hospitals
- Medicare Home Health
- Medicare Nursing Homes and Medicaid Long-Term and Community Care
- Medicare Physicians and Other Health Professionals
- Medicaid Mental Health Services
- Medicare Equipment and Supplies
- Medicare Drug Reimbursement
- Other Medicare Services (lab during inpatient, IDTF, therapy, and CORF)
- Medicare Managed Care Programs
- Medicare Contractor Operations (claims operations)

Within past Work Plans, an example of a current Medicare physician area of review is:

Anesthesia services—Payments for personally performed services

We will review Medicare Part B claims for personally performed anesthesia services to determine whether they were supported in accordance with Medicare requirements. We will also determine whether Medicare payments for anesthesia services reported on a claim with the "AA" service code modifier met Medicare requirements. Physicians report the appropriate anesthesia modifier code to denote whether the service was personally performed or medically directed. (CMS, Medicare Claims Processing Manual, Pub. No. 100-04, ch. 12, § 50) Reporting an incorrect service code modifier on the claim as if services were personally performed by an anesthesiologist when they were not will result in Medicare's paying a higher amount. The service code "AA" modifier is used for anesthesia services personally performed by an anesthesiologist, whereas the QK modifier limits payment to 50 percent of the Medicare-allowed amount for personally performed services claimed with the AA modifier. Payments to any service provider are precluded unless the provider has furnished the information necessary to determine the amounts due. (Social Security Act, §1833(e).)

(OAS; W-00-13-35706; W-00-14-35706; W-00-15-35706; various reviews; expected issue date: FY 2015)

Notice the description of the intent to review services for reason of "identical documentation across services." The information in final parentheses describes the year the rule begins and the expected work timetable.

Coders and other health care professionals are strongly advised to review the Work Plan annually, focusing on the identified OIG risk areas that might be pertinent to your area of practice for potential improvement.

Fraud Risk Prevention

- Consistently review and implement policies and procedures for each participating health insurance plan.

- Set the tone for integrity, honesty, and compliance with the law at all times.

- Before hiring an employee, check the "List of Excluded Individuals" posted on the OIG website. A complete background check is recommended for employees.

- Purchase enough code books and reference materials to meet the needs of the organization, and implement the code updates on the proper dates (e.g., ICD-10-CM is October 1, CPT, and HCPCSII are January 1).

- Clearly outline expectations, including conduct, in job descriptions.

- Allow and encourage employees and physicians to attend educational venues that help them learn more about coding and compliance.

- Schedule communication routinely for the clinical, billing, and coding staff to share information in a nonjudgmental setting. This simple yet very important step will assist with learning, process improvements, contractual renegotiations, the collection of fees, quality of care, and other issues.

Penalties

The OIG is authorized to seek different amounts of civil monetary penalties and assessments based on the type of violation at issue. See the *Code of Federal Regulations*, 42 CFR § 1003.103. For example, in a case of false or fraudulent claims, the OIG may seek a penalty of up to $10,000 for each item or service improperly claimed, and an assessment of up to three times the amount improperly claimed (see the *United States Code*, 42 U.S.C. § 1320a-7a(a)).

Health Insurance Portability and Accountability Act (HIPAA)

HIPAA statutes are extensive and the range of topics much wider than just those associated with health care facilities and organizations. This section offers a brief explanation in hopes of conveying a succinct and simple understanding of HIPAA. There is a plethora of misinformation and misimplementation of the rules, particularly with the privacy standards. When obtaining professional coding advice, ask for guidance in writing.

Transaction and Data Sets (Code Sets)

HHS published two final rules on January 16, 2009, to adopt updated HIPAA standards. In one rule, HHS is adopting X12 Version 5010 and NCPDP Version D.0 for HIPAA transactions. The compliance date for all covered entities was January 1, 2012.

In a separate final rule, HHS modified the standard medical data code sets for coding diagnoses and inpatient hospital procedures by concurrently adopting ICD-10-CM for diagnosis coding and ICD-10-PCS for inpatient hospital procedure coding. These new codes replaced the current ICD-9-CM Volumes 1 and 2 and the ICD-9-CM Volume 3 for diagnosis and procedure codes respectively. The implementation date for ICD-10-CM and ICD-10-PCS was October 1, 2015, for all covered entities.

HIPAA Security

The security rules are site specific, scalable, and, in general, customized for each location. The majority of the rules focus on the security of the electronic protected health data, such as the physical storage, transmission, and access to nonemployees.

HIPAA Privacy

The HIPAA privacy rules have posed an extensive challenge for the health care industry, mostly due to the requirement for patients to be educated and involved in the process. Definitions of some of the terms used in the HIPAA privacy rules include:

Covered entities: Organizations that transmit and share electronic health information.

Protected health information (PHI): Any individually identifiable health information.

Privacy consent: The patient signs a form for an organization that outlines the automatic release of PHI and the options the patient may have. Most consent forms state that the organizations/physicians may release information for care, payment, and for health care operation purposes *without* a written medical release form from the patient.

> **Coding Tip:**
> Patients do not need to sign a medical release form for the transmission of PHI for caring for the patient, payment, or health care operations. This is one of the most misunderstood areas of the HIPAA privacy rules. There are a few exceptions to the concept, such as specialized state laws that supercede the federal HIPAA rules, or for specific care issues such as mental health, sexually transmitted disease data, and certain others.

You should also be familiar with these terms:

- A *privacy officer* is the person who develops and oversees the policies and procedures at the organization.

- *Business associates* are individuals or companies that are given access to PHI at the organization, and have agreed to abide by all policies and procedures for the site. Common business associates are independent medical transcriptionists, for example.

- *Minimum necessary release* means that an organization is expected to release only the information required for the specific purpose—for example, only payment information may be disclosed in payment discussions.

- *Inspection of medical records* means that patients may request a copy of the medical record or to review the information contained in the record. Physicians may choose to release or not, based on the medical care and potential harm to the patient. Physicians may charge for the medical record and for the labor to monitor the medical record. The patient may not alter the medical record in any way, and is not to have a writing instrument while reviewing the chart.

- Patients may request an *amendment* to correct an error in the medical record, and physicians may choose to deny this request with a written notification.

- The Office for Civil Rights is responsible for the *enforcement* of the HIPAA privacy rules, with an overall expectation to educate toward compliance as the first step, and then enforcement levels will be elevated as appropriate. Fines may be $100 per incident, up to $25,000 per year for accidental release. For purposeful distribution of PHI, the fines escalate to $250,000 and potential 10-year imprisonment.

Typical Steps for the HIPAA Privacy Process

The privacy rules require covered entities to manage protected health information using proper techniques. Patients presenting for nonemergency care are usually advised to sign the privacy consent form. Patients who have questions are either quickly advised or the privacy officer is contacted for further clarification. The care is provided, the claim is transmitted, the medical transcription is prepared, and the privacy is maintained. On occasion, the patient or authorized representative requests to amend, review, or have a copy of the medical record. These decisions are typically determined by the privacy officer, or personally by the physician in smaller offices, and the patient request is either honored or denied in writing, specifying the anticipated costs associated with the request.

In comparison with the enormous volume of medical records that are managed throughout the United States, in general, the accidental or the purposeful release of PHI has been minimal since the implementation of HIPAA rules.

Exercise 16.4

1. What are the three parts of HIPAA that affect most physician offices?
2. For HIPAA privacy, can you release a medical record to another health care professional that is caring for the patient without obtaining a written medical release form?
3. What is the name of the enforcement agency for the HIPAA privacy rules?

Summary

The payment cycle includes a team of personnel focusing on the proper payment for professional services. Completion of the advance beneficiary notice is required for all health insurance plans and must be properly completed. Rules for completion of the claim form are under reform, and as the policies evolve, the reforms will need to be implemented.

Physicians and organizations have various contracting options, and these contracts affect the operations, policies, and cash flow, as well as the volume of patients. Avoiding fraud and abuse requires diligent, consistent work efforts by the practice or organization.

References

AHCAE Intensive Chart Auditing Practicum Resource Manual (7th ed.). (2015). Aurora, CO: Association of Health Care Auditors and Educators.

AMA Current Procedural Terminology 2016 professional edition. (2015). Chicago: American Medical Association.

Centers for Medicare and Medicaid Services. Retrieved from https://www.cms.gov.

ICD-10-CM expert for hospitals 2016 edition. (2015). Salt Lake City, UT: Optum360.

National Correct Coding Initiative (NCCI). Retrieved from https://www.cms.gov .OIG Work Plan for 2011. Retrieved from http://www.oig.hhs.gov.

Glossary

A

abortion termination of a pregnancy before the fetus is viable. Spontaneous abortion occurs naturally; also called miscarriage. Therapeutic abortion is induced and is a deliberate interruption of pregnancy (Ch 10).

accept assignment to accept payment received for a claim as full payment after copayment and/or coinsurance amounts have been collected (Ch 14).

account aging a method of identifying how long an account is overdue by the length of time it has been unpaid (Ch 14).

accounts receivable (A/R) the amount of money owed to the medical practice by its patients (Ch 14).

achalasia the inability of muscles to relax (Ch 6).

administration the professional service of giving or rendering, often associated with medications or solutions (Ch 12).

advance beneficiary notice (ABN) notice to health insurance beneficiaries that the program will probably not pay for a service. The patient assumes financial responsibility for paying the provider directly for the service (Ch 15 and Ch 16).

Affordable Care Act a national law that reforms both the health care and health insurance industries to increase the quality, availability, and affordability of private and public health insurance to all Americans (Ch 14).

Alphabetic Index The ICD-10-CM, the alphabetic listing of diagnoses (Ch 2).

American Academy of Professional Coders (AAPC) the professional association for medical coders providing ongoing education, certification, networking, and recognition, with certifications for coders in physicians' offices and hospital outpatient facilities (Ch 1).

American Health Information Management Association (AHIMA) one of the four cooperating parties for ICD-9-CM. Professional association for health information management professionals throughout the country (Ch 1).

American Hospital Association (AHA) one of the four cooperating parties for ICD-10-CM (Ch 2).

anesthesia the pharmacological suppression of nerve function (Ch 6).

anesthesiologist a physician specializing in the evaluation and preparation of a patient for surgery, the introduction of the anesthesia for the procedure, the maintenance phase, and the emergence and postoperative phase (Ch 6).

angioplasty a medical cardiology procedure in which a catheter with an inflatable balloon on the tip is passed through a vessel and inflated at the site of an obstruction within the vessel wall. As the balloon inflates, any soft plaque is flattened against the vessel wall to prevent obstruction of blood flow and to open up the vessel for blood passage (Ch 9).

antepartum time of pregnancy from conception to onset of delivery (Ch 10).

anteverted tipped forward; in gynecology, this term is used to describe the normal position of the uterus (Ch 10).

aorta the main arterial trunk within the circulatory system. All other arteries, except the pulmonary artery, are branches of this main channel. This vessel originates in the left ventricle of the heart and passes upward toward the neck. The carotid (major artery to the brain) and the coronary (major artery to the heart) are branches of the aorta. Blood that has been cleaned and freshly oxygenated flows through the aorta to the various body organs (Ch 9).

aortic semilunar valve located between the junction of the aorta and left ventricle of the heart (Ch 9).

aphakia absence of the crystalline lens of the eye (Ch 6).

arrhythmia an irregular heartbeat due to abnormal electrical activity in the heart (Ch 9).

arthropathy a vague, general term meaning pathology affecting a joint (Ch 8).

Association of Health Care Auditors and Educators (AHCAE) the national association for auditors, educators, clinicians and compliance professionals dedicated to a higher level education and training, auditing certification, recognition and support in both the professional and facility settings (Ch 1 and Ch 16).

atrium upper chamber of the heart (Ch 9).

audit an evaluation of the billing practices within a medical office. Medical billing and insurance records are abstracted and compared to investigate proper billing, coding, and documentation technique and practices (Ch 16).

authorization formal written permission to use or disclose personal health information for reasons other than treatment, payment, or other purposes (Ch 1).

automated laboratories that assay large numbers of samples mechanically (Ch 11).

B

Balanced Budget Act legislation designed to balance the federal budget enacted during the Clinton administration (Ch 16).

bankruptcy a legal declaration of an individual's inability to pay debts (Ch 14).

base units values assigned to each anesthesia CPT code to reflect the difficulty of the anesthesia service, including preoperative and postoperative care and evaluation (Ch 6).

benign lesions a noncancerous injury, wound, or infected patch of skin (Ch 7).

biopsy tissue or organ removal for study or examination (Ch 7).

birthday rule guideline for determination of the primary insurance policy when dependents are covered on two or more policies (Ch 14).

Blue Cross Blue Shield (BCBS) one of the oldest and largest insurance providers providing health benefits nationwide (Ch 15).

brachytherapy a natural or manmade radioactive element that is applied in or around a particular treatment field (Ch 11).

burn an injury to tissue resulting from heat, chemicals, or electricity. The depth or degree of burns is identified as first degree, second degree, and third degree (Ch 7).

C

capitation represents a common managed care payment strategy by which providers are paid according to the number of patients choosing a physician as primary caregiver. The capitation payment is made for a predetermined amount at a predetermined time each quarter or year (Ch 16).

cardiac catheterization the insertion of a catheter into a chamber or vessel of the heart, performed for investigational and interventional purposes of the cardiac chambers and valves or coronary arteries (Ch 9).

cardiomyopathy a condition or general term describing a problem with the heart muscle (Ch 9).

cardioversion an electric shock to the heart muscle, which helps to convert an arrhythmia into a normal or sinus rhythm (Ch 9).

carpal tunnel syndrome a condition that occurs when the tendons and the median nerve that pass through the carpal tunnel in the hands are overused in repetitive movements (Ch 8).

category three-digit representation of a single disease or group of similar conditions, such as category E11, diabetes mellitus. Many categories are divided further into subcategories and subclassifications (Ch 2).

Category II optional alphanumeric codes for quality measures, statistical data research, and development purposes (Ch 4).

Category III required alphanumeric codes for emerging technology instead of unlisted codes (Ch 4).

Category II modifiers alphanumeric modifier codes used with CPT Category II codes only, when specified within the guidelines, reporting instructions and parenthetical notes.

catheter a tubular, flexible instrument for withdrawal of fluids from, or introduction of fluids into, a body cavity (Ch 6).

Centers for Medicare & Medicaid Services (CMS) an administrative agency within the Department of Health and Human Services (DHHS) that oversees Medicare, Medicaid, and other government programs (Ch 1).

certified registered nurse anesthetist (CRNA) a registered nurse licensed by the state of practice who has completed a nurse anesthesia program, credentialed as a CRNA, who provides the same anesthesia services as an anesthesiologist (Ch 6).

CHAMPVA health care program for dependents of disabled veterans or those who died as a result of conditions related to their armed service (Ch 15).

charge slip, superbill, fee ticket, or encounter form three-part form with a record of account information for services performed including charges and payment; can also serve as an insurance reporting form (Ch 14).

chief complaint (CC) a concise statement describing the symptom, problem, condition, diagnosis, or other factor that is the reason for the encounter, usually stated in the patient's words (Ch 5).

circumflex artery a branch of the LCA (left coronary artery), this artery supplies the left atrium of the heart, the rear surfaces of the left ventricle, and the rear portion of the heart's dividing wall or septum (Ch 9).

closed fracture one in which the fracture site does not communicate with the outside environment (Ch 8).

coinsurance a specified amount of insurance determined for each service the patient must pay the health care provider (Ch 15).

computerized tomography (CT) scan this type of radiological procedure is used to scan any part of the body; most useful in scanning brain, lung, mediastinum, retroperitoneum, and liver (Ch 11).

confidentiality the maintenance, protection, security, and restriction of patient information, to only be disclosed to a third party with patient authorization/consent (Ch 1).

consent written or verbal agreement to use, release, or disclose information for treatment, payment, or other reasons (Ch 1).

Consolidated Omnibus Budget Reconciliation Act (COBRA) a law to assist employees in continuing health care coverage in the event of termination of employment, reduction of work hours, divorce, separation, or death of an employee (Ch 15).

consultation a type of service provided by a physician (usually a specialist) whose opinion or advice regarding evaluation and management of a specific problem is requested by another physician or other appropriate source (Ch 5).

contralateral the opposite side (Ch 7).

cooperating parties four agencies who share responsibility for maintaining and updating ICD-10-CM (Ch 2).

coordination of benefits coordination of payment of services submitted on the claim form when a patient is covered by two or more primary medical insurance policies (Ch 15).

coordination of care the arrangement and/or organization of patient care to include necessary referral or contact with other health care providers (Ch 5).

copayment a specified dollar amount a patient or policyholder must pay to the health care provider for each medical service or procedure received, as determined in the insurance contract (Ch 15).

copulation act of sexual intercourse (Ch 10).

counseling the act of providing advice and guidance to a patient and his or her family (Ch 5).

covered service a contracted benefit from the insurer to the provider and patient. For example, while infertility treatment may not be a covered service, testing and treatment until infertility is diagnosed may be a covered service with the insurer (Ch 16).

CPT guidelines within the CPT code book, the guidelines are the pages or paragraphs prior to a series of codes, which provide additional instruction for code use (Ch 4).

CPT modifiers a two-digit number in CPT created to indicate that a service or procedure performed has been altered by some specific circumstance but not changed in its definition or code (Ch 4 and Ch 13).

crossover claim an electronic transfer of information submitted on a Medicare claim to Medicaid or the patient's Medigap carrier (Ch 15).

cycle billing accounts divided alphabetically into groups with each group billed at a different time (Ch 14).

D

debridement a procedure in which foreign material and contaminated or devitalized tissue are removed from a traumatic or infected lesion or wound until the surrounding healthy tissue is exposed (Ch 7).

decubitus ulcer a pressure ulcer; also known as a bedsore or pressure sore. These results from a lack of blood flow and irritation to the skin over a bony projection. As the name indicates, decubiti occur in bedridden or wheelchair-bound patients or from a cast or splint (Ch 7).

deductible a specified amount of covered medical expense that must be paid by the insured to a health care provider before benefits will be reimbursed by the insurance company (Ch 15).

definitive diagnosis diagnosis based on physician findings; the determination of the illness or disease is made by the physician (Ch 7).

dermatitis an inflammation of the upper layers of the skin (eczema). Drugs taken internally can also cause skin reactions, which are considered adverse reactions. Sunburn is classified as dermatitis in ICD-9-CM (Ch 7).

dermis the middle layer of the integument, or skin (Ch 7).

diabetes mellitus a metabolic disease of the endocrine system in which the body does not produce enough insulin, or the cells do not respond to the insulin that is produced (Ch 2).

diagnosis-related groups (DRG) the method of prospective payment used by Medicare and other third-party payors for hospital inpatients (Ch 2).

diagnostic to identify or investigate for purposes of determining a condition or diagnosis (Ch 4).

dilation stretching and opening of the cervix during labor to facilitate the baby's passage through the pelvis; measured in centimeters (Ch 10).

disclosure to reveal, release, transfer, or divulge information outside of the individual or facility holding the information to other parties (Ch 1).

dislocation a complete separation of the bone from its normal position in a joint (Ch 8).

DMEPOS durable medical equipment, prosthetics, orthotics and supplies created by CMS. Examples include wheelchairs, walkers, braces, and colostomy supplies (Ch 3).

downcoding the selection of a lower level code (CPT or HCPCSII) than the supporting documentation (Ch 16).

E

echocardiography (ECHO) is an ultrasound used to visualize the heart, important in the diagnosis of cardiovascular disease and valve disorders (Ch 9).

echography use of ultrasound to evaluate anatomy to aid in diagnosis (Ch 10).

effacement obliteration of the cervix during labor as it shortens from one or two centimeters in length to paper thin, leaving only the external os; expressed as a percentage (Ch 10).

electrocardiogram (EKG or ECG) the recording of the electrical activity of the heart (Ch 9).

electronic medical record (EMR) computer-based medical record or patient chart (Ch 14).

Electronic Prescribing Incentive Program a program developed by the Centers for Medicare and Medicaid Services (CMS) to offer incentives to health care providers to use a qualified electronic prescribing system (Ch 1).

emancipated minor a person under the age of majority, usually 18 to 21 years of age as defined by state statute, who is self-supporting, married, serving in the armed forces, and/or living separate from parents (Ch 14).

endocardium the innermost layer of tissue that lines the chambers of the heart (Ch 9).

endoscopy inspection of organs or cavities by use of a tube through a natural body opening or through a small incision (Ch 6).

end-stage renal disease (ESRD) commonly used term for irreversible kidney failure (Ch 12).

enteral the patient receives feeding or medication into the small intestine (Ch 3).

epidermis the outer layer of the integument, or skin (Ch 7).

epidural located over or on the dural (Ch 6).

eponym a disease, disorder, or procedure named after the person who researched or identified a particular disease or disorder or developed a procedure (Ch 2).

etiology cause of the disease or illness (Ch 2).

evaluation and management services (E/M) the first section of the CPT coding manual that describes visit and special encounter–type services such as office visits, hospital visits, nursing facility visits, and consultations (Ch 5).

examination a critical inspection and investigation, usually following a particular method, performed for diagnostic or investigational purposes and driven by the presenting problem and provider judgment (Ch 5).

excision remove by cutting out (Ch 7).

explanation of benefits (EOB) a summary explaining an insurance company's determination for reimbursements of benefits; for Medicare claims, this is referred to as a Medicare Summary Notice (MSN), some companies use the term remittance advice (RA) (Ch 15).

F

Fair Debt Collection Practices Act a consumer protection policy against abusive collection practices by debt collectors (Ch 14).

False Claims Act federal legislation that prohibits submission of claims for services not rendered or for any services considered fraudulent upon investigation (Ch 16).

fascia the tissue that connects muscles (Ch 7).

fasciocutaneous flap the fasciocutaneous is fibrous tissue beneath the skin; it also encloses muscles and groups of muscles, and separates their several layers or groups. The flap is the placement of portion of tissue or skin and may or not include the fascio. Pedicle, local, or distant are all commonly used flap terms (Ch 7).

Federal Register the official daily *publication* for rules, proposed rules, and notices of federal agencies and organizations, as well as executive orders and documents (Ch 1).

first-listed diagnosis in the outpatient setting, the diagnosis that is the main reason and listed first for the visit. It is usually the diagnosis taking the majority of resources for the visit (Ch 2).

fissure a groove, split, or natural division (Ch 6).

fistula an abnormal tubelike passage from a normal cavity to another cavity or surface (Ch 6).

G

general anesthesia a state of unconsciousness, produced by anesthetic agents, with absence of pain sensation over the entire body (Ch 6).

gestation time in which a woman is pregnant and fetal development takes place (Ch 10).

gravidity term used to indicate the number of pregnancies a woman has had; gravida is used with numerals (e.g., 0, I, II) (Ch 10).

H

HCPCS Level II modifiers two alpha-numeric indicators created and maintained by CMS to provide additional information regarding a procedure, service, or supply (Ch 13).

Healthcare Common Procedure Coding System (HCPCS) coding system that consists of CPT codes (level I) and national codes (level II), used to identify procedures, supplies, medications (except vaccines), and equipment (Ch 1).

Healthcare Common Procedure Coding System Level II (HCPCSII) the second level of the coding system created by CMS for reporting of procedures, services, supplies, medications, equipment, and items (Ch 3).

Health Information Technology for Economic and Clinical Health (HITECH) enacted as part of the American Recovery and Reinvestment Act of 2009 to promote the adoption and meaningful use of health information technology (Ch 1).

Health Insurance Portability and Accountability Act (HIPAA) federal law mandating regulations that govern privacy, security, and electronic transactions standards for health care information (Ch 1).

HIPAA transaction and code sets any set of codes used for encoding data elements, such as tables of terms, medical concepts, diagnosis and procedure codes (Ch 14).

history a record of past events; a systematic account of the medical, emotional, and psychosocial occurrences in a patient's life and of factors in the family, and environment that may have a bearing on the patient's condition (Ch 5).

history of present illness (HPI) a description of the development of the patient's present illness from the first sign and/or symptom to the present (Ch 5).

hyperthermia this procedure uses heat to raise the temperature of a specific area of the body to try to increase cell metabolism and increase the destruction of cancer cells (Ch 11).

I

ICD-10-PCS international Classification of Diseases, 10th Revision, Procedure Classification System (Ch 2 and Ch 9).

immune globulin animal protein with activity similar to that of a human antibody (Ch 12).

implantable cardioverterdefibrillator (ICD) a small battery-powered generator that is implanted in patients who are at risk for sudden cardiac death (Ch 9).

infusion introduction of a solution into tissue or an organ via intravenous therapy (Ch 12).

inhaled solution (INH) the patient inhales the medication, may use respiratory equipment commonly known as the Intermittent Positive Pressure Breathing treatment (Ch 3).

injection a parenteral route of administration during which a needle penetrates the skin or muscle; e.g., subcutaneous injection, intramuscular injection (Ch 12).

injection not otherwise specified (INJ) the patient receives an injection other than the options listed, such as intradermal or an injection directly into anatomy (Ch 3).

insurance fraud intentional, deliberate misrepresentation of information for profit or to gain some unfair or dishonest advantage (Ch 1).

internal derangement a range of injuries of the joint involving the soft tissues such as the synovium, cartilage, and ligaments (Ch 8).

International Classification of Diseases, 9th Revision, Clinical Modification (ICD-9-CM) coding system used to report diagnoses, diseases, and symptoms and reason for encounters for insurance claims (Ch 1).

International Classification of Diseases, 10th Revision, Clinical Modification (ICD-10-CM) coding system to replace ICD-9-CM as of October 1, 2013, to report diagnoses, diseases, and symptoms and reason for encounters for insurance claims (Ch 1).

intra-arterial (IA) the patient receives through the artery system (Ch 3).

intracavitary within a body cavity (Ch 11).

intramuscular (IM) the patient receives an injection into the muscular system. This is the most common method of administration (Ch 3).

intrathecal (IT) the patient receives through the membrane (Ch 3).

intravenous (IV) the patient receives through the venous system (Ch 3).

ipsilateral same side (Ch 9).

L

lactation process of secreting milk from the breasts (Ch 10).

leiomyomas myoma or tumor of muscular tissue involving the nonstriated muscle fibers, also known as fibroid tumors (Ch 10).

limiting charge a percentage limitation on fees that nonparticipating physicians are allowed to bill Medicare patients above the fee schedule amount (Ch 14).

local anesthesia anesthesia confined to one part of the body (Ch 6).

M

magnetic resonance imaging (MRI) this type of radiologic procedure is used to scan brain, spinal cord, soft tissues, and adrenal and renal masses. More superior scan than the CT (Ch 11).

main term the patient's illness or disease. In ICD-10-CM, the main term is the primary way to locate the disease in the alphabetic index. Main terms are printed in boldface type and are even with the left margin on each page (Ch 2).

malignant lesion having the properties of nearby invasive and destructive tumor growth and metastasis; changes in the tissues (Ch 7).

mammography the process of using low-energy x-rays to examine the human breast as both a screening and diagnostic tool (Ch 11).

manifestation an obvious indication or specific evidence that a disease is present (Ch 2).

manual performing something by hand or with the hands (Ch 11).

mastectomy   excision of the breast (Ch 7).

Medicaid   a jointly sponsored federal and state government medical assistance program to provide medical care for persons with incomes below the national poverty level (Ch 15).

medical decision making   the complexity of establishing a diagnosis and/ or selecting a management option (Ch 5).

medical necessity   the justification for an action or service based on the patient's condition, problem, or illness (Ch 16).

Medicare   a federal health insurance program for persons over 65 years of age, retired, on social security benefits, receiving social security disability benefits, or end-stage renal disease coverage (Ch 15).

Medicare Modernization Act   federal law upgrading, streamlining, and revising the Centers for Medicare and Medicaid Services (Ch 16).

Medicare physician fee schedule (MPFS)   a listing of allowable charges for services rendered to Medicare patients (Ch 14).

Medicare Summary Notice (MSN)   a summary explaining Medicare's determination for reimbursement of benefits and other actions on claims. Previously called Explanation of Medicare Benefits (EOMB) (Ch 15).

Medigap   a private, commercial insurance plan purchased by a patient as a supplementary plan to Medicare coverage (Ch 15).

menarche   time when the first menstruation begins (Ch 10).

menopause   time when menstruation ceases (Ch 10).

mitral valve   a two-leafed or cuspid valve shaped like a bishop's miter (head covering), this valve is located between the left atrium and left ventricle. Considered an atrioventricular valve, the mitral valve opens when the atria contract and sends blood into the ventricles. When the ventricles contract, pressure is exerted on the leaflets causing them to balloon upward toward the atria (Ch 9).

modality   application of any therapeutic or physical agent (Ch 12).

moderate (conscious) sedation   a decreased level of consciousness during a procedure without being put completely to sleep. The patient is able to respond to verbal instructions and stimulation (Ch 6).

modifier   a two-digit number placed after the usual procedural code, which represents a particular explanation to further describe the procedure/service or circumstances involved with the procedure (Ch 4 and Ch 13).

Mohs surgery   a highly effective treatment for certain types of skin cancer where the surgeon performs both surgical excision of the skin cancer and microscopic examination of the surgical margins to ensure that all skin cancer cells have been removed (Ch 7).

monthly billing   billing patients at one designated time of the month (Ch 14).

multiple gated acquisition (MUGA)   cardiac blood pool imaging; nuclear and multigated ventriculogram is referred to as an MUGA. This diagnostic tool evaluates left ventricular function, ventricular aneurysms, intracardiac shunting, or other wall motion abnormalities. Technetium radioisotopes "tag" the blood's red cells or serum albumin. With the uptake of the radioactive isotope, a scintillation camera records the radioactivity on its primary left ventricular pass. The second pass includes an ECG and a gated camera used while the patient is manipulated to view all segments of the ventricle. Additional views

may be obtained and observed after administration of sublingual (under the tongue) nitroglycerin or initiation of physical exercise (Ch 9).

muscle flap   a layer of muscle is dissected and moved to a new site (Ch 7).

myocardium   the muscular tissue of the heart (Ch 9).

myocutaneous flap   a muscle flap that contains overlying skin (Ch 7).

N

National Center for Health Statistics (NCHS)   one of the four cooperating parties for ICD-10-CM (Ch 2).

National Correct Coding Initiative (NCCI)   was established by the Centers for Medicare & Medicaid Services and is often referred to as "bundling edits." NCCI is often followed by individual payers that sometimes vary from the CPT definition of the Surgical Package (Ch 4).

National Provider Identifier   an ten-digit number assigned by CMS to identify the provider of service on the CMS-1500 claim form. This number is used to standardize and simplify the use of provider identification to detect and trace fraudulent and abusive submission of claim forms (Ch 15).

nature of the presenting problem (NPP)   A presenting problem may be a complaint, disease, illness, condition, sign or symptom, injury, finding or other reason for an encounter (Ch 5).

NCCI associated modifier   indicates modifiers associated with NCCI that may or may not be allowed to be used with a specified code pair (Ch 13).

neoplasm   any new and abnormal growth of tissue in some part of the body, specifically one in which cell multiplication is uncontrolled and progressive, that may be benign or malignant (Ch 2).

nonparticipating (nonPAR) providers   Medicare nonPAR physicians must not exceed the limiting charge when billing beneficiaries (Ch 14 and Ch 16).

O

occlusion   blockage or obstruction by thrombus or plaque deposits within a blood vessel or passageway (Ch 9).

Office of Inspector General (OIG)   the office that enforces rules and penalties for violations of CMS and federal and state programs (Ch 1 and Ch 16).

Omnibus Budget Reconciliation Act (OBRA) of 1987   a federal law outlining numerous areas of health care, establishing guidelines and penalties (Ch 1).

open fracture   one in which the fracture site communicates with the outside environment (Ch 8).

open reduction internal fixation (ORIF)   a method of surgically repairing a fractured bone, generally involving the use of places and screws or an intra-medullary rod to stabilize the bone (Ch 8).

orally (ORAL)   the patient receives medication through the mouth (orally) (Ch 3).

orthopedics   a medical specialty concerned with the prevention, investigation, diagnosis, and treatment of diseases, disorders, and injuries of the musculoskeletal system (Ch 8).

osteomyelitis   infection or inflammation of the bone or bone marrow. It may be acute, subacute, or chronic (Ch 8).

osteopathic manipulative treatment (OMT) manual treatment performed by the physician for the care of somatic dysfunction and other disorders (Ch 12).

other (OTH) the patient receives any other method not listed (Ch 3).

overpayment excess amount paid in error by the insurer for codes or documentation used to support the claim for payment (Ch 16).

ovulation release of the ovum from the ovary; usually occurs every 28 days (Ch 10).

P

pacemaker electrical (battery-powered) device that helps maintain normal sinus heart rhythm by stimulating cardiac muscles to contract or pump. Pacemakers come in single or dual chamber models and are programmed to sense and correct low heart rates or abnormal rhythms. The devices can be set to a fixed number of beats per minute (Ch 9).

parenteral the patient receives feeding or medication by injection route such as intravenously, subcutaneously, etc., not through the alimentary canal (Ch 3).

parity term used to indicate the number of pregnancies in which the fetus has reached viability; approximately 22 weeks of gestation. May also be used with a series of numbers to indicate the number of full-term infants, pre-term infants, abortions, and living children (e.g., para 0-1-0-1) (Ch 10).

participating (PAR) provider a health care provider who has signed a contract with an insurance company to provide medical services to subscribers in the contract plan (also known as an innetwork provider), and agrees to accept assignment (receives payment directly) from the health insurance program (Ch 14 and Ch 16).

parturition labor and delivery (Ch 10).

past, family, and social history (PFSH) pertinent inquiry of the patient and family's history of allergies, illness, treatments, and surgeries. Social history relates to the patient's occupation, military, education level, sexual history, drug or alcohol use, and other relevant information that may be beneficial to the encounter (Ch 5).

PATH Medicare rules governing payment for physicians at teaching hospitals (PATH) to ensure that claims accurately reflect the level of service provided to patients (Ch 13).

pedicle in skin grafting, it is the stem that attaches to a new growth (Ch 7).

pedicle flap a flap of skin that is lifted from a healthy site, a portion of which is grafted to a new site but remains attached to its blood supply (Ch 7).

pelvic relaxation weakened condition of supporting ligaments of the uterus and bladder; caused by aging, trauma, or excessive stretching from the act of childbirth (Ch 10).

pericardium sac surrounding the heart (Ch 9).

physical status modifier a two-digit amendment to the anesthesia CPT codes that describes the physical status of the patient who is receiving anesthesia (Ch 6).

Physician Quality Reporting System (PQRS) an incentive program for physicians, hospitals, and other health care providers for participation in reporting to CMS on quality performance measures (Ch 1).

Physicians' Current Procedural Terminology (CPT) numeric codes and descriptors for services and procedures performed by providers, published by the American Medical Association (Ch 1).

plaque soft deposits of fatty substances that harden with time and produce rocklike obstructions within vessels. Plaque production occurs due to high-fat dietary intake, sedentary lifestyles, and hereditary tendencies in patients with progressive atherosclerosis (Ch 9).

point of service (POS) the insurance plan encourages the patient to seek health care at a specific location or facility, typically where a contract for less cost has been negotiated (Ch 16).

postpartum time after giving birth (Ch 10).

preexisting condition a medical condition under active treatment at the time application is made for an insurance policy, possibly resulting in an exclusion of that disease or illness (Ch 15).

preferred provider organization (PPO) the health care provider signs a contract to join a group, usually an insurance plan. The physician name is then published in a listing, the listing may be resold, or the patients may receive incentives and discounts when choosing to have the care with a PPO (Ch 16).

presentation manner in which the fetus appears to the examiner during delivery (e.g., breech, cephalic, transverse, vertex) (Ch 10).

principal diagnosis the reason, after study, which caused the patient to be admitted to the hospital (Ch 2).

privacy the right of individuals to keep information from being released or disclosed to others (Ch 1).

privileged information any information communicated by a patient to a provider related to treatment and progress of the patient (Ch 1).

professional courtesy medical treatment free of charge or at a reduced rate, or accepting what insurance pays as full payment to physicians and their families, office employees and their families, and other health care professionals, such as dentists, pharmacists, and clergy, as determined by office policy (Ch 14).

professional services a face-to-face service rendered by a physician or qualified health care professional and reported by a specific CPT code (Ch 5).

prolapse falling or dropping down of an organ from its normal position or location such as the uterus, bladder, vagina, or rectum (Ch 10).

protected health information (PHI) any information identifiable to an individual, such as age, gender, health status, or other demographic information (Ch 1).

provisional diagnosis preliminary diagnosis, including the present signs and symptoms (Ch 7).

psychiatry the branch of medicine that focuses on mental disorder study, treatment, and prevention (Ch 12).

puerperium time after delivery that it takes for the uterus to return to its normal size—usually three to six weeks (Ch 10).

pulmonary artery a major blood vessel that transports blood between the heart and the lungs for oxygenation. Deoxygenated blood is carried from the right ventricle via this vessel, which forks into the right and left lungs. The pulmonary vein then carries freshly oxygenated blood into the left atrium of the heart for passage into the left ventricle and, subsequently, into systemic circulation (Ch 9).

pulmonary semilunar valve a three-leaflet valve, the pulmonic is another semilunar valve. It is situated between the right ventricle and the pulmonary artery. During heart contractions, internal pressure forces this valve to open. Loss of pressure during diastole (heart relaxation) allows the valve to close (Ch 9).

Q

qualitative   tests that detect a particular analyte (Ch 11).

Quality Improvement Organizations (QIO)   organizations contracted by CMS in each state to review medical care, help beneficiaries with complaints, and work to improve the quality of care provided to Medicare beneficiaries by any health care provider or facility (Ch 1).

quantitative   expresses specific numerical amounts of an analyte (Ch 11).

R

radiation absorbed dose (rad)   a unit of measure in radiation (Ch 11).

radiculopathy   disease of the spinal nerve roots (Ch 8).

regional anesthesia   the production of insensibility of a part by interrupting the sensory nerve conductivity from that region of the body (Ch 6).

reimbursement   the act of being paid back or payment in exchange for goods or services (Ch 16).

relative value unit (RVU)   payment component based on physician work, practice expense, and malpractice expense (Ch 14).

remittance advice (RA)   a summary explaining the insurance company's determination for reimbursement of benefits; also referred to as explanation of benefits (Ch 15).

removal   removal of lesions can be by excision, destruction, shaving, or ligation. A biopsy only removes a portion of a lesion (Ch 7).

repair   repair of open wounds or lacerations is classified as simple, intermediate, or complex (Ch 7).

Resource-Based Relative Value System (RBRVS)   a method of predetermining values for physician services for Medicare established in 1992, calculating units based on services performed, practice expenses, and professional liability insurance (Ch 14).

retroverted   tipped back; in gynecology, this term is used to describe the backward displacement of the uterus (Ch 10).

review of systems (ROS)   the obtaining of an inventory of body systems through a series of questions seeking to identify signs and/or symptoms that the patient may be experiencing or has experienced (Ch 5).

ribbons   temporary interstitial placement in clinical brachytherapy (Ch 11).

S

septum   the dividing wall or muscle between the right and left sides of the heart (Ch 9).

sequela   a residual or late effect after the acute phase of an illness or injury (Ch 2).

sequencing   arranging codes in the proper order according to the definitions of principal or first-listed diagnosis (Ch 2).

signature on file   a statement entered on the claim form for authorization purposes, indicating the patient has signed a release of medical information retained in the patient's chart (Ch 15).

skin tag   small, soft, fleshcolored skin flap that appear mostly on the neck, armpits, or groin (Ch 7).

skip   a person who has apparently moved without leaving a forwarding address (Ch 14).

sources   intracavitary placement or permanent interstitial placement in clinical brachytherapy (Ch 11).

sphincter   muscles that constrict an orifice (Ch 6).

stent   following the dilation of an artery, usually by means of balloon angioplasty, the stent is loaded on a special catheter with an expandable balloon. Both devices are threaded into a guide catheter and threaded to the occlusion site. The cardiologist then positions and deploys the stent by expanding the balloon. The stent is composed of a meshlike material that assists in keeping the vessel open and clear of future occlusions (Ch 9).

subcategory   four-digit subcategories are subdivisions of diagnostic categories to provide greater specificity regarding etiology, site, or manifestations (Ch 2).

subclassification   fifth-digit subclassifications are subdivisions of subcategories to provide even greater specificity regarding etiology, site, or manifestation of the illness or disease (Ch 2).

subcutaneous (SC)   the patient receives an injection into the subcutaneous tissue (Ch 3).

T

Table of Drugs   a comprehensive list of non-oral drugs by both technical and brand names that include the route of administration and dose information for reporting purposes (Ch 3).

tabular list   ICD-10-CM is a tabular listing (alpha numerical order) of diseases (Ch 2).

therapeutic   to achieve a therapeutic result or to treat a condition or diagnosis (Ch 4).

toxoids   toxins that are treated and revised, given to stimulate antibody production (Ch 12).

transient   short-term or disappearing after a short amount of time (Ch 2).

TRICARE   health care program for active duty members of the military and their dependents. Previously known as CHAMPUS (Ch 15).

tricuspid valve   diametrically larger and thinner than the mitral valve, three separate leaflets or cusps are found in this critical valve. The anterior, posterior, and septal leaflets are competent only if the right ventricle's lateral wall functions correctly. The septal leaflet is attached to the interventricular septum and is in close proximity to the AV node (Ch 9).

trimester   first, second, and third three-month period of which the pregnancy is divided (Ch 10).

Truth in Lending Act   a consumer-protection act requiring a written statement when there is a bilateral agreement between the physician and patient to pay for a procedure in more than four installments, disclosing finance charges, if any (Ch 14).

U

ulcer   loss of a portion of the skin, penetrating the dermis. Gangrene can be associated with skin ulcers. These are usually due to a vascular disease, as in diabetes (Ch 7).

unbundling   practice of billing multiple procedure codes for a group of procedures that are covered by a single comprehensive CPT code (Ch 16).

upcoding   the action of selecting a higher level of service or procedure code than the documentation or diagnoses support for the purpose of receiving higher reimbursement (Ch 16).

usual, customary, and reasonable (UCR) fees   a method used to average fee profiles to determine what is allowable for reimbursement (Ch 14).

V

vaccine   a suspension of microorganisms that is administered to prevent illness (Ch 12).

various (VAR)   the patient receives the medication using various, often multiple means (Ch 3).

vascular families   arterial, venous, pulmonary, portal, lymphatic (Ch 9).

ventricles   the two lower chambers of the heart are called the ventricles. The right ventricle is two to three times thinner in muscle tissue than the left ventricle. The greater thickness and muscle mass of the left chamber are necessary to exert enough pressure and force to propel blood into systemic circulation (Ch 9).

W

withhold   a percentage held out by the managed care organization as an incentive to keep costs, admissions, and referrals low each year. If the provider follows the plan strategy, the withhold percentage is returned with interest at a predetermined time (Ch 16).

Index